HELLENIC STUDIES 36

HOMER THE CLASSIC

Other Titles in the Hellenic Studies Series

Plato's Rhapsody and Homer's Music
The Poetics of the Panathenaic Festival in Classical Athens

Labored in Papyrus Leaves
Perspectives on an Epigram Collection Attributed to Posidippus
(P.Mil.Vogl. VIII 309)

Helots and Their Masters in Laconia and Messenia
Histories, Ideologies, Structures

Archilochos Heros
The Cult of Poets in the Greek Polis

Master of the Game
Competition and Performance in Greek Poetry

Greek Ritual Poetics

Black Doves Speak
Herodotus and the Languages of Barbarians

Pointing at the Past
From Formula to Performance in Homeric Poetics

Homeric Conversation

The Life and Miracles of Thekla

Victim of the Muses
Poet as Scapegoat, Warrior and Hero
in Greco-Roman and Indo-European Myth and History

Amphoteroglōssia
A Poetics of the Twelfth-Century Medieval Greek Novel

Priene (second edition)

Plato's Symposium
Issues in Interpretation and Reception

http://chs.harvard.edu/publications

HOMER THE CLASSIC

Gregory Nagy

CENTER FOR HELLENIC STUDIES
Trustees for Harvard University
Washington, D.C.
Distributed by Harvard University Press
Cambridge, Massachusetts, and London, England
2009

Homer the Classic by Gregory Nagy
Copyright © 2009 Center for Hellenic Studies, Trustees for Harvard University
All Rights Reserved.
Published by Center for Hellenic Studies, Trustees for Harvard University, Washington, D.C.
Distributed by Harvard University Press, Cambridge, Massachusetts and London, England
Printed in Ann Arbor, MI by Edwards Brothers, Inc.

First corrected printing, 2012.

EDITORIAL TEAM
Senior Advisers: W. Robert Connor, Gloria Ferrari Pinney, Albert Henrichs, James O'Donnell, Bernd Seidensticker
Editorial Board: Gregory Nagy (Editor-in-Chief), Christopher Blackwell, Casey Dué (Executive Editor), Mary Ebbott (Executive Editor), Scott Johnston, Olga Levaniouk, Anne Mahoney, Leonard Muellner
Production Manager for Publications: Jill Curry Robbins
Web Producer: Mark Tomasko
Cover design: Joni Godlove
Production: Kristin Murphy Romano

LIBRARY OF CONGRESS CATALOGING-IN-PUBLICATION DATA:
Nagy, Gregory.
Homer the classic / by Gregory Nagy.
  p. cm. -- (Hellenic studies ; 36)
 Includes bibliographical references and index.
 ISBN 978-0-674-03326-9
 1. Homer--Criticism and interpretation. 2. Epic poetry, Greek--History and criticism. 3. Oral tradition--Greece. I. Title.
  PA4037.N343 2009
  883'.01--dc22

2009034885

CONTENTS

Author's Preface vii
Prolegomena A Classical Text of Homer in the Making 1
Chapter 1 Homer the Classic in the Age of Virgil 73
Chapter 2 Homer the Classic in the Age of Callimachus 187
Chapter 3 Homer the Classic in the Age of Plato 354
Chapter 4 Homer the Classic in the Age of Pheidias 450
Conclusions 589
Abbreviations and Bibliography 601
Index Locorum 625

Author's Preface

The online publication date for this book is 2008, since it was "born digital" in that year on the website of the Center for Hellenic Studies (http://chs.harvard.edu/publications). The print publication date is 2009.

There are many people I want to thank for helping me—so many that I am unable to list them all here. The footnotes, at least, include detailed acknowledgments of some of them. Special thanks go to Valerie Woelfel for her line drawings. In general, I thank my colleagues and friends for all their support. Four names stand out: Christopher Dadian, Soo-Young Kim, Leonard Muellner, and Jill Curry Robbins. My debt to these four is beyond measure.

PROLEGOMENA

A CLASSICAL TEXT OF HOMER IN THE MAKING

P⓼1. The Homeric Koine

P§1 *Homer the Classic* centers on ancient concepts of Homer as the author of a body of poetry that we know as the *Iliad* and *Odyssey*. This body of poetry, this *corpus*, became a classical text, but it started as something else. That something, as I have argued in earlier projects, is oral poetry. In the present project, however, my aim is not to reassess the Homeric corpus as oral poetry. Rather, I aim to show how the Homeric *Iliad* and *Odyssey* became a classic in the days of the Athenian empire and later.

P§2 I will clarify what I mean by the concept of Athenian empire as my argumentation proceeds. I need to say from the start that I could have described the historical reality behind this concept in a variety of alternative ways, steering clear of the English word empire, but I prefer to use this particular word in the light of its derivation from the Roman idea that we translate as 'empire', *imperium*. As for the specific concept of an Athenian empire, I focus on another word, a Greek word:

koinē (κοινή) / plural *koinai* (κοιναί) 'common, standard'

The plural form *koinai* was once used as a substantive in referring to texts of Homer that were 'common, standard'. The concept of a 'common' or 'standard' text of Homer, to which I will refer hereafter simply as Koine, is central to my overall project. It comes closest to capturing what I mean by classic in the title *Homer the Classic*.

P§3 At first glance, my formulation seems anachronistic. Homer, we may be saying to ourselves, does not speak for the Athenian empire. By the time we reach the last chapter of this book, however, we will see that Homer does exactly that: he actually does speak for the Athenian empire—as far as Athenians in the fifth century BCE were concerned. In that age, Homer was

Prolegomena

a classic, an Athenian classic, and Homer's poetry gave meaning not only to civilization in general but to the Athenian empire in particular. The Athenian version of Homer is shaped by the idea of a unified text of Homer, a Homeric Koine. This idea of a Homeric Koine, a text that is both 'common' and 'standard', matches the idea of a society that is both democratic and imperial.

P§4 I plan to show how the multiple *koinai* or 'common' texts of Homer, as they were known in the city of Alexandria around the middle of the second century BCE, stem from a notionally singular Athenian Koine or 'standard' version of Homer that goes as far back as the era of the Athenian empire in the fifth century BCE.

P§5 Beyond the Athenian Koine, the Homeric tradition can be traced all the way back to a poetic *lingua franca* current already in the Bronze Age, in the second millennium BCE. Athenians who lived in the middle of the first millennium BCE imagined this remote age as the era of the so-called Minoan thalassocracy, the maritime empire of King Minos of Crete, who supposedly lived in the second millennium BCE. The very idea of a Homer who knew about such a remote age, however, is beyond reach without an intermediary. For me that intermediary is the idea of Homer in the age of the Athenian empire. That idea converges with what I am calling the Homeric Koine. To grasp that idea is the objective of this book, as reflected in the title *Homer the Classic*.

P(S)2. Twin books about six ages of Homeric reception

P§6 *Homer the Classic* (HC) is complemented by the twin book *Homer the Preclassic* (HPC), which covers the vast prehistoric era that led to the formation of the Homeric Koine. These two books, between the two of them, cover six ages of Homeric reception. These six ages correspond to six lectures I gave in the spring semester of 2002 at the University of California at Berkeley while I was teaching there as the Sather Professor for 2001/2. Here are the six ages, arranged in a sequence going backward in time:

HC ch. 1. Homer the Classic in the age of Virgil

HC ch. 2. Homer the Classic in the age of Callimachus

HC ch. 3. Homer the Classic in the age of Plato

HC ch. 4. Homer the Classic in the age of Pheidias

HPC Part I. A Preclassical Homer from the Dark Age

HPC Part II. A Preclassical Homer from the Bronze Age.

Pⓢ2. Twin books about six ages of Homeric reception

P§7 The first four entries in this list correspond to the titles of the four chapters in *Homer the Classic*. The next two entries correspond to the titles I give to the two parts of the twin book *Homer the Preclassic*. Here I outline the rationale for all six ages. The first four "ages" are of course definable as historical periods, but the last two are prehistoric periods that can only be defined imprecisely and that cover much wider time-spans than the other four. None of these six ages, of and by themselves, has a direct relevance to Homer. They become relevant only if we think of each of them as windows through which we observe the history and prehistory of Homeric poetry. If we look through any one of these six windows, we can see one of six different views of Homer. Through four of the six windows, Homer can be viewed as a classic. Through the other two windows, Homer can be viewed as a classic in the making. Each of the six time-frames I have chosen is different to the extent that Homer and Homeric poetry will have evolved through time.

P§8 The idea of viewing Homer through several different time-frames is consistent with my overall approach to Homer, which goes beyond current debates concerning Homeric "orality" or "literacy."[1] Such debates presuppose some alternative ideas that I do not share. In terms of such ideas, Homer was not really classical or even preclassical: he was primordial. Such a primordial Homer, whether or not his name was Homer, was some kind of primitive; if he was a genius, he was a primitive genius.[2]

P§9 By contrast, the Homer of *Homer the Classic* and *Homer the Preclassic* is more than just a hypothetical person. He is a historical concept. As a concept, Homer is a metonym for the text and the language attributed to Homer in historical times. By metonym I mean an expression of meaning by way of connecting something to something else, to be contrasted with metaphor, which I define for the moment as an expression of meaning by way of substituting something for something else.[3]

P§10 The Homer of Homeric poetry was not just prototypical. He was also definitive in the minds of Greek-speaking people who lived in each of the six time-frames I have chosen for viewing Homer. By the time Greek literature emerged as a historical reality in the sixth and fifth centuries BCE, Homer was already a standard of definition for this literature. In other words, the poetic figure of Homer was already a classic.

---

[1] My approach to such debates is outlined in *HR* 1–3.
[2] For alternatives to such ideas, see Graziosi 2002:90–93. I am in general agreement with her alternative ideas.
[3] *HTL* xi.

Prolegomena

PⓈ3. An evolutionary model

P§11 Before we set out to explore what historical and prehistorical forces could have made Homer such a classic, we must first ask ourselves what it was that made him different in each of these six ages. My answer, in its simplest form, is that Homeric poetry kept evolving throughout the ages. I highlight the word evolving. Here I turn to my earlier work, in which I developed an evolutionary model for the making of Homeric poetry, positing a tentative descriptive framework of five periods, "Five Ages of Homer," as it were. Unlike the six ages I have just listed, which go backward in time, the ages of this evolutionary model go forward in time. To avoid confusion with the six ages, I will from here on speak exclusively in terms of five periods of Homer, not five ages, whenever I refer to my evolutionary model. The details of that model have been worked out in two books I published in 1996.[4] Here I offer an outline, in its simplest form:

> Period 1 of Homer was a relatively most fluid period, with no written texts, extending from the early second millennium BCE to the middle of the eighth century in the first millennium BCE. When I say that this is a most fluid period, I mean that epic was most susceptible to change in this period of its evolution.

> Period 2 of Homer was a more formative or Panhellenic period, still without written texts, extending from the middle of the eighth century BCE to the middle of the sixth.[5]

> Period 3 of Homer was a definitive period, centralized in Athens, with potential texts in the sense of transcripts, extending from the middle of the sixth century BCE to the later part of the fourth. Somewhere near the start of this period, there was a reform of Homeric performance traditions in Athens.

> Period 4 of Homer was a standardizing period, with texts in the sense of transcripts or even scripts, extending from the later part of the fourth century BCE to the middle of the second. Somewhere near the start of this period, there was another reform of Homeric performance traditions in Athens.

---

[4] *PP* and *HQ*.
[5] On the term Panhellenic, see *HQ* 39–42.

Period 5 of Homer was a relatively most rigid period, with texts as <u>scripture</u>, from the middle of the second century BCE onward. This period starts with the completion of the editorial work of Aristarchus of Samothrace on the Homeric texts, not long after 150 BCE or so.

P§12 In this sequence of five periods, we see the intervention of what I call written texts, starting at period 3. The term <u>written text</u>, however, is too imprecise for my purposes, and I introduce the more precise terms <u>transcript</u>, <u>script</u>, <u>scripture</u>.[6] By <u>transcript</u> I mean the broadest possible category of written text: a transcript can be a record of performance, even an aid for performance, but not the equivalent of performance.[7] We must distinguish a transcript from an inscription, which can traditionally refer to itself in the archaic period as just that, an equivalent of performance.[8] As for <u>script</u>, I mean a narrower category, where the written text is a prerequisite for performance.[9] By <u>scripture</u> I mean the narrowest category of them all, where the written text need not even presuppose performance.[10]

P§13 To keep the relative chronology in focus, I now offer a composite outline that correlates the four chapters of *Homer the Classic* and the two parts of *Homer the Preclassic* with my evolutionary model of five periods of Homer:

> HC Chapter 1. Homer in the age of Virgil is to be situated within period 5 of Homer, which I just described as a relatively most rigid period. To repeat, when I say <u>most rigid</u> I mean that Homeric poetry was least susceptible to change in this period of its evolution.
>
> HC Chapter 2. Homer in the age of Callimachus is to be situated in period 4 of Homer, which I have described as a <u>standardizing period</u>. The term <u>standardizing</u> is meant to convey the idea of a movement toward standardization, not the actual achievement of a standard version of Homer. In the course of this standardizing period, there is an exceptional sub-period when the Homeric tradition is found to be in flux, fluctuating between older and newer standards. That sub-

---

[6] See *PP* 110 and following, with working definitions of the descriptive terms <u>transcript</u>, <u>script</u>, and <u>scripture</u>. Chapters 5 / 6 / 7 of *PP* focus respectively on <u>transcript</u> / <u>script</u> / <u>scripture</u>. See also *HQ* 41, where the same descriptive scheme of five consecutive periods is more explicitly situated in an overall evolutionary model.
[7] *HQ* 34–36, 65–69.
[8] *HQ* 34–36, with further citations.
[9] *PP* 153–186, *HQ* 32–34.
[10] *PP* 187–206.

period is what I call the age of Callimachus. The newer standard is represented by the age of Aristarchus in period 5, as explored in HC Chapter 1, while the older standard is represented by the age of Plato in period 3, as explored in HC Chapter 3. The age of Callimachus, as explored in HC Chapter 2, falls between these two standards.

HC Chapter 3. Homer in the age of Plato is to be situated within the later phases of period 3 of Homer, a <u>definitive period</u>. The term <u>definitive</u> is meant to convey the idea of an older standard version of Homer. This idea corresponds to what I call in this book the Koine of Homer.

HC Chapter 4. Homer in the age of Pheidias is to be situated within the earlier phases of period 3 of Homer. In this age as well, the idea of a standard version of Homer corresponds to what I call the Koine of Homer. We will consider the idea of such a Koine in the historical context of Athenian cultural hegemony, with specific reference to the appropriation of Homer by the Athenians. As I will argue, the state of Athens appropriated Homer as an expression of its imperial ideology.

HPC Part 1. Homer in the Dark Age is to be correlated with period 2 and with the later phases of period 1 of Homer.

HPC Part 2. Homer in the Bronze Age is to be correlated with the earlier phases of period 1 of Homer, a relatively most fluid period. To repeat, when I say <u>most fluid</u> I mean that the antecedent of what later became Homeric poetry was most susceptible to change in this period of its evolution.

P§14 Having outlined these six ages of Homer in terms of my evolutionary model, one age after the next, I will now restate my goal in these terms. My goal is to explore what made Homer a classic in the course of these six ages.

P⑤4. Metaphors of rigidity and definitiveness

P§15 I am working with two metaphors in this composite descriptive scheme: <u>rigidity</u> and <u>definitiveness</u>. In terms of the first metaphor, <u>rigidity</u>, we will proceed, overall, from the <u>most rigid</u> to the <u>most fluid</u> period of Homer as we move backward in time. I could have said instead: from <u>least fluid</u> to <u>least rigid</u>.

P⊛4. Metaphors of rigidity and definitiveness

From here on, however, I prefer to say that we are going from the relatively most rigid to the least rigid period of Homer. That is because I want to avoid formulations that oppose the terms rigid and fluid as polar opposites. Such a binary opposition would imply an absolute criterion that forces a choice between rigid and fluid. I need to make it clear that the metaphor of rigidity conveys a relative criterion, designed to measure varying degrees of rigidity or fluidity in the evolution of Homeric poetry. As we will see later on, moreover, there is one era that defies the general trend toward relatively more rigidity as we move forward in time: that era is what I am calling the age of Callimachus, which falls within the broader time frame of period 4. As for why I choose rigidity as the default term rather than fluidity, I will offer an explanation in Chapter 1.

P§16 More important, for the moment, is the second of my two operative metaphors, definitiveness. In this case, my general aim is to examine relative degrees of definitiveness in the status of Homer from one age to the next. I also have a specific aim, which is to trace the history of changes in the meaning of a Greek word that had once upon a time referred to the definitiveness of Homer. The word in question is the adjective *koinos* 'common, standard' and its derivatives, as applied to the transmission of Homer. In the chapters that follow, I will focus on the application of the feminine singular form, *koinē*, to the notionally unified text of Homer. The notion of such a text, such a Koine, will become increasingly relevant to my argumentation as we move historically backward in time from period 5 to period 3 of Homer.

P§17 In period 5, the significance of this word *koinē* was relatively simple, as we will see in Chapter 1 when we view a specific era within the broader time-frame of this period. The era is the age of Virgil. In this era, the singular *koinē* and the plural *koinai* were used to refer to 'common' manuscripts of the text of Homer. In the earlier period 3, by contrast, the significance of this same word *koinē* was far more complex. In the era of the Athenian empire, around the second half of the fifth century BCE, this same word *koinē* meant not only 'common' but 'standard', and these two meanings were not at all opposed to each other. As I hope to show in Chapter 4, this earlier usage reflects the combined cultural heritage of Athenian democracy and Athenian empire, in that the Koine version of Homer was once upon a time not only democratic but imperial.

P§18 I stop here for a moment to observe that the ideas of common and standard become opposites only if the standard loses its definitiveness. In the case of such a loss, the concept of common can become perceived as not standard but substandard, even vulgar.

P§19 For the present, in any case, it is enough for me to stress that the term Koine conveys a relative concept as it applies to Homer. In other words, translations like 'standard' and 'common' are relative criteria, not absolute ones, when we apply them to Homer. Earlier, when I described the so-called period 3 of Homer as definitive and period 4 as standardizing, I intended these descriptions to be understood as relative terms. In order to make this intention of mine more explicit, from here on I will describe periods 3 and 4 simply in terms of relatively more or less definitiveness, and I will extend the description further to period 5, which can be viewed as the relatively most definitive period of them all.

P§20 Having stressed the relativity inherent in my criteria of definitiveness and rigidity, I now proceed to apply them to the concept of Homer as a classic. This time, I am saying a classic, not the classic, because the term classic can be viewed as an absolute only from the synchronic standpoint of each Homeric period taken separately; it needs to be viewed as a relative term, however, from the diachronic standpoint of all Homeric periods taken together.[11]

P§21 By now I have streamlined my evolutionary model to indicate consecutive Homeric periods of increasing definiteness, which can be correlated with increasing rigidity. The one exception to the trend of increasing definitiveness and rigidity, as we will see in some detail when we reach Chapter 2, is the age of Callimachus, situated in period 4.

P§22 Having explained my two criteria of definitiveness and rigidity, I am ready to start with Homer in the age of Virgil, situated in period 5, which I describe as the relatively most definitive and most rigid period of Homer.

P§23 At this point I have reached a crossroads, where I offer readers a choice between two pathways of reading what follows overall. The longer way is to continue reading these Prolegomena, where I proceed to test the criteria of definitiveness and rigidity. The shorter way is to stop here and to skip ahead to Chapter 1 on Homer in the age of Virgil.

P§24 For those readers who have not yet decided at this point whether to go ahead and read the rest of the Prolegomena, I will now say in one sentence what I aim to do here. Essentially, I will be exploring the historical background of the actual text of Homer as we have it, outlining that background by tracing the usage of the word *koinē* with reference to the textual history of Homer. Having read this sentence, some may now decide not to confront the historical

[11] A synchronic standpoint is needed for viewing the current state of an existing structure, while a diachronic standpoint is needed for viewing different phases in the evolution of that structure. In *HR* 1, I offer background on the application of these terms synchronic and diachronic to Homeric studies.

background of the text, or to confront it perhaps only after reading the overall argumentation of the four chapters that follow the Prolegomena. For those who have made such a decision, now is the time to stop and to skip ahead to Chapter 1.

P⑤5. Aristarchus and the Homeric Koine

P§25 The term <u>Koine</u> corresponds to the word *koinē* as it was used by Aristarchus of Samothrace, director of the Library of Alexandria in the middle of the second century BCE, with specific reference to the classical or 'standard' text of Homer. The evidence comes mostly from the usage of the Aristarchean scholar Didymus, who flourished in the first century BCE.[12]

P§26 The idea of a Homeric Koine is approximated by the reality of the base text used by Aristarchus for his editing of Homer. To put it another way, the Homeric Koine was an idea that reached its ultimate form through the efforts of Aristarchus in seeking to build—or, as he thought, rebuild—the best possible base text for his editing of Homer. By <u>base text</u> here I mean simply the text that serves as the basis of the editing process.

P§27 The idea of a Homeric Koine can be reconstructed on the basis of analyzing the use of the actual word *koinē* / *koinai* in ancient sources. As we will see from the Homeric scholia, the word *koinē* / *koinai* was used as a default term for Homeric texts. I will argue that this usage stems from criteria applied by Aristarchus in his *hupomnēmata* 'commentaries' on Homer. By <u>Homer</u> here I mean a definitive base text of Homer, as built or rebuilt by Aristarchus.

P§28 The use of the word *koinē* / *koinai* in the Homeric scholia is complicated and potentially confusing, reflecting different critical trends stemming from different times—as represented by Didymus and Aristarchus. I start by offering an overview of these differences.

P§29 By the time of Didymus, in the first century BCE, the word *koinē* must have lost some of its definitiveness: he must have understood it to mean simply 'common'—and no longer necessarily 'standard'. Some sense of definitiveness was still felt, however, in the earlier time of Aristarchus, in the second century BCE. Faced with multiple *koinai* or 'common' texts of Homer, Aristarchus treated them as if they were all derived from a definitive and

---

[12] In the *Suda*, the life span of Didymus is described thus: γεγονὼς ἐπὶ Ἀντωνίου καὶ Κικέρωνος καὶ ἕως Αὐγούστου 'flourished in the era of Antonius and Cicero, up to the era of Augustus'. Pfeiffer 1968:256 comments on γεγονὼς as 'floruit'. More on Didymus in West 2001:48. By way of comparing dates traditionally ascribed to various scholars in this era, Cameron 1995:191n33 calculates that Didymus was born in 80 BCE and died in 1 BCE.

Prolegomena

notionally singular *koinē* or 'standard' version of Homer. His own base text of Homer was a reconstruction of such a *koinē*.

P§30 Before I proceed to examine specific applications of the term *koinē / koinai* in the Homeric scholia, I need to clarify further my terminology. I am saying that the ancient idea of a singular Koine of Homer, a core text, was tied to the reality of a base text that Aristarchus established for his editing of Homer. But the question remains: what exactly was this reality, as far as Aristarchus himself was concerned?

P§31 The reality of a <u>base text</u> as the editorial point of reference for Aristarchus is not to be confused with the modern idea of an <u>edited text</u> of Homer, where an editor reproduces, word for word, what Homer had supposedly created. We can see the essential difference between an ancient base text and a modern edited text of Homer when we review the methods developed by Aristarchus in confronting the problem of Homeric textual variants.

P§32 When modern editors of Homer are faced with a choice between two or more textual variants, they show in their edited text what they judge to be the correct variant, relegating the supposedly incorrect variant or variants to an <u>apparatus criticus</u>. By contrast, an ancient editor like Aristarchus displayed the sum total of his editorial judgments—that is, his *diorthōsis* 'correction'— only in his *hupomnēmata* 'commentaries', not in his base text.

P§33 But there is more to it. When it came to deciding which variant to show in his base text, Aristarchus allowed the external evidence of Homeric texts described as *koinai* 'common' to override the internal evidence—as he saw it—of Homeric usage. As a rule, he would show in his base text the variant that reflected what he understood to be the *koinē* or 'standard' version of Homer—even if he preferred another variant on the basis of internal evidence.

P§34 What I mean by external evidence is this: Aristarchus actually assembled and collated a wide variety of Homeric texts. This aspect of Aristarchean research is sometimes not recognized.[13] Moreover, as I am about to argue, Aristarchus relied on a consensus of *koinai* texts in order to build—or, as he thought, rebuild—a definitive base text, which for him was tantamount to what I am calling the Koine version of Homer. In other words, Aristarchus posited as his base text of Homer a notionally singular and unified Koine—a *koinē* or 'standard' version that needed to be restored by way of 'correction' or *diorthōsis* of texts. In order to build such a singular *koinē*, Aristarchus would have had to assemble and collate a number of *koinai* texts.

---

[13] For example, West 2001:46–85 thinks that Aristarchus neither collected nor collated Homeric texts. For counterarguments, see *HTL* 87–109; also Rengakos 2002, Montanari 2002a, and 2004a.

P⑤6. Homeric *koinai* and *khariesterai*

P§35 As we see from the reportage of Didymus, mediated by the Homeric scholia, Aristarchus also assembled and collated a number of less common Homeric texts, described as *khariesterai*, that is, 'having more *kharis*' or 'more graceful' than the *koinai* texts.[14] The concept of *kharis*, which conveys the idea of beauty and the pleasure that goes with it, can be translated as 'pleasurable beauty, grace, gracefulness'. Its adjectival form, *kharieis* 'graceful', was for Aristarchean critics a criterion for determining which version of the Homeric text was most likely to be genuinely Homeric. This criterion did not originate with the Aristarchean critics in the first or even in the second century BCE: as we will see later on, it can be traced as far back as the fourth century BCE. For now, however, I concentrate on the actual opposition between *koinai* and *khariesterai*.

P§36 I start with the *khariesterai*. The implied noun that goes with *khariesterai* is *graphai* in the sense of 'texts' (as we see in the explicit combinations ἐν δὲ ταῖς χαριεστέραις γραφαῖς in the scholia for *Odyssey* i 356 and αἱ χαριέστεραι γραφαί in the scholia for *Odyssey* xi 196). From the Homeric scholia, which reflect primarily the reportage of the Aristarchean scholar Didymus, we can see that there were basically two kinds of *khariesterai* texts of Homer:

(1) the editions of two pre-Aristarchean editors of Homer, namely, Zenodotus of Ephesus (third century BCE) and Aristophanes of Byzantium (second century BCE), as well as other texts derived from even earlier figures such as Rhianos of Crete (third century BCE) and Antimachus of Colophon (fifth/fourth centuries BCE)[15]

(2) the so-called *politikai* or 'city editions' stemming from Massalia (Marseille), Chios, Argos, Sinope, Cyprus, and Crete.[16]

---

[14] That Aristarchus actively assembled and collated *khariesterai* texts is argued in *HR* 4–7; see also Rengakos 2002, Montanari 2002a and 2004a.

[15] I offer an overview in *HTL* 87–109.

[16] Again, I offer an overview in *HTL* 87–109. See Rengakos 2002 on scholia A for *Iliad* XIX 386b1, where the testimony of Didymus indicates that Aristarchus himself must have consulted the *politikai* 'city editions'. For the relative dating of the *politikai*, see Citti 1966. For a defense of the authenticity of variant readings found in the *politikai*, see *PP* 147–148, following Citti 1966. For further comments, see Haslam 1997:69–71. West 2001:67 notes that the Homeric scholia nowhere refer to the *politikai* in terms of a *diorthōsis*. So perhaps they are 'uncorrected' texts. In other words, perhaps they are texts that have not undergone the editorial procedures of *diorthōsis* 'correction'. As I note in *PP* 116n46, however, there is one place where the *politikai* are called *ekdoseis* (scholia A for *Iliad* III 10, with reference to the Homer texts from Chios and Massalia).

Prolegomena

The *khariesterai* texts were supposedly better than the texts known as *koinai* 'common' (as we see from the use of *koinai* in the scholia A for *Iliad* IV 170). The *koinai* texts were otherwise known as *dēmōdeis* 'popular' (scholia A for *Iliad* V 881a1).

P§37 In the critical discourse of Aristarchean scholars, *antigrapha* 'copies' of texts judged to be *khariestera* were expected to contain written forms that were *khariestera*, as opposed to copies judged to be *koina*:

P⓵1 Scholia for *Odyssey* xvii 160

ἐν τοῖς χαριεστέροις οὗτοι μόνοι οἱ β' ἀθετοῦνται ... ἐν δὲ τοῖς κοινοτέροις ἀπὸ τοῦ ὣς ἔφατο ἕως τοῦ ἐξ ἐμεῦ.

In the *khariestera* only these two lines are athetized[17] [= *Odyssey* xvii 160–161]. ... But in the *koinotera* [there is athetesis] from ὣς ἔφατο [at the beginning of xvii 150] all the way to ἐξ ἐμεῦ [at the beginning of xvii 165].

P§38 Here the *antigrapha* 'copies' that are *khariestera* athetize[18] only two verses (xvii 160–161), while the *antigrapha* that are *koina* (= *koinotera* by comparison with the *khariestera*) athetize sixteen verses (xvii 150–165).

P§39 For Aristarchus, the existence of Homeric *graphai* 'texts' described as *khariesterai* and therefore judged to be better than other Homeric texts that were *koinai* 'common' did not rule out the possibility that even ordinary texts occasionally contained variants judged to be better. Conversely, variants judged to be ordinary could occur even in supposedly better texts. Examples include some variants that Aristarchus judged to be *koinai* even though he found them in the Homeric *ekdosis* 'edition' of Zenodotus, whose text he judged to be one of the *khariesterai*. Such variants stemming from the *ekdosis* of Zenodotus in the third century BCE were *koinai* in comparison to variants stemming from the *ekdosis* of Aristophanes in the second century, with whom Aristarchus agreed more often than with Zenodotus. Generally, the editions of both Zenodotus (scholia A for *Iliad* II 579; AT for *Iliad* VII 428a1) and Aristophanes (scholia A for *Iliad* II 53a1) adduced variants judged to be *khariesterai*, but Zenodotus was considered to be less consistent and less thorough than Aristophanes—if we apply an Aristarchean standard when it comes to finding *khariesterai* as alternatives to the *koinai* (scholia T for *Iliad* II 53a2).

---

[17] I postpone till P§46 my discussion of the terms athetesis and athetize.
[18] See the previous note.

P§40 The editorial methods of Aristarchus resembled most closely those of Aristophanes.[19] Still, his own methods were superior, because he made a special effort to develop a broader data base of textual variants by way of assembling and collating a variety of texts (*graphai*)—not only *khariesterai* but also *koinai*.

P§41 Through the *khariesterai*, Aristarchus achieved a superior view of degrees of multiformity in the textual history of Homeric poetry. Through the *koinai*, he achieved a superior view of degrees of uniformity. The relative multiformity of the *khariesterai* is a generally recognized fact, but not so the relative uniformity of the *koinai*.

P§42 I will offer a variety of arguments to support what I just said about the *koinai*. In the next paragraph, I begin with an overall formulation, which is meant as an alternative to another formulation that has received wide currency.[20]

P§43 Aristarchus distinguished himself from his predecessors by demonstrating, on the basis of the textual evidence he assembled and collated, that the consensus of the *koinai* texts recovers a Koine text. This Koine was not the real Homer for Aristarchus, but it was the base text from which a real Homer could be reconstructed by way of extensive analysis and debate in his *hupomnēmata* 'commentaries'. The text of the real Homer as he saw it was latent in the relative multiformity of the *khariesterai* texts, and this multiformity could be displayed only in the background, that is, only in his commentaries. By contrast, the text of the Koine was overt in the relative uniformity of the *koinai* texts, and this uniformity could be displayed in the foreground, that is, in the base text. The ultimately real Homer could take shape only through a process of further selection, emerging from a background of relative multiformity in the *khariesterai* texts, while the Koine text had already achieved its shape through a process of consensus, evident in the foreground of relative uniformity in the *koinai* texts. For Aristarchus, an accurate picture of this consensus was the basis for reconstructing the text of a genuine Homer that transcended this consensus. In other words, the Koine as a consensus of *koinai* texts was the basis for reconstructing this supposedly genuine Homer through the variants provided by the *khariesterai* texts.

P§44 Here I need to return to a point I made earlier about the base text of Aristarchus: it approximated such a Koine text. Aristarchus kept out of this base text the special forms he found in the *khariesterai* texts, privileging the

---

[19] Montanari 2002a:124–127.
[20] Haslam 1997:71, following S. West 1967:26.

Prolegomena

consensus emerging from the forms he found in the *koinai* texts. He would express his own editorial preferences only in his *hupomnēmata* 'commentaries'. Only where variations did not affect the content did Aristarchus make decisive choices in the external appearance of his base text. I will consider some of these choices later on, but for now the focus remains on the point I am making about the base text of Aristarchus. This base text approximated the Koine of Homer.

P§45 The rationale of Aristarchus in building or rebuilding such a Koine by way of collecting and collating *koinai* texts can be explained as his active response to two kinds of variation in Homeric textual transmission, (1) "vertical" and (2) "horizontal."[21]

P⑤7. "Vertical" variation and the *numerus versuum*

P§46 Aristarchus included in his base text of Homer even those verses he suspected of being non-Homeric. That is, he included any such verses *if the given verses were strongly attested*. The term strong attestation here refers to situations where attested verses were well represented in the Homeric manuscripts that Aristarchus assembled and collated.[22] Verses that he admitted on these grounds but suspected on other grounds were athetized by him, that is, they were marked by a marginal sign. This sign, also used by his predecessor, Zenodotus, was the *obelos* (–). The *obelos*, placed in the margin to the left of an athetized verse, cross-referred to the relevant analysis of Aristarchus in his *hupomnēmata* 'commentaries', where he would give his reasons for rejecting the given verse as not genuinely Homeric. It is essential to stress, from the start, that verses athetized by Aristarchus were included, not excluded, in his text of Homer—that is, in his base text.

P§47 To be distinguished from the athetized verses are the excluded verses: Aristarchus excluded from his base text of Homer verses he judged to be non-Homeric—*if the given verses were only weakly attested*. The term weak attestation here refers to situations where attested verses were not so well represented in the Homeric manuscripts that Aristarchus assembled and collated.[23] These are the verses known today as the plus verses.[24]

---

[21] I introduced these concepts in Nagy 2000a; see also HTL 54, 56, 59–64, 66, 73.
[22] See also in general Apthorp 1980.
[23] See the previous note.
[24] Apthorp 1980:xv. See also HTL 36. Later on, in ch. 2, I focus on one particular plus verse, *Iliad* XIV 246a. That verse, concerning the Ōkeanos, was excluded from the base text of Aristarchus.

P⒮7. "Vertical" variation and the *numerus versuum*

P§48 Occasionally, we learn from reportage in the Homeric scholia that a given plus verse had been explicitly rejected in the Homer edition of Zenodotus by way of deletion, not by mere athetesis.[25] Here we see an essential difference between the base texts of Zenodotus and Aristarchus. Zenodotus had developed an editorial system that allowed him to choose between either athetizing a suspected verse, by way of an *obelos*, or deleting it, by way of various deletion marks and brief annotations that accompanied these marks.[26]

P§49 The base text of Homer as edited by Zenodotus actually included not only the verses athetized by him but also the plus verses marked with signs indicating the editor's deletion.[27] By contrast, the base text of Homer as edited by Aristarchus excluded the plus verses altogether, and this policy of exclusion eliminated the need for signs indicating deletion.[28] Also eliminated from Aristarchus' base text were comments written into the margins, which were replaced by extensive *hupomnēmata* 'commentaries' written into separate scrolls.[29] The commentaries of Aristarchus were correlated with an expanding set of marginal signs in the base text, indicating a variety of editorial judgments.[30] These signs could help the reader navigate between the base text of Homer as displayed by Aristarchus and the separate text of his commentaries, where all his editorial judgments about all the textual variations could be fully discussed.[31] In short, the base text of Aristarchus was more streamlined than that of Zenodotus. As for the base text of Aristophanes, it was almost as streamlined as that of Aristarchus himself.[32] In what follows, I will explain why I qualify my statement.

P§50 The differences between the length of the base texts of Aristophanes and Aristarchus on the one hand and the length of the base texts of Zenodotus on the other hand are an example of what I call vertical variation.

P§51 The relatively exclusive base text of Aristarchus adhered to a notionally fixed and standard verse-count, and there seems to have been

---

[25] Montanari 2002a:124 says: "The plus-verses present in the Zenodotean text were not his own interpolations but were instead typical of exemplars that were current in his day." West 2001:40n33 offers a list of such plus-verses: *Iliad* I 69ab, III 338a, V 808, VIII 52a–d, X 349, XIII 808a, XIV 136a, XVII 456a, XVIII 156a.
[26] Montanari 2002a:120–125.
[27] Montanari 2002a:124.
[28] Montanari 2002a:124–125.
[29] Montanari 2002a:124.
[30] Montanari 2002a:125.
[31] Montanari 2002a:125.
[32] Montanari 2002a:124.

Prolegomena

a nearly identical verse-count in the base text used by Aristophanes.[33] I say nearly identical rather than identical because, as I will argue, Aristarchus must have surpassed Aristophanes in the assembling and collecting of Homeric texts. Such a fixed verse-count is the *numerus versuum*.[34]

P§52 To justify this working definition of the *numerus versuum*, I recall the fact that Aristarchus included in his base text the verses that he athetized by marking them with an *obelos*. To repeat, this base text was the sum total of non-athetized and athetized verses. Further, this base text represented the consensus of the *koinai* texts that Aristarchus assembled and collated. Such a consensus of many *koinai* texts was the closest approximation of a single *koinē* text, and this notionally single Koine showed a fixed verse-count. To repeat, such a fixed verse-count is the *numerus versuum*.

P§53 What Aristarchus confirmed by way of assembling and collating his samples of *koinai* texts was that they tended to conform to such a fixed verse-count, the *numerus versuum*, whereas the *khariesterai* texts did not (we see examples in the scholia for *Odyssey* i 356, xvii 160). The consistency of this fixed verse-count, the *numerus versuum*, became more and more of a reality in the actual process of assembling and collating more and more samples of *koinai* texts. For Aristarchus, the singularity of the *numerus versuum* emerged out of the plurality of the *koinai* texts. The singularity of this *numerus versuum* corresponded to the singularity of the Homeric Koine. In other words, the Koine that Aristarchus built or rebuilt from the *koinai* texts turned out to be a reality—something that had a fixed verse-count. That is the essence of the *numerus versuum*.

P§54 In short, my argument is that the *numerus versuum* of the base text of Aristarchus and, before him, of Aristophanes, was inherited from a preexisting Homeric Koine. The exactitude of Aristarchus in reconstructing this Koine would have surpassed the exactitude of Aristophanes for this simple reason: Aristarchus assembled and collated more texts than did his predecessor.

P§55 The standard verse-count of the Homeric Koine version of Homer—the *numerus versuum*—was not the same thing as the verse-count of the ostensibly real Homer as reconstructed by Aristarchus the editor. In his commentaries, Aristarchus systematically explained his reasons for rejecting as non-Homeric the verses that he athetized in his base text, marking these verses there with the *obelos*; to be contrasted are the plus verses, which he

---

[33] Montanari 2002a:124.

[34] For an overview of this concept of *numerus versuum*, see PP 138–140, 143–144, 155, following especially Apthorp 1980.

simply excluded from his base text.³⁵ For Aristarchus, the real text of the real Homer was whatever number of verses would be left over after he subtracted the number of verses that he athetized or deleted. Such a text would have a verse-count far lower than the standard verse-count of the standard Homer. That standard Homer was the Koine, and its standard verse-count was the *numerus versuum*.

P§56 The supposedly real Homer of Aristarchus was not the only Homeric text with a verse-count that was far lower than the standard *numerus versuum* of the Koine. If we could subtract the number of verses that Zenodotus had athetized from the total number of verses in his base text of Homer, the resulting verse-count would be even lower. But the essential difference between the verse-counts of Aristarchus and Zenodotus is to be sought elsewhere. As we will see in Chapter 2, the number of verses in the edition of Zenodotus, if we subtracted only the verses he excluded but not the verses he athetized, would have exceeded the number of verses produced by Aristarchus in his own edition, which was a number that corresponded to the *numerus versuum* of the Koine. In terms of the ongoing argumentation, this *numerus versuum* could be recovered only because Aristarchus actually had a working procedure for collating the Homeric texts available to him.

P§57 As for the verse-count of Aristophanes, it would have been based on an earlier form of the procedure that was later to be perfected by Aristarchus. In this respect and in many others as well, the Homer edition of Aristarchus was far closer to the edition of Aristophanes and much farther apart from the edition of Zenodotus.³⁶

P§58 Crates of Mallos, who was director of the library of Pergamon during roughly the same period when Aristarchus was director of the library of Alexandria, was likewise engaged in the editorial practice of athetizing Homeric verses, that is, rejecting verses on the grounds that they are non-genuine, non-Homeric.³⁷ But the number of verses in the base text of Crates—as also of Zenodotus—exceeded the standard verse-count or *numerus versuum* of the Homeric Koine, whereas the base text of Aristarchus adhered to it.³⁸ In contrast to the base text of Aristarchus, which followed the *numerus versuum*, the augmented base text of Crates—as also of Zenodotus—corresponded to what I call the <u>Homerus Auctus</u>. I will explain in Chapter 2 what I mean by

---

³⁵ *HTL* 54, 56, 59–64.
³⁶ Montanari 2002a:124–127.
³⁷ LP (Nagy 1998) 213–228.
³⁸ LP (Nagy 1998) 213–228.

Prolegomena

this term. For now, I simply summarize the emerging patterns of distinctions between the editorial approaches of Crates and Aristarchus:[39]

A) Both men athetized verses, but both included in their texts the verses that they athetized.

B) Aristarchus athetized more verses than Crates.

C) Aristarchus also omitted verses that Crates included; or, to put it differently, Crates had access to texts containing some verses that Aristarchus could not or would not verify on the basis of the texts to which he had access. These extra verses correspond to what I have been calling plus verses.

D) Both men tracked variant readings within the verses, recording them and commenting on them in their formal commentaries (*hupomnēmata / diorthōtika*). Needless to say, the "same" verse containing different variant readings was a "different" verse as far as Aristarchus and Crates were concerned.[40]

E) Aristarchus used a system of signs, affixed at the left-hand margins of his text, to indicate his editorial differences with Crates— as also with his own Alexandrian predecessors, especially with Zenodotus and with Aristophanes of Byzantium.[41]

P§59 Earlier, I noted that the base text of Aristarchus included verses he personally judged to be non-Homeric—*if such verses were strongly attested*. Now I need to stress again that the very concept of a strong attestation was possible only because Aristarchus had assembled and collated texts that he judged to be *koinai* 'common'—not only the less common texts that he judged to be supe-

---

[39] For a general survey, see Fraser 1972 II 674, with reference to the discussion of Pfeiffer 1968:239–242. Pfeiffer sums up this way (p. 242): "Even this short survey of scanty evidence gives the impression that Crates was a serious scholar capable of displaying solid learning who did not disregard the results of previous research, even though it was the work of scholars who were his opponents in principle." See also in general Wachsmuth 1860 and Broggiato 2001.

[40] The editorial disagreements of Crates and Aristarchus extend to the textual tradition of Hesiod and other classics as well. For an illuminating example, see the discussion of the variant readings mentioned by Crates (and also by Zenodotus) at Hesiod *Theogony* 5, as summarized by West 1966:153–154. I do not share, however, West's assumptions about the methodology of Crates: for example, West p. 208 accuses Crates, without justification, of making up a verse (a variant of the medieval manuscript reading adopted by West for *Theogony* 142).

[41] See in general McNamee 1992; also McNamee 1981. Diogenes Laertius 3.66 says that owners of texts featuring margins marked up with signs could get away with charging fees from readers who wished to have access to such texts. I will discuss these signs in ch. 2.

rior and therefore *khariesterai* 'having more *kharis*' or 'more graceful'. As I have argued, the base text of Aristarchus was built from a consensus of manuscript readings found in Homeric texts that Aristarchus judged to be *koinai*, not *khariesterai*. Such a consensus, as we are about to see, was needed as a control not only in the case of <u>vertical variation</u>. It was needed also in the case of <u>horizontal variation</u>.

P⒮8. "Horizontal" variation

P§60 The equivalence of the base text of Aristarchus with the singularity of what I call the Homeric Koine extends beyond patterns of consistency in verse-counts, that is, beyond patterns of conformity to the standard of a *numerus versuum*. Besides confronting the "vertical" textual variations of more or fewer verses in any given sequence of Homeric verses, Aristarchus in his *hupomnēmata* 'commentaries' also confronted the "horizontal" textual variations, that is, variant wordings within the frame of any given verse.[42] For his base text, Aristarchus sought a consensus among <u>horizontal</u> as well as <u>vertical</u> variations.

P§61 Wherever the <u>horizontal variations</u> of wording significantly affected the content of any given Homeric verse, Aristarchus retained in his base text the wording that best reflected the consensus of the *koinai* texts, while he adduced the variant wordings only in his commentaries.[43] That is, he retained in his base text the wording he found in the *koinai* texts—*if that given wording was strongly attested*. The term <u>strong attestation</u> here refers to the testimony of the majority of the Homeric manuscripts that Aristarchus assembled and collated.[44]

P§62 As I noted earlier, only where variations did not significantly affect the content did Aristarchus make his own choices in his base text. Many of these choices had to do with external appearances, as I will show later on. For now, however, I continue to concentrate on the idea of the base text of Aristarchus as a consensus of *koinai* texts. As we will see from the <u>horizontal</u> as well as the <u>vertical</u> dimension of textual variations, there is an equivalence between this base text of Aristarchus and the standard of what I am calling the Homeric Koine.

---

[42] Nagy 2000a.
[43] Nagy 2000a. *HTL* ch. 3.
[44] Relevant are the scholia A for *Iliad* IX 222b; also the scholia A for *Iliad* II 665a and XVI 467c1.

P§63 In some cases, Aristarchus seems to have re-introduced into his base text a Koine reading that had earlier given way to a reading judged to be *khariesteron* 'having more *kharis*' in the base text of his predecessor Aristophanes (scholia A for *Iliad* II 53a1). In such cases, the re-introduction of the Koine reading could have been caused by the availability of more evidence from the *koinai*. What I noted in the case of vertical variations applies also here in the case of horizontal variations: the exactitude of Aristarchus in reconstructing the Koine would have surpassed the exactitude of Aristophanes—to the extent that Aristarchus assembled and collated more texts than did Aristophanes.

P§64 Although Aristarchus conformed to the standard of the Koine, later generations of Aristarcheans preferred a different standard, attributed to Aristarchus himself. In the case of vertical textual variations, there was no serious difference between the two standards, in that the number of verses in the base text of Aristarchus—which included the verses athetized by him but which excluded the plus verses—matched the *numerus versuum* of the Koine. Later generations of Aristarcheans may have agreed or disagreed with the decisions of athetesis made by Aristarchus, but, even if they disagreed, they would not exclude the athetized verses from consideration, just as Aristarchus did not exclude them from his base text. In the case of horizontal textual variations, on the other hand, the variant wordings as reported by Aristarchus in his commentaries could easily infiltrate the base text, actually ousting the wordings inherited by the Koine. Such is the state of affairs already in the time of Didymus. By his time, in the first century BCE, the authority of wordings found in the Koine had already given way to the authority of variant wordings preferred by Aristarchus himself—wordings originally confined to the master's *hupomnēmata* 'commentaries'. For Aristarcheans like Didymus, the preferred readings of Aristarchus became more significant than the received readings of the Koine.

P§65 Such a shift from the Koine standard to an Aristarchean standard is a source of confusion for editors of the Homeric scholia—and even for editors of the Homeric *Iliad* and *Odyssey*. When Aristarchus quoted a *lēmma*, that is, an 'extract' from the Homeric text that provided the headline for editorial discussion in the Aristarchean commentaries, that *lēmma* referred predictably to the wording of his base text, which reflected the Koine (we see an example in the scholia A for *Iliad* I 465b). When Didymus quotes a *lēmma*, on the other hand, we find that such a *lēmma* may refer to variant readings originally reported by Aristarchus in his *hupomnēmata* 'commentaries' (we see an example in the scholia A for *Iliad* XII 404a). The distinction between *lēmmata* derived from the base text and *lēmmata* derived from the commentaries of Aristarchus thus becomes blurred in the Homeric scholia.

P⑤9. Homeric editions attributed to Aristarchus

P§66 The privileging of the Aristarchean standard in the Homeric scholia is linked with the fact that Didymus, one of the primary sources of the scholia, relied heavily on two manuscripts that featured base texts containing alterations derived from the *hupomnēmata* 'commentaries' of Aristarchus. Such alterations, reflecting the preferred readings of Aristarchus, displaced the received readings of the Koine. The two manuscripts in question, in the terminology of Didymus, were *hē Aristarkheios* 'the Aristarchean' and *hē hetera Aristarkheios* 'the other Aristarchean' (scholia A for *Iliad* II 579). The noun implied by these adjectives is *ekdosis* 'edition'. Didymus refers to both of these *ekdoseis* 'editions' as *khariesterai* 'having more *kharis*' (scholia A for *Iliad* II 12a). The combined testimony of these two *ekdoseis* is described as *khariesteron* (scholia AT for *Iliad* VII 428a1). Within this exclusive category of two distinct Aristarchean *ekdoseis* 'editions', we find differences in content. There are occasions, for example, where a variant reading in one of these two *ekdoseis* is different from the variant reading in the other.[45] It also happens that the variant reading preferred in one of the two *ekdoseis* is described as *khariestera* in comparison to the variant reading preferred in the other (scholia A for *Iliad* II 579). It even happens that one of the two *ekdoseis*, in giving a variant reading that differs from the variant reading given in the other, is described as *khariestera* in comparison to the other (scholia for *Odyssey* iv 727).

P§67 The usage of Didymus concerning these two *ekdoseis* 'editions' that he attributes to Aristarchus is relevant to what we learn from the titles of two monographs produced by Aristarchus' successor, Ammonius of Alexandria: (1) περὶ τοῦ μὴ γεγονέναι πλείονας ἐκδόσεις τῆς Ἀριστάρχειου διορθώσεως 'About the fact that there did not exist more [*pleiones*] *ekdoseis* of the Aristarchean *diorthōsis*' (via Didymus in scholia A for *Iliad* X 397–399a) and (2) περὶ τῆς ἐπεκδοθείσης διορθώσεως 'About the *diorthōsis* that underwent an *epekdosis*' (via Didymus in scholia A for *Iliad* XIX 365–368a). I offer comments about each of these two titles, in reverse order:

---

[45] West 2001:61n44 gives a list of the references by Didymus to two distinct readings in these two *ekdoseis* of Aristarchus.

Prolegomena

(1) For a working translation, I use the noun '*epekdosis*' in rendering the concept conveyed by the verb *epekdidonai* (ἐπεκδοθείσης) in the title attached to the second of the two monographs by Ammonius. We find this word *epekdidonai* attested nowhere else in extant Greek texts.

(2) There has been an ongoing debate over the meaning of the title attached to the first of the two monographs. The question is, did Ammonius claim that there did not exist 'more [*pleiones*] *ekdoseis* beyond the existing single *ekdosis*' or 'more [*pleiones*] *ekdoseis* beyond the existing two *ekdoseis*'? If the second of these two interpretations were correct, then ἐπεκδοθείσης in the title of the second monograph would refer to the second of two *ekdoseis* 'editions' supposedly produced by Aristarchus himself. In that case, the coined word '*epekdosis*' in my working translation of ἐπεκδοθείσης would be interpreted to mean something like a 'subsequent edition'.[46] If the first interpretation is correct, however, then Ammonius had in mind simply an ongoing process of *diorthōsis* or '[editorial] correcting', as opposed to two separate *ekdoseis* 'editions'.[47] In terms of this alternative interpretation, the coined word '*epekdosis*' in my working translation of ἐπεκδοθείσης would be interpreted to mean something like a 're-editing' of an already existing 'edition' or *ekdosis*.[48] In what follows, I will support this interpretation, 're-editing'.

P§68 I start by noting that Didymus, who as we saw makes use of two *ekdoseis* that he thinks are Aristarchean, recognizes the divergent thinking of Ammonius, the successor of Aristarchus. In the scholia A for *Iliad* X 397–399a, we see that Didymus distances himself from Ammonius: εἴ τι χρὴ πιστεύειν Ἀμμωνίῳ τῷ διαδεξαμένῳ τὴν σχολήν, ἐν τῷ Περὶ τοῦ μὴ γεγονέναι πλείονας ἐκδόσεις τῆς Ἀριστάρχου διορθώσεως τοῦτο φάσκοντι '... if one should to any extent believe Ammonius, the one who took over the School, in his volume entitled "About the fact that there did not exist more [*pleiones*] than one *ekdosis* of the Aristarchean *diorthōsis*," when he says this ...'.

P§69 Despite the divergence between Didymus and Ammonius in their respective views about the number of *ekdoseis* made by Aristarchus, we can also see an important convergence: Didymus and Ammonius have in common a sustained interest in the question of earlier and later phases in the editorial work of Aristarchus. In the same context that I just cited from scholia A

---

[46] This interpretation, as entertained by West 2001:62–63, is criticized by Montanari 2002a:126n24.
[47] Montanari 2002a:126; see also Nagy 2003b:488, with reference to Montanari 1998:11–20.
[48] Montanari 2002a:126.

P⑤9. Homeric editions attributed to Aristarchus

for *Iliad* X 397-399a, Didymus cites Ammonius as his authority in reporting that Aristarchus preferred one variant in an earlier phase of his editorial work and another variant in a later phase: Ἀμμώνιος δὲ ὁ Ἀριστάρχειος πρῶτον μὲν στιγμαῖς φησι τὸν Ἀρίσταρχον παρασημειώσασθαι αὐτούς, εἶτα δὲ καὶ τελέως ἐξελεῖν 'Ammonius the Aristarchean says that Aristarchus first marked these verses with signs in the margins, but then, at a later point, he took them out completely'.

P§70 What we have just seen is the first of three examples I have found where Didymus consults Ammonius as an authority in determining earlier and later phases in the editorial work of Aristarchus. Two of the three examples, including this first one, involve vertical variation, while the third, as we will see later, involves horizontal variation.

P§71 Now we come to the second of the three examples. Here we find Didymus himself in the act of reporting on different variants found in earlier and later phases of the editorial work of Aristarchus, and in this case he says he finds no relevant report from Ammonius (scholia A for *Iliad* XIX 365-368a1): ὁ δὲ Σιδώνιος ἠθετηκέναι μὲν τὸ πρῶτόν φησιν αὐτοὺς τὸν Ἀρίσταρχον, ὕστερον δὲ περιελεῖν τοὺς ὀβελούς, ποιητικὸν νομίσαντα τὸ τοιοῦτο. ὁ μέντοι Ἀμμώνιος ἐν τῷ Περὶ τῆς ἐπεκδοθείσης διορθώσεως οὐδὲν τοιοῦτο λέγει '[Dionysius] the man from Sidon says that Aristarchus first athetized them [= the verses under consideration], but then, at a later point, removed the obeloi [= the marginal signs indicating athetesis], thinking that such a thing [= what he had athetized] was a poetic creation [of Homer]; Ammonius, on the other hand, in his treatise "About the re-edited [*ep-ekdidonai*] *diorthōsis*," says no such thing'.

P§72 As for the third of the three examples, we find Didymus making a distinction between one horizontal variant (μέγα) found in 'some of the commentaries' of Aristarchus (scholia A for *Iliad* II 111b κατά τινα τῶν ὑπομνημάτων) and a second variant (μέγας) found in 'one of his commentaries that has been corrected for greater accuracy' (ἔν τινι τῶν ἠκριβωμένων ὑπομνημάτων); in this context, Didymus notes that Ammonius and another expert, Dionysodorus, attest the second variant but have nothing to say in addition to what Aristarchus had already said about it: καὶ τοὺς ἀπ' αὐτοῦ δὲ χρωμένους ἔστιν εὑρεῖν τῇ γραφῇ Διονυσόδωρον καὶ Ἀμμώνιον τὸν Ἀλεξανδρέα. ἐπιλέγουσι δὲ οὐδέν· διὸ καὶ τὰς μαρτυρίας αὐτῶν οὐκ ἐγράψαμεν 'and it is possible to ascertain that those who use the way of writing it [= that variant form] that came from him [= Aristarchus] include Dionysodorus and Ammonius of Alexandria, but they have nothing to say in addition, and so I did not write down their testimonies'. To summarize what is being said by

Didymus here (scholia A for *Iliad* II 111b): Ammonius and Dionysodorus use the second of two horizontal variants (μέγας vs. μέγα) adduced by Aristarchus, but they add no further information about this second variant, and so the wording of their testimony is not copied out.

P§73 In the third of these three examples we have just considered, I draw attention to a most significant additional detail. We see Didymus himself making a distinction here not only between earlier and later phases in the editorial work of his predecessor Aristarchus in general but also between earlier and later phases in the predecessor's actual *hupomnēmata* 'commentaries' in particular.[49] This distinction needs to be correlated with another distinction made elsewhere by Didymus—between earlier and later *ekdoseis* corresponding to earlier and later phases of the Aristarchean *hupomnēmata*. According to Didymus, Aristarchus based the earlier phases of his *hupomnēmata* not on an *ekdosis* of his own but on the previous *ekdosis* of Aristophanes (scholia A for *Iliad* II 133a ἐν τοῖς κατ' Ἀριστοφάνην ὑπομνήμασιν Ἀριστάρχου).[50] This statement of Didymus has led to the inference that Aristarchus went on to produce his own *ekdosis* only at a later point in his career, corresponding to a later point in his continuing editorial work as reflected in his *hupomnēmata*.[51] Such an *ekdosis* by Aristarchus would be tantamount to a 'publication' of his own *diorthōsis* 'corrective editing' of Homer. Relatively earlier and later sets of Aristarchean *hupomnēmata*, let us call them H1 and H2, could then be correlated with respectively earlier and later phases of Aristarchus' *diorthōsis*, let us call them D1 and D2. According to one reconstruction, the sequence would be H1 D1 H2 D2.[52] In terms of such a sequence, the claims of Ammonius could be restated this way: he preferred to think of two distinct phases in the history of a single Aristarchean *ekdosis* of Homer, while others claimed—wrongly, according to Ammonius—that there were two distinct *ekdoseis* made by Aristarchus. An heir to such an alternative line of thinking was Didymus,

---

[49] Montanari 2002a:125.
[50] Montanari 2002a:125. The reading given in the edition of Aristophanes was evidently Ἰλίου, which is likewise given in the *lēmma* by scholia A for *Iliad* II 133a; it is also the reading of the vast majority of the medieval manuscripts. Evidently it is the Koine reading, as opposed to the variant Ἴλιον found by Aristarchus and recorded in his earliest *hupomnēmata*.
[51] Montanari 1998:11–20. In Nagy 2000a, reviewing West 1998b, I summarized the relevance of the observations made by Montanari.
[52] Montanari 1998:19. I added in Nagy 2002a the following remark. "But I am not sure that we need to infer, as Montanari does (p. 19), that the contents of D2 were written into the same 'copy' that contained the contents of D1."

P⑨9. Homeric editions attributed to Aristarchus

for whom there existed two *ekdoseis*, one of which was earlier than the other. In fact, Didymus explicitly refers to one of the two Aristarchean *ekdoseis* as *hē protera* 'the previous one' (scholia T for *Iliad* XIX 365-368a2). Moreover, Didymus makes this reference in the same context where he refers also to the work of Ammonius about the '*epekdosis*' of the Aristarchean text. Didymus, then, seems to assume that the second of the two Aristarchean *ekdoseis* available to him is derived from the '*epekdosis*' mentioned by Ammonius.

P§74 We have by now narrowed the differences between Ammonius and Didymus: one spoke of two phases of one *ekdosis* made by Aristarchus, while the other spoke of two *ekdoseis* stemming from two phases in the editorial career of Aristarchus. Clearly the idea of two *ekdoseis* was based on the reality of two distinct texts, and we have evidence from the Homeric scholia that Didymus did use two Aristarchean texts and, further, that these texts were in fact distinct from each other, with one showing earlier features of Aristarchus' editorial work and the other showing later ones.

P§75 In retrospect, the positing of two *ekdoseis* that correspond to two different Aristarchean texts seems a most reasonable explanation. After all, it was not an unknown practice for an editor to publish more than one *ekdosis* in his lifetime, and in fact we have historical documentation of this practice in the era of Hellenistic scholarship.

P§76 A case in point is the information we have about Apollonius of Perga, who flourished in Alexandria during in the second half of the third century BCE. Apollonius produced two editions of portions of his treatise on cone sections, or *Conica*, and what we read about these two editions turns out to be directly comparable to what we read about the Aristarchean editions of Homer. I start with the remarks of Eutocius of Ascalon (who flourished in the first half of the sixth century CE) with reference to his own editorial work on the *Conica* of Apollonius:

P①2 Eutocius *Commentaries on the Conica of Apollonius of Perga* ed. Heiberg vol. 2 p. 176

πλειόνων δὲ οὐσῶν ἐκδόσεων, ὡς καὶ αὐτός φησιν ἐν τῇ ἐπιστολῇ, ἄμεινον ἡγησάμην συναγαγεῖν αὐτὰς ἐκ τῶν ἐμπιπτόντων τὰ σαφέστερα παρατιθέμενος ἐν τῷ ῥητῷ διὰ τὴν τῶν εἰσαγομένων εὐμάρειαν, ἔξωθεν δὲ ἐν τοῖς συντεταγμένοις σχολίοις ἐπισημαίνεσθαι τοὺς διαφόρους ὡς εἰκὸς τρόπους τῶν ἀποδείξεων.

Prolegomena

Since there were a number of ekdoseis [*pleiones ekdoseis*], as Apollonius himself says in his preface,[53] I thought it better to assemble them from whatever source was available and to juxtapose [*paratithesthai*] in the text [*rhēton*] the clearer things, in order to facilitate the understanding of beginners, and to indicate on the outside [= in the margin], in the scholia that have been put together, the evidently different variations of the arguments.[54]

P§77 As we have just seen from the statement of Eutocius, the existence of *pleiones ekdoseis* 'a number of editions' of Apollonius of Perga is known from the testimony of Apollonius. The relevant wording of Apollonius himself has actually survived:

P①3 Apollonius of Perga *Conica* Book 1, prologue lines 1–22 ed. Heiberg vol. 1

Ἀπολλώνιος Εὐδήμῳ χαίρειν. Εἰ τῷ τε σώματι εὖ ἐπανάγεις καὶ τὰ ἄλλα κατὰ γνώμην ἐστί σοι, καλῶς ἂν ἔχοι, μετρίως δὲ ἔχομεν καὶ αὐτοί. καθ' ὃν δὲ καιρὸν ἤμην μετά σου ἐν {5} Περγάμῳ, ἐθεώρουν σε σπεύδοντα μετασχεῖν τῶν πεπραγμένων ἡμῖν κωνικῶν· πέπομφα οὖν σοι τὸ πρῶτον βιβλίον διορθωσάμενος, τὰ δὲ λοιπά, ὅταν εὐαρεστήσωμεν, ἐξαποστελοῦμεν· οὐκ ἀμνημονεῖν γὰρ οἴομαί σε παρ' ἐμοῦ ἀκηκοότα, διότι τὴν περὶ ταῦτα ἔφοδον {10} ἐποιησάμην ἀξιωθεὶς ὑπὸ Ναυκράτους τοῦ γεωμέτρου, καθ' ὃν καιρὸν ἐσχόλαζε παρ' ἡμῖν παραγενηθεὶς εἰς Ἀλεξάνδρειαν, καὶ διότι πραγματεύσαντες αὐτὰ ἐν ὀκτὼ βιβλίοις ἐξ αὐτῆς μεταδεδώκαμεν αὐτὰ εἰς τὸ σπουδαιότερον διὰ τὸ πρὸς ἔκπλῳ αὐτὸν εἶναι οὐ {15} διακαθάραντες, ἀλλὰ πάντα τὰ ὑποπίπτοντα ἡμῖν θέντες ὡς ἔσχατον ἐπελευσόμενοι. ὅθεν καιρὸν νῦν λαβόντες ἀεὶ τὸ τυγχάνον διορθώσεως ἐκδίδομεν. καὶ ἐπεὶ συμβέβηκε καὶ ἄλλους τινὰς τῶν συμμεμιχότων ἡμῖν μετειληφέναι τὸ πρῶτον καὶ τὸ δεύτερον βιβλίον πρὶν {20} ἢ διορθωθῆναι, μὴ θαυμάσῃς, ἐὰν περιπίπτῃς αὐτοῖς ἑτέρως ἔχουσιν.

Apollonius sends his greetings to Eudemus. If you are in good health and if everything else is coming along according to plan, then things must be going quite well for you. As for me, I am doing

---

[53] The expression *pleiones ekdoseis* 'a number of editions' with reference to the editing of the *Conica* by its author, Apollonius of Perga, is comparable to the term *pleiones* in the Homeric scholia, with reference to *ekdoseis* available to Aristarchus (on which see PP 116n48).

[54] My translation of this passage differs from that of Cameron 1990:117.

moderately well myself. Back when I was with you in {5} Pergamon, I observed that you were interested in becoming familiar with my treatise on cone sections [= the *Conica*]. So I have sent you the first volume, having made a *diorthōsis* of it. As for the remaining volumes, I will send them to you after I am satisfied with the results of my reworking. For I think you will remember having heard from me that I had produced a course [*ephodos*] {10} on this subject [= cone sections] at the request of Naucrates the expert in geometry back when he came to Alexandria and visited my school, and that, having treated this subject [= cone sections] in eight volumes and having transmitted them from my course [ἐξ αὐτῆς, where αὐτῆς refers to the *ephodos*] into written form under some pressure, since his ship was scheduled to set sail soon, I did not take the time {15} to clean up [*diakathairein*] the text thoroughly but simply put things together as they occurred to me, intending to come back to them when the time came. So that is why I now always take the opportunity and make an *ekdosis* [= make a publication] of whatever happens to be the current state of my *diorthōsis*. And since it has happened that some others of those who have contact with me had access to the first and the second volumes before {20} they were corrected [*diorthoûn*], do not be surprised, if you happen upon these volumes, that they are different [from the corresponding volumes of the second *ekdosis*].

P§78 In this case, it is made explicit that the author of the two *ekdoseis* intends for the second *ekdosis* to become a replacement of the first in its authoritativeness. Further, it is implied that the first *ekdosis* could potentially retain a claim to authority only if the second *ekdosis* lacked the authorization of the original editor.

P§79 Reflecting on this illustration of the mentality behind the production of a second *ekdosis*, I return to the citations by Didymus of the two monographs attributed to Ammonius: (1) περὶ τοῦ μὴ γεγονέναι πλείονας ἐκδόσεις τῆς Ἀρισταρχείου διορθώσεως 'About the fact that there did not exist more [*pleiones*] *ekdoseis* of the Aristarchean *diorthōsis*' (scholia A for *Iliad* X 397–399a) and (2) περὶ τῆς ἐπεκδοθείσης διορθώσεως 'About the *epekdosis* of the *diorthōsis*' (scholia A for *Iliad* XIX 365–368a). My question is, what would be the motive of Ammonius in denying the existence of a second edition made by Aristarchus himself? In order to formulate an answer, I offer three points for consideration:

Prolegomena

(1) Didymus, even while distancing himself from Ammonius, acknowledges that this distant predecessor of his had been the immediate successor to Aristarchus as director of the Library of Alexandria (scholia A for *Iliad* X 397-399a εἴ τι χρὴ πιστεύειν Ἀμμωνίῳ τῷ διαδεξαμένῳ τὴν σχολήν 'if one is to believe Ammonius, who was the successor to the school [of Aristarchus]').

(2) As director of the Library about a century after Ammonius, Didymus speaks of two Aristarchean texts of Homer, not one, as a basic working reality, and he refers to the two of them as two *ekdoseis*.

(3) Ammonius, in the title of the second of the two monographs in question, likewise speaks of the reality of two Aristarchean texts of Homer, not one, but he refers to the second of the two texts in terms of a *diorthōsis* that underwent an '*epekdosis*': περὶ τῆς ἐπεκδοθείσης διορθώσεως.

P§80 Earlier, I described the verb *ep-ekdidonai* of '*epekdosis*' in terms of a 're-editing'. Here I propose to take a closer look at the use of the prefix *epi-* in *ep-ekdidonai*. I have found a parallel in the usage of Galen (second century CE), specifically, in a work about his own works, both published and unpublished (*De libris propriis liber*). In this work, Galen speaks of *hupomnēmata* of his that he had not initially intended for *ekdosis* or 'publication' and that needed his editorial correction once he decided to go ahead with publication. This process of correction, made necessary because of alleged distortions resulting from unauthorized circulation of Galen's unpublished *hupomnēmata*, is designated by the verb *ep-anorthoûn* and the noun *ep-anorthōsis*:

P①4 Galen *De libris propriis liber* ed. Kühn vol. 19 p. 10 line 4 to p. 12 line 8

φίλοις γὰρ ἢ μαθηταῖς ἐδίδοτο χωρὶς ἐπιγραφῆς ὡς ἂν οὐδὲν πρὸς ἔκδοσιν ἀλλ' αὐτοῖς ἐκείνοις γεγονότα δεηθεῖσιν ὧν ἤκουσαν ἔχειν ὑπομνήματα. . . . φωραθέντων δ' ἁπάντων τῷ χρόνῳ πολλοὶ τῶν αὖθις κτησαμένων ἐπεγράψαντ' ἐμοῦ τοὔνομα καὶ διαφωνοῦντα τοῖς παρ' ἄλλοις οὖσιν εὑρόντες ἐκόμισαν πρός με παρακαλέσαντες ἐπανορθώσασθαι. γεγραμμένων οὖν, ὡς ἔφην, οὐ πρὸς ἔκδοσιν αὐτῶν ἀλλὰ κατὰ τὴν τῶν δεηθέντων ἕξιν τε καὶ χρείαν εἰκὸς δήπου τὰ μὲν ἐκτετάσθαι, τὰ δὲ συνεστάλθαι καὶ τὴν ἑρμηνείαν αὐτήν τε τῶν θεωρημάτων τὴν διδασκαλίαν ἢ τελείαν ὑπάρχειν {p. 11} ἢ ἐλλιπῆ. τὰ γοῦν τοῖς εἰρημένοις γεγραμμένα πρόδηλον δήπου μήτε τὸ τέλειον τῆς διδασκαλίας ἔχειν μήτε τὸ διηκριβωμένον, ὡς ἂν οὔτε δεομένων αὐτῶν οὔτε δυναμένων ἀκριβῶς μανθάνειν πάντα, πρὶν ἕξιν τινὰ σχεῖν ἐν τοῖς ἀναγκαίοις.... τὰ δ' οὖν εἰς ἐμὲ κομισθέντα πρός τινων <u>ἐπανορθώσεως</u> ἕνεκεν ἠξίωσα 'τοῖς εἰσαγομένοις' ἐπιγεγράφθαι·... {p. 12}... ἐν αὐτῷ γὰρ αἱ κατὰ γένος ἀλλήλων αἱρέσεις διαφέρουσαι <u>διδάσκονται</u>· κατὰ γένος δ' εἶπον, ἐπειδὴ καὶ διαφοραί τινες ἐν αὐταῖς εἰσι, καθ' ἃς ὕστερον οἱ εἰσαχθέντες <u>ἐπεκδιδάσκονται</u>.

For my writings were being handed out without an inscribed *epigraphē* to friends or students not for the purpose of <u>ekdosis</u> but as writings done for those same people because they had asked to have <u>hupomnēmata</u> of the things they had heard about. . . . From among all the writings of mine that were misappropriated in the course of time, many of the people who re-acquired them would inscribe on them an *epigraphē* of my name and, upon discovering that these writings did not match the writings that others had, they brought these writings to me and asked me to <u>re-do the anorthōsis</u> [*ep-anorthoûn*]. So, since these writings had been done by me, as I said, not for an <u>ekdosis</u> [= of these writings] but in accordance with the preparation and needs of those who had asked for them, there was of course the likelihood that some parts were expanded and other parts were compressed and that the interpretive and explanatory power of my theories was left either in an integral or in a {11} deficient state. At any rate, the things that had been written for these aforesaid people are evidently not going to have the required perfection of explanatory power or <u>accuracy</u> [*diakriboûn*], since these people neither asked to learn everything <u>with accuracy</u> [*akribōs*]—nor could they if they wanted to before they had some measure of preparation in the basics. . . . In any case, I thought it fitting that some of the writings brought to me by some of them for the sake of <u>re-doing the anorthōsis</u> [*ep-anorthōsis*] should be inscribed with the epigraph *For beginners*. . . . {12} . . . For in this [= this introductory book] the *haireseis* are <u>taught</u> [*didaskesthai*] as they differ from each other, *genos* by *genos*. I just said "*genos* by *genos*" because there are differences in them [= in the *haireseis*], in terms of which at a later point the beginners are <u>thoroughly taught all over again</u> [*ep-ekdidaskesthai*].

P§81 As we see from the contexts of the verb *ep-anorthoûn* and of the noun *ep-anorthōsis*, the correcting that is being done by Galen is a matter of authoritatively 're-doing' something that has already been done before. It is a matter of reapplying a standard of exactness—of what is *akribes* 'exact'. It was this standard of exactness that the editor had applied in the first place.

P§82 This concept of *ep-anorthōsis* is comparable to the concept of '*ep-ekdosis*' as applied by Ammonius in the title of his monograph about the second text of Aristarchus. The term '*ep-ekdosis*', I propose, implies that the original *ekdosis* of Homer by Aristarchus retains its claim to its original authority.

P§83 A moment ago, in reflecting on the mentality of Apollonius in describing his second *ekdosis* of portions of his *Conica*, I drew attention to his attitude about his first *ekdosis*. His wording makes it explicit that the second text replaced the first text as the authorized edition. By contrast, the wording of Ammonius implies that the second text—the '*epekdosis*'—re-establishes the authorization of the editor who produced the first text—the original *ekdosis*.

P§84 The question remains, how do we reconcile the idea of an earlier *ekdosis* and a later '*epekdosis*' of the Homeric text of Aristarchus, as understood by Ammonius in the second century BCE, with the idea of two Aristarchean *ekdoseis* of this Homeric text, as understood by Didymus in the first century?

P§85 In the case of the two Aristarchean *ekdoseis* of Homer as known to Didymus, both are treated as authoritative, but one of the two is considered better, *khariestera*, than the other (scholia for *Odyssey* iv 727). The situation is different in the case of the Aristarchean *ekdosis* and '*epekdosis*' of Homer as known to Ammonius a century earlier. In that case, as we saw, Ammonius prefers to speak of relatively earlier and later phases in the overall editorial work or *diorthōsis* of Aristarchus, evidently as reflected in relatively earlier and later *hupomnēmata*. Further, there is only one *ekdosis* and, by implication, only one authorization by Aristarchus.

P§86 As we saw from the wording of Apollonius of Perga, quoted earlier, *ekdosis* is in and of itself an act, that is, the act of authorization: ὅθεν καιρὸν νῦν λαβόντες ἀεὶ τὸ τυγχάνον <u>διορθώσεως</u> <u>ἐκδίδομεν</u> 'so that is why I now always take the opportunity and <u>make an *ekdosis*</u> [= make a publication] of whatever happens to be the current state of my <u>*diorthōsis*</u>'. A new *ekdosis* as made by Apollonius is a new authorization, presupposing an older authorization that can now be superseded.

P§87 In light of these considerations, I return to my earlier question: what would be the motive of Ammonius in denying the existence of a second edition made by Aristarchus? The answer, I propose, has to do with a crisis of transmission. In what follows, I attempt to reconstruct the circumstances of such a crisis.

PⓈ9. Homeric editions attributed to Aristarchus

P§88 Let us begin with a simple fact. Whatever terminology we apply—second *ekdosis* or '*epekdosis*'—the fact is that the existence of some kind of a second Aristarchean text of Homer was acknowledged not only by Didymus in the first century BCE but also already by Ammonius in the second century BCE. And this second text was a point of contention for Ammonius and his contemporaries.

P§89 In claiming that there was no second *ekdosis* produced by Aristarchus, Ammonius must have been contending with Aristarchean rivals who claimed that they possessed such a second text. In terms of this rival claim, the first text had been replaced by a second text that represented a new *ekdosis* by Aristarchus. As we saw from the passage I cited earlier from Apollonius of Perga, a second *ekdosis* implies the intervention of a living editor who simply replaces an earlier *ekdosis* with a later one. By contrast, if Ammonius denied the existence of a second *ekdosis* produced by Aristarchus himself, then it could be that Aristarchus was no longer living at the time when any kind of a second text was produced. In terms of this formulation, the death of Aristarchus led to divergent editions stemming from a single edition that he had once produced. Such an explanation has been attempted more than once in the history of modern scholarship, starting with Villoison (1788) in the prolegomena for his edition of the *Iliad*.[55] What still needs to be explained, however, is the basic contradiction between the claim of Ammonius about a single *ekdosis* and the counter-claim implied by the very concept of a second *ekdosis*. Why should there be two *ekdoseis* after Aristarchus died if there was only one *ekdosis* when he was still alive? In what follows, I formulate an explanation of this contradiction.

P§90 Ammonius could have claimed that there was only one *ekdosis* if he possessed a unique text of an original *ekdosis* made by Aristarchus himself. Conversely, any Aristarchean rivals of Ammonius could have claimed access to a second *ekdosis*—if they possessed a text supposedly re-edited by Aristarchus himself. In terms of this formulation, the rivals of Ammonius did not possess a unique original text—even if they claimed to possess a second text that was said to be a second *ekdosis* supposedly produced by Aristarchus. Ammonius could have rejected such a second text on the grounds that it had not been authorized by Aristarchus, and he could have produced an alternative text.

---

[55] Villoison 1788:xxvii, followed by Wolf 1795 / 1985:195 (ch. 47). See also Apthorp 1980:132 and West 2001:62n50.

Such an alternative text, produced by Ammonius himself, could have been what he recognized as the true *'epekdosis'* of Aristarchus.

P§91 In this formulation, I have reconstructed the circumstances of a crisis of Homeric transmission in the second century BCE, during the life and times of Ammonius. Even if some details of the reconstruction may be open to question, one detail is for sure: there really was a crisis, since the after-effects are clearly visible from the testimony of Didymus in the first century BCE. Didymus was faced with the reality of a split Aristarchean tradition, that is, with two divergent Aristarchean texts, two divergent *Aristarkheioi ekdoseis*.

P§92 It does not follow, however, that this reality in the era of Didymus is identical with the corresponding reality of two divergent Aristarchean texts in the era of Ammonius, a century earlier. As I will now argue, we cannot assume that the two *Aristarkheioi ekdoseis* used by Didymus were the same texts as (1) the *ekdosis* made by Aristarchus and (2) a later *'epekdosis'* made by Ammonius on the basis of his immediate predecessor's ongoing editorial work.

P§93 In the Homeric scholia, we find telling evidence for arguing against such an assumption. There we see references to variant readings found in the two *Aristarkheioi ekdoseis* used by Didymus that contradict the received readings transmitted in the Koine (I have already noted an example in scholia A for *Iliad* XII 404a). Earlier, I used the term Aristarchean standard with reference to the prioritizing of variant readings preferred by Aristarchus over the received readings of the Koine. As I argued, this standard applies not to what Aristarchus in his own time showed in his base text. In that earlier time, the base text of his own *ekdosis* did not privilege the Aristarchean standard but still followed the Koine standard, as we know from the overall testimony of *lēmmata* transmitted by the Homeric scholia. By contrast, the Aristarchean standard prevailed in the base texts of the two *Aristarkheioi ekdoseis* used by Didymus.

P§94 What, then, were these two *Aristarkheioi ekdoseis* used by Didymus? One possible explanation is that they were (1) a derivative of an alternative *ekdosis* made by Aristarchean rivals of Ammonius and (2) a derivative of the *'epekdosis'* made by Ammonius. In other words, we may be dealing here not with rival claims about the same second text but rather with two different second texts that competed with each other.

P§95 In order to justify the second text, both sides would have claimed the authorization of Aristarchus himself. If Aristarchus had died before the publication of a second *ekdosis*, then those who would claim possession of such a second text would have needed to claim also the authorization of this text by Aristarchus himself. Likewise, Ammonius would have needed to claim that his own second text, as an '*epekdosis*' that he himself produced, was a faithful continuation of the editorial work accomplished by Aristarchus. The actual editor of the '*epekdosis*' would have been Ammonius himself, by virtue of his claim to be the immediate successor of Aristarchus. Similarly, the actual editor of any rival second *ekdosis* would have been a rival of Ammonius.

P§96 The motive for the terminology of Ammonius could then be explained this way: as the editor of an Aristarchean 're-edition' of Homer, Ammonius would have produced a *de facto* new *ekdosis* of Homer, but he chose to describe it instead as a re-edition or '*epekdosis*', derived directly from the authority of his immediate predecessor, Aristarchus himself. We may compare the fact that Aristarchus had produced a *de facto* new *ekdosis* of Homer on the basis of his *hupomnēmata* linked to the previous *ekdosis* of Aristophanes. Just as a *de facto* new *ekdosis* of Homer as produced by Ammonius would have claimed the authorization of Aristarchus, so also any other second *ekdosis* would have been based on a similar but rival claim.

P§97 In the last three paragraphs, we have been considering the possibility that the two *Aristarkheioi ekdoseis* used by Didymus were based on (1) a second *ekdosis* that supposedly stemmed from Aristarchus and (2) an *epekdosis* that likewise stemmed from Aristarchus. This possibility has been offered as an alternative to another possibility that we first considered, that the two *Aristarkheioi ekdoseis* used by Didymus were the same texts as (1) the *ekdosis* made by Aristarchus and (2) a later '*epekdosis*' made by Ammonius on the basis of his immediate predecessor's ongoing editorial work. As we have seen, this other possibility must be rejected, since the evidence produced by the testimony of Didymus himself shows that both of the *Aristarkheioi ekdoseis* of Homer were in fact post-Aristarchean. That is, neither of these two texts as used by Didymus can be derived directly from the editorial work of Aristarchus himself.[56]

P⓼10. The base text of Aristarchus

P§98 I now turn to the question of a first *ekdosis* of Homer produced by Aristarchus. The reality of such a first text is presupposed, as I have argued, by both of the two rival second texts as they existed in the days of Ammonius.

---

[56] For a comparable though slightly different formulation, see Montanari 2002a:127, citing Pfeiffer 1968:217: "Whether Didymus was able to work on copies of these original διορθώσεις of Aristarchus and of his monographs, the συγγράμματα, is an insoluble problem." See also West 2001:66, who says that the two ἐκδόσεις of Aristarchus "were not claimed [by Didymus] to be the master's autographs and accordingly could not be relied on absolutely."

Prolegomena

Both the '*epekdosis*' and the second *ekdosis*, as concepts, presupposed an original *ekdosis*. The question can be formulated this way: if two rival second texts as known to Ammonius became the ultimate sources of the two *Aristarkheioi ekdoseis* as used by Didymus, then what became of the first text, and who inherited it?

P§99 In seeking an answer to this question, I start by repeating my point that the two *Aristarkheioi ekdoseis* used by Didymus stemmed ultimately from an ongoing *diorthōsis* by Aristarchus—and that this word *diorthōsis* refers to the procedure of making editorial judgments without specifying the format of presenting these judgments. In other words, the basis for the *diorthōsis* of Aristarchus was what he said in the *hupomnēmata* 'commentaries', not what he showed in the base text he used as a point of reference for making the judgments recorded in his *hupomnēmata*. To that extent, even our use of the term base text can distract us from understanding the true basis of Aristarchean *diorthōsis*.

P§100 As I was arguing earlier, the base text of Aristarchus was based on the converging uniformity of the *koinai* texts of Homer, not on the diverging multiformity of the *khariesterai* texts. In other words, the base text used by Aristarchus followed a Koine standard, to be contrasted with the base texts of the two *Aristarkheioi ekdoseis* used by Didymus, which followed an Aristarchean standard.

P§101 To be contrasted with Didymus is the contemporary Aristarchean scholar Aristonicus.[57] Unlike Didymus, Aristonicus used a base text that followed the Koine standard. This text, I propose, goes back to the first *ekdosis* of Aristarchus.

P§102 Essential for this proposal is the fact that Aristonicus nowhere distinguishes between two *ekdoseis* of Aristarchus. One explanation that has been offered for this unitary approach of Aristonicus is that "he did not need to seek out the original manuscript or manuscripts of Aristarchus."[58] According to this explanation, Aristonicus had no such need because any copy containing the marginal signs that Aristarchus had used for his editing the text of Homer would have been sufficient.[59] So, supposedly, the approach of Aristonicus to manuscripts of Homer should have been more simplistic than that of his

---

[57] Strabo, born around 64 BCE, refers to Aristonicus refers to Aristonicus as a contemporary of his (1.2.31 C38). See West 2001:47. For an edition of the fragments of Aristonicus' work on the *Iliad*, see Friedländer 1853.
[58] West 2001:65.
[59] West 2001:65 says about the marginal signs of Aristarchus: "they had probably been transcribed into many copies, any of which he [= Aristonicus] could use as the basis for his work."

contemporary Didymus, "who should have pored over them constantly, if they were still extant."[60] I offer an alternative explanation: that Aristonicus actually had direct access to the definitive base text of Aristarchus and to the definitive *hupomnēmata* 'commentaries' of Aristarchus, while Didymus had only indirect access.

P§103 In support of this explanation, I turn to the cumulative evidence provided by the Homeric scholia concerning the work of both Aristonicus and Didymus. I start with Aristonicus.

P§104 As we see from the scholia, the detailed information drawn by Aristonicus from the Aristarchean *hupomnēmata* is systematically correlated with his knowledgeable references to marginal signs that he finds in a base text that he equates implicitly but authoritatively with the edition of Aristarchus. The *lēmmata* that are linked with Aristonicus in the Homeric scholia regularly correspond to the Koine standard that Aristarchus himself had followed for setting up his own base text, not to the Aristarchean standard followed by the two post-Aristarchean *ekdoseis* used by Didymus in Alexandria (I have already noted an example in scholia A for *Iliad* XII 404a).[61]

P§105 In making this distinction between Aristonicus and Didymus, I find it relevant that the information derived from Didymus consistently omits references to the marginal signs of Aristarchus. I propose to explain this pattern of omission by arguing that Didymus, unlike Aristonicus, lacked direct access to the definitive base text that Aristarchus had marked up with marginal signs cross-referring to the master's definitive *hupomnēmata* 'commentaries'. I also find it relevant that Didymus was working in Alexandria while Aristonicus had been relocated from Alexandria to Rome (*Suda* π 3036), along with other Alexandrian scholars like Philoxenus and Seleucus.[62] I propose further that this relocation to Rome involved not only the three Alexandrian scholars themselves but also the definitive base text of Aristarchus, marked with the master's marginal signs.[63] In the days of Aristonicus and Didymus—that is, in the age of Virgil—the most prized Aristarchean texts were to be found in Rome, not in Alexandria.

---

[60] West 2001:65.
[61] I need to emphasize that the Aristarchean standard does not always favor the variants that Aristarcheans found in the master's *hupomnēmata*. Whenever Aristarchus expresses a distinct preference for the Koine reading over a reading he adduces in his *hupomnēmata*, then the base texts of the post-Aristarchean *ekdoseis* can also be expected to show the Koine reading.
[62] So West 2001:47–49.
[63] West 2001:48n8 remarks: "It is curious that these three Alexandrians who went to Rome, Aristonicus, Philoxenus, and Selecucus, all wrote works about Aristachus' critical signs."

Prolegomena

P§106 Back in Alexandria, Didymus lacked direct access not only to the definitive base text but also to the definitive *hupomnēmata* of Aristarchus. That text too was being used by Aristonicus in Rome. As we noted before, the *lēmmata* that are linked with Aristonicus in the Homeric scholia regularly correspond to the Koine standard that Aristarchus himself had followed for setting up his own base text, not to the Aristarchean standard followed by the two post-Aristarchean *ekdoseis* used by Didymus in Alexandria (as we see in scholia A for *Iliad* XII 404a).

P§107 In making this negative argument about Didymus, I am not going so far as to say that he had no Aristarchean texts to consult: in fact the Homeric scholia show that Didymus knows of several different versions of Aristarchean *hupomnēmata*, and he even quotes extensively from these different versions.[64] I argue only that Didymus lacked direct access to the single most definitive version of the Aristarchean *hupomnēmata*—the version that was directly linked to the definitive base text. In support of this negative argument, I point to one particular situation where Didymus seems to have information from the *hupomnēmata* of Aristarchus and yet cannot verify what Aristarchus had actually said in these *hupomnēmata*. In this context, he cites as his only other available sources the two post-Aristarchean *ekdoseis* and some *sungrammata* 'monographs' of Aristarchus (scholia for *Iliad* III 406a1). On the basis of such patterns of citation, I infer that Didymus had access only to abridged versions of the final and definitive Aristarchean *hupomnēmata*.[65] Also, I raise the possibility that the two post-Aristarchean *ekdoseis* used by Didymus were texts that contained in their margins such abridged versions of the information that Aristarchus had provided in his final and definitive *hupomnēmata*.[66] If the two post-Aristarchean *ekdoseis* were formatted to feature in their margins the abridged information extracted from the definitive Aristarchean *hupomnēmata*, then there would have been no need for marginal signs that cross-refer to separate volumes containing such *hupomnēmata*. I see

---

[64] I have already cited two examples at earlier stages of my argumentation. The first was a citation from *hupomnēmata* of Aristarchus for the Homer edition of Aristophanes (Didymus via scholia A for *Iliad* II 133a ἐν τοῖς κατ' Ἀριστοφάνην ὑπομνήμασιν Ἀριστάρχου) and the second was a citation from *hupomnēmata* of Aristarchus that had been 'corrected for greater accuracy' (Didymus via scholia A for *Iliad* II 111b ἔν τινι τῶν ἠκριβωμένων ὑπομνημάτων γράφει ταῦτα κατὰ λέξιν).

[65] What I say here differs slightly from what I said in Nagy 2003b:497–498, which I revised already in HTL 102–104.

[66] On the post-Aristarchean practice of transferring information from *hupomnēmata* into the margins of the edited text, see Wilson 1967 and 1984. See also Cameron 1990:117–118, who stresses that abridgement is generally necessitated by such transfers.

here a possible explanation for the absence of references to the marginal signs of Aristarchus in the information provided by Didymus.

P§108 Despite its limitations, the work of Didymus preserved a vast repertoire of variants assembled by his predecessor Aristarchus, and the preservation of this repertoire ultimately helped transform the Koine standard of the Homeric base text into the Aristarchean standard as represented by the two post-Aristarchean *ekdoseis* used by Didymus. The Aristarchean standard, as we saw, tended to privilege readings that Aristarchus judged to be *khariestera* (hereafter I refer to the word simply in the neuter plural) over readings he judged to be *koina* (again, neuter plural).

P⑤11. The *kharis* of the "real" Homer

P§109 Here I return to the Aristarchean criteria for establishing what is really Homeric and what is not. We saw that the Aristarchean term *khariestera* 'having more *kharis*', that is, 'more graceful', is applied to variant readings in the Homeric text that are more likely to be Homeric. By default, the meaning of *koina*—where the term is contrasted with *khariestera*—is 'common, commonplace, ordinary'—and therefore less likely to be Homeric.

P§110 The comparative form of the term *khariestera* stems from usage that goes back at least as far as the age of Plato in the fourth century BCE.[67] In Chapter 3, which concerns that era, I will highlight a context where the superlative form of the term, *khariestata*, implies a sophistic understanding of Homer that transcends and even challenges a purely civic understanding. For now, however, I continue to concentrate on the distinction between *khariestera* and *koina* as understood by Aristarchus in the second century BCE and by Aristarcheans like Didymus in the first century BCE.

P§111 For Aristarchus, the term *khariestera* as opposed to *koina* was not so much sophistic as it was idealistic—idealistic to the point of impracticability. Despite the implication that the *khariestera* characterized Homer, what must have happened in real practice was that the Aristarchean base text consistently defaulted to the consensus of the *koina*—or, notionally, to a singular Koine. So the base text was highlighting in the foreground the kind of wording that was less likely to be Homeric, while the wording of the supposedly real Homer, along with the variant wordings of any number of supposedly false Homers, was kept in the shade, that is, in the background provided by the *hupomnēmata* 'commentaries' of Aristarchus.

[67] PP 122–124.

P§112 In the days of Didymus, as I noted earlier, variants reported by Aristarchus in his *hupomnēmata* could easily infiltrate the base text, actually ousting the wordings inherited by the Koine. The authority of wordings found in the Koine had given way to the authority of variant wordings preferred by Aristarchus himself—wordings originally confined to his *hupomnēmata*. For Aristarcheans like Didymus, the preferred readings of Aristarchus were more significant than the received readings of the Koine. This shift is exemplified by what I have been calling the Aristarchean standard.

P§113 Whereas the term *khariestera* was a relative criterion for Aristarchus himself, it was approaching the status of an absolute criterion for Didymus. For this follower of the Aristarchean standard, *khariestera* meant not only 'more Homeric' while *koina* meant 'less Homeric'. More directly, *khariestera* implied that the wording of Homer possesses *kharis*, while the wording of non-Homers—of false Homers or pseudo-Homers—must be without *kharis*. Such a dichotomy may have been implied by Aristarchus himself, though the rhetoric of *litotes* built into Aristarchean comments such as *ouk akharis* 'not without *kharis*' (scholia bT for *Iliad* XVI 313) and *ouk akharitōs* 'executed not without *kharis*' (scholia A[im] for *Iliad* XX 188b1) suggests a lack of absolute certainty about *kharis* as a criterion for determining what is Homeric and what is non-Homeric.

P§114 By contrast, we find a sense of absolute certainty in the attitude of Aristarcheans like Didymus. The absolutism carries over even into the comparative degree, as we see in the usage of *khariestera* as reflected in the Homeric scholia. Besides the relativizing sense of the comparative degree—'having more *kharis*' as opposed to 'having less *kharis*'—we can see signs of an absolutizing sense, indicating possession of a quality as opposed to not possessing it at all. In other words, the term *khariestera* can be used to exclude the *koina*. In this case, the possession involves 'having *kharis*' as opposed to 'having no *kharis*', instead of 'having more *kharis*' as opposed to having less *kharis*'.[68] As we see in the reportage of the Homeric scholia concerning the judgments of Didymus, *hai pleious* (scholia A for *Iliad* XII 382a1) and *hai pasai* (scholia T for *Iliad* II 196c2) can be used to mean respectively 'the majority of' and 'all' manuscripts (*graphai*) that are *khariesterai*—not all the versions taken together, which would have included the *koinai*. Along the same line of thinking, the

---

[68] A classic example of such an absolutizing sense is the Homeric Greek *skaioteros* as opposed to *dexios*, meaning 'left' as opposed to 'right', not 'more left' as opposed to 'right'; conversely, *dexiōteros* as opposed to *skaios* means 'right' as opposed to 'left', not 'more right' as opposed to 'left'. See Benveniste 1948.

superlative degree, *khariestatai*, can be used to refer to the aggregate of *khariesterai* (scholia A for *Iliad* II 53a1).

P§115 Why is *kharis*, in the sense of a 'favor' achieved through pleasurable beauty, applied as a criterion for determining the authenticity of a given text attributed to a given author? There is no way to answer this question directly, but I find it useful to compare the use of this same word in an essay by a near-contemporary of Didymus, Dionysius of Halicarnassus, entitled *On Lysias* (sections 10–12).[69] At the summit of a catalogue of objective criteria for judging the authenticity or non-authenticity of texts attributed to Lysias, the author adds, as a *pièce de résistance*, a subjective criterion that he considers to be more important than all the other criteria he has adduced up to this point: if the given text has *kharis*, then the author must be Lysias; if it does not, then the author must be someone who has been mistaken for Lysias. In the context of such a critical choice, the criterion of *kharis* is absolutizing: the text either has or does not have *kharis*, and therefore the author is either Lysias or pseudo-Lysias:

P⓪5 Dionysius of Halicarnassus *On Lysias* 10

> πολλὰ καὶ καλὰ λέγειν ἔχων περὶ τῆς Λυσίου λέξεως, ἣν λαμβάνων καὶ μιμούμενος ἄν τις ἀμείνων γένοιτο τὴν ἑρμηνείαν, τὰ μὲν ἄλλα τοῦ χρόνου στοχαζόμενος ἐάσω, μίαν δὲ ἀρετὴν ἔτι τοῦ ῥήτορος ἀποδείξομαι, κρίνας καλλίστην τε καὶ κυριωτάτην καὶ μόνην αὐτὴν μάλιστα τῶν ἄλλων τὸν Λυσίου χαρακτῆρα δυναμένην βεβαιῶσαι, ἣν ὑπερεβάλετο μὲν οὐδεὶς τῶν ὕστερον, ἐμιμήσαντο δὲ πολλοὶ καὶ παρ' αὐτὸ τοῦτο κρείττους ἑτέρων ἔδοξαν εἶναι τὴν ἄλλην δύναμιν οὐθὲν διαφέροντες· ὑπὲρ ὧν, ἂν ἐγχωρῇ, κατὰ τὸν οἰκεῖον διαλέξομαι τόπον. τίς δ' ἐστὶν ἥδε ἡ ἀρετή; ἡ [τις] πᾶσιν ἐπανθοῦσα τοῖς ὀνόμασι κἀπ' ἴσης χάρις, πρᾶγμα παντὸς κρεῖττον λόγου καὶ θαυμασιώτερον. ῥᾷστον μὲν γάρ ἐστιν ὀφθῆναι καὶ παντὶ ὁμοίως ἰδιώτῃ τε καὶ τεχνίτῃ φανερόν, χαλεπώτατον δὲ λόγῳ δηλωθῆναι καὶ οὐδὲ τοῖς κράτιστα εἰπεῖν δυναμένοις εὔπορον.

I could mention many other fine qualities of Lysias' style which would improve the expressive powers of anyone who adopted and imitated them. But I shall keep my eye on the time, and confine myself to mentioning one more, which I consider to be his finest and most important quality, and the one above all which enables us

---

[69] I owe this reference to Paul Psoinos.

Prolegomena

to establish his peculiar character. None of his successors excelled him in it, but many of those who aspired to it were considered superior to their rivals on the strength of this alone, not because they had greater general ability. But I shall discuss these authors in their proper place, if I have the opportunity. What is this quality? It is his kharis, which blossoms forth in every word he writes, a quality which is beyond description and too wonderful for words.[70] It is very easy and plain for layman and expert alike to see, but to express it in words is very difficult, nor is it easy even for those with exceptional descriptive powers.[71]

P①6 Dionysius of Halicarnassus *On Lysias* 11

καὶ ὅταν διαπορῶ περί τινος τῶν ἀναφερομένων εἰς αὐτὸν λόγων καὶ μὴ ῥᾴδιον ᾖ μοι διὰ τῶν ἄλλων σημείων τἀληθὲς εὑρεῖν, ἐπὶ ταύτην καταφεύγω τὴν ἀρετὴν ὡς ἐπὶ ψῆφον ἐσχάτην. ἔπειτα ἂν μὲν αἱ χάριτες αἱ τῆς λέξεως ἐπικοσμεῖν δοκῶσί μοι τὴν γραφήν, τῆς Λυσίου ψυχῆς αὐτὴν τίθεμαι καὶ οὐδὲν ἔτι πορρωτέρω ταύτης σκοπεῖν ἀξιῶ. ἐὰν δὲ μηδεμίαν ἡδονὴν μηδὲ ἀφροδίτην ὁ τῆς λέξεως χαρακτὴρ ἔχῃ, δυσωπῶ καὶ ὑποπτεύω μήποτ' οὐ Λυσίου ὁ λόγος . . .

Whenever I am uncertain as to the genuineness of any speech that is attributed to him, and find it difficult to arrive at the truth by means of the other available evidence, I resort to this criterion to cast the final vote. Then, if the writing seems to be graced with those additional qualities of kharis, I judge it to be a product of Lysias's genius, and consider it unnecessary to investigate further. But if the style is devoid of pleasure [*hēdonē*] and sensuality [*aphroditē*], I view the speech with a jaundiced and suspicious eye, and conclude that it could never be by Lysias.[72]

P§116 I return to the criterion of *khariestera* as applied by Didymus to Homer. If we compare the criterion of *kharis* as applied by Dionysius of Halicarnassus to Lysias, we may be justified to extrapolate at least this much: Didymus seems to be saying that whatever Homeric variant is judged to 'have more *kharis*' is more likely to be really Homeric than whatever variant has less

---

[70] In the *Iliad*, we see an attestation of the word *kharis* with reference to myrtle blossoms. Analysis in HPC II§425.
[71] Translation after Usher 1974:37–39.
[72] Translation after Usher 1974:41.

kharis. To say too much more than that, however, is to press the comparison too far. After all, we cannot really be certain whether Didymus considered his criterion to be subjective—as was the criterion of Dionysius—or objective. Moreover, despite the sense of certainty and even absolutism that we may detect in some contexts where the criterion of Didymus is applied, other contexts show traces of relativism and even uncertainty about which variant is genuine and which one is false, what is Homeric and what is pseudo-Homeric.

P§117 In fact, from the standpoint of Aristarchus as a collector of Homeric textual variants, the criterion of *khariestera* must have been relative, not absolute. Homeric variants judged to be *khariestera* were relatively rare but mostly multiform whenever they did occur, whereas variants judged to be *koina* were relatively commonplace but at least mostly uniform. In other words, attestations of readings judged to be *khariestera* tended to involve more than one variant, allowing for more options in choosing the supposedly genuine variant, whereas attestations of readings judged to be *koina* allowed for fewer options—or for no option at all. Consequently, the idea of *koinai* as an aggregate of 'common' manuscripts sharing 'common' features must have reinforced the inference that they stemmed from a 'common' source. For Aristarchus, that source was in theory the Koine and in practice the base text of Homer. By contrast, the only thing that the *khariesterai* as an aggregate of special manuscripts would have had in common was their divergence from what was common. Thus the actual choosing of readings taken from texts that were *khariesterai* over readings taken from texts that were *koinai* involved an element of uncertainty for the editor: the more choices he had to make, the more likely it became that he could make a mistake in trying to isolate the supposedly single genuine variant from among a number of false variants. Choosing among *khariesterai* was a matter of relative uncertainty, whereas not choosing and staying with the consensus of the *koinai* was a matter of relative certainty.

P§118 As a rule, Aristarchus chose relative certainty. Here I need to stress again what I said earlier about the *diorthōsis* or editorial procedure of Aristarchus. As a rule, he would show in his base text the variant that reflected what he understood to be the *koinē* or 'standard' version of Homer—even if he occasionally preferred other variants as featured in the *khariesterai*. In his base text, he practiced 'correction' only to the extent of regularizing a single Koine version as he reconstructed it from an aggregate of *koinai*. As I have noted, he confined to his *hupomnēmata* 'commentaries' his information about variants judged to be *khariesterai*. The Koine version remained his base text.

Prolegomena

P§119 As I have also noted, Aristarchus allowed the external evidence of a strong manuscript attestation in *koinai* or 'common' Homeric texts to override the internal evidence—as he saw it—of Homeric diction. Aristarchus preferred the relative certainty of the Koine standard over the relative uncertainty of having to decide among the variants he assembled.

P§120 By contrast with Aristarchus, who preferred to base his editorial work on the relative certainty of the Koine standard, later generations of Aristarcheans preferred the standard of Aristarchus himself—as they understood it. The Aristarchean standard of later Aristarcheans like Didymus became a new certainty that tended to absolutize the master's relativistic editorial criteria. The boundaries between Homeric and pseudo-Homeric forms could now be drawn with a sense of certainty. And yet, this certainty proved to be an illusion, based as it was on the relative uncertainty of Aristarchus himself whenever it came to deciding among the variants he assembled. The Aristarchean standard was itself a grand uncertainty, inviting ever new redrawings of boundaries for distinguishing the real Homer from the amorphous mass of competing pseudo-Homers.

PⓈ12. The Koine standard reaffirmed

P§121 In the practical world of editing Homer, the base text had to remain the point of reference for Aristarchus as editor. To establish this base text as correctly as possible, the editor needed to have access to a representative aggregate of *koinai* or 'common' texts of Homer, derived from an authoritative but relatively 'uncorrected' textual source. The notion that many *koinai* presuppose a singular *koinē* is reflected even in the fluctuations that we occasionally see between plural and singular uses in our sources. For example, mentions of the plural *koinai* in the medieval texts of the Homeric scholia are occasionally matched by mentions of a singular *koinē* in annotations written in papyrus texts of Homer.[73] Such matches have led one expert to draw attention to "the severely reduced nature of the scholia."[74] I should point out, however, that singular *koinē* is also attested in the medieval Homeric scholia (as for example in scholia T for *Iliad* V 461b, scholia A for XII 404a1). Such usages of the singular, relatively more common in the papyri and less common in the medieval scholia, can I think be traced back to the age of Aristarchus. This is not to say that Aristarchus posited a single <u>surviving</u> authoritative text of

---

[73] Haslam 1997:71 and n35.
[74] Haslam 1997:71.

Homer. It is only to say that his base text represented a single uniform *koinē* as reconstructed by 'correcting' a number of multiform *koinai*.[75] To say it another way, Aristarchus produced a standard text from the multiform *koinai*, and such a 'standard' was something he could quite easily have called the *koinē*.

P§122 According to an explanation that differs from the one offered here, the mentions of plural *koinai* in the Homeric scholia refer simply to "the early Ptolemaic papyri that we may see as specimens of the 'common' text(s)."[76] This is to assume, however, that plural *koinai* and the more distinctive singular *koinē* meant 'common' only in the eroded sense of 'vulgar'. It is also to assume that *koinē* is merely a foil, an inferior copy. As I have been arguing, however, the *koinai* provide an authoritative point of departure for the process of scholarly *diorthōsis* 'corrective editing' that ostensibly leads to the edition of a superior text.

P§123 The authenticity of *koinē* readings, where the designation *koinē* is actually made explicit by the scholia, can be confirmed on the basis of two independent criteria: (1) comparative linguistics and (2) oral poetics.[77] But this is not to discredit the authenticity of non-*koinē* readings that the scholia attribute to the *diorthōsis* or 'corrective editing' of scholars like Aristarchus: in many instances, the variant readings attributed to Aristarchus or Aristophanes or Zenodotus can likewise be confirmed on the basis of those same two independent criteria of comparative linguistics and oral poetics.[78] Thus it is unjustified to assume, as some have done, that the variant readings resulting from the *diorthōsis* 'corrective editing' of Alexandrian critics are as a rule scholarly conjectures. Many of these variants stemming from the learned editions prove to be just as authentic, from the standpoint of oral poetics, as the variants stemming from the *koinē* texts in general.[79]

P⑤13. Reading out loud the Homeric Koine

P§124 The Koine standard was not only the textual basis for the *diorthōsis* 'correction' of Homer by Aristarchus. It was also the performative basis, as expressed by the concept of *hē koinē anagnōsis* 'the Koine reading'. In the Homeric scholia, we find examples where this expression refers to a standard

---

[75] This paragraph derives from HTL 22n92.
[76] Haslam 1997:71, following S. West 1967:26. It may be objected that many of the readings of early Ptolemaic papyri reflect readings that Aristarchus would have considered *khariestera*, not *koina*.
[77] Janko 1992:26.
[78] PP 148–149; see also Muellner 1976:58–62 and Bird 1994.
[79] PP 118. When I say learned editions here, I include the *politikai*.

Prolegomena

way of reading out loud the Homeric verses. As we are about to see, what was being read out loud from the textual transmission in the days of Aristarchus reflects linguistic patterns that derive from performative transmission.

P§125 I start with Herodian, an Aristarchean scholar who flourished in the era of Marcus Aurelius (emperor from 161 to 180 CE). Most of the extant information reported by Aristarchus about traditional patterns of pronunciation in Homeric performance is mediated through Herodian, and the accuracy of this information, stemming ultimately from descriptive observations collected by Aristarchus himself, can be validated independently through comparative linguistics.[80] In the descriptions reported by Herodian, as mediated in the Homeric scholia, the expression *hē koinē anagnōsis* 'the Koine reading' refers to the way in which Aristarchus himself read Homeric poetry out loud:

PⓉ7 Scholia A for *Iliad* II 662a1 (Herodian)

{φίλον μήτρωα} κατέκτα: Πτολεμαῖός φησιν ὁ Ἀσκαλωνίτης Ἀρίσταρχον ἀνεγνωκέναι ὁμοίως τῷ ἔκτα σὺν οὐλομένῃ ἀλόχῳ κατὰ συστολήν. Τυραννίων δὲ κατ' ἔκτασιν. οἶμαι δὲ ἀκόλουθον εἶναι ἐκείνῃ τῇ γραφῇ τῇ κομιζομένῃ ὑπ' Ἀριστάρχου ὡς ἔμεν <ὡς> ὅτε δῖον Ἐρευθαλίωνα κατέκτα.[81] ἡ μέντοι κοινὴ ἀνάγνωσις ἡ κατὰ συστολὴν ἀφορμὴν ἔσχε τὴν τῆς ἀποκοπῆς, ὁμοίως τῷ οὖτα κατὰ λαπάρην.

{φίλον μήτρωα} κατέκτα: Ptolemaios Askalonites [p. 42 B.] says that Aristarchus has read it [= the α of κατέκτα] in a way that parallels the expression ἔκτα σὺν οὐλομένῃ ἀλόχῳ [*Odyssey* xi 410], making the vowel [= the α of ἔκτα] short. Tyrannion [F 10 P] reads it as a long. But I think there is an analogy with the reading as preserved by Aristarchus: ὡς ἔμεν <ὡς> ὅτε δῖον Ἐρευθαλίωνα κατέκτα [*Iliad* IV 319]. The Koine reading [*hē koinē anagnōsis*], with a shortening of the vowel, had its point of departure from apocope, as also in the case of οὖτα κατὰ λαπάρην [*Iliad* VI 64].

P§126 According to Herodian, *hē koinē anagnōsis* 'the Koine reading' in this case matches what Aristarchus himself had 'read' (Ἀρίσταρχον ἀνεγνωκέναι), pronouncing the α of κατέκτα in the verse-final phrase φίλον μήτρωα κατέκτα

---

[80] PP 129–132.
[81] I think it is unnecessary to emend the manuscript reading from κατέκτα to κατέκτα<ν>, as we find it in Erbse's edition.

P§13. Reading out loud the Homeric Koine

at *Iliad* II 662 as short rather than long. So this example makes it explicit that such criteria as *hē koinē anagnōsis* 'the Koine reading' stem ultimately not from Herodian but from Aristarchus himself: in other words, Herodian is simply reporting on descriptive facts already collected by Aristarchus. It is important to distinguish these facts of description from the theories of causation adduced by Herodian in his own right. Attempting to explain *why* the Koine reading features the pronouncing of short rather than long α in κατέκτα at *Iliad* II 662, he claims that the cause is an 'apocope' of -ε in a hypothetical form that would look like *κατέκταε, just as οὗτα supposedly results from an 'apocope' of -ε in a hypothetical form that would look like *οὗταε. In terms of comparative linguistics, such a scenario of causation is inadequate, even wrong: the short vowel α of κατέκτα is in fact a formulaic reshaping of morphologically archaic forms of the root κτα-, where the short α is an archaism, not an innovation;[82] similarly, the short vowel α of οὗτα results from a formulaic reshaping of morphologically archaic forms of οὗτα- featuring short α.[83] Still, the actual attestation of the pattern of pronouncing a short vowel α in κατέκτα as reported by Herodian is valuable in and of itself. It indicates that there did in fact exist such a pattern of pronunciation in Homeric poetry—as read aloud by Aristarchus himself. This attestation is all the more valuable because the question of deciding between short or long -α in verse-final κατέκτα does not affect the content or the interpretation of the given verse. The question here is purely a matter of pronunciation, not meaning.

P§127 Another such example of *hē koinē anagnōsis* 'the Koine reading' involves the sequence ΕΠΕΙΣΕ at *Iliad* VI 355. Herodian reports that ΕΠΕΙΣΕ is 'nowadays' read as ἐπεὶ σέ, featuring the non-enclitic pronoun σέ instead of the enclitic σε. He goes on to add, however, that 'the Koine reading' (ἡ κοινὴ ἀνάγνωσις) consistently 'reads' (ἀνέγνω) ΕΠΕΙΣΕ as ἐπεί σε, and he proceeds to adduce several Homeric passages to back up his statement:

P⊙8 Scholia A for *Iliad* VI 355a1 (Herodian)

> τὴν δὲ σέ ἀντωνυμίαν ὀξυτονοῦσι, τουτέστιν ὀρθοτονοῦσιν, ἐπεὶ πρός τί ἐστιν. ἔστι μὲν οὖν ἀληθὲς ὅτι ἀντιδιασταλτική ἐστιν <u>νῦν</u> ἡ ἀντωνυμία· <u>ἡ μέντοι κοινὴ ἀνάγνωσις ἀνέγνω</u> ἐγκλιτικῶς <u>ἀεὶ</u> τὴν τοιαύτην σύνταξιν. ὃ δὲ λέγω, τοιοῦτόν ἐστι· τὸ ἐπεί σε <u>εὑρέθη συνεχῶς οὕτως ἀνεγνωσμένον</u>, ἐγκλιτικῶς <u>ἀεί</u>, μὴ ἐπιφερομένου συνδέσμου, <u>ἐπεί σ' εἴασεν Ἀχιλλεύς, ἐπεί σε πρῶτα κιχάνω, ἐπεί σε</u>

---

[82] Chantraine 1958:381.
[83] Chantraine 1958:380.

φυγὼν ἱκέτευσα, ἐπεί σε λέοντα. οὕτως δὲ καὶ ἐπεί σε μάλιστα πόνος φρένας.

The pronoun σε is pronounced as oxytone, that is, with an acute accentuation, since it is emphatic. In any case, it is true that the pronoun is nowadays non-enclitic. But the Koine reading [*hē koinē anagnōsis*] always reads [*anagignōskein*][84] this kind of syntax by way of enclitic accentuation. Here are some examples of what I am saying: it is found[85] that the combination ἐπεί σε is read this way consistently, always with enclitic accentuation, if there is no linking word that follows: ἐπεί σ' εἴασεν Ἀχιλλεύς [*Iliad* XXIV 684], ἐπεί σε πρῶτα κιχάνω [*Odyssey* xiii 228], ἐπεί σε φυγὼν ἱκέτευσα [*Odyssey* xv 277], ἐπεί σε λέοντα [*Iliad* XXI 483]. So also here: ἐπεί σε μάλιστα πόνος φρένας.

P§128 In the ensuing text of the scholia, the examples of ἐπεί σε are reinforced by further Homeric examples of ἐπεί με, featuring the first person enclitic με instead of the emphatic ἐμέ. As Herodian argues, those who 'read in this way' (οἱ οὕτως ἀνεγνωκότες) ΕΠΕΙΣΕ as ἐπεί σε at VI 355 are following a pattern:

P⓽9 Scholia A for *Iliad* VI 355a1 (Herodian, continued)

καί μοι δοκοῦσι τῷ πρώτῳ προσώπῳ ἀκολουθεῖν οἱ οὕτως ἀνεγνωκότες, πιθανῶς πάνυ· διὰ γὰρ τῆς φωνῆς τὸ πρῶτον πρόσωπον ἐπιδείκνυται τό τε ὀρθοτονούμενον καὶ τὸ ἐγκλιτικόν, εἴ γε ἡ ἐμέ αἰτιατική, ὅτε φυλάσσει τὸ ε, ὀρθοτονεῖται, εἰ δὲ ἀποβάλοι, ἐγκλιτική ἐστιν. εὑρέθη τοίνυν μετὰ τοῦ ἐπεί συνδέσμου παρὰ τῷ ποιητῇ κατὰ ταύτην τὴν σύνταξιν ἀποβάλλουσα τὸ ε· Ἕκτορ, ἐπεί με κατ' αἶσαν, ἐπεί μ' ἀφέλεσθέ γε δόντες. τούτῳ τοίνυν τῷ λόγῳ πιθανὸν ἂν εἴη κατακολουθήσαντας ἡμᾶς ἀναγινώσκειν ἐγκλιτικῶς ἐπεί σε μάλιστα.

I think that those who have read it this way are following the pattern of the first person, and reliably so. The first person—both the accented form and the enclitic form, is made manifest through the word itself. For if the word ἐμέ is accusative, when it keeps the ε it is

---

[84] I am translating ἀνέγνω here as a gnomic aorist; the readership that 'reads' (ἀνέγνω) the text this way is exemplified by an authority like Aristarchus.
[85] I am also translating εὑρέθη as a gnomic aorist; this kind of reading 'is found' (εὑρέθη) by an authority like Aristarchus.

accented with an acute. But if it loses the ε, it is enclitic. In the poet [= Homer], this word is found[86] combined with the conjunction ἐπεί in this syntactical pattern, and it loses the ε: Ἕκτορ, ἐπεί με κατ' αἶσαν [*Iliad* III 59], ἐπεί μ' ἀφέλεσθέ γε δόντες [*Iliad* I 299]. Following this rationale, it would be reliable for us to read, with enclitic accentuation, ἐπεί σε μάλιστα.

P§129 In these examples of ἐπεί με, the form itself guarantees the enclitic construction, whereas in the examples of ἐπεί σε it was only 'the Koine reading' that justified the enclitic pronunciation—as opposed to the emphatic pronunciation corresponding to the way readers 'nowadays' pronounce the sequence ΕΠΕΙΣΕ on the basis of syntactical considerations alone. Herodian explains the Koine reading in terms of analogy: those who read enclitic σε instead of σέ in contexts involving the second person are doing so by analogy with the reading of με instead of ἐμέ in analogous contexts involving the first person. Once again, Herodian is explaining *why* the Koine reading is the way it is. In this case, he is attempting to explain why ἐπεί σε follows the distinct accentual pattern that he describes. In terms of comparative linguistics, the explanation is once again inadequate, even wrong. Still, the actual attestation of the pattern reported by Herodian is once again essential. The attestation shows that there did exist a pattern of pronouncing ἐπεί σε in Homeric poetry as it was read aloud, and that this pattern of reading ἐπεί σε was distinct from the pattern of pronunciation that was current in the Greek language as spoken 'nowadays', ἐπεὶ σέ. By implication, the reader whose Koine reading is reported here by Herodian is once again Aristarchus himself.

P§130 In an abridged version of Herodian's testimony about the Koine reading ἐπεί σε at *Iliad* VI 355, the formulation is worded as follows:

P①10 Scholia b(BCE³)T for *Iliad* VI 355a2

<ἐπεί σε μάλιστα:> ἔστι μὲν νῦν ἀντιδιασταλτικὴ ἡ σέ ἀντωνυμία, καὶ ἐχρῆν αὐτὴν ὀρθοτονεῖσθαι. ἡ δὲ συνήθεια ἐγκλιτικῶς ἀνέγνω.

<ἐπεί σε μάλιστα:> The pronoun σέ is nowadays distinctive [= non-enclitic, as opposed to non-distinctive or enclitic]. And it should have been accented with an acute. But the customary way [*sunētheia*] reads[87] it as an enclitic.

---

[86] Again I am also translating εὑρέθη as a gnomic aorist.
[87] Again I am translating ἀνέγνω as a gnomic aorist.

Prolegomena

P§131 Here in the scholia b at *Iliad* VI 355a2, *hē sunētheia* 'the customary way' functions as the subject of the verb *anegnō* 'reads'. I draw attention to the syntactical parallel with *hē koinē anagnōsis* 'the Koine reading', which functions as the subject of the same verb *anegnō* 'reads' in the scholia A for *Iliad* VI 355a1. As we are about to see, the methodology conveyed by the descriptive term *sunēthēs* 'customary' and its derivatives is relevant to the concept of *hē koinē anagnōsis* 'the Koine reading'. In order to show this relevance, I start with the related concept of *koinē khrēsis* 'Koine usage':

P①11 Scholia b(BCE³E⁴)T^(il) for *Iliad* II 135b (exegetical scholia)

<καὶ δὴ δοῦρα σέσηπε νεῶν καὶ σπάρτα λέλυνται:> ἐν ἑνὶ στίχῳ ἔθηκε τὴν Ἀτθίδα καὶ κοινὴν χρῆσιν.

<καὶ δὴ δοῦρα σέσηπε νεῶν καὶ σπάρτα λέλυνται:> In the same single verse he [= Homer] placed the Attic and the Koine usage [*khrēsis*].

P§132 We see in this description a contrast between τὴν Ἀτθίδα (χρῆσιν) 'Attic usage' and (τὴν) κοινὴν χρῆσιν 'Koine usage'. The point that is being made about this particular verse, *Iliad* II 135, is that it contains the 'Attic' usage of a singular verb with neuter plural subject as well as the 'Koine' usage of a plural verb with neuter plural subject. Moreover, it is claimed that 'Homer' was capable of both 'Koine' and 'Attic' usage, which happen to coexist in this Homeric verse.

P§133 With reference to this same verse, Aristarchus applies the term *sunēthēs* 'customary':

P①12 Scholia A^(im) for *Iliad* II 135a (Aristonicus)

<καὶ δὴ δοῦρα σέσηπε νεῶν καὶ σπάρτα λέλυνται:> ὅτι κατὰ τὸν αὐτὸν στίχον καὶ ἑαυτῷ καὶ ἡμῖν συνήθως ἐξενήνοχε τὸ λέλυνται καὶ σέσηπε.

<καὶ δὴ δοῦρα σέσηπε νεῶν καὶ σπάρτα λέλυνται:> [Aristarchus marks this verse in the margin] because he [= Homer] has produced in the same verse, as is customary [*sunēthōs*] both for him [= Homer] and for us, the λέλυνται and σέσηπε.[88]

---

[88] The form λέλυνται, which comes after σέσηπε in the Homeric verse, is here placed before σέσηπε; I infer that the focus of the commentator's interest is on the plural λέλυνται as an example of both 'Homeric' usage and 'our' usage.

P§134 The comment that I just quoted is ostensibly saying the same thing that was said in the comment previous to this one. In that previous comment, the 'Attic' usage was being contrasted with the 'Koine' usage, and it was claimed that 'Homer' could accommodate both the 'Attic' and the 'Koine' usages. In the comment I just quoted, there is a similar contrast: what is spoken in the time of Homer *sunēthōs heautōi* 'as is customary for him' is supposedly both 'Attic' and 'Koine'. In other words, Homer can accommodate both the 'Attic' and the 'Koine' usages. As for Greek usage in the time of Aristarchus, what is spoken *sunēthōs hēmīn* 'as is customary for us' is implicitly 'Koine', as we will see.

P§135 There is an essential clarification to be added to this description stemming from the ancient grammarians. Applying the methods of comparative linguistics, we can ascertain that the usage of a singular verb with neuter plural subject is the older syntactical pattern, while the substitution of a plural verb is an innovation; moreover, there is nothing intrinsically 'Attic' about the older pattern from the standpoint of Homeric grammar. The pattern seems distinctly 'Attic' only from the hindsight of Aristarchus, in whose own time the Attic literary heritage provided the primary evidence.

P§136 The application of the adverb *sunēthōs* 'as is customary' to 'Koine' as used in the time of Homer is comparable to the application of the adverb *koinōs* 'in a way that is Koine' in the following context:

P⊕13 Scholia H for *Odyssey* vii 132

τοῖ᾽ ἄρ᾽: τόσα ἔσαν, ὡς <u>σπάρτα λέλυνται</u> <u>κοινῶς</u>, τὸ δὲ <u>Ἀττικὸν</u> τοῖα

τοῖ᾽ ἄρ᾽: τόσα ἔσαν, as in the expression σπάρτα λέλυνται, <u>in a way that is common</u> [<u>koinōs</u>], while <u>the Attic</u> form [= as opposed to τόσα] is τοῖα.

P§137 The example that is being cited here by the commentator to illustrate 'Koine' usage, σπάρτα λέλυνται, comes from the same passage that we considered a moment ago (*Iliad* II 135). We saw from the scholia (at *Iliad* II 135b) that such a combination of plural verb with neuter plural subject is considered to be 'Koine' as opposed to 'Attic' usage. Here at *Odyssey* vii (132), the commentator draws attention not only to this 'Koine' usage but also to the 'Attic' usage represented by τοῖα. What is being highlighted is the coexistence of 'Koine' and 'Attic' usages within the same verse. As we saw earlier, the commentary at *Iliad* II (135) highlights a coexistence within that other verse between the 'Koine' syntax of a plural verb featuring a neuter plural subject and the 'Attic' syntax of a singular verb featuring a neuter plural subject. The wording of Eustathius confirms this highlighting:

P⓵14 Eustathius *Commentary* 1.293.12–14 on *Iliad* II 135

> Τὸ δέ <u>δοῦρα σέσηπεν</u> Ἀττικόν· Ἀθηναῖοι γὰρ πληθυντικοῖς οὐδετέροις ἑνικὰ ἐπάγουσι ῥήματα. τὸ μέντοι <u>σπάρτα λέλυνται κοινόν</u>. διὸ καί φασιν οἱ παλαιοί, ὅτι ἑνὶ στίχῳ ἔθηκε τὴν <u>Ἀτθίδα</u> καὶ τὴν <u>κοινὴν χρῆσιν</u>.

> The expression δοῦρα σέσηπεν is <u>Attic</u>. For Athenians produce singular verbs with plural neuters. But the expression σπάρτα λέλυνται is the one that is <u>common</u> [*koinon* = the Koine usage]. That is why the ancients as well say that he [= Homer] put inside one single verse the <u>Attic</u> and the <u>Koine</u> usage [*khrēsis*].

P§138 In what we have seen so far, then, the term *sunēthes* 'customary' refers to Greek usage not only in the time of Aristarchus but also in the time of Homer—that is, in the time of Homer as reconstructed by Aristarchus. The term is descriptive, not prescriptive, as far as Aristarchus is concerned. On the level of internal analysis, he is describing what is 'customary' in Homer by studying the language of the text as a system. On the level of comparative analysis, he is describing what is 'customary' in the Greek usage of his own time in order to shed light on what he understands to be the combined usage of 'Koine' and 'Attic' in the time of Homer.

P§139 A moment ago, we saw the use of the adverb *sunēthōs* 'customary' with the dative of the first person plural to indicate contemporary usage: καὶ ἑαυτῷ καὶ ἡμῖν συνήθως 'in a way that is customary [*sunēthōs*] both for him [= Homer, in the past] and for us [in the present]' (scholia A^im at *Iliad* II 135a). In general, the use of the adjective *sunēthes* 'customary' with the dative of the first person plural indicates contemporary usage. Here is another example:

P⓵15 Scholia A^int for *Iliad* X 461c (Aristonicus)

> <καὶ εὐχόμενος ἔπος ηὔδα:> ὅτι <u>συνήθως</u> ἡμῖν <u>νῦν</u> <u>κέχρηται</u> τῷ <u>εὐχόμενος</u>

> <καὶ εὐχόμενος ἔπος ηὔδα:> [Aristarchus marks this verse in the margin] because he [= Homer] uses this form <u>εὐχόμενος</u> <u>in accordance with the way that is customary</u> [*sunēthōs*] for us <u>nowadays</u>.

P§13. Reading out loud the Homeric Koine

P§140 Besides such examples where contemporary usage happens to match 'Homeric' usage, Aristarchus also finds examples where 'Homeric' usage is clearly distinct from whatever is *sunēthēs* 'customary' for 'us':

Pⓣ16 Scholia A for *Iliad* II 807 (Aristonicus)

ἠγνοίησεν:... οὐ κεῖται δὲ <u>συνήθως ἡμῖν</u> τὸ <u>ἠγνοίησεν</u> ἀλλ' ἀντὶ τοῦ οὐκ ἀπίθησεν

ἠγνοίησεν:... This form <u>ἠγνοίησεν</u> is attested here not <u>in the way that is customary</u> [= <u>sunēthōs</u>] <u>for us</u> but in the sense of an alternative way of saying οὐκ ἀπίθησεν.

Pⓣ17 Scholia A for *Iliad* III 206a (Aristonicus)

σεῦ ἕνεκ' <ἀγγελίης>: ὅτι Ζηνόδοτος γράφει <u>σῆς ἕνεκ' ἀγγελίης</u>. οὐ λέγει δὲ <u>συνήθως ἡμῖν</u>, τῆς σῆς ἀγγελίας χάριν, ἀλλ' ἀγγελίης ἀντὶ τοῦ ἄγγελος.

σεῦ ἕνεκ' <ἀγγελίης>: [Aristarchus marks this verse in the margin] because Zenodotus writes σῆς ἕνεκ' ἀγγελίης. But he [= Homer] does not say it <u>in the customary way</u> [<u>sunēthōs</u>] <u>as we say it</u>, that is, 'for the sake of your *angeliē*', but, rather, he says it as an alternative to *angelos* [= nominative *angeliēs*].[89]

Pⓣ18 Scholia A for *Iliad* III 99a

Ἀργείους καὶ Τρώας [sic:] ὅτι Ζηνόδοτος γράφει <u>Ἀργεῖοι καὶ Τρῶες</u>, ὡς ἀποστροφῆς τοῦ λόγου γεγονυίας πρὸς αὐτούς. ἔστι δὲ τὸ διακρινθῆναι διχῶς χωρισθῆναι. ὁ δὲ Ζηνόδοτος <u>συνήθως ἡμῖν</u> τέταχεν.

Ἀργείους καὶ Τρώας [sic:] [Aristarchus marks this verse in the margin] because Zenodotus writes Ἀργεῖοι καὶ Τρῶες, as if there had

---

[89] The variant reading of Zenodotus here (σῆς ἕνεκ' ἀγγελίης) does not affect the point made by Aristarchus about the syntax of ἀγγελίης—except to the extent that the reading of Zenodotus requires the 'customary' interpretation of a genitive singular of ἀγγελίη whereas the reading favored by Aristarchus (σεῦ ἕνεκ' ἀγγελίης) leaves it open whether ἀγγελίης is the genitive singular of ἀγγελίη or a nominative singular ἀγγελίης. The reading as produced in the *lēmma* can still be a Koine reading even if the interpretation of ἀγγελίης reflects a non-Koine usage.

Prolegomena

taken place a direct address to them [= Argives and Trojans] in the discourse. The form διακρινθῆναι [= διακρινθήμεναι at *Iliad* III 98] is in the sense of 'be divided'. Zenodotus has arranged the wording [= the vocative instead of the accusative] in the way that is customary [*sunēthōs*] for us.

P§141 In all three of these examples, the 'Homeric' usage fails to match the 'customary' usage of Greek as spoken in the time of Aristarchus. In the last two examples, we see Aristarchus arguing in favor of textual variants that correspond to the 'Koine' usage and against variants that correspond to current usage in the time of Aristarchus. In these examples, the variants found in the text of Zenodotus happen to be non-'Koine': as we see from the *lēmmata*, the supposedly 'Homeric' usage is represented by the 'Koine' reading, to be contrasted with readings that correspond to current usage.

P§142 For Aristarchus, the 'Homeric' reading is generally *hē koinē anagnōsis* 'the Koine reading' by default, as we see from this example:

P①19 Scholia A for *Iliad* I 465b1 (Herodian)

> ἄρα τ' ἄλλα: Πτολεμαῖος ὡς τἄργα τἄλλα. ἡ μέντοι κοινὴ ἀνάγνωσις παραπληρωματικὸν ἔλαβε τὸν τέ σύνδεσμον, ἐν ἐκείνῳ δὲ συνεσταλμένον τὸ ἀ ἐφύλαξεν, καθότι ἤδη ἔθος ἐστὶ τῷ ποιητῇ ἐλλείπειν τοῖς ἄρθροις.

> ἄρα τ' ἄλλα: Ptolemaios [Askalonites, p. 41] reads τἄλλα, like τἄργα. But the Koine reading [*hē koinē anagnōsis*] has the conjunction τέ as a filler construction, keeping the α short within that construction. This is in accordance with the Poet's [= Homer's] custom [*ethos*] of leaving out the articles.

P①20 Scholia b(BE³E⁴)T for *Iliad* I 465b2

> τὸ δὲ τἄλλα κατὰ συναλιφὴν ὡς τἄργα·

> The form τἄλλα is by way of contraction, like τἄργα, ...

P①21 Scholia b(BE³)T for *Iliad* I 465b2

> ὁ δὲ Ἡρωδιανὸς τὸν τέ παραπληρωματικὸν ἀποδέχεται, καὶ λείπει τὸ ἄρθρον Ὁμηρικῷ ἔθει.

... but Herodian [2.28.16] accepts [*apodekhetai*] the filler τέ and leaves out the article, in accordance with Homer's custom [*ethos*].

P§143 The expression *apodekhetai* (ἀποδέχεται) 'accepts' in the last example is an indirect indication that Herodian here is following a procedure followed by Aristarchus himself. At a later point, we will encounter this same expression in a context where Aristarchus *apodekhetai* (ἀποδέχεται) 'accepts' as genuine a variant reading of a Homeric verse that is being literally read out loud to him by an *anagnōstēs* 'reader' (scholia A for *Iliad* XVII 75a).[90]

P§144 This stance of Herodian in tending to favor the 'Koine' usage is parallel to the stance of Aristarchus himself when he is faced with an actual choice between textual variants that he would describe as 'Koine' and 'Attic'. In such situations, he tends to favor the 'Koine' variant as more 'Homeric' than the 'Attic' variant. In the scholia A for *Iliad* II 397b, for example, Didymus reports that both of the two Aristarchean 'editions' (*hai Aristarkhou*) show the plural rather than the singular verb in combination with the neuter plural subject, and that Aristarchus in his *hupomnēmata* prefers the variant showing the plural over the variant showing the singular. In the scholia A for *Iliad* II 397a, Aristonicus reports that a given variant showing the plural was Ὁμηρικώτερον 'more Homeric' for Aristarchus than another given variant showing the singular. Similarly in the scholia A for *Iliad* XIII 28b, with reference to another case where Aristarchus prefers the plural over the singular, Aristonicus reports: σύνηθες γὰρ Ὁμήρῳ οὕτως λέγειν 'for it was customary [*sunēthes*] for Homer to say it this way'.[91]

P§145 The last example, where we see the concept of *sunēthes* 'customary' being equated with the concept of 'Homeric', brings me back to the concept of *hē sunētheia* 'the customary way', which as we saw is equated with the concept of *hē koinē anagnōsis* 'the common reading' with reference to 'Homeric' usage.

P§146 In the reportage of Aristarchus, as we saw from the examples I have just surveyed, the term *sunēthēs* 'customary' refers to linguistic usage as described by an ostensibly objective observer. An indication of the degree of objectivity sought by Aristarchus is the fact that his descriptions of Homer's

---

[90] On the semantics of *apodekhesthai* as 'accept as a genuine tradition', see PH 8§§4, 7 (= pp. 217–218, 220).

[91] For Aristarchus, I should note in passing, another example of a contrast between 'Homeric' and 'Attic' usage was the use of the plural instead of the dual, as Aristonicus reports by way of the scholia A for *Iliad* XIII 197.

own customary usage or *sunētheia* are regularly tested against descriptions of usage current in his own time. Such an ideal of objectivity is also what drives the methodology of the Aristarchean scholar Herodian. For him as well, the usage of 'Homer' needs to be compared to the usage that is current. For a telling example, I quote again the passage I quoted at the very beginning of this section:

P①22 Scholia A for *Iliad* VI 355a1 (Herodian)

τὴν δὲ σέ ἀντωνυμίαν ὀξυτονοῦσι, τουτέστιν ὀρθοτονοῦσιν, ἐπεὶ πρός τί ἐστιν. ἔστι μὲν οὖν ἀληθὲς ὅτι ἀντιδιασταλτική ἐστιν <u>νῦν</u> ἡ ἀντωνυμία· <u>ἡ μέντοι κοινὴ ἀνάγνωσις ἀνέγνω</u> ἐγκλιτικῶς <u>ἀεί</u> τὴν τοιαύτην σύνταξιν. ὃ δὲ λέγω, τοιοῦτόν ἐστι· τὸ ἐπεί σε <u>εὑρέθη συνεχῶς οὕτως ἀνεγνωσμένον</u>, ἐγκλιτικῶς <u>ἀεί</u>, μὴ ἐπιφερομένου συνδέσμου, <u>ἐπεί σ' εἴασεν Ἀχιλλεύς, ἐπεί σε πρῶτα κιχάνω, ἐπεί σε φυγὼν ἱκέτευσα, ἐπεί σε λέοντα</u>. οὕτως δὲ καὶ <u>ἐπεί σε μάλιστα πόνος φρένας</u>.

The pronoun σε is pronounced as oxytone, that is, with an acute accentuation, since it is emphatic. In any case, it is true that the pronoun is <u>nowadays</u> non-enclitic. But <u>the Koine reading [*hē koinē anagnōsis*] always reads [*anagignōskein*]</u> this kind of syntax by way of enclitic accentuation. Here are some examples of what I am saying: <u>it is found</u> that the combination ἐπεί σε <u>is read this way consistently, always</u> with enclitic accentuation, if there is no linking word that follows: ἐπεί σ' εἴασεν Ἀχιλλεύς [*Iliad* XXIV 684], ἐπεί σε πρῶτα κιχάνω [*Odyssey* xiii 228], ἐπεί σε φυγὼν ἱκέτευσα [*Odyssey* xv 277], ἐπεί σε λέοντα [*Iliad* XXI 483]. So also here: <u>ἐπεί σε μάλιστα πόνος φρένας</u>.

P§147 In order to make the point that current Greek usage does not match 'Homeric' usage in this particular case, Herodian cites examples of 'Homeric' usage as collected by Aristarchus. These examples show most clearly that 'Homeric' usage is being equated with the 'Koine' usage of Homer in the past, as opposed to current usage in the present. The 'Koine' way of reading ἐπεί σε at *Iliad* VI 355 is being equated with the *sunētheia* of Homer himself in the past, as opposed to the *sunētheia* of Greek speakers in the present:

P⊕23 Scholia b(BCE³)T for *Iliad* VI 355a2

ἐπεί σε μάλιστα· ἔστι μὲν <u>νῦν</u> ἀντιδιασταλτικὴ ἡ σέ ἀντωνυμία, καὶ ἐχρῆν αὐτ ἡν ὀρθοτονεῖσθαι. ἡ δὲ <u>συνήθεια</u> ἐγκλιτικῶς <u>ἀνέγνω</u>.

ἐπεί σε μάλιστα: The pronoun σέ is <u>nowadays</u> distinctive [= non-enclitic, as opposed to non-distinctive or enclitic]. And it should have been accented with an acute. But the <u>customary way</u> [*sunētheia*] reads it as an enclitic.

P§148 So now I have come back full circle to the fact that the scholia b at *Iliad* VI 355a2 feature *hē sunētheia* 'the customary way' as a parallel to *hē koinē anagnōsis* 'the Koine reading' in the scholia A for *Iliad* VI 355a1. Both expressions function as the subject of the verb *anegnō* 'reads'. In this case, to repeat, Herodian is reporting that the 'Koine' usage is different from contemporary usage. Like Aristarchus, he is making the point that the 'Koine' reading occasionally differs from 'customary' usage in his own time.

P§149 Although Aristarchus tends to prefer the 'Koine' variants whenever he is faced with a choice between 'Koine' usage and the 'customary' usage of his own time, there are examples where his preference seems to be headed in the other direction. Here is one such example:

P⊕24 Scholia b(CE³E⁴)T for *Iliad* II 53c (Herodian)

Ἀρίσταρχος τὸ ἷζε ἐκτείνει, <u>ἡ δὲ κοινὴ</u> συστέλλει

Aristarchus stretches out [the pronunciation of] ἷζε, but the <u>Koine</u> makes it short [= ἵζε].

P§150 In this case, the augmented form of the verb (ἷζε) is evidently the variant reflecting the 'customary' usage in the time of Aristarchus, and yet Aristarchus seems to be treating it as 'Homeric' despite the availability of the older unaugmented form of the verb (ἵζε), which is described as 'Koine'. As we see from such examples, the observations of Aristarchus about any given reading are simply a matter of description, not prescription. Sometimes Aristarchus accepts the 'Koine' usages as 'Homeric', and sometimes he does not. Either way, whether or not he prefers the 'Koine' usages, he meticulously reports them.

Prolegomena

P§151 After the age of Aristarchus, however, his descriptions tend to be reinterpreted as prescriptions. Later generations of Aristarcheans can even compete with Aristarchus himself by prescribing what is or is not 'customary' for 'Homer'. For example, where Aristarchus reports variant attestations of syntactical patterns featuring either the presence or absence of 'articles' (ὁ, ἡ, τό, etc.), Didymus prescribes the presence of 'articles' as a mark of 'Homeric' usage, as if Aristarchus had prescribed the opposite:

P⊕25 Scholia T for *Iliad* III 18b1 (Didymus)

αὐτὰρ ὁ δοῦρε δύω: ἄνευ τοῦ ἄρθρου τὸ <u>αὐτὰρ δοῦρε</u> ἐν πάσαις ταῖς <u>χαριεστέραις</u>. ἡ δὲ σὺν τῷ ἄρθρῳ γραφή, καίτοι μὴ οὖσα <u>Ἀριστάρχου</u>, ὅμως ἔχει <u>Ὁμηρικὴν συνήθειαν</u>· ἔθος γὰρ αὐτῷ περὶ τοῦ αὐτοῦ διαλεγομένῳ μεσολαβεῖν τὸ ἄρθρον, ὡς περὶ ἄλλου λέγοντι, ὡς ἐπὶ τοῦ Σαρπηδόνος· <u>αὐτοῦ μὲν ἤμβροτεν, ὁ δὲ Πήδασον οὖτα</u>.

αὐτὰρ ὁ δοῦρε δύω: The sequence αὐτὰρ δοῦρε is without the article in all the <u>khariesterai</u> texts. But writing it with the article, even though it is not the way <u>Aristarchus</u> does it, nevertheless has a <u>Homeric sunētheia</u> about it, since it is a custom [*ethos*] for him [= Homer] to have an intervening article when he is talking about the same person who has been mentioned before, as in the passage about Sarpedon: αὐτοῦ μὲν ἤμβροτεν, ὁ δὲ Πήδασον οὖτα [cf. *Iliad* XVI 466–467].

P⊕26 Scholia <u>b</u>(BCE³) for *Iliad* III 18b2 (Didymus)

τὸ αὐτάρ παρὰ Ζηνοδότῳ καὶ τοῖς ἄλλοις οὐκ ἐπάγεται τὸ ἄρθρον. ὅμως οὖν ἐστι καὶ τοῦτο τῆς <u>Ὁμηρικῆς συνηθείας</u>· ἔθος γὰρ αὐτῷ περὶ αὐτοῦ διαλεγομένῳ μεσολαβεῖν τὸ ἄρθρον, ὡς καὶ περὶ ἄλλου λέγων ποιεῖ· <u>Σαρπηδὼν αὐτοῦ μὲν ἀπήμβροτεν, ὁ δὲ Πήδασον</u>...

The αὐτάρ in the texts of Zenodotus and of others does not introduce the article. Nevertheless, even this [= the use of the article] belongs to the <u>Homeric sunētheia</u>. For it is his [= Homer's] custom [*ethos*] when he is talking about the same person to have an article in the middle, as when he says in connection with another character: Σαρπηδὼν αὐτοῦ μὲν ἀπήμβροτεν, ὁ δὲ Πήδασον...

P§152 Whereas the prescription formulated by Didymus implies that the variant showing the presence of the 'article' is in this case typical of 'Homeric' usage, Aristonicus describes it simply as an example of what is *koinon* 'common'. Here are the reports of Didymus and Aristonicus, as juxtaposed in the Homeric scholia:

P①27 Scholia A for *Iliad* III 18a (Didymus | Aristonicus)

{καὶ ξίφος} αὐτὰρ ὁ δοῦρε: Ἀρίσταρχος ἄνευ τοῦ ἄρθρου, αὐτὰρ δοῦρε. οὕτως καὶ ἡ Ἀριστοφάνους καὶ ἡ Καλλιστράτου καὶ σχεδὸν οὕτως καὶ αἱ χαριέσταται· καὶ ὁ Ἰξίων ἐν τῷ πρώτῳ Πρὸς τὰς ἐξηγήσεις ὁμοίως προφέρεται. ἔχει δὲ τὸν Ὁμηρικὸν χαρακτῆρα καὶ ἡ σὺν τῷ ἄρθρῳ γραφή, καίπερ οὐκ οὖσα Ἀριστάρχειος· σύνηθες γὰρ τῷ ποιητῇ ἐπὶ τῶν αὐτῶν μένοντι ὑπόνοιαν παρέχειν ὡς περὶ ἑτέρου διαλέγοιτο προσθέσει ἄρθρου καὶ μεταλλάξει τοῦ συνδέσμου, ὡς ἐπὶ τοῦ Κύκλωπος κὰδ δέ μιν ὕπνος | ᾕρει πανδαμάτωρ, ὁ δ' ἐρεύγετο οἰνοβαρείων ἀντὶ τοῦ καὶ ἐρεύγετο. {|} Ζηνόδοτος δὲ ἠθέτηκε τοῖς ἑξῆς οὐ συντιθέμενον. δεῖ δὲ κοινὸν παραλαβεῖν αὐτὰρ ὁ δοῦρε δύω ἔχων καὶ νοεῖν τὸ ἄρθρον ἐξ ἐπαναλήψεως παρειλημμένον ἐπὶ τοῦ αὐτοῦ προσώπου.

{καὶ ξίφος} αὐτὰρ ὁ δοῦρε: Aristarchus has it without the article, αὐτὰρ δοῦρε. So also the text of Aristophanes and the text of Callistratus and so also practically all the *khariestatai* texts. Likewise Ixion adduces it in the first volume of his Πρὸς τὰς ἐξηγήσεις. But writing it with the article also has a Homeric character, even though it is not Aristarchean. For it is customary [*sunēthes*] for the Poet when he is staying on the topic of the same [two] entities to provide a hint that he is talking about the other of the two entities by way of adding an article and shifting the conjunction, as in the case of the Cyclops: κὰδ δέ μιν ὕπνος | ᾕρει πανδαμάτωρ, ὁ δ' ἐρεύγετο οἰνοβαρείων [cf. *Odyssey* ix 372-374], where we see ὁ δ' ἐρεύγετο instead of καὶ ἐρεύγετο. [In the corresponding Greek text, I mark this point with the sign "{|}": it is where the testimony of Didymus stops and the testimony of Aristonicus begins.] Zenodotus athetized this verse as not fitting the contiguous verses. But it is necessary to take it the way it is common [*koinon*],[92] αὐτὰρ ὁ δοῦρε δύω ἔχων, and to interpret the article as referring back to the same person to whom reference was made earlier.

---

[92] For the idiom here, compare the wording of the scholia A for *Iliad* VIII 276a1: πιθανώτερον γάρ ἐστι κύριον αὐτὸ παραλαβεῖν 'it is more reliable to take it as proper [= not common]'.

Prolegomena

P§153 The description as reported by Aristonicus, indicating that the variant usage featuring the 'article' is *koinon* 'common', may actually stem from Aristarchus. In other words, it may be Aristarchus himself who is describing as *koinon* 'common' the usage featuring the 'article', that is, the Koine usage. But the question is, did Aristarchus actually find the Koine variant attested in the verse that we know as *Iliad* III 18? In this case, it seems that he did not: otherwise, he would have shown the Koine variant in his base text while conscientiously reporting the alternative variant as found in the *khariesterai*. It is not that Aristarchus removed the 'article' from *Iliad* III 18 in his base text; rather, it appears that he found no 'article' attested for this verse, and he expressed the opinion that Homeric usage had led him to expect an attestation.

P§154 In the era of Aristarchus, the descriptions of what is *sunēthes* 'customary' or *koinon* 'common' in Homer are based on the evidence of variant texts he has at his disposal, not only on the evidence of usage he extrapolates from the language of the texts. In the post-Aristarchean era, however, the opportunities for finding such new textual evidence become increasingly rare, and the various questions about what is *sunēthes* 'customary' or *koinon* 'common' in Homer become increasingly limited to the evidence of usage alone—primarily as described by Aristarchus himself. Accordingly, scholars in the post-Aristarchean era become increasingly dependent on the authority of Aristarchus concerning whatever he describes as *sunēthes* 'customary' or *koinon* 'common'. Such descriptions tend to be reinterpreted by later Aristarcheans as prescriptions of whatever is 'Homeric' pure and simple, as if all the descriptions of Homeric usage were meant to be compared with current usage in what Aristarchus calls 'our' time. In the following passage, for example, the purpose clause implies that the Aristarchean 'editions' of Homer feature readings in the base text that conform to usage that is *sunēthes* 'customary' for 'us':

P①28 Scholia in Papyrus 12 (= *Oxyrhynchus Papyri* 221 second century CE) of Erbse's edition of the Homeric scholia (vol. 5 1977) commenting on *Iliad* XXI 221 (Erbse vol. 5 p. 98, Col. XI line 15)

ἔασον· αἱ Ἀριστάρχ<ε>ιοι οὕτως, ἵνα τὸ <u>σύνηθες ἡμῖν</u> ἦι

ἔασον· This is the way [it is read] by the Aristarchean editions—so that the form may be the one that is <u>customary [*sunēthes*] for us</u>.[93]

---

[93] The οὕτως, indicating 'this is the way it is read', evidently refers to the pronunciation of smooth breathing in ἔασον, as opposed to rough breathing as in ἕασον, a way of reading that yields a different word and a different meaning: see the scholia <u>b</u>T for *Iliad* XXI 221 b1 c1 b2 c2, as opposed to the scholia A for the same verse (where it is said explicitly: ψιλῶς 'with smooth breathing').

P§155 In this example, what is *sunēthes* 'customary' in the current usage is assumed to be the kind of variant that a good Aristarchean should prefer as the truly 'Homeric' usage—as if the criterion of current usage could somehow be applied consistently to a given variant that Aristarcheans prefer as more 'Homeric' than another given variant.

P§156 It all comes down to this: in the post-Aristarchean era, scholars no longer had access to the 'Koine' tradition that had been available to Aristarchus himself when he established his own base text. So they had no independent judgment about what is or is not 'Koine' whenever Aristarchus invokes the concept of *hē koinē anagnōsis* 'the Koine reading'.

P⑤14. Reading Homer out loud to Aristarchus

P§157 In the era of Aristarchus, *hē koinē anagnōsis* 'the Koine reading' (ἡ ... κοινὴ ἀνάγνωσις, as at scholia A for *Iliad* II 662a1 and elsewhere) was actually a matter of reading out loud to Aristarchus the Homeric base text for verification. That is, the Homeric base text was read out loud to Aristarchus as part of the editorial procedure of his *diorthōsis*. In the Homeric scholia, we find indirect references to such reading out loud.

P§158 A case in point is the use of the word *anagnōstēs* 'reader'.[94] In the Homeric scholia, this word is applied in two references to a man called Posidonius, who is described as the *anagnōstēs* 'reader' for Aristarchus (Ποσειδώνιον τὸν Ἀριστάρχου ἀναγνώστην / Ποσειδώνιος ... ὁ ἀναγνώστης Ἀριστάρχου in the scholia A for *Iliad* XVII 75a / VI 511a).

P§159 In one of the two references, where the meaning of a Homeric verse (*Iliad* XVII 75) depends on whether a given word in that verse is syntactically connected with what precedes or with what follows, Aristarchus decides on what he considers to be the correct reading by listening to the reading of 'his' *anagnōstēs* Posidonius:

P①29 Scholia A for *Iliad* XVII 75a (Nicanor)

> Ἕκτορ, νῦν σὺ μὲν ὧδε <θέεις ἀκίχητα διώκων>: μετὰ τὸ ὄνομα στικτέον· προσαγορευτικὴ γάρ ἐστι. τὸ δὲ ἀκίχητα φασὶ Ποσειδώνιον τὸν Ἀριστάρχου ἀναγνώστην τοῖς ἑξῆς προσνέμειν καὶ τὸν Ἀρίσταρχον ἀποδέχεσθαι.

---

[94] For background on this word *anagnōstēs* 'reader', see PP 149–150, 168n49, 176–177, 201.

Prolegomena

Ἕκτορ, νῦν σὺ μὲν ὧδε <θέεις ἀκίχητα διώκων>: It should be punctuated after the noun [= ἀκίχητα], for it is vocative. But they say that the word ἀκίχητα was read by Posidonius the reader [*anagnōstēs*] of Aristarchus as belonging to the words that follow, and that Aristarchus accepted [*apodekhesthai*] this as traditional.

P§160 Evidently the phonology of the reader's performed reading follows one of the two possible ways of performing the verse, and it is said here that Aristarchus accepted (*apodekhesthai*) as traditional the version performed by his reader. In terms of editing, Aristarchus considered the reading of Posidonius to be one of two syntactical variants, and he preferred the variant performed by his reader. The wording of Eustathius confirms the essentials of the approach taken by Aristarchus:

P①30 Eustathius *Commentary* 4.17|18.25-26|1 on *Iliad* XVII 75-76

Τὸ δὲ πλῆρες τῆς ῥηθείσης παροιμιώδους συντάξεως τοιοῦτον· σὺ μὲν ὧδε θέεις, εἶτα ὡς ἄλλης ἀρχῆς, ἀκίχητα διώκων ἵππους, καὶ τὸ ἑξῆς. Ποσειδώνιος δέ, ὁ Ἀριστάρχου ἀναγνώστης, οὕτω λέγει· σὺ μὲν ὧδε θέεις ἀκίχητα, εἶτα· διώκων ἵππους Αἰακίδαο, καὶ τὸν Ἀρίσταρχον ἀποδέχεσθαι τοῦτο.

The filled-out meaning of this sententious utterance goes something like this: σὺ μὲν ὧδε θέεις, and then, as if starting the syntax anew, ἀκίχητα διώκων ἵππους, and then the rest of the syntax in sequence. But Posidonius, the reader [*anagnōstēs*] of Aristarchus, says it this way: σὺ μὲν ὧδε θέεις ἀκίχητα, and then διώκων ἵππους Αἰακίδαο. And it is said that Aristarchus accepted [*apodekhesthai*] this version.

P§161 In contradiction of what is said in scholia A, Eustathius says that Posidonius read ἀκίχητα as going with what precedes syntactically, not with what follows. Either Eustathius or the transmitter of the scholia A has evidently reversed the direction of syntactical linkage. Still, the point remains that Aristarchus considered the reading of Posidonius to be one of two syntactical variants, and that he chose the variant he heard performed by his reader.

P§162 In the other of the two references in the Homeric scholia, it is reported that Posidonius the *anagnōstēs* was reading out loud the wording of the verse that we know as *Iliad* VI 511, pronouncing *rhimpha-e* where we now read ῥίμφα ἑ in the expression ῥίμφα ἑ γοῦνα φέρει:[95]

P①31 Scholia A for *Iliad* VI 511a (Aristonicus)

ῥίμφα <ἑ γοῦνα φέρει>: Ζηνόδοτος ῥίμφ' ἑὰ γοῦνα φέρει. Ποσειδώνιος δὲ ὁ ἀναγνώστης Ἀριστάρχου <ἄνευ> διαιρέσεως τὸ ε ψιλῶς προφέρεται, παρέλκειν αὐτὸ λέγων ὡς ἐν τῷ ἠὲ σὺ τόνδε δέδεξο, καὶ λύεται τὸ σολοικοφανές. ὁ δὲ Ὅμηρος ὑπὸ τῶν γονάτων καὶ ποδῶν φέρεσθαι λέγει· τὸν μὲν ἄρ' ὣς εἰπόντα πόδες φέρον.

ῥίμφα <ἑ γοῦνα φέρει ['lightly his knees carry him along']>: Zenodotus has ῥίμφ' ἑὰ γοῦνα φέρει ['lightly he carries his own knees']. But Posidonius the reader [*anagnōstēs*] of Aristarchus produces the ε without word-division and with smooth breathing, saying that it is suffixed as in the expression ἠὲ σὺ τόνδε δέδεξο [*Iliad* V 228] [where the -ὲ of ἠὲ is 'suffixed']. This way, the problem of the apparent solecism [= as in the reading of Zenodotus] is solved. In Homeric idiom, one can be 'carried' [φέρεσθαι] by one's knees and feet: τὸν μὲν ἄρ' ὣς εἰπόντα πόδες φέρον [*Iliad* XV 405].

P①32 Scholia A^im for *Iliad* VI 511b (exegetical scholia)[96]

<ῥίμφα ἑ γοῦνα φέρει:> μετέβη τὴν πτῶσιν· τὸ γὰρ ἓ αὐτόν σημαίνει.

<ῥίμφα ἑ γοῦνα φέρει:> He [= Homer] omitted the declined form. For the ἓ means 'him'.

---

[95] West 2001:55 thinks that Posidonius pronounced *rhimphea*, that is, ῥίμφεα. Such an interpretation cannot be justified, I think, on the basis of what we read in the original Greek of the scholia for *Iliad* VI 511. In the same discussion, West claims that Posidonius was "the author of opinions on the articulation of Zenodotus' text." But I see no specific association between Posidonius and the text of Zenodotus per se. In fact, the reading of Posidonius represents an alternative to the reading of Zenodotus. What the Greek says in the scholia for *Iliad* VI 511a is that Posidonius reads ε where Zenodotus had read ἑά. Further, Posidonius pronounces the . . .*a-e* of ῥίμφα ἑ in a way that parallels the way he pronounces the *ē-e* of ἠὲ at *Iliad* V 228.

[96] I follow here the attribution given by Erbse.

Prolegomena

P⊕33 Scholia T for *Iliad* VI 510–511a1 (Aristonicus | exegetical scholia)

ὁ δ' ἀγλαΐηφι <πεποιθὼς ῥίμφα ἑ γοῦνα φέρει>: ἀντὶ τοῦ τοῦτον. {|} καὶ τὸ ἕ ἀντὶ τοῦ αὐτόν, φημὶ τὸ ῥίμφα †1. | Ποσειδώνιος δὲ ψιλῶς τὸ ἕ προφέρεται καί φησιν αὐτὸ πλεονάζειν ὡς ἐν τῷ ἠὲ σύ.

ὁ δ' ἀγλαΐηφι <πεποιθὼς | ῥίμφα ἑ γοῦνα φέρει>: The ἕ is in place of 'him'. [In the corresponding Greek text, I mark this point with the sign "{|}": it is where the testimony of one source stops and the testimony of another source begins.] The ἕ is in place of 'him'. I say 'ῥίμφα †1. | Posidonius produces the ἕ with smooth breathing and says that it [= the ἕ] is pleonastic, as [the -ὲ] in the expression ἠὲ σύ [*Iliad* V 228].

P⊕34 Eustathius *Commentary* 2.377|378.19–21|1–3 on *Iliad* VI 510–511

Τινὲς δέ φασι τὸν τοῦ Ἀριστάρχου ἀναγνώστην Ποσειδώνιον ῥίμφαε λέγειν ἐν ἑνὶ τρισυλλάβῳ μέρει λόγου, πλεονάσαντος, φησίν, ἐν παρολκῇ τοῦ ε, ὡς ἐν τῷ ἠὲ σὺ τόνδε δέδεξο. καὶ αὐτοὶ μὲν τοιαῦτα. Ὁ δὲ Ὁμηρικὸς ἀνὴρ ἥδιον ἀκούοι ἂν καὶ νῦν καινοφωνοῦντος ἐλλόγως τοῦ ποιητοῦ τὰ ἀστεῖα ταῦτα σολοικοφανῆ ἥπερ ἀνέχοιτο Ἀττικῶς φθεγγομένων ἀκροᾶσθαι τῶν ἐπιδιορθουμένων αὐτόν

And some people say that the reader [*anagnōstēs*] for Aristarchus, Posidonius, said ῥίμφαε, as if it were a trisyllabic word, with a pleonastic suffixation of ε, he says, as in the expression ἠὲ σὺ τόνδε δέδεξο. Well, that is the kind of thing that these people say. But a man who knows his Homer would more gladly hear, even today, the Poet's neologizing of these elegant words, though they appear to be solecisms, instead of putting up with listening to Attic-sounding speakers who try to correct him [= the Poet].

P§163 In the last of these passages that I just quoted, Eustathius is evidently distancing himself from the methodology of Aristarchus, who tests the usage of 'Homer' by comparing 'Attic' and other supposedly extraneous evidence.

P§164 The rationalizing explanation given by Posidonius for the pronunciation, that the *-e* is 'pleonastic' like the *-e* of the conjunction *ē-e* (ἠὲ), may be diachronically invalid, but the actual need for a rationalization indicates the reality of the traditional way in which this Homeric verse was performed for Aristarchus by 'his' reader. The variant reading adduced by Zenodotus, by contrast, is ῥίμφ' ἑὰ γοῦνα φέρει. From the short-term perspective of the immediate context in *Iliad* VI 511, this version as adduced by Zenodotus is the *lectio facilior*.[97] From the long-term perspective of Homeric diction involving analogous phraseology, however, Aristarchus preferred the *lectio difficilior*.[98] The pronunciation of his *anagnōstēs*, who read *rhimphae*, helped Aristarchus reconstruct the syntactically and morphologically valid wording ῥίμφα ἑ.[99] Such a pronunciation, even if Posidonius himself interpreted it wrongly, is I think a plausible reflex of the diachronically valid wording ῥίμφα ἑ, which was evidently the interpretation of Aristarchus. Moreover, the reading ῥίμφα ἑ is evidently the Koine version, reinforced here by the Koine pronunciation *rhimphae* of the official reader or *anagnōstēs*.[100] It is the Koine reading, the *koinē anagnōsis*.[101]

P§165 The explanation I have offered here is at odds with another explanation, formulated as follows: "Evidently Aristarchus had Zenodotus' text read aloud to him by Posidonius, who had to decide between alternative articulations. Aristarchus occasionally thought it worth noting his choices and giving him credit for them."[102] As I have just argued, there is no reason to infer that it was specifically the text of Zenodotus that had been read out loud for Aristarchus by Posidonius.[103] Nor is it justified to assume that Posidonius was arbitrary in following one of two alternative articulations. The point of the Aristarchean testimony about the reading of Posidonius to Aristarchus is that the reading of this *anagnōstēs* was a traditional reading. Aristarchus accepted the readings of Posidonius as traditional: such is the force of the expression *apodekhesthai* 'accept as traditional'.

P§166 This editorial practice, where an *anagnōstēs* 'reader' reads out loud to an editor a text to be approved by the editor, is reflected in a traditional formula attested in texts dated to later periods. The formula consists of a geni-

---

[97] This way, ῥίμφ' ἑὰ γοῦνα φέρει allows the subject of φέρει to agree with the subject marked by the following participle πεποιθώς.
[98] Scholia for *Iliad* VI 511a: ὁ δὲ Ὅμηρος ὑπὸ τῶν γονάτων καὶ ποδῶν φέρεσθαι λέγει 'in Homeric idiom, one can be "carried" (φέρεσθαι) by one's knees and feet'.
[99] The sequence φημὶ τὸ ῥίμφα †<ι> in the scholia for *Iliad* VI 510–511a1 may perhaps be restored as a direct quotation from Posidonius: φημὶ τὸ ῥίμφαε 'I say *rhimphae*'.
[100] As we saw earlier, Eustathius (*Iliad* commentary vol. 2 pp. 377 / 378 lines 19–21 / 1–3) expresses his own preference for this version, ῥίμφα ἑ γοῦνα φέρει, which he contrasts negatively with what he describes as the strained 'Attic' version represented by ῥίμφ' ἑὰ γοῦνα φέρει, which results from what he calls *epidiorthōsis*.
[101] See my note above on the concept of ἡ ... κοινὴ ἀνάγνωσις 'the Koine reading'.
[102] West 2001:55.
[103] See the notes above.

tive absolute construction, ἐκδόσεως παραναγνωσθείσης in combination with the use of the dative case in referring to the editor:

P①35 *Explicit* for the commentary of Eutocius of Ascalon (sixth century CE) on Book I of Archimedes *On Sphere and Cylinder* (ms. Laurentianus 28.4)[104]

> Εὐτοκίου Ἀσκαλωνίτου ὑπόμνημα εἰς τὸ πρῶτον τῶν Ἀρχιμήδους περὶ σφαίρας καὶ κυλίνδρου, ἐκδόσεως παραναγνωσθείσης τῷ Μιλησίῳ μηχανικῷ Ἰσιδώρῳ ἡμετέρῳ διδασκάλῳ
>
> The commentary [*hupomnēma*] of Eutocius of Ascalon to the first volume of the works of Archimedes *On Sphere and Cylinder*, and the ekdosis had been read out loud to the Milesian engineer Isidore, my teacher, for cross-checking [*paranagignōskein*][105]

P§167 My interpretation of *paranagignōskein* here, 'read out loud for cross-checking', needs further comment. The contexts of some earlier attestations of *paranagignōskein* indicate that the text that is being read out loud is a model text in the making, that is, it is a text that becomes a model through the actual process of cross-checking and correcting. I have discussed such contexts in my previous work.[106] Here I concentrate on specialized contexts where the model text is being read out loud to its editor, whose task is to cross-check this text with other texts in order to correct any mistakes. In the wording I just cited, the editor of the text of Archimedes is Isidore of Miletus.[107] The model text that Isidore edited is in this case the actual text of Archimedes that is being read back to Isidore for cross-checking and correction.[108] The process of cross-checking may involve reading from—or remembering from—parallel texts, leading to corrections and, ultimately, approval by the editor.

P§168 I proceed to examine some further examples of this formula:

---

[104] See Cameron 1990:103–107.
[105] On Isidore of Miletus, the 'Milesian Engineer', who along with Anthemius of Tralles was commissioned by Justinian in 532 CE to design and build the new Hagia Sophia, see Cameron 1990:103–104. On the editing procedures of Eutocius, see the data assembled by Cameron pp. 116–118 with reference to Eutocius' edition of the *Conica* of Apollonius of Perga: scholars who prepared a ninth-century Arabic translation collated Eutocius' edition of Books 1–4 with earlier versions of the text and found that Eutocius made important 'corrections'. In his commentary, Eutocius often refers to variants found 'in some copies [*antigrapha*]' (ἔν τισιν ἀντιγράφοις).
[106] PP 174–176. See also the contexts of *paranagignōskein* assembled by Cameron 1990:124–125.
[107] Cameron 1990:118–120. Commenting on the Doric dialectal features and the technical terminology inherent in the textual tradition of Archimedes, Cameron p. 120 offers the opinion that "both dialect and terminology had already been largely modernized before Isidore's day."
[108] Cameron 1990:118.

P①36 From the heading to Book 3 of the commentary by Theon of Alexandria on Ptolemy's *Almagest* (ms. Laurentianus 28.18)[109]

Θέωνος Ἀλεξανδρέως εἰς τὸ τρίτον τῆς μαθηματικῆς Πτολεμαίου Συντάξεως <u>ὑπόμνημα ἐκδόσεως παραναγνωσθείσης</u> τῇ φιλοσόφῳ θυγατρί μου Ὑπατίᾳ

The <u>commentary [*hupomnēma*]</u> of Theon of Alexandria to the third volume of the *mathēmatikē Suntaxis* of Ptolemy, <u>and the *ekdosis* had been read out loud to</u> my philosopher daughter Hypatia <u>for cross-checking [*paranagignōskein*]</u>.

P§169 The role of Theon's learned daughter Hypatia can be better understood in the light of the formula describing the role of Theon himself:

P①37 From the headings to Books 1 and 2 of Theon's commentary on Ptolemy's *Almagest*[110]

Θέωνος Ἀλεξανδρέως τῆς παρ' αὐτοῦ γεγενημένης <u>ἐκδόσεως</u> εἰς τὸ πρῶτον τῆς Συντάξεως Πτολεμαίου <u>ὑπόμνημα</u>

Θέωνος Ἀλεξανδρέως τῆς παρ' αὐτοῦ γεγενημένης <u>ἐκδόσεως</u> εἰς τὸ δεύτερον τῆς Συντάξεως Πτολεμαίου <u>ὑπόμνημα</u>

The <u>commentary [*hupomnēma*]</u> of Theon of Alexandria of the <u>edition [*ekdosis*]</u> made by him of the first / second volume of the *Suntaxis* of Ptolemy

P§170 Just as the father edited Books 1 and 2 of Ptolemy's *Almagest*, so also the daughter edited Book 3: for the first two books, Theon produced both the edition and the commentary, but for the third he produced only the commentary while Hypatia produced the edition.[111] As we see in the more expanded wording that describes the contribution of the daughter, the actual process of editing involved the reading out loud of the text to the editor. This process is mentioned explicitly only when the person who produced the commentary or *hupomnēma* is different from the person who produced the edition or *ekdosis*.

P§171 Unlike the roles of Isidore and Hypatia, who produced only the *ekdosis* 'edition' but not the *hupomnēma* 'commentary' for their respective

---

[109] Cameron 1990:106.
[110] Cameron 1990:111.
[111] Cameron 1990:115, who adds that he has no way of determining whether Hypatia also edited the text of the remaining ten books of the *Almagest*.

Prolegomena

texts, the role of Theon is directly comparable to that of Aristarchus, in that he produced both *ekdosis* and *hupomnēma* for the Homeric texts. And, like Theon, Aristarchus must have had the text read out loud to him for the purpose of cross-checking. The process of cross-checking leads to *diorthōsis* 'correction' and, ultimately, approval, so that the edited text becomes the model text.[112]

P⒮15. Conclusions: the Homeric Koine as a classical text

P§172 I conclude that the base text of the edition of Homer by Aristarchus was at least notionally the Koine version. I conclude also that the criteria of Aristarchus in editing Homer were relatively more rigid than those established by one of his predecessors as director of the Library of Alexandria, Zenodotus of Ephesus, who was active over a hundred years earlier, in the age of Callimachus.

P§173 It is all-important for me to stress, however, that the criteria of Zenodotus as editor of Homer were rigid in their own right. They can be considered relatively less rigid only if we compare them to the later criteria of Aristophanes and to the still later criteria of Aristarchus himself. The earlier criteria of Zenodotus, by comparison with those of his own contemporaries in the age of Callimachus, turn out to be almost as rigid as those of Aristophanes, Aristarchus, and later Aristarcheans such as Didymus in the age of Virgil.

P§174 The Homeric *koinē*, equated by Aristarchus with the base text he used for editing Homer, was rigid not only because it was the 'definitive' or 'standard' Homer: it was rigid also because it was the 'common' Homer, the 'vulgate' Homer. This last term 'vulgate' tends to be misunderstood and misused nowadays. The casual reader of Homeric scholarship is often led to believe that the 'vulgate' Homer was unstable and even chaotic—or let us say fluid. As I will argue in Chapter 3, however, the Homeric *koinē* or 'vulgate' was the opposite: it was relatively stable, orderly, and even rigid. To put it more precisely, the Homeric *koinē* was *notionally* rigid, that is, it was thought to be unchangeable in terms of its reception, from the standpoint of those who

---

[112] I revise the interpretation I gave in the original version of *PP* 175–176n83 for the formula ἐκδόσεως παραναγνωσθείσης plus dative, and I offer the following rewording (see also Davidson 2001b:410n19): "I interpret the formula ἐκδόσεως παραναγνωσθείσης plus dative to mean 'and the edition [*ekdosis*] was read out loud (by reader X) for (editor) Y'." I withdraw my translation 'with the edition [*ekdosis*] read out loud, as a model, by X'. I rewrite as follows the rest of *PP* 175–176n83: "The *ekdosis* 'edition' in question is the text of the work about which the commentary is written, not the commentary itself, and this text is 'corrected' by the one who 'has it read out loud' [corrected from 'reads it out loud as a model'] (this editor is sometimes but

P⑤15. Conclusions: the Homeric Koine as a classical text

considered Homer to be their common possession, their own standard Homer. The way I have just spoken about the vulgate Homer is meant to evoke the way Saint Jerome spoke about the vulgate Bible.[113]

P§175 In contemplating the reality of multiple *koinai* and the ideal of a singular *koinē* of Homer, I see an analogy with the *vulgata* or 'vulgate' of the Bible.[114] In Jerome's *Epistle to Sunnia and Fretela*, the word *koinē*, which he glosses in Latin as the *vulgata* or 'vulgate', is applied to two 'common' Greek versions of the Hebrew Bible, one of which is the *editio* or 'edition' of one Lucian while the other is the *editio* of Origen of Alexandria (late second to mid-third century CE)—that is, the Septuagint as edited in the *Hexapla* of Origen.[115] As in the usage of the Homeric scholia, there is an element of negative comparison here as well: conceding that the Greek term *koinē* is applicable to both of the Greek-language biblical 'editions' in question, Jerome goes on to contrast the 'old corrupt edition' of Lucian with the 'uncorrupted and immaculate' version resulting from the edition of Origen, which serves as the source for Jerome's Latin vulgate translation:

P①38 Jerome *Epistles* 106.2

> quaeritis a me rem magni operis, et majoris invidiae; in qua scribentis non ingenium, sed <u>eruditio</u> comprobetur; ut dum ipse cupio de caeteris judicare, judicandum me omnibus praebeam: et in opere Psalterii juxta digestionem schedulae vestrae, ubicumque inter Latinos Graecosque contentio est, quid magis Hebraeis conveniat, significem. In quo illud breviter admoneo, ut sciatis aliam esse <u>editionem</u>, quam Origenes et Caesariensis Eusebius, omnesque Graeciae tractatores κοινήν, id est <u>communem</u> appellant, atque <u>vulgatam</u>, et a plerisque nunc Λουκιανός dicitur; aliam Septuaginta interpretum, quae in ἑξαπλοῖς codicibus reperitur, et a nobis in Latinum sermonem fideliter versa est, et Jerosolymae atque in Orientis ecclesiis decantatur.... <u>κοινή autem ista, hoc est communis, editio ipsa est quae et septuaginta</u>, sed hoc interest inter utramque

---

not always the same person as the commentator), with variant readings placed at the margins of the 'edited' text (Cameron 1990:116–117). I suggest that the idea of 'reading out loud' is a way of expressing the process of establishing a definitive text as if it were a speech-act."

[113] The next three paragraphs are a revised version of what I offer in *HTL* 20–21.
[114] So I agree basically with Allen 1924:317.
[115] Jerome *Epistles* 106.2, as discussed by Allen 1924:317, 319. See in general Neuschäfer 1987. See also Lührs 1992:8 on Origen's editorial policy of avoiding personal emendations or conjectures in editing the text of the Septuagint.

Prolegomena

> quod κοινή pro locis et temporibus et pro voluntate scriptorum vetus corrupta editio est, ea autem quae habetur in ἑξαπλοῖς et quam nos vertimus ipsa est quae in eruditorum libris incorrupta et immaculata septuaginta interpretum translatio reservatur.

You ask me about a matter of great importance, which is a source of even greater invidiousness. In this matter it is not the inborn gifts of the one who is writing but his erudition [*eruditio*][116] that is being tested. The result is that, in wishing to make judgments about others, I am setting myself up to be judged by all. Juxtaposing what is in my work on the Psalter with a listing of your queries, wherever there is a difference between the Latin and Greek texts I will indicate what agrees more with the Hebrew texts. In this matter, I caution you about something, just briefly. Here is what you have to understand. There is an edition that Origen, Eusebius of Caesarea, and all those who are experts in the Greek tradition call the Koine edition, that is, the common edition, the vulgate edition, and most people nowadays call it the Lucianus edition. Then there is another edition [= the Septuagint], which comes from the Seventy Interpreters, which is found in the hexapla codices and which I faithfully translated into the Latin language. This is the edition that is liturgically sung in Jerusalem and in other congregations of the East. That Koine of yours [= the Lucianus edition that you are using], that is, the common edition, is the same thing as the edition of the Seventy [= the Septuagint = the edition that I am using], but there is this difference between the two: that the Koine—in line with different times and different places and different whims of people who wrote it down—is an old corrupt edition, whereas by contrast the one that is contained in the hexapla and which I have translated is the same thing as the actual translation [into Greek from Hebrew] that has been conserved in the books of the erudite [*eruditi*][117] without corruption and without blemish—that is, the translation by the Seventy interpreters.

P§176 In other words, the 'edition' of the Septuagint that Jerome uses as his own textual source—that is, the edition of Origen as found in the fifth

---

[116] On Jerome's concept of *eruditio*, see the next note.

[117] Jerome's concept of 'the books of the erudite [*eruditi*]' corresponds to the Aristarchean concept of the *khariesterai*.

P⑤15. Conclusions: the Homeric Koine as a classical text

column of his six-column display or *hexapla*—is the same thing as the *koinē* to the extent that it is 'common' in the sense of 'general' or even 'universal', but it transcends the designation of *koinē* to the extent that it is a 'corrected' text, freed from 'corruptions' associated with the other *koinē* text that is 'common' in the sense of 'vulgar'.

P§177 For Jerome, then, the word *koinē* has the aura of an authoritative but relatively 'uncorrected' text. Similarly in the case of Aristarchus, I am saying that his category of *koinai* or 'common' texts of Homer is notionally derived from an authoritative but relatively 'uncorrected' textual source—a Koine in the sense of a 'standard' version. As I have argued in earlier work and will argue further in the chapters that follow, especially in Chapter 3, such an authoritative but relatively 'uncorrected' Koine is the Homeric tradition as it existed in Athens in the fourth century.[118]

P§178 A piece of evidence that supports my reconstructing a fourth-century Athenian Koine is the fourth-century Athenian usage of the adjective *koinos / koinē* as 'common' in the ideological sense of 'general, standardized, universalized'.[119] As I have argued in earlier work, such a meaning of Koine would fit the *Iliad* and *Odyssey* as "owned" by the Athenian State, on the occasion of seasonally recurring performances at the Festival of the Panathenaia.[120]

P§179 In my earlier work, I described such a notionally single text, such a single Koine, in terms of an Athenian "City Edition" of Homer.[121] But the very idea of an Athenian "City Edition" can be called into question on the grounds that Aristarchus never refers to such a thing. According to this line of reasoning, there never was an Athenian "City Edition," since Aristarchus would most likely have preferred it over other editions—if such a thing had ever existed.[122] It all depends, however, on what we mean when we speak of Aristarchus' preferences. In one sense, Aristarchus preferred readings judged

---

[118] *PP* 187–200, following (in part) Jensen 1980:109. This possibility is entertained but rejected by Haslam 1997:71.

[119] See Lycurgus *Against Leokrates* 102 and Demosthenes 18.170; also Isaeus 7.16, on the care taken in the legitimizing of texts recorded by the state of Athens: only after full verification 'are they to be written down into the *koinon grammateion*' (εἰς τὸ κοινὸν γραμματεῖον ἐγγράφειν). This usage confirms that the expression ἐν κοινῷ goes with *both* γραψαμένους *and* φυλάττειν in "Plutarch" *Lives of the Ten Orators* 841f (as discussed in *PP* 175n77): in this context, what is recorded and preserved by the Athenian state in standardized form is the corpus of tragedies attributed to Aeschylus, Sophocles, and Euripides. See also Bollack 1994.

[120] *PP* 189. For the moment, this formulation is unaffected by the existing distinction between the feast of the Great Panathenaia, celebrated every fourth year, and the feast of the Lesser Panathenaia, celebrated in the other years.

[121] *PP* 187–190.

[122] I am paraphrasing here (and disagreeing with) the formulation of Haslam 1997:71.

Prolegomena

to be *khariesterai* over readings that were *koinai*. In another sense, however, the overall practice of Aristarchus can be described as just the opposite: we have seen that he chose as a rule to retain in his base text the readings he judged to be *koinai*. In that sense, he did indeed prefer what I have just described as an Athenian "City Edition." Still, I now think it would be better not to use the word edition in this context. After all, the Homeric Koine was for Aristarchus not an edition but rather a preedition. For Aristarchus, the Koine was a tradition that still needed to be edited. The Homeric scholia make it clear that Aristarchus' criterion for distinguishing a superior from an inferior *ekdosis* or 'edition' was the variable scholarly quality of the editing process, that is, of *diorthōsis* or 'correction'—in the sense of restoring 'genuine' or 'original' readings to a 'corrupted' text.

P§180 To the extent that the *koinē* Homer is 'common' in the uneroded and privileged sense of a 'general, standardized, universalized' text stemming from an earlier past, we can expect Aristarchus to value it; to the extent that this same *koinē* is 'common' in the eroded and non-privileged sense of 'vulgar', we can expect him to prefer the more 'corrected' editions from the more recent past, including those of Aristophanes and Zenodotus. This pattern of preference could only be expected to intensify in the post-Aristarchean era, by which time the privileged sense of *koinē* would have eroded further.

P§181 In Jerome's *Letters* (106.2), as we saw, he speaks about achieving a perfect biblical text by correcting any mistakes that may have corrupted or stained the *vulgata* or 'vulgate'. Correction, he says, recovers a *vulgata* that is *incorrupta et immaculata*, freed of all corruptions and stains. Implicitly, the *vulgata* had been authoritative from the start, and that is why it was worthy of serving as a base text in the first place. The base text simply needed to be corrected in order to become the master text. In the passage from the *Letters* of Jerome that I am citing, the Greek word that Jerome says is equivalent to this authoritative base text, this *vulgata*, is *koinē* / κοινή.

P§182 I propose to illustrate this essential concept of the Koine as an authoritative base text by showing a snapshot image that I invoke as a metaphor for the fixity sought by Jerome for the vulgate Bible. The image I have in mind is in the neighborhood where I live. It is a bronze statue that sits in front of the Croatian Embassy on Massachusetts Avenue in Washington, District of Columbia (Figure 1).

P§183 The statue represents Saint Jerome, or "Jerome the Priest," as the lettering inscribed at the base of the statue calls him. We see him seated on top of a block of stone, wearing nothing, hunched over a codex of the Bible, the Latin vulgate version of which is primarily his own achievement—the result of

P⒮15. Conclusions: the Homeric Koine as a classical text

his own agonizing efforts at perfection. I walk past Jerome every time I head for Sheridan Circle. There he sits, day after day, stooped over his beloved text, lost in his thoughts as he seeks ever to find the exact meaning of the Book. The rigidity of the bronze that freezes Jerome in this moment of deep concentration extends from the fixity of the text he is forever reading. Oblivious to his external surroundings, he sits there in all his nakedness, all exposed to the elements, rain or shine, and unwittingly inviting the gaze of gawking passers-by. Day in and day out, he just sits there, steadfastly indifferent to all that comes and goes outside his inner world of words, those perfect words of perfection in the making.

P§184 With this image in mind, I conclude my argument about the Homeric Koine as 'corrected' by Aristarchus, which had become the definitive Homeric text of later ages, including the age of Virgil.

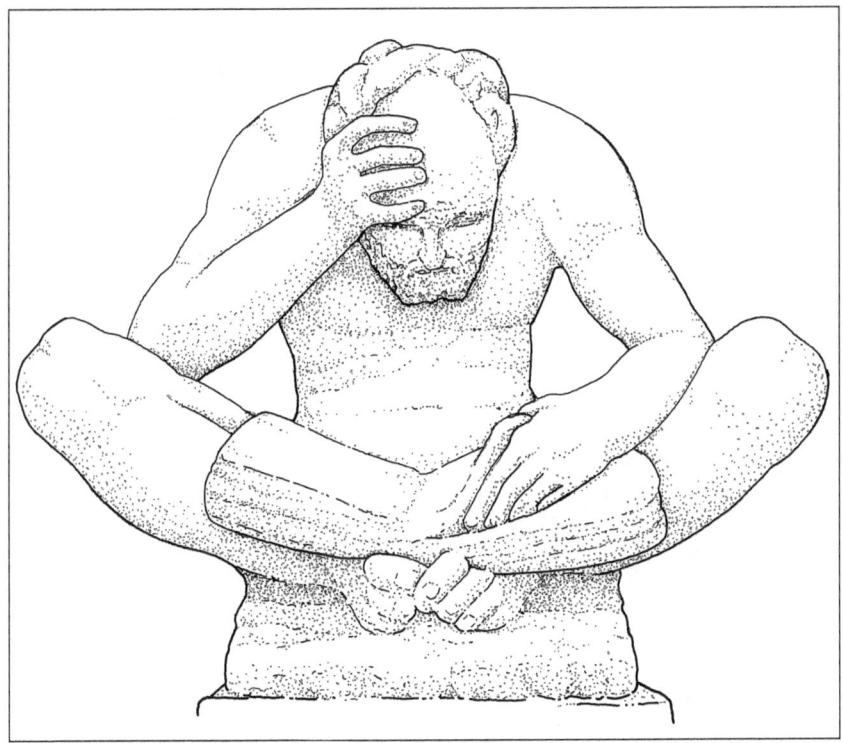

Figure 1. Sculpture: Ivan Meštrović (1883-1962), St. Jerome the Priest, 1954. Bronze, over life size. Located in front of the Embassy of the Republic of Croatia, Washington, DC.

Prolegomena

P§185 Aristarchus accepted the already rigid Athenian Koine version of Homer as his base text not because he thought it went back directly to Homer. In fact, we have seen that Aristarchus distanced himself from the Koine by imposing even more rigid criteria for determining what is or is not Homeric. Still, Aristarchus adhered to the Koine version as his point of departure, as a base text that required massive editorial correction, *diorthōsis*, which he displayed fully in his commentaries. Although Aristarchus' narrower system of preferred readings—his *diorthōsis*—has not survived *as a system*, the broader system of the Koine textual tradition that he used as his base text, which was still relatively narrower than the augmented base text used by Zenodotus and Crates, has indeed survived, by and large, in the so-called medieval vulgate, that is, in the overall medieval manuscript tradition of Homer.[123] It has also survived, by and large, in papyri dating from the post-Aristarchean period. It has even survived in Homeric quotations dating from that later period. These survivals represent the classical text of Homer.

---

[123] The point that I am making here can easily be misunderstood if we translate *koinē* simply as 'vulgate', without further clarification.

CHAPTER ONE

HOMER THE CLASSIC IN THE AGE OF VIRGIL

1Ⓢ1. An esthetics of rigidity

1§1 The poetry of Virgil, I take it as a given, rivals that of Homer. Historically, Virgil the Classic even displaced Homer the Classic in the Latin culture of the Roman empire (though not in the Greek)—already in the age of Virgil. But the question is: what is it exactly about the poetry of Virgil that made it rival the poetry of Homer in the first place—not so much as a Latin alternative but as an <u>absolute classic</u> in its own right? The answer, essentially, is to be found in the poetry of Virgil himself, especially in his epic masterpiece, the *Aeneid*.

1§2 As we can see from Virgil's use of—and references to—Homer in the *Aeneid*, Homer was clearly a poetic model for Virgil, but this Homer in the age of Virgil had become too limited—too rigid—for the Roman poet. Virgil had to go beyond Homer the Classic in his own age in order to succeed as a rival.

1§3 Let us proceed now to the age of Virgil. In this age the text of Homer— and therefore the poetry of Homer—was defined by the editorial norms of the Library of Alexandria, which I have already surveyed in the Prolegomena. I have more to say in the twin book *Homer the Preclassic* about these and other editorial norms. For now, however, I focus on the simple fact that the Homer of Aristarchus was the definitive Homer in the age of Virgil. This fact is relevant to Virgil's artistic goal, which was, to rival Homer in definitiveness. It is also relevant to another fact: that Virgil became, by hindsight, "Virgil the Classic," rivaling Homer the Classic.

1§4 But what exactly was Homer to Virgil? For him, the Homer of Aristarchus was not only definitive: Homer had already become overdefined. Definitiveness had gone too far by the time of Virgil. In his time, Homer must have seemed too rigid, too perfect.

1§5 By saying "too rigid" I risk making the metaphor of rigidity sound negative. That is not at all my intention. I need to affirm that Homeric poetry treats rigidity as a positive esthetic value. This poetry can picture itself as absolutely rigid, and such absolute rigidity is seen as beautiful and even ideal, the essence of perfection. I am about to give an example, taken directly from the Homeric *Iliad*.

1§6 Before I go any further, though, I need to affirm that Virgilian poetry likewise treats rigidity as a positive esthetic value. As we will see presently, Virgilian poetry can also picture itself as absolutely rigid, and again this absolute rigidity is seen as beautiful and even ideal, the essence of perfection. Still, the relatively less rigid Homer of earlier times, as in the age of Callimachus, must have seemed more accommodating for poets like Virgil who hoped to imitate Homer and thereby rival him. As we will see later on, Virgil's imitation of Homer can draw from more fluid phases of Homer in order to achieve its own rigidity.

1§7 In order to avoid any further negative connotations of rigidity, let me proceed to offer some specialized metaphors that convey the idea of absolute rigidity—without the negative associations conveyed by the word <u>rigid</u> in English. In my previous work, I have found it apt to use the metaphor of <u>crystallization</u>.[1] Another apt metaphor is <u>freezing</u>, as in the expression <u>freeze-frame</u> used by filmmakers. Far less suitable is the word <u>stereotyping</u>. Perhaps least suitable is <u>sclerosis</u>. Less unsuitable, on the other hand, is <u>rigor mortis</u>—provided we appreciate the aestheticizing of death within the <u>freeze-frame</u> of a perfect moment.

1Ⓢ2. Sculpting a perfect Homeric moment

1§8 The notion of a stop-motion picture at the moment of death brings me finally to the Homeric example I have in mind. As we set out to visualize the picture, however, it is essential for me to reiterate: I am not saying that Homeric poetry is rigid. I am saying only that it can idealize itself as absolutely rigid. Here, then, is my example from the *Iliad*. It is a passage where Homeric poetry pictures itself in terms of absolute rigidity. The operative metaphor, this time, is that of <u>petrifaction</u>:

1Ⓣ1 *Iliad* II 299–332

    299 τλῆτε φίλοι, καὶ μείνατ' ἐπὶ χρόνον ὄφρα δαῶμεν
    300 ἢ ἐτεὸν Κάλχας μαντεύεται ἦε καὶ οὐκί.

[1] *HQ* 109.

1⑤2. Sculpting a perfect Homeric moment

301 εὖ γὰρ δὴ τόδε ἴδμεν ἐνὶ φρεσίν, ἐστὲ δὲ πάντες
302 μάρτυροι, οὓς μὴ κῆρες ἔβαν θανάτοιο φέρουσαι·
303 χθιζά τε καὶ πρωΐζ' ὅτ' ἐς Αὐλίδα νῆες Ἀχαιῶν
304 ἠγερέθοντο κακὰ Πριάμῳ καὶ Τρωσὶ φέρουσαι,
305 ἡμεῖς δ' ἀμφὶ περὶ κρήνην <u>ἱεροὺς κατὰ βωμοὺς</u>
306 <u>ἔρδομεν ἀθανάτοισι τεληέσσας ἑκατόμβας</u>
307 καλῇ ὑπὸ πλατανίστῳ ὅθεν ῥέεν ἀγλαὸν ὕδωρ·
308 ἔνθ' <u>ἐφάνη</u> <u>μέγα σῆμα</u>· δράκων ἐπὶ νῶτα δαφοινὸς
309 <u>σμερδαλέος</u>, τόν ῥ' <u>αὐτὸς Ὀλύμπιος ἧκε</u> φόως δέ,
310 <u>βωμοῦ ὑπαΐξας</u> πρός ῥα πλατάνιστον ὄρουσεν.
311 ἔνθα δ' ἔσαν στρουθοῖο νεοσσοί, νήπια τέκνα,
312 ὄζῳ ἐπ' ἀκροτάτῳ πετάλοις ὑποπεπτηῶτες
313 ὀκτώ, ἀτὰρ μήτηρ ἐνάτη ἦν ἣ τέκε τέκνα·
314 ἔνθ' ὅ γε τοὺς <u>ἐλεεινὰ</u> κατήσθιε τετριγῶτας·
315 μήτηρ δ' ἀμφεποτᾶτο <u>ὀδυρομένη</u> φίλα τέκνα·
316 τὴν δ' ἐλελιξάμενος πτέρυγος λάβεν <u>ἀμφιαχυῖαν</u>.
317 αὐτὰρ ἐπεὶ κατὰ τέκνα φάγε στρουθοῖο καὶ αὐτήν,
318 τὸν μὲν <u>ἀρίζηλον</u> θῆκεν θεὸς ὅς περ <u>ἔφηνε</u>·
319 <u>λᾶαν γάρ μιν ἔθηκε</u> Κρόνου πάϊς ἀγκυλομήτεω·
320 ἡμεῖς δ' ἑσταότες <u>θαυμάζομεν</u> οἷον ἐτύχθη.
321 ὡς οὖν <u>δεινὰ</u> πέλωρα θεῶν εἰσῆλθ' ἑκατόμβας,
322 Κάλχας δ' αὐτίκ' ἔπειτα <u>θεοπροπέων</u> ἀγόρευε·
323 τίπτ' ἄνεῳ ἐγένεσθε κάρη κομόωντες Ἀχαιοί;
324 ἡμῖν μὲν τόδ' <u>ἔφηνε</u> <u>τέρας</u> μέγα μητίετα Ζεὺς
325 ὄψιμον ὀψι<u>τέλεστον</u>, <u>ὅου κλέος οὔ ποτ' ὀλεῖται</u>.
326 ὡς οὗτος κατὰ τέκνα φάγε στρουθοῖο καὶ αὐτήν
327 ὀκτώ, ἀτὰρ μήτηρ ἐνάτη ἦν ἣ τέκε τέκνα,
328 ὣς ἡμεῖς τοσσαῦτ' ἔτεα πτολεμίξομεν αὖθι,
329 τῷ δεκάτῳ δὲ πόλιν αἱρήσομεν εὐρυάγυιαν.
330 κεῖνος τὼς ἀγόρευε· <u>τὰ δὴ νῦν πάντα τελεῖται</u>.
331 ἀλλ' ἄγε μίμνετε πάντες ἐϋκνήμιδες Ἀχαιοὶ

Chapter One

332 αὐτοῦ εἰς ὅ κεν ἄστυ μέγα Πριάμοιο ἕλωμεν.

299 Endure, my near and dear ones, and stay as long as it takes for us to find out
300 whether Calchas is prophesying something that is true or not.
301 For I know this well in my heart, and you all
302 are witnesses, those of you who have not been carried off by the demons of death.
303 It is as if it was yesterday or the day before, when the ships of the Achaeans at Aulis
304 were gathered, portending doom to Priam and the Trojans.
305 Standing around a spring, <u>at a sacred altar,</u>
306 <u>we were sacrificing perfect [*teléessai*]² hecatombs to the immortal ones</u>
307 under a beautiful plane tree, in a place where sparkling water flowed.
308 Then there <u>appeared [*phainesthai*] a great sign [*sēma*], a serpent</u> [*drakōn*] with blood-red markings on its back.
309 <u>Terrifying it was.</u>³ The <u>Olympian [= Zeus] himself had sent it</u> into the zone of light.
310 <u>It darted out from underneath the altar</u>, and it rushed toward the plane tree.
311 Over there were the nestlings of a sparrow, helpless young things.
312 In the highest branch amidst the leaves they were hiding in fear,
313 eight of them. The ninth was the mother that had hatched the young ones.
314 Then it devoured them, <u>in a way that is pitiful</u> [*eleeina*],⁴ while they were chirping.

---

² As we see from this context, the word *telos* can be used to express the idea of <u>perfection</u> in sacrifice.
³ The narrative here draws attention to the theme of terror. More in a moment.
⁴ The narrative here draws attention to the theme of pity. More in a moment.

315	And their mother was fluttering above, <u>lamenting</u> [*oduresthai*] for her dear little things.
316	Then it threw its coils around her, catching her by the wing as she was <u>wailing over</u> [*amphiakhuia*]⁵ them.
317	And when it devoured the young ones of the sparrow and the mother as well,
318	the same god that had <u>made</u> it <u>visible</u> [*phainein*] now made it <u>most visible</u> [*arizēlos*].⁶
319	For the son of crafty Kronos <u>now made it into stone</u>.⁷
320	We just stood there, <u>struck with awe</u> [*thauma*] at what happened,
321	how such <u>frightful</u>⁸ portents invaded the hecatombs of the gods.
322	Then, right away, Calchas spoke, <u>speaking the words of seers</u> [*theopropeîn*]:
323	"Why are you speechless, Achaeans with the elaborate hair?
324	Zeus, master of craft, <u>made visible</u> [*phainein*] this great <u>portent</u> [*teras*].
325	It is late in coming, late in <u>reaching its outcome</u> [*telos*], and <u>its fame</u> [*kleos*] <u>will never perish</u>.
326	Just as this thing devoured the young ones of the sparrow and the mother as well,
327	eight in number, while the mother made it nine, the one that hatched the young ones,
328	so also we will wage war for that many years in number,
329	and then, on the tenth year, we will capture the city with its broad streets."

---

⁵ The *amphi-* of *amphi-akhuia* in the sense of 'wailing over' a loved one is comparable in its associations with the *amphi-* of *amphi-khumenē* (Odyssey viii 527) in the sense of 'weeping over' a loved one.

⁶ More in a moment about the translation 'most visible'.

⁷ This verse was athetized by Aristarchus. More in a moment.

⁸ Again the narrative draws attention to the theme of terror. More in a moment.

330   Thus spoke that man. <u>And now I see that all these things are reaching their outcome</u> [<u>telos</u>].⁹
331   So come now, all of you, hold your place, all you Achaeans with the fine shin-guards,
332   stay here until we capture the great city of Priam.

1§9 The narrative of the *Iliad* is quoting the words of Odysseus, who in turn is quoting the words of Calchas the seer. These embedded quotations recall an incident that took place in the first year of the ten-year Trojan War. This incident, as Odysseus relates, was interpreted by Calchas as a portent. This portent of the nine birds and the serpent prompts the seer Calchas to respond with an oracular utterance, a prophecy. The seer responds not only to the portent. He responds also to the vision of the portent, and that vision is represented as something eternal—that is, something made eternal by the medium of poetry. I have studied this passage before in another work, concentrating on the interaction we see here between the media of poetry and prophecy.¹⁰ Here I concentrate on two other aspects of the passage. First, I will analyze the portent of the nine birds and the serpent as a poetic vision, a scene of terror and pity that takes place in the unexpected setting of an ongoing sacrifice. As we will see, this poetic vision captures the entire story of the Trojan War in one single frozen motion picture. Second, I will analyze the references in this passage to the ending of the story—a story that ends on a theme of terror and pity. As we will also see, this ending of the story is represented as the ultimate defining point of the epic that is currently in progress.

1§10 Here I must interrupt the flow of my argumentation in order to highlight the combined themes of <u>terror and pity</u> in this Homeric story. I find it pertinent to recall here a well-known formulation of Aristotle, who speaks of the emotions of <u>terror</u> (<u>phobos</u>) and <u>pity</u> (<u>eleos</u>) as essential aspects of tragic poetry (*Poetics* 1449b24–28). What is less well known is that these same two emotions are essential aspects of Homeric poetry as well.¹¹

1§11 Now I restart the argumentation, offering an analysis of the poetics built into the ominous vision of the serpent and the birds in *Iliad* II. The setting

---

⁹ The particle δή here has an "evidentiary" force, indicating that the speaker has just <u>seen</u> something, in other words, that the speaker has achieved an insight just a moment ago ('aha, now I see that . . .'). See Bakker 1997:74–80, 2005:146.

¹⁰ HR 25–27.

¹¹ Shankman 1983. See especially his p. 108, with reference to the poetics of terror and pity in *Odyssey* xvii 415–444, as observed by Shankman's teacher, Elroy Bundy, in a course that Bundy gave on the Aristotelian theory of criticism in the spring of 1973.

is a sacrifice (306) at a sacrificial altar (305). When the serpent appears, the wording that describes its appearance, *phainesthai* 'appear, be made visible' (308), expresses the idea of a sacred epiphany. The epiphany was caused by the Plan of Zeus (309). The god is later described by the seer as the agent of the epiphany: the middle verb *phainesthai* 'appear, be made visible' now becomes the active verb *phainein* 'cause to appear, make visible', and the subject of the verb is Zeus himself as the active agent of the epiphany (318, 324). Now let us proceed to the poetic aspects of the vision, with specific reference to the poetics of terror and pity. When the serpent first makes its appearance, it is described as 'terrifying' (309 *smerdaleos*); it is a 'terrifying' thing (*deina*), says the narrating Odysseus, that portents like this should intrude upon an ongoing sacrifice (321). And the serpent proceeds to devour the eight little birds 'in a way that is pitiful' (314 *eleeina*). As the little birds are being swallowed, one after the other, the mother bird is pictured as 'lamenting' (314 *oduromenē*) while fluttering helplessly over the nest.[12] This scene of holy terror reaches its critical moment when the serpent lunges at this ninth bird, striking her in midair and swallowing her as well. At that precise moment, marked by the emotions of terror and pity, the same god who had sent the serpent, Zeus himself (309), now turns it into stone (319).

1§12 Calchas the seer instantly responds to the vision with this formulation: just as surely as the serpent, who is the tenth and last part in the ten-part sequence of the vision, has devoured the nine birds, so will the Achaeans destroy the city of Troy in the tenth year of the ten-year sequence of the story of the Trojan War (326–329). Responding to the petrifaction of the serpent in *Iliad* II, the voice of the seer Calchas is being quoted by Odysseus, and, ultimately, by Homeric poetry, and this prophetic voice equates the petrified serpent with the Troy story all told. At the moment of the equation, however, that Troy story is still in the process of being narrated. The narration is in progress, it is current, and it will not be over until it is over. Once it is really over, then and only then will the narration become rigid like the petrified serpent—and permanent. The storytelling itself is animated or live—in the parlance of modern technology—and it must remain animated until the story is fully told. The petrified serpent is a prophecy of this fulfillment, and it too is animated and life-like in the sense that it predicts the live performance of the narration all the way to the very end, which is the outcome of the narration.

---

[12] On the picturing of a lamenting woman as a grieving mother bird that has lost her nestlings, see Euripides *Trojan Women* (146–151 and 826–830), with the commentary of Dué 2006:140–141.

Chapter One

And the word that conveys the idea of reaching an ending or outcome is *teleîn* (325, 330), which I have been translating so far as 'reach an outcome'.

1§13 So the portent of the nine birds and the serpent in *Iliad* II is a prophetic vision of the Troy story. Just as the vision of the seer Calchas concentrates on the ending of the vision, which is the tenth part of a ten-part sequence of nine birds and a serpent, so also the Troy story concentrates on the tenth year of its own sequence of ten years, and on a particular moment of terror and pity in that tenth year, the capture of the city. The tenth year marks the moment when the action is arrested. And the serpent—as the tenth part of the visionary sequence—marks the moment when the motion is arrested. The climactic moment of terror and pity in the vision of the serpent and the birds is marked by the petrifaction.

1§14 What is the technical term for a seer's response to such a vision? In Homeric diction, oracular statements uttered by *theopropoi* 'seers' like Calchas are conventionally signaled by the word *hupokrinesthai* (ὑποκρίνεσθαι) 'respond'. This word designates a verbal response to an ominous event or portent that is <u>seen</u> by someone. That is, *hupokrinesthai* designates a verbal message that responds to a visual message. Having examined every Homeric attestation of this verb *hupokrinesthai*, I can report what I have found: just as the poetic words of an oracular prophecy are expected to match exactly the realities of the future that is being 'seen' by a seer, so also the poetic words of Homeric narrative are expected to match exactly the realities of the past.[13] The epic poetry of Homer figures itself as the fulfillment of the prophecies made in its own past, and to that extent the epic is coextensive with oracular poetry: just as oracular poetry guarantees the future, epic poetry can guarantee the past. This mentality is embedded in Homeric references to seers:

1①2 *Iliad* XII 228

> ὧδε χ' <u>ὑποκρίναιτο θεοπρόπος</u>
>
> thus would a <u>seer</u> [*theopropos*] <u>respond</u> [*hupokrinesthai*].

1§15 In the Homeric context I just quoted, the speaker's point is that his quoted words are the same words that a *theopropos* 'seer' would use in response—that is, if such a seer were to <u>see</u> what the speaker has just seen. The equation of the speaker's wording with some seer's potential wording rein-

---

[13] HR 23, 29, 32, 34.

forces not only the credibility but also the exactness of the Homeric wording that generates the speaker's wording in the first place.¹⁴

1§16 In the passage about the nine birds and the serpent, it is essential that Calchas speaks as a *theopropos* 'seer' when he interprets the vision:

1①3 *Iliad* II 322

> Κάλχας δ' αὐτίκ' ἔπειτα <u>θεοπροπέων</u> ἀγόρευε
>
> Then, right away, Calchas spoke, <u>speaking the words of seers</u> [*theopropeîn*].

1§17 The words of the seer need to be remembered exactly and quoted back exactly, as they are indeed quoted back at *Iliad* II 323-329. It is a necessity for the words to be quoted back exactly, since the realities will turn out exactly the way the seer had foretold them. But the exact recovery of the words is a necessity not only for the seer but also for the poet. When the words of the seer's oracular poetry are quoted back exactly by the figure of Odysseus at II 323-329, that act of quoting becomes a demonstration or proof of the unchangeability of these poetic words.¹⁵

1§18 This idea of unchangeability is conveyed by the words of Odysseus that frame what he had just quoted. I focus on the verse featuring the verb *teleîn*, which is derived from the noun *telos* 'outcome' and which I have been translating as 'reach an outcome [*telos*]':

1①4 *Iliad* II 330

> τὰ δὴ νῦν πάντα <u>τελεῖται</u>
>
> And now I see that all these things <u>are reaching their outcome</u> [*telos*].

1§19 The recurring sameness of Homeric quotations, as signaled by such oracular words as *hupokrinesthai* 'respond', corresponds to the recurring sameness of the given vision that calls for the question that calls for the response. In the case of the words of the seer Calchas as quoted back by the *Iliad* at II 323-329, the sameness of the original vision—as retold—is concretized¹⁶ in the image of petrifaction: Zeus turns the serpent into stone at the critical moment when it has just devoured the nine birds (II 319). In doing so, the same god

---

¹⁴ HR 23, 29, 32, 34.
¹⁵ HR 23, 29, 32, 34.
¹⁶ I draw attention to the etymology of this word.

Chapter One

who had made the original epiphany has now made the centerpiece of that epiphany into a permanent landmark:[17]

1①5 *Iliad* II 318

> τὸν μὲν ἀρίζηλον θῆκεν θεὸς ὅς περ ἔφηνε
> The same god that had made it visible [*phainein*] now made it most visible [*arizēlos*].

1⑤3. Variations on a perfect Homeric moment

1§20 Aristarchus, the premier Alexandrian commentator on Homer, athetizes the next verse:

1①6 *Iliad* II 319

> λᾶαν γάρ μιν ἔθηκε Κρόνου πάϊς ἀγκυλομήτεω·
> For the son of Kronos, the one with the oblique plans, now made it into stone.

1§21 Aristonicus, an Aristarchean scholar who flourished in the age of Virgil, well over a century after Aristarchus, has this to say about the verse, in the scholia A for *Iliad* II 319 (a1): ἀθετεῖται 'it is athetized'—that is, this verse is athetized by Aristarchus. Such an athetesis by Aristarchus should not be misunderstood to mean that verse 319 of *Iliad* II is a substandard verse. From the standpoint of the history of Homeric textual transmission, as surveyed in the Prolegomena, it is just the opposite: this verse, like the many hundreds of other verses athetized by Aristarchus, belongs to the standard version of Homer, the Koine. Moreover, Aristarchus featured this verse in the text of his own edition of Homer. This verse would have looked like any other verse in the edition of Aristarchus—except for one small detail. Aristarchus placed a mark in the left-hand margin next to all verses that he athetized. That sign is the *obelos* (–).

1§22 Here I return to the conclusions I formulated in the Prolegomena concerning the editorial policy of Aristarchus. In cases where this editor was

---

[17] I used the work landmark here with reference to the petrified serpent in view of other examples of landmark poetics involving the theme of petrifaction. The premier example is the story of the petrifaction of the ship of the Phaeacians, as narrated in *Odyssey* xiii 160–164. See Nagy 2001c.

1§3. Variations on a perfect Homeric moment

uncertain whether a given Homeric verse was genuinely Homeric, he had two choices, in terms of his own editorial system:

(1) If he found the given verse only weakly attested in the available manuscripts, he would omit the verse from his base text.

(2) If he found the given verse strongly attested, then he would keep the verse in his base text, marking that verse with an *obelos* (-), the sign of athetesis, in the left-hand margin.

As I argued in the Prolegomena, the base text of Homer as established by Aristarchus was designed to reflect as accurately as possible the standard version of Homer, the Koine. Aristarchus confined to his *hupomnēmata* 'commentaries' whatever information and opinions he had about non-Koine variant readings, which in many cases he thought were more likely to be Homeric than the readings he featured in his own base text.

1§23 Applying what I formulated in the Prolegomena about the editorial policies of Aristarchus, I reaffirm what I just said about the verse at *Iliad* II 319 as I quoted it. To put it in the most simple terms, this verse stems from the base text of Aristarchus. And, like all other verses in that base text, verse 319 of *Iliad* II stems from the Koine tradition.

1§24 The Homeric scholia report another relevant detail about verse 319 of *Iliad* II. So far, we have seen that this verse must have been strongly attested in the standard Homer texts available to Aristarchus. But now we will see that it was also attested in a Homer text that particularly interested Aristarchus—the Homer edition of Zenodotus, who predates Aristarchus by well over a century. According to Zenodotus (scholia A for *Iliad* II 318), the verse that we know as II 319 was connected in meaning to an epithet in the previous verse 318. That epithet is *aridēlos* (ἀρίδηλον) 'most visible', with reference to the petrified serpent. To quote the wording of Aristonicus (scholia A for II 318 1): ὅτι Ζηνόδοτος γράφει ἀρίδηλον καὶ τὸν ἐχόμενον προσέθηκεν '[Aristarchus disagrees with the reading of Zenodotus] because Zenodotus writes ἀρίδηλον in his text, and he [= Zenodotus] added the line that follows'.[18]

---

[18] In the Homeric A scholia, the use of ὅτι 'because' as the word that introduces information derived from Aristonicus is a conventional way of indicating that 'Aristarchus writes a marginal sign in the margin because . . . '. In this case ὅτι was keyed to the marginal sign of the *diplē periestigmenē* (>:) placed at the left of *Iliad* II 318 in the base text of Aristarchus, and this placement of the sign is still attested in the Venetus A manuscript of the *Iliad*. Then there was the marginal sign of an *obelos* (-) placed at the left of *Iliad* II 319, and this placement is also still attested in the Venetus A.

Chapter One

1§25 I must take a moment to offer some words of caution here about the wording of Aristonicus, which can be misleading. When Aristonicus says that Zenodotus had 'added' the next verse, that is, verse 319 as we know it, he is speaking retrospectively: by hindsight, Aristarcheans like Aristonicus in the age of Virgil make it seem as if Zenodotus had 'added' such verses—as if the verses athetized by Aristarchus had come from outside the manuscript tradition of Homer. From the standpoint of Aristarchus himself over a century earlier, however, the verses that he athetized had not been <u>added</u> by previous editors like Zenodotus.[19] Rather, as I showed in the Prolegomena, Aristarchus was simply expressing his own editorial opinion that such verses should now be <u>subtracted</u> from the corpus of verses supposedly composed by Homer himself. Moreover, as I also showed in the Prolegomena, such editorial opinions of Aristarchus were confined to his *hupomnēmata* 'commentaries'. Aristarchus did not actually subtract from his base text the verses that he athetized. To repeat, the base text of Aristarchus continued to reflect the standard manuscript tradition of Homer.

1§26 Returning to verse 318 of *Iliad* II, I repeat the testimony of Aristonicus concerning what Aristarchus found in the edition of Zenodotus: in that Homeric text, the epithet of the serpent was spelled ἀρίδηλον—which would have been pronounced ἀρίδδηλον.[20] In the standard Homeric texts consulted by Aristarchus, the epithet was spelled ἀρίζηλον, and it was evidently this spelling that Aristarchus featured in the base text of his own edition. These two phonological byforms *ari-dēlos* and *ari-zēlos* are parallel in morphology, but the meaning is transparent only in the phonological byform *ari-dēlos*—'most visible'.[21]

1§27 It is essential to keep in mind that such information about the Homeric textual variation ἀρίζηλον / ἀρίδηλον, as mediated by the Homeric scholia, is derived ultimately from the *hupomnēmata* of Aristarchus. In these *hupomnēmata*, as we see further from the abridged reportage of the Homeric scholia, Aristarchus linked his discussion of the variants ἀρίζηλον and ἀρίδηλον at verse 318 with yet another variant, ἀίζηλον. Whereas *arizēlos* and *aridēlos* mean 'most visible', *aïzēlos* means the opposite, 'invisible'. In this case, unfortunately, the abridgment in the scholia is so severe that the actual mention of the variant ἀίδηλον has dropped out, though the basic argument adduced by Aristarchus in favor of this reading has been preserved. I will

---

[19] In making this point, I agree with Montanari 2008.
[20] On the pronunciation ἀρίδδηλον, see Chantraine *DELG* s.v. ἀρίζηλος, with further citations.
[21] Again, Chantraine *DELG* s.v. ἀρίζηλος.

1§3. Variations on a perfect Homeric moment

confront the argument in a moment, but first I need to stress the morphological validity of the variant *aïzēlos*, which is a phonological byform of *aïdēlos* just as *arizēlos* 'most visible' is a phonological byform of *aridēlos* 'most visible' at verse 318: the form *a-ïzēlos* / *a-ïdēlos* must have the basic meaning 'invisible' (derived from earlier **a-widēlos*).[22]

1§28 Next I turn to the argumentation of Aristarchus. The basic meaning of *a-ïdēlos* / *a-ïzēlos* as 'invisible' helps explain why Aristarchus was interested in the variant reading ἀίζηλον 'invisible' as an alternative to ἀρίζηλον 'most visible' at verse 318 of *Iliad* II. Even in their abridged form, the Homeric scholia show clearly what Aristarchus said in his *hupomnēmata* about the meaning of this variant. I give here the wording of scholia A: λέγει μέντοι γε ὅτι ὁ φήνας αὐτὸν θεὸς καὶ ἄδηλον ἐποίησεν 'he [= Homer] says that the same god that had made it [= the serpent] visible [= *phainein*] also made it invisible [*a-dēlos*]' (scholia A for *Iliad* II 318 1). The point is reinforced by the wording of scholia T for verse 319: ἀθετεῖται· πιθανώτερον γὰρ αὐτὸν καθάπαξ πεποιηκέναι ἀφανῆ τὸν καὶ φήναντα θεόν '[This verse] is athetized [by Aristarchus]: for it is more plausible that the same god who made it [= the serpent] visible [= *phainein*] should straightaway make it disappear [= make it *a-phanēs* 'invisible'].

1§29 So the variant verse at *Iliad* II 318 would look like this:

1Ⓘ7 *Iliad* II 318 (variant reading attested by Aristarchus)

τὸν μὲν <u>ἀίζηλον</u> θῆκεν θεὸς ὅς περ <u>ἔφηνε</u>

And the god that had <u>made</u> it [= the serpent] <u>visible</u> [<u>*phainein*</u>] now made it <u>invisible</u> [<u>*a-ïzēlos*</u>].

1§30 This version of *Iliad* II 318 is evidently incompatible with II 319 as we have it, which tells about the petrifaction of the serpent. The theme of making the serpent disappear is evidently incompatible with the theme of making the serpent into stone:

1Ⓘ8 *Iliad* II 318–319

τὸν μὲν <u>ἀρίζηλον</u> θῆκεν θεὸς ὅς περ <u>ἔφηνε</u>·
<u>λᾶαν γάρ μιν ἔθηκε</u> Κρόνου πάϊς ἀγκυλομήτεω

---

[22] Chantraine *DELG* s.v. ἄδηλος. He discusses both the morphology and the meaning of *a-ïdēlos*, reconstructing an active sense of 'causing someone or something to become invisible' alongside the intransitive sense of 'invisible'. I propose that the meaning 'invisible' is attested also in the figurative sense of 'inconspicuous, undistinguished' in Homeric contexts where *aïdēlos* is applied as an insult to morally undistinguished characters (as in *Odyssey* xxii 165).

Chapter One

> The same god that had made it visible [*phainein*] now made it most visible [*arizēlos*].
>
> For the son of Kronos, the one with the oblique plans, now made it into stone.

1§31 Some modern commentators have attempted to discredit the standard version I just quoted. One of these commentators claims that the contrast being made at verse 318 in this version is "rather pointless," and he expresses his preference for the alternative version adduced by Aristarchus.[23] This commentator implies that the standard version conveys a redundancy, which we may paraphrase this way: "the snake was made visible by the god who had made it visible." But such a paraphrase blunts the point of the intensifying prefix *ari-* in the compound *ari-zēlos* 'most visible'. I translate *ari-* as 'most' rather than 'very' in order to convey a rhetoric of extreme intensification here, which serves to express a competitively outstanding quality. Hence my translation: 'The same god that had made it visible [*phainein*] now made it most visible [*arizēlos*]'. I maintain, then, that the standard version of verses 318–319 of *Iliad* II makes just as much sense as the non-standard version of verse 318 minus verse 319.

1§32 Although Aristarchus personally preferred a configuration of textual variants that expresses the idea that Zeus made the serpent appear and then disappear, it is clear that he recognized the reality of the alternative configuration of variants expressing the idea that Zeus made the serpent appear and then made that appearance permanent by turning it into a physical landmark. It is also clear that he recognized that this alternative configuration of variants was considered the standard Homeric version even in his own time. The clearest indication of this recognition, as we saw earlier, is the fact that he included verse 319 of *Iliad* II in his base text instead of omitting it. In other words, the verse that signals the non-disappearance of the serpent occupies a place in the base text of Aristarchus, even though he athetizes it. Similarly at verse 318, Aristarchus featured in his base text the variant *arizēlos* 'most visible' as the epithet of the serpent, again indicating its non-disappearance, relegating to the *hupomnēmata* his comments on the variant *aizēlos* 'invisible'—which he linked in his commentary with his proposal to athetize verse 319. As we noted earlier, the linkage is self-evident: if the serpent disappears after its epiphany, then the subsequent verse describing the petrifaction of the serpent is out of place. But this non-Koine version, which features a scene of epiphany

---

[23] Kirk 1985:149.

1⑤3. Variations on a perfect Homeric moment

followed by disappearance, simply could not be formatted as the true Homeric alternative to the Koine version, which features a scene of epiphany followed by petrifaction. I must stress again: even though Aristarchus preferred the non-Koine version, he kept the Koine version in the base text of his edition.[24]

1§33 Elsewhere too, Aristarchus reacts in a comparable way to a scene of petrifaction. A relevant case in point is the myth of Niobe as retold in another most memorable passage of the *Iliad*. Although it is important for my short-term argumentation to consider this passage right away, those readers who are more interested in my long-term argumentation may prefer to postpone what follows here in §§33–36 for another occasion and to shift forward to §37 in their reading. For those readers who prefer to stay on course with the short-term argumentation, I now proceed to consider the passage about the myth of Niobe:

1①9 *Iliad* XXIV 601–620

601 νῦν δὲ μνησώμεθα δόρπου.
602 καὶ γάρ τ' ἠΰκομος Νιόβη ἐμνήσατο σίτου,
603 τῇ περ δώδεκα παῖδες ἐνὶ μεγάροισιν ὄλοντο
604 ἓξ μὲν θυγατέρες, ἓξ δ' υἱέες ἡβώοντες.
605 τοὺς μὲν Ἀπόλλων πέφνεν ἀπ' ἀργυρέοιο βιοῖο
606 χωόμενος Νιόβῃ, τὰς δ' Ἄρτεμις ἰοχέαιρα,
607 οὕνεκ' ἄρα Λητοῖ ἰσάσκετο καλλιπαρῄῳ·
608 φῆ δοιὼ τεκέειν, ἣ δ' αὐτὴ γείνατο πολλούς·
609 τὼ δ' ἄρα καὶ δοιώ περ ἐόντ' ἀπὸ πάντας ὄλεσσαν.
610 οἳ μὲν ἄρ' ἐννῆμαρ κέατ' ἐν φόνῳ, οὐδέ τις ἦεν
611 κατθάψαι, λαοὺς δὲ λίθους ποίησε Κρονίων·
612 τοὺς δ' ἄρα τῇ δεκάτῃ θάψαν θεοὶ Οὐρανίωνες.
613 ἣ δ' ἄρα σίτου μνήσατ', ἐπεὶ κάμε δάκρυ χέουσα.
614 νῦν δέ που ἐν πέτρῃσιν ἐν οὔρεσιν οἰοπόλοισιν
615 ἐν Σιπύλῳ, ὅθι φασὶ θεάων ἔμμεναι εὐνὰς
616 νυμφάων, αἵ τ' ἀμφ' Ἀχελώϊον ἐρρώσαντο,

---

[24] See also Montanari 2008, who shows that the reasoning of Aristarchus was influenced by the earlier reasoning of Aristotle about these same lines 318–319 of *Iliad* II (Aristotle F 145 ed. Rose via the commentary of Porphyry on the *Iliad* (vol. I, pp. 32–33 ed. Schrader).

617 ἔνθα λίθος περ ἐοῦσα θεῶν ἐκ κήδεα πέσσει.
618 ἀλλ' ἄγε δὴ καὶ νῶϊ μεδώμεθα δῖε γεραιὲ
619 σίτου· ἔπειτά κεν αὖτε φίλον παῖδα κλαίοισθα
620 Ἴλιον εἰσαγαγών· πολυδάκρυτος δέ τοι ἔσται.

601 But now the two of us [= Achilles speaking to Priam] must think of eating.
602 Even Niobe, the one with the beautiful hair, thought of eating grain,
603 the one who had twelve children, and all of them were killed in the palace,
604 six daughters and six sons in the bloom of youth.
605 Apollo killed the sons, shooting from his silver bow.
606 He was angry at Niobe—and the daughters were killed by Artemis, shooter of arrows—
607 angry because she [= Niobe] tried to make herself equal to Leto, the one with the beautiful cheeks.
608 She [= Niobe] said that she [= Leto] gave birth to two, while she herself produced many.
609 So the two of them [= Apollo and Artemis], only two though they were, destroyed the many.
610 They [= the children of Niobe] lay there in their gore for nine days, and there was no one
611 to bury them. The people had been turned into stone by the son of Kronos.
612 Then on the tenth day they [= the children of Niobe] were given a burial by the sky-dwelling gods themselves.
613 And she [= Niobe] thought of eating, since she was exhausted by her shedding of tears,
614 and now, somewhere amidst the rocks, on the desolate heights,
615 in Sipylos, where they say the goddesses have places to sleep
616 —the goddess nymphs, the ones who dance on the banks of the Akhelōios—

1ⓢ3. Variations on a perfect Homeric moment

617   there does she [= Niobe], though she has been turned into stone, digest her sorrows inflicted by the gods.
618   So too now the two of us must think, radiant old man,
619   of eating grain. And then, after that, for your dear child you may weep again,
620   after you have brought him to Troy. And there will be many tears shed for him.

1§34 In the logic of this complex simile, Niobe weeps, then consumes grain, and then resumes her weeping as she continues to 'digest' her sorrows for all eternity: so also Priam weeps, then is invited to eat grain, and then he too will resume his own weeping. The point is, 'even' Niobe ate grain, though the sorrows she had to 'digest' were eternal. Her sorrows, in the rhetoric of the simile spoken by Achilles, are overwhelmingly greater than the sorrows of Priam over the death of Hector—or than the sorrows of Achilles over the death of Patroklos. The sorrows of Niobe are in fact so overwhelming that she continues to weep eternally even after the gods turn her into stone. A petrified figure should be drained of emotion, as we see from the logic of the narrative contained in the simile: when the population in the realm of Niobe is petrified, there can be no weeping, no mourning, and therefore no funeral, so that the gods themselves must conduct a funeral and bury the children of Niobe. But Niobe, even after she is petrified, is like a human figure in that she continues to dissolve into tears. So overwhelming are her sorrows. Unlike the dissolving of a human figure in mourning, however, this petrified figure dissolves for eternity because her tears come from an inexhaustible source. Relevant is the use of the word *tēkesthai* 'dissolve' in Sophocles' *Antigone* (828) picturing a weeping Niobe in a state of petrifaction. This word, as we will see later, conjures the image of a cold mountain stream that flows without interruption from the heights where Niobe turned into stone; her tears are the uninterrupted source of that eternal stream.[25]

1§35 In this Koine version as it comes down to us by way of the medieval manuscript tradition, we see at verse 611 that all the people in the realm of Niobe were turned into stone after her sons and daughters were destroyed by Apollo and Artemis, so that they could not bury Niobe's children; then, at verses 614–617, we see further that Niobe herself was turned into stone.

---

[25] The visualization of Niobe is associated with a cold stream flowing down a mountainside (Dué 2006:161).

Chapter One

Commenting on all five of these verses in his *hupomnēmata*, Aristarchus argues that verse 611 is genuinely Homeric while verses 614–617 are not, and he athetizes all four of these supposedly non-Homeric verses (scholia A for *Iliad* XXIV 614–617a 1). It would be a mistake to infer, however, that verses 614–617 had no prehistory of their own. Aristarchus reports that there was indeed a version of the story where Niobe herself became petrified, and he ascribes this version to poets later than Homer, referring to them as the *neōteroi* 'newer ones'; by contrast, according to Aristarchus, the supposedly older poet Homer did not have such a version (scholia A for *Iliad* XXIV 613a 1).

1§36 I postpone till Chapter 2 my examination of Homeric textual variations where Aristarchus assigns one variant to Homer as the older poet and the other variant or variants to poets whom he considers to be *neōteroi* 'the newer ones'. As we will see, the Koine tends to include and accommodate variants that Aristarchus ascribes to the *neōteroi*, whereas Aristarchus isolates such variants as non-Homeric and even post-Homeric accretions—though he continues to include and accommodate them in his base text, which as I showed in the Prolegomena is meant to correspond as closely as possible to the Koine as he understood it.

1§37 I return to the standard or Koine version of the vision of the nine birds and the serpent. The petrified serpent at verse 319 of *Iliad* II, like some splendid statue sculpted by natural forces, radiates a permanent vision matching the permanent words that give it meaning. Such words provide the permanent response to the question posed by the permanent vision. It is this kind of definitive response that we see conveyed by the word *hupokrinesthai*, conveying the idea of prophetic words responding to prophetic visions.

1§38 What, then, is this permanent and perfect vision? It is a moment of terror and pity, and it captures in essence the story of Troy. This single moment pertains not only to the birds and the serpent that devoured them: it pertains to an audience that is getting caught up in the story of Troy's capture. That captivating story, if we are to use the exact word for story of Troy in Greek, is *Ilias*, that is, the '*Iliad*'.[26]

1Ⓢ4. Metaphors of unchangeability

1§39 I describe the Homeric vision of the petrified serpent as a statue sculpted by natural forces. That is because I see a metaphor at work in the sculpting of real statues that is comparable to the metaphor inherent in the vision of the

---

[26] *BA*² Preface §17 (= p. xii).

1§4. Metaphors of unchangeability

petrified serpent. The unchangeability of the petrified serpent is a metaphor for the notional unchangeability of the verbal art that reports it. We can see a comparable notion of unchangeability in the sculpting of real statues. I give two examples.

1§40 The first example has to do with the wording inscribed on a bronze statue dated to somewhere between 490 and 480 BCE. The statue has disappeared, but the base and its inscription have survived. Here is the inscription:

1ⓣ10 *CEG* 286 [*IG* I³ 533]. Inscription for a bronze statue dedicated by Antiphanes

πασιν ισ' ανθροποι|ς hυποκ|ρινομαι hοστις ε[ρ|ο]ται · |
hος μ' ανεθεκ' ανδ|ρον· Αντι|φανες δεκατεν

I respond [*hupokrinomai*] equally²⁷ to all men, whoever asks me:
Who among men dedicated me?²⁸ Antiphanes did, as a tithe.²⁹

1§41 The mentality of unchangeability, where the response to the question inherent in a vision is always an equivalent thing said in equivalent words, is signaled here, as in Homeric diction, by the word *hupokrinesthai*. In this case, of course, it is also signaled by the fact that the response is written down in the inscription. The letters will not change, just as the words of oracular response will not change. Still, I contend that the actual writing down of the words is not at all the cause of the notional unchangeability of this inscription but simply an effect. So also with the word *hupokrinesthai*: the usage of this word can be viewed as the effect, not the cause, of the notional unchangeability of oracular poetry and, by extension, of Homeric poetry.³⁰

1§42 Continuing to focus on the inscription featuring the word *hupokrinesthai*, I note that the letters of this inscription give potential voice to the words of response. I say potential because the voice is not inherently built into the inscription. In the mentality of early Greek poetic inscriptions, including this one, readers who happen to read a given inscription have to lend their own

---

²⁷ In my previous work, I translated *isa* here at *CEG* 286 [*IG* I³ 533] as 'in the same way' (*HR* 30, with further citations). Now I prefer to translate 'equally'. When I say 'equally', I mean notional equality, which is not necessarily real equality.
²⁸ On the use of the relative pronoun for expressing an indirect question, see *PH* 8§7n34 (= pp. 220–221).
²⁹ This translation follows what I give in *HR* 30n14, where I attempt to improve on my earlier translation in *HQ* 35n25. I now think that the genitive plural construction 'among men' must go with 'who', not with 'Antiphanes'.
³⁰ *HR* ch. 1.

voice by reading the letters aloud, so that these letters may then transmit the words that the inscribed object is saying.[31] The speaker is not the inscription itself, nor is it the actual writing in a more general sense. Rather, the speaker is the dedicated art object, which—or 'who'—is conventionally marked as the 'I' of the discourse. The words of this discourse are inherent in the dedicated art object, and it is the actual vision of the object that leads to asking it any question in the first place: who are you and why are you here? The response of the art object—I am such-and-such an object and I have been dedicated by so-and-so—is likewise dependent on the vision, which had set the framework of the question in the first place. The dedicated art object can always give the equivalent response because it always gets the equivalent question, given shape by the unchangeability of the vision that radiates from the object.

1§43 In this case, then, the unchanging response is notionally spoken by the dedicated art object, the statue, who is the 'I' that responds to all the questions that come from all those who engage with the vision of the statue. Yes, the mentality of unchangeability is reinforced by the writing down of these words. Still, notionally, these words of response would be constant even without writing, since they are predicated on the overall vision of the statue.

1§44 The usage of *hupokrinesthai* in Homeric Greek, as also in the inscription we have just read, helps explain the meaning of the classical Greek word *hupokritēs* 'actor', derived from *hupokrinesthai*. This theatrical word can be better understood by juxtaposing it with another theatrical word, *theatron* 'theater', composed of verb-root *thea-* 'have a vision' and noun-suffix *-tron*, indicating an instrument; thus the whole word can be interpreted etymologically as 'instrument for having a vision [*thea-*]'. The etymological implications of these two words, *theatron* and *hupokritēs*, can be interpreted together. The audience of theater, of *theatron*, which is the instrument for achieving *thea*, or vision, literally sees a vision of a character, such as the Antigone of Sophocles in the drama that is named after her, and this vision of Antigone can then speak for itself. Moreover, the word for 'audience' is *theatai* 'spectators'. Thus the mask-wearing actor who is the visualization of, say, Antigone is a *hupokritēs* of the theatrical vision of Antigone and of the whole drama that is the *Antigone* of Sophocles. Such an interpretation of the two words *theatron* and *hupokritēs* taken together is illustrated in this striking turn of phrase concerning the acting of the character of Antigone by the noted actors Theodoros and Aristodemos:

---

[31] Svenbro 1988.33–52 (= 1993:26–43), esp. pp. 36–38 (= 29–31); also Day 1989.

1§4. Metaphors of unchangeability

1①11 Demosthenes 19.246

Ἀντιγόνην δὲ Σοφοκλέους πολλάκις μὲν Θεόδωρος, πολλάκις δ' Ἀριστόδημος <u>ὑποκέκριται</u>

... many times <u>has</u> Theodoros, many times <u>has</u> Aristodemos <u>acted</u> [perfect of <u>hupokrinesthai</u>] the Antigone of Sophocles.³²

1§45 Just as writing is not a necessity for expressing a fixed message emanating from a fixed mental image, so also the physical reality of a work of art is not a necessity for achieving such a fixed image. In other words, you don't need a painting or a statue to express a fixed mental image any more than you need letters to write down what it looks like.

1§46 I now turn to my second example illustrating the notion of unchangeability in the sculpting of real statues. As in the case of the petrified serpent in the standard version of the Homeric narrative, we are about to see a freeze-frame of a perfect moment. In this case, however, the moment is one of happiness, not of terror and pity. Such a perfect moment is captured by Herodotus in his retelling of a story told by Solon about two young men, Kleobis and Biton, who performed a superhuman feat at the Heraia, the festival of the goddess Hera in their native city of Argos:

1①12 Herodotus 1.31.3–5

ταῦτα δέ σφι ποιήσασι καὶ <u>ὀφθεῖσι</u> ὑπὸ τῆς <u>πανηγύριος</u> <u>τελευτὴ</u> τοῦ βίου ἀρίστη ἐπεγένετο, διέδεξέ τε ἐν τούτοισι ὁ θεὸς ὡς ἄμεινον εἴη ἀνθρώπῳ τεθνάναι μᾶλλον ἢ ζώειν. Ἀργεῖοι μὲν γὰρ περιστάντες ἐμακάριζον τῶν νεηνιέων τὴν ῥώμην, αἱ δὲ Ἀργεῖαι τὴν μητέρα αὐτῶν, οἵων τέκνων ἐκύρησε. Ἡ δὲ μήτηρ <u>περιχαρὴς</u> ἐοῦσα τῷ τε ἔργῳ καὶ τῇ φήμῃ, στᾶσα ἀντίον τοῦ ἀγάλματος εὔχετο Κλεόβι τε καὶ Βίτωνι τοῖσι ἑωυτῆς τέκνοισι, οἵ μιν ἐτίμησαν μεγάλως, τὴν θεὸν δοῦναι τὸ ἀνθρώπῳ τυχεῖν ἄριστόν ἐστι. Μετὰ ταύτην δὲ τὴν εὐχὴν ὡς <u>ἔθυσάν</u> τε καὶ <u>εὐωχήθησαν</u>, <u>κατακοιμηθέντες</u> <u>ἐν αὐτῷ τῷ ἱρῷ</u>

---

³² The verb *hupokrinesthai* can take as its direct object not only the name of the character in the drama but also the name of the drama itself. There is an example to be found in the same context that we have just considered. Just before he speaks of the *Antigone* of Sophocles, Demosthenes (19.246) is speaking of a drama by Euripides, the *Phoenix*, which is named after the hero Phoenix. Demosthenes refers to this drama as *drāma* (δρᾶμα), and he uses the noun *drāma* here as a direct object of the verb *hupokrinesthai*: ταῦτα μὲν γὰρ τὰ ἰαμβεῖ' ἐκ Φοίνικός ἐστιν Εὐριπίδου· τοῦτο δὲ τὸ <u>δρᾶμ'</u> οὐδεπώποτ' οὔτε Θεόδωρος οὔτ' Ἀριστόδημος <u>ὑπεκρίναντο</u> 'these iambic lines [that I have just quoted] come from the *Phoenix* of Euripides: neither Theodoros nor Aristodemos ever <u>acted</u> [*hupokrinesthai*] this particular <u>drāma</u>'.

οἱ νεηνίαι οὐκέτι ἀνέστησαν, ἀλλ' ἐν τέλεϊ τούτῳ ἔσχοντο. Ἀργεῖοι δέ σφεων εἰκόνας ποιησάμενοι ἀνέθεσαν ἐς Δελφοὺς ὡς ἀνδρῶν ἀρίστων γενομένων.

After they [= Kleobis and Biton] had done these things and had been seen [op-] doing these things by everyone participating in the festival [panēguris], the very best ending [teleutē] of life followed up for them.[33] And in all this the god made it clear that it is better for a man to be in a state of death than in a state of life.[34] For the men of Argos, standing around the two youths, declared them blessed [makares] for having such physical strength, while the women of Argos declared the mother of the youths blessed for having such children as these two. And the mother, with feelings of utmost happiness [perikharēs] about what had been done and about what had been said about the things that had been done, stood before the statue [= of Hera] and prayed on behalf of Kleobis and Biton, her two children, who had given her such great honor [timē]. She prayed that the goddess [= Hera] should give them [= the two youths] the very best thing that can happen to a human. After this prayer, the people sacrificed [thuein] and feasted [euōkheîn], and the youths went to sleep [katakoimâsthai] right then and there in the sacred precinct [of Hera]. And they [= the two youths] never got up [an-histasthai] again, but were held fast [ekhesthai] in this outcome [telos]. And the people of Argos made likenesses [eikōn plural] of them and dedicated these at Delphi, saying that these were images of men who had become the very best of men.

1§47 Amidst the sacrificing and the feasting, as the two youths fall asleep inside the sacred precinct of the goddess, the euphemistic wording highlights the idea that they will be permanently encapsulated in the perfect state that they had reached at this precise moment in the story of their lives: οὐκέτι ἀνέστησαν 'they never got up again' (1.31.5). Now they are held fast forever, in exactly the state of the moment, and the wording captures perfectly the earlier point I was making about a freeze frame: ἐν τέλεϊ τούτῳ ἔσχοντο 'they were held fast [ekhesthai] in this outcome [telos]' (1.31.5). The verb ekhein 'hold' in the middle voice, ekhesthai, is used here in the sense of capturing a snapshot

---

[33] The visualizing of this scene, as indicated here by op- 'see', is essential to the narrative. Relevant is the insightful analysis by Danielle Arnold Freedman (1998:11–13).
[34] On the mystical subtext of this formulation, see PH 8§§45–48 (= pp. 243–247).

1ⓢ4. Metaphors of unchangeability

moment, such as the moment captured by the photographer's expression <u>hold it right there</u>.[35] In other words, the two youths die at the perfect moment—in a perfect <u>pose</u>.

1§48 My choice of the word <u>pose</u> here is based on the meaning of the noun derived from the verb *ekhesthai* 'hold', that is, *skhēma* (σχῆμα) 'pose', derived from *ekhesthai*, as in Herodotus' expression ἐν τέλεϊ τούτῳ ἔσχοντο 'they were held fast [*ekhesthai*] in this outcome [*telos*]' (1.31.5). This word *skhēma*—from which the English word 'scheme' is derived, can indeed mean the 'pose' of a dancer or even the 'pose' of a statue.[36] So we see the two youths settling into a perfect and eternal pose, which becomes a visible sign of their *telos*.

1§49 I propose here to take a closer look at this word *telos* (τέλος), which I have been translating as 'outcome' and which can also be translated as 'end', 'ending', 'completion', 'fulfillment'. To these translations I add another: 'coming full circle'. In terms of a straight line, *telos* is the 'end' of that line; in terms of a circle, however, *telos* is a 'coming full circle'.[37] In terms of a process, *telos* is the achieving or <u>perfecting</u> of that process. In Homeric Greek, as we will see later, the noun *telos* and its corresponding verb *teleîn* convey the perfection inherent in the perfect tense.

1§50 In the case of Herodotus' narrative of Solon's narrative, it reaches its own *telos* in an aetiology. By <u>aetiology</u> here I mean a myth that motivates an institutional reality, especially a ritual.[38] In this case the aetiology has to do with the rituals and the ritual objects connected with the hero cult of Kleobis and Biton at Argos. The ritual objects are the statues of the two young men, and their status as cult heroes is evidently visualized in the form of these statues. As we learn from Herodotus, the outcome of the story of these two young men is formalized in these statues. The perfect pose of their perfect moment, rigid to the point of *rigor mortis*, is captured by the creation of their statues. And the two statues have actually survived: you can see them today in the Museum at Delphi (Figure 2).[39]

---

[35] *PH* 1§39n111 (= p. 38). Freedman (1998:13) describes this moment as "photographic."
[36] *PH* 1§39n111 (= p. 38). Relevant is a poem by Dioscorides in the *Anthology* (7.37), as analyzed by Fantuzzi 2007a.
[37] The form from which Greek *telos* and related forms derive cannot be reduced to a single Indo-European root. As the discussion proceeds, we will see that there are two roots involved in the formation of *telos* and related forms: *k^wel-* and *tel-*. The first of these two roots conveys the idea of 'come full circle'.
[38] For more on this definition of <u>aetiology</u>, see *BA* 16§2n2 (= p. 279).
[39] It does not affect my argument whether or not Kleobis and Biton were the original referents at the time when these statues were made. What matters is that they were truly the referents <u>as far as the Argives were concerned</u>, with reference to the time of Herodotus' own narration.

Chapter One

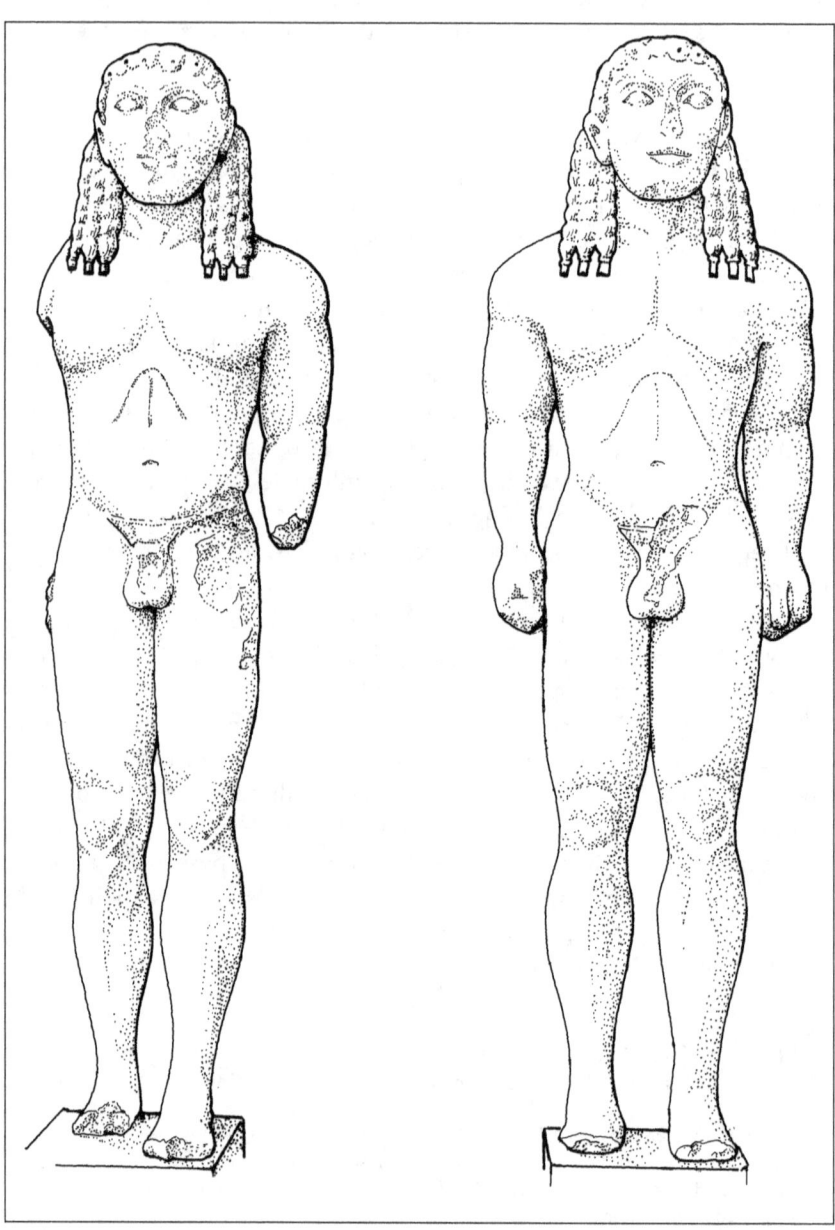

Figure 2. Pair of sculptures: [Poly]medes of Argos, "Kleobis and Biton." Marble, free standing, height approx. 2.2 m. Archaic, ca. 580 BCE. Delphi, Archaeological Museum, 467 and 1524.

1§51 In the context of the Herodotean narrative, a perfect moment of happiness was experienced by all who took part in the festival of Hera, and this moment became concretized in the form of the statues. In the context of the Homeric narrative, by comparison, a perfect moment of terror and pity is experienced by all who take part in the narrative about the capture of Troy, and it becomes concretized in the form of the petrified serpent.

1Ⓢ5. Homeric poetry as visual art

1§52 The petrified serpent of *Iliad* II is not a statue, since it was made not by the art of sculptors but by the art of poets—or, to say it in terms of Homeric poetry, it was made by a god as viewed by the art of poets. Although the artifice of a sculptor as an artisan is like the artifice of a poet as an artisan, in that both kinds of artisans produce artifacts that are by definition artificial, what makes the artifice of the poet unlike the artifice of the sculptor is the way in which the poet can imagine his artifact as natural, not artificial. The poet's work of art can be natural if it is like the god's work of art, which is natural as well as artificial. What we see here is the idea that the verbal art of Homeric poetry can create a visual artifact that is natural. This visual artifact could have been a statue—or let us say a piece of three-dimensional artwork— if it had not already been created by verbal art. The verbal art of Homeric poetry demonstrates that it can bypass the visual arts of sculpture, painting, and so on. I am talking about poetic imagination.[40]

1§53 Here I return to the actual wording of the poetic visualization in this Homeric passage, drawing attention again to the epithet *arizēlos* describing the marvel of the petrified serpent:

1①13 *Iliad* II 318

τὸν μὲν ἀρίζηλον θῆκεν θεὸς ὅς περ ἔφηνε

The same god that had made it visible [*phainein*] now made it most visible [*arizēlos*].

1§54 That the petrified serpent is a work of art is made explicit by this epithet *arizēlos*. To back up this formulation, I compare a detail from the City of War as pictured on the Homeric Shield of Achilles in *Iliad* XVIII. In this detail we see a visualization of the gods Ares and Athena:

---

[40] See Ferrari 1997, who shows that metaphor in the verbal art of Aeschylus is independent of visual art.

Chapter One

1①14 *Iliad* XVIII 516–519

> οἳ δ' ἴσαν· ἦρχε δ' ἄρά σφιν Ἄρης καὶ Παλλὰς Ἀθήνη
> ἄμφω χρυσείω, χρύσεια δὲ εἵματα ἕσθην,
> καλὼ καὶ μεγάλω σὺν τεύχεσιν, ὥς τε θεώ περ
> ἀμφὶς <u>ἀριζήλω·</u> <u>λαοὶ δ' ὑπολίζονες ἦσαν</u>.

> And they [= warriors represented on the Shield] were on their way. Leading them were Ares and Pallas Athena.
> They were both golden. And they were wearing golden clothing.
> Beautiful and immense they were in their armor, gods that they are,
> <u>most visible</u> [*arizēlō*], side by side. <u>But the warriors were smaller in size</u>.

1§55 The two gods, marked as *arizēlō* at verse 519, are described as larger than life-size, by contrast with the human figures who are framing them. These humans are the <u>supporting cast</u>, as it were, of the gods; they are therefore <u>smaller in size</u> than the gods, as signaled by *hup-olizones* at verse 519.[41] The proportion matches the inherent distinction between larger-than-life-size statues of gods and the life-size humans who must worship them. In terms of the metaphor we see at work here in the Shield passage, larger-than-life size means immortality. There is also an inherent metonymy: because the Olympians are immortal, they are <u>artificial</u> as well as <u>natural</u>. As I argued in my work on the Homeric epithet *aphthitos* 'unwilting, imperishable', living things in the divine realm are *aphthita*, imperishable and <u>artificial</u> as well as <u>natural</u>, by contrast with the human realm, where living things are *phthita*, perishable and only <u>natural</u>.[42] In Homeric poetry, anything immortal is perfectly <u>artificial</u> as well as <u>natural</u>.[43]

1§56 This Homeric passage, showing the gods Ares and Athena in all their golden radiance, has given me the first opportunity to view the Homeric Shield of Achilles. The Shield, a verbal picture that claims to show a perfect

---

[41] I deliberately use the expression <u>supporting</u> to convey the idea underlying the prefix *hupo-*.
[42] Nagy 1974:244, 250–255; BA 6§11 (= p. 102), §30 (= pp. 116–117); 7§§1–2 (= pp. 118–120); 10§§1–18 (= pp. 174–188); PH 0§5n10 (= p. 3); 6§3n9 (= p. 147).
[43] PH 8§15 (= p. 225), 8§46n126 (= pp. 244–245), 10§9n21(= p. 278), 10§11n27 (= p. 280).

1ⓢ5. Homeric poetry as visual art

world of visual art, the work of the god Hephaistos himself, will be an essential point of interest in *Homer the Classic*—as well as in *Homer the Preclassic*. Much has been said about the Shield, and there is surely a universe of things still waiting to be said, so vast is the subject. And yet, the vastness of it all should not deter me from attempting to capture the essence of the Shield as a form of visual communication. For me an ideal point of entry into the world of images radiating from the Shield is the epithet *arizēlō* 'radiant', which shows the gods Ares and Athena in their golden state of perfection.

1§57 It is important that the same epithet applies to the petrified serpent, likewise *arizēlos* 'radiant', in *Iliad* II 318. Zeus had sent it as an epiphany, *ephēne* (318), and, once the serpent is petrified, it becomes *arizēlos* 'radiant' (318). This epithet marks the petrified serpent as a permanent vision, pictured by the poetry as a perfect work of art, not only a perfect work of nature. The petrified serpent may seem like a natural rock formation, but it is at the same time a work of art, made by Zeus himself—by the god who had produced the vision in the first place, *ephēne*. The verbal art of Homeric poetry captures this concretized vision, signaling the petrified serpent as *arizēlos*.

1§58 Now I go one step further by arguing that the petrified serpent in *Iliad* II is a concretized three-dimensional visualization of the *telos* of composition-in-performance. So far, I have translated *telos* as the 'outcome' of the story in the making, of the composition-in-performance. As we will see, however, such a *telos* is more than an outcome. It is a perfect outcome. And, as we will also see, it is perfection itself.

1§59 The petrifaction of the serpent in *Iliad* II, as a three-dimensional visualization, is made to seem natural as well as artificial—to the extent that it cannot be equated explicitly with artifacts produced by the art of sculpture or metalwork or other three-dimensional handiwork—not to mention the two-dimensional handiwork of painting and the like. But there remains an implicit equation of petrifaction with divine art pure and simple, in that the petrified serpent is a product of a verbal art that re-creates the divine art. In its depiction of the petrified serpent, verbal art can claim to be natural as well as artificial, since it bypasses the referential world of artifacts hand-made by human artisans. The petrified serpent may seem like a three-dimensional work of art, but the artistry is conveyed purely by verbal art.

1§60 The question remains: how can there be such a thing as arrested motion within the medium of performance, which is to be understood as continuing motion? In a performance medium, after all, poetry is in the making. It is alive and in motion. This motion can be seen as static only after

Chapter One

the story is told. What, then, is the answer? It is to be found in the vision of the petrified serpent: its arrested motion, within the motion that is the performance, is a prophetic vision of the notionally unchangeable 'outcome' of the performance, its *telos*.

1§61 As I observed earlier, the notion of an unchangeable 'outcome' is conveyed by the words of Odysseus that frame what he had just quoted. I highlight again the verb *teleîn*, derived from the noun *telos*:

1①15 *Iliad* II 330

> τὰ δὴ νῦν πάντα <u>τελεῖται</u>
>
> And now I see that all these things <u>are reaching their outcome</u> [= verb <u>*teleîn*</u>, from *telos*].

1§62 We may compare this wording with the wording of the prophecy itself:

1①16 *Iliad* II 324–325

> ἡμῖν μὲν τόδ' <u>ἔφηνε</u> <u>τέρας</u> μέγα μητίετα Ζεὺς
>
> ὄψιμον ὀψι<u>τέλεστον</u>, ὅου κλέος οὔ ποτ' ὀλεῖται
>
> Zeus the planner <u>made visible</u> [*phainein*] this great <u>portent</u> [*teras*].
>
> It is late in coming, late in <u>reaching its outcome</u> [*telos*], and its fame [*kleos*] will never perish.

1§63 The word *opsiteleston* 'late in reaching its outcome [*telos*]' makes it explicit that the *telos* 'outcome' of the narrative as signaled by the *teras* 'omen' will have to wait till later—till the performance is complete. The word *kleos* 'fame', further, makes it explicit that the narrative equates itself with the plot of the Troy story. The usages of the verb *teleîn* 'bring to *telos*' in Homeric diction indicate clearly, by way of contrasting imperfective and perfective tenses, whether the narrative is still in progress or whether it is being considered a finished composition. The present imperfective *teleîtai* 'is reaching its outcome' here in *Iliad* II 330—and the imperfect *eteleieto* 'was reaching its outcome' in *Iliad* I 5—refer to the story of Troy as it is being told, in progress, as it is heading toward a finish.[44] By contrast, the perfect *tetelesmenon* 'having reached its outcome' refers to the story after it is told, that is, as it turns out after the narrative is finished. A case in point is *Odyssey* xix 547 where the

---

[44] I offer a detailed commentary on these passages in *HPC* I§§263 and following.

1ⓢ5. Homeric poetry as visual art

talking eagle of Penelope's dream prophesies that this dream (*hupar*) will come to fulfillment—that it will be *tetelesmenon* (verb *teleîn*).[45] All these usages of *teleîn* 'reach an outcome' are relevant to the status of Zeus as the absolute referent in the poetic form of the *humnos* 'hymn'.[46]

1§64 By contrast with the petrified serpent in *Iliad* II, the Shield of Achilles in *Iliad* XVIII is an explicit, not implicit, equation of three-dimensional artwork—in this case, metalwork—with the artwork of poetry. The divine creativity that produced the petrified serpent was overtly natural; by contrast, the divine creativity that produces the Shield is overtly artificial, since it is seen as an artistic product achieved by the divine artisan himself, Hephaistos the metalworker. The Homeric gods, in their artistic creativity, are not confined to the natural world. As ultimate masters of the artistic world, not just the natural world, the gods can express the world of nature as a work of art in its own right. For the Homeric gods, all nature is a work of art. Moreover, the Shield of Achilles, as a masterpiece of metalwork created by the divine artisan Hephaistos, expresses the whole world as a work of art.

1§65 In the history of literature, the Shield of Achilles is considered the premier example of ecphrasis. For a working definition, I say that ecphrasis is an act of verbal art shown in the act of depicting non-verbal art—such as painting, sculpting, or, as in this case, bronzework. Verbal art is different from the visual art of artisans. As a specific example, I take the art of bronzeworkers, who make bronze shields that have pictures on them made of bronze—or of even more precious metal, such as gold. Of course, verbal art cannot produce real bronze shields that have real pictures on them, but it can indeed produce an idealized shield, and the pictures on such a shield will of course be idealized as well.

1§66 Such a distinction is relevant to the picturing of the immortal gods Ares and Athena on the Shield as larger than mortals. Since everything is already idealized by the verbal art on the Shield, including mortals, the immortals need to be distinguished from mortals in some special way—in this case, by making the mortals relatively smaller in size. In addition, the immortals are made of gold and marked by a special epithet, *arizēlō* 'radiant', which draws attention to the idealization of the immortals—and away from the idealization of the mortals likewise pictured on the Shield. Unlike mortals, who are natural outside of art, the immortals are forever artificial as well as natural,

---

[45] *HR* 24, 26–29.
[46] Again, *HPC* I§§263 and following.

both inside and outside of art, and so they must always be seen as perfect works of art.[47]

1§67 The same kind of thing can be said about the petrified serpent of *Iliad* II, likewise marked as *arizēlos* 'radiant'. The epithet applies only after petrifaction. The serpent, once petrified, becomes like the immortals, since from here on it too must be seen as a perfect work of art forever. In this case, the art that shows the petrified serpent is explicitly verbal art, and the non-verbal art of, say, a sculptor is bypassed altogether. In the case of the Shield, the art that shows the golden immortals is likewise verbal, even if it pretends to be the non-verbal art of a virtuoso bronzeworker.[48]

1§68 My emphasis on verbal art, as an alternative to visual art, brings me to a most celebrated essay by Gotthold Ephraim Lessing, originally published in 1766 (Berlin), entitled *Laocoön: an Essay on the Limits of Painting and Poetry* (*Laokoon, oder über die Grenzen der Mahlerey und Poesie*).[49] In the title of this essay, we notice that Lessing says painting or, in the original German, Malerei (Mahlerey), but he really means, as we see from the essay itself, all non-verbal arts that produce objects of art—for example sculpture as well as painting.

1§69 The central thesis of Lessing's essay is that painting (in his generalized sense of painting), as a vehicle of the imagination, concentrates on a unique moment in any action, while the verbal art of poetry expresses the given action as a continuum. I aim to extend the formulation of Lessing by arguing that verbal art as well, being a vehicle of the imagination, can concentrate on a unique moment—without depending on painting as a point of reference.

1§70 In the example of the petrified serpent in *Iliad* II, for example, we have seen Homeric poetry actually visualizing itself as a unique moment, in the form of a stop-motion picture. The emotions of this moment are terror and pity. The picture of this one single moment of terror and pity is like a snapshot (hold-it-right-there).[50] It is a way of capturing the entire story of Troy's capture.

1§71 Words like snapshot or even picture imply only images that are two-dimensional, but I mean to include the three-dimensional as well when I speak of the power of verbal art in Homeric poetry. From here on, I will use picture

---

[47] The exceptions to this formulation of what happens 'always' have to do with epiphanies of gods in human form.

[48] The noun *khalkeus* 'bronzeworker' can designate any kind of 'metalworker', not just workers in *khalkos* 'bronze'. In *Odyssey* iii 432, for example, the referent of *khalkeus* is a smith who works in gold, not in bronze.

[49] For references to this work of Lessing, I use the 1984 edition of the 1962 translation by E. A. McCormick.

[50] I note again the term "photographic" as used by Freedman 1998:13.

to refer to three-dimensional as well as two-dimensional images. This kind of usage requires some effort. Whenever you use the noun image in everyday English, you may have noticed that you tend to picture in your mind images that are only two-dimensional. You have a better chance of imagining three-dimensionally when you use the verb imagine, in a concentrated effort to keep from lapsing back into a two-dimensional frame of mind.

1§72 In saying this I rely on the insights of cognitive psychology. I take it that the human capacity for imagining, as a process, tends to default to a two-dimensional vision of images that are projected on the "screen" of the mind's eye.[51] It requires a special effort to be able to imagine three-dimensionally.[52]

1§73 In various cultures, we can track the evolution of various traditions that train the mind to break free of its innate two-dimensional constraints and to pass into the realm of three-dimensional imagination. When I speak of traditions that train the mind to imagine, three-dimensionally as well as two-dimensionally, I am of course thinking primarily of the verbal arts, especially of song and poetry. In the verbal arts, two-dimensional imagination needs to integrate the sense of seeing with the sense of hearing. Seeing must be verbalized in order to be shared. A shared vision depends on verbalization. As for three-dimensional imagination, it needs to integrate the sense of touch with the sense of seeing.[53] The sense of touch can activate the mind to imagine what is three-dimensional, solid, and substantial—moving beyond what is two-dimensional, "thin," insubstantial. In some cultural contexts, the metaphorical world of the two-dimensional can be seen as a foil for the virtuosity of three-dimensional imagination. For example, the two-dimensional can be seen as thin and filmy—to be contrasted with dense and solid as positive terms for the three-dimensional.[54]

1§74 All this is not to say that a two-dimensional object of art, as produced by the fine arts, is less imaginative than a corresponding three-dimensional object. It can even be said that a two-dimensional work of art actually requires more imagination than a three-dimensional one. Along this line of thinking, in any case, verbal art requires the most imagination. And the greater the imaginative power, the greater the art.

1§75 Here is an example taken from the medium of film. In a work by the French *auteur* Jean-Jacques Beineix, *Betty Blue* (1986), the character Zorg wants to capture 'all of it' for the character Betty. He tries to use his words, a verbal

---

[51] Kosslyn 1994.
[52] Scarry 1999.
[53] Scarry 1999.
[54] For an example of the use of the term filmy, see Scarry 1999:10.

art of sorts, to make things three-dimensional—to break out of the filmy two-dimensionality of the film screen that defines his existence. Here are the words used by the character Zorg in his attempt to break into the three-dimensional:

From *Betty Blue* (1986, directed by Jean-Jacques Beineix), Zorg shows 'perfection' to Betty . . .

> Z: <u>Look</u>! See the little wall?
>
> B: The little Wall of China?
>
> Z: The one that stands at the lake. And that big rock, <u>see</u>?
>
> B: That big thing?
>
> Z: Yeah. And isn't that little house over there nice?
>
> B: But what are you driving at?
>
> Z: I love this place. [J'adore ce coin.]
>
> B: You're right. It's <u>perfect</u>. <u>Everything in its place</u>. Fantastic.
>
> Z: <u>It's all for you, all of it</u>! It starts at the wall and goes beyond the rock. And the house is in the middle.
>
> B: But . . .
>
> Z: And—sh! That's not all . . . [55]

In Zorg's attempt to show perfection to Betty, we see an ironic contrast between the ideal three-dimensional macrocosm desired by Zorg <u>and by his director-filmmaker</u> and the all-too-insubstantial and "filmy" two-dimensional microcosm of the "silver screen." The words and the camera angles keep trying to push out of the two-dimensional frame.

1ⓢ6. A rethinking of terms for artistic imagination

1§76 I now restate my ongoing argument, rethinking it in terms that suit the poetics of imagination. My thesis is that the imaginative power of Homeric poetry is essential for understanding the reception of Homer the Classic in the poetic world of Virgil.

---

[55] My translation from the original French. For details about the film: http://www.imdb.com/title/tt0090563/

1§7. Virgil's sculpting of a perfect Homeric moment

1§77 Before I proceed to read carefully an example I selected from Virgil's poetry, I need to set up two signposts:

A) First, I offer a long-term observation on the Latin word *pictura* 'picture, painting' and on related words. When Virgil and other Augustan poets say *pictura*, we do not need to worry whether this word refers to the two-dimensional art of painting or to the three-dimensional art of sculpture. As with Lessing's usage of <u>Malerei</u> (<u>Mahlerey</u>), the Latin word *pictura* can refer to the visual arts in general—not only to painting or sculpture. Later on in this chapter, I will show examples taken from the *Aeneid* of Virgil. So also in Greek poetry, the word *poikilia*, meaning 'variety, patterning', refers to all visual arts, even though its root *poik-*, related to the root *pic-* of Latin *pictura*, is associated mostly with the art of painting. Before we even get to see the examples of Greek *poikilia* and Latin *pictura*, I need only to stress here, already at this early point in my argumentation, that I will be including metalwork—especially bronzework—within the general category of sculpture.

B) The second signpost is about another essential form of visual arts. Besides painting and sculpting—including all manner of metalwork—there is weaving. As we will see, both Latin *pictura* and Greek *poikilia* can refer to weaving.

1§7. Virgil's sculpting of a perfect Homeric moment

1§78 Moving past these two signposts, I proceed to search for a place where the poetry of Virgil most clearly imagines itself as a single moment. My intended point of comparison in the poetry of Virgil is something as close as possible to what we have seen in the poetry of Homer, that is, the way in which the whole *Iliad*—in its etymological sense of 'Troy story'—imagines itself as a single moment, through the image of the petrified serpent. What makes my attempt to compare Virgil and Homer different from most other attempts is that I see comparable levels of artistry in both. I am ready to say that whatever artistry we admire in Virgil the Classic is already at work in Homer, considered a classic in Virgil's age. In other words, I choose not to say that Virgil has accomplished an artistic feat that he thinks Homer has failed to accomplish. Rather, he is trying to accomplish something that he knows has already been accomplished by Homeric poetry. This proposition is difficult to accept only for those who

Chapter One

refuse to appreciate the Homeric accomplishment in the first place. Here I take the opportunity of criticizing those who think there must be some kind of unintended or unconscious genius in Homer, just waiting to be systematized by later poets. I hold that the poetic systematization was in fact already in place and at work in Homer. Homeric poetry already had its own poetics.

1§79 Book 2 of Virgil's *Aeneid* is the place where I find a passage most directly comparable to the Homeric passage about the nine birds and the serpent. Virgil designed his passage, as I hope to show, with a preconceived understanding of Homer as a Classic—and I think his passage was meant to rival the artistic feat already accomplished by this classical 'Homer'. I have in mind *Aeneid* 2 199–227, where we see Aeneas in the act of narrating to the queen Dido and her Carthaginian subjects his own entrancing visualization of events leading up to the capture of Troy. As we will see, the visualization is entrancing because it is driven by an ominous vision that emanates from the mind of the narrator and enters the minds of his listeners.[56] Aeneas has just reached a point in his narration where the Trojan hero Laocoön has been chosen 'by lot', that is, *ad hoc*, to serve as priest of Poseidon / Neptune (201). At this point, Laocoön is in the act of sacrificing a bull to the god at an altar[57] when, suddenly, twin serpents come into view (203).[58] And, as they come into view, the ominous vision begins to control the narration. The twin serpents are swimming over a calm sea (203 *tranquilla per alta*) from the direction of Tenedos, which is the island where the main force of the Achaeans is hidden away from view. The Achaeans at Tenedos are waiting to join the other Achaeans hiding inside the Wooden Horse at the gates of Troy, and all are ready to penetrate the city's walls.[59] The twin serpents, swimming at full

---

[56] Relevant is the commentary in Nagy 1972:50 on the Greek word *thelgein* in the sense of put into a trance by way of conjuring a vision. In the analysis that follows, I will have more to say about this word.

[57] In the *Laocoön* of Sophocles (F 370 ed. Radt), we see a description of the altar.

[58] The artistic motif of twin serpents, as we see it here in Virgil's *Aeneid* (2.203 and following), occurs elsewhere as well in the *Aeneid* (7.450, 8.289, 8.697).

[59] In the version as narrated by Aeneas, the Wooden Horse is at this point still outside the city walls. In terms of this same version of the story of Troy, as we know from Servius (on *Aeneid* 2.13, 2.241, 3.351), the lintel over the Scaean Gate of Troy contained the corpse of Laomedon, father of Priam, and the sacred power of this corpse protected Troy from destruction. When the Wooden Horse was brought inside the city walls of Troy through the Scaean Gate, this lintel had to be lifted, and the power of the corpse was thus canceled. See Robertson 1970, who connects this theme with a theme represented in a grand painting by Polygnotus, housed in the Lesche of the Cnidians at Delphi (Pausanias 10.27.3): this painting, dated to the mid-fifth century BCE, pictured the destruction of Troy, and one of the details it showed was the removal of the corpse of Laomedon by Sinon and Ankhialos.

speed, are aiming for the shore, their menacing heads erect, protruding well above the waves left behind in their wake (207 *superant undas*).[60] Once they reach shore, they speed toward Laocoön. As I said, we have just seen Laocoön in the act of sacrificing, as an *ad hoc* priest of Poseidon / Neptune.[61] But now the epiphany of the two serpents has interrupted the story that would have told the sequence of the sacrifice. This interruption has canceled the meaning of the sacrifice and has substituted the meaning of the epiphany that we see in progress. And the interruption is signaled by the word *ecce* 'behold!' (203). This word demands a visualization of the epiphany.[62]

1§80 We saw something similar happening in *Iliad* II. It was the scene showing the epiphany of a serpent sent by Zeus. There too, a sacrifice was in progress, and I will return in a minute to the details of that sacrifice, as interrupted by that other epiphany of a serpent. But now I have in the meantime interrupted my own retelling of the ongoing epiphany of the twin serpents in *Aeneid* 2. So, I return to this epiphany at the point where I stopped: just now, the serpents have finally reached the place where Laocoön is sacrificing at the altar. Immediately, each of the two serpents devours one of the priest's two children. Like the mother bird in the epiphany of *Iliad* II, Laocoön is helpless. He struggles in vain against the overwhelming force of the twin serpents, which now proceed to sting him and choke him to death.[63] It is a scene of terror and pity (199 *miseris... tremendum*; 204 *horresco referens*; 212 *diffigimus visu exsangues*; 215 *miseros*). And it rivals the scene of terror and pity in *Iliad* II.

1§81 We see in this scene not just an opportunity for rivalry between Virgil and Homer. The newer classic complements and thus validates the older classic, and that is part of the rivalry. Homeric poetry as an oral poetic tradi-

---

[60] In the Latin, it is emphasized that the upper halves of the serpents, in all their immensity, protrude from the water. At a later point, I will refer to a sculpted figure of a serpent with its upper half practically standing, waist-high, next to a sculpted figure of the goddess Athena.

[61] I repeat here a significant detail: Laocoön was chosen *sorte* 'by lot' as priest of Poseidon / Neptune. In one version of the Laocoön story, he was a hereditary priest of Apollo. Comments by Williams 1972:229. It is as if the priest of Apollo were a stand-in for the priest of Poseidon.

[62] Austin 1964:101 on *ecce* 'behold!' in *Aeneid* 2.203 notes the interruption and then proceeds to show other instances of *ecce autem* as a "formula" that marks in each case "an unexpected interruption of action in progress." I agree, except that the action is more than an action here: it is a ritual procedure. On this point, I refer to my discussion in *PP* 43–53 on the root *deuk-*. Austin 1964:101 adds, with reference to *Aeneid* 2.202, that Laocoön was "performing a ritual act at the appointed place for it." Then he goes on to say that "the word marks the importance of the occasion and the correctness of the ceremonial act, thus increasing the dreadfulness of what is to come." I will have more to say on ritual correctness when I analyze *Aeneid* 3.307, where Andromache is making ritual offerings to Hector's shade at the moment when Aeneas approaches her.

[63] The actual moment of death is left unspoken.

Chapter One

tion stems from a comparable principle of poetic rivalry: the performance of the moment rivals all previous performances because it fulfills them in the here and now. Virgil the Classic clarifies this aspect of Homer the Classic.

1§82 The rival passages in *Aeneid* 2 and *Iliad* II both center on a moment when a ritual goes wrong—when the master-plan of the ritual is interrupted. In both the Virgilian and the Homeric passages, that same moment of interruption activates another master-plan, which is the overarching plot of the master-narrative. Let me test this formulation by taking a second look at the passage about the nine birds and the serpent in *Iliad* II. This time I focus on this question: how was the epiphany of the serpent introduced into the narrative? Here again is my translation of the relevant verses I have already quoted:

1⊕17 *Iliad* II 299–310 (once again: enter the serpent . . .)

299 Endure, my near and dear ones, and stay as long as it takes for us to find out
300 whether Calchas is prophesying something that is true or not.
301 For I know this well in my heart, and you all
302 are witnesses, those of you who have not been carried off by the demons of death.
303 It is as if it was yesterday or the day before, when the ships of the Achaeans at Aulis
304 were gathered, portending doom to Priam and the Trojans.
305 Standing around a spring, at a sacred altar,
306 we were sacrificing perfect [*teléessai*] hecatombs to the immortal ones
307 under a beautiful plane tree, in a place where sparkling water flowed.
308 Then [*entha*] there appeared [*phainesthai*] a great sign [*sēma*], a serpent [*drakōn*] with blood-red markings on its back.
309 Terrifying it was. The Olympian [= Zeus] himself had sent it into the zone of light.
310 It darted out from underneath the altar, and it rushed toward the plane tree.

1§83 As we compare this part of the passage in *Iliad* II with the rival passage in *Aeneid* 2, we may now observe some details in *Iliad* II that may easily be overlooked. We notice how the serpent slips into view from a dark hole underneath the altar (319).⁶⁴ Sent by Zeus, this serpent emerges from the darkness and heads for the light (309). The word *entha* 'then' (308), which signals the epiphany as expressed by the very next word, *ephanē* 'there appeared' (308), interrupts the sequence of a ritual sacrifice. This sacrifice of the Achaeans has just been interrupted by a portent that portends the overarching plot of the master-narrative, the story of Troy.

1§84 As we now take a second look at *Aeneid* 2, we may observe comparable details that may easily be overlooked here as well. I note again how the word *ecce* 'behold!' (203), which signals the epiphany of the two serpents, interrupts the narration—and the rationale—of the ritual.⁶⁵ I must add that the function of *ecce* here in *Aeneid* 2 203 transcends the Latin usage and connects with the Homeric function of *entha* 'right then and there' in introducing the epiphany of the serpent in *Iliad* II 308. The epiphany of this serpent is relevant to the look of the serpent, by which I mean the power of a serpent to entrance its victims simply by looking at them. The notion of such a power is evident in the etymology of the word that is used for 'serpent' here in *Iliad* II: that word is *drakōn* (308). Etymologically, *drakōn* 'serpent' is 'the one who looks' (from *derkesthai* 'look').⁶⁶

1§85 An essential question remains to be answered. What kind of master-plan, what overarching narrative, is being signaled by the epiphany of the twin serpents in *Aeneid* 2? And what divinity is actually sending this epiphany? The answer has to do with the master-plan of the plot driving the overarching narration of Virgil's *Aeneid*, which is a frame for the inner narration of Aeneas as performed for the queen Dido and her Carthaginian subjects. This inner narration seems to be driven by the plot of the *Iliou Persis*. This traditional title marks the story of Troy as retold in what is known as the <u>epic Cycle</u>.⁶⁷ The *Iliou Persis* or 'The Destruction of Troy', attributed to the poet Arctinus of Miletus, survives for us only in meager fragments, but we have at least the plot summary of Proclus. I quote here the entire text of that summary, following the page- and line-numbering of Allen's Oxford Classical Text volume V of Homer (1912):

---

⁶⁴ Similarly, as we will see later, Virgil's serpents dart into Athena's holy of holies on the acropolis.
⁶⁵ I have already noted the interruptive usage of *ecce* here and elsewhere in Latin poetry.
⁶⁶ Chantraine DELG s.v. δέρκομαι.
⁶⁷ This is the first time I use the term <u>epic Cycle</u>. I offer a working definition of this term in PP 74, 150.

Chapter One

1①18 Arctinus of Miletus *Iliou Persis* plot summary by Proclus pp. 107–108 ed. Allen

16 Ἕπεται δὲ τούτοις Ἰλίου πέρσιδος βιβλία δύο Ἀρκτίνου Μιλησίου περιέχοντα τάδε. ὡς τὰ περὶ τὸν ἵππον οἱ Τρῶες ὑπόπτως ἔχοντες περιστάντες βουλεύονται ὅ τι χρὴ ποιεῖν· καὶ τοῖς μὲν δοκεῖ κατακρημνίσαι αὐτόν, τοῖς δὲ
20 καταφλέγειν, οἱ δὲ ἱερὸν αὐτὸν ἔφασαν δεῖν τῇ Ἀθηνᾷ ἀνατεθῆναι· καὶ τέλος νικᾷ ἡ τούτων γνώμη. τραπέντες δὲ εἰς εὐφροσύνην εὐωχοῦνται ὡς ἀπηλλαγμένοι τοῦ πολέμου. ἐν αὐτῷ δὲ τούτῳ δύο δράκοντες ἐπιφανέντες τόν τε Λαοκόωντα καὶ τὸν ἕτερον τῶν παίδων διαφθείρουσιν. ἐπὶ
25 δὲ τῷ τέρατι δυσφορήσαντες οἱ περὶ τὸν Αἰνείαν ὑπεξῆλθον εἰς τὴν Ἴδην. καὶ Σίνων τοὺς πυρσοὺς ἀνίσχει τοῖς Ἀχαιοῖς, πρότερον εἰσεληλυθὼς προσποίητος. οἱ δὲ ἐκ Τενέδου προσπλεύσαντες καὶ οἱ ἐκ τοῦ δουρείου ἵππου ἐπιπίπτουσι τοῖς πολεμίοις καὶ πολλοὺς ἀνελόντες τὴν πόλιν κατὰ
30 κράτος λαμβάνουσι. καὶ Νεοπτόλεμος μὲν ἀποκτείνει Πρίαμον ἐπὶ τὸν τοῦ Διὸς τοῦ ἑρκείου βωμὸν καταφυγόντα.

p. 108 Μενέλαος δὲ ἀνευρὼν Ἑλένην ἐπὶ τὰς ναῦς κατάγει, Δηΐφοβον φονεύσας. Κασσάνδραν δὲ Αἴας ὁ Ἰλέως πρὸς βίαν ἀποσπῶν συνεφέλκεται τὸ τῆς Ἀθηνᾶς ξόανον. ἐφ' ᾧ παροξυνθέντες οἱ Ἕλληνες καταλεῦσαι βουλεύονται τὸν
5 Αἴαντα. ὁ δὲ ἐπὶ τὸν τῆς Ἀθηνᾶς βωμὸν καταφεύγει καὶ διασῴζεται ἐκ τοῦ ἐπικειμένου κινδύνου. ἔπειτα ἐμπρήσαντες τὴν πόλιν Πολυξένην σφαγιάζουσιν ἐπὶ τὸν τοῦ Ἀχιλλέως τάφον. καὶ Ὀδυσσέως Ἀστυάνακτα ἀνελόντος, Νεοπτόλεμος Ἀνδρομάχην γέρας λαμβάνει. καὶ τὰ λοιπὰ
10 λάφυρα διανέμονται. Δημοφῶν δὲ καὶ Ἀκάμας Αἴθραν εὑρόντες ἄγουσι μεθ' ἑαυτῶν. ἔπειτα ἀποπλέουσιν οἱ Ἕλληνες, καὶ φθορὰν αὐτοῖς ἡ Ἀθηνᾶ κατὰ τὸ πέλαγος μηχανᾶται.

1§7. Virgil's sculpting of a perfect Homeric moment

16 After the preceding [= four scrolls of the *Little Iliad*, by Lesches of Lesbos] there follow two scrolls of the *Iliou Persis*, by Arctinus

of Miletus, containing the following. With regard to the things concerning the Horse, the

Trojans, suspicious about the horse, stand around wondering what they should

do. Some think it should be pushed off a cliff, while others

20 think it should be burned down, and still others say that it should be dedicated as sacred [*hieros*] to Athena.

In the end, the opinion of the third group wins out. They turn

to merriment, feasting as if they had been freed from the war.

At this point two serpents appear and

destroy Laocoön and one of his sons. At the sight of

25 this marvel, Aeneas and his followers get upset and withdraw

to Mount Ida. Sinon lights signal fires for the Achaeans.

He had previously entered the city, using a pretext. And they [= the Achaeans], some of them sailing from Tenedos

[toward Troy] and others of them emerging from the Wooden Horse, fall upon

their enemies. They kill many, and the city

is taken by force. Neoptolemos kills

Priam, who has taken refuge at the altar of Zeus Herkeios.

p. 108 Menelaos finds Helen and takes her back down to the ships, after

slaughtering Deiphobos. Ajax son of Oileus takes Kassandra by

force, dragging her away from the wooden statue [*xoanon*] of Athena. At the sight

of this, the Achaeans get angry and decide to stone

5 Ajax to death, but he takes refuge at the altar of Athena, and so

is preserved from his impending destruction. Then

Chapter One

        the Achaeans put the city to the torch. They slaughter Polyxena on the
        tomb of Achilles. Odysseus kills Astyanax,
        and Neoptolemos takes Andromache as his prize. The rest
10   of the spoils are distributed. Demophon and Akamas find Aithra
        and take her with them. Then the Greeks sail off [from Troy],
        and Athena begins to plan destruction for them at sea.

1§86 It is commonly thought that Virgil adapted his version of the Troy story mainly from the epic Cycle, more specifically, from the *Iliou Persis* of Arctinus of Miletus. I highlight here the most relevant parts of Proclus' plot summary of this *Iliou Persis*: we read of an <u>epiphany</u> of <u>two serpents</u> (Arctinus of Miletus *Iliou Persis* 107.23 <u>δύο δράκοντες ἐπιφανέντες</u>), who kill Laocoön along with one of his children (23–24). Aeneas and his followers, understanding this as a *teras* 'portent' that portends the capture of Troy (25), decide to withdraw from Troy and relocate to Mount Ida (25–26).[68] Right after the exit of Aeneas, the Proclus plot summary of the *Iliou Persis* mentions the character Sinon for the first time (26). Even his name says it all: he is the agent of destruction (Greek *sinesthai* 'harm, hurt') for Troy. Sinon, having already gained entrance within the walls of Troy by pretending not to be what he really is (27 πρότερον εἰσεληλυθὼς προσποίητος), aids the Achaeans who are now seen emerging from within the Wooden Horse (as I infer from the compressed wording of Proclus).[69]

1§87 There are remarkable similarities between this version of the Troy story, drawn from the epic Cycle, and the version of *Aeneid* 2. Still, the dissimilarities are just as remarkable. Moreover, we find still other dissimilarities in still other versions, especially with reference to the fate of Laocoön and his children: in one version, as we have seen, only one of the children is killed; in

---

[68] A fragment from the *Laocoön* of Sophocles (F 373 ed. Radt) shows six verses of a messenger speech reporting the departure of Aeneas from Troy: the hero is carrying his lame father on his back and is accompanied by a large retinue (see also Dionysius of Halicarnassus *Roman Antiquities* 1.48). Another fragment from the *Laocoön* (F 370) shows two verses describing the altar at which Laocoön sacrifices. Yet another fragment (F 371) features a choral lyric passage containing four lines of a prayer to Poseidon, addressed as ruler of the *Aigaios* (*pontos*) 'Aegean (sea)'.

[69] In Virgil *Aeneid* 2.259, it is Sinon who opens the door of the Wooden Horse that lets the Achaeans out: *laxat claustra Sinon*. Austin 1964:121 remarks that "Virgil gives Sinon a far more dramatic part than that of mere call-boy; the drama of the Horse began with him and with him it ends." I think that the *Iliou Persis* of Arctinus, as we can see even from the summary of Proclus, already contained this "drama."

another, both children die, but Laocoön survives;[70] in some of these versions, moreover, the serpents are envisioned as *pleusantes* 'swimming' not from Tenedos but from Kalydnai.[71]

1§88 Such variations are characteristic of Homer the Classic in the age of Callimachus and earlier, not Homer the Classic in the age of Virgil. One variant detail stands out, because it turns out to be indispensable for Virgil's *Aeneid*: Aeneas and his followers must not depart from Troy immediately after the portent of the twin serpents, but only after the city has already been set on fire. Some might think that Virgil invented the postponement of Aeneas' departure. I see no such invention, and I am about to argue that this detail in the *Aeneid* derives from a genuine epic tradition, involving a sacred statue of Athena, known as the Palladium, situated on the acropolis of Troy.

1⑤8. A statue of Athena in the epic Cycle and beyond

1§89 A most remarkable thing about the Palladium is that we find it mentioned nowhere in our text of Homer, either in the *Iliad* or in the *Odyssey*. Moreover, it is hardly ever mentioned in modern Homeric and Virgilian studies. The reasons are easy to appreciate. The Palladium seems non-Homeric—at least, on the surface—and the surviving information about it seems confused. The confusion stems from the vast number of variant myths and rituals surrounding the Palladium. The sheer variety, in its vastness, bewilders the modern mind. I maintain that this variety, in and of itself, is an important historical fact—and it can help provide an explanation for the absence of the Palladium in Homer as we know Homer—and as Virgil knew Homer. I also maintain that the Palladium is in fact not absent but very much present in

---

[70] In Quintus of Smyrna 12.390–500, Laocoön is not killed by the serpents, but he is blinded; in "Apollodorus" *Library* epitome 5.18, the two children are both devoured, but the fate of the father is not made explicit.

[71] Scholia for Lycophron 347; also Servius on *Aeneid* 2.204, reporting the version of Bacchylides (F 9 ed. Snell / Maehler p. 88). See Sophocles *Laocoön* (F 372 ed. Radt, with apparatus). Strabo (13.1.46 C604) says that the island of Tenedos has a *polis Aiolis* 'Aeolian city', with a *hieron* 'sacred space' of Apollo Smintheus, and that the island is flanked by two smaller islands called *Káludnai*; he adds that, according to another version, the entire island of Tenedos is called *Káludna*. I note with interest that Servius refers to Calydnae in the plural (*a Calydnis insulis*). The variation between singular *Kaludna* and plural *Kaludnai* is comparable to the variation between a single serpent and twin serpents in describing the attendant(s) of the goddess Athena. In the version of Bacchylides, according to Servius, the serpents were turned into humans (*de serpentibus a Calydnis insulis venientibus et in homines conversis*). The twin serpents were apparently given names: Porkis and Khariboia (Sophocles *Laocoön* F 372 ed. Radt; via scholia for Lycophron 347).

Chapter One

Homeric poetry—as an <u>absent signifier</u>. As we will see, Virgil was aware of such an absent signification and wove it into his *Aeneid*.

1§90 The essentials of the story of the Palladium, its aetiology, can be found in the *Library* of "Apollodorus" (3.12.3):[72] there we read that it was a three-dimensional image of Athena, which fell from the sky in response to Ilos, who prayed to Zeus for a signal when he founded Ilion, that is, Troy.[73] This image is described by "Apollodorus" as a primitive—or, better, primal—statue: it was three cubits high, holding a spear in its right hand and a distaff or spindle in its left (again, *Library* 3.12.3).[74] In terms of this sacred narrative, the original resting place of the Palladium was Troy. The statue signaled not only the foundation but also the continuity of the city. Myth had it that Troy could not be captured so long as the Palladium remained there (Servius commenting on Virgil *Aeneid* 2.166). The capture of Troy thus depended on the taking of the Palladium from Troy. Here is where a vast variety of different versions enters the picture. The burning question was: who took the Palladium from Troy and where was its "final resting place"?[75]

1§91 The farther back we go in time, the more hotly contested was the possession of the Palladium, this sign that fell from the sky, as a source of wealth, power, and prestige for those who possessed it. Possessing the Palladium was essential not only for the survival or destruction of one city, Troy, but also for the foundation or re-foundation of other cities—if Troy was destroyed and never rebuilt. It is a historical fact that many régimes in many different cities of the ancient world claimed to possess the Palladium. A moment ago, however, I added this qualification: <u>if Troy was to be destroyed and never rebuilt</u>. This qualification was necessary because one city that claimed to possess the Palladium was Troy itself—by which I mean the "New Troy" that was actually rebuilt as a new Ilion sometime around the eighth century BCE and that lasted all the way into the classical Roman period and beyond.[76]

1§92 For purposes of validating the possession of the Palladium, the myths and rituals connected with it had to keep evolving to fit the ever-

---

[72] See also the Tzetzes scholia for Lycophron 355. For an overall view of the sources, the commentary of Frazer 1929 IV 260 on Ovid *Fasti* 6.421 is most useful.

[73] See also Dictys of Crete 5.5. Later on, we will see other versions where the Palladium came not to Ilos but to his father, Dardanos.

[74] Hedreen 2001:28.

[75] I borrow the expression "final resting place" from Frazer 1929 IV 260 on Ovid *Fasti* 6.421.

[76] For a glimpse of the historical and archaeological evidence surrounding the Palladium as venerated in New Ilion in the Troad during the Hellenistic as well as Roman periods, see Rose 2006:148.

evolving cultural politics of the here and now. The burning question, in the ongoing competition to appropriate this statue, centered on the last days of Troy before it was captured and set on fire by the Achaeans. So let us return to this question: who took the Palladium from Troy and where did they take it?

1§93 According to the local mythology of the city of Argos, it was Diomedes who captured the Palladium from the acropolis of Troy and ultimately brought the sacred object to the city of Argos as its final resting place (Pausanias 2.23.5). There are many variations in telling about how, when, and why Diomedes took the Palladium from the acropolis of Troy, and many of the variant stories involve Odysseus as a partner of Diomedes in the quest to take it. According to some of these variant stories, the partnership modulates into an intense rivalry. As we are about to see, there are even versions where Odysseus is represented as scheming to keep the Palladium for himself. The basic idea of a partnership linking Diomedes with Odysseus in capturing the Palladium is attested in the epic Cycle. There is a brief reference in the Proclus plot outline of the *Little Iliad* that says simply: καὶ μετὰ ταῦτα σὺν Διομήδει τὸ παλλάδιον ἐκκομίζει ἐκ τῆς Ἰλίου 'and after this [= after Odysseus infiltrates Troy in a previous adventure] he [= Odysseus] along with Diomedes takes out [*ek-komizein*] the Palladium from Ilion' (Lesches of Lesbos[77] *Little Iliad* 107.7-8).[78]

1§94 According to the local mythology of the city of Athens, which rivals the local mythology of the city of Argos, the final resting place of the Palladium was not Argos but Athens. Here is a summary of this Athenian mythology as reported by a variety of sources:

> Diomedes, sailing home from Troy with the Palladium in his possession, happened to stop over at the Athenian seaport of Phaleron. Mistaken for an enemy, Diomedes was attacked by the Athenians, led by a hero called Demophon. The Palladium was taken by mistake from Diomedes, and thus it found its final resting place in Athens. It was housed in the ancient building used for trials involving

---

[77] I say Lesbos instead of specifying the city in Lesbos, whether Mytilene or Pyrrha. As I show in HPC II§31, the poetic traditions of Lesbos were federal in that they transcended the individual traditions of cities like Mytilene and Pyrrha.

[78] This retelling assumes a positive attitude about the role of Odysseus in his partnership with Diomedes; according to the logic of the narrative as it plays out here, the infiltration of Troy by Odysseus in partnership with Diomedes would not have succeeded if Odysseus had not already succeeded in an earlier adventure when he infiltrated Troy all by himself (as we have already seen). Also, the use of the word *ek-komizein* assumes a positive attitude about the actual taking of the Palladium: in terms of this word, the Palladium was not stolen but carried to safety. On the usage of *komizein* in the sense of 'rescuing' something precious and sacred, see LP (Nagy 1998) 197n38.

Chapter One

involuntary homicide; by metonymy, the building itself was called Palladium.[79]

1§95 In Virgil's time, the canonical final resting place of the Palladium was the *aedes* of Vesta in Rome,[80] and only the Vestal Virgins were allowed to see it.[81] The question is, who brought the Palladium to Rome after the capture of Troy? A contemporary of Virgil, Dionysius of Halicarnassus, says it explicitly: according to Dionysius, Aeneas was the one who rushed up to the acropolis of Troy and snatched the Palladium from the fires of destruction at the very last moment, as the city was going up in flames; then he brought the Palladium with him to Italy, along with other sacred objects he rescued from the acropolis of Troy (*Roman Antiquities* 1.69.2).

1§96 Such a version of the myth is perfectly suited to the ideology of the Roman empire in the age of Augustus.[82] It links Augustus with the heroes of Troy, since his adoptive father Julius Caesar was a notional descendant of Aeneas by way of Ascanius, otherwise named Iulus, the son of Aeneas. Our source is Strabo (13.1.27 C594–595).[83] As we will soon see, however, the actual rescuing of the Palladium by Aeneas is a theme that predates—and is thus originally independent of—any such Roman appropriation.

1§97 Possession of the Palladium was evidently essential for Rome—at least, for earlier phases of Roman history as also for at least some later phases, including the eras of Cicero and Virgil. Referring to the Palladium, which he also calls a *signum*, Cicero recalls an incident in early Rome when a *pontifex* rescued this sacred object from a fire in 241 BCE and lost his eyesight (*pro Scauro* 48).[84] Judging from such an early date, I infer that the Palladium had been in Italy, in Cicero's mind, ever since Aeneas had taken it there. The aetiology that justified the Roman appropriation of the Palladium must have evolved over time, but the basic idea remained the same: Rome possessed the Palladium as an expression of its own identity as an empire. In the same context where Cicero mentions the rescue of the Palladium from a fire in Rome, he refers to it as 'that Palladium which is kept in Vesta's guardianship as the pledge of our

---

[79] Frazer 1929 IV 263 collects the sources, including Pausanias 1.28.8–9, Polyaenus 1.5, Harpocration (s.v. ἐπὶ Παλλαδίῳ), and the Suda (s.v. ἐπὶ Παλλαδίῳ).

[80] Dionysius of Halicarnassus *Roman Antiquities* 1.69, 2.66.5; Plutarch *Camillus* 20; Pausanias 2.23.5.

[81] Frazer 1929 IV 260 collects the sources, including Plutarch *Camillus* 20.

[82] For an overview of the historical and archaeological evidence concerning the Roman appropriation of myths and rituals related to New Ilion in the age of Augustus and beyond, see Rose 2006:152–153.

[83] See also Frazer 1929 IV 265.

[84] See also Austin 1964:84.

1§8. A statue of Athena in the epic Cycle and beyond

safety and empire [*imperium*]' (*pro Scauro* 48).[85] For my overall argumentation, the link between the idea of empire and the Palladium is essential. By the time we reach Chapter 4, it will be clear that such cultural agenda of the Roman empire reflect the earlier cultural agenda of the Athenian empire.

1§98 The Palladium in Athena's temple on the acropolis of Troy can be imagined to look like the archaic statue of Athena Polias in the temple of Athena Polias on the acropolis of Athens.[86] Pausanias mentions that statue (1.26.4), and he also reports a myth that tells how it had fallen from the sky (1.26.6). We have already noted a similar myth about the Palladium at the acropolis of Troy: it too had fallen from the sky ("Apollodorus" *Library* 3.12.3).

1§99 When Aeneas narrates in Virgil's *Aeneid* the destruction of Troy, his narrative as embedded within Virgil's framing narrative is true to the Roman version of the myth about the Palladium. Things are different, however, in the narrative of Sinon that is embedded within the framing narrative of Aeneas. From the standpoint of the framing narrative, the embedded narrative of Sinon is a fabrication devised by Sinon for the purpose of persuading the Trojans to take the Wooden Horse within their city walls. Taken out of its embedded context, however, the narrative by Sinon about the Palladium matches a non-Roman version of the myth about the Palladium. In the wording of the narrative of Sinon as embedded in the framing narrative told by Aeneas in Virgil's *Aeneid*, we see clear references to this alternative non-Roman version (2.162–175, 182). According to this alternative version of the myth, the two heroes Diomedes and Odysseus together captured the Palladium from the Trojans by infiltrating the citadel of Troy even before the capture of the city. Once captured by the Achaeans, the Palladium reacts by radiating a variety of ominous signs (2.171–175), and it even comes alive, that is, it undergoes mechanical animation as it starts to brandish its shield and spear (2.175 *parmamque ferens hastamque trementem*). In this case, the signs of the goddess conjure the ways in which Athena Promakhos is represented on the acropolis of Athens.[87] From here on, according to this version of the myth as reused by Sinon, the goddess will no longer look favorably upon the Achaeans (2.170

---

[85] See Frazer 1929 IV 262–263, with further citations. See also Dionysius of Halicarnassus *Roman Antiquities* 2.66.4.
[86] For observations about the relevant archaeological evidence in New Ilion, see Rose 2006:148.
[87] Hedreen 2001:28 refers to iconographical representations of the Palladium as looking like the Athena Promakhos of the acropolis in Athens. Earlier, I noted that Athena in the acropolis of Athens can also be visualized as Athena Polias. In ch. 4 I have more to say about the various different representations of Athena on the acropolis of Athens.

aversa deae mens). The Wrath of Athena is about to afflict them. I will have more to say presently about this theme of Athena's anger.

1§100 This alternative version of the myth about the Palladium, as narrated by Sinon in the narrative embedded within the framing narrative of Aeneas in *Aeneid* 2, matches what we find in the epic known as the *Little Iliad* of Lesches of Lesbos (Proclus summary p. 107.7-8).[88] As for the canonical Roman version of the myth about the Palladium, as narrated by Aeneas in his framing narrative, we will now see that it matches what was narrated in the epic known as the *Iliou Persis* of Arctinus of Miletus.

1§101 For background, I start by focusing on three alternative versions of the myth of the Palladium as it was current in the age of Virgil. These three are made explicit in the relevant wording of Ovid's *Fasti* (6.433-435): it was Diomedes or Odysseus or Aeneas—one of these three—who took possession of the Palladium (*seu genus Adrasti seu furtis aptus Ulixes | seu pius Aeneas eripuisset eam | auctor in incerto, res est Romana . . .*). The first two heroes would have done so as an act of theft, while the third hero did it out of piety. The third of these three versions, according to which Aeneas 'snatched' the Palladium from destruction (*eripuisset*), is based on a preconceived notion: the Palladium that had been taken earlier by Diomedes or by Odysseus or by both from the acropolis of Troy must have been something other than the real thing. It must have been false.

1§102 This notion, that there had been a false Palladium as well as a real one, stems from ancient traditions. The story was told in the *Iliou Persis* of Arctinus of Miletus (F 1), as we know from the retelling of Dionysius of Halicarnassus (*Roman Antiquities* 1.69.3). According to this story, the Palladium was stolen by Diomedes and Odysseus—but that object was an *eikōn* 'likeness', which had been made to look exactly like the real thing in order to fool any thief, while the real Palladium was stored in an *abaton* 'inner sanctum', where it remained till Troy went up in flames.[89] We may compare versions of the Troy story that tell about the *eidōlon* 'likeness' of Helen in Troy, while the real Helen stayed in Sparta—or at least in Egypt, according to other versions.[90]

---

[88] With reference to the provenience of Lesches, as I have already indicated earlier (1§93), it is preferable to say <u>Lesbos</u> instead of <u>Mytilene</u> or <u>Pyrrha</u>.

[89] Burgess 2001:142 takes note of this reference to the stealing of the Palladium in *Iliou Persis* F 1. As he points out, "the event occurs only in the *Little Iliad* section of Proclus." To put it another way, the event is recorded only in that section of the Proclus summaries. When it comes to the plot of the *Iliou Persis*, the reference to the Palladium may have taken the form of a narrative flashback.

[90] PH 14§13 (= p. 419).

1§8. A statue of Athena in the epic Cycle and beyond

1§103 As we have just seen from the retelling of Dionysius, the story about the Palladium in the *Iliou Persis* of Arctinus of Miletus claimed that a false copy had been stolen by the Achaeans while the real thing remained in a secret place on the acropolis of Troy. The outcome of this story in the retelling of Dionysius is that the Palladium stayed on the acropolis of Troy until the city was about to be captured:

1Ⓣ19 Dionysius of Halicarnassus *Roman Antiquities* 1.69.3

Ἀρκτῖνος δέ φασι ὑπὸ Διὸς δοθῆναι Δαρδάνῳ Παλλάδιον ἓν καὶ εἶναι τοῦτο ἐν Ἰλίῳ μέχρις ἡ πόλις ἡλίσκετο κεκρυμμένον ἐν ἀβάτῳ.

Arctinus [of Miletus] says about this one [real] Palladium that it had been given by Zeus to Dardanos, and that it was in Ilion all the way up to the time when the city was being captured,[91] hidden in an inner sanctum.

It is of special interest here that the original recipient of the Palladium is specified as Dardanos, not Ilos.

1§104 The narrative in the *Iliou Persis* about the two Palladia, the false and the real, could accommodate the canonical Roman version of the myth:[92] as Dionysius notes (1.69.2), it was of course the genuine Palladium and not the *eikōn* 'likeness' that Aeneas had rescued just before Troy went up in flames.[93] Once the Palladium is rescued by Aeneas, its destiny is clear from the standpoint of the Roman version: as Dionysius goes on to say, Aeneas took the Palladium with him to Rome.

1§105 But where did Aeneas take the Palladium in the version of the myth as narrated in the *Iliou Persis* of Arctinus of Miletus? Dionysius does not say. The dichotomy of the false and the real Palladium in the narrative of the *Iliou Persis* indicates that its own version of the myth of the Palladium conflicted with other versions. The variety of conflicting versions in the archaic period is evident from the examples given by Strabo (13.1.53 C608).

---

[91] The imperfect of ἡλίσκετο may imply that someone did rescue the Palladium before the final capture: I could translate 'was about to be captured'. The rescuer would be none other than Aeneas. I will return to this point in a moment.

[92] In the descriptions of Dionysius of Halicarnassus (especially *Roman Antiquities* 2.66.5), the Palladium is named together with the other *hiera* 'sacred objects' that Aeneas brought from Troy to Italy. See Austin 1964:84.

[93] As for Virgil's version in the *Aeneid*, he chooses not to follow through on various different Roman traditions about the Roman appropriation of the Palladium. And why should he? After all, the narrator of his version is Sinon, and that character's narration is "fiction" in any case. Austin 1964:83–84 gives a survey of variant traditions concerning the fate of the Palladium.

Chapter One

1§106 In reporting about the plot of the *Iliou Persis* of Arctinus of Miletus, Dionysius mentions a telling detail that provides an answer to my question about the destiny of the Palladium in that epic. In the *Iliou Persis*, as we saw a moment ago, it was Dardanos rather than his son Ilos who had been given the Palladium by Zeus. The significance of this variation is obviously political as well as poetic: though only Priam could be traced back genealogically to Ilos, son of Dardanos, both Priam and Aeneas could be traced back to Dardanos. So the possession of the Palladium by Aeneas as the descendant of Dardanos could qualify him to rule a "New Troy," just as he had been qualified to rule the "Old Troy" if it had not been for the genealogical superiority of Priam.

1§107 A place that figured as such a "New Troy" was the city of Scepsis, located in the highlands of Mount Ida. According to Demetrius of Scepsis as mediated by Strabo (13.1.52 C607), this city was ruled by Aeneas after the Trojan War; then it was ruled jointly by Ascanius the son of Aeneas and by Scamandrius the son of Hector; then it was ruled by their descendants, who were an 'oligarchy'; and then it was ruled by a 'democracy' that included immigrants from the city of Miletus.

1§108 The city of Scepsis was the rival of another "New Troy," a city that was actually named New Ilion. According to the *Trōïka* of Hellanicus (*FGH* 4 F 31) as mediated by Dionysius of Halicarnassus (*Roman Antiquities* 1.45.4–1.48.1), the city of New Ilion was ruled jointly by Ascanius the son of Aeneas and by Scamandrius the son of Hector; then it was ruled jointly by their descendants; and then, as we learn from the scholia T for the *Iliad* (XX 307–308a1), it was ruled exclusively by the descendants of Scamandrius the son of Hector after the descendants of Aeneas were expelled.

1§109 The epic of the *Iliou Persis*, attributed to Arctinus of Miletus, evidently validates the "New Troy" of Scepsis at the expense of the "New Troy" called New Ilion. As we have seen, the Palladium in the *Iliou Persis* is linked with Dardanos, not with Ilos. This link is decisive, since a link with Ilos would have favored only the descendants of Priam whereas a link with Dardanos favors not only the descendants of Priam (by way of Hector) but also the descendants of Aeneas.

1§110 In terms of the *Iliou Persis*, the power of a dynasty founded by Aeneas depended on the appropriation of the Palladium and on the appropriation of Aeneas himself as the genealogical 'beginning' of that dynasty.[94]

---

[94] It is in this sense of 'beginning' that *arkhē* means also 'empire'.

1§8. A statue of Athena in the epic Cycle and beyond

Attempts made by various cities to appropriate Aeneas as a dynastic ancestor were thus linked with the appropriation of the Palladium.[95]

1§111 Let us look again at the moment in the narrative of the *Iliou Persis* of Arctinus of Miletus when Aeneas along with his followers withdraws from Troy and moves to the highlands of Mount Ida (Proclus summary p. 107.25–26). By taking this action, Aeneas is responding in two ways to the portent of the death of Laocoön: he not only avoids the pollution that leads to the destruction of Troy but he also sets the stage for the founding of a "New Troy." In the logic of this narrative, Aeneas must relocate the Palladium from the "Old Troy" to the "New Troy" that is Scepsis.

1§112 This version of the Aeneas myth reflected the prestige of the city of Scepsis as a relocated "New Troy." But there was an alternative version that reflected the prestige of the city of New Ilion as an alternative "New Troy" that was not relocated but built on the ruins of the "Old Troy." As we have seen, the descendants of Aeneas had an initial role in the rule of both cities in both versions of the Aeneas myth (Hellanicus *FGH* 4 F 31), but they were eventually ousted from New Ilion (scholia T for *Iliad* XX 307–308a1). As I argue in the twin book *Homer the Preclassic*, this ouster shows that the prestige of New Ilion as the "New Troy" that was founded at the site of the "Old Troy" eventually overshadowed the prestige of Scepsis as a rival "New Troy."[96] Even later, the prestige of Scepsis was further overshadowed by the prestige of Rome as another rival "New Troy," supposedly founded by Aeneas himself. Rome's new link to the descendants of Aeneas would have fatally weakened any older link to Scepsis.[97]

1§113 It is in this context that I introduce an aberrant reference to the Palladium myth involving the city of New Ilion in the Roman era. This version, as reported by Appian (*Mithridateios* 8.53), concerns what happened when this city was captured by the Roman general C. Flavius Fimbria in 85 BCE, during the war against Mithridates.[98] After the Romans burned the temple of Athena, the supposedly real Palladium was found there, all intact: it had been hidden within a wall.[99] From Troy the Palladium was then transferred to Rome (Servius on *Aeneid* 2.166). Comparing this version with the version we have already seen, where Cicero refers to an incident in 241 BCE involving

---

[95] On the appropriation of Aeneas as dynastic ancestor of Julius Caesar, I cite again Strabo 13.1.27 C594–595. See also Frazer 1929 IV 265 and, in general, Gruen 1992.
[96] *HPC* II§§171–181.
[97] *HPC* II§§182.
[98] For historical and archaeological background, see Rose 2006:151–152.
[99] See Frazer 1929 IV 262, with reference to Appian *Mithridateios* 8.53; Frazer also gives references to other sources on the destruction: Livy *Periochae* 83; Strabo 13.1.27 C594; Dio Cassius 30–33 F 104 ed. Cary.

Chapter One

the Palladium in Rome, I infer that Appian's version about the Palladium was based on claims that ultimately became discredited.

1§114 Unlike the *Iliou Persis* of Arctinus of Miletus, the *Aeneid* of Virgil omits—as we have already noted—the detail about the withdrawal of Aeneas to Mount Ida in response to the portent of the death of Laocoön. In Virgil's retelling, Aeneas stayed in Troy till the final hours, when he rushed up to the acropolis and rescued the Palladium before Troy went up in flames. As far as we can tell, however, an actual rescue of the Palladium could have happened even in the narrative of the *Iliou Persis* of Arctinus of Miletus: that is, Aeneas could be imagined as returning to Troy in the final hours to rescue the Palladium while the old city went up in flames.[100]

1§115 To sum up, Virgil follows the plot of the *Iliou Persis* of Arctinus of Miletus in the framing narrative of Aeneas in *Aeneid* 2 but he follows the plot of the *Little Iliad* of Lesches of Lesbos in the embedded narrative of Sinon. The story of Sinon as embedded within the larger story of Aeneas in *Aeneid* 2 is of course "false" in the immediate context, since Sinon "invents" such details as the mantic utterance of the Achaean seer Calchas. Still, Sinon's "lies" may represent alternative "truths"—if they derive from a genuine epic tradition. We may compare the "Cretan lies" of the Homeric *Odyssey*. These "lies" are "false" short-range, in that Odysseus is "lying" to his interlocutors in each immediate context, but they are "true" long-range, since the Cretan epic traditions behind these "lies" turn out to validate the master narrative of the *Odyssey*.[101]

1§116 One commentator observes that the death of Laocoön, as narrated by Aeneas to the queen Dido and her Carthaginian subjects in *Aeneid* 2, "clinched" Sinon's "fiction," making it believable for the Trojans.[102] This "clinching" was of course valid for the Trojans only short-range. Long-range, the death of Laocoön signaled their doom. I say signaled because the death of Laocoön is not just an epic event in *Aeneid* 2. It is also an epiphany, a portent. As an epic event, it makes the Trojans believe something that is false—for them. As an epiphany or portent, however, the death of Laocoön signals or portends something that is true—both for the Achaeans, who will set Troy on fire, and for Aeneas and his followers, who will have to abandon Troy, sooner or later. Longer-range, the death of Laocoön "clinches" a version of the Troy story that derives from the epic Cycle and that validates the overall plot of the *Aeneid*. As

---

[100] Such a version could be posited also for the *Laocoön* of Sophocles. *Aeneid* 2 may show traces.
[101] *BA* 12§§14–15 (= pp. 234–236), Nagy 1985 §73.
[102] I am using the expression of Austin 1964:93. At p. 92 on *Aeneid* 2.189, he reminds us that Sinon is reporting the words of Calchas. Austin says that Sinon's version of Calchas' instructions is "bogus."

1⑤8. A statue of Athena in the epic Cycle and beyond

we will see, the death of Laocoön signals—that is, portends—an overarching epic theme that is shaded over in the Homeric *Iliad* but highlighted in the epic Cycle. That theme is the Wrath of Athena.

1§117 Just as the death of Laocoön is not just a narrative event but a portent, so too is the appearance of the Wooden Horse. When Sinon reports the words of the seer Calchas, who says that Athena wants the Horse to penetrate the walls of Troy as a compensation for the stealing of the Palladium by the Achaeans (*Aeneid* 2.183-184), his words are of course a fiction in the immediate context, but they become a genuine portent, an unintended prophecy that must be fulfilled by the overall plot of the Troy story. I said the plot of the Troy story, not the plot of the *Aeneid* itself. Once the Horse enters Troy, the city will go up in flames, and the revenge of Athena against the Trojans will have been fulfilled; once Troy goes up in flames, Athena can now start to have revenge against the Achaeans as well. This second round of revenge compensates for the taking of the Palladium—as also for other outrages committed against the goddess.[103] The fulfillment of this second round of revenge is formally predicted at the point where the narrative of the *Iliou Persis* of Arctinus of Miletus draws to a close. Here is the relevant wording: ἔπειτα ἀποπλέουσιν οἱ Ἕλληνες, καὶ φθορὰν αὐτοῖς ἡ Ἀθηνᾶ κατὰ τὸ πέλαγος μηχανᾶται 'then the Greeks sail off [from Troy], and Athena begins to plan destruction for them at sea' (*Iliou Persis* 108.11-13).[104] It is the Wooden Horse that inaugurates the two-fold revenge of Athena.

1§118 The revenge of Athena against the Achaeans / Argives is actually retold, however briefly, in *Odyssey* iii 132-135: Zeus planned for them a *nostos* 'homecoming' that was *lugros* 'baneful' (132), because some of them were 'unthinking and unjust' (133), and they were marked for destruction because of the *mēnis* 'anger' of Athena against them (135). It is significant that some Achaeans seem to be exempted from the destruction caused by the Wrath of Athena.[105] Similarly with the Trojans: Aeneas, rescuer of the Palladium, has been exempted from the destruction of the Trojans.

1§119 The theme of Athena's two-fold revenge, first against the Trojans and then against the Achaeans, is integrated into Homeric poetry. The essential

---

[103] When Cassandra holds on to the *xoanon* of Athena for sacred protection, Ajax the son of Oileus forcibly drags her away, *xoanon* and all (*Iliou Persis* Proclus summary p. 108.2-3). I take it that the *xoanon* is distinct from the Palladium.

[104] This type of ending is a typical rhapsodic "cliffhanger." For this concept, see PR 63-65.

[105] There are interesting attenuations here: not all of the Achaeans will be punished. Ultimately, Odysseus will be reconciled with Athena in the *Odyssey*. Moreover, as we will see later, the heroes of the Athenians cannot even be identified with the Achaeans.

Chapter One

passage is *Odyssey* viii 504-512, part of the '*Iliou Persis*' as retold by Demodokos, blind singer of the Phaeacians.[106] We see here the Trojans debating about three possible choices of what to do with the gift Horse: to take it apart with 'pitiless bronze' (507), or to throw it off the heights of 'a steep rock' (508), or to leave it inside Troy (509). In this version the Horse is already inside the walls.[107] The wording of each of the three alternatives is suggestive:

1①20 *Odyssey* viii 504-512

αὐτοὶ γάρ μιν Τρῶες ἐς <u>ἀκρόπολιν</u> ἐρύσαντο.

505 ὣς ὁ μὲν ἑστήκει, τοὶ δ' ἄκριτα πόλλ' ἀγόρευον
ἥμενοι ἀμφ' αὐτόν· τρίχα δέ σφισιν ἥνδανε βουλή,
ἠὲ διατμῆξαι <u>κοῖλον δόρυ νηλέϊ χαλκῷ</u>,
ἢ κατὰ πετράων βαλέειν ἐρύσαντας ἐπ' <u>ἄκρης</u>,
ἢ ἐάαν μέγ' <u>ἄγαλμα</u> θεῶν <u>θελκτήριον</u> εἶναι,

510 τῇ περ δὴ καὶ ἔπειτα <u>τελευτήσεσθαι ἔμελλεν</u>·
<u>αἶσα</u> γὰρ ἦν ἀπολέσθαι, ἐπὴν πόλις ἀμφικαλύψῃ
δουράτεον μέγαν ἵππον, . . .

> For they themselves pulled it [= the Wooden Horse] into the acropolis.[108]

---

[106] Burgess 2001:199n34, with reference to Cook 1999:15n29. Erwin Cook writes me (6 27 03): "In my [. . .] article 'Active and Passive Heroics,' p. 159, I note that in telling the story of his return, Odysseus picks up the Trojan War story where Demodokos leaves off in good rhapsodic fashion, and in my note, 29, go on to say: 'This observation is relevant to G. Nagy's argument, in *Poetry as Performance. Homer and Beyond* (Cambridge 1996) chap. 3, that the Homeric epics display awareness of the principle of rhapsodic succession. In *Od.* 8, Demodokos narrates a quarrel between Akhilleus and Odysseus that most likely belonged to the *Kypria* tradition (on which, see W. Kullmann, *Die Quellen der Ilias*, Hermes Einzelschriften 14 [Wiesbaden 1960] 100). This is followed by Odysseus' participation in athletic games with the Phaiakian youths and his pointed refusal to compete in the foot race, an event that he won in the games of *Il.* 23. Demodokos then sings the story of the Wooden Horse, known from the *Iliou Persis*, and the narrator continues with a simile that dramatizes the immediate aftermath of that story. Odysseus himself continues the narrative with his Apologoi, thus bridging the *Iliou Persis* and the *Nostoi*. It is, moreover, Odysseus himself who requested the Wooden Horse story, so that he is responsible for the fact that these stories are related in their proper sequence.' That there are no less than five narrative segments related in order seems to me a massive confirmation of your position here."

[107] I take it that the Wooden Horse is on the acropolis, and the wording *akrē* reinforces this idea.

[108] So the Wooden Horse is within the acropolis already, not as in *Aeneid* 2.

1§8. A statue of Athena in the epic Cycle and beyond

505 So there it was, standing there, while they [= the Trojans] were saying many different things
sitting around it. There were three different plans:
to cut open the <u>hollow wood with pitiless bronze</u>[109]
or to throw it off the rocky heights after pulling it up to the <u>peak</u> [of the acropolis],[110]
or to leave it, great <u>artifact</u> [<u>agalma</u>][111] that it was, as a <u>charm</u> [<u>thelktērion</u>] of the gods[112]
510 —which, I now see it, was exactly the way <u>it was sure to</u> [<u>mellein</u>] <u>reach an outcome</u> [<u>teleutân</u>],
because it was <u>fate</u> [<u>aisa</u>] that the place would be destroyed,
once the city had enfolded in itself
the great Wooden Horse.

1§120 The third of the three alternatives, to 'leave' the Horse within the walls of Troy (viii 509), is not just an alternative, like the other two. It connects with the plot of the master-narrative that is the Troy story. The connection of this alternative to the plot of the Troy story is signaled in the *Odyssey* through the usage of *teleîn* 'reach an outcome [*telos*]' and *mellein* 'is sure to' (viii 510).[113] The *telos* that is the capture of Troy, as an inevitable outcome of the narrative in progress, signals the chain reaction of events that lead to this inevitable outcome. This chain reaction of events, as made explicit here in the *Odyssey* (viii 510–512), is motivated in the *Aeneid* through the portent of the killing of Laocoön by the twin serpents. This portent "clinches" not only the *Aeneid* but also, ultimately, the Homeric version of the Troy story as retold here in three verses from the *Odyssey* (viii 510–512). Virgil the Classic connects with Homer the Classic.

1§121 It is relevant to ask: how exactly is the Wooden Horse an *agalma*, an 'artifact'? As we read in the *Odyssey* (viii 509), this *agalma* is a *thelktērion* 'charm' of the gods. By comparing this Greek story of the Wooden Horse with similar stories attested around the world, we find a common theme in this "inter-

---

[109] I draw attention to the word *doru* here. This word evokes what Laocoön does when he drives a bronze-tipped spear into the wood.
[110] As I noted before, the epithet *akrē* is evocative of the acropolis.
[111] It is like a substitute for the Palladium. The statue of Athena in her temple on the acropolis of Troy is called an *agalma* in a song of Alcaeus (F 298.21).
[112] The wording here is particularly suggestive, especially the use of the word *thelktērion* 'charm', the meaning of which I will analyze in what follows.
[113] On *mellein* in the sense of 'is sure to', see Bakker 2005:97–101, 107–108, 111–112.

Chapter One

national tale type": the purpose of such a "gift horse" is <u>to enchant those to whom it is given as a gift</u>.¹¹⁴ It is relevant that the noun *thelktērion* 'charm' is derived from the verb *thelgein*, which means 'put a trance on' or 'enchant' or 'charm'. More than that, the contexts of *thelgein* in Homeric poetry include one particular way of being metaphorically 'entranced' or 'enchanted' or 'charmed'—through the beauty and the pleasure of poetry (*Odyssey* xvii 521). And one particular way of being physically 'entranced' or 'enchanted' or 'charmed' is <u>through the eyes</u>: in Homeric diction, the eyes are conventionally featured as the direct object of *thelgein* (*Iliad* XIII 435, 343; *Odyssey* v 47, xxiv 3).¹¹⁵ The prehistory of the meaning of *thelgein* has its uncertainties, but the most plausible etymological explanation is that this Greek verb is cognate with the Lithuanian verb *žvelgiù* 'look'.¹¹⁶ If this explanation is valid, then the meaning of *thelgein* has to do with <u>visual attraction</u>.¹¹⁷ That is, *thelgein* conveys the basic idea of being riveted by a vision, a vision of something that enchants those who see it, putting them into a trance. That kind of vision is an <u>inner vision</u>, the vision of the imagination, activated by the sound of verbal art. What I just said is relevant to what I we saw earlier in the epiphany of the serpent that was turned into stone in *Iliad* II. The <u>look</u> of that serpent, as we noted, is relevant to the etymology of the word that is used for 'serpent' there and elsewhere in Greek: that word is *drakōn* (*Iliad* II 308). Etymologically, *drakōn* 'serpent' is 'the one who looks' (from *derkesthai* 'look').¹¹⁸

1§122 How, then, can we imagine the Wooden Horse of *Odyssey* viii 509 as a work of art? Destined to go up in flames along with the old city of Troy, the Horse could not be imagined as a permanent work of art, in the sense of a sacred art object like the Palladium, which will supposedly last forever. It could not be a substitute, as a sacred art object, for the Palladium. Nor could it be a substitute for the requirement of returning the Palladium to the acropolis: the Wrath of Athena against the Achaeans could not be canceled by a substitution of the Wooden Horse for the Palladium. Unlike the Palladium, the Wooden Horse was destined to go up in flames, along with the old city of Troy. And yet, the Horse was indeed recognized as a permanent work of art, destined to enchant forever as an *agalma* 'artifact', a sacred art object, in the sense that it is made as a permanent work of <u>verbal</u> art. It achieves its substantiality as

---

[114] Hansen 2002:169–176 (the number for the tale type is AT 854).
[115] Nagy 1972:50.
[116] Chantraine *DELG* s.v. θέλγω.
[117] Nagy 1972:50.
[118] Chantraine *DELG* s.v. δέρκομαι.

1§8. A statue of Athena in the epic Cycle and beyond

a work of the poetic imagination. Its maker, aided by Athena herself, was the ultimate artisan of *epea* (*epos* plural) whose name is none other than *Epeios*.[119]

1§123 The story of the Wooden Horse in Virgil's *Aeneid* affirms not only the tradition of the epic Cycle but also the tradition of Homer the Classic—as represented by *Odyssey* viii 509. This affirmation was made possible by the portent of the twin serpents that killed Laocoön. And the narration of this portent in *Aeneid* 2 is a moment that connects Virgil the Classic with Homer the Classic.

1§124 But the question is, can we really say that Virgil's narration is a moment? Here we return to the central thesis of Lessing's essay, *Laocoön*. We have seen Lessing argue that Malerei or painting, in his generalized sense of the word as a vehicle of the imagination, concentrates on a unique moment in any action, while the verbal art of poetry expresses that given action as a continuum. To repeat, my aim is to extend the formulation of Lessing by arguing that verbal art too, as a vehicle of the imagination, can concentrate on a unique moment—without depending on 'painting' as a point of reference. In the case of Homeric poetry, I have found such a moment in *Iliad* II, where we see the portent of the nine birds and the serpent. In the case of Virgilian poetry, I argue for a comparable moment in *Aeneid* 2, where we see the portent of Laocoön and the twin serpents. But the question remains: is the Virgilian narration really a moment?

1§125 Continuing my search for an answer, I propose to have a look at yet another version of the Laocoön story. This version is mediated by the visual art of sculpture. I am referring to "the Vatican group," a set of marble statues dated to somewhere around the middle or second half of the first century BCE, depicting the death of Laocoön and his children.[120] It was discovered in 1506 CE near the Baths of Titus and is currently housed in the Vatican Museum. In the judgment of Pliny the Elder (*Natural History* 36.37), this work of sculpture was superior to all other paintings and sculptures in his time—*opus omnibus et picturae et statuariae artis praeferendum*. Although there is some uncertainty over whether Virgil knew the work—or an earlier version of the work (perhaps a painting),[121] I have my own reasons for feeling certain that he did in fact know it—or a version of it.[122] But it is far more important for now to examine this art object simply as an independent witness. Let us look at an image of the statue (Figure 3).

---

[119] Detailed analysis at 2§282 below.
[120] Austin 1964:96.
[121] Austin 1964:96 mentions the possibility of an earlier version, a lost painting that may be dated as early as the fourth century BCE, "of which the sculptors of the Vatican group were aware."
[122] Lessing was inclined to think that the Vatican group was post-Virgilian; see Austin 1964:96.

Chapter One

Figure 3. Sculpture: The Laocoön group. Roman freestanding marble copy, perhaps after Agesander, Athenodorus, and Polydorus of Rhodes. 1st c. CE. Marble. Vatican Museums.

1§126 As we contemplate the image, I stress the essential: we behold here a unique moment of terror and pity. The question is, how do we compare this moment with the poetic visualization of Laocoön and the two serpents in Virgil's *Aeneid* and, ultimately, with the visualization of the nine birds and the serpent in the Homeric *Iliad*?

1§127 For the moment, I will block in my mind the Iliadic image and restrict my field of vision to the two Roman visualizations of the death of Laocoön—the Vatican group sculpture and Virgil's verses in *Aeneid* 2. I will also restrict my terminology to two media, <u>poetry</u> and <u>painting</u>. It will not affect my argument whether the three-dimensional artwork of the Vatican group was modeled on the two-dimensional artwork of an older painting, or whether Virgil used as a model either the painting or the sculpture or both. In examining the dichotomy of <u>poetry</u> and <u>painting</u> as formulated by Lessing, I am also giving myself a chance to renew my own long-standing interest in this dichotomy, dating back to a work I published over a quarter of a century ago. In that work, I had started with a dictum of Simonides as mediated by Plutarch (*On the glory of the Athenians* 346f): as the saying goes, <u>painting is silent poetry, but poetry is talking pictures</u>.[123]

1§128 Lessing draws attention to some details in the sculpture—or "painting"—of the death of Laocoön that differ markedly from the version captured by the poetry of Virgil. "Virgil winds the serpents twice around the body and neck of Laocoön and has their heads project high above him" (*Aeneid* 2.218-219).[124] "This picture," Lessing continues, "satisfies our imagination fully; the most essential parts of the body are squeezed to the point of strangulation, and the venom is aimed toward the face."[125] By contrast, the artist of the sculpture needs the pain in these "essential parts" of the priest's body to be fully visible, in order to show his "suffering nerves and laboring muscles."[126] The priest must be seen in his nakedness.[127] For the second time now, we have seen a priest stripped naked to the world in all his vulnerability.

1§129 In the sculpture, the coils of the twin serpents gravitate toward the lower rather than the upper parts of the priest's body. As Lessing interprets it, the sculpture "transferred all the coils from the body and neck to thighs and feet, where they could conceal and squeeze as much as necessary without detriment to the expression, and where at the same time they could awaken the idea of suddenly arrested flight and a kind of immobility..."[128]

1§130 In this most arresting moment of eternally arrested mobility, in this stop-motion picture of terror and pity, we see the two legs of Laocoön and the coils of the twin serpents intertwined forever. The moment captured

---

[123] Nagy 1974:21. See also Lessing [1984] 4.
[124] Lessing [1984] 36-37.
[125] Lessing [1984] 37.
[126] Lessing [1984] 37.
[127] Lessing [1984] 38.
[128] Lessing [1984] 37.

Chapter One

Figure 4. Relief sculpture: Athena Parthenos defeats the giant Alkyoneus. From the Great Altar of Zeus, Pergamon. Marble, ca. 180 BCE. Staatliche Museen zu Berlin, Pergamonmuseum.

by such an artistic vision is I think a perfect analogue to the moment when the serpent in *Iliad* II is turned into stone—when the imaginative power of Homeric poetry creates its own piece of three-dimensional artwork. It is also a moment that signals further meanings, heretofore unexplored, in the representations of Laocoön's death. Let me anticipate my conclusion: in this image of Laocoön in agony, showing twin serpents intertwined with his twin legs, I see a reference to traditional imagery derived from a central myth in the calendar of the Athenian city state. That myth narrates the battle of the *gigantes* 'giants' against the goddess Athena and the other Olympian gods, who established cosmic order by defeating the rebellious giants. That primal battle is called the Gigantomachy or *gigantomakhia* (Figures 4, 5, 6).[129]

1§131 I fold in here a rudimentary outline of the overall myth of the Gigantomachy, in order to help clarify the connections I see between its imagery and the imagery of the Laocoön sculpture. The myth tells how the giants, generated by the primal goddess Earth, rebelled against the gods who

---

[129] I note, en passant, the example of serpent-legged monsters throwing rocks, as mentioned by Hardie 1985:24; below the waist, they look like Laocoön entwined by serpents.

1⑤8. A statue of Athena in the epic Cycle and beyond

Figure 5. Relief panels from square column bases: anguiped Giants battle with the Olympian gods. Marble, ca. 200 CE. From a temple in the Severan Forum, Lepcis Magna (Libya). Tripoli, Jamahiriya Museum, 225.

Chapter One

Figure 6. Marble sarcophagus: Gigantomachy, with anguiped Giants. From Rome, Porte Pignattara, probably 2nd century BCE. Vatican, Museo Pio-Clementino, 549.

dwell on Mount Olympus. The giants attempted to storm the heavens but were repelled by the Olympians, chiefly by Zeus and by his daughter, Athena, goddess of Athens; Athena had been born on the same day that marks her victory over these giants.[130] Once the earth-born prodigies start to lose their struggle against the sky-born Olympians, their legs begin to turn into serpents. In surviving pictorial representations of the Gigantomachy, some of the struggling giants are shown still having human legs to stand on while others of the giants are already showing serpents where we expect to see legs, and I interpret this variation as a dynamic representation of their devolution—from the status of aspiring sky-dwellers back to the status of the earth-bound denizens they really are. I show here one such pictorial representation (Figure 7).

1§132 Once the Olympian gods start winning the battle, the giants find themselves having no leg to stand on. Their resistance collapses. The twin serpents we see extending from their lower bodies may now be allowed to follow the natural instincts of serpents and slip back, head first, into the hollows of the same mother Earth that had generated them in the first place.[131]

1§133 In this light, I need to take a second look at the Vatican group sculpture of Laocoön's death, capturing the moment when this *ad hoc* priest of Poseidon is being punished for unwittingly resisting the will of Athena by

---

[130] The mythological synchronicity linking the day of Athena's birth and the day of her defeating the giants needs to be stressed. I will have more to say about this synchronicity in ch. 4.

[131] Douglas Frame reminds me that the figure of the prototypical Athenian king Cecrops is conventionally pictured as *diphuēs* 'double-natured': his upper half is human but his lower half is serpentine (a rare example of an explicit reference is the wording in the scholia for Aristophanes *Wasps* 438).

1§8. A statue of Athena in the epic Cycle and beyond

Figure 7. Attic red-figure calyx krater: Giants repelled from Olympus by the Olympians. The panorama is based on a masterpiece of metalwork by Pheidias, situated inside the concave interior surface of the gigantic shield of Athena Parthenos in the Parthenon of Athens. Attributed to the Pronomos Painter, ca. 425-375 BCE. Naples, Museo Archeologico Nazionale, 815.

opposing the penetration of the Wooden Horse within the walls of Troy. The coils of the twin serpents intertwining with his own legs make him look like some earth-born giant struggling in vain against the overriding will of the Olympians (Figure 8, as Figure 3 above).

1§134 For Lessing, the representation of Laocoön's death in sculpture becomes a perfect example of the ways in which "painting" has the power to capture a single moment, as opposed to poetry. All along, I have been arguing that poetry has that same power. So I come back to my question: does Virgil's poetry in his description of Laocoön's death possess that kind of imaginative power? If it does, then Virgil the Classic has indeed validated Homer the Classic in the age of Virgil.

1§135 To answer my own question, I need to start with another question. After the twin serpents kill the priest of Poseidon / Neptune in *Aeneid* 2, I ask: what happens to them? At the very next sighting, the twin serpents are seen heading for the acropolis of Troy, up to the sacred precinct of Athena that looms over the city; one mighty leap, and the next thing you know they have

133

Chapter One

Figure 8 (as Figure 3 above). The Laocoön group.

slipped inside the temple on high, and now we see them nestled at the feet of the goddess—that is, at the feet of the statue of the goddess.

1①21 Virgil *Aeneid* 2.225–227

at gemini lapsu <u>delubra ad summa</u> dracones

1⑤8. A statue of Athena in the epic Cycle and beyond

effugiunt saevaeque petunt Tritonidis arcem,
sub pedibusque deae <u>clipeique sub orbe</u> teguntur.

But then the twin serpents slip away and <u>to the sacred spaces way up high</u>
they flee, heading straight for the citadel of fierce Athena,
and, at the feet of the goddess, <u>under the orb [*orbis*] of her Shield</u>,
they find cover.

1§136 So now we see that the twin serpents from Tenedos had slipped into the acropolis of Troy even before the Wooden Horse penetrated the city's walls—and before the Achaeans waiting at Tenedos—along with the Achaeans waiting inside the Horse—converge to begin their work of destruction.[132] What is the point of this narrative detail about the serpents? What was Virgil imagining? His wording does not say it explicitly, but the idea must be that the twin serpents of *Aeneid* 2, once they had slipped inside the acropolis and nestled next to the statue of the goddess in her sacred precinct, were now turned into statues themselves.

1§137 Essential for such a vision is the surviving testimony about the statue of Athena Polias on the acropolis in Athens. According to the testimony of Phylarchus (*FGH* 81 F 72), the goddess was attended by two serpents. Our immediate source for this testimony is Photius (*Lexicon* s.v. οἰκουρὸν ὄφιν), who observes that other sources like Aristophanes (*Lysistrata* 759) and Herodotus (8.41.2) indicate a single serpent (οἰκουρὸν ὄφιν· τὸν τῆς Πολιάδος φύλακα· καὶ Ἡρόδοτος, Φύλαρχος δὲ αὐτοῦ δύο). As for the tradition about two serpents, it is reported also in the ancient lexicographical tradition as subsumed under the name of Hesychius:

1①22 Hesychius s.v. οἰκουρὸν ὄφιν

τὸν τῆς Πολιάδος φύλακα δράκοντα. καὶ οἱ μὲν ἕνα φασίν, οἱ δὲ δύο
ἐν τῷ ἱερῷ τοῦ <u>Ἐρεχθέως</u>. τοῦτον δὲ φύλακα τῆς ἀκροπόλεώς φασι,
ᾧ καὶ μελιτοῦτταν παρατίθεσθαι

---

[132] Contrast Quintus of Smyrna 12.488, on which Austin 1964:108 comments: "the serpents vanish into Apollo's temple (i.e. the tradition is followed that Virgil abandoned, see [Austin] p. 95). On Laocoön's first appearance he is shown as coming *summa ab arce* (41): now the serpents who have killed him go *summa ad delubra*, perhaps a deliberate pattern of events."

On the expression *oikouros ophis* 'serpent that guards the dwelling [*oikos*]':[133] it is the serpent [*drakōn*] who is the guardian [*phulax*] of the goddess [= Athena] Polias. Some say that there is one such serpent while others say that there are two in the sacred space of Erekhtheus. And they say that he [= such a serpent] is a guardian [*phulax*], and that an offering of a barley-cake kneaded with honey is offered to him.

1§138 As we are about to see, Erekhtheus is the name of the cult hero whose sacred space, the *Erekhtheion* or Erechtheum, was contiguous with the sacred space of the goddess Athena Polias on the acropolis in Athens. There is a reference to the hero cult of this Erekhtheus in *Iliad* II 547, where he is described as a prototypical human: born of the goddess Earth and 'nursed' (548 *threpse*) by the goddess Athena, he is said to be worshipped by the Athenians in a festive setting of seasonally recurring sacrifices. The link between Athena Polias and this cult hero Erekhtheus on the acropolis of Athens is reflected also in another Homeric reference, in *Odyssey* vii 81.[134] At some point after the embedding of these references to Erekhtheus in the Homeric tradition, however, the figure of this cult hero underwent a mitosis. The one figure with one name becomes two figures with two names. In the evolution of Athenian myths and rituals, the name Erikhthonios displaced the name Erekhtheus in occupying the older role of the prototypical human conceived by the goddess Earth, while the name Erekhtheus was reassigned to the newer role of a dynastic grandson of Erikhthonios, as we see from the references made by Pausanias (1.2.6 and 1.5.3 respectively on Erekhtheus and Erikhthonios). In terms of this pattern of displacement and reassignment, as we see most clearly from the narrative of "Apollodorus" (*Library* 1.187–189), Erikhthonios now became the name of the prototypical human who was begotten by the god Hephaistos, born of the goddess Earth, and 'nursed' (1.189 line 2 *etrephen*) by the goddess Athena. At one point, Pausanias says ostentatiously that he knows the myth about the relationship of Erikhthonios and Athena (1.14.6); at an earlier point, he refers to Erikhthonios as begotten by the god Hephaistos and born of the goddess Earth (1.2.6). All the same, the whole cult complex that housed the myths and rituals concerning Erikhthonios and the goddess Athena Polias continued to be defined by the name Erekhtheus, as we see from

---

[133] The expression οἰκουρὸν ὄφιν 'serpent that guards the dwelling' comes from Aristophanes *Lysistrata* 759.
[134] *HTL* 159–160.

1⑤8. A statue of Athena in the epic Cycle and beyond

the context of the reference made by Pausanias to the whole sacred space as the *Erekhtheion* or Erechtheum (1.26.5).

1§139 Unlike the linking of the old statue of Athena Polias with the oscillating figure of Erekhtheus / Erikhthonios, the newer statue of Athena Parthenos was linked exclusively with Erikhthonios. This newer statue, made by the Athenian master sculptor Pheidias, was inaugurated in the Parthenon, the new temple of Athena Parthenos, in 438 BCE. While we have conflicting reports about two serpents or a single serpent attending the statue of Athena Polias in her old temple on the acropolis of Athens, it is clear that only one serpent attended the statue of Athena Parthenos in her new temple, the Parthenon. In his eyewitness account of the statue of Athena Parthenos in the Parthenon, Pausanias identifies the statue of the single serpent attending the goddess as Erikhthonios himself:

1①23 Pausanias 1.24.5-7

> αὐτὸ δὲ ἔκ τε ἐλέφαντος τὸ ἄγαλμα καὶ χρυσοῦ πεποίηται. μέσῳ μὲν οὖν ἐπίκειταί οἱ τῷ κράνει Σφιγγὸς εἰκών [. . .] καθ' ἑκάτερον δὲ τοῦ κράνους {6} γρῦπές εἰσιν ἐπειργασμένοι. [. . .] καὶ γρυπῶν {7} μὲν πέρι τοσαῦτα εἰρήσθω· τὸ δὲ ἄγαλμα τῆς Ἀθηνᾶς ὀρθόν ἐστιν ἐν χιτῶνι ποδήρει καί οἱ κατὰ τὸ στέρνον ἡ κεφαλὴ Μεδούσης ἐλέφαντός ἐστιν ἐμπεποιημένη· καὶ Νίκην τε ὅσον τεσσάρων πηχῶν, ἐν δὲ τῇ χειρὶ δόρυ ἔχει, καί οἱ πρὸς τοῖς ποσὶν ἀσπίς τε κεῖται καὶ πλησίον τοῦ δόρατος δράκων ἐστίν· εἴη δ' ἂν Ἐριχθόνιος οὗτος ὁ δράκων. ἔστι δὲ τῷ βάθρῳ τοῦ ἀγάλματος ἐπειργασμένη Πανδώρας γένεσις. πεποίηται δὲ Ἡσιόδῳ τε καὶ ἄλλοις ὡς ἡ Πανδώρα γένοιτο αὕτη γυνὴ πρώτη·

> The statue [*agalma*][135] itself is made of gold and ivory. In the middle of the helmet is placed a likeness of Sphinx. [Pausanias here gives a cross-reference to a later excursus on the Sphinx.] On each side of the helmet there are griffins worked in. [Pausanias here gives an excursus on griffins.] Enough said about griffins. The statue [*agalma*] of Athena is standing, wearing a khiton [*khitōn*] that extends to her feet. On her chest is the head of Medusa, made of ivory. She has [in one hand] a [figure of] Nike, around four cubits in height, and she holds in her [other] hand a spear. A shield [*aspis*] is positioned at her

---

[135] The statue of Athena in her temple on the acropolis of Troy is called an *agalma* in a song of Alcaeus (F 298.21).

Chapter One

feet. And near the spear is a serpent [*drakōn*].¹³⁶ Now this serpent [*drakōn*] would be Erikhthonios. And on the surface of the base of the statue is a relief of the genesis of Pandora. The story of the genesis of this first woman Pandora is told by Hesiod in his poetry as well as by others.

1§140 The wording makes it clear that Pausanias is well aware of the highly charged mysticism of what he was saying when he says that the serpent who attends Athena Parthenos is none other than the autochthonous hero of Athens, Erikhthonios. The potential optative, which I translate as 'would be', marks the speaker's self-awareness at a sacral moment of contemplation. He is touching on a matter of the greatest importance.

1§141 To help visualize the goddess Athena and her serpent attendant, I offer some reconstructions of the statue of Athena Parthenos, in the company of the statue serpent (Figure 9).

1§142 The question arises, how did Virgil imagine the statue of Athena on the acropolis of Troy? Since this statue was attended by the two serpents who killed Laocoön, I propose that it resembled the old statue of Athena Polias in the old temple of the goddess. In one version, as we saw earlier (Phylarchus *FGH* 81 F 72), Athena Polias was attended by two serpents.

1§143 It still remains to ask, however, how these two serpents were visualized as statues. In a search for answers, I start here by drawing attention to a detail clearly visible in the reconstructions of the single serpent attending Athena Parthenos: both in the Toronto reconstruction and in the surviving miniature copies of Athena Parthenos, you can see a statue serpent at the feet of the goddess, standing erect near the inside of her shield. You can see how this serpent, stationed at the feet of the goddess, is literally being shielded by the Shield of Athena, finding cover there. In describing the reconstructed modern serpent this way, I have in mind the image shown by Virgil, who sees the twin serpents finding cover under the orb of Athena's shield.

1§144 Looking at the figure of the serpent shielded by the Shield of Athena in the picture of the Toronto reconstruction, we see that this figure actually blocks the view of the concave space inside the Shield. I doubt that this aspect of the reconstruction is correct.¹³⁷ Any blocking of the view to be seen inside that concave space would have been unthinkable in the era of Classical Athens, the age of Pheidias. There was a masterpiece to be seen there. Inside

---

[136] I draw attention to the wording of Pausanias concerning the position of the serpent: 'near the spear', not 'near the shield'.

[137] See my earlier remark about the proximity of the serpent to the spear.

1§8. A statue of Athena in the epic Cycle and beyond

that concave space, within the inner surface of the Shield of Athena, was a masterpiece of metalwork, and the metalworker was none other than Pheidias himself. This metalwork, primarily in gold, pictured the Gigantomachy, the battle of the gods and giants. I will treat more fully in Chapter 4 this lost masterpiece of Pheidias, along with its grand theme, the Gigantomachy. But I highlight already here a fact that we will consider more thoroughly in Chapter 4. The fact is, there was at the same time another masterpiece of artwork representing the Gigantomachy. Besides the metalworked version of the Gigantomachy, representing a classical moment frozen in time, there was also a woven version, rewoven every four years at the feast of the quadrennial Great Panathenaia.[138] This other version was woven into the *peplos* or 'robe' presented to the goddess Athena at the climax of a sacred procession in her honor. The woven version, which can be seen as an ongoing classical process in contrast to the single classical moment sculpted by Pheidias, figures prominently not only in Chapter 4 but also in the twin book *Homer the Preclassic*. As I argue there, this version is relevant to the Homeric visualization of the *peplos* or 'robe' that the women of Troy present to the statue of the goddess Athena in her temple situated on the acropolis of Troy in *Iliad* VI.[139] This Homeric visualization is in turn relevant to Virgil's visualization of the same statue in *Aeneid* 2.

1§145 A question needs be raised in the light of Virgil's image of the two serpents. What would be the conventional poetic way of imagining the moment signaled by the verse in *Aeneid* 2 203 when we behold for the first time Virgil's twin serpents? The visual force of this verse shines forth already in the first word, *ecce* 'behold!'. Some may think that the poet's visualization of this moment depends merely on his familiarity with the conventions of "fine arts" in his own life and times: as one commentator remarks about this verse, "any old picture of the sea-serpent will well illustrate Virgil here."[140] I argue, to the contrary, that the artistic convention of picturing these twin serpents is far more specific in its referential power. We have already seen an ancient poetic precedent in the epic Cycle, which shows an epiphany of two serpents instead of one (Arctinus of Miletus *Iliou Persis* 107.23 δύο δράκοντες ἐπιφανέντες). As arresting as the image of these serpents may be, what I find even more arresting about their epiphany is something that is missing from the picture in the *Aeneid*. The absent signifier is the goddess Athena herself.

---

[138] Here and hereafter, I note the distinction between the quadrennial Great Panathenaia, celebrated every fourth year, and the annual Lesser Panathenaia, celebrated in the other years.
[139] *HPC* II§298.
[140] Page 1894:224.

Chapter One

Figure 9. Plaster model: Reconstruction of Pheidias' chryselephantine statue of Athena Parthenos on the acropolis of Athens, with serpent. Reconstruction by G. P. Stevens and Sylvia Hahn, ca. 1970. Ontario, Canada. Royal Ontario Museum.

1§8. A statue of Athena in the epic Cycle and beyond

Here I turn to the visual arts. There is a painting that actually pictures Athena as riding on a chariot drawn by two serpents on the occasion of a grand ceremonial entrance. In this painting, three Olympian goddesses are arriving to participate in a primal occasion known as the Judgment of Paris: they are Hera, Aphrodite, and Athena.[141] Each of the three goddesses is making an individualized ceremonial entrance. Hera is shown arriving on the scene riding in a chariot drawn by horses; Aphrodite pulls up in a chariot drawn by adolescent 'cupids', that is, by Erotes; and then there is Athena, who makes her own grand ceremonial entrance riding in a chariot drawn by twin serpents (Figures 10a and 10b).

1§146 The fact that the two serpents who kill Laocoön have their own names in the *Laocoön* of Sophocles (F 372 ed. Radt) reinforces the idea that they, too, like the two divine horses of Hera and the two divine Erotes of Aphrodite, are a divine chariot team. All three divine chariot teams of all three goddesses are divine counterparts of a conventional chariot team of two horses driven by a conventional chariot-driver. The specialized role of the serpents as the chariot team of Athena is what generates the idea of two serpents instead of one serpent – such as the single serpent who is stationed next to Athena Parthenos in the Parthenon. Similarly, the specialized role of the Erotes as the chariot team of Aphrodite is what generates the idea of two Erotes instead of one Eros – such as the single god Eros who is pictured in the Hesiodic *Theogony* (120, 201).[142]

1§147 A moment ago, I quoted Pausanias saying, with ostentatious ritual reverence, that the single serpent stationed next to Athena Parthenos in the Parthenon 'would be' the primordial Athenian cult hero Erikhthonios. We see here the single serpent of Athena being personalized as an archetypal male companion, but twin serpents are stylized as her chariot team. Analogously, Eros as a single god figures as a male attendant of Aphrodite, while twin Erotes are stylized as her own chariot team. I see yet another analogy in the myths of the dawn goddess Eos: she is said to have a son called *Phaethōn* in the Hesiodic *Theogony* (987), but she also has a chariot team drawn by divine twin horses named *Phaethōn* and *Lampos* in the Homeric *Odyssey* (xxiii 246).[143]

1§148 Besides the grand ceremonial entrances, by chariot, of the three goddesses involved in the Judgment of Paris, there are other such scenes as well. In Homeric poetry, the most spectacular of all such chariot-powered

---

[141] There is an evocative reference to the Judgment of Paris in *Iliad* XXIV 28-30.
[142] Eros is a primordial god in "Orphic" traditions: *Orphic Fragment* 28 ed. Kern (further references in West 1966:195).
[143] *GM* 249-250.

Chapter One

Figure 10a. Attic red-figure pyxis lid: panorama of all three goddesses arriving in their chariots drawn by customized chariot-teams. Unattributed, ca. 425-375 BCE. Copenhagen, National Museum, 731.

Figure 10b. Copenhagen pxyis: detail, Athena riding on chariot drawn by two serpents.

1⑤8. A statue of Athena in the epic Cycle and beyond

arrivals is the grand ceremonial entrance of the god Poseidon on the battlefield in *Iliad* XIII. He is shown riding in his horse-drawn chariot, skimming effortlessly over the surface of the sea as he heads for the scene of battle in Troy:

1①24 *Iliad* XIII 23–31

    ἔνθ' ἐλθὼν ὑπ' ὄχεσφι τιτύσκετο χαλκόποδ' ἵππω
    ὠκυπέτα χρυσέῃσιν ἐθείρῃσιν κομόωντε,
25 χρυσὸν δ' αὐτὸς ἔδυνε περὶ χροΐ, γέντο δ' ἱμάσθλην
    χρυσείην εὔτυκτον, ἑοῦ δ' ἐπεβήσετο <u>δίφρου</u>,
    βῆ δ' ἐλάαν <u>ἐπὶ κύματ'</u>· ἄταλλε δὲ κήτε' ὑπ' αὐτοῦ
    πάντοθεν ἐκ κευθμῶν, οὐδ' ἠγνοίησεν ἄνακτα·
    γηθοσύνῃ δὲ θάλασσα διίστατο· τοὶ δὲ πέτοντο
30 ῥίμφα μάλ', <u>οὐδ' ὑπένερθε διαίνετο χάλκεος ἄξων</u>·
    τὸν δ' ἐς Ἀχαιῶν νῆας ἐΰσκαρθμοι φέρον ἵπποι.

    Arriving there [= at Aigai], he [= Poseidon] harnessed to his chariot his two bronze-hooved horses

    —swift they were, with golden manes streaming from their heads—

25 and he put on his golden armor, which enveloped his skin, and he seized his whip,

    golden it was, beautifully made, and he stepped on the platform of his <u>chariot</u>,

    and off he went <u>over the waves</u>, and the sea creatures were frolicking underneath as we went along.

    They came out from all their hiding places down below, recognizing their lord and master.

    Gladly did the sea part as they [= the divine horses] were speeding ahead.

30 So lightly they moved that <u>the wetness did not touch from below the bronze axle</u>

    as he [= Poseidon] was being conveyed toward the ships of the Achaeans by his prancing horses.

Chapter One

1§149 I suspect that a grand ceremonial arrival of Athena in the *Iliou Persis* of Arctinus of Miletus could have been expressed in words that matched closely the words expressing Poseidon's arrival here in the Homeric *Iliad*. In the version as shaped by Virgil, however, the divine chariot-rider and her chariot are invisible. Only the twin serpents, the team that draws her chariot, are visible to the Trojans. Athena produces an epiphany that keeps her out of the picture, as an absent signifier. In fact, the goddess is not really absent: she is only hidden, invisible. It is her agency that sends the twin serpents, who are then reunited with her after their deed is done, after they destroy Laocoön. The goddess Athena is invisible as she drives her chariot drawn by twin serpents, but she is visible as the statue that forms an ensemble with the twin serpents that become statues that attend her. Athena is invisible at the moment of her agency in killing Laocoön, just as she is invisible at the moment of her agency in preventing the killing of Agamemnon by Achilles in *Iliad* I. But the instruments of her agency are visible as live serpents at the moment of this agency—and as statues of serpents after the moment is over. Similarly, Athena herself is a statue when the moment of her agency is over.

1§150 Given the fragmentary state of the epic Cycle as we have it today, we have no way of being certain whether Virgil was following the *Iliou Persis* when he imagined the twin serpents petrified as statues at the foot of Athena's own statue in her sacred precinct on top of the Trojan acropolis. It remains a question whether Virgil's poetic imagination captured a moment that corresponds to a moment that comes from the *Iliou Persis*. Such questions, in any case, are secondary for my argumentation. The primary question centers on Virgil's rivalry with Homeric poetry. My point remains that the petrifaction of the twin serpents in *Aeneid* 2 is a scene that rivals, as an artifact of poetic imagination, the scene of the petrified serpent in *Iliad* II.

1§151 As an artifact, the petrified serpent of *Iliad* II is not a creation of the visual art of sculpture: it is exclusively a creation of verbal art. The petrified serpents of *Aeneid* 2 seem at first glance different in this regard: they are juxtaposed with the sculpture of the goddess, and, to that extent, they must become part of the sculpture as an artistic ensemble. On second thought or, better, at second glance, however, the vision is blurred. The artificial and the natural are no longer readily distinguishable: even the sculpture of the goddess is pictured in Virgil's words as the goddess herself, not as a piece of artwork in and of itself. What notionally animates the art is the creative impulse of the artist—whether that artist's medium is sculpture or poetry or both. There is a paradox here: animation is realized in the absolute rigidity of a single moment captured by the art. This absolute rigidity of the moment, of a single eternity, embodies the perfect self-expression of the art.

1⑤9. Ovidian variations on a theme of rigidity in art

1§152 The paradox of animation, as realized in the absolute rigidity of artistic perfection, is illuminated by the poetry of another artist of Virgil's age. I have in mind the story of Pygmalion in Ovid's *Metamorphoses*. This poet's use of the Latin words *rigidus* 'rigid' and *rigor* 'rigidity' captures the metaphor of absolute rigidity as perfection.

1①25 Ovid *Metamorphoses* 10.238–297

      Sunt tamen obscenae Venerem Propoetides ausae
      esse negare deam; pro quo sua numinis ira
240 corpora cum fama primae vulgasse feruntur,
      utque pudor cessit, sanguisque induruit oris,
      in <u>rigidum</u> parvo <u>silicem</u> discrimine <u>versae</u>.
      Quas quia Pygmalion aevum per crimen agentis
      viderat, offensus vitiis, quae plurima menti
245 femineae natura dedit, sine coniuge caelebs
      vivebat thalamique diu consorte carebat.
      interea <u>niveum</u> mira feliciter arte
      <u>sculpsit</u> <u>ebur</u> formamque dedit, qua femina nasci
      nulla potest, <u>operisque sui concepit amorem</u>.
250 <u>virginis est verae facies, quam vivere credas,</u>
      <u>et, si non obstet reverentia, velle moveri.</u>
      ars adeo latet arte sua. miratur et haurit
      pectore Pygmalion simulati corporis ignes.
      saepe manus operi temptantes admovet, an sit
255 corpus an illud ebur, nec adhuc ebur esse fatetur.

Chapter One

[oscula dat reddique putat loquiturque tenetque][144]
et[145] credit tactis digitos insidere membris
et metuit, pressos veniat ne livor in artus,
et modo blanditias adhibet, modo grata puellis
260 munera fert illi conchas teretesque lapillos
et parvas volucres et flores mille colorum
liliaque pictasque pilas et ab arbore lapsas
Heliadum lacrimas; ornat quoque vestibus artus,
dat digitis gemmas, dat longa monilia collo,
265 aure leves bacae, redimicula pectore pendent:
cuncta decent; nec nuda minus formosa videtur.
conlocat hanc stratis concha Sidonide tinctis
adpellatque tori sociam adclinataque colla
mollibus in plumis, tamquam sensura, reponit.
270 Festa dies Veneris tota celeberrima Cypro
venerat, et pandis inductae cornibus aurum
conciderant ictae nivea cervice iuvencae,
turaque fumabant, cum munere functus ad aras
constitit et timide "si, di, dare cuncta potestis,
275 sit coniunx, opto," non ausus "eburnea virgo"
dicere, Pygmalion "similis mea" dixit "eburnae."
sensit, ut ipsa suis aderat Venus aurea festis,
vota quid illa velint et, amici numinis omen,
flamma ter accensa est apicemque per aera duxit.
280 ut rediit, simulacra suae petit ille puellae
incumbensque toro dedit oscula: visa tepere est;
admovet os iterum, manibus quoque pectora temptat:
temptatum mollescit ebur positoque rigore
subsidit digitis ceditque, ut Hymettia sole

---

[144] For a questioning of the authenticity of verses 256: Tarrant 2005:75n15.
[145] For the possibility of reading *sed* instead of *et* here: Tarrant 2005:75n15.

19. Ovidian variations on a theme of rigidity in art

285 cera remollescit tractataque pollice multas
flectitur in facies ipsoque fit utilis usu.
dum stupet et dubie gaudet fallique veretur,
rursus amans rursusque manu sua vota retractat.
<u>corpus erat</u>! saliunt temptatae pollice venae.
290 tum vero Paphius plenissima concipit heros
verba, quibus Veneri grates agat, oraque tandem
ore suo non falsa premit, dataque oscula virgo
sensit et erubuit timidumque ad lumina lumen
attollens pariter cum caelo vidit amantem.
295 coniugio, quod fecit, adest dea, iamque coactis
cornibus in plenum noviens lunaribus orbem
illa Paphon genuit, de qua tenet insula nomen.

But the obscene Propoetides dared to say that Venus
is not a goddess. To compensate for this, through the wrath of the goddess,
240 they are said to have been the first to prostitute their bodies along with their fame.
and, as their sense of shame receded and the blood of their faces hardened,
into <u>rigid stone</u> they were <u>turned</u>. You could barely tell them apart from the stone.
Because Pygmalion had seen these women spending an eternity in a state deserving of reproach,
and because he was deeply offended by their shameful faults, so many of which the mind
245 of females has by nature inherited, he chose to live unmarried, without a spouse.
That is how he lived for the longest time, without someone to share with him his bed.
Meanwhile a <u>snow-white</u> figure, with an artistry that must be marveled at, did he successfully

sculpt. It was an <u>ivory</u> figure, and he gave it a beautiful form. With this kind of beauty no woman can be born,

not a single one can, <u>and he conceived a love for his own handiwork</u>.

250 <u>Its looks are the looks of a real girl, and you would think that she is alive</u>

<u>and, if modesty were not in the way, you would think it is desiring to be moved</u>.

That is how much his art is hiding behind his art. Pygmalion marvels at it and inhales

in his heart the flames of love for something that looks like a body.

Often he places his hands on the work to test whether it is a

255 body, that thing, or ivory. And he just cannot admit that it is ivory.

He gives it kisses and thinks his kisses are returned. He speaks to it, holds on to it

and thinks he is feeling his fingers press down on the limbs when he touches them;[146]

and then he gets scared that bruises might show on the parts where he pressed too hard.

One moment, he tries to use fond words of love. The next moment, things that please girls,

260 gifts, does he bring to that thing—gifts like shells and smooth precious stones

and little birds and flowers of thousands of different colors,

and lilies and colored balls, and dripping from trees,

the teardrops of the Heliades. He adorns its limbs also with precious fabrics.

He gives its fingers rings with gems on them, and he gives its neck a long necklace.

265 Smooth pearls hang from its ears and chains hang from its neck to adorn its breasts.

---

[146] See the previous two notes.

All these adornments enhance her beauty. But she looks no less beautiful when she is nude.[147]

He lays her on a bed spread with coverlets <u>dyed with the extract from murex shells from Sidon</u>,[148]

and calls her his bedmate. He rests her reclining head

on soft, downy pillows, as if she could feel the softness.

270 And now the day of the festival of Venus had come, celebrated throughout all of Cyprus,

yes, it had come. Heifers with their expansive horns covered with gold

had fallen from the blow of the sacrificial axe aimed at their snow-white throat,

and the altars smoked with incense. Pygmalion, having performed his sacrifice at the altar,

stood and hesitantly prayed: "If you, O gods, are able to grant everything,

275 I wish that the wife . . . "—not daring to say "<u>ivory virgin</u>,"

Pygmalion went ahead and said— . . . "that my wife could be just like the ivory one."[149]

But she sensed—golden Venus did, for she herself was present at her festival—

what that prayer meant; and, as an omen of favorable divine presence,

three times did the flame [of sacrifice] burst forth and shoot high up into the air.

280 When he returned he went straight for the image of his girl,

and, bending over the bed, he kissed her. She seemed warm to the touch.

Again he moved his lips to her flesh, and with his hands also he touched her breasts.

---

[147] Suddenly there is a shift from neuter ('it') to feminine ('she'), from the inanimate to the animate.

[148] Here in Ovid *Metamorphoses* 10.266, we see that the provenience of purple is traditionally associated with the city of Sidon in Phoenicia.

[149] Ovid's wording achieves a "hesitation effect" in what Pygmalion says. See the next note.

Chapter One

> The <u>ivory</u> <u>softens</u> to the touch and, its <u>hardness</u> [*rigor*] set aside,
> gives in and yields to his fingers, as wax from Hymettus, under the sun,
> 285 softens and, molded by the thumb, into many different
> appearances is reshaped, becoming usable by way of being used.
> In his amazement, rejoicing but still in doubt, fearing he is deluded,
> the lover tests his hopes with his hand again and again.
> <u>Yes, it was a real body</u>! The veins were pulsing to the touch of his testing thumb.
> 290 Then did the hero from Paphos conceive the most fully-formed words
> with which to give thanks to Venus, and lips that were at last
> not false lips did he press with his own lips. And the kisses given by him the girl
> could feel, and she blushed, while the timid light of her eyes toward the lights
> she raised, seeing at the same time the sky and her lover.
> 295 The goddess was present for the marriage she made, and, with the filling
> of the crescent moon into a full orb for the ninth time,
> she [= the wife of Pygmalion] gave birth to a daughter, Paphos, and the island takes its name from her.

1§153 In these verses of Ovid, we see distinctions being made between art and nature, between the artificial and the natural. The rigidity of petrifaction is imagined as natural, to be distinguished from the rigidity of sculpture, which is seen as artificial. And the artificial rigidity of sculpture is being ostentatiously distinguished from the natural softness of the living body.

1§154 Let us re-examine the narrative in terms of these distinctions. The sculptor Pygmalion is horrified to see women being turned into stone. As natural beings, they have failed to see the divinity of Aphrodite, viewing her divine sexuality only in terms of their own human sexuality. The "natural" petrifaction of the women is pictured as a negative consequence of natural female sexuality. Pygmalion reacts to this petrifaction by canceling all contact with female sexuality, with the natural. So he avoids sex with "live" women (I am thinking here of the metaphor of "live" performance). He makes something artificial as a substitute or compensation for the natural, sculpting the ideal female. She—or it—is an ivory statue, and she is absolutely rigid. The "natural" petrifaction of real females in all their sexuality inspires an artificial creation, the sculpting of the ideal female as an <u>ivory virgin</u>. This image of an <u>ivory virgin</u> invites an unholy equation with the ivory statue of Athena the virgin, Athena Parthenos, on the acropolis of Athens. Any direct equation, however, is playfully canceled by the poetry of Ovid.[150] By contrast with the divine sexuality of Aphrodite, Athena is a model of divine asexuality. Mistaking divine sexuality for human sexuality was dangerous enough, but now an even more dangerous possibility emerges: the sculptor conceives a desire to change divine asexuality into human sexuality. Pygmalion starts wishing for the statue to become "live." The story works toward a wish-fulfillment. The sculptor prays that the gods grant his wish that his sculpture should become "live." He does not dare to say directly that the *eburnea virgo*, evoking visions of the ivory statue of Athena Parthenos on the acropolis, should be his wife. He says it only indirectly. The sculpting of the ideal female inspires a male desire for the softening of her absolute rigidity. Once the softening of the *rigor* gets underway, the absolute and the asexual become the real and the sexual. The statue becomes a real woman. This softening cancels the poetics of perfection implied by the absolute rigidity of the 'ivory virgin'. In the end, it is no longer a matter of art after all. At first glance, the statue loses its rigidity (*rigor*) as it responds to the loving touch of the artist. At second glance, however, that loving touch comes from a lover, no longer from an artist.

1§155 By contrast with Ovid's false Athena Parthenos, a playful challenge to the paradoxical idea of rigidity as animation, I view Virgil's image of the true Athena at Troy attended by her twin serpents as a serious effort to elaborate on this same idea of rigidity and to link it with the making of poetry. This true Athena resembles not the Athena Parthenos of the Parthenon but the

---

[150] Relevant is the "hesitation effect" in *Metamorphoses* 10.275-276, where we read "*sit coniunx, opto,*" *non ausus* "*eburnea virgo*" | *dicere, Pygmalion* "*similis mea*" *dixit* "*eburnae.*" In my translation, I attempt to simulate this effect: 'I wish that the wife . . .—not daring to say "ivory virgin," Pygmalion went ahead and said—" . . . that my wife could be just like the ivory one."' The hesitation effect is achieved not only by not saying 'I wish that my wife were the ivory virgin' and instead saying 'I wish that my wife could be just like the ivory virgin'. It is achieved also by postponing the 'my'. And then by not saying 'virgin' at all.

Chapter One

Athena Polias of the *Erekhtheion* or Erechtheum. In Virgil's imagination, this true Athena is the Palladium.

1Ⓢ10. A poet's lasting response to permanent beauty

1§156 I return to the metaphor of absolute rigidity as a sign of perfection in art. This metaphor, as we have seen, is alive in Virgil's poetry. And the model is to be found in Homeric poetry. It is the perfect and permanent mental image of the petrified serpent in *Iliad* II. This image is to be visualized forever in the same way, reflecting on the perfection that is the story of Troy, in a single gloriously beautiful moment of terror and pity. Such an exquisite moment is brought back to life once again in the poetry of Virgil. The depiction of the death of Laocoön in *Aeneid* 2 demonstrates Virgil's own appreciation of Homer the Classic.

1§157 In Homeric poetry, a perfect and permanent mental image demands a response worthy of a seer, of a poet. In *Iliad* II, as we have seen, such a response is conveyed directly by the seer Calchas, and, indirectly, by the poet who narrates what the seer had seen and had said. The word that expresses such a response, as we have also seen, is *hupokrinesthai*.

1§158 The responsiveness of *hupokrinesthai*, to repeat, is a matter of performance. The very act of performing can be considered an act of interpretation, as we see from such modern usages as French *interpréter* in the sense of perform—as when you sing a composition or play it on a musical instrument. In this light, let us consider the idea inherent in usages of *krinein*, from which the compound form *hupokrinesthai* is derived. This verb *krinein*, in the active voice, can be translated as 'interpret' when combined with the noun *opsis* 'vision' as its object (Herodotus 7.19.1-2) or with *enupnion* 'dream' as its object (Herodotus 1.120.1).[151] It is a question of interpreting-in-performance. In the middle voice, *hupokrinesthai* suggests that the performer is interpreting for himself as well as for others.[152] The basic idea of *hupokrinesthai*, then, is to see the real meaning of what others see and to quote, as it were, what this vision is really telling them.[153]

1§159 Here I return to my initial observations about the responsiveness of Homeric poetry as conveyed by *hupokrinesthai*: the framing words of Homer require the same responsive mentality as required by the framed

---

[151] Koller 1957:101.
[152] Koller 1957:102.
[153] Most of this paragraph is taken from what I wrote in *HR* 37-38.

words of heroes and gods as quoted by the poetry. The performance of Homer as a speaker mirrors the performances of the heroes and gods whose speeches he frames.[154] Homer as the framing narrator mirrors the poetic virtuosity of his framed epic characters, especially Achilles.[155] The responsive mentality of speakers in Homeric song extends ultimately to Homer himself, who becomes re-enacted again and again in the traditions of performance.[156]

1§160 The responsiveness of Homeric poetry, as conveyed by *hupokrinesthai*, is parallel to the responsiveness of theatrical poetry, as likewise conveyed by the same word *hupokrinesthai*. Earlier, I argued for the relevance of theatrical contexts of *hupokrinesthai* in the sense of 'act', as in 'act the role of a persona', and of *hupokritēs* in the sense of 'actor'. Now I am arguing that Homer himself is such a 'persona' in his own right. In that sense, Homer is the embodiment of theater.

1§161 I will postpone till Chapter 3 an examination of contexts where the concept of performing the 'persona' of Homer is explicitly analogized with the concept of acting in theater, and I concentrate here simply on the analogies implicit in theatrical usages of relevant words. Besides *hupokrinesthai* 'act' and *hupokritēs* 'actor', I recall here a third relevant word, which I have already analyzed at an earlier stage of my argumentation. It is the ancient Greek word for 'theater', *theatron*, composed of the verb-root *thea-* 'have a vision' and noun-suffix *-tron*, indicating an instrument. Etymologically, the word can be interpreted as meaning 'instrument for having a vision [*thea-*]'.

1⒮11. Virgil as theatrical spectacle

1§162 The relevance of the Greek word *theatron* to Homer is comparable to the relevance of the Latin word *spectaculum* to Virgil. Earlier, I said that Homer, as a master of visualization, is the embodiment of theater. I am now ready to argue that the same can be said of Virgil, as a master of visualization in his own right.

1§163 To start the argumentation, I propose to take a brief look at the visual arts. In one celebrated mosaic, we see a staging of Virgil in the company of the Muses. The picture shows Virgil seated on a throne, with scroll in hand,

---

[154] This point is argued most effectively by Martin 1989; see esp. pp. 231–239.
[155] Martin 1989:220–230.
[156] I offer a fuller argumentation in *HR* 38.

Chapter One

attended by the Muses Clio, goddess of history, and Melpomene, goddess of tragedy.[157]

1§164 Next I turn to the staging of Virgil in the verbal arts. In the passage I am about to quote from the *Dialogus* of Tacitus, Virgil himself has just been spotted in a crowd. He is in the midst of an audience of spectators attending a theatrical performance. The spectators have just been listening to the sound of Virgil's verses being performed, and then, suddenly, there is a sighting of Virgil himself amidst the crowd of spectators. The crowd's reaction is instantaneous. The spectacle of the theater becomes instantly transformed into the spectacle of Virgil himself. The sound of Virgil has become the sight of Virgil in person. Virgil has become the embodiment of theater:

1ⓣ26 Tacitus *Dialogus* 13.1-2

Ac ne fortunam quidem vatum et illud felix contubernium comparare timuerim cum inquieta et anxia oratorum vita. licet illos certamina et pericula sua ad consulatus evexerint, malo securum et quietum Virgilii secessum, in quo tamen neque apud divum Augustum <u>gratia</u> caruit neque apud populum Romanum <u>notitia</u>. testes Augusti epistulae, testis ipse populus, qui auditis <u>in theatro</u> Virgilii versibus surrexit universus et forte praesentem spectantemque Virgilium veneratus est sic quasi Augustum.

I have no fears[158] about comparing the good fortune of poets, and the happiness they feel in the company they keep [*contubernium*], to the anxious and troubled life of orators. <u>They</u> may be propelled to the consulship by way of their struggles and the risks they take; but *I* prefer the peace and serenity of Virgil's withdrawal from public life—and he did not go without <u>favor</u> [*gratia*] in the eyes of *divus* Augustus or <u>fame</u> [*notitia*] in the eyes of the Roman people. The letters of Augustus bear witness, and the people themselves bore witness, who all stood up when they heard the verses of Virgil <u>in the theater</u>, thus venerating the poet—who happened to be present in the audience—as though he was Augustus himself.[159]

---

[157] Mosaic showing Virgil and the two Muses. Early third century CE. From Hadrumentum (modern Sousse), Tunisia. Tunis, Musée National du Bardo.
[158] The figure of Maternus is speaking.
[159] My translation is based on that of Winterbottom in Russell and Winterbottom 1972:439.

1Ⓢ12. Virgil's imperial poetry

1§165 In this passage taken from the *Dialogus* of Tacitus, the private and reclusive figure of the poet Virgil stands in sharp contrast to the public and dominating figure of the emperor Augustus. And yet, the public reacts to the poet as if he were the emperor. The emperor is not the only public figure. So too is the poet. The private sphere of the poet is just as imperial as the public sphere of the emperor. Why? It is because the poet's poetry has the same imperial prestige as the emperor's power—in terms of a codependency claimed by both sides. The word for this codependency, as we saw in the passage taken from the *Dialogus* of Tacitus, is *gratia*, which I translate for the moment as 'favor'.

1§166 This word *gratia* clarifies why I said age of Virgil in the title of this chapter, not age of Augustus. I highlight the poetry of Virgil, not the *imperium* of Augustus. But the fact remains that Virgil's golden age of poetry was also an imperial age, and the poetry depended on imperial *gratia* 'favor', as the words of Tacitus make clear. To become the people's favorite was not enough. The emperor's favor was also needed. The poetry of Virgil was imperial as well as popular. Because this poetry was popular, however, it was needed by the imperial power. That power depended on the *gratia* 'favor' of the popular poet. This poetic *gratia* was not just a 'favor' to be returned. The word *gratia* conveys not only the idea of favor ('graciousness') but also the ideas of pleasure ('gratification') and beauty ('gracefulness'). Implicitly, poetry returns the favor ('graciousness') of power by offering the pleasure ('gratification') of beauty ('gracefulness'). Something very similar can be said, as I argue in the twin book *Homer the Preclassic*, about the *kharis* 'favor' returned by the poetry of Homer in the glory days of the Athenian empire.[160]

1§167 Aside from what I quoted from the *Dialogus* of Tacitus, there is another passage that refers to the performance of Virgil's verses in theater. In the commentaries of Servius to Virgil's *Eclogues* (6.11), we are told of performances, in theater, of selections from Virgil's *Eclogues*.[161] This information about the choice of Virgil's *Eclogues* for performance in theaters is relevant to what we are told in the *Dialogus*. The pastoral setting of the *Eclogues* is the key. In the passage I quoted from the *Dialogus*, such a pastoral setting is the actual subtext of the reference to Virgil. In other words, Virgil is imagined as inter-

---

[160] HPC E§200.
[161] See also Suetonius *Life of Virgil* 26–27 and Ovid *Tristia* 2.519–520. For a reference to the spontaneous generation of instant celebrity in the public setting of theatrical performances, see Cicero *Pro Sestio* 115–116.

Chapter One

acting with the Muses in a pastoral setting that mirrors the *Eclogues*. When the speaker in the *Dialogus* speaks about the happiness that poets feel in their *contubernium* 'companionship' with others, the poet he has in mind is Virgil, and his 'companions' are none other than the Muses in a pastoral setting:

1①27 Tacitus *Dialogus* 13.5

> Me vero <u>dulces</u>, ut Vergilius ait, <u>Musae</u>, remotum a sollicitudinibus et curis et necessitate cotidie aliquid contra animum faciendi, <u>in illa sacra illosque fontes</u> ferant. . . .
>
> As for me, may the <u>Muses sweet to the taste</u>, as Virgil says, carry me away, far away from the worries and cares and obligations of performing each and every day something that goes against my spirit—far away <u>to those sacred places, to those sacred springs</u>. . . .

The speaker here is referring to the words of Virgil's *Georgics*, where the poet is pictured as the main participant in the sacred rites of the Muses, celebrated at their sacred spring:

1①28 Virgil *Georgics* 2.475–477, 485–486

> Me vero primum <u>dulces</u> ante omnia <u>Musae</u>,
> quarum <u>sacra</u> fero ingenti percussus amore,
> accipiant . . .
> rura mihi et rigui placeant in vallibus <u>amnes</u>,
> <u>flumina</u> amem silvasque inglorius
>
> As for me, may it happen first and foremost that the <u>Muses, sweet to the taste</u> beyond everything else,
> they whose <u>sacred rites</u> I carry out, struck as I am with an overwhelming love,
> —may it happen that they accept me as their very own . . .[162]
> May the countryside be pleasing to me, also the moistening <u>waters</u> in the valleys.
> Let me love the <u>streams</u> and the forests, though I be unknown to fame [*gloria*].

---

[162] At this point, the poet prays to the Muses to tell him about the workings of the cosmos (Virgil *Georgics* 2.477–482); then the poet shifts from contemplating the cosmos (2.483–484) to participating in the joys of the countryside (2.485–486).

1ⓢ12. Virgil's imperial poetry

1§168 Although the speaker in the *Dialogus* seems to be referring to the passage I just quoted from the *Georgics*, Virgil himself is referring to the Muses in his *Eclogues*. Moreover, he is referring to the Muses of his own *Eclogues* in poetic terms that suit most closely the Muses of the Hesiodic *Theogony*. I offer here an overview of those parts of the *Theogony* that are relevant to Virgil's allusion in the passage I just quoted.

1§169 The Hesiodic *Theogony* begins with the naming of the Muses local to Mount Helicon (verses 1-2), who are pictured as dancing (3-4) around the source of a sacred spring (3), next to which is an altar of Zeus (3-4). These local Muses of Mount Helicon are pictured as a choral ensemble (7-8) who are both dancing (8) and singing with a beautiful voice (10). The Muses proceed to teach Hesiod their song (22), enjoining him to perform it (33). In order to get this song started, the poet is told that that he must begin with the Muses and end with the Muses (34), and in fact we have already heard at the beginning of the song that Hesiod has indeed already begun with the Muses (1-2). These Muses of Mount Helicon, as they perform their song, are heard by Zeus himself in the heights of Mount Olympus (37). There is an emphasis on the 'voicing' of the Muses' song (39 φωνῇ and αὐδή, 41 ὀπί, 43 ὄσσαν) and on the 'sweetness' of this voice that literally 'flows' from their mouths, as if from a spring (39-40): τῶν δ' ἀκάματος ῥέει αὐδὴ | ἐκ στομάτων ἡδεῖα 'inexhaustible is the sweet voice that flows from their mouths'.

1§170 The ultimate source of this song, equated with the *Theogony* in the course of its being performed, is the authority of Zeus as king of the immortals (71-74), and it emanates from there to the Olympian Muses (75-79), especially to the Muse Kalliope, whose own authority literally flows to kings (75-93).[163] The metaphor of fluidity becomes explicit in the following description of the ideal king who is favored by the Muses:

1ⓣ29 Hesiod *Theogony* 83-84

> τῷ μὲν ἐπὶ γλώσσῃ γλυκερὴν <u>χείουσιν</u> ἐέρσην,
>
> τοῦ δ' ἔπε' ἐκ στόματος <u>ῥεῖ</u> μείλιχα
>
> For this man [= for this ideal king] they [= the Muses] <u>pour</u> [*kheîn*] sweet dew,
>
> and from his [= the king's] mouth <u>flow</u> [*rheîn*] sweet words.

---

[163] The idea that the Olympian Muse Kalliope authorizes kings is related to another idea: that Kalliope is the mother of Orpheus (as in Apollonius of Rhodes *Argonautica* 23-25). I analyze the relationship between these ideas in HPC E§109.

Chapter One

1§171 Whereas the authority of kings flows from Zeus, the authority of poets flows from the authority of the Muses, and of Apollo as their choral leader:

1①30 Hesiod *Theogony* 94-97

> ἐκ γάρ τοι Μουσέων καὶ ἑκηβόλου Ἀπόλλωνος
> ἄνδρες ἀοιδοὶ ἔασιν ἐπὶ χθόνα καὶ κιθαρισταί,
> ἐκ δὲ Διὸς βασιλῆες· ὁ δ' ὄλβιος, ὅντινα Μοῦσαι
> φίλωνται· <u>γλυκερή</u> οἱ ἀπὸ στόματος <u>ῥέει αὐδή</u>.

> The Muses and far-shooting Apollo are the sources
> for the existence of singers [*aoidoi*] and players of the lyre [*kitharis*] on this earth.
> And Zeus is the source for the existence of kings. Blessed [*olbios*] is he whom the Muses
> love. And a <u>sweet</u> <u>voice</u> [*aud*ḗ] <u>flows</u> [*rheîn*] from his mouth.

1§172 As in the previous passage that I quoted from the Hesiodic *Theogony* (35-45), we see in this passage as well the metaphor of fluidity: the voice of the Muses, sweet as it is, literally 'flows' from their mouths (97).

1§173 In Hesiodic poetry, then, the ideal king and the ideal poet are both kingly. So also in the poetics of Virgil: the ideal emperor and the ideal poet are both imperial. Further, as we saw in the *Dialogus*, the *gratia* of the poet and the *gratia* of the emperor are coextensive. Virgil's poetic *gratia* is an imperial *gratia*. Virgil's poetry is imperial poetry. In the twin book *Homer the Preclassic*, we see how the <u>cosmos and imperium</u> of the age of Augustus comes alive in the words of Virgil, whose imperial poetry becomes the global theater staged by the Roman empire.[164]

1§174 To say that the poetry of Virgil was imperial is not to deny that this poetry was a humane and civilizing force. It is not my aim to raise moral questions about Virgil's imperial poetry. Here I will go only so far as to say that I do feel morally troubled by the historical realities of the Roman empire—and of empires in general. That is because I am persuaded that humanity faces moral decisions precisely in the context of historical realities, and that these realities cannot be invoked as an excuse to rationalize any failure in one's own personal moral decisions. Still, a questioning of Virgil's moral decisions is surely beyond

---

[164] HPC E§§ 152-157.

my reach here. For the moment, I simply accept Virgil's imperial poetry as a historical given. Virgil's poetry is its own historical reality.[165]

1§175 Virgil's poetry accepts the reality of the Roman empire, but it also presupposes an ideal that transcends this reality. As I just said, Virgil's imperial poetry was meant to be seen as a humane and civilizing force. So the poetics of terror and pity, and the compassion evoked by such poetics, can be seen as a hallmark of Roman imperial poetry.

1§176 As I have observed in this chapter, the poetics of terror and pity can also be seen as a hallmark of Homeric poetry. And, as I will argue in Chapter 4, Homeric poetry too became imperial in its own right. The Athenian empire, in appropriating Homeric poetry, will make it imperial. In the process, the poetics of terror and pity will become a hallmark of Athenian imperial poetry, and here I mean not only Homer but also classical tragedy. This Athenian hallmark, as I will also argue in Chapter 4, is in fact a model for Virgil. In using the term terror and pity, I have in mind a passage about these emotions in the *Poetics* of Aristotle (1449b24–28). Although Aristotle in this passage is thinking of tragedy, not of Homeric poetry, we must keep in mind that he thinks of Homeric poetry as a prototypical form of tragedy in its own right (*Poetics* 1459a37–b16). I will have more to say about this topic when we reach Chapter 3, but I must highlight already now the word used here by Aristotle in observing the emotions of terror and pity. That word is *pathos*, in the sense of 'emotion'. The emotions of terror and pity are captured by that single word as it is used today, pathos.

1§177 So far, I have concentrated on two epic scenes of pathos—of terror and pity. One scene was a stop-motion picture of the serpent who turned into stone in *Iliad* II and the other scene, of the serpents who turned into statues in *Aeneid* 2. The petrified serpent in *Iliad* II is viewed by the seer—and by the poetry of the *Iliad*—as a generalized metonym for all the pathos of the Trojan War. A similar view is achieved in Virgil's epic vision of the petrified serpents in *Aeneid* 2. From here on, I will refer to all this pathos as the sorrows of the Trojan War.

---

[165] There is a most striking example in Virgil's *Aeneid* (6.851): *tu regere imperio populos, Romane, memento* 'keep in mind, O Roman, that you must rule over the peoples of the world with your *imperium*'.

Chapter One

1⑤13. *Sunt lacrimae rerum*

1§178 Virgil's epic vision extends further. As I will now argue, he views the sorrows of the Trojan War as a foundation for comprehending the genesis of the Roman empire. I begin with a passage showing a general scene of the Trojan War as pictured by Virgil. I mean literally pictured. The actual medium of the visual art that is being represented in this passage is not precisely specified, but it is in any case called *pictura*. This picture, as we are about to see, is a veritable panorama of the Trojan War as a spectacle to end all spectacles:

1①31 Virgil *Aeneid* 1.441–493

    lucus in urbe fuit media, laetissimus umbrae,
    quo primum iactati undis et turbine Poeni
    effodere loco signum, quod regia Iuno
    monstrarat, caput acris equi; sic nam fore bello
445 egregiam et facilem victu per saecula gentem.
    hic templum Iunoni ingens Sidonia Dido
    condebat, donis opulentum et numine divae,
    aerea cui gradibus surgebant limina nexaeque
    aere trabes, foribus cardo stridebat aënis.
450 hoc primum in luco nova res oblata timorem
    leniit, hic primum Aeneas sperare salutem
    ausus et adflictis melius confidere rebus.
    namque sub ingenti lustrat dum singula templo
    reginam opperiens, dum quae fortuna sit urbi
455 artificumque manus inter se operumque laborem
    miratur, videt Iliacas ex ordine pugnas
    bellaque iam fama totum vulgata per orbem,
    Atridas Priamumque et saevum ambobus Achillem.
    constitit et lacrimans 'quis iam locus', inquit, 'Achate,
460 quae regio in terris nostri non plena laboris?
    en Priamus. sunt hic etiam sua praemia laudi,
    sunt lacrimae rerum et mentem mortalia tangunt.

1⑤13. Sunt lacrimae rerum

solve <u>metus</u>; feret haec aliquam tibi <u>fama</u> salutem'.
sic ait atque <u>animum pictura pascit inani</u>
465 multa gemens, largoque umectat <u>flumine</u> vultum.
namque videbat uti bellantes Pergama circum
hac fugerent Grai, premeret Troiana iuventus;
hac Phryges, instaret curru cristatus Achilles.
nec procul hinc Rhesi niveis tentoria velis
470 agnoscit <u>lacrimans</u>, primo quae prodita somno
Tydides multa vastabat caede cruentus,
ardentisque avertit equos in castra prius quam
pabula gustassent Troiae Xanthumque bibissent.
parte alia fugiens amissis Troilus armis,
475 infelix puer atque impar congressus Achilli,
fertur equis curruque haeret resupinus inani,
lora tenens tamen; huic cervixque comaeque trahuntur
per terram, et versa pulvis inscribitur hasta.
interea ad <u>templum</u> non aequae Palladis ibant
480 crinibus <u>Iliades</u> passis <u>peplum</u>que ferebant
suppliciter, tristes et tunsae pectora palmis;
<u>diva solo fixos oculos aversa tenebat.</u>
ter circum Iliacos raptaverat <u>Hectora</u> muros
exanimumque auro corpus vendebat Achilles.
485 tum vero ingentem gemitum dat pectore ab imo,
ut spolia, ut currus, utque ipsum corpus amici
tendentemque manus <u>Priamum</u> conspexit inermis.
se quoque principibus <u>permixtum</u> agnovit <u>Achivis</u>,
Eoasque acies et nigri Memnonis arma.
490 ducit Amazonidum lunatis agmina peltis
Penthesilea furens mediisque in milibus ardet,
aurea subnectens exsertae cingula mammae
bellatrix, audetque viris concurrere virgo.

Chapter One

There was a grove in the middle of the city, most lush in shade.
It was here that, in the beginning, after being tossed around by waves and swirling winds, the Phoenicians
dug up the sign [*signum*] that queenly Juno
had pointed out, the head of a fierce horse; for this is the way it was to be, that in war
445 they would be outstanding and that their way of life would be well cared for, this nation [of Carthaginians].
Here an enormous temple, dedicated to Juno, was being set up by <u>Sidonian</u>[166] Dido.
She was the founder. It was well endowed with gifts and with the aura of the goddess.
Made of bronze was its threshold, looming over the steps that led up to it.
Made of bronze were its lintel-beams, and its hinges creaked on doors made of bronze.
450 It was in this grove that, for the first time, something totally new presented itself to him, and it released him from his <u>fear</u>,
smoothing it away.[167] It was here for the first time that Aeneas dared to hope for salvation and,
in this act of daring, have more confidence that his adverse situation would get better.
For as he looks up <u>from the ground level</u> of the immense temple, <u>scanning with his eye</u> [*lustrare*][168] <u>every single thing one by one</u> [*singula*]

---

[166] I note here the theme of an "epic detour," which I analyze in *HPC* I§§184–186, II§367. Just as Carthage is an epic detour for Aeneas in the *Aeneid*, so also is Sidon an epic detour for Paris in the *Iliad*.
[167] Here we see the first reference to the <u>fear</u> experienced by Aeneas in this context.
[168] The metaphor of performing a lustration—*lustrare*—depends on the ritual symbolism of the Roman concept of *templum*. The *templum* is a mapping of the sky on the earth, which is circular and directionless until the quadrilateral sky gives it direction—the four directions—thereby giving it orientation, order. I offer a detailed analysis in *GM* 107-111. When a priest performs a lustration within a sacred place, that is, within a *templum*, he is making a sacred sequence by making sacred connections modeled on the connections of the heavenly bodies within the cosmic order that is the sky. In contemplating the sky, the observer is making mental connections that correspond to ritual connections made in performing a lustration.

1§13. Sunt lacrimae rerum

while he is waiting for the queen, seeing what good fortune befell the city [of Carthage]

455 as he contemplates the mutual[169] handiwork of the artisans and the labor of their workmanship,

he is filled with wonder. He sees in due order [*ex ordine*][170] the battles of Troy,

the wars that have become public knowledge by way of a fame [*fama*] that by now extends throughout the entire orb [*orbis*] of the world.

He sees the sons of Atreus, and Priam, and Achilles, who is savagely angry at both.

Then he stops and says, with tears streaming [*lacrimare*] down his face: "What place, Achates,

460 what region on earth is now not saturated with the story of our pain [*labor*]?

Look! It is Priam! So you see here once again that things requiring praise have their own reward.[171]

There are tears [*lacrimae*] that connect with the real world [*res* plural], and things that happen to mortals touch [*tangere*] the mind [*mens*].

Dissolve your fears: this fame [*fama* = the fame of the story of our pain] will bring for you too a salvation of some kind."

---

[169] The idea of mutuality in workmanship, as expressed here, may be an indirect allusion to the ideology of the building program of Pericles on the acropolis of Athens in the fifth century BCE. This ideology can be reconstructed from a relatively late source, Plutarch's *Pericles* 13.13, where we read that Athena, goddess of artisans, was imagined in the act of 'lending a hand' to the handiwork of artisans in executing the building program of Pericles. Commentary at 4§§114–118 below. This Athenian ideology may have inspired a parallel Roman ideology in the poetics of the *Aeneid*, where a doomed building program of the past, in the Carthage of Dido, is imagined as a foil for a successful building program of the present, in the Rome of Augustus.

[170] The syntax of *ex ordine* 'in due order' is relevant to the morphology of the technical word *ex-ordium*, which refers to the 'initial threading' of the weave and, by metaphor, to the *pro-oimion* of a verbal weave. See PR 80. On the concept of *ordo* 'order' as a metaphor derived from the process of weaving, see PR 78, 80. Elsewhere, I examine metaphors of weaving that extend to sculpting. The 'order' of the sculpted images of the temple, as a quadrilateral superimposition from the sky, imposes a logic on the sequence of looking at the details that are being narrated by the sculpture. By contemplating the order of the details in the temple, Aeneas is metaphorically performing an act of lustration.

[171] In other words, the particular things that Aeneas sees 'here' bear out, 'once again', a universal formula, that 'things worthy of praise have their own reward'.

163

Chapter One

So he speaks, <u>feasting</u> [*pascere*] his <u>mind</u> [*animus*] on the <u>insubstantial picture</u> [*pictura*],

465 and he groans over and over, flooding his face with a vast <u>stream</u> of tears.

For he saw how, as they fought round the walls of Pergamon,

the Greeks were on the run in one zone, with the Trojan youth closing in on them,

while in another zone it was the Phrygians who were on the run, and attacking them in his chariot was the man wearing the crest on his helmet, Achilles.

Not far away the tents of Rhesus, with canvas as white as snow,

470 he recognizes, <u>as tears continue to stream</u> [*lacrimare*] down his face. These tents, betrayed during the first hour of sleep,

did the son of Tydeus destroy, stained with the gore of all those he slaughtered,

and he drove the fiery war-horses [of Rhesus] away [from Troy] and into the camp [of the Achaeans] before

they could taste Trojan fodder or drink of the waters of the river Xanthos.

Elsewhere Troilus, with his armor thrown away as he was fleeing,

475 ill-starred boy, and ill-matched in conflict with Achilles,

is carried along by his horses and, fallen backward, clings to the <u>empty</u> [*inanis*] chariot,

still holding on to the reins. His neck and hair are dragged over the ground, and the dust is inscribed by his inverted spear.

Meanwhile, to the <u>temple</u> [*templum*][172] of a not impartial Pallas Athena were proceeding

480 the <u>Trojan women</u> with streaming tresses, and they were carrying the <u>peplos</u>,

---

[172] The art of the temple of Juno now begins to represent the art of the temple of Athena.

1§13. *Sunt lacrimae rerum*

> in the mode of suppliants, sadly, and beating their breasts with the flat of the hand.
> <u>With averted face the goddess kept her eyes fixed on the ground.</u>
> Three times had Achilles dragged <u>Hector</u> around the walls of Troy
> and he was now selling the lifeless body for gold.
>
> 485 And then it was that, from the depths of his heart, he [= Aeneas] heaved an enormously heavy groan,
> as the spoils of war, as the chariot, as the body of his friend—yes, his body—
> met his gaze,¹⁷³ and so too the sight of an unarmed <u>Priam</u>, supplicating with outstretched hands.
> Himself, too, <u>all mixed into the thick of battle with the Achaean princes</u>, he [= Aeneas] recognized,
> and the battle line of Eos the dawn-goddess, featuring the armor of shining-black Memnon.
>
> 490 Leading the crescent-shielded battle lines of the Amazons
> is Penthesileia in all her martial fury, glowing in the heat of battle and surrounded by her thousands of fellow she-warriors,
> wearing a golden cincture that binds her exposed breast,
> she-warrior that she is, and she dares to compete against men, this virgin.¹⁷⁴

1§179 The composite picturing of the sorrows of the Trojan War, as conveyed by the word *pictura* at verse 464, is described here as *inanis* or 'insubstantial'. This epithet, as I read it, conveys the idea that the picturing is not the actual 'substance' of the real things that happened at Troy. This is not to say, however, that the picturing is not real or that the things being pictured are

---

¹⁷³ So the vision of the dragging of Hector's corpse behind the chariot of Achilles is a primary impetus for the sorrow of Aeneas here.
¹⁷⁴ The choice of the theme of Penthesileia as the closure of this ecphrasis by Virgil may be a way of cross-referring to the theme of Penthesileia as the beginning of the *Aithiopis*. One version of the *Aithiopis* began at the closure of the *Iliad*, where the last word of the last verse of the *Iliad* narrative, *hippodamoio* 'horse-tamer' (referring to Hector) was replaced by the first words of the *Aithiopis* narrative, *ēlthe d' Amazōn* 'and an Amazon came' (*Iliad* XXIV 804).

not real. They are very much for real. The decisive word is *pascit* 'nourishes' in the same verse: the viewer is said to be 'nourishing' his mind or *animus* by virtue of looking at the *pictura*, by feasting his eyes on what is being pictured. The viewer is forming a mental picture, and that picture derives from the substance of the real things that happened at Troy, as mediated by the *pictura*. The *pictura* is the act of mediation, not the mediated thing itself. As the mediation, that is, as the medium, the *pictura* can be said to lack the substance of the real things it mediates, which are exterior. Nevertheless, the use of the verb *pascit* 'nourishes' makes it clear that the mental 'nourishment' of feasting the eyes on the *pictura* comes from exterior stimuli that are quite real. Those real exterior stimuli can even be invisible, as we see from the following passage, taken from Lucretius, where the eye 'feasts' on atoms that convey pleasant visions as contrasted with atoms that convey unpleasant ones:

1ⓣ32 Lucretius *De rerum natura* 2.418–420

> neve bonos <u>rerum</u> similes constare colores
> semine constituas, oculos qui <u>pascere</u> possunt,
> et qui conpungunt aciem <u>lacrimare</u>que cogunt

> Nor should you think that the good colors of the <u>real world</u> [<u>res</u> plural], colors that <u>nourish</u> [= are a feast for] the eyes, are similarly constituted in their atomic seed as the [bad] colors [of the real world], which cause a sharp sting [for the eyes] and compel the shedding of <u>tears</u>.[175]

1§180 In this description, the exterior stimuli come from invisible particles, but these particles are still part of the real world.[176] I am using the word <u>real</u> here in the sense of its etymology as an adjective derived from the noun *res*, which refers here and elsewhere in Lucretius and Virgil to the world of reality.

1§181 The medium of the *pictura* at verse 464 of *Aeneid* 1 is making contact between the mental faculty of the *animus* and reality—the reality of the sorrows experienced in the Trojan War. The idea of actual contact is made clear earlier in the use of *mens* 'mind' at verse 462. There as well as elsewhere,

---

[175] In translating this particular passage, I gave up on my usual practice of simulating the original verse-boundaries.

[176] Pagliaro 1953:174–175.

mens is a synonym of *animus*.[177] A clear example is this poetic formulation, where the *mens* or *animus* is pictured as residing in the *pectus* 'chest':

1ⓣ33 Lucretius *De rerum natura* 3.136-144

    136 nunc <u>animum</u> atque <u>animam</u> dico coniuncta teneri
            inter se atque unam naturam conficere ex se,
            sed caput esse quasi et dominari in corpore toto
            consilium, quod nos <u>animum</u> <u>mentem</u>que vocamus.
    140 idque situm media regione in <u>pectoris</u> haeret.
            hic exultat enim <u>pavor</u> ac <u>metus</u>, haec loca circum
            laetitiae mulcent: hic ergo <u>mens</u> <u>animus</u>quest.
            cetera pars <u>animae</u> per totum dissita <u>corpus</u>
            paret et ad numen <u>mentis</u> momenque movetur

    136 The <u>*animus*</u> and the <u>*anima*</u>, I say, are held joined together one with the other,
            and form one single nature of themselves,
            but the chief and dominant thing in the whole <u>body</u> [<u>*corpus*</u>]
            is still that faculty of reasoning that we call the <u>*animus*</u> or <u>*mens*</u>,
    140 which is lodged in the middle region of the <u>chest</u> [<u>*pectus*</u>].
            Here is where <u>fear</u> and <u>terror</u> flourish; it is around these places
            that moments of happiness offer their caresses; here, then, is the <u>*mens*</u> or <u>*animus*</u>.
            The remaining part of the <u>*anima*</u> is scattered throughout the whole <u>body</u> [<u>*corpus*</u>],
            but it obeys and is <u>moved</u> [<u>*movēre*</u>] according to the assent and the motion of the <u>*mens*</u>.

1§182 Like *animus* at verse 464 of *Aeneid* 1, the word *mens* at verse 462 there designates the mental faculty that perceives reality by distinguishing it from the unreal. And, at verse 462, the reality of the Trojan War and all its sorrows

---

[177] Pagliaro 1953:176-179. For an outstanding example of *mens* and *animus* used together in Virgil, I cite *Aeneid* 6.11.

Chapter One

are making contact with the mind of Aeneas. I quote again the overall context of verses 462 and 464:

1ⓣ34 Virgil *Aeneid* 1.459–465

    constitit et <u>lacrimans</u> 'quis iam locus', inquit, 'Achate,
460 quae regio in terris nostri non plena <u>laboris</u>?
    en Priamus. sunt hic etiam sua praemia laudi,
    <u>sunt lacrimae rerum</u> et <u>mentem mortalia tangunt</u>.
    solve <u>metus</u>; feret haec aliquam tibi <u>fama</u> salutem'.
    sic ait atque <u>animum pictura pascit inani</u>
465 multa gemens, largoque umectat <u>flumine</u> uultum.

    Then he stops and says, <u>with tears streaming</u> [*lacrimare*] down his face: "What place, Achates,
460 what region on earth is now not saturated with the story of our <u>pain</u> [*labor*]?
    Look! It is Priam! So you see here once again that things requiring praise have their own reward.
    There are <u>tears</u> [*lacrimae*] that connect with the <u>real world</u> [*res* plural], and things that happen to mortals <u>touch</u> [*tangere*] the <u>mind</u> [*mens*].
    Dissolve your <u>fears</u>: this <u>fame</u> [*fama*; = the fame of the story of our pain] will bring for you too a salvation of some kind."
    So he speaks, and <u>feasting</u> [*pascere*] his <u>mind</u> [*animus*] on the <u>insubstantial picture</u> [*pictura*],
465 and he groans over and over, flooding his face with a vast <u>stream</u> of tears.

1§183 The particular things that Aeneas sees 'here' (461) in the artwork of artisans bear out, 'once again', a universal formula, that 'things requiring praise have their own reward' (again, 461). In other words, real things that happen in our universe deserve and demand to be credited by the artwork of artisans. This universal formula is then extended by way of a parallel universal formula, which says that the reality of the universe is somehow connected with the shedding of tears (462). The neuter plural *mortalia*, which I translate as 'things that happen to mortals', is a universalizing reference to the *res* 'things' (as in *rerum*) in the real world that connect with the shedding of tears, and these realities are further connected with the mental faculty of the *mens* or *animus*. The mental connection here is a matter of genuine contact with things that are real. These real things literally touch the *mens*. The mind is touched by these real things mediated through the art of the artisans (462), and it feasts on this reality (464). In the poetic world inherited by Virgil, the experience of touching, like feasting, cannot be insubstantial. If something touches and is touched, it must be substantial, real. What is substantial may be either visible or invisible, like the atom, but it must be a *corpus* 'body':

1①35 Lucretius *De rerum natura* 1.304

> tangere enim et tangi, nisi corpus, nulla potest res
>
> No thing [*res*] can touch [*tangere*] and be touched [*tangere*]
>   unless it is a body [*corpus*].

1§184 So the cause of the tears of Aeneas is real, substantial, even though the real Hector and the real Priam and all the other Trojans he mourns are absent from the medium of the *pictura*, which is thus sadly *inanis* 'insubstantial'. The hero's loved ones are sadly missing from the vehicle of the *pictura*.

1§185 The pathos of desiring what is not there is subjectively replicated in the inner world of the *pictura* that is being scanned by the eye of Aeneas: at verse 476, the beautiful Troilus has just been struck down by Achilles and falls from his chariot, which is pictured as rushing onward but now *inanis*, that is, sadly deprived of its beautiful rider. Troilus is now pathetically absent or missing from the vehicle. The void left by Troilus in the vehicle of the chariot is comparable to the void left in the metaphorical vehicle of a picture that conveys realities sadly no longer inside the picture. The real men and women who suffered and died at Troy are no longer present in a picture that is now sadly *inanis* 'insubstantial' because it lacks their presence. Enhancing the pathos is the understanding that the imagined temple of Juno, picturing the destruction of Troy, will likewise no longer exist once Carthage itself is destroyed by the Roman empire of the future.

1§186 Although the *pictura* of Troy's destruction is described as insubstantial in the *Aeneid*, the tears of Aeneas are substantial and therefore not at all in vain, since the sorrows of the Trojan War have made real contact with his mind, that is, with his *animus* or *mens*. In other words, the mind of the hero is moved with genuine emotion in this context. This emotion is contrasted in a later context with another emotion experienced by Aeneas. In that later context, the hero's mind will remain unmoved by the tears of the queen Dido, and so his tears will now be insubstantial, not substantial:

Chapter One

1①36 Virgil *Aeneid* 4.449

> mens immota manet, lacrimae volvuntur inanes
>
> The mind [*mens*] [= of Aeneas] remains unmoved [*movēre*] but tears [*lacrimae*] keep rolling from his eyes—tears that are insubstantial [*inanes*].

1§187 Though the tears of Aeneas reveal a deeply felt response to the reported tears of Dido, they are nevertheless *inanes* 'insubstantial'. This time, the hero's feeling comes implicitly from his *anima*, not from his *animus* or *mens*. The part of Aeneas that is his *mens* 'mind' is in this instance not moved. It fails to make contact with the alluring sorrows of the beautiful queen.

1§188 We can find a reason for this failure in the poetic formulation of Lucretius, for whom the *mens* or *animus* is only a part of the *anima*. It is the part that resides in the *pectus* 'chest', which is the seat of emotions controlled by reason. Those emotions are real, and that is why they can literally touch the mind that is lodged in the heart, that is, in the middlemost part of the *pectus* 'chest'. An example of such real emotions is what a father feels when he is kissed by a loving son:

1①37 Lucretius *De rerum natura* 3.896

> et tacita pectus dulcedine tangent
>
> ... and they [= the kisses] will touch [*tangere*] the heart [*pectus*] with a silent sweetness.

1§189 By contrast with such real emotions, the part of Aeneas that is so deeply moved by the reported tears of Dido is not the mind that is lodged in his heart. The *anima* of Aeneas is moved, but not his controlling *animus*. Being moved by this deluding emotion causes Aeneas to weep just as intensely as he had wept before, but the emotion he now feels is caused by something insubstantial, not substantial, and so the tears he now sheds are *inanes* 'insubstantial', not substantial. The hero's tears for Dido are thus in vain, whereas his tears for Hector and Priam and all the other doomed Trojans were not in vain.

1§190 Like the tears of Aeneas, the tears of Andromache, another survivor of Troy's destruction, are not in vain. The first time we see her in the *Aeneid*, Virgil pictures her in the act of weeping for her lost husband Hector and her lost infant son Astyanax, both killed in the war:

1①38 Virgil *Aeneid* 3.303–305

> libabat cineri Andromache Manesque vocabat

1⑤13. Sunt lacrimae rerum

Hectoreum ad tumulum viridi quem caespite <u>inanem</u>

et geminas, <u>causam</u> <u>lacrimis</u>, sacraverat aras

Andromache was pouring libations for the ashes and invoking the spirits of the dead,

at the tomb of Hector which, with its covering of green grass, <u>empty</u> [<u>inanis</u>] though it was,

she consecrated, along with twin altars for burning sacrifices [for Hector and Astyanax], a <u>cause</u> for her <u>tears</u> [<u>lacrimae</u>].[178]

1§191 The *causa* 'cause' of the tears shed by Andromache is substantial, real, in contrast with the tomb of her loved ones. That tomb is literally an 'empty tomb', a <u>cenotaph</u>. That tomb is sadly *inanis* 'insubstantial', since the beloved bodies of Hector and Astyanax are absent, missing, from this place made sacred by Andromache's rituals.

1§192 So also when Aeneas weeps for the Trojans as he contemplates the picturing of their sorrows, the cause of the tears he sheds is substantial, real, even though the real Hector and all the other Trojans he mourns are absent, missing, from the medium of the *pictura*, described as sadly *inanis* 'insubstantial' at verse 464 of *Aeneid* 1.[179]

1§193 The causation of the tears is only implicit, not explicit, in the syntax of the expression *sunt lacrimae rerum* 'there are tears [*lacrimae*] that connect with the real world' at verse 462 of *Aeneid* 1. The genitive case of *rerum*, the plural noun referring to the 'real things' that are the cause of the tears, expresses merely the idea of a connection between the cause and the effect. The actual causation is then made explicit by the universalizing thought that follows in the same verse, namely, that 'real things' suffered by mortals make contact with the mind: *et mentem mortalia tangunt* 'and things that happen to mortals touch the mind'. Then and only then are the cause and the effect to be understood as exactly that, cause and effect.

1§194 What makes this universalizing formula apply to the here-and-now of Aeneas as he awaits his audience with the queen of Carthage is the *pictura* that nourishes his eye with the sorrows of the Trojan War (464). It is the medium of this *pictura* that makes possible the mental contact between the

---

[178] For a comparable theme, see Euripides *Trojan Women* 740–779, where Andromache laments for Astyanax. For the child's funeral, his grandmother dresses him in the clothes that were woven for his wedding (1218–1220). See Dué 2006:145.

[179] Pagliaro 1953:175.

universalizing formula and the specific situation. It is the *pictura* that mentally connects the reality of human suffering with the reality of the tears that respond to this suffering. Only after the mental connection is made can the controlling mind finally release the flood of tears that respond to the countless sufferings of humankind.

1§195 I continue to focus on the word *inanis* 'insubstantial' describing the *pictura* of the Trojan War at verse 464 of *Aeneid* 1, corresponding to *inanis* 'insubstantial' describing the tomb of Hector and Astyanax at verse 304 of *Aeneid* 3. Just as the material substance of the human body is sadly missing from the tomb of Hector and Astyanax, so also the material substance of the artwork that supposedly created the *pictura* seen by Aeneas is sadly missing from the artwork of Virgil's poetry, which is of course what really created the *pictura* in the first place. Pointedly, there is no specific indication of the material substance that is being used in the art of creating the *pictura* seen by Aeneas. Moreover, as I noted earlier, the material substance of this imagined *pictura* in the imagined temple of Juno would in any case no longer exist once Carthage is destroyed by Rome.

1§196 The question remains, how are we to imagine the artwork of this *pictura* at verse 464 of *Aeneid* 1? The word *pictura* will not give us a specific answer. Like the German word Malerei (*Mahlerey*) used by Lessing in his essay *Laocoön*, Latin pictura can refer to painting, sculpture, and a variety of other kinds of picturing. As we have seen already, *pictura* can even refer to the kind of picturing achieved by way of the verbal arts exclusively—without any access to the material substances required by any of the conventional visual arts. And yet, despite the generality of associations, there is a specific answer to the question. As we will see when we reach Chapter 4, the *pictura* of *Aeneid* 1 is to be imagined as a masterpiece of relief sculpture.[180]

1⑤14. The sorrows of Andromache

1§197 The verbal art of Virgil pictures the sorrows of the Trojan War not only in the *pictura* seen by Aeneas at the temple of Juno in *Aeneid* 1. In *Aeneid* 3, Virgil's words picture these sorrows again. This time, however, the medium of the picturing is different. This time, Virgil's words achieve a theatrical restaging of a single scene of terror and pity in the Homeric *Iliad*. That scene pictures Andromache at the dramatic moment of hearing the news of Hector's death in *Iliad* XXII. As we will see, the centerpiece of that scene is a piece of

---

[180] 4§251.

1⑤14. The sorrows of Andromache

fabric that Andromache is weaving when she hears the news. So also in the scene restaged by Virgil in *Aeneid* 3, the centerpiece is a piece of fabric that is woven by Andromache, and the artistry of her weaving is expressed by way of a word derived from *pictura*.

1§198 In what follows, then, I will be looking at a scene in the *Aeneid* that centers on the sorrows of Andromache. In each of the four chapters of *Homer the Classic* and in each of the two parts of the twin book *Homer the Preclassic*, I focus on one such scene.

1§199 In *Aeneid* 3 294–355, Virgil produces a theatrical restaging of what happened to Andromache in the Homeric *Iliad*.[181] As the scene opens, we see Aeneas making his way uphill from the harbor of Buthrotum and heading toward that city's acropolis on high (293). Along the way, he sees a grove, and in that grove he recognizes Andromache herself in the act of sacrificing at the cenotaph of Hector and Astyanax. I repeat here the wording:

1①39 Virgil *Aeneid* 3.303–305

> libabat cineri Andromache Manesque vocabat
> Hectoreum ad tumulum viridi quem caespite <u>inanem</u>
> et geminas, <u>causam</u> <u>lacrimis</u>, sacraverat aras
>
> Andromache was pouring libations for the ashes and
>   invoking the spirits of the dead,
> at the tomb of Hector which, with its covering of green grass,
>   <u>empty</u> [<u>inanis</u>] though it was,
> she consecrated, along with twin altars for burning sacrifices
>   [for Hector and Astyanax], a <u>cause</u> for her <u>tears</u> [<u>lacrimae</u>].

1§200 The description *inanis* that applies here to the tomb of Hector and Astyanax is metonymic, since it applies also to the whole setting of the scene. That setting, the city of Buthrotum in Epirus, is a replica of the original Troy. Buthrotum is a virtual New Troy, featuring the same landmarks and the same names attached to the landmarks: like the original Troy, this new version features the rivers Xanthos (350) and Simoeis (302), the citadel called Pergamon / Pergama (350), the Scaean Gates (351), and so on, though the new setting seems miniature in comparison to the greatness of the old setting (349–350). In fact, this New Troy cannot be the real Troy, since it is devoid of the Trojans and therefore *inanis*, just as the tomb of Hector and Astyanax is

---

[181] On the Andromache scenes of the *Iliad*, see in general Lohmann 1988; also Segal 1971.

Chapter One

inanis, that is, devoid of their bodies. The only Trojans in this New Troy are two survivors of the original Troy, Andromache and Helenos. They had been brought to Buthrotum as captives enslaved by Neoptolemos, destroyer of Troy, who is also known as Pyrrhos. After the unexpected death of Pyrrhos, Andromache and Helenos become the queen and king of a New Troy, which can now become a restaging of the real Troy. And the centerpiece of the whole scene will be the weaving of Andromache herself, as expressed by the word *pictura*. Besides the *pictura* seen by Aeneas in the temple of Juno, Andromache has created her own *pictura* of all the sorrows of the Trojan War. As Aeneas and his retinue prepare to leave the New Troy, they are offered parting gifts by Helenos and Andromache, including the following gift of Andromache to the son of Aeneas, Ascanius (whose alternative name is Iulus):

1①40 Virgil *Aeneid* 3.482–491

> nec minus Andromache <u>digressu</u> maesta supremo
> fert <u>picturatas</u> auri <u>subtemine</u> <u>vestis</u>
> et Phrygiam Ascanio chlamydem (nec cedit honore)
> 485 <u>textilibus</u>que <u>onerat</u> donis, ac talia fatur:
> "accipe et haec, <u>manuum</u> tibi quae <u>monimenta</u> mearum
> sint, puer, et longum Andromachae testentur <u>amorem</u>,
> coniugis Hectoreae. cape dona extrema tuorum,
> o mihi sola mei super Astyanactis <u>imago</u>.
> 490 sic oculos, sic ille manus, sic ora ferebat;
> et nunc aequali tecum pubesceret aevo."

> Next [= after Helenos had given parting gifts],[182] Andromache, mournful over the final <u>parting of company</u>,[183]
> brings <u>fabrics</u> [*vestis* plural] <u>pattern-woven</u> [*picturatae*] with traverse threading [*subtemen*] of gold
> to Ascanius, and also a Phrygian *chlamys*—she is second to none in honoring him [= Ascanius]

---

[182] The wording *nec minus* expresses the idea that the parting gifts about to be given by Andromache are just as wondrous as the parting gifts just given by Helenos.

[183] That is, Aeneas and his followers are finally taking leave of Andromache and of her new husband Helenos, who stay behind in the new Troy at Buthrotum in Epirus.

1§14. The sorrows of Andromache

495 Weighing him down [*onerare*] with a mass of woven [*textilis* neuter plural] gifts, she speaks to him words that go like this:

"Receive these things too,[184] as reminders [*monimenta*] of the work of my hands.

Let them be exactly that, reminders, young boy. Let them bear witness to the long-standing love [*amor*] of Andromache,

wife of Hector.[185] You must take these final gifts given to you by your own people [= your Trojan kinfolk],

you who are for me the only image [*imago*] of my Astyanax that is left for me to have.

Yes, this is just the way he moved: his eyes, his hands, his face...

And now he would be the same age as you, blossoming as an adolescent."

1§201 The adjective *picturatae* 'pattern-woven', applied to the plural of the noun *vestis* 'fabric' at verse 483 of *Aeneid* 3, is derived from the noun *pictura*, which refers not only to the process of painting but also to a kind of fabric work that highlights the virtuosity of patterning (as in Apuleius *Florida* 15 *tunicam picturis variegatam* 'a tunic variegated with patterned fabric work').[186] This kind of pattern-weaving is achieved by way of a *subtemen*. The noun *subtemen* (/ *subtegmen*), which means 'traverse threading', is derived from the verb *texere* 'weave' and designates a process of interweaving the horizontal threading or weft with the vertical threading or warp, thus creating the ongoing foregrounded narrative of the pattern-weaving. Here the foregrounding is in gold, while elsewhere it can be in purple (Tibullus 3.7.121 *fulgentem Tyrio subtemine vestem* 'fabric gleaming with Tyrian traverse threading').

1§202 These *vestes* 'fabrics' woven by Andromache would have clothed Astyanax, son of Hector and Andromache, if he had lived to grow up to manhood as had Ascanius, son of Aeneas and Creusa. The clothing that will never fit Astyanax will now fit Ascanius, just as it had once fit Hector, who is called the *avunculus* 'uncle' of Ascanius (*Aeneid* 3.343). This relationship

---

[184] That is, receive these gifts that are added to the gifts given by Helenos.
[185] Andromache calls herself wife of Hector, though she is now married to another son of Priam, the Trojan Helenos, who has become the new king of the New Troy.
[186] For an introduction to the concept of pattern-weaving, as expressed by the Latin noun *pictura* and by the verb from which it is derived, *pingere*, see Barber 1991:359n2.

Chapter One

with the Trojan kinfolk is at the heart of a mother's need to give 'these final gifts' to a maternal nephew, who will thus become reconnected to his own people. By implication, the *vestes* 'fabrics' that had been *picturatae* 'pattern-woven' by Andromache for Hector and then for Astyanax to wear are now to be worn by the maternal 'nephew' Ascanius, who will take the place of Astyanax in wearing *monimenta* 'reminders' that connect with the epic past of the Trojan War. By way of this gift of textiles woven by Andromache, a gift so generous that its sheer weight almost overburdens the recipient (495 *onerare* 'weigh down'), Ascanius has received a direct connection with this epic past. Andromache's onerous gift of textiles to Ascanius is Virgil's metaphor for the burden of this epic past, which is the poet's own onerous gift to the notional descendant of Ascanius (whose alternative name is Iulus), that is, to Caesar Augustus, who is the ultimate patron of Virgil's Roman epic.

1§203 This Virgilian usage of *picturatae vestes* 'pattern-woven fabrics' as a metaphor for the poetic burden of the epic past is an evocation of Homeric poetry. I quote here the relevant Homeric narrative in *Iliad* XXII, starting from the moment when the lamenting Hecuba announces the news of Hector's death to Andromache. At that moment, Andromache is weaving a fabric:

1ⓣ41 *Iliad* XXII 437–515

437 Ὣς ἔφατο κλαίουσ', ἄλοχος δ' οὔ πώ τι πέπυστο
Ἕκτορος· οὐ γάρ οἵ τις ἐτήτυμος ἄγγελος ἐλθὼν
ἤγγειλ' ὅττί ῥά οἱ πόσις ἔκτοθι μίμνε πυλάων,
440 ἀλλ' ἥ γ' ἱστὸν <u>ὕφαινε</u> μυχῷ δόμου ὑψηλοῖο
<u>δίπλακα πορφυρέην, ἐν δὲ θρόνα ποικίλ' ἔπασσε</u>.
κέκλετο δ' ἀμφιπόλοισιν ἐϋπλοκάμοις κατὰ δῶμα
ἀμφὶ πυρὶ στῆσαι τρίποδα μέγαν, ὄφρα πέλοιτο
Ἕκτορι θερμὰ λοετρὰ μάχης ἐκ νοστήσαντι
445 νηπίη, οὐδ' ἐνόησεν ὅ μιν μάλα τῆλε λοετρῶν
χερσὶν Ἀχιλλῆος δάμασε γλαυκῶπις Ἀθήνη.
κωκυτοῦ δ' ἤκουσε καὶ οἰμωγῆς ἀπὸ πύργου·
τῆς δ' ἐλελίχθη γυῖα, χαμαὶ δέ οἱ ἔκπεσε <u>κερκίς</u>·
ἣ δ' αὖτις δμῳῇσιν ἐϋπλοκάμοισι μετηύδα·
450 δεῦτε δύω μοι ἕπεσθον, ἴδωμ' ὅτιν' ἔργα τέτυκται.

1⑤14. The sorrows of Andromache

αἰδοίης ἑκυρῆς ὀπὸς ἔκλυον, ἐν δ' ἐμοὶ αὐτῇ
<u>στήθεσι πάλλεται ἦτορ ἀνὰ στόμα</u>, νέρθε δὲ γοῦνα
<u>πήγνυται</u>· ἐγγὺς δή τι κακὸν Πριάμοιο τέκεσσιν.
αἲ γὰρ ἀπ' οὔατος εἴη ἐμεῦ ἔπος· ἀλλὰ μάλ' αἰνῶς
455 δείδω μὴ δή μοι θρασὺν Ἕκτορα δῖος Ἀχιλλεὺς
μοῦνον ἀποτμήξας πόλιος πεδίον δὲ δίηται,
καὶ δή μιν καταπαύσῃ ἀγηνορίης ἀλεγεινῆς
ἥ μιν ἔχεσκ', ἐπεὶ οὔ ποτ' ἐνὶ πληθυῖ μένεν ἀνδρῶν,
ἀλλὰ πολὺ προθέεσκε, τὸ ὃν μένος οὐδενὶ εἴκων.
460 Ὣς φαμένη μεγάροιο διέσσυτο <u>μαινάδι</u> ἴση
παλλομένη κραδίην· ἅμα δ' ἀμφίπολοι κίον αὐτῇ
αὐτὰρ ἐπεὶ πύργόν τε καὶ ἀνδρῶν ἷξεν ὅμιλον
ἔστη παπτήνασ' ἐπὶ τείχεϊ, τὸν δὲ νόησεν
ἑλκόμενον πρόσθεν πόλιος· ταχέες δέ μιν ἵπποι
465 ἕλκον ἀκηδέστως κοίλας ἐπὶ νῆας Ἀχαιῶν.
τὴν δὲ κατ' ὀφθαλμῶν ἐρεβεννὴ νὺξ ἐκάλυψεν,
ἤριπε δ' ἐξοπίσω, ἀπὸ δὲ ψυχὴν ἐκάπυσσε.
τῆλε δ' ἀπὸ κρατὸς βάλε δέσματα σιγαλόεντα,
ἄμπυκα κεκρύφαλόν τε ἰδὲ πλεκτὴν ἀναδέσμην
470 κρήδεμνόν θ', ὅ ῥά οἱ δῶκε χρυσῆ Ἀφροδίτη
ἤματι τῷ ὅτε μιν κορυθαίολος ἠγάγεθ' Ἕκτωρ
ἐκ δόμου Ἠετίωνος, ἐπεὶ πόρε μυρία ἕδνα.
ἀμφὶ δέ μιν γαλόῳ τε καὶ εἰνατέρες ἅλις ἔσταν,
αἵ ἑ μετὰ σφίσιν εἶχον ἀτυζομένην ἀπολέσθαι.
475 ἣ δ' ἐπεὶ οὖν ἔμπνυτο καὶ ἐς φρένα θυμὸς ἀγέρθη
ἀμβλήδην γοόωσα μετὰ Τρῳῇσιν ἔειπεν·
Ἕκτορ ἐγὼ δύστηνος· ἰῇ ἄρα γεινόμεθ' αἴσῃ
ἀμφότεροι, σὺ μὲν ἐν Τροίῃ Πριάμου κατὰ δῶμα,
αὐτὰρ ἐγὼ Θήβῃσιν ὑπὸ Πλάκῳ ὑληέσσῃ
480 ἐν δόμῳ Ἠετίωνος, ὅ μ' ἔτρεφε τυτθὸν ἐοῦσαν
δύσμορος αἰνόμορον· ὡς μὴ ὤφελλε τεκέσθαι.

> νῦν δὲ σὺ μὲν Ἀΐδαο δόμους ὑπὸ κεύθεσι γαίης
> ἔρχεαι, αὐτὰρ ἐμὲ στυγερῷ ἐνὶ πένθεϊ λείπεις
> χήρην ἐν μεγάροισι· πάϊς δ' ἔτι νήπιος αὕτως,
> 485 ὃν τέκομεν σύ τ' ἐγώ τε δυσάμμοροι· οὔτε σὺ τούτῳ
> ἔσσεαι Ἕκτορ ὄνειαρ ἐπεὶ θάνες, οὔτε σοὶ οὗτος.
> ἤν περ γὰρ πόλεμόν γε φύγῃ πολύδακρυν Ἀχαιῶν,
> αἰεί τοι τούτῳ γε πόνος καὶ κήδε' ὀπίσσω
> ἔσσοντ'· ἄλλοι γάρ οἱ ἀπουρίσσουσιν ἀρούρας.
> 490 ἦμαρ δ' ὀρφανικὸν παναφήλικα παῖδα τίθησι·
> πάντα δ' ὑπεμνήμυκε, δεδάκρυνται δὲ παρειαί,
> δευόμενος δέ τ' ἄνεισι πάϊς ἐς πατρὸς ἑταίρους,
> ἄλλον μὲν χλαίνης ἐρύων, ἄλλον δὲ χιτῶνος·
> τῶν δ' ἐλεησάντων κοτύλην τις τυτθὸν ἐπέσχε·
> 495 χείλεα μέν τ' ἐδίην', ὑπερῴην δ' οὐκ ἐδίηνε.
> τὸν δὲ καὶ ἀμφιθαλὴς ἐκ δαιτύος ἐστυφέλιξε
> χερσὶν πεπλήγων καὶ ὀνειδείοισιν ἐνίσσων·
> ἔρρ' οὕτως· οὐ σός γε πατὴρ μεταδαίνυται ἡμῖν.
> δακρυόεις δέ τ' ἄνεισι πάϊς ἐς μητέρα χήρην
> 500 Ἀστυάναξ, ὃς πρὶν μὲν ἑοῦ ἐπὶ γούνασι πατρὸς
> μυελὸν οἶον ἔδεσκε καὶ οἰῶν πίονα δημόν·
> αὐτὰρ ὅθ' ὕπνος ἕλοι, παύσαιτό τε νηπιαχεύων,
> εὕδεσκ' ἐν λέκτροισιν ἐν ἀγκαλίδεσσι τιθήνης
> εὐνῇ ἔνι μαλακῇ θαλέων ἐμπλησάμενος κῆρ·
> 505 νῦν δ' ἂν πολλὰ πάθῃσι φίλου ἀπὸ πατρὸς ἁμαρτὼν
> Ἀστυάναξ, ὃν Τρῶες ἐπίκλησιν καλέουσιν·
> οἶος γάρ σφιν ἔρυσο πύλας καὶ τείχεα μακρά.
> νῦν δὲ σὲ μὲν παρὰ νηυσὶ κορωνίσι νόσφι τοκήων
> αἰόλαι εὐλαὶ ἔδονται, ἐπεί κε κύνες κορέσωνται
> 510 γυμνόν· ἀτάρ τοι εἵματ' ἐνὶ μεγάροισι κέονται
> λεπτά τε καὶ <u>χαρίεντα</u> τετυγμένα χερσὶ γυναικῶν.
> ἀλλ' ἤτοι τάδε πάντα καταφλέξω πυρὶ κηλέῳ

1⑤14. The sorrows of Andromache

οὐδὲν σοί γ' ὄφελος, ἐπεὶ οὐκ ἐγκείσεαι αὐτοῖς,
ἀλλὰ πρὸς Τρώων καὶ Τρωϊάδων κλέος εἶναι.
515 Ὣς ἔφατο κλαίουσ', ἐπὶ δὲ στενάχοντο γυναῖκες.

437 So she [= Hecuba] spoke, lamenting, but the wife [= Andromache] had not yet heard anything,
Hector's wife: for no true messenger came to her
and told her any news, how her husband was standing his ground outside the gates.[187]
440 She [= Andromache] was weaving [*huphainein*] a web in the inner room of the lofty palace,
a purple [*porphureē*][188] fabric that folds in two [= *diplax*], and she was inworking [*en-passein*][189] patterns of flowers [*throna*] that were varied [*poikila*].[190]
And she called out to the attending women, the ones with the beautiful tresses [*plokamoi*], in the palace
to set a big tripod on the fire, so that there would be
a warm bath for Hector when he had his return [*nostos*] from battle.[191]
445 Unwary [*nēpiē*] as she was, she did not know [*noeîn*] that, far from the bath,
the hands of Achilles had brought him [= Hector] down. It was the work of Athena, the one with the look of the owl.
She [= Andromache] heard the wailing and the cries of *oimoi* coming from the high walls [*purgos*].

---

[187] The news must be subjectivized here: Andromache is expecting to hear news of Hector, how he is standing his ground, and in her present state of mind she is not yet ready for the news that Hector has already been killed.
[188] In ch. 4, I consider also a variant reading: besides *porphureē* 'purple', *marmareē* 'gleaming' is also attested here at *Iliad* XXII 441.
[189] Metaphorically, *en-passein* is to 'sprinkle': PR 93.
[190] In HPC II§§373–374, I analyze the technical meanings of the words having to do with pattern-weaving in this verse.
[191] The wording here at *Iliad* XXII 444 needs to be compared with the wording at *Iliad* XVII 207, where Zeus expresses his Plan for Hector and Andromache: the return (*nostos*) of Hector from battle will be altogether different. On the inherent irony of the wording here, see Grethlein 2007.

Chapter One

Her limbs shook, and she dropped on the ground her shuttle.

And then she stood among the women slaves attending her, the ones with the beautiful tresses, and she spoke to them:

450 "Come, I want two of you to accompany me. I want to see what has happened.

I just heard the voice of my venerable mother-in-law, and what I feel inside is that

my heart is throbbing hard in my chest right up to my mouth, and my knees down below

are frozen stiff. I now see that something bad is nearing the sons of Priam.

If only the spoken word had been too far away for me to hear. But I so terribly

455 fear for my bold Hector at the hands of radiant Achilles.

I fear that he has got him cut off from the rest, putting him on the run toward the open plain,

and that he has put a stop to a manliness that has gone too far, the cause of so much sorrow.

It was a thing that had a hold over him, since he could never just stand back and blend in with the multitude of his fellow warriors.

Instead, he would keep on running ahead of the rest of them, not yielding to anyone as he pushed ahead with his vital force [*menos*]."

460 So speaking she rushed out of the palace, same as a maenad [*mainás*],[192]

with heart throbbing. And her attending women went with her.

But when she reached the tower and the crowd of warriors,

she stood on the wall, looking around, and then she noticed him.

There he was, being dragged right in front of the city. The swift chariot team of horses was

---

[192] I will have more to say later about Andromache as a 'maenad'.

465 dragging him, far from her caring thoughts, back toward the hollow ships of the Achaeans.

Over her eyes a dark night spread its cover,

and she fell backward, gasping out her life's breath [*psukhē*].

She threw far from her head the splendid adornments that bound her hair

—her frontlet [*ampux*], her snood [*kekruphalos*], her plaited headband [*anadesmē*],

470 and, to top it all, the headdress [*krēdemnon*] that had been given to her by golden Aphrodite

on that day when Hector, the one with the waving plume on his helmet, took her by the hand and led her

out from the palace of Eëtion, and he gave countless courtship presents.

Crowding around her stood her husband's sisters and his brothers' wives,

and they were holding her up. She was barely breathing, to the point of dying.

475 But when she recovered her breathing and her life's breath gathered in her lung,

she started to sing a lament in the midst of the Trojan women, with these words:

"Hector, I too am wretched. For we were born sharing a single fate,

the two of us—you in Troy, in the palace of Priam,

and I in Thebe, the city at the foot of the wooded mountain of Plakos

480 in the palace of Eëtion, who raised me when I was little

—an ill-fated father and a daughter with an equally terrible fate. If only he had never fathered me.

But now you [= Hektor] are headed for the palace of Hades inside the deep recesses of earth,

that is where you are headed, while I am left behind by you, left behind in a state of hateful mourning [*penthos*],

Chapter One

      a widow in the palace. And then there is the child, not yet bonded to you, so young he is,

485 whose parents we are, you and I with our wretched fate. Neither will you be for him,

      no you will not, Hektor, of any help, since you died, nor will he be of any help for you

      even if he escapes the attack of the Achaeans, with all its sorrows,

      still, for the rest of his life, because of you, there will be harsh labor for him,

      and sorrows. For others will take his landholdings away from him. The time of bereavement

490 leaves the child with no agemates as friends.

      He bows his head to every man, and his cheeks are covered with tears.

      The boy makes his rounds among his father's former companions,

      and he tugs at one man by the mantle and another man by the tunic,

      and they pity him. One man gives him a small drink from a cup,

495 enough to moisten the boy's lips but not enough to moisten his palate.

      But another boy whose parents are living hits him and chases him from the banquet,

      beating him with his fists and abusing him with words:

      "Get out, you! Your father is not dining with us!"

      And the boy goes off in tears to his widowed mother,

500 the boy Astyanax, who in days gone by, on the knees of his father,

      would eat only the marrow or the meat of sheep that were the fattest.

      And when sleep would come upon him after he was finished with playing,

      he would go to sleep in a bed, in the arms of his nurse,

1ⓈⓈ14. The sorrows of Andromache

> in a soft bed, with a heart that is filled in luxury.
> 505 But now he [= our child] will suffer many things, deprived of his father,
> our child Astyanax, as the Trojans call him by name.
> That is what he is called because you all by yourself guarded the gates and long walls.
> But now, you are where the curved ships [of the Achaeans] are, far from your parents,
> and you will be devoured by writhing maggots after the dogs have their fill of you.
> 510 There you lie, naked, while your clothes are lying around in the palace.
> Fine clothes they are, marked by <u>pleasurable beauty</u> [*kharis*], the work of women's hands.
> But I will incinerate all these clothes over the burning fire.
> You will have no need for them, since you will not be lying in state, clothed in them.[193]
> But there is to be fame [*kleos*] [for you] from the men and women of Troy."
> 515 So she [= Andromache] spoke, weeping, and the women mourned in response.

1§204 In the age of Virgil, this picturing of Andromache weaving her fabrics is understood as a Homeric metaphor for epic narration, as revealed by Virgil's reference in his own epic to the *picturatae vestes* 'pattern-woven fabrics' of Andromache. This reference, as we have seen, is a metaphor for the burden of the epic past.

1§205 More than that, this reference is a metaphor for the burden of the epic past of Homeric poetry. As we are about to see, Virgil's wording actually evokes the passage I just quoted from *Iliad* XXII, showing Andromache in the act of pattern-weaving her web. The *picturatae vestes* 'pattern-woven fabrics'

---

[193] This prophecy of Andromache turns out to be mistaken: after Priam is granted his request to recover the body of Hector, Achilles himself arranges for Hector's body to be covered with various fabrics, two *pharea* and one *khitōn*, which had been brought by Priam as ransom for the body of Hector. The relevant wording can be found in *Iliad* XXIV 580-581. Comments by Grethlein 2007:38.

Chapter One

that Andromache gives to Ascanius in the *Aeneid* are pictured as a continuation of the patterns she had been weaving for Hector in the *Iliad* at the very moment when the news of her husband's death reached her. Virgil's evocation of that Iliadic moment is confirmed by other details that evoke the same moment. The most revealing of these details involve pictorial impressions of Andromache in the New Troy of Buthrotum in Epirus. Just as Andromache swooned when she saw Hector dead in the *Iliad* (XXII 466-474), she now swoons when she sees Aeneas alive in the *Aeneid* (3.306-309). To see Aeneas is to recall the Old Troy. The exact moment before Andromache fell into her swoon in the *Iliad*, she looked like a woman possessed, a *mainás* 'maenad' (XXII 460 μαινάδι).[194] Now that she recovers from her swoon in the *Aeneid*, she looks once again like a woman possessed, a *furens* (3.313 *furenti*).

1§206 Virgil's epic poetry is returning to the picture of Andromache at that Iliadic moment by evoking what Andromache herself pictures. The weaving of Andromache is her way of picturing her own world. It is her way of not losing sight of the picture. She pictures herself inside that picture, which is a picture of returning to the picture. It is an act of infinite regression, infinite retrospection.

1§207 I see an analogy in another picture, based on a historical moment in the formative stages of imperial Rome. It is a picture of a doomed couple, Brutus and Porcia. We are about to see, in infinite regression, a picture looking back at a picture of another doomed couple, Hector and Andromache:

1①42 Plutarch *Brutus* 23.2-5

> ὅθεν ἡ Πορκία μέλλουσα πάλιν εἰς Ῥώμην ἀποτραπέσθαι, λανθάνειν μὲν ἐπειρᾶτο περιπαθῶς ἔχουσα, γραφὴ δέ τις αὐτὴν προύδωκε, τἆλλα γενναίαν οὖσαν. ἦν γὰρ ἐκ τῶν Ἑλληνικῶν διάθεσις, προπεμπόμενος Ἕκτωρ ὑπ᾽ Ἀνδρομάχης, κομιζομένης παρ᾽ αὐτοῦ τὸ παιδίον, ἐκείνῳ δὲ προσβλεπούσης. ταῦτα θεωμένην τὴν Πορκίαν ἡ τοῦ πάθους εἰκὼν ἐξέτηξεν εἰς δάκρυα, καὶ πολλάκις φοιτῶσα τῆς ἡμέρας ἔκλαιεν.

> As Porcia was preparing to return from there [= from the headquarters of Brutus] to Rome, she tried to conceal her extreme emotional state, but a certain painting [*graphē*] gave her away, in spite of her

---

[194] Earlier in the *Iliad*, in an analogous context (VI 389), Andromache is pictured as μαινομένῃ ἐϊκυῖα 'looking like a woman possessed' as she rushes toward the walls of Troy to see for herself the fate of the Trojans on the battlefield. For more on the theme of Andromache as a 'maenad', see Signore 2006.

1ⓢ14. The sorrows of Andromache

noble character. The subject [of the painting] was derived from Greek traditions. It showed Hector at the moment when Andromache is saying goodbye to him as he goes off [to war] and she is taking back from his arms their little child <u>while her gaze is riveted on him [= Hector]. As Porcia was gazing at all this, the picture [eikōn] of the emotion [pathos] caused her to dissolve into tears, and she kept on revisiting it many times a day and weeping over it.</u>[195]

1§208 The story goes on to compare Porcia with Andromache, who was sent back to her weaving after her own final farewell to Hector:

1ⓣ43 Plutarch *Brutus* 23.5–6

Ἀκιλίου δέ τινος τῶν Βρούτου φίλων τὰ πρὸς Ἕκτορα τῆς Ἀνδρομάχης ἔπη διελθόντος·

Ἕκτορ, ἀτὰρ σύ μοί ἐσσι πατὴρ καὶ πότνια μήτηρ

ἠδὲ κασίγνητος, σὺ δέ μοι θαλερὸς παρακοίτης

Iliad VI 429–430

μειδιάσας ὁ Βροῦτος "ἀλλ' οὐκ ἐμοί γ'" εἶπε "πρὸς Πορκίαν ἔπεισι φάναι τὰ τοῦ Ἕκτορος·

<ἀλλ' εἰς οἶκον ἰοῦσα τὰ σαυτῆς ἔργα κόμιζε,>

ἱστόν τ' ἠλακάτην τε καὶ ἀμφιπόλοισι κέλευε·

Iliad VI 490–491

σώματος γὰρ ἀπολείπεται φύσει τῶν ἴσων ἀνδραγαθημάτων, γνώμῃ δ' ὑπὲρ τῆς πατρίδος ὥσπερ ἡμεῖς ἀριστεύσει." ταῦτα μὲν ὁ τῆς Πορκίας υἱὸς ἱστόρηκε Βύβλος.

And when Acilius, one of the friends of Brutus, quoted the verses spoken by Andromache to Hector,

Hector, you are for me my father and my mother the queen

and my brother as well as my vibrant partner in lovemaking

Iliad VI 429–430

Brutus smiled and said: "But it does not even occur to me that I should say to Porcia the verses spoken by Hector:

---

[195] This detail about revisiting a picture of sadness, over and over again, was first pointed out to me by David Konstan.

> But you [= Andromache] go back to the household and attend to your own work,
>
> that is, the loom and the shuttle, giving orders to the handmaidens [who work for you].
>
> *Iliad* VI 490–491

Even if she may not be physically up to performing deeds of valor that equal those of men, when it comes to her powers of mind, she can perform the greatest deeds of valor just like me." This story about Porcia was told by her son Bibulus.

1§209 The idea of being sent back to your weaving is being equated in this story with the idea of being sent back, again and again, to the original picture. We see here a poetics of retrospection, which is already at work in Homeric poetry. In an exquisite moment, we see Andromache herself returning again and again to the original picture of her last farewell to Hector:

1①44 *Iliad* VI 496

> ἐντροπαλιζομένη, θαλερὸν κατὰ δάκρυ χέουσα
>
> She was turning her head back again and again, shedding tears thick and fast.[196]

1§210 Andromache and Hector have just parted, turning away from each other and heading in opposite directions. He is going off to die while she is going back to her weaving. As she is being led away, Andromache keeps turning her head back again and again, *entropalizomenē*, hoping to catch one last glimpse of the receding view of her doomed husband.[197]

1§211 Just as Andromache is shaping her last mental image of her last parting with Hector, so also the poetry of epic is shaping the last mental image of Andromache in its own act of retrospective, of returning to the fixed image. Every time Homeric poetry is performed, it can return once again to the picture of Andromache in the act looking back to see if she can capture one last glimpse of Hector. It is a world of tears, and there is a world of beauty in these tears. To quote Virgil once again, *sunt lacrimae rerum*. To look back on this world is to look back on perfection, in all its frozen beauty. Homeric poetry is like that: it looks back on its own crystallized perfection.

---

[196] A related image is *Iliad* VI 484, where Andromache is described as δακρυόεν γελάσασα 'smiling through her tears'.

[197] There is a comparable image in Euripides *Hecuba* 939.

CHAPTER TWO
HOMER THE CLASSIC
IN THE AGE OF CALLIMACHUS

2ⓢ1. An esthetics of fluidity

2§1 Homeric poetry imagines itself as rigid—that is, unchanging like the petrified serpent in Iliad II. That is what I was arguing in Chapter 1. But there is more to it. As I will now argue in Chapter 2, this three-dimensional vision of arrested motion is being expressed by something ever changing and—paradoxically—fluid. That something is performance. More specifically, that something is Homeric narration, which shows its oral poetic heritage of changeability in performance. Homeric poetry deploys a metaphor that forcefully expresses this changeability. It originates from the idea of fluidity, the opposite of rigidity. We are about to see a variety of poetic examples emanating from the summit of Hellenistic poetry, the age of Callimachus, around the third century BCE. From these examples, we will learn how Homeric poetry can also picture itself as fluid instead of rigid in its powers of narration.

2§2 In the age of Callimachus, even the textual tradition of Homer is fluid by comparison with the textual tradition of Homer in the later age of Aristarchus. The Homer of Aristarchus, who flourished in the second century BCE, about a hundred years after Callimachus, stands in sharp contrast: it represents the most rigid editorial criteria for judging what is or is not genuinely Homeric, and those criteria were rigorously applied by later Aristarchean scholars like Didymus, who flourished in the age of Virgil.

2§3 Not only does Homeric poetry seem to be fluid in the age of Callimachus. It was actually pictured as fluid by poets of that age, and such pictures of fluidity complement the antithetical pictures of Homeric rigidity. In order to see more clearly the interaction of fluidity and rigidity as complementary

Chapter Two

metaphors for the making of Homeric poetry, I propose here to take one more look at a picture created by the poetry of Virgil. In Chapter 1, I touched on Virgil's uncanny vision of Athena's two serpents turning into statues in *Aeneid* 2. Once they kill Laocoön and his two sons, the serpents become visual effects complementing the visual effect of Athena's own statue. Virgil's poetry has shaped a sculptural ensemble that pictures Athena attended by her twin serpents, residing together inside her temple situated on the heights of the acropolis of Troy.

2§4 Virgil's picture evokes one of the most exquisite sights anywhere to be seen in the classical world. This sight, a vision to be imagined in its broadest classical outlines, was a most celebrated sculptural ensemble, created by Pheidias of Athens. Its permanent place was meant to be Athens. Pausanias (1.24.7) saw it there and described it. It was a sculptural ensemble that pictured Athena Parthenos, the 'virgin goddess', attended by a single serpent; the Parthenos and her serpent attendant resided together inside her newest temple situated on the heights of the acropolis of Athens, that is, inside the Parthenon or 'place of the virgin'. This vision of Athena as Parthenos or 'virgin goddess' inside her temple on the acropolis of Athens was complemented, as we saw in Chapter 1, by the vision of Athena as Polias or 'city goddess' inside another temple of hers on the same acropolis; in this complementary setting, an old and most venerable wooden statue of the goddess was attended by the simulacra of two serpents, not one (Phylarchus *FGrH* 81 F 72, by way of Photius *Lexicon* s.v. οἰκουρὸν ὄφιν, and Hesychius s.v. οἰκουρὸν ὄφιν). These two complementary aspects of the goddess Athena on the acropolis of Athens, one of which was most old and interiorized while the other was forever new and exteriorized, could merge as a composite sculptural vision in Virgil's composite poetic evocation. Virgil's poetic vision could be further enhanced by a variety of mediated versions of the statue of Athena Parthenos; in Virgil's day, the most presigious of these mediated versions was the statue of Athena Parthenos inside her temple situated on the heights of the acropolis of Pergamon, which was evidently modeled on the Parthenos in the Parthenon of Athens.

2§5 Virgil's poetic vision of the statue of Athena evokes more than a sculptural classic. It evokes also a classic of poetry, Homer. Virgil's vision has a distinctly Homeric touch to it. As we saw in Chapter 1, the Roman poet's picturing of the twin serpents that turned into statues in *Aeneid* 2 rivals the Homeric picturing of the serpent that turned into stone in *Iliad* II.

2§6 As I look for a unifying idea behind these two rival pictures, what I see is motion suddenly followed by stop-motion. I see something that lives and moves in one moment, and then, the very next moment, something that suddenly stops moving. Does this something stop living as well? No, the vitality of its motion has not at all stopped. Only the motion has stopped. The single petrified serpent and the twin sculpted serpents retain their vitality in the art that made them. They keep on living in the art that stopped their motion. They are stop-motion pictures of vitality, of motion itself. The verbal art of poetry is saying here something essential about the visual art of making statues. The rigidity of statues, or of stylized statues like Homer's petrified serpent, is not really *rigor mortis* after all. The statue retains signs of life in motion. The rigidity of the statue retains the vitality of narration in progress, in motion.

2§7 The idea of such vitality, the vitality of narration, is what I see being shared by Homeric metaphors of fluidity and rigidity. We can see the interaction of fluidity and rigidity when we think in terms of a sequence of go followed by stop, or of flow followed by freeze. And the idea of a stop-motion picture presupposes the idea of a motion picture. The rigid presupposes the fluid. More than that, the idea of a motion picture presupposes another idea, that the motion itself must have an origin, a beginning. The flow needs to have a source.

2ⓢ2. Homeric *humnos*

2§8 How, then, is fluidity a metaphor for Homeric narration? This question presupposes another question, which must override the first: how does the poet begin a narration in the first place? To say it metaphorically, what is the source for the flow of narration? For answers, I look to a word that captures perfectly the idea of a perfect beginning for narration. It is *humnos* / ὕμνος 'hymn'.

2§9 I will examine how this word is used in Hellenistic poetry, especially in the *Hymns* of Callimachus, and in Homeric poetry. This usage of *humnos* is relevant to the word's Homeric usage, which will be essential for understanding Homer as a classic in the age of Callimachus of Cyrene. I will also examine the relevant usage of two other eminent poets of that age, Apollonius of Rhodes and Theocritus of Syracuse.

2§10 In order to understand the usage of *humnos* in Callimachus, it is important to notice that Homeric poetry actually refers to itself, in its own usage, as *humnos*. I am thinking here not about the use of this word *humnos* in the *Homeric Hymns*. Granted, that usage is important as well for my argument, since Homer in the age of Callimachus was conventionally understood to be

Chapter Two

the author of the *Homeric Hymns* as well as the author of the *Iliad* and *Odyssey*.[1] Still, the question is: where in the *Iliad* or the *Odyssey* does Homeric poetry actually refer to itself as a *humnos*? The answer is not necessarily self-evident, even for experts in Homeric poetry. I will leave this question unanswered until we finish looking at other relevant contexts of *humnos*.

2§11 I start with contexts of *humnos* in Callimachus. First and most important, Callimachus begins the collection of his own *humnoi* with a *humnos* addressed to Zeus in his *Hymn 1*. Then, in *Hymn 2*, he proceeds to Apollo. Here is a most revealing passage from Callimachus' *Hymn 2*, his *Hymn to Apollo*:

2①1 Callimachus *Hymn to Apollo* 28-31

> τὸν χορὸν ὡπόλλων, ὅ τι οἱ κατὰ θυμὸν ἀείδει,
> τιμήσει· δύναται γάρ, ἐπεὶ Διὶ δεξιὸς ἧσται.
> οὐδ' ὁ χορὸς τὸν Φοῖβον ἐφ' ἓν μόνον ἦμαρ ἀείσει,
> ἔστι γὰρ εὔυμνος· τίς ἂν οὐ ῥέα Φοῖβον ἀείδοι;

> The chorus [*khoros*] will be honored by Apollo because it sings [*aeidein*] in a way that suits his heart.
> Yes, he will honor the chorus, for he has the power. After all, he is seated at the right hand of Zeus.
> Nor will the chorus [*khoros*] sing Phoebus [= Apollo] for one day only,
> since he is good for hymning [*eu-humnos*]. Who would not fluently [*rhea*] sing Phoebus?

2§12 In this *humnos*, which is *Hymn 2* in the canonical order of *humnoi* composed by Callimachus, Apollo is positioned immediately next to Zeus, just as the *Hymn to Apollo* of Callimachus—that is, *Hymn 2*—is positioned immediately next to the *Hymn to Zeus*—that is, next to *Hymn 1*. Such sequencing is basic to the poetics of *humnos*, as we can see by concentrating on two essential words that I highlighted in what I just quoted, both having to do with the word *humnos*:

1. Callimachus *Hymn to Apollo* 31: Apollo is to be hymned *rhea* (ῥέα) 'fluently'.

---

[1] I have made this argument about the authorship of Homer more than once, for example in *PP* 62, where I explicitly use the word 'author'.

2. Callimachus *Hymn to Apollo* 31: Apollo is *eu-humnos* (εὔυμνος) 'good for hymning'.

In what follows, I will analyze these two words one at a time.

2ⓢ3. The fluidity of the *humnos*

2§13 In verse 31 of Callimachus' *Hymn to Apollo*, we have seen that the god Apollo is to be hymned *rhea* 'fluently'. This metaphor of fluency is driven by the basic idea of starting from a perfect beginning. The image derives naturally from the process of flowing, as when water flows from its source. With the right beginning, the words of a *humnos* are fluent, flowing, fluid. The relevant forms are these:

rheîn / ῥεῖν 'flow' (verb)

rhoos / ῥόος 'flow' (noun)

rhea / ῥέα 'easily, fluently, fluidly' (adverb)

Also, by way of "folk etymology," the goddess *Rhea* (or *Rheiē* or *Rheē*), mother of Zeus, is 'fluidity'.[2]

2§14 The *Hymns* of Callimachus abound in these metaphors: 'fluency' is the mark of the *humnos*, especially in the *Hymn to Apollo* and in the *humnos* that precedes it, the *Hymn to Zeus*.[3] The first and inaugural *humnos* of Callimachus, the *Hymn to Zeus*, actually metaphorizes itself as 'fluidity' by "folk-etymologizing" the name of Zeus' mother, *Rhea*, as the cosmic force that initiates the 'flow' of rivers and springs (*rhoos* at verse 15, *rheîn* at verse 17)—a force that is realized at the precise moment when the goddess gives birth to Zeus (*Rheiē* / *Rheē* at verses 10 / 20).[4]

---

[2] What I mean by folk etymology is explained in *HTL* ch. 6.

[3] As we will see at a later point, some traditional features of Zeus are predicated on traditional features of his divine son, Apollo, but the predication can be mythologized in reverse order, as if the features of Apollo were modeled on his divine father, Zeus. Such a pattern of reversal applies also to the divine daughter of Zeus, Athena. In "Orphic" traditions, for example, Zeus himself is figured as a weaver (Pherecydes of Syros B 2 DK).

[4] In the *Hymn to Zeus* by Callimachus, where Rhea gives birth to Zeus in concert with Earth, the words that refer to the birth are *kheîn* 'pour' and *kheuma* 'pouring' (32). On the "Orphic" connotations of such words designating the 'flowing' or 'pouring' of fresh water, I will have more to say at a later point. The word *rhoos* is also prominently featured in Callimachus *Hymn to Apollo* 108, referring to the diluted 'Assyrian stream' as a foil for the undiluted source of water for bees that make honey for Demeter. I hope to pursue elsewhere the interweaving of "Orphic" and "Cretan" traditions in the *Hymn to Zeus* by Callimachus.

Chapter Two

2§15 The association of the word *humnos* with the idea of fluidity is made explicit in the Hesiodic *Theogony*. In fact, the idea of fluidity is the ultimate source of self-definition for this poetic composition. As I am about to argue, the Hesiodic *Theogony* defines itself as one single continuous gigantic *humnos* that 'flows' perfectly. In order to make this argument, I offer here a brief analysis of the relevant wording, starting from the beginning of the *Theogony* and proceeding all the way to verse 104, where the persona of Hesiod offers a formal salutation to the Muses of Mount Olympus. We have already considered the first 104 verses of the Hesiodic *Theogony* in Chapter 1, where I analyzed the function of Hesiodic poetry as an authorization of royal power. Now, as we take a closer look at the wording of these first 104 verses, we are about to see that this validation takes the form of a *humnos*.

2§16 The singing of the Hesiodic *Theogony* begins with the naming of the Muses local to Mount Helicon (verses 1-2), who are pictured as dancing (3-4 πόσσ' ἁπαλοῖσιν | ὀρχεῦνται) around the source of a sacred spring (3), next to which is an altar of Zeus (3-4). More specifically, these local Muses of Mount Helicon are pictured as a choral ensemble (7-8 ἀκροτάτῳ Ἑλικῶνι χοροὺς ἐνεποιήσαντο, | καλοὺς ἱμερόεντας) who are both dancing (8 ἐπερρώσαντο δὲ ποσσίν) and singing with a beautiful voice (10 περικαλλέα ὄσσαν ἱεῖσαι)—and who are thereby performing a *humnos* (11 ὑμνεῦσαι). The subject of their *humnos* is Zeus (11), followed by the other gods (11-21), including Apollo and his sister Artemis (14). The Muses proceed to teach Hesiod their song (22), enjoining him to perform it (33). Just as the Muses were performing a *humnos* (11 ὑμνεῦσαι), Hesiod must now perform a *humnos* in his own right (33 ὑμνεῖν), and the subject of this *humnos* is to be 'the genesis [*genos*] of the gods', that is, a theogony (33 ὑμνεῖν μακάρων γένος αἰὲν ἐόντων). In order to get this *humnos* started, the poet is told that he must begin with the Muses and end with the Muses (34), and we have already heard at the beginning of the song that Hesiod has already begun with the Muses (1-2). Before he starts all over again with the Muses, there is a rhetorical moment of hesitation, where the performer, signaling that he is about to make a decision in the midst of performance, asks himself at verse 35 how he should proceed.[5] Such a rhetorical moment of hesitation can be described as an <u>aporetic crisis</u>. At a later point, we will encounter two other such moments in another example of a *humnos*, which is the *Homeric Hymn* (3) *to Apollo*. For now, however, I concentrate on the moment of hesitation in the Hesiodic *Theogony*. The aporetic crisis at verse 35

---

[5] I have analyzed Hesiod *Theogony* 35 in some detail in *GM* 181-201. In a forthcoming project, I hope to update my analysis.

2⑤3. The fluidity of the *humnos*

of the *Theogony* marks the point where the master of the *humnos* decides to start all over again with the Muses, and it is precisely at this point that the idea of fluidity becomes explicit. I quote the relevant verses, starting with the verse declaring the aporetic crisis:

2①2 Hesiod *Theogony* 35-45

35 ἀλλὰ τίη μοι ταῦτα περὶ δρῦν ἢ περὶ πέτρην;
τύνη, <u>Μουσάων ἀρχώμεθα</u>, ταὶ Διὶ πατρὶ
<u>ὑμνεῦσαι</u> τέρπουσι μέγαν νόον ἐντὸς Ὀλύμπου,
εἴρουσαι τά τ' ἐόντα τά τ' ἐσσόμενα πρό τ' ἐόντα,
<u>φωνῇ</u> <u>ὁμηρεῦσαι</u>, τῶν δ' ἀκάματος <u>ῥέει αὐδὴ</u>
40 ἐκ στομάτων ἡδεῖα· γελᾷ δέ τε δώματα πατρὸς
Ζηνὸς ἐριγδούποιο θεᾶν ὀπὶ λειριοέσσῃ
σκιδναμένῃ, ἠχεῖ δὲ κάρη νιφόεντος Ὀλύμπου
δώματά τ' ἀθανάτων· αἱ δ' ἄμβροτον <u>ὄσσαν ἱεῖσαι</u>
θεῶν γένος αἰδοῖον πρῶτον κλείουσιν ἀοιδῇ
45 <u>ἐξ ἀρχῆς</u>,

35 But why should I care about these things that keep on going around an oak or a rock?[6]

Come, let me <u>begin</u> [*arkhesthai*] with the <u>Muses</u>, who please Zeus the father

as <u>they sing their humnos</u> [*humneîn*], pleasing his great mind [*noos*] as he abides in Olympus.

They tell of things that are, that will be, and that were before,

making <u>things fit together</u> [*homēreuein*] with their sound. And their <u>voice</u> [*audē*] <u>flows</u> [*rheîn*] without ever wearing out,

40 coming sweetly from their mouths.[7] Glad is the palace of father

---

[6] From the standpoint of local creation myths, humankind was generated out of oak trees (another variant: ash trees) or out of rocks: see *GM* ch. 7.
[7] The metonymy that comes to life in associating the *stomata* 'mouths' of the Muses with their voices is part of an extended metonymy centering on an eroticized sense of desire as evoked by the voice of the singer.

Chapter Two

> Zeus the loud-thunderer over the delicate voice of the goddesses
> as it spreads far and wide. It echoes off the peaks of snowy Olympus
> and the dwellings of the immortals. And they [= the Muses], sending forth [*hienai*] an immortal voice [*ossa*],
> give fame [*kleos*] with their song first to the genesis [*genos*] of the gods, a matter of reverence,
> 45   starting from the beginning [*arkhē*]...

2§17 We see here that the Muses of Mount Helicon, as they perform their *humnos* (37 ὑμνεῦσαι), are heard by Zeus himself in the heights of Mount Olympus (37). There is an emphasis on the 'voicing' of the Muses' song (39 φωνῇ and αὐδή, 41 ὀπί, 43 ὄσσαν) and on the 'sweetness' of this voice that literally 'flows' from their mouths, as if from a spring (39-40). Then it is repeated that the subject of the Muses' song is to be 'the genesis [*genos*] of the gods', that is, a theogony (44 θεῶν γένος αἰδοῖον πρῶτον κλείουσιν ἀοιδῇ), but this time the Muses sing the sequence in terms of a chronological rather than a hierarchical priority, starting 'from the beginning', from the children of Gaia and Ouranos (45 ἐξ ἀρχῆς, οὓς Γαῖα καὶ Οὐρανὸς εὐρὺς ἔτικτεν), not from Zeus, who is now mentioned as second in chronological sequence, coming after earth and sky and the rest (47 δεύτερον αὖτε Ζῆνα). This time, there is also a further detail: after the Muses sing the gods as their first subject, they sing as their next subject 'the genesis [*genos*] of men and of giants' (50 αὖτις δ' ἀνθρώπων τε γένος κρατερῶν τε Γιγάντων).[8] And this song that they perform is explicitly a *humnos* (51 ὑμνεῦσαι). From here on, the Muses of the Hesiodic *Theogony* are invoked not as the local goddesses of Mount Helicon but as the Panhellenic goddesses of Mount Olympus, daughters of Zeus and Mnemosyne (52-62).[9] As the Muses ascend Mount Olympus (68), assuming Panhellenic status, they are both singing and dancing (69 μολπῇ).[10] We see in this context a highlighting of their singing per se (68 ὀπὶ καλῇ) and of their dancing per se (70 ἐρατὸς δὲ ποδῶν ὕπο δοῦπος ὀρώρει). Such singing and dancing, as we saw already at the beginning of the *Theogony* (8-10), is tantamount to a performance by a *khoros* 'choral ensemble' (7 χοροὺς ἐνεποιήσαντο), and such a

---

[8] At a later point, I will have more to say about Athenian agenda implicit in this reference to giants.
[9] *GM* 57–59.
[10] The verb *melpesthai* and the noun *molpē* convey the combination of singing and dancing: *PH* 12§29n62 (= p. 350) and n64 (= p. 351).

performance is pictured there as a *humnos* (11 ὑμνεῦσαι), at that early moment when the Muses are still Heliconian and not yet Olympian. So also at the later moment of the *Theogony* that we are now considering, the performance by the choral ensemble of singing and dancing Olympian Muses is pictured as a *humnos* (70 ὑμνεύσαις).

2§18 The ultimate source of this Olympian *humnos*, equated with the *Theogony* in the course of its being performed, is the authority of Zeus as king of the immortals (71-74), and it emanates from there to the Olympian Muses (75-79), especially to the Muse Kalliope (79-80).[11] Further, the authority emanates from the Muses to kings (75-93). Literally, the authority flows from them. The metaphor of fluidity becomes explicit in the following description of the ideal king who is favored by the Muses:

2①3 Hesiod *Theogony* 83-84

> τῷ μὲν ἐπὶ γλώσσῃ γλυκερὴν χείουσιν ἐέρσην,
> τοῦ δ' ἔπε' ἐκ στόματος ῥεῖ μείλιχα
>
> For this man [= for this ideal king] they [= the Muses] pour [*kheîn*] sweet dew,
> and from his [= the king's] mouth flow [*rheîn*] sweet words.

2§19 The wording goes on to specifiy that the authority of kings flows from Zeus, while the authority of poets flows from the authority of the Muses, and of Apollo as their choral leader:

2①4 Hesiod *Theogony* 94-97

> ἐκ γάρ τοι Μουσέων καὶ ἑκηβόλου Ἀπόλλωνος
> ἄνδρες ἀοιδοὶ ἔασιν ἐπὶ χθόνα καὶ κιθαρισταί,
> ἐκ δὲ Διὸς βασιλῆες· ὁ δ' ὄλβιος, ὅντινα Μοῦσαι
> φίλωνται· γλυκερή οἱ ἀπὸ στόματος ῥέει αὐδή.
>
> The Muses and far-shooting Apollo are the sources
> for the existence of singers [*aoidoi*] and players of the lyre [*kitharis*] on this earth.

---

[11] As I noted earlier, the idea that the Olympian Muse Kalliope authorizes kings is related to another idea: that Kalliope is the mother of Orpheus (as in Apollonius of Rhodes *Argonautica* 23-25). I analyze the relationship between these ideas in *HPC* E§109.

Chapter Two

> And Zeus is the source for the existence of kings. Blessed [*olbios*] is he whom the Muses
> love. And a <u>sweet voice</u> [*audē*] <u>flows</u> [*rheîn*] from his mouth.

2§20 As in what I quoted earlier from the Hesiodic *Theogony* (35-45), we see here once again the metaphor of fluidity: the voice of the Muses, sweet as it is, literally 'flows' from their mouths (97). Once again, the theme of fluidity expresses the idea that the *humnos* must have a perfect beginning. The *humnos* flows from a perfect source, and so it becomes the perfect performance. In this context as well, the actual performance is equated with the making of the *humnos* (101 ὑμνήσει).

2§21 Finally, as I anticipated at the beginning, we come to verse 104 of the *Theogony*. It is at this point that the persona of Hesiod gets to offer his formal salutation to the Muses of Mount Olympus.[12]

2Ⓢ4. Perfecting the *humnos*

2§22 I hold off till later an examination of the precise wording of the poet's salutation to the Muses in the *Theogony* (104). For the moment, I proceed instead to the second of the two words I had highlighted in Callimachus' *Hymn to Apollo* (31): Apollo is *eu-humnos* (εὔυμνος) 'good for hymning'. What this means, I argue, is that the god is pictured as the perfect subject for the *humnos* or 'hymn'. And, as the perfect subject, the god makes the hymn itself notionally perfect.

2§23 To make this argument about the concept of a god as a perfect hymnic subject, I begin by comparing the two occurrences of the same word *eu-humnos* (εὔυμνος) 'good for hymning' in the *Homeric Hymn* (3) *to Apollo*. Both occurrences involve a verse that declares an aporetic crisis in the form of an aporetic question:[13]

2①5 *Homeric Hymn* (3) *to Apollo* verses 19 and 207

πῶς γάρ[14] σ' <u>ὑμνήσω</u> πάντως εὔυμνον ἐόντα

---

[12] For a most helpful commentary that covers the first 115 verses of the Hesiodic *Theogony*, see Pucci 2007.

[13] PR 82, with reference to the term <u>aporetic question</u> used by Race 1990:104. See also Bundy 1972:47.

[14] At verse 19 of the *Homeric Hymn to Apollo*, the manuscript reading is γάρ, while at 207, it is τ' ἄρ.

2§4. Perfecting the *humnos*

> For how shall I <u>hymn</u> you, you who are so <u>absolutely [*pantōs*] good for hymning [*eu-humnos*]</u>?[15]

2§24 Faced with the absoluteness of the god, the performer experiences a rhetorical hesitation: how can I make the subject of my *humnos* something that is perfect, absolute? The absoluteness of this hymnic subject is signaled by the programmatic adverb *pantōs* 'absolutely', which modifies not only the adjective *eu-humnos* 'good for hymning' but also the entire phrasing about the absoluteness of the subject.[16] The absoluteness of the god Apollo is continuous with the absoluteness of the *humnos* that makes Apollo its subject. This *Homeric Hymn* is saying about itself that it is the perfect and absolute *humnos*. As such, it is not only the beginning of a composition but also the totality of the composition, authorizing everything that follows it, because it was begun so perfectly. And the source of the perfection is the god as the subject of the *humnos*. As we will see from here on, this idea of the <u>hymnic subject</u> as the source of poetic perfection is all-pervasive in the history and prehistory of the *humnos*. Such is the theology, as it were, of the *humnos*.

2§25 The need for a perfect beginning in a *humnos* is precisely what motivates the aporetic questions of the *Homeric Hymn (3) to Apollo*, at verses 19 and 207. So also at verse 35 in the Hesiodic *Theogony*, as we saw earlier, there is an aporetic question, motivated by a need for a perfect beginning. I repeat here only the essentials. The *Theogony* begins when the persona of Hesiod says, at the beginning, ἀρχώμεθ' ἀείδειν 'let me begin [*arkhesthai*] to sing' (verse 1). He begins by singing the hymnic subject of the Muses of Mount Helicon (verses 1-2), who are performing a *humnos* (11 ὑμνεῦσαι). The Muses proceed to teach Hesiod their song (22), enjoining him to perform it (33). Just as they were performing a *humnos* (11 ὑμνεῦσαι), Hesiod must now perform a *humnos* in his own right (33 ὑμνεῖν), and the subject of this *humnos* is to be 'the genesis [*genos*] of the gods', that is, a theogony (33 ὑμνεῖν μακάρων γένος αἰὲν ἐόντων). In order to get this *humnos* started, the poet is told that that he must

---

[15] PR 82-83. Koller 1956:197 argues that the rhetorical strategy of this aporetic question at *Homeric Hymn to Apollo* 19 / 207 is a substitute for another strategy, which is the gesture of a metabasis or 'switch' to the consequent, that is, to the rest of the song. At a later point, I will have more to say about metabasis. Koller (p. 197) notes that the aporetic question of *Homeric Hymn to Apollo* 19 / 207 comes after *khaire / khairete* 'hail and take pleasure' at 14 /166, which is a performative gesture that calls on Leto and on the Delian Maidens respectively to reciprocate the pleasure that they have experienced from what has been said so far. At a later point, I will have more to say about *khaire / khairete*. I suggest that the aporetic question is intended to lead to a new beginning—as an alternative to a smooth transition to the consequent.

[16] On the syntax of *pantōs* 'absolutely' as an overall modifier of absolute phraseology, see for example Solon F 4.16 ed. West and the commentary in Nagy 1985:59-60, *PH* 9§7n38 (= p. 256).

begin with the Muses and end with the Muses (34), and, as we have already seen at the beginning of the song, he has indeed already begun with the Muses (1-2). Before Hesiod starts all over again with the Muses, there is a moment of rhetorical hesitation: signaling that he is about to make a decision in the midst of performance, he asks himself how to proceed, declaring an aporetic crisis (35). At this moment of hesitation, he is in effect asking himself: why am I going around in circles, looking for the origins (35)? Then, in the very next verse, he begins all over again by telling himself: Μουσάων ἀρχώμεθα 'let me begin [*arkhesthai*] with the Muses' (36). We now see that the figure of Hesiod has decided, after the moment of hesitation that leads to his aporetic question (35), to start all over again with the Muses (36), but now the Muses are no longer who they were when the poet had started, by invoking them as they sang and danced at the heights of Mount Helicon: rather, the Muses are now headed for the heights of Mount Olympus (52-62).

2§26 There are similar shifts taking place after the two aporetic questions in the *Homeric Hymn* (3) *to Apollo*. Before the first such question (19), we hear that Apollo is recognized as god of Delos, his birthplace (16-18). But then, right after this question, we hear that Apollo is recognized as god in every conceivable place (20 and following). Although the god is now said to be worshipped everywhere, the main place of Apollo's worship is pictured as Delos even after the first aporetic question—that is, until we come to a moment of hesitation expressed in the second aporetic question (207). After that question, the main place of Apollo's worship shifts to Delphi. Now the Muses of the *Homeric Hymn* (3) *to Apollo* are the Panhellenic Muses of Mount Olympus. Before the shift, as we are about to see, the Muses of the *Homeric Hymn* (3) *to Apollo* are not yet the Olympian Muses. Rather, they are the local Muses of Delos, the Delian Maidens.

2⑤5. Homer's hymnic encounter with the Delian Maidens

2§27 The main speaker of the *Homeric Hymn* (3) *to Apollo*, who is not named in the *Hymn*, was understood to be Homer. Thucydides, who quotes extensively from the *Hymn* as it was known in his time, says explicitly that the author of the *Homeric Hymn to Apollo* is *Homēros* (Ὅμηρος) 'Homer' (3.104.4). In this *Hymn*, a choral ensemble of Delian Maidens is described as encountering the main speaker, Homer himself, who calls on the ensemble to 'respond', *hupokrinesthai*, to anyone who asks about him:

2⑤5. Homer's hymnic encounter with the Delian Maidens

2①6 *Homeric Hymn (3) to Apollo* 156-178

  πρὸς δὲ τόδε μέγα <u>θαῦμα</u>, ὅου κλέος οὔποτ' ὀλεῖται,
  κοῦραι Δηλιάδες Ἑκατηβελέταο θεράπναι·
  αἵ τ' ἐπεὶ ἄρ πρῶτον μὲν Ἀπόλλων' <u>ὑμνήσωσιν</u>,
  αὖτις δ' αὖ Λητώ τε καὶ Ἄρτεμιν ἰοχέαιραν,
160 μνησάμεναι ἀνδρῶν τε παλαιῶν ἠδὲ γυναικῶν
  <u>ὕμνον</u> ἀείδουσιν, θέλγουσι δὲ φῦλ' ἀνθρώπων.
  πάντων δ' ἀνθρώπων φωνὰς καὶ κρεμβαλιαστὺν
  <u>μιμεῖσθ'</u> ἴσασιν· φαίη δέ κεν αὐτὸς ἕκαστος
  φθέγγεσθ'· οὕτω σφιν καλὴ <u>συνάρηρεν</u> ἀοιδή.
165 ἀλλ' ἄγεθ' ἱλήκοι μὲν Ἀπόλλων Ἀρτέμιδι ξύν,
  <u>χαίρετε</u> δ' ὑμεῖς πᾶσαι· ἐμεῖο δὲ καὶ μετόπισθε
  μνήσασθ', <u>ὁππότε κέν τις</u> ἐπιχθονίων ἀνθρώπων
  ἐνθάδ' <u>ἀνείρηται</u> ξεῖνος ταλαπείριος ἐλθών·
  ὦ κοῦραι, <u>τίς</u> δ' ὕμμιν ἀνὴρ ἥδιστος ἀοιδῶν
170 ἐνθάδε πωλεῖται, καὶ <u>τέῳ</u> <u>τέρπεσθε</u> μάλιστα;
  ὑμεῖς δ' εὖ μάλα πᾶσαι <u>ὑποκρίνασθαι</u> ἀφ' ἡμέων·[17]
  τυφλὸς ἀνήρ, <u>οἰκεῖ</u> δὲ <u>Χίῳ</u> ἔνι παιπαλοέσσῃ,
  τοῦ πᾶσαι μετόπισθεν ἀριστεύουσιν ἀοιδαί.
  ἡμεῖς δ' ὑμέτερον κλέος οἴσομεν ὅσσον ἐπ' αἶαν
175 ἀνθρώπων στρεφόμεσθα πόλεις εὖ ναιεταώσας·
  οἱ δ' ἐπὶ δὴ πείσονται, ἐπεὶ καὶ ἐτήτυμόν ἐστιν.
  αὐτὰρ ἐγὼν <u>οὐ λήξω</u> ἑκηβόλον Ἀπόλλωνα
  <u>ὑμνέων</u> ἀργυρότοξον ὃν ἠΰκομος τέκε Λητώ.

---

[17] I read here ὑποκρίνασθαι (infinitive used as imperative) not ὑποκρίνασθε (imperative). And I read ἀφ' ἡμέων not ἀμφ' ἡμέων (both textual variants are attested in the medieval manuscript tradition).

Chapter Two

> And on top of that, there is this great thing of <u>wonder</u>
> [*thauma*],[18] the fame [*kleos*] of which will never perish:
> the Delian Maidens, attendants [*therapnai*] of the one who
> shoots from afar.
> So[19] when they <u>make</u> Apollo their <u>humnos</u>[20] first and foremost,
> and then Leto and Artemis, shooter of arrows,
> 160   they keep in mind men of the past and women too,
> as they sing the <u>humnos</u>, and they enchant all different kinds
> of humanity.
> All humans' voices and rhythms[21]
> they know how to <u>re-enact</u> [*mimeîsthai*].[22] And each single
> person would say that his own voice
> was their voice. That is how their beautiful song has each of
> its parts <u>fitting together</u> [*sun-arariskein*] in place.
> 165   But come now, may Apollo be gracious, along with Artemis;

---

[18] This word *thauma* 'thing of wonder' conveys a spectacular visual experience. Comparable is the *thauma* of the serpent as analyzed in ch. 1. In the *Lives of Homer*, as I show in HPC I§§120–123, the same word *thauma* marks the universal response to Homer's poetry.

[19] The particle ἄρα / ῥα / ἄρ 'so, then' has an "evidentiary" force, indicating that the speaker notionally <u>sees</u> what is simultaneously being spoken. See Bakker 2005:80, 84, 97–100, 104, 146, 172n33.

[20] On the occasion of singing a *humnos*, the god who is being sung in the *humnos*—who is the subject of the humnos—is metonymically equated with the humnos itself: by metonymy, the god <u>is</u> the song.

[21] A variant reading here is *bambaliastus*. See PH 1§48n130 (= p. 43). The noun *krembaliastus* indicates the creation of rhythm by way of musical instruments of percussion, such as *krotala*, and this rhythm is distinctly choral: see the argumentation of Peponi 2009, who also adduces iconographical evidence showing the Muses themselves in the act of singing and dancing while playing on *krotala*.

[22] Here in *Homeric Hymn to Apollo* 163, I take special note of the verb *mimeîsthai* 're-enact, imitate', derived from *mimos* 'mime'; the derivative noun *mimēsis* and its relatives have distinctly choral and even theatrical associations. See PP 80–81. On the psychology of "empathy" in such re-enactment by way of choral song and dance, see Peponi 2009:60–68.

and you all also, <u>hail and take pleasure</u> [*khairete*],²³ all of you [Maidens of Delos]. Keep me, even in the future,

in your mind, <u>whenever someone</u>, out of the whole mass of earthbound humanity,

comes here [to Delos], after arduous wandering, as a guest entitled to the rules of hosting, and <u>asks this question</u>:

"O Maidens, <u>who</u> is for you the most pleasurable of singers

170   that wanders here? <u>In whom</u> do you <u>take</u> the most <u>delight</u> [*terpesthai*]?"

Then you, all of you [Maidens of Delos], must very properly <u>respond</u> [*hupokrinesthai*]²⁴ about me:²⁵

"It is a blind man, and he <u>dwells</u> [*oikeîn*] in <u>Chios</u>, a rugged land, and all his songs will in the future prevail as the very best."

And I²⁶ in turn will carry your fame [*kleos*] as far over the earth

175   as I roam, throughout the cities of men, with their fair populations.

And they will all believe—I now see—since it is genuine [*etētumon*].

As for me, <u>I will not leave off</u> [*lēgein*] <u>making</u> far-shooting Apollo

---

²³ I translate *khaire* / *khairete* here at *Homeric Hymn to Apollo* 166 as 'hail and take pleasure'. The verb *khairein* is related to the noun *kharis*, which is analogous to the Latin noun *gratia* in combining the ideas of pleasure ('gratification') and beauty ('gracefulness') by way of reciprocity ('graciousness'), as I argued in ch. 1. The imperative *khaire* / *khairete* is used in contexts of marking the beginning or ending of a personal encounter, which I render by way of 'hail!'. In the *Homeric Hymns*, *khaire* / *khairete* marks a transition from focusing on a god or on an aspect of a god to focusing on the rest of the song. See also Calame 2005:26-28.
²⁴ The infinitive ὑποκρίνασθαι, as I noted above, is used here as an imperative.
²⁵ In a quotation made by Thucydides (3.104.5) from the *Homeric Hymn to Apollo*, we find in the corresponding verse not ἀφ' ἡμέων 'about me' but ἀφήμως. This variant reading ἀφήμως is not corrupt, as we see from the entry in the lexicographical tradition represented by Hesychius: ἀφήμως· ἐν κόσμῳ, ἡσυχῇ. The interpretation ἐν κόσμῳ, ἡσυχῇ 'in an orderly or serene way' seems to be a guess, however, based on the context of verse 171. A more likely interpretation is 'without naming names', since the adjective ἄφημος was understood to be a synonym of ἀπευθής (as we see in the scholia to Aratus 1.270.2 ed. Martin 1974). This word ἀπευθής is used in the sense of 'without information', as in *Odyssey* iii 88 and 184. When the Delian Maidens are asked to respond to the question 'who is the singer?' they respond without naming names, that is, without giving information about the singer's name. I propose that the textual variants ἀφ' ἡμέων and ἀφήμως are authentic formulaic variants.
²⁶ Literally, 'we'.

my humnos,²⁷ the one with the silver quiver, who was born of Leto with the beautiful hair.

2§28 The context of the word *hupokrinesthai* 'respond' here at verse 171 of the *Homeric Hymn* (3) *to Apollo* needs to be compared to the contexts of the same word in the *Iliad* and *Odyssey*. From the analysis I presented in Chapter 1, we can see that this word has mantic and even riddling connotations. Also, it conveys the idea of fixity, rigidity, as we saw in the case of an inscription recording the fixed response made by a statue to any questions addressed to it (*CEG* 286). It is with this background in mind that I analyze the 'response' of the Delian Maidens as spoken first by the main speaker of the *Hymn*, who quotes what the Maidens will respond. As I will argue, the same quoted response is imagined as radiating from the same speaker—let us for the moment continue to call him 'Homer'—as if from some statue, over and over again for eternity.

2ⓢ6. Homer as theatrical spectacle

2§29 There is an element of theatrical spectacle in the quoted Homeric response of the *Homeric Hymn* (3) *to Apollo*, and this element is implicit in the use of *hupokrinesthai* 'respond' at verse 171. As I have already argued in Chapter 1, the 'responsion' conveyed by this verb *hupokrinesthai* is performative, not just interpersonal. Further, we have already seen there the usages of *hupokrinesthai* and *hupokritēs* in the sense of 'act' and 'actor' in the context of the *theatron* 'theater'. Now we see that the *Homeric Hymn* (3) *to Apollo* makes the theatricality explicit, at verse 163, by way of the word *mimeîsthai* 're-enact'.²⁸ In earlier work, I have argued that the Delian Maidens of the *Homeric Hymn* (3) *to Apollo* are in effect offering to make a *mimēsis* of Homer, that is, to 're-enact' him, and Homer responds by making a *mimēsis* of them.²⁹ Here I hope to expand on my earlier argumentation.

2§30 To begin, I must take a moment to review the relationship between poets and Muses. In archaic Greek poetry, formulaic descriptions of the Muses are closely related to formulaic descriptions of the generic poet or *aoidos* 'singer'.³⁰ The characteristics of the Muses, as defined in formulas describing

---

[27] Once again, the god who is being sung in the *humnos*—who is the subject of the *humnos*—is metonymically equated with the *humnos* itself: by metonymy, the god is the song.

[28] See the note above on *Homeric Hymn to Apollo* verse 163.

[29] *PH* 12§71 (= pp. 375–376); *PP* 82. My arguments there can be used to complement the arguments of Peponi 2009:60–68 about the psychology of "empathy" in the choral performance of the Delian Maidens.

[30] *BA* 17§9 (= pp. 296–297).

2⑤6. Homer as theatrical spectacle

them, reflect the characteristics of the *aoidos* in a variety of performative contexts.[31]

2§31 These performative contexts include situations where the *aoidos* is interacting with a *khoros* 'chorus', that is, with a singing and dancing ensemble. The *partheneia* of Alcman are a case in point: here we see a variety of ritual situations where the *aoidos* is interacting with a chorus composed of elite local girls of Sparta who, at the moment of singing and dancing, are notionally re-enacting the singing and dancing of local goddesses (as in Alcman PMG 1).[32]

2§32 As we saw earlier, the Muses themselves can be idealized as a *khoros* 'chorus' of local goddesses who perform their choral song and dance in a locale that is sacred to them.[33] When the Muses in the Hesiodic *Theogony* are imagined as starting the performance of their song, which is a "theogony" in its own right and thus a model for Hesiod the *aoidos*, they perform in the mode of a *khoros* of local goddesses singing and dancing in a locale sacred to them, Mount Helicon (*Theogony* 3-4, 70).

2§33 The relationship between the *aoidos* of the Hesiodic *Theogony* and the chorus of Heliconian Muses is matched by the relationship between the *aoidos* of the *Homeric Hymn to Apollo* and the Delian Maidens, as we see it dramatized in the passage I just quoted and translated from the *Homeric Hymn (3) to Apollo*. These Maidens, described as the *therapnai* 'attendants' of the god Apollo (157), are addressed by the poet of this *Homeric Hymn* with the hymnic salutation *khairete* (166), in conjunction with the god Apollo (165).[34] I translate this salutation as 'hail and take pleasure', and I have already given my reasons in my note on the verse containing the salutation (166): the verb *khairein* is related to the noun *kharis*, which conveys the idea of 'favor' or 'graciousness' in the sense of <u>reciprocated beauty and pleasure</u>.[35] With his salutation of *khairete* (166), the *aoidos* is asking the Delian Maidens to accept the *kharis* 'favor' of his song and to give him their 'favor', their *kharis*, in return. The hymnic salutation *khaire / khairete* is used in the *Homeric Hymns* to address the given god / gods presiding over the performance of each given hymn. Similarly in the Hesiodic *Theogony*,

---

[31] The ritual identification of the *aoidos* 'singer' with the Muses is made explicit in the designation of the generic *aoidos* as Μουσάων θεράπων '*therapōn* of the Muses'. On *therapōn* 'attendant' in the earlier sense of 'ritual substitute', see BA 18§1-9 (= pp. 301-307), with special reference to the use of the epithet Μουσάων θεράπων '*therapōn* of the Muses' in the Life of Archilochus and Life of Aesop traditions. On the Hesiodic model of Μουσάων θεράπων '*therapōn* of the Muses' (*Theogony* 100), see GM 47-51.

[32] PH 12§20 (= pp. 346-347); PP 53-54, 57, 89-90, 92, 96.

[33] See also GM 57-58.

[34] See also GM 58.

[35] See also PR 82n37.

Chapter Two

the figure of Hesiod addresses the Muses with the hymnic salutation *khairete* (104) in the context of naming them, in conjunction with Apollo, as the divine sources of poetic power (94-95). In the *Homeric Hymn to Apollo*, the *aoidos* who addresses the Delian Maidens with the hymnic salutation *khairete* is imagined as Homer himself. To repeat, Thucydides (3.104.4) says explicitly that the author of the *Homeric Hymn to Apollo* is Homer.

2§34 I focus on the fact that the figure of Homer addresses the Delian Maidens with the hymnic salutation *khairete* in the *Homeric Hymn (3) to Apollo* (166) just as the figure of Hesiod addresses the Olympian Muses with the hymnic salutation *khairete* in the *Theogony* (104). The parallelism indicates that Homer is in effect addressing the local Muses of Delos, who are divine in their own right. It is not a contradiction, however, to maintain that the Delian Maidens are simultaneously envisioned as members of a local *khoros* 'chorus' of girls or women.[36] As I argued a moment ago, the role of divinity can be appropriated by members of a chorus during choral performance. That is to say, the Delian Maidens as a choral ensemble can re-enact the local Delian Muses.[37]

2§35 Homer's dramatized encounter with the Delian Maidens is comparable to Hesiod's dramatized encounter with the local Muses of Mount Helicon (*Theogony* 22-34), which leads to the transformation of their local theogony into the Panhellenic *Theogony* sung by Hesiod—and to their own transformation into the Panhellenic Muses of Mount Olympus (verses 52 and thereafter).[38] The Panhellenization of the Heliconian Muses is a matter of reciprocation:

---

[36] See Peponi 2009:54-55, 66n71. Also Calame 2001:30, 104, 110. Thucydides 3.104.5 refers to this chorus as *gunaikes* 'women'; accordingly, it may be too restrictive to say 'Delian Maidens', if the categories of choral groupings included women as well as unmarried 'maidens'; in that case, it may be preferable to use a more inclusive translation, 'Deliades'.

[37] See my note for *Homeric Hymn to Apollo* verse 163 at 2§27. The designation of the Delian Maidens as *therapnai* 'attendants' of the god Apollo in the *Homeric Hymn to Apollo* (157) is comparable to the designation of the generic *aoidos* 'singer' as *therapōn* 'attendant' of the Muses (Μουσάων θεράπων), as in the Hesiodic *Theogony* (100). Since the feminine form *therapnē* is related to the masculine *therapōn*, I suggest that the Delian Maidens as choral performers are surrogates of Apollo and, by extension, of his choral ensemble of Muses, just as the generic *aoidos* 'singer' in the *Theogony* is a surrogate of the Muses, and by extension, of their choral leader Apollo. On Apollo as a metonym for Apollo and the Muses in choral contexts, see *PH* 12§§29 (= pp. 350-351) and 58 (= p. 370). On *therapōn* 'attendant' in the earlier sense of 'ritual substitute', I refer again to *BA* 18§1-9 (= pp. 301-307), with special reference to the use of the epithet Μουσάων θεράπων '*therapōn* of the Muses' in the Life of Archilochus and Life of Aesop traditions. On the Hesiodic model of Μουσάων θεράπων '*therapōn* of the Muses' (*Theogony* 100), I refer again to *GM* 47-51. With reference to the word *therapnai* 'attendants', consider also the Laconian place-name Therapna (Serapna), which I interpret as a metonym like *Mukēnē*, *Thēbē*, and so on (on these place names, see *HTL* 163).

[38] See *GM* 58.

they are transformed into Olympian Muses because they transform Hesiod, who is implicitly a generic *aoidos* 'singer' and master of *kleos* 'fame' (*Theogony* 99-101).[39] They transform Hesiod into a Panhellenic figure in his own right, who articulates a single *Theogony* that notionally supersedes all other potential theogonies in its truth value (22-34).[40] Further, the local *humnos* of the Heliconian Muses has been transformed into the Panhellenic *humnos* of the Olympian Muses. As I have already argued earlier, the Hesiodic *Theogony* ultimately defines itself as one single continuous gigantic *humnos*.

2§36 Similarly in the *Homeric Hymn (3) to Apollo*, the dramatized encounter of the *aoidos* with the local Delian Maidens leads to the transformation of their local *humnos* 'hymn' to Apollo (ὑμνήσωσιν at 158, ὕμνον at 161) into the Panhellenic *Hymn to Apollo* sung by a man described as 'the most pleasing of all singers [*aoidoi*]' (169). This *aoidos* 'singer' is further described, in the words of the Delian Maidens, as a blind man whose home is on the island of Chios (172). His *aoidai* 'songs', as the words of the Delian Maidens prophesy, will be supreme, performed throughout the cities of humankind (173-175).

2§37 This *aoidos* of the *Homeric Hymn (3) to Apollo*, like Hesiod, is a master of *kleos* 'fame': he speaks about the *kleos* of the hymn performed by the Delian Maidens (*Hymn to Apollo* 156), and he promises that he will spread that *kleos* (174) throughout all the cities he visits (173-175). The Panhellenization of the Delian Maidens, like the Panhellenization of the Heliconian Muses, is a matter of reciprocated *kleos*. The description of the blind *aoidos* from Chios who will spread the *kleos* of the Delian Maidens throughout the cities of humankind (172-175) starts with a quotation spoken by the Delian Maidens (172-173) in response to an unnamed wanderer, 'someone' (*tis*) who arrives in Delos and asks the Delian Maidens this question: who is the best *aoidos* of all? (169-170). When the Delian Maidens 'respond' (ὑποκρίνασθαι 171) to the question of this unnamed wanderer, of this 'someone', it is the quotation of their performed words that reciprocates the *kleos*: the quoted response of the Maidens (173-175) identifies the best *aoidos* with the *aoidos* who quotes their response about him, who will confer *kleos* on the Delian Maidens as he wanders throughout the cities of humankind.

2§38 In the riddling language of the *Homeric Hymn (3) to Apollo*, the unnamed wanderer to Delos, this 'someone' whose question to the Delian Maidens is quoted in the *Hymn* (169-170), can be the same persona as the

---

[39] I quote *Theogony* 99–101 at a later point. In this context, Hesiod as generic *aoidos* 'singer' is called '*therapōn* of the Muses'.
[40] HQ 124–128.

unnamed *aoidos* 'singer' of the *Hymn* who quotes the response of the Delian Maidens (172-173), who is the same persona as the unnamed *aoidos* who will now wander from Delos to all the cities of humankind, a bearer of the *kleos* 'fame' that is reciprocated between him and the Maidens (174-175). This composite unnamed persona is the figure of Homer himself.

2§39 The identity of Homer in the *Homeric Hymn* (3) *to Apollo* is expressed by way of riddling and even mantic speech. The description of the 'someone' who has reached Delos after arduous wanderings (167-168) anticipates the response (174-175) to the question 'who?' (169-170). That response (174-175) pictures the master singer who wanders throughout the cities of humankind. But this master singer is not explicitly named as Homer. Instead, his identity is implicit in the riddle posed by the question: he is the answer to the question 'who?'—but he is also the 'someone' that asks the question 'who?' The response of the Delian Maidens is Homer's own response, since their response is quoted by him. The singer who leaves Delos with an answer loops back to the singer who arrives at Delos with a question.[41] This looping effect has its own significance: each time this wandering singer arrives at Delos, he becomes a regeneration of Homer as he sings in Delos. Each time the figure of Homer is pictured as singing in Delos, the Delian Maidens authorize him all over again. The eternal return of Homer is made possible by the notionally eternal recycling of his songs.

2§40 Here I come back full circle to what I said earlier, that the Delian Maidens of the *Homeric Hymn* (3) *to Apollo* are in effect offering to make a *mimēsis* 're-enactment' of Homer, and that Homer responds by making a *mimēsis* 're-enactment' of them. In the mythical world of the *Homeric Hymn to Apollo*, epic performance is being assimilated to a theatrical performance by an idealized chorus of local Muses, the Delian Maidens.

2Ⓢ7. The naming of Homer

2§41 The interaction of the Delian Maidens with Homer is expressed in this description of these singing local Muses:

---

[41] In the *Homeric Hymn to Apollo* (168), according to the version quoted by Thucydides 3.104.5, the wanderer who arrives at Delos is described as *allos*—seemingly some person 'other' than the speaker. Even in terms of this variant, my formulation holds: this seemingly 'other' person becomes the same person as the speaker—once the response of the Delian Maidens to that 'other' person is actually quoted by the speaker.

2⑤7. The naming of Homer

2①7 *Homeric Hymn* (3) *to Apollo* 164

οὕτω σφιν καλὴ <u>συνάρηρεν</u> ἀοιδή

That is how their beautiful song has each of its parts <u>fitting together</u> [*sun-arariskein*] in place.

2§42 The collocation here of *sun-* 'together' and *arariskein* 'fit' is parallel, I submit, to the collocation of *homo-* 'together' and *arariskein* 'fit' in this other description of singing Muses:

2①8 Hesiod *Theogony* 39

φωνῇ <u>ὁμηρεῦσαι</u>

<u>making things fit together</u> [*homēreuein*] with their sound

There is a similar usage of *arariskein* 'fit' in this further description of the singing Muses:

2①9 Hesiod *Theogony* 29

<u>ἀρτιέπειαι</u>

having words [*epos* plural] <u>fitted</u> [*arariskein*] together

2§43 The theme of Hesiod's interaction with these singing Muses is embedded in his poetic name, which is *Hēsiodos* (Ἡσίοδος *Theogony* 22). I interpret the etymology of this name as *hēsi-wodos, meaning 'he who emits the voice'. The first part of this compound formation *hēsi-wodos comes from the root of the verb *hienai* (ἱέναι) 'emit', while the second part comes from the root of the noun *au̯dē* (αὐδή) 'voice'.[42] There is a semantic correspondence between this etymology and the description of the singing Muses as ὄσσαν ἱεῖσαι 'emitting the voice' (*Theogony* 10, 43, 65, 67), which applies to them in a choral context (7-8, 63). An analogous point can be made about the etymology of the poetic name of Homer, *Homēros* (Ὅμηρος, Thucydides 3.104.4). I argue that the morphology of this name can be explained as a compound formation *hom-āros meaning 'he who fits [the song] together', composed of the prefix *homo-* (ὁμο-) 'together' and the root of the verb *arariskein* (ἀραρίσκειν).[43] There is a semantic correspondence between this etymology and the description of the singing Muses as φωνῇ ὁμηρεῦσαι 'fitting things together [*homēreuein*]

---

[42] *GM* 47n32.
[43] *BA* 17§§9-13 (= pp. 296-300). The meaning 'fitting together' is linked with the metaphorical world of the craft of woodworking.

with their sound' (*Theogony* 39) and ἀρτιέπειαι 'having words [*epea*] fitted [*arariskein*] together' (*Theogony* 29), again in an analogous choral context.⁴⁴

2§44 This etymology of *Homēros* comes to life in the words describing Homer interacting with the singing Delian Maidens, whom I have compared earlier with the singing Heliconian Muses of Hesiod:

2①10 *Homeric Hymn (3) to Apollo* 164

οὕτω σφιν καλὴ <u>συνάρηρεν</u> ἀοιδή

That is how their beautiful song has each of its parts <u>fitting together</u> [<u>sun-arariskein</u>] in place.

2§45 I see in this theatrical moment of interaction the signature, as it were, of Homer himself—that is, of *Homēros* (Ὅμηρος) as a *nomen loquens* designating the one 'who fits the song together'.⁴⁵

2⑤8. Homer's perfect *humnos*

2§46 With this background in place, I am ready to consider the *mimēsis* of Homer by the Delian Maidens. The *Homeric Hymn to Apollo*, conceived as a perfect and absolute *humnos*, becomes a perfect and absolute *mimēsis* of Homer. Here I concentrate on three passages that signal this *mimēsis*. In the first passage, we see the Delian Maidens beginning their performance of the *humnos* by making the god Apollo continuous with the *humnos*:

2①11 *Homeric Hymn (3) to Apollo* 158

αἵ τ' ἐπεὶ ἄρ πρῶτον μὲν Ἀπόλλων' <u>ὑμνήσωσιν</u>

So when they <u>make</u> Apollo their <u>humnos</u> first and foremost

In the second passage, we see the Delian Maidens continuing their performance of the *humnos* by making the subject of their song not only the god Apollo (158) and his divine sister and mother, Artemis and Leto (158-159), but also the 'men and women of the past':

---

⁴⁴ *PH* 12§66 (= pp. 372-373).

⁴⁵ *BA* 17§§9-13 (= pp. 296-300), including a discussion of an alternative explanation by Durante 1976:194-197. See also West 1999, who argues that the name of Homer, *Homēros*, is merely a back-formation derived from *Homēridai*, and that Homer is a "fictitious person" (p. 372). I offer a different argument in *HPC* I§142.

2○12 *Homeric Hymn (3) to Apollo* 160-161

> μνησάμεναι ἀνδρῶν τε παλαιῶν ἠδὲ γυναικῶν
> <u>ὕμνον</u> ἀείδουσιν
>
> they keep in mind men of the past and women too,
> as they sing the <u>humnos</u>

In the third passage, we now see 'Homer' himself performing the *humnos*, making the god Apollo continuous with his *humnos*:

2○13 *Homeric Hymn (3) to Apollo* 177-178

> αὐτὰρ ἐγὼν οὐ <u>λήξω</u> ἑκηβόλον Ἀπόλλωνα
> <u>ὑμνέων</u>
>
> As for me, I will not <u>leave off</u> [*lēgein*] making the far-shooting
> Apollo my *humnos*.

2§47 Of course, 'Homer' has been the *ex post facto* performer of the *humnos* to Apollo from the very start, by way of interacting with the Delian Maidens as they perform their *humnos*. The interaction is signaled when Homer tells the Delian Maidens: ὑποκρίνασθαι ἀφ᾽ ἡμέων 'make response [*hupokrinesthai*] from me' (*Homeric Hymn to Apollo* 171). The first time I translated this phrase, I rendered the meaning of *apo-* in the expression ἀφ᾽ ἡμέων as 'about me'—literally, 'from us'.[46] The 'response' of the Delian Maidens comes <u>from</u> Homer, but it is also <u>about</u> Homer, since Homer is identified by his audience through the voice of the Delian Maidens. Now, if we could hear what the Delian Maidens are pictured as singing when they sing their *humnos* at verse 161, what would be their 'response', their *hupokrisis*, to the question asked by Homer? That 'response', signaled by the word *hupokrinesthai* at verse 171, is to be found in the two verses, 172-173, where the Delian Maidens answer the singer's question by saying these words:

2○14 *Homeric Hymn (3) to Apollo* 172-173

> τυφλὸς ἀνήρ, οἰκεῖ δὲ Χίῳ ἔνι παιπαλοέσσῃ,
> τοῦ πᾶσαι μετόπισθεν ἀριστεύουσιν ἀοιδαί.
>
> "It is a blind man, and he dwells in Chios, a rugged land,
> and all his songs will in the future prevail as the very best."

---

[46] 2§27.

2§48 I translate not 'will in the future be best' but 'will in the future prevail as the very best'. This response is a prophecy—as expressed by *metopisthen* 'in the future'. In the logic of the prophecy, a reference is being made to the songs of Homer himself in the future. These songs are prefigured as absolutely fixed in their ultimate permanence. That is, the songs of Homer are imagined as becoming a fixed text in the fullness of time. The figure of Homer himself can now be viewed as the sum total of his notionally perfect songs. He can now become static, no longer fluid. As I argue in the twin book *Homer the Preclassic*, this Homer is imagined to be the author of the *Iliad* and *Odyssey* as possessed by the 'descendants of Homer', the *Homēridai*.⁴⁷

2§49 Once the collective voice of the Delian Maidens has been quoted about Homer, the solo voice of the figure of Homer himself can take over. Homer proceeds to speak by continuing the *humnos* that the collective voice of the Delian Maidens had started together with him. I quote again the third passage:

2ⓣ15 *Homeric Hymn* (3) *to Apollo* 177-178

αὐτὰρ ἐγὼν οὐ <u>λήξω</u> ἑκηβόλον Ἀπόλλωνα

<u>ὑμνέων</u>

As for me, I will not <u>leave off</u> [*lēgein*] making the far-shooting Apollo

my <u>humnos</u>.

2§50 The exchange that we have just seen dramatized here between Homer the soloist and the choral ensemble of Delian Maidens is technically a choral exchange. The *humnos* that had started off as a collective expression of the choral ensemble is now being continued as the individual expression of Homer himself. As I have already argued, this exchange between Homer and the choral ensemble of the Delian Maidens is parallel to the exchange in the Hesiodic *Theogony* between Hesiod and the choral ensemble of Heliconian Muses. An individuated member of an ensemble speaks to the ensemble and quotes them, so that the collective quotation of the ensemble may now validate his individuality.⁴⁸

2§51 After the exchange of Homer with the choral ensemble of Delian Maidens, whom I have described as the local Muses of Delos, and after the

---

⁴⁷ *HPC* I§§141-156.
⁴⁸ As Marco Fantuzzi points out to me, there is a comparable theme to be found in *Hymn* 5 of Callimachus, *The Bath of Pallas*.

declaration of Homer that he will not leave off making Apollo the subject of his *humnos* (as we have just seen in *Hymn to Apollo* 177-178), Apollo himself takes leave of the island of Delos and ascends to Olympus (186 ἔνθεν δὲ πρὸς Ὄλυμπον . . .), where he begins his interaction with the choral ensemble of Panhellenic Muses, who are described as singing with a beautiful voice (189 πᾶσαι ἀμειβόμεναι ὀπὶ καλῇ). What the Muses sing is a *humnos* (190 ὑμνεῦσιν), which involves not just singing but also dancing (196 ὀρχεῦντ'): the description focuses on the dancing performed by goddesses accompanying the Muses, specifically, by the *Kharites* or 'Graces' and the *Hōrai* or 'Seasons' (194 ἐϋπλόκαμοι Χάριτες καὶ ἐΰφρονες Ὧραι),[49] along with the goddesses Harmonia, Hebe, and Aphrodite (195); joining in the song and dance is Artemis herself (197-199; the use of μεταμέλπεται at 197 indicates that the goddess is imagined as singing as well as dancing).[50] The god Apollo himself is pictured as the leader of this Olympian choral performance as he plays the *kithara* (201) and dances (202-203 καλὰ καὶ ὕψι βιβάς, αἴγλη δέ μιν ἀμφιφαείνει | μαρμαρυγαί τε ποδῶν). Thus the *humnos* of the *Homeric Hymn (3) to Apollo*, which started as the performance of what I have been calling the local Muses of Delos, has been transformed into the performance of the Olympian Muses led by the god Apollo himself.[51] We saw a comparable transformation in the Hesiodic *Theogony*, where the *humnos* of the Heliconian Muses becomes the *humnos* of the Olympian Muses.

2§52 At this point in the *Homeric Hymn (3) to Apollo*, where the subject of the *humnos* is being transformed from the Apollo of Delos to the Apollo of Delphi, the second of the two aporetic questions in the *Hymn* is activated. After the first aporetic question, as we already saw, the perspective shifts from Apollo as god of Delos to Apollo as god of all Hellenes, though the hymnic subject remains Apollo at Delos. After the second aporetic question, the perspective shifts from Apollo at Delos to Apollo at Delphi:

2①16 *Homeric Hymn (3) to Apollo* 207

πῶς τ'ἄρ[52] σ' ὑμνήσω πάντως εὔυμνον ἐόντα

---

[49] The epithet of the *Kharites* 'Graces' here, *eu-plokamoi* 'with their tresses beautifully plaited', is relevant the description of Euphorbos as a *beau mort* in the *Iliad*. I analyze that description in *HPC* II§425.

[50] *PH* 12§29n62 (= p. 350) and n64 (= p. 351).

[51] As Marco Fantuzzi points out to me, there is a comparable theme to be found in *Hymn 2* of Callimachus, the *Hymn to Apollo*.

[52] At verse 19, the location of the first aporetic question, the manuscript reading is γάρ, while at 207, the location of the second, it is τ'ἄρ.

Chapter Two

> For how shall I <u>hymn</u> you, you who are so <u>absolutely [*pantōs*] good for hymning</u>?

2§53 Not only is there a shift from Apollo at Delos to Apollo at Delphi as the point of concentration for the *Homeric Hymn (3) to Apollo*. The ongoing *humnos* has by now become an Olympian performance. We see the god Apollo himself emerging as the leader of a choral ensemble of Olympian Muses, joined by all the other Olympian gods, and this joint Olympian choral performance becomes the essence of the perfect *humnos*. At this moment, Apollo emerges as the absolutely perfect model of the *humnos*. His performance makes him the perfect maker of the *humnos*, not only the perfect subject of this *humnos*. As the perfect maker of what must be the perfect *humnos*, he becomes the model for the eternal remaking of his *humnos*, season after season.[53] This *humnos* must not stop. It must keep looping back to its perfect beginning. It is as the continuator of this *humnos* that Homer experiences his two aporetic crises in the *Homeric Hymn (3) to Apollo*. Just as Apollo takes the lead in the performance of a *humnos* by a choral ensemble of Olympian Muses, we have seen Homer already taking the lead in the performance of that same *humnos* by a choral ensemble of Delian Maidens.

2ⓢ9. A prototype of *humnos* in the *Poetics* of Aristotle

2§54 In the *Homeric Hymn (3) to Apollo*, we see a self-representation of a performer in the act of taking the lead in the performance of a *humnos* by a choral ensemble and thereby becoming a soloist. The performer is Homer, and the divine model for his individuation out of a *khoros* 'chorus' is Apollo himself. What the poetry represents as a single act on the part of the performer can also be viewed as a complex process of evolution, where the figure of the soloist takes shape only by virtue of evolving out of the ensemble. Such a view is compatible with the theorizing of Aristotle about the *humnos* as a choral prototype of epic and tragedy.

2§55 In the *Poetics*, Aristotle reconstructs a prehistoric dichotomy between the ethics of proto-poets who are *semnoteroi* or 'more stately' and the ethics of would-be proto-poets who are by comparison *eutelesteroi*, that is, 'of less value'. According to this construct, poets who are *semnoteroi* are those

---

[53] In ch. 4, I will examine a parallel sacred model: the goddess Athena is the perfect maker of her own robe or peplos, and she thus becomes the model for the eternal remaking of her peplos, season after season. And the seasonally recurring occasion of this remaking is the festival of the Panathenaia.

engaged in the *mimēsis* or 're-enactment' of actions that are *kala* 'noble' and that are performed by those who are *kaloi* 'noble', while poets who are *euteles-teroi* 'of less value' are characterized by actions that are *phaula* 'base' and are performed by those who are *phauloi* 'base'. Here is the wording of Aristotle:

2Ⓣ17 Aristotle *Poetics* 1448b25-27

> οἱ μὲν γὰρ <u>σεμνότεροι</u> τὰς καλὰς <u>ἐμιμοῦντο</u> πράξεις καὶ τὰς τῶν τοιούτων, οἱ δὲ εὐτελέστεροι τὰς τῶν φαύλων, πρῶτον ψόγους ποιοῦντες, ὥσπερ ἕτεροι <u>ὕμνους</u> καὶ <u>ἐγκώμια</u>.

> The <u>more stately</u> ones [= <u>semnoteroi</u>] <u>made mimēsis</u> [1] of noble deeds and [2] of the deeds of [other] such stately ones, while the ones who were of less value [made *mimēsis*] of the deeds of the base. In the beginning, the latter made invectives [*psogoi*], while the former made <u>humnoi</u> and <u>enkōmia</u>.

2§56 I highlight two points that Aristotle is making here in the *Poetics* (1448b27): first, *humnoi* 'hymns' and *enkōmia* 'encomia, celebrations, songs of praise' are the undifferentiated prototypes of epic and tragedy, and, second, both these prototypes involve *mimēsis* 're-enactment'.[54] Of special relevance is a third point that Aristotle makes elsewhere in the *Poetics*: it is not only the prototypical *humnoi* and *enkōmia* but also epic and tragedy that involve the *mimēsis* 're-enactment' of the noble by the noble, as we see in several passages (1448a1-2, 26-27; 1448b34-36; 1449b9-10, 17-20, 24-28). In these passages, the word for 'noble' is *spoudaioi*, meaning literally 'the serious ones'.

2§57 The idea that the *spoudaioi* 'serious ones' and the *semnoteroi* 'more stately ones' are engaging in *mimēsis* 're-enactment' of what is noble is relevant to the use of the word *mimeîsthai* 're-enact' in the *Homeric Hymn* (3) *to Apollo* (verse 163). Here the performers of *mimēsis* are none other than the Delian Maidens, whose 'seriousness' or 'stateliness' is a given. And the *mimēsis* is taking place in the context of a *humnos*. For Aristotle, *mimēsis* takes place in prototypical *humnoi* that have not yet become differentiated into epic and tragedy. Here in the *Homeric Hymn to Apollo*, we see an approximation of such a model, to the extent that it resembles both epic and tragedy: this *Hymn* is like epic because it has the same meter as epic and because its diction is closely related to epic diction, while it is like tragedy because it is theatrical, as I have already argued with regard to the usage of the term *hupokrinesthai* 'respond', which refers to the quoted words of the Maidens in the *Hymn* (verse 171). As

---

[54] *PH* 6§91 (= pp. 197-198).

Chapter Two

for the usage of the term *mimeîsthai* 're-enact' in the *Hymn* (verse 163), it is in fact explicitly theatrical.[55]

2§58 In my previous work, I have argued that the use of a theatrical word like *mimeîsthai* in the *Homeric Hymn* (3) *to Apollo* (verse 171) reveals an early phase of an ongoing symbiosis of two elements: one is the Homeric tradition as it evolved at the Athenian festival of the Panathenaia and the other is the theatrical tradition of drama as it evolved at the Athenian festival of the City Dionysia.[56] Now I will argue that such symbiosis was facilitated by the medium of the *humnos* 'hymn' / *enkōmion* 'encomium, celebration, song of praise'— whether or not Aristotle is right in thinking of this medium as an undifferentiated prototype of epic and tragedy.[57]

2§59 From Aristotle's point of view, the prototypical medium of the *humnos* / *enkōmion* was a choral medium. This medium's eventual differentiation into epic and tragedy involved the individuation of its leading performers. That is, the performances of soloists emerged out of an ensemble of choral performers. Further, there was a differentiation of roles: a speaker of words was singled out from among an ensemble of singers and dancers. Such differentiation, as we are also about to see, is conveyed by Aristotle's use of the technical term *ex-arkhein*, in the sense of 'leading' a chorus. For Aristotle, the *ex-arkhōn* or 'leader' of a chorus was a prototypical actor in drama, whose *lexis* or 'speech' was differentiated from the rest of the singing and the dancing by the chorus.

2§60 In the *Poetics*, Aristotle develops this theory of differentiation in the broader context of reconstructing the prehistory of the four dramatic genres of the City Dionysia in Athens: tragedy, comedy, dithyramb, and satyr drama. In terms of Aristotle's reconstruction, all four of these dramatic genres resulted from progressive differentiations of earlier and less differentiated

---

[55] PP 80–81.
[56] PP 81. The symmetry of the Panathenaia and the City Dionysia as the two most important festivals of the Athenians is evident in a formulation by Demosthenes in the *First Philippic* (4.35).
[57] Aristotle's use of the terms *humnos* 'hymn' / *enkōmion* 'encomium, celebration, song of praise' is comparable to Plato's use of the terms *humnos* and *enkōmiazein* in the *Timaeus* (21a): τὴν θεὸν ... ἐν τῇ <u>πανηγύρει</u> δικαίως τε καὶ ἀληθῶς ... <u>ὑμνοῦντας ἐγκωμιάζειν</u> 'rightly and truthfully <u>celebrating</u> [*enkōmiazein*] the goddess on this the occasion of her <u>festival</u> [*panēguris*], ... making her the subject of a *humnos*'. I draw attention to the use of the verb *enkōmiazein* 'celebrate' with the accusative case of the divinity who presides over the festival and who is the subject of the *humnos* that inaugurates the festival. In this case, the divinity is Athena, presiding over the festival of the Panathenaia. <u>There is a mythological parallelism between the *humnos* as a notionally prototypical song and the *peplos* of Athena as a notionally prototypical fabric.</u> Analysis in *HPC* I§201.

forms of choral performances.[58] By choral performances I mean the singing and dancing of choral ensembles on festive occasions.

2§61 The case of the *dithurambos* 'dithyramb' is particularly telling. We see an earlier and less differentiated form of the dithyramb attested in the historical context of archaic Corinth, where this dramatic genre was aetiologized as an invention of Arion, a singer hailing from the city of Methymna in Lesbos, who was renowned for his virtuosity in singing while accompanying himself on the *kithara*; this aetiology of the dithyramb, linked with the celebrated myth of Arion's ride on a dolphin, is familiar to Classicists from the retelling of Herodotus (1.23-24).[59]

2§62 The archaic Corinthian form of the dithyramb was evidently related to an ostentatiously grotesque and wanton form of singing and dancing performed by "padded dancers" represented in archaic Corinthian vase-paintings, which feature not only "padded dancers" in the company of dolphins but even "padded dolphins."[60] A comparable theme in Athenian vase-paintings is the image of choral performers riding on dolphins.[61] In its earlier and less differentiated phases, then, the dithyramb shows a continuum rather than a break between "low art" and "high art," between grotesquerie and gracefulness, between wantonness and stateliness.[62] Only in the case of later and more differentiated phases of the dithyramb was there a need felt for expressing the seriousness of choral compositions attributed to Arion as opposed to the ostentatious frivolity of choral performances by masqueraders. That is the point of a remark preserved in the *Suda* about Arion (s.v.): this poet is credited with making the dithyramb 'more tragic'.[63]

2§63 In the scholia for Pindar's *Olympian* 13 (with reference to lines 18-19) we find a related remark about Arion as the inventor of the dithyramb in Corinth:

2①18 Scholia for Pindar *Olympian* 13.26b

αἱ τοῦ Διονύσου διθυράμβων ἐν Κορίνθῳ ἐφάνησαν χάριτες, τουτέστι τὸ σπουδαιότατον τῶν Διονύσου διθυράμβων ἐν Κορίνθῳ πρῶτον ἐφάνη· ἐκεῖ γὰρ ὡράθη ὁ χορὸς ὀρχούμενος· ἔστησε δὲ αὐτὸν πρῶτος Ἀρίων ὁ Μηθυμναῖος, εἶτα Λάσος ὁ Ἑρμιονεύς.

---

[58] PH 13§§6-21 (= pp. 384-392).
[59] PH 3§§9-10 (= pp. 87-88), 12§7 (= p. 341). On the term aetiology: PH 1§50 (= p. 44).
[60] Steinhart 2007:202-203.
[61] Nagy 2007a:123.
[62] Nagy 2007a:123-124.
[63] Steinhart 2007:210-211.

"The kharites [graces] of the dithyrambs of Dionysus appeared in Corinth."[64] That is, the most serious [spoudaion] aspect of the dithyrambs of Dionysus appeared first in Corinth. For that is where the dancing chorus [of dithyrambs] was first seen. And the first person to set it up [= set up such a chorus] was Arion of Methymna; the second to have done it was Lasus of Hermione.

2§64 There is a connection being made here in the scholia between the 'gracefulness' of the dithyramb, as expressed by the plural of *kharis* in the sense of 'pleasurable beauty', and its 'seriousness', as expressed by *spoudaion*. A similar connection is already being made in the original words of Pindar as paraphrased by the scholia.[65] The description of Arion's dithyramb as something that is *spoudaion* 'serious' is strikingly similar to what we have already seen in Aristotle's *Poetics*: he describes epic and tragedy as a *mimēsis* 're-enactment' of actions that are *spoudaia* 'serious' by those who are *spoudaioi* 'serious' (again, 1448a1-2, 26-27; 1448b34-36; 1449b9-10, 17-20, 24-28).

2§65 The idea that the dithyrambs of Arion are more 'serious' than the less differentiated choral forms of this dramatic genre is relevant to the point made by Aristotle in the *Poetics* concerning the development of (1) tragedy and (2) comedy out of forms that he links with choral singing and dancing led by two kinds of performers:

(1) performers of dithyrambs (1449a10-11): ἡ μὲν ἀπὸ τῶν ἐξαρχόντων τὸν διθύραμβον 'one of the forms [derives] from those who lead [ex-arkhein] the dithyramb'

(2) performers wearing costumes outfitted with phallic appendages (1449a12-14): ἡ δὲ ἀπὸ τῶν τὰ φαλλικὰ ἃ ἔτι καὶ νῦν ἐν πολλαῖς τῶν πόλεων διαμένει νομιζόμενα 'the other of the forms [derives] from those who wear phallic appendages—and this is a custom that persists in many of the city states'.

2§66 Aristotle is positing here an early phase of drama where proto-tragedy and proto-comedy are already differentiated, but these prototypes are seen as forms that have not yet reached the ultimate forms of tragedy and comedy, since tragedy has not yet been differentiated from the dithyramb while the satyr drama has not yet been differentiated from comedy. By implication, there is a still earlier phase where tragedy / dithyramb are not yet

---

[64] The wording here is the scholiast's paraphrase of lines 18-19 of Pindar's *Olympian* 13.
[65] *PH* 3§9 (= p. 87), 13§17 (= p. 389).

2Ⓢ9. A prototype of *humnos* in the *Poetics* of Aristotle

differentiated from satyr drama / comedy. Such an earlier phase is reflected in a follow-up remark in the *Poetics* of Aristotle concerning the evolution of tragedy from (1) an undifferentiated medium that is both grand and serious as well as non-grand and non-serious into (2) a differentiated medium that is exclusively grand and serious:

2①19 Aristotle *Poetics* 1449a19-21

ἐκ μικρῶν μύθων καὶ λέξεως γελοίας διὰ τὸ ἐκ σατυρικοῦ μεταβαλεῖν ὀψὲ <u>ἀπεσεμνύνθη</u>

[Tragedy,] developing out of slight plots and laugh-provoking diction on account of its derivation from a form having to do with satyrs, <u>became</u>, in the fullness of time, <u>stately</u> [*aposemnunesthai* = become *semnē*].

2§67 Aristotle's idea that tragedy evolves into something that is *semnon* 'stately' is tied to his thinking of epic and tragedy as the *mimēsis* 're-enactment' of the noble by the noble, to be contrasted with comedy, which is the re-enactment of the base by the base. In one particular context, as we have seen, he uses the word *semnoteroi* 'more stately' with reference to proto-poets who make *mimēsis* of noble deeds, and, in this context, he links the forms of epic and tragedy to a proto-form of *humnoi* 'hymns' and *enkōmia* 'encomia, celebrations, songs of praise'; in that same context, he contrasts epic and tragedy with the existing form of comedy, linking that form with a proto-form of *psogoi* 'invectives' (*Poetics* 1448b25-27).

2§68 I highlight the wording used by Aristotle in referring to those who 'lead' the singing and dancing of the dithyramb in the *Poetics* (1449a10-11): ἡ μὲν ἀπὸ τῶν <u>ἐξαρχόντων</u> τὸν <u>διθύραμβον</u> 'one of the forms [derives] from those who <u>lead</u> [*ex-arkhein*] the <u>dithyramb</u>'. This term *ex-arkhein* 'lead' signals an individuated act of performance that leads into a distinctly collective or choral act of performance. Relevant is this striking attestation of the term in a fragment of Archilochus:

2①20 Archilochus F 120 ed. West

ὡς Διωνύσου ἄνακτος καλὸν <u>ἐξάρξαι</u> μέλος
οἶδα <u>διθύραμβον</u> οἴνῳ συγκεραυνωθεὶς φρένας

To <u>lead</u> [*ex-arkhein*] the beautiful song [*melos*] of the lord Dionysus,

217

Chapter Two

the <u>dithyramb</u>, I know how to do it, thunderstruck as I am with wine.

2§69 These verses of Archilochus are composed in a meter known as the trochaic tetrameter catalectic, which Aristotle in the *Poetics* describes as a medium associated with the speaking parts, as it were, of early choral drama: he says that this meter later became displaced by another meter as a medium for the speaking parts, the iambic trimeter, which became dissociated from the choral aspects of drama, especially from the dancing (*Poetics* 1449a22-24, *Rhetoric* 3.1404a31-33). In other words, the medium of the trochaic tetrameter catalectic is undifferentiated in its combining of speaking parts and dancing parts, whereas the medium of the iambic trimeter is differentiated in its restriction to speaking parts. Aristotle's linking of the trochaic tetrameter catalectic with dance may well be extrapolated from such self-references as we find in the fragment I have just quoted from Archilochus (F 120), where the figure of Archilochus exhibits a distinctly choral personality: his individuated singing as the choral leader or *ex-arkhōn* of the dithyramb leads into the collective singing and dancing of the dithyramb by the chorus. The wording here corresponds to Aristotle's model of the *ex-arkhontes* of dithyramb who figure as prototypes of actors in tragedy.[66]

2§70 Archilochus figures as the choral leader or *ex-arkhōn* not only of the dithyramb but also of other media. We are about to see another striking attestation of the choral term *ex-arkhein* 'lead' in another fragment of Archilochus. Here again, the meter is trochaic tetrameter catalectic, but this time the choral medium is not the dithyramb but the paean. Once again we see an act of individuated singing that leads into the collective singing and dancing of the chorus:

2①21 Archilochus F 121 ed. West

αὐτὸς <u>ἐξάρχων</u> πρὸς αὐλὸν Λέσβιον <u>παιήονα</u>

I myself, <u>leading [*ex-arkhein*]</u> the <u>paean</u> from Lesbos, to the sound of the *aulos*.

In this case, the individuated singing is accompanied by a musical instrument, the *aulos*.

2§71 The ultimate model for the choral leader of the paean is the god Apollo himself, as we are about to see in a passage taken from the *Homeric Hymn* (3) *to Apollo*. The prototypical chorus that is chosen for Apollo's proto-

---

[66] *PH* 12§49 (= pp. 363-364).

typical performance as choral leader of the paean is a group of Cretan sailors whom the god has just coopted as his future attendants at Delphi. The choral performance of the paean is introduced with a narrative of the preliminaries (*Hymn to Apollo* 502-513): when the Cretans land at the harbor of Delphi, they immediately build on the beach an altar (*bōmos* at verse 508) for the god, and at this altar they proceed to make sacrifice (*thuein* at 509) and to dine at the sacrificial feast. After they are finished with their dining and general feasting, they proceed to the heights of Mount Parnassus, where Apollo's sanctuary awaits them, and their procession takes the form of a choral paean led by the god himself:

2①22 *Homeric Hymn* (3) *to Apollo* 514-523

βάν ῥ' ἴμεν· ἦρχε δ' ἄρα σφιν ἄναξ Διὸς υἱὸς Ἀπόλλων
515 φόρμιγγ' ἐν χείρεσσιν ἔχων ἐρατὸν κιθαρίζων
καλὰ καὶ ὕψι βιβάς· οἱ δὲ ῥήσσοντες ἕποντο
Κρῆτες πρὸς Πυθὼ καὶ ἰηπαιήον' ἄειδον,
οἷοί τε Κρητῶν παιήονες οἷσί τε Μοῦσα
ἐν στήθεσσιν ἔθηκε θεὰ μελίγηρυν ἀοιδήν.
520 ἄκμητοι δὲ λόφον προσέβαν ποσίν, αἶψα δ' ἵκοντο
Παρνησὸν καὶ χῶρον ἐπήρατον ἔνθ' ἄρ' ἔμελλεν
οἰκήσειν πολλοῖσι τετιμένος ἀνθρώποισι·
δεῖξε δ' ἄγων ἄδυτον ζάθεον καὶ πίονα νηόν.

> They [= the Cretans] went ahead. And leading them was the lord, son of Zeus, Apollo.
> 515 having a phorminx in his hands and playing on it a lovely tune
> while gracefully taking high steps. They followed him in rhythm,
> the Cretans, in the direction of Delphi, and they sang the paean song
> —the kinds of paean songs the Cretans have. For them the Muse
> places in their hearts, goddess that she is, a sweet-sounding song.

Chapter Two

> 520   Without getting tired, they approached on foot the peak and, the next thing you know, they reached
> Parnassus and the lovely place where he [= Apollo] was to
> make his home, receiving honor from a multitude of mortals.
> He took them [= the Cretans] and showed them his inner sanctum, most holy, as well as his well-endowed temple.

2§72 As we see from this description, the individuated performance of the choral leader or *ex-arkhōn* is not only the act of singing, which is only implied in this case, but also the act of dancing, along with instrumental accompaniment, all of which leads into a collective performance by the singing as well as dancing chorus. It is made explicit here that the chorus as led by Apollo is singing as well as dancing the paean that they perform. We see a similar emphasis on singing as well as dancing in Pindar's *Nemean 2*, at the moment when the chorus of performers, imagined as the citizens of the city in assembly, is called upon to 'begin' or 'lead off', *ex-arkhein*, by singing an individuated song that leads into collective singing and dancing:

2①23 Pindar *Nemean* 2.23-25

> τόν, ὦ πολῖ|ται, κωμάξατε Τιμοδήμῳ σὺν εὐκλέϊ νόστῳ·| ἁδυμελεῖ δ' ἐξάρχετε φωνᾷ
>
> Him [= Zeus, presiding over the festival of the Némea] you O citizens of the city must celebrate [*kōmazein*] for the sake of Timodemos, at the moment of his homecoming marked by genuine fame [*kleos*], and, in sweet-sounding song, you must lead off [*ex-arkhein*] with your voice.

2§73 I highlight here the collocation of *ex-arkhein* 'begin, lead off' with *phōnē* 'voice': the choral singing and dancing is 'begun' by way of a kind of singing that gives 'voice' to the words of song. I note also in passing the idea of a group engaged in festive celebration as conveyed by the noun *kōmos*, from which the parallel concepts of *kōmazein* 'celebrate' and *enkōmion* 'celebration, song of praise' are derived.

2§74 The use of the word *ex-arkhein* to mark an individuated performance that leads into the collective performance of a *khoros* 'chorus' is found also in this idealized representation adorning the Shield of Achilles:

2⑨9. A prototype of *humnos* in the *Poetics* of Aristotle

2①24 *Iliad* XVIII 590-604

590 Ἐν δὲ <u>χορὸν</u> <u>ποίκιλλε</u>⁶⁷ περικλυτὸς ἀμφιγυήεις,
τῷ ἴκελον οἷόν ποτ' ἐνὶ Κνωσῷ εὐρείῃ
<u>Δαίδαλος</u> ἤσκησεν καλλιπλοκάμῳ <u>Ἀριάδνῃ</u>.
ἔνθα μὲν ἠίθεοι καὶ παρθένοι ἀλφεσίβοιαι
<u>ὀρχεῦντ'</u> ἀλλήλων ἐπὶ καρπῷ χεῖρας ἔχοντες.
595 τῶν δ' αἳ μὲν λεπτὰς ὀθόνας ἔχον, οἳ δὲ χιτῶνας
εἴατ' ἐϋννήτους, ἦκα στίλβοντας ἐλαίῳ·
καί ῥ' αἳ μὲν καλὰς <u>στεφάνας</u> ἔχον, οἳ δὲ μαχαίρας
εἶχον χρυσείας ἐξ ἀργυρέων τελαμώνων.
οἳ δ' ὁτὲ μὲν θρέξασκον ἐπισταμένοισι πόδεσσι
600 ῥεῖα μάλ', ὡς ὅτε τις τροχὸν ἄρμενον ἐν παλάμῃσιν
ἑζόμενος κεραμεὺς πειρήσεται, αἴ κε θέῃσιν·
ἄλλοτε δ' αὖ θρέξασκον ἐπὶ στίχας ἀλλήλοισι.
πολλὸς δ' <u>ἱμερόεντα</u> <u>χορὸν</u> περιίσταθ' ὅμιλος
τερπόμενοι· μετὰ δέ σφιν <u>ἐμέλπετο</u> θεῖος <u>ἀοιδὸς</u>
605 φορμίζων·⁶⁸ δοιὼ δὲ κυβιστητῆρε κατ' αὐτοὺς
<u>μολπῆς</u> <u>ἐξάρχοντος</u>⁶⁹ ἐδίνευον κατὰ μέσσους.

---

⁶⁷ Variant reading: ποίησε.
⁶⁸ Here at verses 604-605, I follow the reading τερπόμενοι· μετὰ δέ σφιν ἐμέλπετο θεῖος ἀοιδὸς | φορμίζων, which is not attested in the medieval manuscript tradition but was restored by F. A. Wolf in his 1804 edition of the *Iliad*. The relevant verse-numbering of 604-605 in current editions of the *Iliad* goes back to the Wolf edition. The restoration is based on what we read in Athenaeus 5.181c about the treatment of this passage in the edition of Aristarchus: reportedly, that editor accepted the reading τερπόμενοι· μετὰ δέ σφιν ἐμέλπετο θεῖος ἀοιδὸς | φορμίζων at *Odyssey* iv 17-18, where it is still attested in the medieval manuscript tradition, while rejecting the same reading in the corresponding passage at *Iliad* XVIII 604-605. I will have more to say about this reading in my footnote for my translation of verses 604-605.
⁶⁹ Here at verse 606, I follow the reading ἐξάρχοντος reported by Athenaeus 5.180d, who notes that Aristarchus argued for the reading ἐξάρχοντες, which is what we find in the medieval manuscripts both here at *Iliad* XVIII 606 and at *Odyssey* iv 18. Athenaeus defends ἐξάρχοντος, and his wording indicates that this reading was attested as a textual variant. I will have more to say about these alternative readings in my footnote for my translation of verse 606.

Chapter Two

> 590   The renowned one [= Hephaistos], the one with the two strong arms, pattern-wove [*poikillein*] in it [= the Shield] a *khoros*.⁷⁰
>
> It [= the *khoros*] was just like the one that, once upon a time in far-ruling Knossos,
>
> Daedalus made for Ariadne, the one with the beautiful tresses [*plokamoi*].
>
> There were young men there,⁷¹ and girls who are courted with gifts of cattle,
>
> and they all were dancing with each other, holding hands at the wrist.
>
> 595   The girls were wearing delicate dresses, while the boys were clothed in khitons
>
> well-woven, gleaming exquisitely, with a touch of olive oil.
>
> The girls had beautiful garlands [*stephanai*], while the boys had knives
>
> made of gold, hanging from knife-belts made of silver.
>
> Half the time they moved fast in a circle, with expert steps,
>
> 600   showing the greatest ease, as when a wheel, solidly built, is given a spin by the hands
>
> of a seated potter, who is testing it whether it will run well.
>
> The other half of the time they moved fast in straight lines, alongside each other.
>
> A huge assembly stood around the place of the *khoros*, which evokes desire,
>
> and they were all delighted. In their midst sang and danced [*melpesthai*]⁷² a divine singer [*aoidos*],

---

⁷⁰ This word *khoros* can designate either the place where singing and dancing takes place or the group of singers and dancers who perform at that place. The relationship of the place with the group that is the *khoros* is metonymic.

⁷¹ The 'there' is both the place of dance and the place in the picture that is the Shield.

⁷² The verb *melpesthai* and the noun *molpē* convey the combination of singing and dancing: PH 12§29n62 (= p. 350) and n64 (= p. 351).

2§9. A prototype of *humnos* in the *Poetics* of Aristotle

605   playing on the phorminx.⁷³ Two special dancers among them
      were swirling as he led [*ex-arkhein*]⁷⁴ the singing and dancing
      [*molpē*] in their midst.

---

⁷³ As I said in my footnote for the original Greek of verse 605, Aristarchus rejected the reading τερπόμενοι· μετὰ δέ σφιν ἐμέλπετο θεῖος ἀοιδὸς | φορμίζων '. . . and they were all delighted. In their midst sang and danced a divine singer, playing on the phorminx . . .' at *Iliad* XVIII 604–605 (the verse-numbering goes back to the Wolf edition) but accepted it at *Odyssey* iv 17–18, where it is still attested in the medieval manuscript tradition. Instead of the two verses that take up the space of 604–605, τερπόμενοι· μετὰ δέ σφιν ἐμέλπετο θεῖος ἀοιδὸς | φορμίζων, δοιὼ δὲ κυβιστητῆρε κατ' αὐτοὺς '. . . and they were all delighted. In their midst sang and danced a divine singer, | playing on the phorminx. Two special dancers among them . . .', Aristarchus preferred to read simply one verse, τερπόμενοι· δοιὼ δὲ κυβιστητῆρε κατ' αὐτοὺς '. . . and they were all delighted. Two special dancers among them . . .', with one verse instead of two verses taking up the same narrative space. I note that the wording τερπόμενοι· μετὰ δέ σφιν ἐμέλπετο θεῖος ἀοιδὸς | φορμίζων '. . . and they were all delighted. In their midst sang and danced a divine singer, | playing on the phorminx . . .', which is the wording attested at *Odyssey* iv 17–18 and restored at *Iliad* XVIII 604–605, can be independently authenticated on the basis of the wording attested at *Odyssey* xiii 27–28, where we read τερπόμενοι· μετὰ δέ σφιν ἐμέλπετο θεῖος ἀοιδὸς | Δημόδοκος '. . . and they were all delighted. In their midst sang and danced the divine singer, | Demodokos'. The evidence of this passage from *Odyssey* xiii is missing in the reportage of Athenaeus about the editorial decisions of Aristarchus. And it is missing also from the argumentation of Revermann 1998, who reasons that the wording μετὰ δέ σφιν ἐμέλπετο θεῖος ἀοιδὸς | φορμίζων 'In their midst sang and danced a divine singer, | playing on the phorminx' at *Iliad* XVIII 604–605 results from what he calls "rhapsodic intervention" (p. 37). The problem with this kind of reasoning is that it fails to account for the formulaic nature of such an "intervention." The evidence of the wording in the relevant passages here indicates that both the shorter and the longer versions of *Iliad* XVIII 604–605 result from formulaic composition. Both the shorter and the longer versions are formulaic variants.

⁷⁴ As I said in the footnote for the Greek text of this verse, I follow here the alternative reading ἐξάρχοντος reported by Athenaeus 5.180d, who notes that Aristarchus argued for the reading ἐξάρχοντες, which is what we find in the medieval manuscripts both here at *Iliad* XVIII 606 and at *Odyssey* iv 18. As I also said in that footnote, the wording of Athenaeus indicates that we are dealing here with two textual variants, ἐξάρχοντος and ἐξάρχοντες. And both of these forms can be shown to be formulaic as well as textual variants. As we saw from the contexts of *ex-arkhein* in other passages that I quoted earlier, this word marks an individuated performance that leads into the collective performance of the chorus. The variants ἐξάρχοντος and ἐξάρχοντες indicate two different scenarios corresponding to the longer and the shorter versions of the wording. According to the shorter version as signaled by ἐξάρχοντες, it is the two specialized dancers whose performance leads into the choral singing and dancing. According to the longer version as signaled by ἐξάρχοντος, which is the reading I adopt here, it is the lyre-singer joined by the two specialized dancers whose combined performance leads into the choral singing and dancing. The second of these two scenarios resembles what happens when Demodokos the lyre-singer is joined by specialized dancers in their combined performance at *Odyssey* viii 256–266. I repeat the wording attested at *Odyssey* xiii 27–28, where we read τερπόμενοι· μετὰ δέ σφιν ἐμέλπετο θεῖος ἀοιδὸς | Δημόδοκος 'and they were all delighted. In their midst sang and danced the divine singer, | Demodokos'.

Chapter Two

2§75 The verb *melpesthai* and the noun *molpē* in this context, as we know from other contexts, refers to both singing and dancing.[75] Similarly in the *Homeric Hymn* (3) *to Apollo*, we saw a self-representation of a performer in the act of taking the lead in the performance of a choral ensemble and thereby becoming a soloist. In that case, the performer is Homer, and the divine model for his individuation out of a *khoros* 'chorus' is Apollo himself.

2§76 The use of the word *ex-arkhein* to mark the beginning of singing and dancing in a *khoros* 'chorus' is also evident in this description of Artemis as a model for the choral performance of a *humnos*:

2ⓣ25 *Homeric Hymn* (27) *to Artemis* 11–20

<blockquote>

αὐτὰρ ἐπὴν τερφθῇ θηροσκόπος ἰοχέαιρα
εὐφρήνῃ δὲ νόον, χαλάσασ' εὐκαμπέα τόξα
ἔρχεται ἐς μέγα δῶμα κασιγνήτοιο φίλοιο
Φοίβου Ἀπόλλωνος Δελφῶν ἐς πίονα δῆμον
15 <u>Μουσῶν</u> καὶ <u>Χαρίτων</u> καλὸν <u>χορὸν</u> ἀρτυνέουσα.
ἔνθα κατακρεμάσασα παλίντονα τόξα καὶ ἰοὺς
<u>ἡγεῖται</u> <u>χαρίεντα</u> περὶ χροΐ <u>κόσμον</u> ἔχουσα,
<u>ἐξάρχουσα</u> <u>χορούς</u>· αἱ δ' ἀμβροσίην <u>ὄπ' ἱεῖσαι</u>
<u>ὑμνεῦσιν</u> Λητὼ καλλίσφυρον ὡς τέκε παῖδας
20 ἀθανάτων βουλῇ τε καὶ ἔργμασιν ἔξοχ' ἀρίστους.

But when she has taken her pleasure [of hunting], that
    stalker of wild animals, that shooter of arrows,
and has cheered her mind, she loosens the string of her well-
    curved bow
and goes into the great palace of her dear brother
Phoebus Apollo, in the well-endowed district of Delphi,
15   and she gets set to arrange the beautiful <u>choral ensemble</u>
    [<u>khoros</u>] of the <u>Muses</u> and <u>Kharites</u>.
And there, after she hangs up [on a peg] her curved bow and
    her quiver of arrows,

</blockquote>

---

[75] *PH* 12§29n62 (= p. 350) and n64 (= p. 351).

she begins to lead [hēgeîsthai] [the choral ensemble], and
the adornment [kosmos] she wears enveloping her flesh is
delightfully graceful [kharieis]
as she leads off [ex-arkhein] the songs and dances of the
choral ensemble [khoros].[76] And they [= the Muses and the
Kharites], sending forth [hienai] a voice that is immortal,
make Leto their humnos [humneîn], the one with the beautiful
ankles, [as they sing] how once upon a time she gave birth
to children

20 who were by far the best of the immortals in both the things
they planned and the things they did.

2§77 Here the khoros, that is, the choral ensemble composed of the Muses and the 'Graces' or Kharites (15 Μουσῶν καὶ Χαρίτων καλὸν χορόν), is not just dancing: the wording makes it explicit that they are 'emitting an immortal voice' (18 ἀμβροσίην ὄπ' ἱεῖσαι) when they perform the humnos (19 ὑμνεῦσιν). Enveloped in a kosmos 'adornment' that is kharieis 'graceful' (17 χαρίεντα περὶ χροΐ κόσμον ἔχουσα), Artemis is 'leading' (17 ἡγεῖται) the choral ensemble. The goddess begins by 'leading off', an action expressed by the choral verb ex-arkhein, with the noun khoroi as the object (18 ἐξάρχουσα χορούς). Artemis here stands out as a choral model for performing a humnos focusing on her and her family. As a choral model, she resembles her divine brother Apollo, who as we saw figures as the ultimate maker as well as recipient of humnoi that honor him.

2§78 As the recipient of humnoi that honor her, the goddess can be pictured as the object of the verb of singing, as we see in this verse from another Homeric Hymn to Artemis:

2①26 Homeric Hymn (9) to Artemis 8

αὐτὰρ ἐγώ σε πρῶτα καὶ ἐκ σέθεν ἄρχομ' ἀείδειν

As for me, I sing you first of all and from [ex-] you do I start off [arkhesthai] to sing.

---

[76] I interpret the plural of khoros here as a metonymic way of concretizing the performance by the chorus: whereas the singular of khoros would have indicated singing and dancing in general, the plural indicates specific instances of singing and dancing. Hence the translation 'songs and dances of the chorus'.

Chapter Two

2§79 The accusative *se* 'you' referring to Artemis here matches the accusative *ton* 'him' referring to Zeus in what I quoted earlier from an athletic victory song composed by Pindar:

2①27 Pindar *Nemean* 2.23-25

> τόν, ὦ πολῖ|ται, κωμάξατε Τιμοδήμῳ σὺν εὐκλέϊ νόστῳ·| ἀδυμελεῖ δ' ἐξάρχετε φωνᾷ
>
> Him [= Zeus, presiding over the festival of the Némea] you O citizens of the city must celebrate [*kōmazein*] for the sake of Timodemos, at the moment of his homecoming marked by genuine fame [*kleos*], and, in sweet-sounding song, you must lead off [*ex-arkhein*] with your voice.

2§80 Moreover, the expression *ek sethen* '[starting] from you' depending on *arkhom' aeidein* 'I begin to sing' in the *Homeric Hymn to Artemis* is parallel to the expression *hothen* '[starting] from the point where' depending on *aoidoi arkhontai* 'singers begin' at the beginning of the same victory song composed by Pindar:

2①28 Pindar *Nemean* 2.1-3

> Ὅθεν περ καὶ Ὁμηρίδαι | ῥαπτῶν ἐπέων τὰ πόλλ' ἀοιδοί | ἄρχονται, Διὸς ἐκ προοιμίου.
>
> [starting] from the point where [*hothen*] the *Homēridai*, singers, most of the time begin [*arkhesthai*] their stitched-together words, from the *prooimion* of Zeus ...

2§81 This Pindaric passage imitates the beginning of a *Homeric Hymn to Zeus*. I will have more to say in a moment about Pindar's imitation, and about the meaning of the word *prooimion*, which I have left untranslated, but for now I simply emphasize the parallelism of the wording here with the wording of the *Hymn to Artemis*. The parallelism with *ek sethen* '[starting] from you', with reference to Artemis, indicates that the referent of *hothen* '[starting] from the point where' is Zeus himself. The performance starts with the god and is a continuation from the god. Such continuity, as we will now see, is the essence of *humnos*.

2ⓢ10. Convergences and divergences in the meanings of *humnos* and *prooimion*

2§82 The idea that Zeus is the point of departure marked by the expression *hothen* '[starting] from the point where' in Pindar's *Nemean 2* is conveyed by the expression Διὸς ἐκ προοιμίου '[starting] from the *prooimion* of Zeus'. In order to show the logic behind this expression, I will need to produce a working definition of *prooimion*, but I can do that only after I highlight the divergences as well as the convergences in meaning between this word and the word *humnos*.

2§83 To say that Zeus is the song's point of departure in Pindar's *Nemean 2* is equivalent to saying that the point of departure is the *prooimion* of Zeus, in that the *prooimion* starts with the god and is a continuation from the god. Further, the continuity that is started by the *prooimion* becomes the continuum that is the *humnos*.[77] In this formulation, I am highlighting a basic divergence between the meanings of *prooimion* and *humnos*: whereas the word *prooimion* refers only to the start of the continuum, the word *humnos* refers to both the start of the continuum and the continuum itself. To put it another way, the naming of the god is a metonymy—of and by itself—from the standpoint of the *prooimion* that starts off with the naming of the god, and the whole process of starting and then continuing is the essence of *humnos*. In the logic of the *humnos*, there is further metonymy: the god who presides over the occasion of performance becomes continuous with the occasion and thus becomes the occasion.

2§84 A moment ago, I said that the beginning of Pindar's *Nemean 2* amounts to an imitation of a *Homeric Hymn to Zeus*. To back up this assertion, I will now focus on the word *Homēridai* 'descendants of Homer' at the beginning of Pindar's victory song. I repeat here the relevant wording, which shows that the *Homēridai* conventionally begin their singing with what is called a *prooimion* of Zeus:

2ⓣ29 Pindar *Nemean* 2.1-3

Ὅθεν περ καὶ Ὁμηρίδαι | ῥαπτῶν ἐπέων τὰ πόλλ' ἀοιδοί | ἄρχονται, Διὸς ἐκ προοιμίου).

---

[77] *PH* 12§§33-43 (= pp. 353-360), following Koller 1956, who argues that the *prooimion* is particularly suited to lead into the performative genre of the *nomos*. See also Obbink 2001:73.

Chapter Two

[starting] from the point where [*hothen*] the <u>Homēridai</u>, singers, most of the time <u>begin</u> [*arkhesthai*] their <u>stitched-together</u> words, from the <u>prooimion</u> of Zeus ...

2§85 In this Pindaric passage, we find precious indications of conventions characteristic of *Homēridai* or 'descendants of Homer' as performers of Homer. In earlier work, I have analyzed these conventions in some detail, and here I merely highlight the relevant aspects of that analysis.⁷⁸

2§86 First I focus on the word *hothen* '[starting] from the point where', which signals the sequence of agenda in the performance once the performance has begun. As we see from the wording I have just quoted, *hothen* 'from the point where' unexpectedly takes first place in this song, and the name of the god who is signaled as the actual beginning unexpectedly takes second place. As we also see from what I have just quoted, it is only in the middle of the initial wording that we find the actual word for this beginning, *arkhesthai* 'begin'. Then, toward the ending of the whole song, we find for the second time a word for 'begin':

2①30 Pindar *Nemean* 2.23-25

τόν, ὦ πολῖ|ται, <u>κωμάξατε</u> Τιμοδήμῳ σὺν εὐκλέϊ νόστῳ·| ἀδυμελεῖ δ' <u>ἐξάρχετε</u> φωνᾷ

Him [= Zeus, presiding over the festival of the Némea] you O citizens of the city must <u>celebrate</u> [*kōmazein*] for the sake of Timodemos, at the moment of his homecoming marked by genuine fame [*kleos*], and, in sweet-sounding song, <u>you must lead off</u> [*ex-arkhein*] with your voice.

2§87 This word *ex-arkhein* 'begin'—here in the sense of 'lead off'—presupposes that a word like *hothen* 'from the point where' will follow as a signal for continuing the poetic agenda of the song, but here, at the end of the song, the *hothen* is missing because the wording has come to an end. Or is it really missing? The word *hothen* is in fact not missing if the wording of the song does not come to an end here but instead loops back to the beginning, that is, to the beginning of the song, where the *hothen* is actually located.⁷⁹ In other words, the *prooimion* in Pindar's imitation expresses a beginning that cycles back into

---

⁷⁸ PH 12§39 (= pp. 356-357), especially n95; PP 62-63 (where I revise my earlier interpretation of Διὸς ἐκ προοιμίου: not 'from Zeus Prooimios' but 'from the *prooimion* of Zeus').

⁷⁹ PP 63 on Pindar *Nemean* 2.1, following Kurke 1991:43; see also PH 12§39n95 (= p. 357), with further citations of other interpretations.

itself instead of allowing for a continuation of the poetic agenda introduced by the *prooimion*.

2§88 By contrast, a *prooimion* of Zeus performed by the *Homēridai* would be expected to begin not with a word like *hothen* 'from the point where' but with *arkhomai* 'I begin' or its equivalent. Such a beginning is typical of the *Homeric Hymns*. As just one of many possible examples, I cite the beginning of the *Homeric Hymn to Demeter*:

2①31 *Homeric Hymn (2) to Demeter* 1

Δήμητρ' ἠΰκομον σεμνὴν θεὰν ἄρχομ' ἀείδειν

I begin [*arkhesthai*] to sing Demeter with the beautiful hair, stately goddess.

2§89 This example shows why I said earlier that Pindar in his *Nemean 2* imitates a virtual *Homeric Hymn to Zeus*. As we can now see, a *prooimion* of Zeus is the equivalent of a *humnos* 'hymn' to Zeus. The *Homeric Hymn (3) to Apollo* is in fact a perfect parallel: it refers to itself in terms of a *humnos* (verses 158, 161, 178), while Thucydides refers to it explicitly as a *prooimion* (3.104.4). Similarly, when Socrates is said to compose a *Hymn to Apollo* in prison while awaiting his execution, his composition is called a *prooimion* (Plato *Phaedo* 60d).[80]

2§90 The convergence in meanings between *humnos* and *prooimion* as poetic terms extends to the metaphorical world that generated the poetic terminology. As I have argued in earlier work, both *humnos* and *prooimion* are derived from roots referring to the making of fabric.

2§91 In the case of the noun *humnos* / ὕμνος, conventionally translated as 'hymn', the most convincing explanation is that it derives from the verb root of *huphainein* / ὑφαίνειν, meaning 'weave'.[81] Alternatively, it may derive from

---

[80] The act of composing this *Hymn to Apollo* is expressed by way of the word *poieîn* 'make', not *graphein* 'write' (Plato *Phaedo* 60de); in this context, the art of poetic composition and performance is called *mousikē* (60e and 61a-b), on which see *PH* 3§1n1 (= p. 82). I will have more to say later about *mousikē*. (On Plato's consistent use of *poieîn* and not *graphein* in such contexts, I refer to my analysis in *HPC* I§61.) In the same passage (*Phaedo* 60d–61b), it is said that Socrates composed not only a *Hymn to Apollo* but also Aesopic fables in verse; on formal connections between Apollonian and Aesopic discourse, see *PH* 11§§19–21 (= pp. 323–325).

[81] On *humnos* / ὕμνος as derived from the verb root *webh- / *ubh-, as in *huphainein* / ὑφαίνειν 'weave', see Schmitt 1967:300. In Bacchylides *Epinicians* 5.9–10, *humnos* / ὕμνος 'hymn' is attested as the object of *huphainein* / ὑφαίνειν 'weave', as if it meant 'the thing woven'.

a different verb root, referring to the stitching together of distinct pieces of cloth to make a unified article of clothing'.[82]

2§92 In the case of the compound noun *prooimion* / προοίμιον, conventionally translated as 'proemium', the element *-oim-* / -οιμ- is derived from a root that we find also attested in two simple nouns, *oimos* / οἶμος and *oimē* / οἴμη. The Attic by-form of *prooimion* / προοίμιον, which is *phroimion* / φροίμιον, elucidates the prehistory of the root: we must reconstruct it not as **oim-* but as **hoim-*, from **soim-*. This reconstruction helps elucidate the surviving contexts of both *oimos* / οἶμος and *oimē* / οἴμη, which do not always give a clear picture of the basic meaning of either form.[83] In some contexts, the meaning seems to be 'song',[84] while in others it seems to be 'way, pathway'.[85] With the help of comparative evidence, however, the primary meaning of *oimos* and *oimē* can be reconstructed as 'thread, threading', and the meanings 'song' or 'way, pathway' can be explained as secondary: that is, 'song' and 'way, pathway' are metaphorical generalizations derived from the meaning 'thread, threading'.[86] And it is such a primary meaning 'thread, threading' that we find in comparable forms attested in other Indo-European languages: for example, the form *soimos that we reconstruct from Greek *oimos* is attested as Old Icelandic *seimr*, meaning 'thread'.[87] In terms of such a primary meaning, the etymology of the compound noun *prooimion* 'prooemium' can be interpreted as a metaphor referring to the 'initial threading' of a song. A close semantic parallel to the etymology of Greek *prooimion* 'proemium' as an 'initial threading' of a song is the etymology of Latin *exordium*, which likewise means 'proemium' in poetic and rhetorical contexts: the meaning of this noun as well

---

[82] In terms of this explanation, the verb root of *humnos* / ὕμνος would be **syu-*, the derivatives of which mean 'sew' in some Indo-European languages (for references, see PR 70–72). From the standpoint of Indo-European linguistics, still other explanations are possible (for an overview, see Vine 1999:575–576, who also offers his own explanation). Whichever explanation ultimately proves to be right from the standpoint of Indo-European linguistics, it is worth noting that the association of the noun *humnos* with the verb *huphainein* in archaic Greek poetry (see the previous note) was probably in effect already in prehistoric phases of the Greek poetic language. I continue to think that this association does in fact point to the right etymology.

[83] For a survey of contexts, see Chantraine DELG s.vv. οἶμος and οἴμη.

[84] For example, *oimē* can be translated as 'song' in *Odyssey* viii 74 and xxii 347.

[85] For example, *oimos* can be translated as 'way' in Hesiod *Works and Days* 290. In the case of the form δύσοιμος in Aeschylus *Libation-Bearers* 945, it is explained in Hesychius (s.v.) as δύσοδος.

[86] PR 72, 81. See also PP 63n20, with reference to Durante 1976:176–177, who disagrees with Chantraine DELG s.vv. οἶμος and οἴμη. Chantraine concludes that the basic meanings of *oimos* and *oimē* are distinct, but the contexts that he adduces point to an opposite conclusion, as noticed already by Pagliaro 1953:34–40.

[87] For this and other examples, see Durante 1976:176.

can be traced back to the basic idea of an 'initial threading'.[88] The poetic and rhetorical concepts of both Greek *prooimion* and Latin *exordium* in the sense of 'proemium' have a common Indo-European ancestry.

2§93 Pursuing the argument that *oimos* / *oimē* / *prooimion* and *humnos* are all derived from roots referring to the making of fabric, I note that the word *oimos* is formulaically interchangeable with the word *humnos* at verse 451 of the *Homeric Hymn* (4) *to Hermes*, where we see the attestation of both οἶμος ἀοιδῆς and ὕμνος ἀοιδῆς in the manuscript tradition; at a later point, we will also consider the cognate expression ἀοιδῆς ὕμνον at verse 429 of *Odyssey* viii. I interpret the combinations of *humnos* and *oimos* with *aoidē* 'song' to mean respectively the 'weaving' of song and the 'threading' of song. Relevant to this interpretation is the context of *oimē* at verse 74 of *Odyssey* viii: as we will see later when we examine this context, there is a metaphorical reference here to the intial part of performing a song, that is to the 'initial threading' of a song. To sum up, the meaning of *oimos* or *oimē* as 'song' results from a metaphorical extension: the idea of making song is being expressed metaphorically through the idea of making fabric. As for contexts where *oimos* and *oimē* seem to mean 'way, pathway', I argue that such a meaning is likewise a result of metaphorical extension: here the general idea of moving ahead from one point to another is being expressed metaphorically by applying the specific idea of threading one's way from one point to another.[89]

2§94 Such etymological connections with the metaphorical world of making fabric are parallel to the poetic connection of the *prooimion* of Zeus with the overt metaphor of *rhapta epea* 'stitched-together words' in Pindar's *Nemean 2*, which in turn is connected with a latent metaphor embedded in the etymology of the word *rhapsōidos* 'rhapsode', a compound formation composed of the morphological elements *rhaptein* 'stitch together' and *aoidē* 'song'.[90]

2§95 I round out my observations on Pindar's imitation of the *prooimion* of Zeus by highlighting two points that will be relevant to the argumentation that follows. The first point is simple: Pindar's wording shows that the performance of the *Homēridai* is linked with the performance of *rhapsōidoi*

---

[88] See PP 63n20, with reference to Durante 1976:177 on Latin *ex-ordium* as a semantic equivalent of Greek *pro-oimion*. Also PR 72, 81.

[89] Whereas the metaphorical extension here goes from the specific (threading) to the general (going, moving ahead), we can also find examples of a reverse metaphorical extension, from the general to the specific, as in the case of *metabainein* 'moving ahead'. A point of comparison is the Turkish musical term *makam*, in the sense of 'step'. I offer further observations in the excursus at 2§311 further below.

[90] PP 61–79.

'rhapsodes'.⁹¹ The second point, which will concern the word *prooimion*, is more complex: in contexts where we see this word *prooimion* applied as an equivalent of *humnos*, it refers to a notionally perfect beginning of a rhapsodic performance, which is envisioned as the stitching together of distinct pieces of cloth to make a unified article of clothing.⁹²

2§96 I have more to say in Chapter 3 about the *Homēridai* and about rhapsodic performances of Homer. And I have more to say about the *Homēridai* in the twin book *Homer the Preclassic*, where I argue that this lineage, claiming to be the 'descendants of Homer', was central to the definition of Homer in Athens—in the late sixth century BCE and thereafter.⁹³ For now I simply concentrate on the idea of a *prooimion* of Zeus as performed rhapsodically by *Homēridai*, which is the equivalent of a virtual *Homeric Hymn to Zeus*.

2ⓢ11. The poetics of metabasis in the Homeric Hymns

2§97 As we have seen from examining the form of song designated by the words *humnos* and *prooimion*, the act of creating such a song is not just a matter of artistic composition. It is also a matter of artistic performance. As we have also seen, such performance is perceived as a notionally perfect 'beginning', expressed by the word *arkhein / arkhesthai*, which signals the invocation of the god or goddess who presides over the occasion of performance. But now the question is, what does such a perfect beginning introduce? To ask the question in another way, what is the consequence of a perfect beginning, especially as conveyed by the word *humnos*? For an answer, I turn to the *Homeric Hymns*, which show how the *humnos* can make reference to its own hymnic consequent. It is done by way of a performative device that I call metabasis.

2§98 As we will see from the attestations of this device in the *Homeric Hymns*, a *humnos* is not just the perfect beginning of a performance. It is also the signal of a perfect transition to the rest of the performance. By metonymy, the *humnos* includes the rest of the performance, proceeding sequentially all the way to the conclusion of the whole performance. If the performance is sequential, consequential, you know it was started by a *humnos* and you know

---

⁹¹ Relevant is the link between the *Homēridai* and rhapsodes performing at the Panathenia in Athens, as signaled in Plato *Ion* 530d.
⁹² PR 80–81.
⁹³ HPC I§§141 and following. As I argue there, the *Homēridai* were an ultimate source for the *Lives of Homer* tradition. From the standpoint of the *Homēridai* in the late sixth century BCE, Homer was both the author of the *Iliad* and *Odyssey* as performed at the Panathenaia and the author of what we know as the *Homeric Hymn to Apollo*.

2§11. The poetics of metabasis in the Homeric Hymns

it is really a *humnos*. Such consequentiality is indicated by the verb *metabainein*, which I translate as 'move ahead and shift forward' and to which I will refer short-hand by way of the term metabasis. As we are about to see, the metabasis is a formal feature of the *humnos*. Here are three most telling examples from the *Homeric Hymns*:

2①32 *Homeric Hymn* (5) *to Aphrodite* 292-293

> χαῖρε θεὰ Κύπροιο ἐϋκτιμένης μεδέουσα·
> σεῦ δ' ἐγὼ ἀρξάμενος μεταβήσομαι ἄλλον ἐς ὕμνον.

> Hail and take pleasure [*khaire*], goddess, queen of well-founded Cyprus.
> But, having started off from you, I will move ahead and shift forward [*metabainein*] to the rest of the *humnos*.

2①33 *Homeric Hymn* (9) *to Artemis* 7-9

> καὶ σὺ μὲν οὕτω χαῖρε θεαί θ' ἅμα πᾶσαι ἀοιδῇ·
> αὐτὰρ ἐγώ σε πρῶτα καὶ ἐκ σέθεν ἄρχομ' ἀείδειν,
> σεῦ δ' ἐγὼ ἀρξάμενος μεταβήσομαι ἄλλον ἐς ὕμνον.

> So, with all this said, I say to you [= Artemis] now: hail and take pleasure [*khaire*], and along with you may all the other goddesses [take pleasure] from my song.
> As for me, I sing you first of all and from you do I start off [*arkhesthai*] to sing.
> And, having started off from you, I will move ahead and shift forward [*metabainein*] to the rest of the *humnos*.[94]

2①34 *Homeric Hymn* (18) *to Hermes* 10-12

> καὶ σὺ μὲν οὕτω χαῖρε Διὸς καὶ Μαιάδος υἱέ·
> σεῦ δ' ἐγὼ ἀρξάμενος μεταβήσομαι ἄλλον ἐς ὕμνον.
> χαῖρ' Ἑρμῆ χαριδῶτα διάκτορε, δῶτορ ἐάων.

---

[94] Note the wording in the beginning of this hymn, in verse 1: Ἄρτεμιν ὕμνει Μοῦσα 'make Artemis, O Muse, the subject of my *humnos*'.

Chapter Two

> So, with all this said, I say to you [= Hermes] now: hail and take pleasure, son of Zeus and Maia.
> And, having started off from you, I will move ahead and shift forward [*metabainein*] to the rest of the *humnos*.
> Hail and take pleasure [*khaire*], Hermes, giver of pleasurable beauty [*kharis*], you who are conductor [of *psukhai*] and giver of good things.

2§99 The transition in each of these passages, as marked by *metabainein* 'move ahead and shift forward', is predicated on the idea of a perfect beginning, as marked by *arkhesthai* 'begin', linked with the genitive case of the noun referring to the god who presides over the festive occasion of performance. The idea is, 'I begin, starting from the god'. The process of transition or metabasis, signaled by the verb *metabainein*, is activated by the hymnic salutation *khaire / khairete*, which I interpret as 'hail and take pleasure'. Implicit in these imperative forms of the verb *khairein* is the meaning of the related noun *kharis*, which conveys the idea of a 'favor' achieved by reciprocating the pleasure of beauty. Making this idea explicit, I now offer this paraphrase of *khaire / khairete* in the context of all its occurrences in the *Homeric Hymns*:

> Now, at this precise moment, with all this said, I greet you, god (or gods) presiding over the festive occasion, calling on you to show favor [*kharis*] in return for the beauty and the pleasure of this, my performance.

What drives the performative gesture of *khaire / khairete* is the fundamental idea that the reciprocal favor of *kharis* is the same beautiful thing as the pleasure that it gives.

2§100 This idea of *kharis*, implicit in the attested contexts of *khaire / khairete* in the *Homeric Hymns*, is made explicit in the last verse (5) of the *Homeric Hymn (24) to Hermes*, where the performer does not say *khaire* to the presiding god Hermes but instead asks him to confer *kharis* upon the singing (χάριν δ' ἅμ' ὄπασσον ἀοιδῇ). In the last verse (12) of another *Homeric Hymn (18) to Hermes*, which we just saw quoted above, the performer says *khaire* to Hermes in the context of addressing him as 'giver of *kharis*' (χαῖρ' Ἑρμῆ χαριδῶτα).[95]

---

[95] The salutation *khaire* in this verse 12 in the *Homeric Hymn (18) to Hermes* is a reapplication of the salutation *khaire* in verse 10. Between these two verses is verse 11, where we see the formula for metabasis: σεῦ δ' ἐγὼ ἀρξάμενος μεταβήσομαι ἄλλον ἐς ὕμνον 'and, having started off from you, I will move ahead and shift forward [*metabainein*] to the rest of the *humnos*'. The last verse, containing the reapplication of *khaire*, has the effect of deferring the metabasis, as we will see later.

234

2⑤11. The poetics of metabasis in the Homeric Hymns

In *Homeric Hymn* (26) *to Dionysus*, the singer follows up his performative gesture *khaire* at verse 11 by asking the god, at verses 12-13, to grant that the singer may return to the same performative occasion over and over again, that is, season after season, *hōra* after *hōra*, for a multitude of years; proleptically, presuming that his request will be granted, the singer in the first person plural describes himself at verse 12 as *khairontes*, that is, taking pleasure reciprocally, just as he calls on the god to take pleasure.

2§101 After the signal *khaire / khairete* in the *Homeric Hymns*, the actual process of metabasis can be activated. This process is made explicit in the expression we have just seen in the three passages that I quoted, μεταβήσομαι ἄλλον ἐς ὕμνον 'I will move ahead and shift forward [*metabainein*] to the rest of the *humnos*' (*Homeric Hymns* 5.292-293, 9.7-9, 18.10-12). The word *humnos* in the wording ἄλλον ἐς ὕμνον in the *Homeric Hymns* marks the whole performance, so that ἄλλον ἐς ὕμνον means not 'extending into another performance' but 'extending into the rest of the performance'.[96] So also the expression ἄλλης... ἀοιδῆς in other *Homeric Hymns* means not 'another song' but 'the rest of the song':

2①35 *Homeric Hymn* (2) *to Demeter* 494-495

> πρόφρονες ἀντ' ᾠδῆς βίοτον θυμήρε' ὀπάζειν.
> αὐτὰρ ἐγὼ καὶ σεῖο καὶ ἄλλης μνήσομ' ἀοιδῆς.
>
> You [= Demeter and Persephone] be favorably disposed, granting me a livelihood that fits my heart's desire, in return for my song.
> As for me, I will keep you in mind along with the rest of the song.

2①36 *Homeric Hymn* (3) *to Apollo* 545-546

> Καὶ σὺ μὲν οὕτω χαῖρε Διὸς καὶ Λητοῦς υἱέ·
> αὐτὰρ ἐγὼ καὶ σεῖο καὶ ἄλλης μνήσομ' ἀοιδῆς
>
> So, with all this said, I say to you [= Apollo] now: hail and take pleasure [*khaire*], son of Zeus and Leto.
> As for me, I will keep you in mind along with the rest of the song.

---

[96] *PH* 12§33 (= pp. 353–354), following Koller 1956:174–182; see also Bakker 2005:144 (in disagreement with Clay 1997:493).

Chapter Two

2①37 *Homeric Hymn (4) to Hermes* 579-580

> Καὶ σὺ μὲν <u>οὕτω χαῖρε</u> Διὸς καὶ Μαιάδος υἱέ·
> <u>αὐτὰρ ἐγὼ</u> καὶ σεῖο καὶ <u>ἄλλης</u> μνήσομ' <u>ἀοιδῆς</u>
>
> So, <u>with all this said</u>, I say to you [= Hermes] now: <u>hail and take pleasure</u> [<u>khaire</u>], son of Zeus and Maia.
> <u>As for me, I</u> will keep you in mind along with <u>the rest of the song</u>.

2①38 *Homeric Hymn (6) to Aphrodite* 19-21

> <u>Χαῖρ</u>' ἑλικοβλέφαρε γλυκυμείλιχε, δὸς δ' ἐν <u>ἀγῶνι</u>
> νίκην τῷδε φέρεσθαι, ἐμὴν δ' ἔντυνον ἀοιδήν.
> <u>αὐτὰρ ἐγὼ</u> καὶ σεῖο καὶ <u>ἄλλης</u> μνήσομ' <u>ἀοιδῆς</u>.
>
> <u>Hail and take pleasure</u> [<u>khaire</u>], you [= Aphrodite] with the spiral glances, you the honey-sweet. Grant that in the <u>competition</u> [<u>agōn</u>]
> that is at hand I may win victory. Arrange my song.
> <u>As for me, I</u> will keep you in mind along with <u>the rest of the song</u>.

2①39 *Homeric Hymn (10) to Aphrodite* 4-6

> <u>Χαῖρε</u> θεὰ Σαλαμῖνος ἐϋκτιμένης μεδέουσα
> εἰναλίης τε Κύπρου· δὸς δ' ἱμερόεσσαν ἀοιδήν.
> <u>αὐτὰρ ἐγὼ</u> καὶ σεῖο καὶ <u>ἄλλης</u> μνήσομ' <u>ἀοιδῆς</u>.
>
> <u>Hail and take pleasure</u> [<u>khaire</u>], goddess, ruling over Salamis with its good foundation,
> and over all Cyprus, island in the sea. Grant me a song that is full of charm.
> <u>As for me, I</u> will keep you in mind along with <u>the rest of the song</u>.

2①40 *Homeric Hymn (19) to Pan* 48-49

> Καὶ σὺ μὲν <u>οὕτω χαῖρε</u> ἄναξ, ἵλαμαι δέ σ' ἀοιδῇ·

2⑤11. The poetics of metabasis in the Homeric Hymns

αὐτὰρ ἐγὼ καὶ σεῖο καὶ ἄλλης μνήσομ' ἀοιδῆς.

So, with all this said, I say to you [= Pan] now: hail and take pleasure [*khaire*], and I beseech you with my song.

As for me, I will keep you in mind along with the rest of the song.

2①41 Homeric Hymn (25) to the Muses and Apollo 6-7

Χαίρετε τέκνα Διὸς καὶ ἐμὴν τιμήσατ' ἀοιδήν·
αὐτὰρ ἐγὼν ὑμέων τε καὶ ἄλλης μνήσομ' ἀοιδῆς.

Hail and take pleasure [*khairete*], children of Zeus. Give honor [*timē*] to my song.

As for me, I will keep you in mind along with the rest of the song.

2①42 Homeric Hymn (27) to Artemis 21-22

Χαίρετε τέκνα Διὸς καὶ Λητοῦς ἠϋκόμοιο·
αὐτὰρ ἐγὼν ὑμέων καὶ ἄλλης μνήσομ' ἀοιδῆς

Hail and take pleasure [*khairete*], children of Zeus and of Leto with the beautiful hair.

As for me, I will keep you in mind along with the rest of the song.

2①43 Homeric Hymn (28) to Athena 17-18

Καὶ σὺ μὲν οὕτω χαῖρε Διὸς τέκος αἰγιόχοιο·
αὐτὰρ ἐγὼ καὶ σεῖο καὶ ἄλλης μνήσομ' ἀοιδῆς.

So, with all this said, I say to you [= Athena] now: hail and take pleasure [*khaire*], daughter of Zeus who has the aegis.

As for me, I will keep you in mind along with the rest of the song.

2①44 Homeric Hymn (29) to Hestia 13-14

Χαῖρε Κρόνου θύγατερ, σύ τε καὶ χρυσόρραπις Ἑρμῆς.
αὐτὰρ ἐγὼν ὑμέων τε καὶ ἄλλης μνήσομ' ἀοιδῆς.

> Hail and take pleasure [*khaire*], daughter of Kronos. Both you and Hermes as well, the one with the golden wand.
>
> As for me, I will keep you in mind along with the rest of the song.

2ⓣ45 *Homeric Hymn* (30) *to Gaia* 17-19

> Χαῖρε θεῶν μήτηρ, ἄλοχ' Οὐρανοῦ ἀστερόεντος,
> πρόφρων δ' ἀντ' ᾠδῆς βίοτον θυμήρε' ὄπαζε·
> αὐτὰρ ἐγὼ καὶ σεῖο καὶ ἄλλης μνήσομ' ἀοιδῆς.

> Hail and take pleasure [*khaire*], mother of the gods, wife of Ouranos of the stars.
>
> Be favorably disposed, and grant me a livelihood that fits my heart's desire, in return for my song.
>
> As for me, I will keep you in mind along with the rest of the song.

2ⓣ46 *Homeric Hymn* (33) 18-19 *to the Dioskouroi*:

> Χαίρετε Τυνδαρίδαι ταχέων ἐπιβήτορες ἵππων·
> αὐτὰρ ἐγὼν ὑμέων καὶ ἄλλης μνήσομ' ἀοιδῆς.

> Hail and take pleasure [*khairete*], Tundaridai, mounters of swift horses.
>
> As for me, I will keep you in mind along with the rest of the song.

2§102 In this inventory of hymnic moments of metabasis, two details need to be highlighted, both of which will be relevant to later stages of the argumentation. First, I note that each of these moments of metabasis begins with the wording αὐτὰρ ἐγώ 'As for me, I . . .'. Second, each verse that begins with this wording is preceded and activated by the performative gesture of *khaire* / *khairete* or by a periphrasis of that gesture.[97]

---

[97] Here I offer an inventory of cases where we find a periphrasis for *khaire* / *khairete*. The metabasis at *Homeric Hymn* 2.495 is preceded at 2.494 not by *khaire* but by an elaborate periphrasis. As for 30.17-18, we find both *khaire* and a similar periphrasis. At 10.4-5, we find both *khaire* and a different periphrasis. At 6.19-20, we find both *khaire* and yet another different periphrasis, which features a reference to the winning of a prize at an *agōn* 'competition', making explicit the actual occasion of performance.

2Ⓢ11. The poetics of metabasis in the Homeric Hymns

2§103 In all the cases of the hymnic salutation *khaire* / *khairete* that we have seen so far, this wording—or a periphrasis of this wording—has been followed by a metabasis. In other cases, however, the verse containing the wording *khaire* / *khairete* is not followed by any explicit metabasis (*Homeric Hymn* 7.58, 11.5, 13.3, 14.6, 15.9, 16.5, 17.5, 21.5, 22.7, 26.11).[98] The question is, are we to assume that the *humnos* in these other cases comes to a stop, or is there some other form of continuation?

2§104 In two cases of *khaire* / *khairete*, what follows is not a metabasis but a formula that serves as a substitute for metabasis.[99] Both cases occur in the *Homeric Hymn* (3) *to Apollo*, verses 14 and 166, where the word *khaire* / *khairete* 'hail and take pleasure' is used to salute respectively the goddess Leto and the Delian Maidens.[100] After the salutations at verses 14 and 166, the speaker goes on to say:

2①47 *Homeric Hymn* (3) *to Apollo* verses 19 and 207:

πῶς γάρ[101] σ' ὑμνήσω πάντως εὔυμνον ἐόντα

For how shall I <u>hymn</u> you, you who are so <u>absolutely</u> [*pantōs*] <u>good for hymning</u>?

2§105 Earlier, I described the wording framed in this verse as an aporetic question.[102] What this question achieves is a shift in perspective about the god as a hymnic subject. After the first aporetic question, as we already saw, the perspective shifts from Apollo as god of Delos to Apollo as god of all Hellenes, though the hymnic subject remains Apollo at Delos. After the second aporetic question, the perspective shifts from Apollo at Delos to Apollo at Delphi. Although there is a shift in perspective about the place where Apollo is worshipped, the hymnic subject still remains Apollo. These shifts that take place after the two separate moments of aporetic crisis are not a matter of shifting the subject, because the subject of the god remains the same.[103] That

---

[98] At *Homeric Hymn* 20.8, 23.4, and 24.5, we see periphrases for *khaire*, and no metabasis follows. At *Hymn* 13.3, the expression ἄρχε δ' ἀοιδήν 'start the singing' may conceivably refer to the starting of a subject different from the one that was started at 13.1, but it could also refer to the restarting of the same subject that was started at 13.1. At *Hymn* 18.12, the verse containing the *khaire* may have the effect of canceling the metabasis expressed in the previous verse, 18.11.

[99] Koller 1957:197. See also PR 82n37.

[100] The verse containing the salutation to the Delian Maidens at *Homeric Hymn* (3) *to Apollo* 166 has already been quoted at 2§27, with commentary on the meaning of *khairete* in the context of that salutation.

[101] At verse 19, the manuscript reading is γάρ, while at 207, it is τ'ἄρ.

[102] 2§§23 and following.

[103] 2§§52 and following.

Chapter Two

is, the Apollo of Delos is notionally the same god as the Apollo of Delphi.[104] To sum up, when the hymnic salutation *khaire / khairete* is followed by an aporetic question, there is a shift in perspective but not in subject.

2§106 Following up on this formulation, let us consider once again the hymnic salutations *khaire* and *khairete* at verses 14 and 166 in the *Homeric Hymn (3) to Apollo*. These salutations, as we have seen, are addressed to the goddess Leto as mother of Apollo and to the Delian Maidens respectively, and they are followed by declarations of aporetic crisis, addressed to Apollo at verses 19 and 207. Both Leto and the Delian Maidens are centrally linked to the main subject, the god Apollo, and the *Hymn* continues to concentrate on the main subject of Apollo by way of the two declarations of aporetic crisis. These declarations expand as well as extend the hymnic subject of Apollo, so that the god may reciprocate the augmented pleasure experienced from what continues to be said about him.

2§107 The continuation of the hymnic subject of Apollo, as signaled by the two declarations of aporetic crisis at verses 19 and 207, indicates a deferral of metabasis. This deferral is made explicit after the second hymnic salutation, *khairete* at *Homeric Hymn (3) to Apollo* 166, which is followed by *autar egōn* 'as for me, I . . .' at verse 177.[105] We expect a metabasis here at 177, as signaled by *autar egōn*, but the potential metabasis is deferred by way of an explicit declaration that cancels any metabasis at the moment. The speaker declares his intention, which is, 'I will not leave off [*lēgein*]':

2ⓣ48 *Homeric Hymn (3) to Apollo* 177-178

αὐτὰρ ἐγὼν οὐ λήξω ἑκηβόλον Ἀπόλλωνα
ὑμνέων

As for me, I will not leave off [*lēgein*] making the far-shooting Apollo

my *humnos*.

2§108 The phrasing *autar egōn* 'As for me, I . . .' at verse 177 could have induced a metabasis,[106] but the *Homeric Hymn (3) to Apollo* was not yet ready for

---

[104] In terms of politics, however, as I note in *HPC* I§27, the Apollo of Delos was in fact worlds apart from the Apollo of Delphi.

[105] Verses 166 and 177 of the *Homeric Hymn (3) to Apollo*, containing respectively the wording *khairete* 'hail and take pleasure' and the wording *autar egōn* 'as for me, I . . .', have already been quoted at 2§27.

[106] Martin 2000b:407n20.

2ⓢ11. The poetics of metabasis in the Homeric Hymns

it.[107] Instead of a metabasis at 177, there is a prolongation of the first subject, which thus remains the only subject. That subject is Apollo. Only when we reach the end of the *Hymn*, at verse 546, do we finally get to see a metabasis, introduced by a final *autar egō* 'As for me, I...', following a final *khaire* addressed to Apollo at 545:

2①49 *Homeric Hymn* (3) *to Apollo* 545-546

> Καὶ σὺ μὲν <u>οὕτω χαῖρε</u> Διὸς καὶ Λητοῦς υἱέ·
> <u>αὐτὰρ ἐγὼ</u> καὶ σεῖο καὶ <u>ἄλλης</u> μνήσομ' <u>ἀοιδῆς</u>
>
> So, <u>with all this said</u>, I say to you [= Apollo] now: <u>hail and take pleasure [*khaire*]</u>, son of Zeus and Leto.
> <u>As for me, I</u> will keep you in mind along with <u>the rest of the song</u>.

2§109 Once the hymnic salutation *khaire* / *khairete* is actually followed by a metabasis, what happens after the metabasis? As we are now about to see, the metabasis signals a shift in subject, not only in perspective. Metabasis is a device that signals a shift from the subject of the god with whom the song started—what I have been calling the hymnic subject—and then proceeds to a different subject—in what must remain notionally the same song. Ideally, the shift from subject to different subject will be smooth. Ideally, the different subject will be consequential, so that the consequent of what was started in the *humnos* may remain part of the *humnos*. This way, the transition will lead seamlessly to what is being called 'the rest of the song'. In other words, the concept of *humnos* is the concept of maintaining the song as the notionally same song by way of successfully executing a metabasis from the initial subject to the next subject. The initial subject of the god and the next subject are linked as one song by the *humnos* in general and by the device of hymnic metabasis in particular. What comes before the metabasis is the *prooimion*, the beginning of the *humnos*. What comes after the metabasis is no longer the *prooimion*—but it can still be considered the *humnos*.

2§110 We are ready to observe what kinds of different subjects can follow a metabasis that follows a hymnic salutation *khaire* / *khairete* that finally takes leave of a god initially invoked by a *humnos*. In two of the *Homeric Hymns*, the subject of the narration that follows the metabasis is made explicit:

---

[107] As I have already noted, the deferral of *metabasis* at verse 177 in the *Homeric Hymn to Apollo* is also signaled by the aporetic question that follows, at verse 207.

Chapter Two

2①50 *Homeric Hymn (31) to Helios 17-19*

χαῖρε ἄναξ, πρόφρων δὲ βίον θυμήρε' ὄπαζε·
ἐκ σέο δ' ἀρξάμενος κλήσω μερόπων γένος ἀνδρῶν
ἡμιθέων ὧν ἔργα θεοὶ θνητοῖσιν ἔδειξαν.

Hail and take pleasure [*khaire*], lord, and be favorably disposed, granting me a livelihood that suits my heart.

Taking my start from you I will give fame to the lineage [*genos*] of men,

heroes [*hēmitheoi*] that they are,[108] whose deeds [*erga*] have been shown by gods to mortals.[109]

2①51 *Homeric Hymn (32) to Selene 17-20*

χαῖρε ἄνασσα θεὰ λευκώλενε δῖα Σελήνη
πρόφρον ἐϋπλόκαμος· σέο δ' ἀρχόμενος κλέα φωτῶν
ᾄσομαι ἡμιθέων ὧν κλείουσ' ἔργματ' ἀοιδοὶ
Μουσάων θεράποντες ἀπὸ στομάτων ἐροέντων.

Hail and take pleasure [*khaire*], queen goddess, you with the white arms, shining Selene.

Be favorably disposed, you with the beautiful tresses [*plokamoi*]. Taking my start from you I will sing the glories [*klea*][110] of men,

singing of heroes [*hēmitheoi*][111] whose deeds [*ergmata*] singers celebrate with fame [*kleos*].

---

[108] On the special poetics of the word *hēmitheoi* 'demigods' in the sense of 'heroes', see EH §§66–73.

[109] The first of two kinds of narration here in *Hymn* 31.18–19, which is the narration of the *erga* 'deeds' of *hēmitheoi* 'heroes' (19), is linked with a second kind, which is the narration of their *genos* 'genesis, genealogy' (18). The second kind of narration corresponds to the meaning of the name *Melēsigenēs* 'he who is concerned with genealogy [*genos*]'—which is actually the name of Homer before he is renamed as Homer in the *Life of Homer* traditions. Analysis in HPC II§§13 and following.

[110] The word *kleos* is abstract in the singular, meaning 'fame', but it becomes concrete in the plural, *klea*, meaning 'things that are famed', which I will render hereafter as 'glories'.

[111] On the special poetics of the word *hēmitheoi* 'demigods' in the sense of 'heroes', I refer again to EH §§66–73.

2§11. The poetics of metabasis in the Homeric Hymns

They [= the singers] are attendants [*therapōn* plural] of the
Muses,[112] and the sounds that come from their mouths
evoke desire.[113]

2§111 These verses, taken from *Homeric Hymns* 31 and 32, are the most explicit examples of a central theme that tends to be less explicit in other *Homeric Hymns*. This theme concerns the power of the *humnos* to set in motion, by way of metabasis, a perfect narration about heroes, about the *erga* / *ergmata* 'deeds' of heroes (31.19 / 32.19). To sing these deeds is to confer *kleos* 'fame' (κλήσω 31.18 / κλέα 32.18). As I am about to argue, such a narration is the narrative of epic. In other words, the *humnos* may introduce an entire epic narrative.

2§112 The narrating of the epic deeds of heroes is mentioned even in the Hesiodic *Theogony*, which as we have already seen defines itself as one single continuous gigantic *humnos*. Toward the conclusion of its self-definition, the *Theogony* makes it explicit that the potential subjects of a poet's *humnos* are not only gods but also heroes and their famous deeds:

2①52 Hesiod *Theogony* 99-101

αὐτὰρ ἀοιδὸς
Μουσάων θεράπων κλεῖα προτέρων ἀνθρώπων
ὑμνήσει μάκαράς τε θεοὺς οἳ Ὄλυμπον ἔχουσιν

As for the singer [*aoidos*],
attendant [*therapōn*] of the Muses, he will sing the glories
[*klea*] of mortals of previous times,
making them [= the *klea* of mortals] the subject of his
humnos,[114] as well as the blessed gods who hold the stronghold of Olympus.

2§113 The narratives represented by the *klea* 'glories' of such heroes correspond to the catalogue-style narratives of heroic genealogies that follow

---

[112] On the significance of the expression '*therapōn* of the Muses', see BA 17§6 (= p. 295).
[113] The metonymy that comes to life in associating the *stomata* 'mouths' of poets—and of Muses—with their voices is part of an extended metonymy centering on an eroticized sense of desire as evoked by the voice of the singer. The eroticized theme of longing or *pothos* for heroes of the past is part of this extended metonymy: Nagy 2001e xxvii n20.
[114] I highlight the collocation of *humnein* with *klea* here in Hesiod *Theogony* 100-101. The verb *humnein* 'make X the subject of a *humnos*' takes as its direct object the subject of the song, and that subject is the *klea* 'glories' of heroes.

the *Theogony* as we know it, starting with verses 965 and following. Likewise, the narratives represented by what is called the *genos* of heroes in *Homeric Hymn* 31.18 correspond to the same kind of catalogue-style heroic genealogies. A further point of comparison is the fact that the narrating of the *genos* 'genesis' of the gods in *Theogony* 33 and 44 is equivalent to the narrating of the 'genealogies' of the gods, which is the essence of theogony. But there is more to it. As we see from *Homeric Hymn* 31.19, the *genos* 'genesis' of heroes is actually equated with the *erga* 'deeds' of heroes, and the latter term is evidently appropriate to the epics of heroes, not only to their heroic genealogies. The general reference to the *ergmata* 'deeds' of heroes in *Homeric Hymn* 32.19, without any specific reference to their *genos* or 'genealogies', shows that epic is the general category of the *klea* 'glories' of heroes, and that the catalogue-style narratives of heroic genealogies that we find in *Theogony* verses 965 and following is only a subcategory. In view of this comparative evidence, the reference in *Theogony* 100 to the *klea* 'glories' of mortals can be taken to be a general reference to epic. In sum, the relevant wording in *Homeric Hymns* 31 and 32 shows that the *humnos* has the power to 'move ahead and shift forward', by way of metabasis, to an epic narration as its hymnic consequent.

2§114 Even the *Theogony*, as a *humnos* in its own right, has the potential to 'move ahead and shift forward' to a form of heroic narrative as its own hymnic consequent. In the version of the *Theogony* as we have it, that hymnic consequent takes on the specific form of heroic genealogies that begin where the divine genealogies leave off. In theory, however, the *Theogony* could also 'move ahead and shift forward' to a hymnic consequent that takes on the general form of epic. I say "in theory" because it seems at first impossible to imagine any consequent that could match, in its amplitude, a *humnos* as ample—as gigantic—as the Hesiodic *Theogony*. On second thought, however, there is one possible match: the gigantic dimensions of the Hesiodic *Theogony* as a *humnos* match the gigantic dimensions of the Homeric *Iliad* and *Odyssey* as epics.[115] But then the question is: can we imagine a historical context where the Hesiodic *Theogony* could possibly have served as a *humnos* that 'moves ahead and shifts forward' to, say, the Homeric *Iliad*? What prevents an answer is the historical fact that the performance traditions of the *Iliad* are linked to Homer as the originator, whereas the performance traditions of the *Theogony* as we know it are linked to Hesiod. It would be another matter, however, if we asked the question in another way: can we imagine a historical context where

---

[115] BA^2 Preface §19n1 (= p. xiii), following Slatkin 1987 and Muellner 1996:45 (also 94–132).

2ⓢ11. The poetics of metabasis in the Homeric Hymns

a theogony could possibly have served as a *humnos* that 'moves ahead and shifts forward' to an epic about Troy, even to a Homeric *Iliad*?

2§115 For an answer to this revised question, it is essential to recall the primary subject of the Hesiodic *Theogony*, that is, Zeus himself. In effect, the *Theogony* as we have it is a gigantic Hesiodic Hymn to Zeus.[116] Accordingly, what we should be looking for as the *humnos* that 'moves ahead and shifts forward' to a Homeric *Iliad* is a gigantic Homeric Hymn to Zeus. In fact, we have already seen indications of such a *humnos*. Here I return to the concept of a "virtual" Homeric Hymn to Zeus as narrated by the *Homēridai* and as imitated by Pindar. As we saw earlier from the wording of Pindar's imitation, the beginning of such a *humnos* is technically a *prooimion*:

2ⓣ53 Pindar *Nemean* 2.1-3

Ὅθεν περ καὶ Ὁμηρίδαι | ῥαπτῶν ἐπέων τὰ πόλλ' ἀοιδοί | ἄρχονται, Διὸς ἐκ προοιμίου).

[starting] from the point where [*hothen*] the *Homēridai*, singers, most of the time begin [*arkhesthai*] their stitched-together words, from the *prooimion* of Zeus . . .

2§116 Technically, such a *prooimion* for a Homeric Hymn to Zeus, performed by the *Homēridai* as descendants of Homer, introduces as its hymnic consequent an epic that is performed by Homer himself as the ancestor of the *Homēridai*.[117] Such an epic is still a part of the *humnos*, though it is distinct from the *prooimion* that introduced it. Further, just as the epic is only the 'next' part of the *humnos*, the *prooimion* is only its 'first' part. In this sense, a Homeric Hymn to Zeus—or any Homeric Hymn—is only the first part of a *humnos*. Any Homeric Hymn is a *prooimion*—but without being a complete *humnos*. For a *humnos* to be complete, the *prooimion* must lead to a metabasis which must lead to a hymnic consequent.

2§117 Besides Pindar's imitation, there is an actual attestation of a Homeric Hymn to Zeus. It is highly compressed, consisting of only four verses:

2ⓣ54 Homeric *Hymn* (23) *to Zeus*

Ζῆνα θεῶν τὸν ἄριστον ἀείσομαι ἠδὲ μέγιστον
εὐρύοπα κρείοντα τελεσφόρον, ὅς τε Θέμιστι

---

[116] As for the first ten verses of the Hesiodic *Works and Days*, they amount to a miniature Hesiodic Hymn to Zeus. See GM 63.

[117] The idea of Homer as ancestor of the *Homēridai* is examined in HPC I§§138 and following.

245

Chapter Two

ἐγκλιδὸν ἑζομένη πυκινοὺς ὀάρους ὀαρίζει.
Ἴληθ' εὐρύοπα Κρονίδη κύδιστε μέγιστε.

I will sing Zeus as my subject, best of the gods, and most great,
whose sound reaches far and wide, the ruler, the one who brings things to their outcome [*telos*], the one who has Themis
attentively seated at his side, and he keeps her company with regular frequency.
Be propitious, you whose sound reaches far and wide, son of Kronos, you who are most resplendent and most great.

I describe this composition as "a *Hymn to Zeus*" not "the *Hymn to Zeus*" because there is no reason to assume the existence of only one such *humnos*. In the extant corpus of *Homeric Hymns*, we find multiple versions of *humnoi* addressed to divine addressees: there are for example three *Hymns to Dionysus* (*Homeric Hymn* 1, with an undetermined number of verses; *Hymn* 7, with 59 verses; *Hymn* 26, with 13 verses), three *Hymns to Aphrodite* (*Homeric Hymn* 5, with 293 verses; *Hymn* 6, with 21 verses; *Hymn* 10, with six verses), two *Hymns to Artemis* (*Homeric Hymn* 9, with 9 verses; *Hymn* 27, with 22 verses).

2Ⓢ12. An eternal deferral of epic in a *humnos* by Callimachus

2§118 To be contrasted with the *Homeric Hymn* (23) *to Zeus* is a virtual *Homeric Hymn to Zeus* by Callimachus: it is his *Hymn* (1) *to Zeus*, consisting of 94 verses. I qualify my description "Homeric" by adding "virtual," since we find a striking feature in this *Hymn to Zeus* by Callimachus that stands in sharp contrast to the *Homeric Hymns*. This *Hymn* by Callimachus not only lacks a metabasis to another subject. It also defers the possibility of such a metabasis, and the deferral is eternal:

2Ⓣ55 Callimachus *Hymn* (1) *to Zeus* 91-94

χαῖρε μέγα, Κρονίδη πανυπέρτατε, δῶτορ ἑάων,
δῶτορ ἀπημονίης. τεὰ δ' ἔργματα τίς κεν ἀείδοι;
οὐ γένετ', οὐκ ἔσται· τίς κεν Διὸς ἔργματ' ἀείσει;

2ⓈS12. An eternal deferral of epic in a *humnos* by Callimachus

χαῖρε, πάτερ, χαῖρ' αὖθι· δίδου δ' ἀρετήν τ' ἄφενός τε.

Hail and take great pleasure [*khaire*] mightily, son of Kronos,
the highest of them all, giver of good things,
giver of freedom from pain. Who could sing your deeds [*ergmata*]?
No one like that ever was or ever will be. Who could sing the deeds [*ergmata*] of Zeus?
Hail and take pleasure [*khaire*], Father. Once again, hail [*khaire*]! And give me excellence and wealth.

2§119 This deferral must be contrasted with the two deferrals of metabasis in the *Homeric Hymn (3) to Apollo*. As we have seen, the hymnic salutations *khaire* and *khairete* at verses 14 and 166 of this *Hymn*, which are addressed respectively to the goddess Leto as mother of Apollo and to the Delian Maidens, are followed by aporetic questions addressed to Apollo at verses 19 and 207. As we have also seen, these questions have the effect of prolonging the first subject, which thus remains the only subject. That subject is Apollo. Only when we reach the end of the *Homeric Hymn (3) to Apollo*, at verse 546, do we finally get to see a metabasis, introduced by a final *autar egō* 'as for me, I. . . .', following a final *khaire* addressed to Apollo at verse 545. The contrast here with Callimachus' *Hymn to Zeus* is striking: there, the metabasis never comes. In that *Hymn* by Callimachus, the first subject remains the only subject, and that is Zeus. The metabasis that is potentially activated by *khaire* 'hail and take pleasure' at verse 91 of Callimachus' *Hymn to Zeus* never takes place, and instead the *humnos* proceeds to another *khaire* at verse 94, and then to yet another *khaire* at verse 94. After the first of the three occurrences of *khaire* at verse 91 comes an aporetic question at verse 92: who could possibly sing the *ergmata* 'deeds' of Zeus? But the only decision that follows the aporetic question at verse 92 is the decision to proceed to another aporetic question at verse 93, where the question is repeated: who could possibly sing the *ergmata* 'deeds' of Zeus? And the only decision that follows the repeated aporetic question is the decision to make a repetition of *khaire* at verse 94, to be followed by yet another repetition of *khaire* at verse 94.

2§120 By deferring a metabasis from the subject of Zeus in a would-be "Homeric" *Hymn to Zeus*, the Callimachean *Hymn to Zeus* defers for all time to come the hymnic consequent of a "Homeric" epic. Not only does this Callimachean *Hymn* lack a metabasis. In point of fact, all six of the *Hymns* of

Chapter Two

Callimachus lack a metabasis. Like the *Hymn* (1) *to Zeus*, the five other *Hymns* of Callimachus also feature the hymnic salutation *khaire* toward the end, anticipating a metabasis, but the metabasis never comes. The absence of metabasis in the Callimachean *Hymns* 2, 3, 4, 5, 6 is not remarkable in and of itself, since we have seen that a number of attested *Homeric Hymns* likewise lack an overt metabasis. What is remarkable, however, is the ostentatious negation of metabasis in Callimachus' *Hymn to Zeus*. As I have been arguing about Pindar's imitation of a virtual *Homeric Hymn to Zeus*, what makes such a *humnos* "Homeric" is that a *Hymn to Zeus*—as supreme god among all other gods—is the *prooimion* of choice for the descendants of Homer, the *Homēridai*. Zeus as the supreme god is evidently the preferred subject for a *humnos* that 'moves ahead and shifts forward' to the supreme epic as its hymnic consequent. From the standpoint of the poetics of such a *humnos*, that supreme epic would be an epic by Homer himself, ancestor of the *Homēridai*.

2§121 From the standpoint of Callimachean poetics, however, the making of a perfect new *Hymn to Zeus* does not imply a need to make a perfect new epic to follow it. As we saw, the infinite deferral of metabasis in the *Hymn to Zeus* by Callimachus has the effect of deferring infinitely the making of such a perfect new epic. Still, as I will now argue, the notional perfection of the *Hymn* implies a need for another kind of perfection. There is a necessity to perfect the text of the old epic, that is, the epic of Homer.

2§122 In the age of Callimachus, the perfect text of Homer is imagined as virtual, not real. The reality of a perfect text has not yet happened. Such a reality is to be deferred until some future moment when a perfect text is finally achieved. And such an achievement can only be realized through an ongoing and never-ending process of *diorthōsis* or 'corrective editing'. In the age of Callimachus, the text of Homer is perceived as still imperfect. Its eventual perfection is the implied promise of the *Homeric Hymns* as reinterpreted in the *Hymns* of Callimachus.

2ⓢ13. The fluidity of the Homeric tradition in the age of Callimachus

2§123 What was so imperfect about the old text of Homer? That perceived imperfection, I submit, had to do with the fluidity of the Homeric textual tradition in the age of Callimachus. A sign of that fluidity was the scholarly notion, current in this period, that the Homeric text accommodated non-Homeric elements. These notionally non-Homeric elements can be described as Cyclic, Hesiodic, and Orphic.

2§124 The order in which I list these elements here is meant to indicate a chronological sequence in the evolution of Homeric poetry, and the list proceeds from later to earlier phases. I present at length the rationale for positing this sequence in the twin book, *Homer the Preclassic*. Here I simply offer a working definition for all three.

2§125 By <u>Cyclic</u> I mean the poetry of the epic Cycle as understood by Aristotle, for whom the Cycle was categorically non-Homeric and even post-Homeric. I reserve for Chapter 3 my discussion of Aristotle's explicit comments concerning the distinctions he sees between Homer and the epic Cycle. And I reserve for the twin book *Homer the Preclassic* my discussion of a preclassical era—what I call there the Dark Age—when the Cycle was considered Homeric: in that era, Homer was viewed as the notional author of all epic, as represented by the concept of the epic Cycle before it became historically differentiated from the *Iliad* and *Odyssey*.[118]

2§126 By <u>Hesiodic</u> I mean the poetry of the *Theogony* and the *Works and Days*, ascribed to Hesiod. But the term <u>Hesiodic</u> also includes, beyond the *Theogony* and the *Works and Days*, such "pseudo-Hesiodic" suites as the *Catalogue of Women*.[119] As the discussion proceeds, we will see that there was relatively less overlap of Homeric traditions with the Hesiodic than there was with the Cyclic and the Orphic.

2§127 By <u>Orphic</u> I mean the poetry attributed to the mystical figure of Orpheus. I note from the start that this poetry was not as clearly defined in the ancient world as the poetry of the Cyclic and Hesiodic traditions, and there are traces of overlap with those traditions.[120]

2§128 Seeking a more precise definition of <u>Orphic</u>, I find it useful to start with Plato. I will wait till Chapter 3 before I consider in detail what Plato himself thought of Orpheus and Orphic poetry, restricting here my field of vision to Plato's general reportage of conventional views about this poetry.

2§129 From Plato's works, we will see that poetry ascribed to Orpheus was conventionally associated with *humnos*—both the word and the concept. Such poetry, as we will also see, is fundamentally mystical in nature. The idea of Orpheus as a prototypical master of mystical *humnoi* highlights various dissimilarities between Homeric and Orphic poetry—insofar as these two

---

[118] *HPC* I§§169–170.

[119] *GM* 56.

[120] For example, we may consider the "Cyclic" *Theogony* as reflected in "Apollodorus": see West 1983:121–126, especially p. 125, where he infers that "this Cyclic theogony itself went under the name of Orpheus."

categories of poetry are described by Plato. In terms of these descriptions, what was Orphic was non-Homeric, just as Cyclic and Hesiodic poetry were non-Homeric.

2§130 At first sight, Orphic poetry seems to be post-Homeric as well as non-Homeric. In the twin book *Homer the Preclassic*, however, I show that the poetry associated with Orpheus stems from a pre-Homeric tradition—that is, if we define pre-Homeric in terms of earlier periods when Orphic poetry was not yet differentiated from what later became Homeric poetry. And what applies to the relative dating of Orphic poetry applies to Cyclic and Hesiodic poetry as well: all three traditions seem to be post-Homeric at first sight, but various aspects turn out to be pre-Homeric. In *Homer the Preclassic*, I develop further the rationale for what I just said about all three traditions. For now, however, I confine myself to the Orphic traditions.

2§131 In searching for pre-Homeric aspects of Orphic traditions, I start with various convergences between Orphic and Homeric poetry, which tend to be shaded over by Plato. A premier example of such a convergence is the mystical cosmic stream named Ōkeanos. In introducing the concept of such a stream, I choose a most conventional description, as captured by these words of Plato:

2①56 Plato *Phaedo* 112e

> τὰ μὲν οὖν δὴ ἄλλα πολλά τε καὶ μεγάλα καὶ παντοδαπὰ <u>ῥεύματά</u> ἐστι· τυγχάνει δ' ἄρα ὄντα ἐν τούτοις τοῖς πολλοῖς τέτταρ' ἄττα <u>ῥεύματα</u>, ὧν τὸ μὲν μέγιστον καὶ ἐξωτάτω <u>ῥέον</u> <u>περὶ κύκλῳ</u> ὁ καλούμενος <u>Ὠκεανός</u> ἐστιν.
>
> There are many and various great <u>streams</u> [*rheumata*] of all kinds in the world, but among these there happen to be four <u>streams</u> [*rheumata*] to be noted in particular, and among these four the greatest is the one that <u>flows</u> [*rheîn*] <u>around</u> the world at the outermost periphery in a <u>circle</u> [*kuklos*], and that stream is called the <u>Ōkeanos</u>.

2§132 In the next Platonic passage to be quoted, we are about to see that this stream Ōkeanos is explicitly connected with the idea of cosmic fluidity, which converges with the theory of Heraclitus about a universe that is perpetually in flux (Heraclitus A 5 DK, by way of Plato *Cratylus* 402a). We are also about to see the same poetic word-play we had seen earlier in the *Hymn to Zeus* by Callimachus, whose words connected the metaphorical fluidity of the *humnos* with the name of the mother of Zeus, *Rhea*. Moreover, our upcoming

Platonic passage shows that the Homeric Ōkeanos is explicitly associated with an Orphic Ōkeanos:

2①57 Plato *Cratylus* 402a-d

ΣΩ. Γελοῖον μὲν πάνυ εἰπεῖν, οἶμαι μέντοι τινὰ πιθανότητα ἔχον.

ΕΡΜ. Τίνα ταύτην;

ΣΩ. Τὸν Ἡράκλειτόν μοι δοκῶ καθορᾶν παλαί᾽ ἄττα σοφὰ <u>λέγοντα</u>, ἀτεχνῶς τὰ ἐπὶ Κρόνου καὶ <u>Ῥέας</u>, <u>ἃ καὶ Ὅμηρος ἔλεγεν</u>.

ΕΡΜ. Πῶς τοῦτο <u>λέγεις</u>;

ΣΩ. <u>Λέγει</u> που Ἡράκλειτος ὅτι 'πάντα χωρεῖ καὶ οὐδὲν μένει', καὶ <u>ποταμοῦ ῥοῇ ἀπεικάζων τὰ ὄντα λέγει</u> ὡς 'δὶς ἐς τὸν αὐτὸν ποταμὸν οὐκ ἂν ἐμβαίης'.

ΕΡΜ. Ἔστι ταῦτα. {b}

ΣΩ. Τί οὖν; δοκεῖ σοι ἀλλοιότερον Ἡρακλείτου νοεῖν ὁ τιθέμενος τοῖς τῶν ἄλλων θεῶν προγόνοις '"<u>Ῥέαν</u>" τε καὶ "Κρόνον"'; ἆρα οἴει ἀπὸ τοῦ αὐτομάτου αὐτὸν ἀμφοτέροις <u>ῥευμάτων</u> ὀνόματα θέσθαι; ὥσπερ αὖ <u>Ὅμηρος</u>

<u>Ὠκεανόν</u> τε θεῶν <u>γένεσίν</u>" φησιν "καὶ μητέρα Τηθύν·

Iliad XIV 201 and 302

οἶμαι δὲ καὶ <u>Ἡσίοδος</u>. λέγει δέ που καὶ <u>Ὀρφεὺς</u> ὅτι

<u>Ὠκεανὸς</u> πρῶτος <u>καλλίρροος</u> ἦρξε γάμοιο, {c}
ὅς ῥα κασιγνήτην ὁμομήτορα <u>Τηθὺν</u> ὄπυιεν.

ταῦτ᾽ οὖν σκόπει ὅτι καὶ ἀλλήλοις συμφωνεῖ καὶ πρὸς τὰ τοῦ Ἡρακλείτου πάντα τείνει.

ΕΡΜ. Φαίνῃ τί μοι λέγειν, ὦ Σώκρατες· τὸ μέντοι τῆς Τηθύος οὐκ ἐννοῶ ὄνομα τί βούλεται.

ΣΩ. Ἀλλὰ μὴν τοῦτό γε ὀλίγου αὐτὸ λέγει ὅτι <u>πηγῆς ὄνομα ἐπικεκρυμμένον ἐστίν</u>. τὸ γὰρ διαττώμενον καὶ {d} τὸ ἠθούμενον πηγῆς ἀπείκασμά ἐστιν· ἐκ δὲ τούτων ἀμφοτέρων τῶν ὀνομάτων ἡ <u>Τηθὺς</u> τὸ ὄνομα σύγκειται.

ΕΡΜ. Τοῦτο μέν, ὦ Σώκρατες, κομψόν.

Chapter Two

SOCRATES: I have something ridiculous to say, though it is plausible.

HERMOGENES: What is that?

SOCRATES: I think I can picture Heraclitus speaking [*legein*] some ancient [*palaia*] wise [*sopha*] things that go back to the time of Kronos and Rhea—things that Homer also was speaking [*legein*].

HERMOGENES: What do you mean when you are saying [*legein*] this?

SOCRATES: Heraclitus says [*legein*], if I have it right, that "all things are in motion and nothing is stationary." He compares the universe to the stream [*rhoē*] of a river and says [*legein*] that "you cannot go into the same river twice."[121]

HERMOGENES: Yes, this is the way he says it.

SOCRATES: Well, then, do you think that he was thinking [*noeîn*] differently from Heraclitus—(when I say 'he') I mean the one who established [*tithesthai*] the names of Rhea and Kronos for the ancestors of the gods? So do you think it was purely automatic that he established [*tithesthai*] the names of streams [*rheumata*] for both of them? Consider where Homer says

> Ōkeanos, the genesis [*genesis*] of gods, and mother Tethys[122]
>
> *Iliad* XIV 201 and 302

And I think that Hesiod says the same thing.[123] And, if I have it right, Orpheus says that

> Ōkeanos, with his beautiful streams [*kalli-rrhoos*], was the first to start a marriage,[124]
>
> and he married his sister Tethys, who was his mother's daughter.[125]
>
> *Orphic Fragment* 22 ed. Bernabé

---

[121] Here we see the main testimony for Heraclitus A 6 DK. See also West 1983:118, who thinks that Plato is "playfully" arguing here "that more than one of the older poets anticipated the Heraclitean doctrine of flux."
[122] See *Iliad* XIV 201 and 302.
[123] Hesiod *Theogony* 337.
[124] The depersonalized becomes personalized, as if for the first time.
[125] On these two Orphic verses, see Janko 1992:181.

2§13. The fluidity of the Homeric tradition . . .

So when you look at these wordings you see that they are in agreement with one another and that they are all heading in the direction of Heraclitus.

HERMOGENES: I think that there is something in what you say [*legein*], Socrates, but I do not register in my mind [*en-noeîn*] what the name of Tethys means.

SOCRATES: Well, this name comes very close to saying what it is. It is a mystical name of a spring,[126] since that which is strained [διαττώμενον] and filtered [ἠθούμενον] sounds like a spring, and the name Tethys is composed of these two words.

HERMOGENES: The explanation is quite elegant, Socrates.

2§133 Here we see an explicit reference to the Orphic affinities of Homeric poetry. And the poetry of Orpheus is linked here with whatever is generative, as symbolized by the generative—and fluid—power of the Ōkeanos that surrounds the earth.

2§134 Later on, I will take a closer look at the Homeric verse embedded in this Platonic passage, *Iliad* XIV 201 / 302 (Ὠκεανόν τε θεῶν γένεσιν καὶ μητέρα Τηθύν). For now, however, I simply view the passage as a whole, highlighting two facts. First, the passage deals with two subjects: cosmogony and initiation into mysteries. Second, there are verses being quoted from 'Homer', 'Orpheus', and Heraclitus in an overall mystical context.

2§135 These two facts are relevant to what we find in the *Derveni Papyrus*, which has been dated around 340 to 320 BCE.[127] This text, which is a commentary on poetry attributed to Orpheus, centers on two subjects: cosmogony and initiation into mysteries.[128] Moreover, the anonymous commentator of the *Derveni Papyrus* quotes from 'Homer',[129] 'Orpheus',[130] and Heraclitus.[131] It is clear that the commentator understands his main poetic source to be Orpheus

---

[126] Note the mystical language implied by ἐπικεκρυμμένον: *epi-kruptesthai* is to 'hide the meaning'.
[127] Kouremenos, Parássoglou, and Tsantsanoglou 2006. On the dating, see Tsantsanoglou and Parássoglou 1988; see also Funghi 1997:26.
[128] Obbink 1997. See especially his p. 54, where he justifies the opinion, expressed by Pfeiffer 1968:139n1, that the *Derveni Papyrus* is a pre-Alexandrian *hupomnēma* 'commentary' on Orphic poetry.
[129] *Derveni Papyrus* column 26 adduces verses that match *Odyssey* viii 335 and *Iliad* XXIV 527–528. See Obbink 1997:41n4, who argues persuasively that the commentator considered these verses not Homeric but Orphic: "no doubt he [= the commentator] held that Homer had borrowed these lines from Orpheus' poem." See also Böhme 1988 and 1989.
[130] *Derveni Papyrus* column 22 adduces a number of verses from the Orphic *Hymns*. See in general Obbink 1997.
[131] *Derveni Papyrus* column 4 adduces Heraclitus B 3 and B 94 DK.

Chapter Two

(δηλοῖ, column 26 lines 2 and 5).¹³² Moreover, in one of his quotations from Orphic poetry, he says specifically that he is quoting from 'what has been said in the <u>humnoi</u>' (ἔστι δὲ καὶ ἐν τοῖς "<u>Ὕμνοις</u> εἰρ[η]μένον, column 22 line 11). So the mystical medium of Orphic poetry is specified as *humnos*. One expert has raised the possibility "that the theogonic poem treated by the commentator was at the time of his writing still primarily an oral poem: it must have existed solely in an oral, rhapsodically transmitted state not more than a generation or so before the writing of the papyrus."¹³³ At one point, the anonymous commentator of the *Derveni Papyrus* insists on the importance of interpreting correctly the *huponoia* 'meaning' of the poet.¹³⁴ This mentality resembles that of a rhapsode, such as the figure of Ion in Plato's *Ion*, who claims expertise in interpreting correctly the *dianoia* 'meaning' of Homer himself (530b-c).¹³⁵

2§136 As we saw from Plato's wording in the *Cratylus* (402a-d), quoted a moment ago, the idea of initiation into the mysteries is expressed by the theme of a secret name given to the mystical *pēgē* 'source' of initiation. The etymologizing of the name of Tethys is unscientific from the standpoint of modern historical linguistics, but the actual idea conveyed by the false etymology, *pēgē* as 'source', reveals a conventional mentality deriving from traditions of initiation.

2§137 The same theme of a secret name given to a source of initiation recurs in yet another relevant Platonic passage:

2①58 Plato *Theaetetus* 179e-180d

> ΘΕΟ. παντάπασι μὲν οὖν. καὶ γάρ, ὦ Σώκρατες, περὶ τούτων τῶν Ἡρακλειτείων ἤ, ὥσπερ σὺ λέγεις, '<u>Ὁμηρείων</u> καὶ ἔτι <u>παλαιοτέρων</u>, αὐτοῖς μὲν τοῖς περὶ τὴν Ἔφεσον, ὅσοι προσποιοῦνται ἔμπειροι, οὐδὲν μᾶλλον οἷόν τε διαλεχθῆναι ἢ τοῖς οἰστρῶσιν. ἀτεχνῶς γὰρ κατὰ τὰ συγγράμματα φέρονται, τὸ δ' ἐπιμεῖναι ἐπὶ λόγῳ καὶ ἐρωτήματι καὶ ἡσυχίως {180a} ἐν μέρει ἀποκρίνασθαι καὶ ἐρέσθαι ἧττον αὐτοῖς ἔνι ἢ τὸ μηδέν· μᾶλλον δὲ ὑπερβάλλει τὸ οὐδ' οὐδὲν πρὸς τὸ μηδὲ σμικρὸν ἐνεῖναι τοῖς ἀνδράσιν ἡσυχίας. ἀλλ' ἄν τινά τι ἔρῃ, ὥσπερ ἐκ φαρέτρας <u>ῥηματίσκια</u> <u>αἰνιγματώδη</u> ἀνασπῶντες ἀποτοξεύουσι, κἂν τούτου ζητῇς λόγον λαβεῖν τί εἴρηκεν, ἑτέρῳ

---

¹³² Obbink 1997:41n4.
¹³³ Obbink 1997:41n2.
¹³⁴ Funghi 1997:29, where she also remarks that the surviving fragments of Orphic literature reveal "an inclination not to crystallize the written discourse but rather to perpetuate an 'open' text."
¹³⁵ PR 29-30.

πεπλήξῃ καινῶς μετωνομασμένῳ. περανεῖς δὲ οὐδέποτε οὐδὲν πρὸς οὐδένα αὐτῶν· οὐδέ γε ἐκεῖνοι αὐτοὶ πρὸς ἀλλήλους, ἀλλ' εὖ πάνυ φυλάττουσι τὸ μηδὲν βέβαιον ἐᾶν εἶναι {b} μήτ' ἐν λόγῳ μήτ' ἐν ταῖς αὐτῶν ψυχαῖς, ἡγούμενοι, ὡς ἐμοὶ δοκεῖ, αὐτὸ <u>στάσιμον</u> εἶναι· τούτῳ δὲ πάνυ πολεμοῦσιν, καὶ καθ' ὅσον δύνανται πανταχόθεν ἐκβάλλουσιν.

ΣΩ. Ἴσως, ὦ Θεόδωρε, τοὺς ἄνδρας μαχομένους ἑώρακας, εἰρηνεύουσιν δὲ οὐ συγγέγονας· οὐ γὰρ σοὶ ἑταῖροί εἰσιν. ἀλλ' οἶμαι τὰ τοιαῦτα τοῖς μαθηταῖς ἐπὶ σχολῆς φράζουσιν, οὓς ἂν βούλωνται ὁμοίους αὑτοῖς ποιῆσαι.

ΘΕΟ. Ποίοις μαθηταῖς, ὦ δαιμόνιε; οὐδὲ γίγνεται τῶν {c} τοιούτων ἕτερος ἑτέρου μαθητής, ἀλλ' αὐτόματοι ἀναφύονται ὁπόθεν ἂν τύχῃ ἕκαστος αὐτῶν ἐνθουσιάσας, καὶ τὸν ἕτερον ὁ ἕτερος οὐδὲν ἡγεῖται εἰδέναι. παρὰ μὲν οὖν τούτων, ὅπερ ᾖα ἐρῶν, οὐκ ἄν ποτε λάβοις λόγον οὔτε ἑκόντων οὔτε ἀκόντων· αὐτοὺς δὲ δεῖ <u>παραλαβόντας</u> ὥσπερ πρόβλημα ἐπισκοπεῖσθαι.

ΣΩ. Καὶ μετρίως γε λέγεις. τὸ δὲ δὴ πρόβλημα ἄλλο τι <u>παρειλήφαμεν</u> παρὰ μὲν τῶν <u>ἀρχαίων</u> μετὰ ποιήσεως {d} ἐπικρυπτομένων τοὺς πολλούς, ὡς ἡ <u>γένεσις</u> τῶν ἄλλων πάντων 'Ὠκεανός τε καὶ Τηθὺς <u>ῥεύματα</u> <ὄντα> τυγχάνει καὶ οὐδὲν <u>ἕστηκε</u>, παρὰ δὲ τῶν <u>ὑστέρων</u> ἅτε <u>σοφωτέρων</u> ἀναφανδὸν ἀποδεικνυμένων, ἵνα καὶ οἱ <u>σκυτοτόμοι</u> αὐτῶν τὴν σοφίαν μάθωσιν ἀκούσαντες καὶ παύσωνται ἠλιθίως οἰόμενοι τὰ μὲν <u>ἑστάναι</u>, τὰ δὲ <u>κινεῖσθαι</u> τῶν ὄντων, μαθόντες δὲ ὅτι πάντα <u>κινεῖται</u> τιμῶσιν αὐτούς;

THEODORUS: By all means, I agree, since the idea of having a dialogue with the people in Ephesus themselves who profess to be knowledgeable about these followers of Heraclitus—or, as you say, of Homer or of still more ancient [*palaioi*] men—is like having a dialogue with people who are under the influence of a gadfly's sting.[136] In synchronization with their own writings they are literally in motion, and their capacity for staying still in order to pay attention to a piece of discourse [*logos*] or to a question or to a serene interchange of question and answer amounts to less than

---

[136] The speaker here is agreeing with Socrates that the two of them must follow through in tracing back to their source the principles that are being garbled by the followers of Heraclitus who are based 'in Ionia', especially in Ephesus (Plato *Theaetetus* 179d).

Chapter Two

nothing, or rather even a minus quantity is too strong an expression for the absence of the least modicum of serenity in these men. When you ask a question, they draw from their quiver <u>initiatory formulas</u> [<u>rhēmatiskia</u>] that are <u>full of riddles</u> [<u>ainigmatōdē</u>] to shoot at you, and if you try to obtain some account [<u>logos</u>] of what these things mean to say, you will be instantly shot by another little formula, newly rephrased for the occasion. You will never get through to any of them, nor, for that matter, do they ever get through to each other, but they take very good care to leave nothing solid either in discourse [<u>logos</u>] or in their own life of the spirit [<u>psukhē</u>]. I suppose they think that would be something <u>stationary</u> [<u>stasimon</u>]—a thing they will fight against to the last and do their utmost to banish from the universe.

SOCRATES: Perhaps, Theodorus, you have seen these men in the act of making war and never met them in their peaceful moments. I say this because it is obvious to me that they are no friends of yours. But I would think that they must take time out to explain such matters to those disciples whom they want to look just the way they are.

THEODORUS: Disciples? What disciples? What on earth has possessed you? Why, for such people there is no such thing as being a disciple of anyone else. They are self-generated, and each one of them gets his divine inspiration from wherever he happens to be, and not one of them thinks that the other one understands anything. So, as I was going to say, you can never get an accounting [<u>logos</u>] from them, either with or without their consent. We must ourselves <u>take the tradition</u> [<u>paralambanein</u>] as a given and try to solve it like a problem.

SOCRATES: What you say is quite reasonable. As for the problem, isn't it that <u>we have</u> on the one hand <u>a tradition</u> [<u>paralambanein</u>] that derives from the <u>ancient ones</u> [<u>arkhaioi</u>], who hid their meaning [<u>epi-kruptesthai</u>][137] from the *hoi polloi* by way of poetry [<u>poiēsis</u>]—a tradition that says that the <u>genesis</u> [<u>genesis</u>] of all things, <u>Ōkeanos and Tethys</u>, happen to be <u>flowing streams</u> [<u>rheumata</u>] and that nothing <u>is static</u> [<u>hestanai</u>]?[138] And that we have, on the other hand, a tradition that derives from the ones who came after [the ancient

---

[137] Note the mystical language: *epi-kruptesthai* is to 'hide the meaning'.
[138] What is fluid is not rigid or 'static'.

ones], that is, from the later ones [*husteroi*], who are more wise [*sophoi*] [than the ancient ones] and who make their explanations quite openly, in order that even leatherworkers [*skutotomoi*] may hear and understand their wisdom [*sophia*]¹³⁹ and, abandoning their simple understanding that some things are static [*hestanai*] while other things are in motion [*kineîsthai*], may hold in respect those who teach them that all things are in motion [*kineîsthai*]?

2§138 In this passage, the idea that everything is fluid—or, more generally, that there is no hard and fast dichotomy between rigidity and fluidity—is being treated as a mystical tradition originating from both Orphic and Homeric poetry. This mystical idea is a 'tradition' (as expressed by the wording παρειλήφαμεν at 180c) derived from the *arkhaioi* 'ancient ones', who communicate by way of poetry to the initiated few (180c-d παρὰ μὲν τῶν ἀρχαίων μετὰ ποιήσεως ἐπικρυπτομένων τοὺς πολλούς). The *arkhaioi* 'ancient ones' are contrasted with the *husteroi* 'later ones', who express their ideas about fluidity and rigidity for all to hear, without any mystery (180d). The contrast here is between earlier thinkers who depend on mystical sources and later thinkers who depend on non-mystical sources. Plato's wording leaves it ambiguous whether Homer himself belongs to the earlier mystical sources or to the later non-mystical sources. As I will argue, Homer is mystical only if he is left undifferentiated from Orpheus. If that is the case, Homer's followers belong to the *arkhaioi* 'ancient ones'. If, however, he is differentiated from Orpheus, then Homer's followers become the *husteroi* 'later ones'. It is made explicit that there are thinkers who are *palaioteroi* 'more ancient' than the thinkers who specialize in Homer (179e Ὁμηρείων καὶ ἔτι παλαιοτέρων). The primary source of such relatively 'more ancient' thinkers, as we can see from all the relevant Platonic contexts taken together, was Orpheus, whose poetry was conventionally thought to be older than the poetry of Homer.

2§139 There is no need to infer that Plato himself thought of Orpheus as genuinely more ancient than Homer. Still, Plato's wording regularly features Orpheus as a predecessor of Homer in conventional references to the ancient poets. Further, Plato's wording consistently characterizes Orpheus as a mystical figure, whereas the figure of Homer is mystical only in contexts where he is not being differentiated from the 'more ancient' Orpheus.

2§140 Pursuing the idea of Orpheus as a master of mysteries, I draw attention to the use of the adjective *ainigmatōdē* 'full of riddles' applied to

---

[139] For the moment, I translate *sophia* simply as 'wisdom'. As the argumentation develops, I will modify this translation in accordance with earlier meanings of the word.

Chapter Two

rhēmatiskia 'initiatory formulas' in this passage that I just quoted from Plato's *Theaetetus*. We may compare the word *ainigmatōdēs* 'riddling' applied to the 'Orphic' poem that is being interpreted by the anonymous commentator of the *Derveni Papyrus* (column 7 line 5).[140] In the passage from the *Theaetetus*, we see not only the theme of initiation but also the content of the mystery of this initiation: it concerns a contrast between *kineîsthai* 'to be in motion' and *hestanai* 'to be static', which is comparable to a contrast between the metaphors of fluidity and rigidity—metaphors I have been tracing since the beginning of Chapter 1. Elsewhere in the *Theaetetus* of Plato, the idea of *kineîsthai* 'to be in motion' is explicitly correlated with the idea of fluidity, and an undifferentiated Homer is specified as the source for such a correlation. In fact, the Homeric verse that is cited as the specific context is the same verse about the Ōkeanos that we have already seen quoted elsewhere by Plato, that is, *Iliad* XIV 201 / 302:

2①59 Plato *Theaetetus* 152e

ἔστι μὲν γὰρ οὐδέποτ' οὐδέν, ἀεὶ δὲ γίγνεται. καὶ περὶ τούτου πάντες ἑξῆς οἱ σοφοὶ πλὴν Παρμενίδου συμφερέσθων, Πρωταγόρας τε καὶ Ἡράκλειτος καὶ Ἐμπεδοκλῆς, καὶ τῶν ποιητῶν οἱ ἄκροι τῆς ποιήσεως ἑκατέρας, κωμῳδίας μὲν Ἐπίχαρμος, τραγῳδίας δὲ <u>Ὅμηρος</u>, <ὃς> εἰπών—

Ὠκεανόν τε θεῶν γένεσιν καὶ μητέρα Τηθύν

Iliad XIV 201 / 302

—πάντα εἴρηκεν ἔκγονα <u>ῥοῆς</u> τε καὶ <u>κινήσεως</u>· ἢ οὐ δοκεῖ τοῦτο λέγειν;

For nothing ever is, and things are always becoming. In this matter let us take it for granted that, with the exception of Parmenides, the whole series of wise men [*sophoi*] agree—Protagoras, Heraclitus, Empedocles—and among the poets the ones that are first and foremost in each of the two kinds of poetry [*poiēsis*], Epicharmus in comedy, and <u>Homer</u> in tragedy. When Homer says [*legein / eipeîn*] . . .

Ōkeanos, genesis of the gods, and mother Tethys

Iliad XIV 201 / 302

---

[140] I find it significant that the *Derveni Papyrus* column 20 line 1 refers to initiations that take place [*en*] *polesin* 'in cities', to be contrasted with privatized initiations (column 20 line 3 and following).

he has just said [eirēkenai] that all things are the offspring of a flowing stream [rhoē] and of motion [kinēsis]. Or don't you think that is what he is saying [legein]?

2§141 I will save the details for Chapter 3, where I focus on the divergences between Orpheus and Homer in Plato, not on the convergences. For now, it is enough to say that Plato's choices in emphasizing either the divergences or the convergences between Orpheus and Homer need to be understood as a function of his own philosophical agenda. In terms of such agenda, the point remains that Orpheus is being viewed as older than Homer, and that his poetry is differentiated as mystical.

2§142 The association of Ōkeanos with the mysticism of Orphic poetry is highlighted by this Orphic hymn to Ōkeanos:[141]

2①60 *Orphic Hymn* 83 ed. Kern

> Ὠκεανὸν καλέω, πατέρ' ἄφθιτον, αἰὲν ἐόντα,
> ἀθανάτων τε θεῶν γένεσιν θνητῶν τ' ἀνθρώπων,
> ὃς περικυμαίνει γαίης περιτέρμονα κύκλον·
> ἐξ οὗπερ πάντες ποταμοὶ καὶ πᾶσα θάλασσα
> 5 καὶ χθόνιοι γαίης πηγόρρυτοι ἰκμάδες ἁγναί.
> κλῦθι, μάκαρ, πολύολβε, θεῶν ἅγνισμα μέγιστον,
> τέρμα φίλον γαίης, ἀρχὴ πόλου, ὑγροκέλευθε,
> ἔλθοις εὐμενέων μύσταις κεχαρημένος αἰεί.

> I invoke Ōkeanos, the imperishable [aphthitos] Father, the one who always is,
> the genesis [genesis] of immortal gods and mortal humans,
> the one who makes water flow as a circle [kuklos][142] that sets a limit all the way around the Earth,

---

[141] See also Broggiato 2001:179–180, with reference to the earlier work of Helck 1905; defending Helck's position, Broggiato also adduces the newer evidence of *Orphic Fragment* 49 ed. Kern (= P.Berol. 13044; 383 T etc., ed. Bernabé), which features lines that are cognate with corresponding lines in the *Homeric Hymn to Demeter*.

[142] The equation of Ōkeanos with an earth-encircling *kuklos* is relevant to the usage of Latin *orbis* with reference to cosmological contexts.

> and the one from whom originate all rivers and the entire sea,[143]
> 5 as well as the sacred liquids that flow out of the Earth from springs.
> Hear me, blessed one, beneficent is so many ways, the most holy thing to contemplate that comes from the gods,
> you who are the near and dear setting of the limit of Earth, the beginning of the Vault of the Sky [*polos*], the one whose pathways are fluid,
> come with a mind that is benign toward your initiates [*mustai*], showing favor [*kharizesthai*] to them always.

2§143 Plato himself evidently taps into the conventional idea that such Orphic discourse is an older source of mystical knowledge about the genesis of the cosmos. We see an elaboration of this idea in Plato's *Timaeus*, in the context of an extended narrative about the work of the cosmic Demiurge:

2①61 Plato *Timaeus* 40d-41a

> περὶ δὲ τῶν ἄλλων δαιμόνων εἰπεῖν καὶ γνῶναι τὴν γένεσιν μεῖζον ἢ καθ' ἡμᾶς, πειστέον δὲ τοῖς εἰρηκόσιν ἔμπροσθεν, ἐκγόνοις μὲν θεῶν οὖσιν, ὡς ἔφασαν, σαφῶς δέ που τούς γε αὐτῶν προγόνους εἰδόσιν· ἀδύνατον οὖν θεῶν {ε} παισὶν ἀπιστεῖν, καίπερ ἄνευ τε εἰκότων καὶ ἀναγκαίων ἀποδείξεων λέγουσιν, ἀλλ' ὡς οἰκεῖα φασκόντων ἀπαγγέλλειν ἑπομένους τῷ νόμῳ πιστευτέον. οὕτως οὖν κατ' ἐκείνους ἡμῖν ἡ γένεσις περὶ τούτων τῶν θεῶν ἐχέτω καὶ λεγέσθω. Γῆς τε καὶ Οὐρανοῦ παῖδες Ὠκεανός τε καὶ Τηθὺς ἐγενέσθην, τούτων δὲ Φόρκυς Κρόνος τε καὶ Ῥέα καὶ ὅσοι μετὰ {41a} τούτων, ἐκ δὲ Κρόνου καὶ Ῥέας Ζεὺς Ἥρα τε καὶ πάντες ὅσους ἴσμεν ἀδελφοὺς λεγομένους αὐτῶν, ἔτι τε τούτων ἄλλους ἐκγόνους· ἐπεὶ δ' οὖν πάντες ὅσοι τε περιπολοῦσιν φανερῶς καὶ ὅσοι φαίνονται καθ' ὅσον ἂν ἐθέλωσιν θεοὶ γένεσιν ἔσχον, λέγει πρὸς αὐτοὺς ὁ τόδε τὸ πᾶν γεννήσας τάδε· "θεοὶ θεῶν, ὧν ἐγὼ δημιουργὸς πατήρ τε ἔργων, δι' ἐμοῦ γενόμενα ἄλυτα ἐμοῦ γε μὴ ἐθέλοντος . . . [the speech of the Demiurge continues].

---

[143] On the notion of the Ōkeanos as the source of all fresh-water streams and the salt-water ocean, I will have more to say at a later point.

2ⓈI3. The fluidity of the Homeric tradition...

To speak [*legein* / *eipeîn*] and to know the genesis [*genesis*] of the other divinities [*daimones*]¹⁴⁴ is something so great as to go beyond our competence, but we must believe those who have spoken [*legein* / *eirēkenai*] before us, since they are descendants of the gods [*theoi*]—that is what they say—and they must surely have known their own ancestors. So it is not possible to disbelieve the children of the gods [*theoi*], even if they speak [*legein*] without giving probable or certain proofs [*apodeixis* plural], and, since they declare that the messages they perform [*apangellein*] are internal to their lineage [*oikeia*], we must follow their tradition [*nomos*] and believe them. So then, according to them, the genesis [*genesis*] of these gods [*theoi*] is to be this way and is to be told [*legein*] by us as follows. The children generated from Earth and Ouranos were Ōkeanos and Tethys, and their children were Phorkys and Kronos and Rhea and all that generation, and the children of Kronos and Rhea were Zeus and Hera and all those who are said [*legesthai*] to be their siblings, and others who were the descendants of these. Now when all of them, both those who visibly appear in their trajectories and those other gods who appear only when they want to, had their genesis [*genesis*], the one who generated all this in its entirety [= the Demiurge] spoke [*legein*] to them as follows: "Gods and gods who are generated from gods, I speak to you who are the work [*ergon* plural] generated by me as your Artificer [Demiurge] and as your Father, and I tell you that all the things generated by me cannot be undone, if I do not want them to be undone."¹⁴⁵

2§144 In Plato's recasting of Orphic traditions about the genesis of the cosmos, we can see that the world-encircling stream of Ōkeanos has a vital role. It—or he—is imagined as the genesis of all. Here I highlight an essential point of confluence between the Orphic and the Homeric traditions.¹⁴⁶ The same theme of the Ōkeanos as the genesis of all is well attested in Homeric

---

[144] The context is this: first to be spoken of were divinities who are visible; next to be spoken of are these 'other' divinities or *daimones* who are visible only when they wish to make themselves visible.

[145] Translation after Jowett 1895. For more on this Platonic passage, see Janko 1992:181.

[146] Janko 1992:181 argues that the references in *Iliad* XIV 201 and 246 to Ōkeanos and Tethys derive "from a theogony, one, moreover, wherein Ōkeanos and [Tethys] are the primeval parents ([XIV 201, 246]), not merely the parents of all waters (as at [Hesiod *Theogony* 337-370; see also *Iliad* XXI 196-197])."

261

Chapter Two

poetry—even in the rigid Homer adopted by Aristarchus as his base text. For example, let us consider this Homeric verse:

2ⓣ62 *Iliad* XIV 246

Ὠκεανός, ὅσπερ γένεσις πάντεσσι τέτυκται

... Ōkeanos, who has been fashioned as genesis for all ...

2§145 In this Homeric verse, the mysticism inherent in the idea of Ōkeanos is implicit, not explicit, because the immediate context concerns mainly the idea that Ōkeanos is an ancestor of all the gods, Zeus and Hera included.[147] But even this immediate context is cognate with Orphic traditions. In the passage from Plato's *Cratylus* (402a-c) that I quoted earlier, there are two embedded Orphic verses that make it explicit that Ōkeanos and Tethys are the parents of all the gods:

2ⓣ63 *Orphic Fragment* 22 ed. Bernabé

Ὠκεανὸς πρῶτος καλλίρροος ἦρξε γάμοιο,

ὅς ῥα κασιγνήτην ὁμομήτορα Τηθὺν ὄπυιεν.

Ōkeanos, with his beautiful streams [*kalli-rrhoos*], was the first to start a marriage,[148]

and he married his sister Tethys, who was his mother's daughter.[149]

2§146 These consecutive Orphic verses, as quoted in Plato's *Cratylus* (402a-c), are evidently cognate with the Homeric verse quoted by Plato in the very same context:

2ⓣ64 *Iliad* XIV 201 / 302

Ὠκεανόν τε θεῶν γένεσίν καὶ μητέρα Τηθύν·

---

[147] Janko 1992:180 comments on *Iliad* XIV 200-207: Hera's announced intention, to reconcile Ōkeanos and Tethys, "parodies her real intent and alludes to a threat to the cosmic order of the sort that she herself now poses." I agree with Janko (here and at pp. 168-172) that these verses may "recall" traditions about the sacred wedding of Zeus and Hera near the streams of Ōkeanos (Janko p. 171, with references to Pherecydes *FGH* 3 F16 and Euripides *Hippolytus* 742-751, with notes by Barrett 1964:303; see also Crane 1988:144-147). I also agree with Janko (p. 179) when he says that Hera's story is an *ad hoc* invention only in the short term. That is, from the standpoint of the framing narrative, Hera is making up the story; in the long term, however, this story is based on traditions that are already established.

[148] The depersonalized becomes personalized, as if for the first time.

[149] On these two Orphic verses, I cite again Janko 1992:181.

Ōkeanos, the genesis [*genesis*] of gods, and mother Tethys

2§147 The ultimate context, in any case, concerns the idea that Ōkeanos is the generative force behind—or under—everything that exists on the face of the earth.[150]

2Ⓢ14. Variations on a theme of Ōkeanos in the Homeric text of Crates

2§148 In order to understand the cosmological traditions that shaped the primal idea of Ōkeanos, it is important to consider the base text of Homer as edited by Crates of Mallos, which differed significantly from the base text of Homer as edited by Aristarchus, director of the library of Alexandria. Crates, like Aristarchus, flourished in the second century BCE, and he was director of the rival library of Pergamon. The era of Crates is also the era of the Great Altar of Zeus at Pergamon, featuring the relief sculpture depicting the primal battle of the gods and giants.[151] Of all the ancient editors of Homer, I think of Crates as representing a most fluid Homer, just as surely as Aristarchus represents a most rigid Homer. In the ancient world, the many real differences between these two rival editors of Homer were conventionally reduced to a single overarching contrast between Crates the Pergamene as 'anomalist' and Aristarchus the Alexandrian as 'analogist'.[152] The two men also differed—sometimes radically so—in their interpretations of Homer as reflected in their commentaries. Unlike Aristarchus, Crates was given to allegorizing Homer, and his allegoresis of cosmological themes in Homer turns out to be strikingly similar to the allegoresis of cosmological themes in poetry attributed to Orpheus as analyzed by the anonymous commentator of the *Derveni Papyrus*.[153]

2§149 The following passage illustrates, in microcosm, the differences between Aristarchus and Crates as editors and interpreters of Homer:

---

[150] I agree with Janko 1992:181 about the Orphic theogony (he surveys the available testimony, including that of the *Derveni Papyrus*): it was not, as some argue, merely an extrapolation from Homer. Rather, "it is simpler to suppose that the Iliadic and Orphic theogonies both adapt a myth which made the primeval waters, perhaps with Night as their parent, the origin of the world." (In his parenthetical comment about Night, Janko is following West 1983:116-121; I disagree, however, with their opinion that Night is the parent.)

[151] The *terminus post quem* for the Altar has been dated at 165 BCE. See Hardie 1985:23n79.

[152] Such an antithesis between Crates as 'anomalist' and Aristarchus as 'analogist' is of course an exaggeration: *HTL* 47-48.

[153] Pfeiffer 1968:292; see also Funghi 1997:30.

Chapter Two

2①65 Plutarch *On the face in the moon* 938d

ἀλλὰ σύ, τὸν Ἀρίσταρχον ἀγαπῶν ἀεὶ καὶ θαυμάζων, οὐκ ἀκούεις Κράτητος ἀναγινώσκοντος

Ὠκεανός, ὅσπερ γένεσις πάντεσσι τέτυκται

(*Iliad* XIV 246)

ἀνδράσιν ἠδὲ θεοῖς, πλείστην <τ'> ἐπὶ γαῖαν ἵησιν.

(*Iliad* XIV 246a)

But you are always so enamored of Aristarchus and so impressed with him that you do not hear [*akouein*][154] Crates as he reads out loud [*anagignōskein*]:[155]

... Ōkeanos, who has been fashioned[156] as genesis[157] for all

(*Iliad* XIV 246)

men and gods, and he flows over the Earth in all her fullness.[158]

(*Iliad* XIV 246a)

2§150 The first of these two verses as quoted by Plutarch corresponds to *Iliad* XIV 246—with verse-initial Ὠκεανοῦ, continuing the syntax of verse 245 as we have it—while the second, "XIV 246a," has been omitted from the text proper of modern editions of the *Iliad*.[159] Evidently, the base text of Homer as established by Aristarchus excluded this plus verse, while the base text as established by Crates included it.

---

[154] For *akouein* 'hear' in the sense of 'have a piece of writing read out loud', see *PP* 33n94, with reference to Aelian *De natura animalium* 5.38.
[155] For *anagignōskein* 'read out loud' in the technical sense of an editorial speech-act, see *PP* 149-150, 174-177, especially pp. 175-176n83.
[156] The wording τέτυκται 'has been fashioned' implies that Ōkeanos is a work of art.
[157] The wording γένεσις 'genesis' implies that Ōkeanos is a primal generating force—an idea that seems at first to contradict the other idea that Ōkeanos is itself generated as a work of art. There is no contradiction here, however, from the standpoint of a mentality that imagines the activity of primal figures as a model for any activity directed toward them, as in the case of the "sacrificing god": for references to important new work on the subject, see *PP* 57.
[158] I will save for another project a justification of my translation of πλείστην <τ'> ἐπὶ γαῖαν ἵησιν as 'and he flows over the Earth in all her fullness'.
[159] For example, *Iliad* XIV 246a is relegated to the apparatus criticus of the Oxford Classical Text of Allen and Monro (ed. 3, 1920) as also of West (2000a). It is missing altogether from the *Iliad* edition of van Thiel (1996).

2§151 For the first time since the Prolegomena to these chapters, I have used the term plus verse. As we will now see, the concept of the plus verse actually depends on the concept of the base text, as I outlined it in the Prolegomena, and this dependency turns out to be essential for undertanding the history and prehistory of the Homeric tradition.

2§152 For Crates (F 20), what I am calling the plus verse of *Iliad* XIV 246a provided evidence for a cosmic theory—that the Ōkeanos was the salt-water ocean covering the earth, which was supposedly spherical.[160] According to the theory of Crates, the earth was spherical, at the center of a universe that was likewise spherical.[161] Crates evidently interpreted in a modernizing sense the expression πλείστην ... ἐπὶ γαῖαν at *Iliad* XIV 246a: '[which flows] over most of the earth'. In other words, the salt-water ocean covers most of the spherical earth.[162] This theory was opposed by Aristarchus, who viewed the Homeric Ōkeanos as a fresh-water river surrounding an Earth that is circular and flat.[163]

2§153 This dispute between Crates and Aristarchus over definitions of the Ōkeanos was linked to their disagreement concerning the double-verse variant XIV 246-246a adopted by Crates and the single-verse variant XIV 246 adopted by Aristarchus in their respective base texts of Homer. What was at stake, in this dispute between Crates and Aristarchus, was no trivial matter. In this case, in fact, the stakes were of cosmic proportions. Both sides of the dispute were attempting to establish their theories of the cosmos by way of deciding the rightness or wrongness of different variants in the text of Homer.[164] I find it ironic that I am describing this ancient state of affairs in an era when it appears fashionable to dismiss Homeric textual variations as "trivial," "banal," and even "boring."[165] There are further ironies in the fact that today's editions

---

[160] Here and elsewhere, my numbering of the fragments of Crates follows the edition of Broggiato 2001.

[161] Broggiato 2001:lii.

[162] See also the Orphic fragment quoted above.

[163] See Broggiato 2001:179 and Wachsmuth 1860:44; also Porter 1992:88-103, especially p. 92 on Crates' interpretation of the Shield of Achilles in *Iliad* XVIII 481-489 as an *imago mundi*. In terms of Crates' theory (F 29, via the Geneva [Ge] scholia for *Iliad* XXI 195), the outermost realms of the salt-water ocean were not salt water but fresh water. More on this point later. To that extent, Crates' theory was still in accord with the earlier idea of the Ōkeanos as a fresh-water river encircling the universe.

[164] Most of what follows here in this paragraph and in the next was initially presented in LP (Nagy 1998) 221.

[165] Pelliccia 1997: "trivial" (p. 45) and "banal" (p. 46). Citing as his authority S. West 1988:40, Pelliccia asserts (p. 46): "the variant recordings that we know of from the papyri and the indirect sources ... are for the most part too boring and insignificant to imply that they derived from a truly creative performance tradition." Counterarguments in Nagy 2001a.

Chapter Two

of Homer tend to slight such textual variations as signaled—and interpreted—by Crates. Today's scholarship may well have singled out Crates for his scientific foresight in envisioning a spherical earth instead of a circular one—had he not based his reasoning on the text of Homer. We today find it most difficult to envision an era of intellectual history when the prestige of all higher learning centered on the study of Homer. The fact that Crates today is associated mostly with Homeric textual criticism has even diminished his potential status as a literary critic. And yet there is enough evidence from what little survives of Crates' Homeric criticism to aclaim him as a most perceptive and sensitive literary critic, one whose interpretations equal, and perhaps even surpass, those of "Longinus," author of the essay *On the Sublime*.[166]

2§154 Even from the standpoint of Homeric criticism, the editorial decisions of Crates reflect a solid grounding in the textual evidence. We may often wish to disagree with his specific points of interpretation, but the textual variants that he adduces cannot be dismissed as mere inventions. From an analysis of the formulaic composition of *Iliad* XIV 246a, for example, we can see that there is nothing non-Homeric per se about the form of this verse as adduced by Crates.[167] Nor is there anything non-Homeric per se about the contents.[168] Moreover, from a formulaic point of view, the verse does not even necessarily convey a vision of a salt-water ocean—let alone a spherical earth, as argued by Crates.

2§155 From the standpoint of Homeric poetry as a formulaic system, the mythological essence of Ōkeanos is self-evident: he is a cosmic fresh-water river-god who encircles Earth, pervading her with fresh-water springs that he sends up mysteriously from below.[169] Restating this essence in a depersonalized way, we can say that the earth is irrigated all over its surface by an upward flow that emanates ultimately from this cosmic earth-encircling river Ōkeanos.[170] From the standpoint of Homeric poetry, then, the phrase πλείστην

---

[166] An effective argument for such an assessment is made by Porter 1992:95–107.
[167] Broggiato 2001:179n151, with reference to *Iliad* XIII 632 and *Odyssey* xi 239 and *Iliad* XXI 158.
[168] LP (Nagy 1998) 220.
[169] See especially *Iliad* XXI 195–197. For an overview of Homeric contexts, see *GM* 99n61. For Near Eastern parallels, see Janko 1992:182, especially on the Babylonian god Apsū, the god of fresh waters, who is the consort and son of Tiāmat, goddess of the salt sea. See also West 1983:120–121.
[170] In Euripides *Hippolytus* 121–130, a fresh-water spring that flows from a rock is pictured as emanating ultimately from the Ōkeanos. Barrett (1964:184–185) argues convincingly that Euripides took this detail from the local lore of Trozen: Pausanias (2.31.10) speaks of a spring there that is known for not drying up even in periods of drought when all other local springs fail.

2§14. Variations on a theme of Ōkeanos ...

... ἐπὶ γαῖαν at *Iliad* XIV 246a can be interpreted as '[who flows] throughout the Earth in all her fullness'.

2§156 The meaning of *Iliad* XIV 246-246a needs to be situated within the context of the ongoing Homeric narrative. In XIV 246, the immediate point is this: Ōkeanos is a primal ancestor of the gods Zeus and Hera. In XIV 246a, this theme is developed further: Ōkeanos is a primal force that ultimately generated humans as well as gods, and it pervades the earth. This theme is actually implicit already in XIV 246, even without the explicit amplification of XIV 246a: the adjective πάντεσσι 'all' in XIV 246 implies that Ōkeanos is the father of not only 'all' gods but also, by extension, 'all' men. There is a parallel idea in Homeric references to Zeus himself as the 'father' of gods and men, *patēr andrōn te theōn te* (*Iliad* I 544, etc.). Further, the noun γένεσις in the same verse XIV 246, which I translated above by using the English borrowing 'genesis', implies a depersonalized cosmic power that generates not only all gods and all men but also all things. The idea that Ōkeanos is the 'genesis' of all is ultimately not so much the expression of an interpersonal relationship, such as parenthood in the immediate narrative context, but of a depersonalized cosmic creation, a cosmogony. Thus the adjective πάντεσσι is in fact all-inclusive, even without XIV 246a.[171] I should add that there is nothing non-Homeric about picturing the Ōkeanos simultaneously as an anthropomorphic father of gods and as a cosmic source for everything on earth.[172] The cosmogonic themes of *Iliad* XIV 246-246a, less explicit as read by Aristarchus (without 246a) and more explicit as read by Crates (with 246a), are deeply rooted in the Homeric tradition.[173]

2§157 The more explicit Homeric readings of Crates reflect, more clearly than the corresponding readings of Aristarchus, an Orphic phase in the evolution of the Homeric tradition. I propose that Crates derived such verses from a Homerus Auctus.

---

[171] As Charles Murgia points out to me, when plural adjectives meaning 'all' are being used substantively in ancient Greek (that is, without an accompanying noun), they can be expected to refer—by default—to all relevant persons, not to all things. So also, I would add, in English: for example, 'of all' is by default 'of all persons', not 'of all things'. Nevertheless, if I say in English 'genesis of all', the depersonalized implications of 'genesis' extend to 'all' as well. So also with γένεσις πάντεσσι τέτυκται at *Iliad* XIV 246: the depersonalization of γένεσις ... τέτυκται 'has been fashioned as a genesis' extends to what is the result of the genesis: the Ōkeanos is pictured as the ultimate source of everything, not only of all gods or even of all gods and all humans.

[172] Compare the oscillation, in *Iliad* XXI, between the heroic theme of Achilles fighting the river god and the cosmic theme of fire fighting water, as discussed in *HQ* 145.

[173] Janko 1992:190 describes *Iliad* XIV 246a as "a very suspect plus-verse," but he gives no reasons for rejecting this verse.

Chapter Two

2ⓢ15. Homerus Auctus

2§158 I coin this term <u>Homerus Auctus</u> as a way of referring to a Homeric tradition that is seemingly augmented by other traditions. These other traditions, as I will now argue, were primarily Orphic, Hesiodic, and Cyclic.

2§159 Up to now, I have been using the term <u>Orphic</u> primarily in a descriptive sense, with reference to the poetic and hermeneutic traditions ascribed by the ancient world to Orpheus.[174] The same goes for my use of the term <u>Hesiodic</u>. As for the term <u>Cyclic</u>, I used it to indicate traditions associated with what I have been calling the epic Cycle. From here on, however, I will use <u>Orphic</u>, <u>Hesiodic</u>, and <u>Cyclic</u> primarily in an evolutionary sense. And I will argue that Orphic or Hesiodic or Cyclic elements in Homer are intrinsic, not extrinsic, to the evolution of Homeric poetry. That is, the seemingly augmented elements of what I am calling the Homerus Auctus are Homeric in their own right. They need to be differentiated as Orphic or Hesiodic or Cyclic elements only with reference to the rigid Homer of Aristarchus, as distinct from the more fluid Homer of Crates.

2§160 For the moment, I will continue to concentrate exclusively on the Orphic elements of what I am calling the Homerus Auctus. So I return to *Iliad* XIV 246a, which I described as a <u>plus verse</u> included by Crates and excluded by Aristarchus. This verse shows the expansiveness of the tradition represented by the Orphic elements of the Homerus Auctus. We see that Ōkeanos is not only a primordial ancestor of Zeus and Hera: he is also the ultimate source of all things on earth. Taken together, the two verses of *Iliad* XIV 246 and 246a about the Ōkeanos convey an integral Orphic cosmos, which I have already been reconstructing from the references to Ōkeanos in Plato. The picture of Ōkeanos that emerges from a combination of the verses 246 and 246a in *Iliad* XIV is a unified vision of a world-encircling and ever-flowing cosmic stream, the generative powers of which are simultaneously personalized and depersonalized.

2§161 In terms of Plato's own Homeric quotations about the Ōkeanos, the unified Orphic vision of this cosmic stream originates from Homer as well as from Orpheus, that mysterious poet who is ostensibly earlier than Homer. Here I return to the first passage in my earlier survey of passages concerning the circularity and fluidity of Ōkeanos:

---

[174] Helck 1905:30–31. On the Orphic traditions in their ultimate textual form, see West 1983.

2⓵66 Plato *Phaedo* 112e

τὰ μὲν οὖν δὴ ἄλλα πολλά τε καὶ μεγάλα καὶ παντοδαπὰ <u>ῥεύματά</u> ἐστι· τυγχάνει δ' ἄρα ὄντα ἐν τούτοις τοῖς πολλοῖς τέτταρ' ἄττα <u>ῥεύματα</u>, ὧν τὸ μὲν μέγιστον καὶ ἐξωτάτω <u>ῥέον</u> <u>περὶ κύκλῳ</u> ὁ καλούμενος <u>Ὠκεανός</u> ἐστιν

There are many and various great <u>streams</u> [*rheumata*] of all kinds in the world, but among these there happen to be four <u>streams</u> [*rheumata*] to be noted in particular, and among these four the greatest is the one that <u>flows</u> [*rheîn*] <u>around</u> the world at the outermost periphery in a <u>circle</u> [*kuklos*], and that stream is called the <u>Ōkeanos</u>.

2§162 This visualization brings us back full-circle to where we started. The Ōkeanos is seen here as the circular frame for an integral Orphic cosmos.

2§163 An integral Orphic cosmos, as I have been reconstructing it from the references to Ōkeanos in Plato, is visible in other Homeric verses besides *Iliad* XIV 246-246a. A most telling example is the Shield of Achilles in *Iliad* XVIII. In Chapter 1, I described the Shield as a verbal picture that aims to show a perfect world of visual art, the metalwork of the Olympian god Hephaistos himself. Here I extend the description, showing its Orphic dimensions.

2§164 The Shield of Achilles pictures the cosmos, as seen through the narrative of the Homeric *Iliad*, and this cosmos is defined by an outermost limit, which is the cosmic circular stream of Ōkeanos:

2⓵67 Close-up from *Iliad* XVIII 478-609, the Shield of Achilles:

478 <u>ποίει</u> δὲ πρώτιστα σάκος μέγα τε στιβαρόν τε
479 <u>πάντοσε δαιδάλλων</u>, περὶ δ' <u>ἄντυγα</u> βάλλε φαεινὴν
480 <u>τρίπλακα μαρμαρέην</u>, ἐκ δ' ἀργύρεον τελαμῶνα.

. . .

482 ποίει <u>δαίδαλα</u> πολλὰ ἰδυίῃσι πραπίδεσσιν.
483 Ἐν μὲν γαῖαν ἔτευξ', ἐν δ' οὐρανόν, ἐν δὲ θάλασσαν,
484 ἠέλιόν τ' ἀκάμαντα σελήνην τε πλήθουσαν,
485 ἐν δὲ τὰ τείρεα πάντα . . .

. . .

607 Ἐν δ' ἐτίθει ποταμοῖο μέγα σθένος <u>Ὠκεανοῖο</u>
608 <u>ἄντυγα</u> πὰρ πυμάτην σάκεος πύκα ποιητοῖο.

Chapter Two

609 Αὐτὰρ ἐπεὶ δὴ τεῦξε σάκος μέγα τε στιβαρόν τε, . . .

478 First of all <u>he</u> [= Hephaistos] <u>was making</u> the Shield, huge and massive,

479 <u>fashioning it from inside out in every direction</u>, and around it he was putting a <u>rim</u> that is radiant,

480 <u>having three folds</u> [*triplax*] and <u>radiant</u>. And he [made] a silver sling that was hanging from . . .

. . .

482 And he was making many <u>variegated</u> things with his knowledgeable thinking.

483 In it he fashioned the earth, in it the sky, in it the sea,

484 And the sun that does not wear out, and the moon in her fullness,

485 And in it he [fashioned] all the celestial signs.

. . .

607 And he was putting in it the mighty power of the river <u>Ōkeanos</u>

608 along the last <u>rim</u> of the Shield compactly made.

609 And when he had fashioned the huge and massive Shield . . .

2§165 From this selection of ten verses from the Shield of Achilles, we can see that the narrative of the Shield, as a verbal artifact, centers on the whole world—the cosmos. The cosmos is of central concern in the divine metalworker's artistic creation: Hephaistos begins his metalwork by figuring earth, sky, sea, sun, moon, and stars (XVIII 482-485), and it is out of this thematic centralization of the cosmos that all other themes radiate. I say <u>radiate</u> because the divine metalworker begins his work of art from the center, continuing outward toward the periphery, 'in every direction' (479 πάντοσε δαιδάλλων). The periphery frames not only the cosmos but also the narrative of the Shield: at the very beginning, the same verse that describes the radiant diffusion of the artwork 'in every direction' (479) describes also the periphery or *antux* 'rim' (479) that frames this artwork. This *antux* 'rim', which marks the beginning of the narrative of the Shield (479), marks also its end (608). The same word, *antux*, is used at both the beginning and the end. This signaling of both the beginning and the end with the same wording for the periphery, *antux*, follows the narrative rules of ring composition. According to these rules, which are typical of Homeric poetry, the linear movement of narration in the dimension of time, from beginning to end, corresponds to a circular movement of narration in the dimension of space—a timeless coming-full-circle. The outermost circle of the rim, this *antux* that encircles the cosmos, is the Ōkeanos (607-608), envisioned as a fresh-water cosmic stream described elsewhere as flowing in a circle, that is, flowing 'back on itself' (ἀψορρόου Ὠκεανοῖο XVIII 399, XX 65).

2§166 In Hesiodic poetry, the river Ōkeanos is implicitly compared to a cosmic serpent that encircles the world: in *Theogony* 791, Ōkeanos is imagined as εἰλιγμένος 'coiling' around the earth nine times.[175] I translate the verb *helissein* of εἰλιγμένος as 'coiling' here in the light of a Hesiodic passage where the river Kephisos is explicitly described as εἰλιγμένος 'coiling' like a *drakōn* 'serpent' as it winds its way through Orkhomenos (Hesiod F 70.23 καί τε δι' Ἐρχομενοῦ εἰλιγμένος εἶσι δράκων ὥς).[176]

2§167 In Orphic poetry, the comparison of the river Ōkeanos to a cosmic serpent is explicit: just before the mystical description of Ōkeanos that I already quoted from Plato's *Phaedo* (112e), we find this generalized mystical reference to cosmic rivers:

2①68 Plato *Phaedo* 112d

ἔστι δὲ ἃ παντάπασιν <u>κύκλῳ</u> <u>περιελθόντα</u>, ἢ ἅπαξ ἢ καὶ πλεονάκις <u>περιελιχθέντα</u> περὶ τὴν γῆν ὥσπερ οἱ <u>ὄφεις</u>.

There are some cosmic rivers that <u>come around</u> in a complete <u>circle</u> [*kuklos*], <u>coiling around</u> [*peri-helissein*][177] the Earth, like <u>serpents</u> [*ophis* plural], either one time or many times over.

The use of the word *ophis* 'serpent' here is relevant to the derivative form Ophiōn (Ὀφίων), which is the name of the primal ruler of the cosmos in the cosmogonic song of Orpheus as represented in the *Argonautica* of Apollonius of Rhodes (1.496-511). In the beginning of beginnings, according to the song of Orpheus, the ruler of Olympus was this Ophiōn, along with Ophiōn's consort, Eurynome the Ōkeanis (Ὠκεανίς) 'daughter of Ōkeanos' (1.503-504); when this primal couple were overthrown by Kronos and Rhea, they were cast into the streams of the river Ōkeanos (1.505-506). As one commentator remarks,

---

[175] Janko 1992:190, in disagreement with West 1966:374.
[176] See also *Orphic Hymn* 11.15 ed. Kern: Ὠκεανός τε πέριξ † ἐν ὕδασι † γαῖαν ἑλίσσων.
[177] The usage of *peri-helissein* 'coil around' (περιελιχθέντα) here in Plato's *Phaedo* (112d) supports my interpretation of *helissein* as 'coil' with reference to the participle εἰλιγμένος describing the river Ōkeanos in Hesiod *Theogony* 791.

Chapter Two

"Ophion is in a sense a suitable substitute for Oceanus."[178] The fusion of Ophiōn and Ōkeanos is evident in the confluence implied by the fall of the cosmic serpent into the cosmic river:

2①69 Apollonius of Rhodes *Argonautica* 1.503-506

>   ἤειδεν δ' ὡς πρῶτον <u>Ὀφίων</u> Εὐρυνόμη τε
>   <u>Ὠκεανὶς</u> νιφόεντος ἔχον κράτος Οὐλύμποιο·
>   ὥς τε βίῃ καὶ χερσὶν ὁ μὲν Κρόνῳ εἴκαθε τιμῆς,
>   ἡ δὲ <u>Ῥέῃ</u>, ἔπεσον δ' ἐνὶ κύμασιν <u>Ὠκεανοῖο</u>·

> And he [= Orpheus] sang how, in the beginning, <u>Ophiōn</u> and Eurynome,
> she who is <u>daughter of Ōkeanos</u>, had power over snow-capped Olympus,
> and how, with violent hands, Kronos forced him [= Ophiōn] to give up his privilege [*timē*],
> and Rhea forced her [= Eurynome] to give up hers. And they [= Ōkeanos and Eurynome] were then cast down into the waters of the <u>Ōkeanos</u>.

In non-Greek traditions, there is a wide variety of comparable imagery concerning cosmic serpents that encircle the world.[179] A most striking example is a Phoenician bowl found at Praeneste: cosmic themes pervade this bowl, "whose circular decoration strikingly resembles that of [Achilles'] shield," and which features "a snake encircling the whole."[180]

2§168 The river Ōkeanos, encircling the Shield of Achilles in *Iliad* XVIII 607-608, signals that the world of this Shield, as a work of art, is at the same time rigid and fluid. The rigidity of the Shield is of course conveyed by its three-dimensional metallic essence, consisting primarily of bronze.[181] Its fluidity is conveyed by the waters of the river Ōkeanos, which encircles it and thereby defines it. We see a parallel confluence of metallic rigidity and encircling fluidity in the Hesiodic tradition, as in this description of the Shield of Herakles:

---

[178] West 1983:127.
[179] For references, see Janko 1992:190. For further references, see Onians 1951:315–317.
[180] Janko 1992:190.
[181] The symbolism of the bronze essence of the Shield is analyzed in *HPC* II§§54 and following.

2⑤15. Homerus Auctus

2①70 Hesiodic *Shield of Herakles* 314-315

ἀμφὶ δ' ἴτυν ῥέεν Ὠκεανὸς πλήθοντι ἐοικώς,
πᾶν δὲ συνεῖχε σάκος πολυδαίδαλον·

And the Ōkeanos flowed [*rheîn*] around the rim, looking just like a river in full flow,[182]
and it kept together the entire shield, in all its many complexities.

2§169 Such a confluence of opposites, where the rigidity of metalwork is being defined ultimately by the fluidity that 'keeps it all together', or 'contains it all', is evidently a mystical idea. We have in fact just seen such an idea expressed in the Orphic tradition, as recovered from the wording of Plato. In terms of this wording, the idea of a distinction between *hestanai* 'to be static' and *kineîsthai* 'to be in motion' is overridden by the idea of a non-distinction or mystical fusion, where everything is ever in motion. According to this overriding idea, everything becomes fluid because there is ultimately no hard and fast distinction between rigidity and fluidity. To put it another way: if indeed fluidity ultimately defines rigidity, then, in the end, 'everything is fluid'. As we have already seen, this mystical formula amounts to a secret of initiation into Orphic mysteries. But by now we can see that there is more to it: this formula was not only Orphic, it was also Homeric and Hesiodic. Or, to put it diachronically, this formula must have been Homeric and Hesiodic as far back as the time when the theme of the Ōkeanos became part of what ultimately became the Homeric and Hesiodic traditions. Such a remote time predates the ages of Homer we have considered so far, and it even predates the still earlier ages to be considered in the next two chapters. As I argue in the twin book, *Homer the Preclassic*, such a time dates back to what I call in that book the Dark Age

2§170 The mysticism of the Homeric Ōkeanos is evident not only in the idea of fusing the rigidity of metalwork in the Shield of Achilles with the fluidity of a cosmic stream that encircles and ultimately defines both the Shield and the whole world. It is evident also in the overall idea of identifying this cosmic stream with a cosmic serpent that encircles the whole world. The very idea of such a serpent is in and of itself a fusion of rigidity and fluidity. The fluidity is explicit in the picturing of the fresh-water stream Ōkeanos as a serpent, while the rigidity is implicit in the picturing of this same stream as the

---

[182] On the participle *plēthōn* (from *plēthein* 'be full') as an epithet of rivers in full flow, see *Iliad* V 87, XI 492.

Chapter Two

rim of an artifact made of metal—an artifact that tells the whole story of Troy in microcosm. We have in fact already seen another artifact that likewise tells this whole story. That was the petrified serpent of the *Iliad*, described as *arizēlos* 'radiant' once the serpent was petrified (*Iliad* II 318). In Chapter 1, I compared the Homeric context of *arizēlos*, epithet of the petrified serpent, with another Homeric context: it was a detail in the Shield of Achilles, showing the gods Athena and Ares presiding over war itself in the City of War, where the two war gods are said to be *arizēlō* 'radiant' in their metallic perfection (*Iliad* XVIII 519). In *Homer the Preclassic*, I show how this combination of Athena and Ares stems from traditions that are traceable all the way back to the Bronze Age.[183]

2§171 As I noted in Chapter 1, the context of the epithet *arizēlō* 'radiant' in the Shield of Achilles (XVIII 519) can be seen as an ideal point of entry into the entire world of images radiating from the Shield. It is essential that the same epithet *arizēlos* 'radiant' applies to the petrified serpent precisely because Zeus had sent it as an epiphany, *ephēne* (II 318), conveying the whole story of Troy's capture. In both these instances of *arizēlos*, the epithet marks an everlasting vision, pictured by Homeric poetry as a perfect and permanent work of art.

2§172 We have already seen how the rigidity of the petrified serpent in *Iliad* II foretells the eventual rigidity of the *Iliad* as a whole, which is still fluid—a narrative in the making—at the moment of the serpent's petrifaction. The *Iliad* remains fluid and does not become rigid until the *telos* 'outcome' of the entire narrative has been reached. The metaphor of rigidity applies in a similar way to the Shield of Achilles, where we see an interplay with the metaphor of fluidity as signaled by the Ōkeanos, that ever-flowing periphery that frames the cosmos as expressed by the Shield of Achilles.

2§173 The mystical interplay between rigidity and fluidity in the Shield of Achilles is not only cosmological but also narratological. Immediately after the beginning of the narrative of the Shield, which begins by figuring the natural cosmos of earth, sky, sea, sun, moon, and stars (XVIII 482-489), the continuity is sustained by the figuring of the human cosmos—that is, of society—organized here along the lines of two modes of existence equated with two cities (XVIII 490).[184] The first is the City of Peace (XVIII 491-508) and the second is the City of War (XVIII 509-540). There follows an extended general narrative about the human cosmos (XVIII 541-606). Then comes the conclusion of the whole narrative, marked explicitly by the periphery of the narrative, the Ōkeanos

---

[183] *HPC* II§409.
[184] On *kosmos* as a marker of human society—what I call here the 'human cosmos'—see *PH* 5§17n45 (= p. 145), especially with reference to the usage of *kosmos* in Pindar F 194 ed. Snell / Maehler.

(XVIII 607), which is equated with the outermost rim or *antux* of the Shield as an artifact (XVIII 608). Taking the narrative about the human cosmos as a whole, I focus on the way in which this narrative continues where the narrative about the natural cosmos leaves off. Here is the wording that introduces the continuity of narration.

2①71 *Iliad* XVIII 490-491

> Ἐν δὲ δύω ποίησε πόλεις μερόπων ἀνθρώπων
> καλάς. ἐν τῇ μέν ...
>
> There in the inside he made two cities of radiant humans,
> beautiful cities. In the first one, ...

2§174 The narrative about the first of the two cities, the City of Peace, begins with a picture of a wedding (XVIII 491-496), to be followed by a picture of a litigation (XVIII 497-508). In the passage I am about to quote, I highlight only a part of the narrative, about the litigation, but my observations apply to the entire narrative about the human cosmos on the Shield of Achilles.

2①72 *Iliad* XVIII 497-501

> λαοὶ δ' εἰν ἀγορῇ ἔσαν ἀθρόοι· ἔνθα δὲ <u>νεῖκος</u>
> <u>ὠρώρει</u>, δύο δ' ἄνδρες <u>ἐνείκεον</u> εἵνεκα ποινῆς
> ἀνδρὸς <u>ἀποφθιμένου</u>· ὃ μὲν <u>εὔχετο</u> πάντ' ἀποδοῦναι
> 500 δήμῳ πιφαύσκων, <u>ὃ δ' ἀναίνετο μηδὲν ἑλέσθαι</u>·
> ἄμφω δ' <u>ἱέσθην</u> ἐπὶ ἴστορι <u>πεῖραρ</u> ἑλέσθαι.
>
> The people were gathered together in the assembly place,
>   and there a <u>dispute</u> [*neikos*]
> <u>had arisen</u>, and two men <u>were disputing</u> [*neikeîn*] about the
>   blood-price
> for a man who had <u>died</u> [*apo-phthinesthai*]. The one <u>made a</u>
>   <u>claim</u> [*eukhesthai*] to pay back in full,
> 500 making a public declaration to the district, <u>but the other was</u>
>   <u>refusing</u> [*anainesthai*] <u>to accept anything</u>.
> Both <u>were eagerly heading for</u> [*hiesthai*] an arbitrator, to get
>   a <u>limit</u> [*peirar*].[185]

---

[185] Commentary in *HR* ch. 4.

Chapter Two

2§175 What is perhaps most striking about this passage, and about the entire narrative continuum of the Shield, is the mystical fluidity of its metallic action. The action is shown in progress, as expressed by the dominantly imperfective aspect of the verbs (ἐνείκεον, εὔχετο, ἀναίνετο, ἰέσθην). Also, the referential world is generalized, not specific. For example, the two litigants and the onlookers who participate in the litigation are all unidentified, unbound by any single time and place. The generality is universalizing. If the referents were to become identified, the universality would be lost: the fluidity of the ongoing action would become arrested, crystallized into rigidity. Once the story was told, its action would become rigid, frozen forever in the final retelling. In particular, the two unidentified litigants would be frozen forever in their respective stances, once they became identified as the Achilles and the Agamemnon of the *Iliad* all told. In modern representations, the litigants of the Shield can indeed be explicitly identified as Achilles and Agamemnon (Figures 11a and 11b).

2§176 Keeping in mind the idea that the story of the *Iliad*, once told, is destined to solidify to the point of inflexibility, rigidity, let us recall one more time the frame of this story, as pictured in the Shield of Achilles. That frame is the river Ōkeanos, surrounding the rim of the Shield. Here, by way of contrast, is the idea of a story forever in flux.

2§177 The Ōkeanos has no source of its own: it is self-sustaining, self-perpetuating. It is the source of all other sources, that is, of all fresh-water springs in the cosmos that it encompasses. Just as the Ōkeanos has no beginning, it has no ending, that is, no *telos* in the linear sense of 'end'. It conveys, instead, the circular sense of *telos*, that is, 'coming full circle'. Because it always comes full circle, flowing back upon itself at whatever point it restarts, it is ever-flowing. The Shield of Achilles, a study in the ultimate rigidity of metalwork, is framed by the ultimate fluidity that is the Ōkeanos.

2§178 Such coexistence of fluidity and rigidity, which I have described as Orphic in its mysticism, is also Homeric. All along, I have been arguing that a verse like *Iliad* XIV 246 cannot be differentiated as Homeric or Orphic, even if Aristarchus might have set aside as distinctly Orphic a verse like *Iliad* XIV 246a. Moreover, even a verse like *Iliad* XIV 246a, stemming from a Homerus Auctus as edited by Crates in Pergamon, need not be dismissed as an interpolation from Homeric editions that had been contaminated, as it were, by Orphic traditions. The Homerus Auctus need not be viewed as an editorial conflation of incompatible texts but as a preedited corpus of undifferentiated oral traditions that later became differentiated into distinct textual traditions that we recognize as Orphic, Hesiodic, Cyclic, and even Homeric.

2⑤16. Principles of anomaly and analogy in editing Homer

2§179 In taking stock of the intellectual legacy of Crates as a textual critic of Homer, it is important to consider the distinction made by Varro (*De lingua latina* 8.23 and 9.1) concerning the principles of <u>anomaly</u> and <u>analogy</u> as respectively espoused by Crates and Aristarchus. This distinction has led to assumptions that reinforce a negative opinion about Crates—that he is the kind of editor who will apply the principle of anomaly to admit into his edition of Homer practically any reading that suits his allegorizing theories.[186] A careful reexamination of the variants attributed to him, as in the case of the Iliadic passage on the Ōkeanos, leads to a more positive opinion.[187] Similarly, the principle of analogy as practiced by Aristarchus has led to the assumption that Aristarchus will level out anomalous variants in the name of regularity.[188] And yet, it can be shown that Aristarchus was scrupulous in avoiding regularization of variants at the expense of the manuscript evidence.[189]

2§180 In the long run, it is more important to appreciate the convergences rather than the divergences between the approaches of Crates and Aristarchus to Homeric textual criticism. In fact, the intellectual histories of the Aristarchean / Alexandrian and Cratetean / Pergamene "schools" reveal their own tendencies of eventual convergence. An ideal case in point is the Stoic Panaetius, who considered himself a disciple of Crates (Strabo 14.5.16 C676) and who at the same time praised Aristarchus as a *mantis* 'seer' who knew the *dianoia* 'meaning' of Homer (Athenaeus 14.634c).[190] Dionysius Thrax, on the other hand, even though he may have been a disciple of Aristarchus, was strongly influenced by the Cratetean approach to "the variety of forms in the spoken language, the *sunētheia* ['habituation']."[191] The excellence of Crates in his approach to linguistic "irregularity" was generally acknowledged in the ancient world.[192] His holistic approach to the Homeric corpus in all its potential "irregularities" can be viewed, I suggest, in the same light.

2§181 The approach of Crates is compatible with the Homerus Auctus—a more expansive and therefore more unwieldy and anomalous corpus. But we

---

[186] For example, see West 1966:208.
[187] See in general Porter 1992:85–103.
[188] For a survey of such assumptions, see *PP* 128–129.
[189] See Ludwich 1884/1885:92, 97, 109, 114; also *PP* 129n99.
[190] Porter 1992:70; Pfeiffer 1968:232, 245, 270. See also Fraser 1972 I 471 and IIb 682n225 on the converging Alexandrian / Attalid connections of Apollodorus of Athens, originally a disciple of Aristarchus.
[191] Pfeiffer 1968:245.
[192] Pfeiffer 1968:245.

Chapter Two

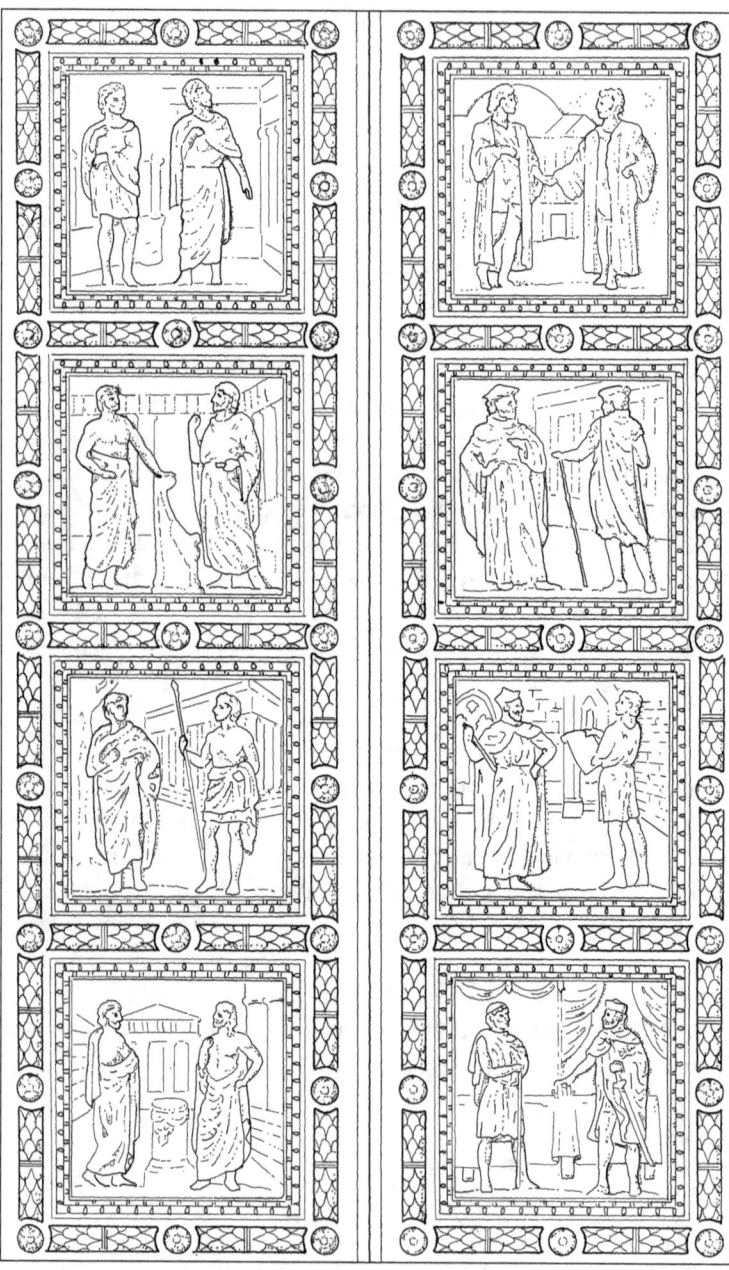

Figure 11a. Monumental bronze doors, with relief panels depicting the evolution of Western justice. Designed by Cass Gilbert and John Donnelly, Sr.; sculpted by John Donnelly, Jr. Installed 1935. Supreme Court of the United States, Washington, DC.

2⑤16. Principles of anomaly and analogy in editing Homer

Figure 11b. Bronze doors of the Supreme Court: detail, Achilles and Agamemnon.

should not assume that his approach is what caused the existence of a more anomalous Homer. Rather, I think it is better to say that the approach of his rival Aristarchus made Homer a less expansive and therefore less unwieldy corpus.

2§182 We must keep in mind that Crates, like Aristarchus, athetizes, and in some instances we may even be shocked by his daring, as when he athetizes the *prooimia* of both the *Theogony* and the *Works and Days* of Hesiod.[193] But athetesis does not of and by itself make a difference in the expansiveness of the Homeric text, since both Crates and Aristarchus leave in rather than leave out whatever they athetize. The difference is in the plus verses, which Aristarchus leaves out but Crates leaves in. Again, we must keep in mind that Crates simply leaves things in: it is not that he puts things in. Conversely, we may say that Aristarchus does not leave things out passively by ignoring them: he takes things out actively by calling attention to them. That is what we see in *Iliad* XIV 246 minus 246a, as read by Aristarchus, and in *Iliad* XIV 246 plus 246a, as read by Crates.

2§183 I have already noted that the traditional orientation of *Iliad* XIV 246-246a as read out loud by Crates is decidedly Orphic, reflecting the poetic and hermeneutic traditions ascribed by the ancient world to Orpheus.[194] My

---

[193] On the athetizing by Crates of the *prooimia* of the Hesiodic *Theogony* and *Works and Days*, see LP (Nagy 1998) 218.
[194] See also Helck 1905:30–31.

thesis is that Crates derived such verses from a Homerus Auctus, a Homeric tradition augmented by Orphic traditions; moreover, I argue for the preexistence of plus verses emanating from Homeric editions that had been contaminated, as it were, by these Orphic traditions.

2§184 As far as scholars like Crates of Pergamon were concerned, such Orphic plus-verses in the Homeric textual tradition were not "contaminations" at all, if he—unlike Aristarchus and Aristotle—accepted the view that Orpheus as well as Musaeus lived before Homer.[195] It seems clear to me that Pergamene editorial practice included Orphic plus verses in the Homeric text, as contrasted with the Alexandrian (at least, Aristarchean) practice of excluding them—that is, omitting them altogether from the text, instead of merely athetizing them. Such conflicting editorial practices are reflected, I think, in the following ancient witticism:

2ⓣ73 Seneca *Epistle* 88.39[196]

> annales evolvam omnium gentium et quis primus carmina scripserit quaeram? Quantum temporis inter Orphea intersit et Homerum, cum fastos non habeam, computabo? Et Aristarchi ineptias, quibus aliena carmina conpunxit, recognoscam et aetatem in syllabis conteram?
>
> Shall I unroll the annals of the world's history and try to find out who first wrote poetry? Shall I make an estimate of the number of years that separate Orpheus and Homer, although I do not have the records [*fasti*]? And shall I investigate the absurd writings of Aristarchus, where he 'skewered' [*conpunxit*][197] other men's verses, and wear my life away on syllables?

2§185 Before I conclude this section, I need to stress once again that I have been using the term Orphic in an evolutionary sense. Using the term Orphic is not at all the same thing as accepting the idea of a poet named Orpheus who preceded Homer. Still, it is relevant to note the prevalence of a received opinion about the priority of Orpheus over Homer. In terms of this opinion, certain poetic traditions, considered peripheral and posterior to Homer by the

---

[195] *PH* 8§2n10 (= p. 216).
[196] Thanks to Jed Wyrick, who writes (2 15 1998): "I think that there is a clear contrast here between two different kinds of 'absurd' approaches to learning—the one involving Orpheus, and the other, Aristarchus."
[197] We see here a playful reference to Aristarchus' editorial practice of marking athetesis by way of the sign known as the *obelos* or 'skewer' (–).

likes of Aristarchus, originated from a mythical singer named Orpheus. Such Orphic poetry, as I have been arguing, was in some ways undifferentiated from Homeric poetry. From an evolutionary point of view, the Orphic poetry that we find included in the Homerus Auctus was in some ways really older, not newer, than the poetry ascribed exclusively to Homer by Aristarchus.

2Ⓢ17. Homer and the neoterics

2§186 The opposing idea of Aristarchus, that Orphic poetry was something newer than Homeric poetry, can be linked to the term *neōteroi*, meaning 'newer' or 'neoteric'. This term neoteric was applied by Aristarchus to poets who were judged to be 'newer' than Homer.[198] For Aristarchus, non-Homeric meant post-Homeric. From here on, I will use the term neoteric in this sense, without prejudging whether the neoteric poets were really 'newer' than Homer.

2§187 A particularly noteworthy follower of Aristarchus in applying the criterion of *neōteroi* was Apollodorus of Athens.[199] A striking example of such an application is a Cologne papyrus (*P.Col.* inv. 5604) that shows Apollodorus commenting on a manuscript he found: this manuscript, he says, contained an otherwise unknown epic called the *Meropis* (*SH* 903A), and he describes the anonymous author as *neōteros tis* 'someone newer' on the basis of the *idiōma* 'idiom' of this poet's interests in chosing poetic topics (ἐδόκει δέ μοι τὰ ποήμα|[τα] νεωτέρου τινὸς εἶναι ... τὸ ἰδίωμα τῆς ἱστορίας).[200]

2§188 Here it is relevant to consider a basic editorial principle attributed to Aristarchus, *Homēron ex Homērou saphēnizein* 'clarify Homer on the basis of Homer'.[201] This principle was founded on the premise that the real Homer must be systematically isolated from the supposedly non-Homeric accretions represented by the *neōteroi* or 'newer' poets—the neoterics. Aristarchus' system, especially as reported by the Aristarchean scholar Didymus in the first century BCE, remains our main source for the working distinction between the

---

[198] The term *neōteroi* reflects the usage of Aristarchus himself, not only of the Aristarcheans who came after him—or of the scholiasts who report on the opinions of the Aristarcheans. See Severyns 1928:33–34n4.

[199] On Apollodorus as a disciple of Aristarchus, see Apollodorus *FGH* 244 T 1; see also the comments of Pfeiffer 1968:261 and Rusten 1982:32n10.

[200] Henrichs 1993:188–189; see also Rusten 1982:32.

[201] The wording comes from Porphyry, *Homeric Questions* [*Iliad*] 297.16 ed. Schrader 1890; see also scholia D for *Iliad* V 385. On the Aristarchean provenience of the wording, see Porter 1992:70–74 (who effectively addresses the skepticism of Pfeiffer 1968:225–227).

neōteroi or 'neoteric' poets and the supposedly oldest poet of them all, Homer as the original poet.[202]

2§189 These newer poets were imagined as authors of post-Homeric wordings—words or groups of words or even verses—that somehow found their way into the Homeric texts. In the *hupomnēmata* 'commentaries' of Aristarchus, these supposedly post-Homeric wordings were traced back to such 'newer' sources as Hesiod and the poets of the epic Cycle.[203]

2§190 As we just saw in the case of *Iliad* XIV 246a, Aristarchus occasionally excluded overtly 'Orphic' verses from his edition. Thus Orpheus too, like Hesiod and the poets of the Cycle, was evidently a 'newer' poet in the age of Aristarchus, though the question of Orphic accretions was evidently not a major concern for this editor.[204]

2ⓢ18. Variations on a theme of Ōkeanos in the Homeric text of Zenodotus

2§191 The question of Orphic accretions was a major concern, however, for Zenodotus of Ephesus, the first official director of the Library of Alexandria, who flourished in the age of Callimachus. As we are about to see, the edition of Homer by Zenodotus tended to screen out Homeric verses he suspected of being Orphic in origin. One of these verses contains a most important mention of the Ōkeanos, and the excluding of this verse by Zenodotus illustrates a major difference between his Homeric edition and that of Aristarchus.

2§192 The anti-Orphic editorial stance of Zenodotus can best be understood in the light of the generally anti-neoteric stance of Aristarchus a century later. In the case of Aristarchus, the category of poets he judged to be *neōteroi* 'newer' than Homer extended well beyond the archaic era of shadowy figures like Orpheus, all the way into the Hellenistic era. Even poets like Callimachus and his Alexandrian contemporaries were considered *neōteroi*, that is, 'newer'

---

[202] Severyns 1928:81 shows that Aristarchus relied on the poets of the Cycle as a main source for attestations of neoteric usage, and that the precision of his work on the Cycle and on other poetic sources is often blurred by the reportage of later Aristarcheans like Didymus.

[203] On Hesiod as *neōteros* according to the Aristarcheans, see Severyns 1928:39, 89; on the poets of the Cycle as *neōteroi*, see especially Severyns p. 63, who argues that Aristarchus considered the Cycle to be a major component of this neoteric category.

[204] In Severyns 1928, where we have an exhaustive survey of mentions of *neōteroi* in the Homeric scholia, I find no mention of Orpheus or Orphica.

or 'neoteric', in their own right.²⁰⁵ A most notable exponent of such neoteric poets in the Hellenistic era, besides Callimachus himself, was Apollonius of Rhodes, who succeeded Zenodotus of Ephesus as director of the Library of Alexandria: though Apollonius, unlike Zenodotus, did not produce an edition of Homer, he was most influential in reshaping the idea of Homer. Another notable exponent of such neoteric poets was Theocritus of Syracuse, likewise a contemporary of Callimachus and Apollonius. Later on, I will illustrate an aspect of Theocritus' neoterism by examining the poetics of *Idyll* 1.

2§193 As we have just seen, the term *neōteroi* in the sense of 'neoterics' was actually being applied to these scholar-poets who flourished in the age of Callimachus.²⁰⁶ And the term is implicit in the reference made by Cicero (*Tusculan Disputations* 3.19.45) to the *poetae novi* 'new poets', whom he further describes as *cantores Euphorionis* 'singers of Euphorion'; Euphorion of Chalkis, a scholar-poet who was made director of the Library of Antioch around 220 BCE, specialized in imitating Callimachus.²⁰⁷

2§194 Callimachus and other such poets of his era were 'newer' or 'neoteric' not only because they cultivated those aspects of Homeric poetry that were later rejected as post-Homeric in the age of Aristarchus. Already in the age of Callimachus himself, such neoteric aspects of Homer were being rejected by Zenodotus in his own edition of Homer. For example, Zenodotus made a point of keeping Homer free from what he evidently considered to be Orphic interpolations. Paradoxically, this was happening in the age of Callimachus, when neoteric poets were actually cultivating the poetry of Orpheus: a prime example is the cosmogony sung by Orpheus in the *Argonautica* of Apollonius of Rhodes (1.503-506). Another example, as we will see later on, is the *humnos* sung by Thyrsis in *Idyll* 1 of Theocritus.

2§195 A fitting monument to the editorial anti-neoterism of Zenodotus is his radical move of athetizing—that is, marking as non-Homeric—the entire sequence of verses that narrated the images displayed on the Shield of Achilles (XVIII 483-608).²⁰⁸ By 'athetized', I mean that Zenodotus made markings in the

---

²⁰⁵ Rengakos 2000.
²⁰⁶ For a survey of references dating back to the Hellenistic era, I cite again Rengakos 2000, especially p. 333 on the criticism leveled at Callimachus *Aetia* Book 1 F 13 by Apollodorus of Athens FGH 244 F 157 ed. Jacoby II B p. 1089 line 34; via Strabo 1.2.37 C44: among the neoterisms of Callimachus mentioned here by Apollodorus is the poet's equation of Corcyra with the island of the Phaeacians. More on this equation in the Conclusion, C§§4-7 below.
²⁰⁷ Pfeiffer 1968:150.
²⁰⁸ Aristonicus reports (via scholia A for *Iliad* XVIII 483a): ὅτι Ζηνόδοτος ἠθέτηκεν ἀπὸ τούτου τοῦ στίχου τὰ λοιπά '[Aristarchus marks with the sign >:] because Zenodotus has athetized the rest of this passage, starting with this verse'.

Chapter Two

left margin next to the suspected verses in his text of Homer to indicate that he considered these verses to be non-Homeric; his mark of athetesis, as we have seen, was the *obelos* (−). By dissociating the world of the Shield from the world of Homer, Zenodotus also dissociated the Ōkeanos, the cosmic river that ever encircles and defines the Shield in *Iliad* XVIII 607-608.

2§196 The fact that Zenodotus dissociated the Ōkeanos from the world of Homer was evidently part of an overall editorial plan. Zenodotus in his edition of Homer systematically athetized those aspects of the *Iliad* that he judged to be Orphic. An explicit example is a sequence of verses at *Iliad* XXI 194-197. At verse 196, we see a relative clause describing Ōkeanos as the source of all fresh-water springs and rivers. Zenodotus rejected as non-Homeric the preceding verse, 195, where Ōkeanos is named as the referent of the relative clause.[209] This way, the referent shifts from the river Ōkeanos to the river Akhelōios, which is named at verse 194. Zenodotus' rejection of verse 195 was not the result of some arbitrary editorial decision: there is external evidence for an alternative textual tradition of the *Iliad* where this verse 195 was in fact missing, and there is also external evidence for an alternative poetic tradition where Akhelōios rather than Ōkeanos figures as the primal stream that generates all other streams.[210]

2§197 It is important to keep in mind that Zenodotus did not actually leave out of his text of Homer the verses concerning the images on the Shield in *Iliad* XVIII, even if he judged the whole passage to be Orphic and therefore non-Homeric. Throughout the Shield passage, Zenodotus actually attests variations within the sequence of the verses that he athetizes.[211] The fact that Zenodotus only athetized the world of the Shield, instead of leaving it out altogether, is a most straightforward indication that all these verses of the Shield were conventionally thought to belong to the Homeric textual tradition—at least, in the age of Zenodotus and Callimachus.

2§198 Unlike Zenodotus, Aristarchus refrained from actually athetizing the verses describing the images on the Shield in *Iliad* XVIII 483-608. So he did not athetize the verses about the Ōkeanos at XVIII 607-608; nor did he athe-

---

[209] According to the scholia Ge (Geneva), Zenodotus athetized *Iliad* XXI 195. That is, he did not actually omit this verse.

[210] Pausanias 8.38.10 follows a version of *Iliad* XXI 194–197 that does not include the verse we know as XXI 195, where the Ōkeanos is privileged over the Akhelōios as the primal river. For more on the Akhelōios, see D'Alessio 2004.

[211] I await the publication of a work by Alex Beecroft on the variants adduced by Zenodotus in athetized verses.

2§18. Variations on a theme of Ōkeanos …

tize the verse about Ōkeanos in *Iliad* XXI 195.[212] Here we have the clearest indication that all these verses were conventionally thought to belong to the Homeric tradition—even in the age of Aristarchus.[213]

2§199 Viewing the differences between Zenodotus and Aristarchus in their editorial treatment of Homeric passages involving the Ōkeanos, we can see that Zenodotus was more extreme than Aristarchus in his efforts to distinguish Orphic from Homeric elements. At the other extreme was Crates of Pergamon. As we saw earlier, his text of Homer seems to have kept the supposedly Orphic elements indistinguishable from the Homeric.

2§200 There is more to be said about the specific differences between the Homeric texts of Zenodotus and Aristarchus with reference to the Ōkeanos. I start by reviewing the general differences between Zenodotus and Aristarchus as editors of Homer.

2§201 In the scrolls of his Homeric *hupomnēmata* 'commentaries', Aristarchus analyzed extensively the textual problems underneath the surface of his text of Homer—which was a base text produced in the scrolls of his Homeric edition.[214] Keyed into the text of his Homeric commentaries was a system of critical signs written into the left margins of his Homeric base text. The signs in the base text were placed to the left of each Homeric verse to be analyzed in the commentaries, with different signs indicating different problems to be discussed. An Aristarchean contemporary of Didymus, Aristonicus, specialized in studying the system of critical signs used by Aristarchus in his base text, and we find in the Homeric scholia numerous references to the testimony of Aristonicus. I am about to focus on a case where Aristonicus provides crucial information about differences between the Homeric editions of Zenodotus and Aristarchus with reference to the Ōkeanos.

2§202 In the scrolls of his Homeric *hupomnēmata*, Aristarchus debated extensively with Zenodotus, and in the scrolls of his Homeric base text he placed a special sign to the left of any given Homeric verse where he explicitly disagreed with the editorial judgment of Zenodotus about the contents of that verse. That critical sign was the *diplē periestigmenē* (>:).[215] This usage of the

---

[212] According to the Homer commentary preserved in *Oxyrhynchus Papyri* 221 column ix = Papyrus XII ed. Erbse, Aristarchus considered the verse at *Iliad* XXI 195 to be genuine, while Seleucus athetized it. See also Broggiato 2001:192.
[213] For a general discussion, see Pasquali 1962:225–227.
[214] I am reviewing here what I presented in the Prolegomena, P§§98–108.
[215] In the prolegomena of the D scholia of Codex Z (p. 55, ed. Montanari 1979), the use of the *diplē periestigmenē* (>:) is described as follows: τῇ δὲ περιεστιγμένῃ πρὸς Ζηνόδοτον τὸν διορθωτήν '[Aristarchus] used the *periestigmenē* with reference to [corrections made by] Zenodotus as corrector [*diorthōtēs*]'.

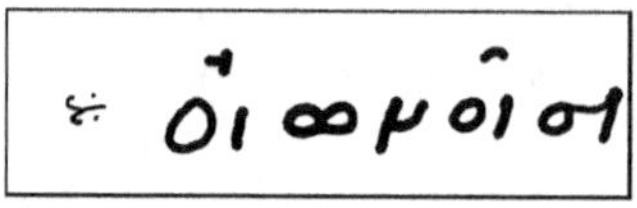

Chapter Two

> ⁚ ὂι ∞ μ ὂι ⲟ⳿

Figure 12. The so-called "Venetus A" manuscript of the Iliad: detail, *diplē periestigmenē* (>:) at the left margin, next to Iliad I 5. Venice, Biblioteca Marciana, Codex Marcianus Graecus 454.

diplē periestigmenē (>:) is preserved in the tenth-century Venetus A codex of the *Iliad*. A case in point is the fifth verse of the very beginning of the *Iliad*, as we see it transmitted by the Venetus A (Figure 12).

2§203 Where Aristarchus happened to disagree with editors other than Zenodotus, another kind of marginal sign was placed to the left of the given Homeric verse. That marginal sign was the simple *diplē* (>). Like the *diplē periestigmenē* (>:), the simple *diplē* (>) served as an indication that Aristarchus adduced in his commentaries a variant reading, provided by someone other than Zenodotus, which differed from the reading he preferred to keep in his own text of Homer.

2§204 In his Homeric commentaries, Aristarchus debated extensively with his near-contemporary and rival, Crates of Mallos, who as we saw was director of the Library of Pergamon.[216] Unlike the disagreements of Aristarchus with Zenodotus, which were marked by the *diplē periestigmenē* (>:), his disagreements with Crates and others were marked by the simple *diplē* (>).[217] The distinction between this less specific *diplē* (>) and the more specific *diplē periestigmenē* (>:) implies that the disagreements Aristarchus had with Crates and others were less important than those he had with Zenodotus, who

---

[216] Broggiato 1998:41 and 2001:134–135. For a seminal discussion, see Helck 1905:50, arguing that Aristarchus was in general disputing the editorial decisions of Crates, not the other way around.

[217] Wachsmuth 1860:30. Helck 1905:66 focuses on an instance of a *diplē* marking an Aristarchean disagreement with Crates (this one is not discussed by Wachsmuth), at *Iliad* XXI 323, where the argumentation of Crates seems more persuasive than that of Aristarchus. See also the summation by Helck at p. 76, where he argues in general that Aristarchus tended to go on record as disagreeing with Crates, and that instances of counterarguments generally involve Crates' disciples, not Crates himself. See also Aristonicus, by way of the A scholia, concerning the *diplē* attached to *Iliad* XX 7.

flourished a century earlier than Aristarchus and Crates.[218] Or, I would prefer to say, the disagreements of Aristarchus with Zenodotus were more important for the Aristarcheans than his disagreements with the likes of Crates. For my own argumentation, however, the disagreements of Aristarchus with Crates are just as important as his disagreements with Zenodotus.

2§205 What is more important for now is not the obvious fact that the Homer edition of Aristarchus was dissimilar from the Homer editions of both Zenodotus and Crates. Far more important, the 'corrected' Homer texts of Zenodotus and Crates were dissimilar from each other as well, not only from the 'corrected' Homer text of Aristarchus. Such dissimilarities, however, can only be reconstructed by way of observing the actual disagreements of Aristarchus with these two other editors, Zenodotus and Crates.

2§206 With this background in place, I am ready to focus on the disagreement between Aristarchus with Zenodotus over the attestation of Ōkeanos in a verse I have already noted, *Iliad* XXI 195. The disagreement was articulated in the Homeric *hupomnēmata* 'commentaries' of Aristarchus, as paraphrased later on in the Homeric scholia. Ancient readers of Homer would have been alerted to this disagreement, as marked in the margin of Aristarchus' base text of the *Iliad*, which featured the critical signs referring to specific points in the editor's commentaries. I repeat, these Aristarchean commentaries were published in scrolls separate from the scrolls featuring the base text of the *Iliad*. The marginal sign of the *diplē periestigmenē* (>:) to the left of the verse in question, *Iliad* XXI 195, would have sent the reader to the corresponding *lēmma* or 'extract' featuring the key wording of that verse; that key wording served as the heading for the corresponding commentary on that verse, as found

---

[218] In the prolegomena of the D scholia of Codex Z (p. 54, ed. Montanari 1979) we read this fuller description of the *diplē periestigmenē*: ἡ δὲ περιεστιγμένη πρὸς τὰς γραφὰς τὰς Ζηνοδοτείους καὶ Κράτητος καὶ αὐτοῦ Ἀριστάρχου καὶ τὰς διορθώσεις αὐτοῦ 'the *periestigmenē* was used with reference to the texts of Zenodotus and Crates—as also of Aristarchus himself and his own corrections [*diorthōseis*]'. See West 2001:54n22. This longer description needs to be compared to the shorter description, which I have already quoted (p. 55, ed. Montanari 1979). I think there may be a way to reconcile the two quoted descriptions of the *diplē periestigmenē*, both the shorter and the longer versions (on the problem, see in general Pfeiffer 1968:240). According to the shorter description, the *diplē periestigmenē* marked disagreements with Zenototus in particular. Moreover, as we saw in the immediately preceding note, the simple *diplē* was used in contexts where Aristarchus was reported to disagree with Crates, not with Zenodotus. Perhaps the *diplē periestigmenē* was used to signal the disagreements of Aristarchus with Crates only in contexts where Aristarchus was already disagreeing with Zenodotus and where the reading of Crates happened to match the reading of Zenodotus (I say happened to match because there is some debate over whether or not Crates systematically referred to Zenodotus: see Broggiato 1998:141-142; see also Broggiato 2001:134-135).

Chapter Two

in the separate scroll containing the commentaries of Aristarchus.[219] In the discussion headed by the *lēmma*, the reader would find that the commentator disagreed with the editorial rationale of Zenodotus—not necessarily with the Homer text of Zenodotus. The *ad hoc* discussion by Aristarchus in his commentary on *Iliad* XXI 195, as signaled by the marginal sign (>:) in his text of Homer and by the *lēmma* οὐδὲ βαθυρρείταο in his corresponding commentary on this verse of Homer, is in this case preserved by Aristonicus.

2§207 The relevant testimony of Aristonicus, Aristarchus, and Zenodotus concerning this matter has survived in both the Venetus A scholia and the Geneva (Ge) scholia for the *Iliad*. According to the Venetus A scholia, Aristonicus explained that Aristarchus marked the verse that we know as *Iliad* XXI 195 with a *diplē periestigmenē* (>:) because Aristarchus had disagreed with Zenodotus. The point of Aristarchus' disagreement, as marked by this sign, is 'because Zenodotus did not write it [out]', ὅτι Ζηνόδοτος αὐτὸν οὐκ ἔγραφεν. In the Venetus A scholia, the wording leaves it unclear whether Zenodotus omitted the line or simply athetized it. In the Geneva scholia, the reason given by Aristonicus for the disagreement of Aristarchus with Zenodotus is worded this way: ὅτι Ζηνόδοτος τοῦτον ἠθέτηκεν ἄρας '[Aristarchus disagreed] because Zenodotus athetized the line, taking it out'. The Geneva scholia go on to say: τοῦτον οὐ γράφει Μεγακλείδης 'Megaclides does not write out this line'. Megaclides was an expert in Homer who flourished in the fourth centuy BCE, and he is described as a 'Peripatetic' by Tatian (*To the Greeks* 31.2). In the case of Megaclides, it seems that his text of Homer simply did not contain the verse XXI 195, and it is possible that he was not aware that the verse existed.[220] In the case of Zenodotus, however, I will argue that he was very much aware of the verse and kept it in the text of his edition, but he marked it with a sign indicating his opinion that the verse should be rejected.

2§208 As a counterweight to the stance of Zenodotus, the Geneva scholia for *Iliad* XXI 195 adduce direct quotations from Crates of Pergamon—more precisely, from his *Homērika* (Crates F 29). From these quotations, it is clear that Crates defended XXI 195 as well as other Homeric verses that could be used to prove, as far as he was concerned, that the Ōkeanos and not the Akhelōios is the primal cosmic body of water—because it is the same thing as the salt sea we know as the ocean. As we learn from the Geneva scholia, Crates adduced the fifth-century thinker Hippon (38 B 1 DK) to back up his own argument that

---

[219] Montanari 2002a:125.

[220] Broggiato 2001:193 accepts the opinion of Janko 1992:28 that Megaclides "ignored" *Iliad* XXI 195. I agree that this is possible, but it does not necessarily follow that Zenodotus also "ignored" it.

this salt sea, this ocean, had at its extremities not salt water but fresh water—explicitly 'drinkable' (*poton*), which somehow still supplied all the fresh-water sources of the earth. This way, even Crates' modernizing image of the Ōkeanos as the ocean could be said to match the archaizing image of the Ōkeanos as a fresh-water earth-encircling cosmic river.[221]

2§209 The explanation of Aristonicus, as we saw it reported in the Homeric scholia, implies that Zenodotus had made an annotation in his text of Homer in order to indicate his reasons for rejecting *Iliad* XXI 195. Zenodotus' reasoning was evidently paraphrased and then disputed in the commentary of Aristarchus as reported by Aristonicus, and Aristarchus seems to have given his own counterargument for retaining the verse. Here is the wording that goes back to Aristonicus in the Geneva scholia for *Iliad* XXI 195: ὅτι Ζηνόδοτος αὐτὸν οὐκ ἔγραφεν· γίνεται γὰρ ὁ Ἀχελῷος πηγὴ τῶν ἄλλων πάντων '[Aristarchus disagreed] because Zenodotus did not write it out [= the suspected verse], on the grounds that the Akhelōios is the source [*pēgē*] of all the others [= rivers]'.

2§210 I need to stress that Zenodotus himself had two different ways of rejecting a suspected verse in his text of Homer. Evidence shows that he was systematic in choosing between either <u>athetizing</u> a suspected verse, by way of an *obelos*, or <u>deleting</u> it altogether, by way of various deletion signs and brief annotations that accompanied these signs in his text.[222] Such a distinction, however, tended to get blurred in later reportage of Zenodotus' editorial decisions, as we see in this case when we look at the differences between the reports of the Venetus A and the Geneva scholia.

2§211 I need to stress also, once again, that the alternative version of *Iliad* XXI 194-197 as defended by Zenodotus was based on alternative traditions attested independently of what we know as Homeric poetry. According to those independent traditions, Akhelōios, like Ōkeanos, was pictured as a cosmic river that supplies all fresh-water sources on earth.[223] In other words, Akhelōios and Ōkeanos are variant mythological constructs. As we will now see, these two cosmic rivers could even coexist as respectively older and newer generations of cosmic river-gods in poetic traditions attributed to Orpheus.

2§212 In the Venetus A scholia for *Iliad* XXI 195, we see that Aristarchus, after giving a reason for Zenodotus' rejection of that verse, proceeds to justify his own retention of the verse. Here is the reasoning offered by Aristarchus:

---

[221] See Broggiato 2001:192.
[222] Montanari 2002a:120–125
[223] On this subject, see D'Alessio 2004.

Chapter Two

ἔστι δὲ καθ' Ὅμηρον ὁ Ὠκεανὸς ὁ ἐπιδιδοὺς πᾶσι τὰ ῥεύματα· διὸ καὶ κατὰ τιμήν φησιν· "οὔτε τις οὖν ποταμῶν ἀπέην νόσφ' Ὠκεανοῖο" [*Iliad* XX 7] 'but according to Homer [= in terms of Homeric diction] it is the Ōkeanos who supplies the flow to all [= the rivers]; so, it is in terms of a ranking system that he [= Homer] says . . .'. At this point Aristarchus adduces the internal evidence of a verse that he quotes from the *Iliad* (XX 7), the wording of which implies that Ōkeanos is the one and only primal cosmic river.

2§213 From what we have seen so far, it appears that Zenodotus accepted the idea that the primal cosmic river was exclusively the Akhelōios for Homer, while Aristarchus argued that it was exclusively the Ōkeanos. But there is reason to think that Homeric poetry accommodated both names. I have been arguing that *Iliad* XXI 195, which privileges Ōkeanos, was indeed part of the textual tradition of Homer both before and after Zenodotus, despite that editor's rejection of the verse as probably Orphic and therefore supposedly non-Homeric. Also, the internal evidence of Homeric poetry shows that Akhelōios was accommodated by this poetry as an alternative to the Ōkeanos, although it ultimately became subordinated to it.

2§214 The fact that Aristarchus defended *Iliad* XXI 195, despite its Orphic and therefore supposedly non-Homeric characteristics—and despite his general editorial stance of rejecting supposedly non-Homeric verses—is linked to another aspect of Aristarchean editorial method: Homeric verses suspected of neoterism could not be omitted merely on the grounds of neoteric content. If any verse suspected of neoterism was strongly attested, Aristarchus preferred to defend such a verse and to make a case for the possibility that it was not neoteric after all. Only weakly attested neoteric verses were omitted by Aristarchus, as in the case of the supposedly Orphic verse at *Iliad* XIV 246a, which was privileged by Crates but omitted by Aristarchus. Neoteric verses that were strongly attested—even if Zenodotus had been inclined to reject them as probably Orphic—could still be defended by Aristarchus, who was evidently ready to infer that such strongly attested verses could still turn out to be genuinely Homeric after all.

2§215 Before I proceed, I must stress that I consistently use the term neoteric from the standpoint of Aristarchus, not from my own standpoint. I do not prejudge whether poets judged to be neoteric by Aristarchus were really 'newer' than Homer, or whether the poetic forms judged to be neoteric by Aristarchus were really 'newer' than the poetic forms judged to be Homeric. The same goes for poets and poetic forms judged to be neoteric by Zenodotus.

2§216 While Zenodotus was preoccupied with isolating those verses that he judged to be Orphic accretions in the Homeric text, the contemporary neoteric poets—among them, Apollonius—were preoccupied with privileging in their own poetry those same supposedly Orphic accretions. A prime example is a passage we have already seen in Apollonius *Argonautica* 1.503-506. Here I retell briefly the Orphic themes that we find in this passage. Orpheus sings his cosmogony and starts the theogonic sequence of his narrative by singing about Eurynome, the daughter of Ōkeanos and the wife of a distinctly Orphic figure, Ophiōn the cosmic serpent; after Ophiōn and the daughter of Ōkeanos are overthrown respectively by Kronos and Rhea the old gods are cast into the streams of Ōkeanos. There is more about Ophiōn in the poetry of another eminent neoteric, Callimachus himself (F 177.7-8).

2§217 After the age of Callimachus, in the age of Aristarchus, the Alexandrian editorial preoccupation with Orpheus and Orphic accretions had evidently waned, and Aristarchus was more preoccupied with isolating verses he judged to be Cyclic accretions in the Homeric text. For Aristarchus, it was the poets of the epic Cycle who became primary exponents of the category known to him as the *neōteroi*.[224] Occasionally, Aristarchus even criticized his predecessor Zenodotus for not being vigilant enough in isolating the neoterisms of the epic Cycle.[225] And just as Zenodotus seemed to be less preoccupied with the alleged neoterisms of the Cycle, so also the contemporary neoteric poets—among them, Callimachus—were less preoccupied with cultivating in their own poetry those aspects of Homeric poetry that seemed to be Cyclic. A salient example is the celebrated wording of Callimachus: ἐχθαίρω τὸ ποίημα τὸ κυκλικόν 'I detest the Cyclic poem' (*Epigram* 28.1).

2§218 A moment ago, I stated that Aristarchus seemed to be less preoccupied with Orphic than with Cyclic elements in Homer. Looking at Homeric poetry from an evolutionary point of view, however, I would prefer to reformulate this statement. On the basis of both the textual and the contextual evidence available to him, Aristarchus must have found the supposedly Orphic elements in Homer to be far more difficult to isolate as neoterisms than the Cyclic elements. I infer that Orphic elements were in some ways contextually more embedded—and therefore older—than Cyclic elements in the evolution of Homer the Classic. Conversely, Cyclic elements were more easily separable—and therefore newer—than Orphic elements.

2§219 In *Homer the Preclassic*, I treat the differences in degrees of embeddedness between Orphic and Cyclic elements in Homer. Here my aim is simply to stress that the 'Homeric' elements of Homeric poetry do not necessarily

---

[224] Severyns 1928:63.
[225] See especially Severyns 1928:44, 46, 98-99.

represent the oldest layers of this poetry. Whatever elements in Homeric poetry seem to be Orphic and Cyclic may turn out to be genuine traces of still older layers of that poetry. Of these two older layers, the Cyclic elements were differentiated from 'Homeric' poetry more systematically than the Orphic elements. Whatever Cyclic elements Aristarchus may have found embedded in the Homeric textual tradition would have been more easy for him to isolate, whereas most of the Orphic elements had already been isolated by Zenodotus. For Aristarchus, the methods used by Zenodotus to isolate Orphic elements in the Homeric text must have seemed too radical, whereas the same editor's methods in isolating Cyclic elements seemed too superficial.

2§220 In short, Zenodotus and Aristarchus were dissimilar in their emphasis on what to isolate as neoteric. For the earlier editor, it was mainly the Orphic aspects of Homer that were targeted. For the later editor, it was mainly the Cyclic aspects.

2§221 Here I need to stress once again a fundamental difference between Zenodotus and the neoteric poets of the Hellenistic era who imitated the neoterisms isolated by Zenodotus. Although these poets may have followed Zenodotus in treating accretive elements in Homer as examples of non-Homeric poetry, they were antithetical to Zenodotus in their cultivation of this poetry for its own sake. For them this kind of poetry was worth cultivating precisely because it was judged to be non-Homeric. For the likes of Callimachus and Apollonius, Homer was not the only Classic as an exponent of epic. The 'newer' poets—as represented by Cyclic and Hesiodic and Orphic poetry—were also Classics in their own right.

2§222 The earlier Alexandrians in the age of Callimachus appreciated Homeric poetry in broader terms than the later Alexandrians in the age of Aristarchus. In the eyes of the earlier Alexandrians, the Homeric text included non-Homeric—that is, neoteric—elements. For them the Homeric text was a neoteric Homer, transcending the classic Homer. This neoteric Homer of Callimachus, Apollonius, and Theocritus was closer to the edition of Crates than to the edition of Aristarchus. And, as we have seen, this Homer in the age of Callimachus was textually far more fluid than the Homer of the Aristarcheans.

2§223 Despite the anti-neoteric editorial stance of Zenodotus, the actual text of his Homeric edition must have seemed neoteric, retrospectively, by comparison with the corresponding text of Aristarchus. Despite the marginal marks and annotations devised by Zenodotus for the purpose of prescribing the rejection of neoteric elements—whether by athetesis or by outright deletion—his text of Homer included all these elements. In its inclusiveness, the Homeric text of Zenodotus could serve as an all-encompassing bible, as it were, for neoterics and anti-neoterics alike.

2§224 By contrast, the Homeric edition of Aristarchus shaded over the neoteric elements, thereby highlighting what he considered to be the core text of Homer. These neoteric elements, like other variant readings, could not be studied in the scrolls containing the Homeric base text as presented by Aristarchus; instead, such study was relegated to his *hupomnēmata* 'commentaries', written in separate scrolls.

2§225 As I noted earlier, the base text of Homer as edited by Aristarchus was adorned with critical signs that cross-referred to the *hupomnēmata* of the editor. It was in these *hupomnēmata* that the reader could find out about textual variants in general. Among these variants, the neoteric elements figured most prominently. In these *hupomnēmata*, Aristarchus offered a critical analysis of what he judged to be the rightness or wrongness of the core version as juxtaposed with all available textual variants found in other versions—and as juxtaposed also with any conjectures made by critics, including himself. Unfortunately, the corpus of variant readings assembled by Aristarchus has not survived as a corpus, since the Homeric *hupomnēmata* of Aristarchus have not been preserved in their textual integrity.[226] What survives from these commentaries is an unwieldy mass of excerpts and reports made by Aristonicus, Didymus, and other Aristarchean scholars, whose own works in turn survive only in the form of sporadic excerpts and reports made by scholiasts in the Homeric scholia.[227] The unfortunate outcome is that Aristarchus' collection of neoteric elements, a most important component of the variant readings reported by him, has been for the most part irretrievably lost.[228] The Aristarchean editorial policy of shading over the supposedly peripheral neoteric elements in order to highlight the core text of Homer resulted ultimately—and unintentionally—in the relegation of this periphery into a permanent outer darkness. Against this background of darkness, the non-neoteric core text of Homer continued to shine forth to the public at large.

2§226 This Homeric core text, surrounded by a periphery of neoteric elements that Aristarchus relegated to his *hupomnēmata* 'commentaries', was the Koine. The Homeric Koine, as approximated by the base text of Aristarchus in the second century BCE, stands in stark contrast with the Homerus Auctus, as approximated by the base text of Zenodotus in the age of Callimachus in the third century BCE. By contrast with the base text of Aristarchus, the base

---

[226] For an overall assessment of Aristarchus' methods in collecting Homeric textual variants, see HTL ch. 5.
[227] I offer an overall survey in HTL ch. 1.
[228] For a tracing of the broad outlines of this Aristarchean collection of neoteric variants, as indirectly reflected in the usage of the Hellenistic poets, see Rengakos 2000.

text of Zenodotus was more inclusive—and encumbered—even though the editorial criteria of Zenodotus himself were in some ways more exclusive than those of Aristarchus. When it came to discriminating between ostensibly Homeric and non-Homeric verses, Zenodotus was more exclusive in that he tended to athetize more verses than did Aristarchus, at least when it came to verses judged to be Orphic accretions. An extreme example, as we saw, is the fact that Zenodotus athetized the entire narrative of the Shield of Achilles in *Iliad* XVIII. Conversely, Aristarchus tended to athetize more verses than did Zenodotus when it came to passages judged to be Cyclic accretions. Overall, the number of verses athetized by Aristarchus on the grounds that they are Cyclic accretions tends to be exceeded, as I argued, by the number of verses athetized by Zenodotus on the grounds that they are Orphic accretions. In any case, both editors retained in their base texts the verses they athetized.

2§227 The notionally genuine Homer, as 'corrected' by the system of athetesis developed by Zenodotus, may have been more exclusive than the notionally genuine Homer of Aristarchus, but the point remains that the base text of Zenodotus was more inclusive, since it included not only the athetized verses marked with an *obelos* but also the plus verses marked with deletion signs and featuring brief comments written into the margins. In other words, the base text of Zenodotus must have encompassed the same kinds of augmentation encompassed by the base text of Crates, which was the equivalent of what I have been calling the Homerus Auctus.[229] By contrast, the base text of Aristarchus retained only the verses he athetized, not the plus verses, and this base text was the equivalent of the Homeric Koine.

2ⓢ19. Variations in the consequences of hymnic metabasis

2§228 The fluctuation between the Homerus Auctus and the 'corrected' Homer of editors like Zenodotus in the age of Callimachus can be viewed as a poetic challenge as well as a scholarly problem for poet-scholars like Callimachus. Here I return to *Hymn* 1 of Callimachus, which I have described as his virtual *Homeric Hymn to Zeus*. As we saw, the infinite deferral of metabasis in this *Hymn to Zeus* by Callimachus implies that the poet defers the poetic challenge of making a perfect new Homeric text. On the other hand, scholars like Zenodotus in the age of Callimachus accepted the scholarly challenge of perfecting the old Homeric text. Such an ongoing process of perfecting the text is the essence of *diorthōsis* or

---

[229] In displaying the Homerus Auctus, the base text of Zenodotus was different from the base text of Crates in one important way: Zenodotus followed an editorial policy of marking for deletion the plus verses that Crates later chose to leave undeleted.

2⑤19. Variations in the consequences of hymnic metabasis

'corrective editing'. As I will now argue, such *diorthōsis* is viewed by Callimachus as a non-poetic or meta-poetic variation on the theme of imagining the consequences of hymnic metabasis. Proceeding from there, I will also consider other variations we can find in the consequences of hymnic metabasis—variations that are decidedly poetic.

2§229 So far, we have seen that Callimachus defers the making of a metabasis in his *Hymns*. This is not to say, however, that he never successfully executed a hymnic metabasis. We find a splendid poetic execution in the ending of Callimachus' *Aetia*, in the last three verses of the conclusion of Book 4, the last of four scrolls:

2①74 Callimachus *Aetia* Book 4 F 112.7-9

χαῖρε, σὺν εὐεστοῖ δ' ἔρχεο λωϊτέρῃ.
χαῖρε, Ζεῦ, μέγα καὶ σύ, σάω δ' [ὅλο]ν οἶκον ἀνάκτων·
αὐτὰρ ἐγὼ Μουσέων πεζὸν [ἔ]πειμι νομόν.

Hail and take pleasure [*khaire*], and return the next time,
   bringing even better well-being.[230]
And you too, Zeus, hail and take pleasure [*khaire*], in a big
   way. Keep in safety the entire royal household.
As for me, I [*autar egō*] will enter the pasture of the Muses
   where one walks on foot.[231]

2§230 As we saw in the *Homeric Hymns*, the expression *autar egō* 'As for me, I . . .' signals an upcoming metabasis after the hymnic salutation *khaire* 'hail and take pleasure'. The hymnic metabasis, then, is quite clear here. The hymnic consequent of the metabasis, however, is opaque and riddling. On one hand, the word *nomos* evidently means 'pasture'—a meaning reinforced by the textual transmission of the oxytone accentuation *nomós*.[232] On the other hand, an alternative word *nómos*, with an alternative non-oxytone ("barytone") accentuation, is implied by the immediate context of the metabasis here, in that *nómos* is a poetic term for a lyric genre, the prosaic term for which is *kitharōidikos nomos* 'citharodic nome'.[233] I refer to my earlier work for details about this lyric genre, where I emphasize the essential fact that the

---

[230] Because of the fragmentary nature of the text, the poetic moment of naming the god or hero being saluted here has been lost.
[231] On the textual basis for reading *nomós* 'pasture' and not the expected *nómos* 'nome' (more on which later on), see Obbink 2001:73n29.
[232] See the note immediately above.
[233] Obbink 2001:73.

Chapter Two

kitharōidikos nomos was conventionally introduced by a hymnic metabasis.[234] That is to say, a hymnic metabasis could introduce as its hymnic consequent not only epic, as we have seen so far, but also a variety of other genres, among which the *kitharōidikos nomos* 'citharodic nome' figures as the most salient example. I emphasize here the lyrical essence of this genre, because it stands in sharp contrast to the description of the *nomos* that is being introduced by the metabasis of Callimachus at the conclusion of his *Aetia*. The *nomos* projected as the hymnic consequent of this Callimachean metabasis is the opposite of the lyrical. It is non-lyrical, non-musical: it is *pezos* 'pedestrian'. The metabasis of Callimachus projects as its consequent not lyric poetry, not even poetry, but 'pedestrian' prose. That 'pedestrian' prose, I submit, is the prose of Alexandrian scholarship, which enables the Alexandrian scholar to range all over the 'pasture of the Muses'.

2§231 There are scholarly as well as poetic implications in this poetic pronouncement by Callimachus. For now, however, I confine myself to the poetics, concentrating on a single point: that the hymnic metabasis is capable of projecting, as its hymnic consequent, genres other than epic. A salient example, as we have just seen, is the *kitharōidikos nomos* 'citharodic nome'. I now proceed to examine two other examples, involving other genres.

2§232 The first example is a fragment from a song of Simonides (F 11 ed. 2 West) celebrating the victory of the Hellenes who fought the Persians at the battle of Plataea in 479 BCE. This song (for the moment, I use "song" in the broadest possible sense of the word) shows the characteristics of a *humnos*: after glorifying the deeds of the Achaean heroes at Troy in verses 11-18, the speaker of the song turns to Achilles and addresses him in the second person as a cult hero, greeting him with the hymnic salutation *khaire* 'hail and take pleasure' at verse 19, which is followed by a metabasis signaled by the expression *autar egō* 'as for me, I ...' at verse 20, which activates as its hymnic consequent a narration of the glorious deeds of the Hellenes who fought at Plataea, starting with the Spartans at verse 25.[235]

2§233 The second example is a fragment from Empedocles:

2①75 Empedocles B 35 DK (= F 201 ed. Bollack)

αὐτὰρ ἐγὼ παλίνορσος ἐλεύσομαι ἐς πόρον ὕμνων,
τὸν πρότερον κατέλεξα, λόγου λόγον ἐξοχετεύων,

---

[234] PH 12§§40–42 (= pp. 357–359).
[235] For a brief commentary on the relevant themes in Simonides F 11 ed. 2 West, see Obbink 2001:72–73.

2⓼19. Variations in the consequences of hymnic metabasis

20 κεῖνον· ἐπεὶ Νεῖκος μὲν ἐνέρτατον ἵκετο βένθος
    <u>δίνης</u>, ἐν δὲ μέσηι Φιλότης στροφάλιγγι γένηται,
    ἐν τῆι δὴ τάδε πάντα συνέρχεται ἓν μόνον εἶναι,
    οὐκ ἄφαρ, ἀλλὰ θελημὰ συνιστάμεν' ἄλλοθεν ἄλλα.
    τῶν δέ τε μισγομένων <u>χεῖτ</u>' ἔθνεα μυρία θνητῶν·
25 πολλὰ δ' ἄμεικτ' ἔστηκε κεραιομένοισιν ἐναλλάξ,
    ὅσσ' ἔτι Νεῖκος ἔρυκε μετάρσιον· οὐ γὰρ ἀμεμφέως
    τῶν πᾶν ἐξέστηκεν ἐπ' <u>ἔσχατα</u> <u>τέρματα</u> <u>κύκλου</u>,
    ἀλλὰ τὰ μέν τ' ἐνέμιμνε μελέων τὰ δέ τ' ἐξεβεβήκει.
    ὅσσον δ' αἰὲν ὑπεκπροθέοι, τόσον αἰὲν ἐπήιει
30 ἠπιόφρων Φιλότητος ἀμεμφέος ἄμβροτος ὁρμή·
    αἶψα δὲ θνήτ' ἐφύοντο, τὰ πρὶν μάθον ἀθάνατ' εἶναι,
    ζωρά τε τὰ πρὶν ἄκρητα διαλλάξαντα κελεύθους.
    τῶν δέ τε μισγομένων <u>χεῖτ</u>' ἔθνεα μυρία θνητῶν,
    παντοίαις ἰδέηισιν ἀρηρότα, θαῦμα ἰδέσθαι.

As for me, I [*autar egō*], starting again [*palin-orsos*], will now come back to the watercourse [*poros*][236] of my *humnoi*,

the one [= the *poros*] that I had pronounced in due order before,[237] as I stream-channeled [*okheteuein*] one set of words from another.[238]

20 That is the one [= the *poros*]. When Strife [*Neikos*] came to the lowest depth

of the swirling stream [*dinē*], and Bonding [*Philotēs*] was generated in the middle of the swirl,

and it is in her, now I see, that all these things came together to become a single thing,

---

[236] On the meaning of *poros* (in such contexts) as 'watercourse', not 'path', see Bollack 1969:194; also Obbink 2001:73n28.
[237] What was said 'before' corresponds to the wording we see in Empedocles B 17. The verbal correspondences are studied by Bollack 1969:195.
[238] I translate *okheteuein* as 'stream-channeling': the metaphor derives from techniques of irrigating the land. The sequence of consonants and vowels here in line 19 imitates the flow of elements in what is said ... ἔλεξα λόγου λόγον ἐξ ... [... *elexalogōlegonex* ...]. See Bollack 1969:195.

> not all at once, but different things coming together willingly from different directions.
>
> And from the things that were being mixed together there poured [*kheîn*] forth countless groupings of things mortal.
>
> 25 But many other things stayed as they were, unmixed, in alternation with the things that were being mixed together,
>
> I mean, all the things that Strife [*Neikos*] was still holding back, keeping them in suspension. For it did not happen that, without taking exception,
>
> the entirety of them stood outside toward the outermost limits of the circle [*kuklos*],
>
> but some of the members were staying on the inside while others had gone out to the outside.
>
> As much as they kept on running away toward the outside all the time, so much did it keep on coming toward them all the time,
>
> 30 I mean, the immortal onrush, with a disposition that is kind and gentle, of Bonding [*Philotēs*] herself, the one who does not take exception.
>
> Then, all of a sudden, things were becoming mortal that had previously learned to be immortal,
>
> and things that had been pure and unmixed before had now changed their ways.
>
> And from the things that were being mixed together there poured [*kheîn*] forth countless groupings of things mortal.
>
> They were fashioned in all manner of shapes, a wonder to behold.

2§234 This passage from Empedocles makes it explicit at verse 18 that the speaker's discourse is a matter of singing songs that are *humnoi*. Moreover, the wording *autar egō* 'as for me, I . . .' in the same verse signals a metabasis, which as we saw is characteristic of *humnoi*.

2§235 There are also other passages to be found in Empedocles that reveal characteristics of *humnoi*. A case in point is the following:[239]

---

[239] For more on this passage, see Obbink 2001:70–71.

2§19. Variations in the consequences of hymnic metabasis

2①76 Empedocles B 131 DK

εἰ γὰρ ἐφημερίων ἕνεκέν τινος, ἄμβροτε Μοῦσα,
ἡμετέρας μελέτας <ἅδε τοι> διὰ φροντίδος ἐλθεῖν,
εὐχομένωι νῦν αὖτε παρίστασο, Καλλιόπεια,
<u>ἀμφὶ θεῶν μακάρων</u> ἀγαθὸν <u>λόγον</u> <u>ἐμφαίνοντι</u>.

If for the sake of any ephemeral being, immortal Muse,
it <pleased> you to care about what concerned me,
then, I pray to you, come now once again and stand by me, Kalliope,
as I <u>make visible</u> [*en-phainein*] the genuine <u>wording</u> [*logos*] about [*amphi*] the blessed gods.[240]

2§236 In this passage, Empedocles B 131 DK, I draw attention to the invocation of Kalliope as the speaker's primary Muse of inspiration. This detail is characteristic of Orphic traditions. As I show in the twin book *Homer the Preclassic*, the Muse Kalliope is particularly associated with Orphic *humnoi*, and it is relevant that Kalliope is claimed as the mother of Orpheus, as in the *Argonautica* of Apollonius of Rhodes (verses 23-25).[241]

2§237 Also in the passage quoted earlier, Empedocles B 35 DK, we find characteristics of Orphic traditions. Overall, the mysticism of this passage is Orphic, as we see from the form of the *humnoi* to which the speaker is referring at verse 18. Most telling is the hymnic metabasis that we see in the same verse. This metabasis signals not a change of subject but a return to the same subject as before. The speaker is saying at verses 19-20 that he will start over again, and the restarting is described in metaphorical terms as the channelling of a continuous flow of water. Further, the flow of water is metaphorically equated with the flow of the speaker's *humnoi*. As we are about to see, the idea of a hymnic subject that returns to itself after the metabasis is characteristic of Orphic *humnoi* in particular. This idea will bring us back to our starting point,

---

[240] In HPC I§208 I analyze other attestations, in a hymnic context, of the preposition *amphi* 'about' in combination with the genitive case of gods named as the subject of a *humnos*. On *amphi* plus genitive in the sense of 'about' (a given subject), see also *Homeric Hymn* (4) *to Hermes* 172. As for the use of *en-phainein* 'make visible' here in Empedocles B 131.4 DK, it is comparable to the use of *phainein* 'make visible' with reference to the visualization of Demodokos in narrating his version of the epic *Iliou Persis* in *Odyssey* viii 499—after performing a hymnic metabasis signaled at viii 492 by *metabainein* and at viii 499 by *theou arkheto*.
[241] HPC I§280.

Chapter Two

that is, the metaphor of the *humnos* as an eternally recycled *rhoos* 'flow' in the Callimachean *Hymn to Zeus*.

2⑤20. Theocritus and the mystical circularity of the song of Thyrsis

2§238 The mystical theme of an eternally recycled *rhoos* 'flow' recurs in a poem composed by another Alexandrian poet-scholar in the age of Callimachus. The poet is Theocritus of Syracuse, and the poem is his *Idyll* 1. Here the idea of an eternal flow of fresh spring water is once again being equated with the making of a *humnos*. We start with a verse that is notionally the final verse in a *humnos*:

2①77 Theocritus 1.145

<u>χαίρετ'</u>· <u>ἐγὼ δ'</u> ὔμμιν καὶ <u>ἐς ὕστερον</u> ἅδιον ᾀσῶ.

Hail and take pleasure [*khairete*]. As for me, I [*egō de*] will sing for you even more sweetly <u>in times to come</u>.

2§239 The hymnic salutation *khairete* 'hail and take pleasure' is being addressed here to the Muses. The wording *egō de* 'as for me, I . . .' is the equivalent of *autar egō* 'as for me, I . . .', which as we saw signals a metabasis in the making of a *humnos*.

2§240 I draw attention to my translation of ἅδιον here in verse 145 of Theocritus 1 as an adverb, 'more sweetly', not as a substantival adjective, 'a more sweet thing [= song]'. In what follows, I will justify this translation as I proceed to analyze this verse as a poetic act of metabasis.

2§241 Verse 145 in *Idyll* 1 of Theocritus marks the end of a song within a song. It is the last verse of a song about Daphnis, extending from verse 64 all the way through verse 145. This song within a song is notionally being performed by a figure called Thyrsis.[242] The inner song, just like the outer song that frames it, is a poem that pretends to be a song in its own right—though both the inner song and the outer song that frames it are composed in the non-singing recitative medium of the meter generalized by Homeric poetry, dactylic hexameter.

2§242 Earlier, at verse 61 of *Idyll* 1, the song of Thyrsis explicitly refers to itself as a *humnos*.[243] As we have already seen, this equation is borne out by formal features of the song, such as the hymnic salutation *khairete* 'hail and

---

[242] In Theocritus 1, the song of Thyrsis about Daphnis seems to be modeled on the poetry of Stesichorus about Daphnis: see Hunter 1999:65.

[243] This *humnos* is described at verse 61 of Theocritus 1 as 'evoking desire' (*ephimeros*).

2§20. Theocritus and the mystical circularity of the song of Thyrsis

take pleasure', addressed to the Muses at verse 145, which is the last verse of the song about Daphnis. From what we already know about the usage of *khairete* in *humnoi*, we would expect this hymnic salutation to signal here that the song about Daphnis has been a *humnos* all along. As we saw earlier in the *Homeric Hymns*, the hymnic salutation *khairete* activates a potential transition to the rest of the performance. What we expect to follow the hymnic *khairete* is a hymnic metabasis, and, after the metabasis, a hymnic consequent that continues as part of the *humnos*. And, true to form, a metabasis does in fact follow the salutation *khairete*: as we saw in the passage I just quoted, the hymnic salutation and the hymnic metabasis coexist in verse 145. But then the question is: what has happened to the hymnic consequent that we are expecting after the hymnic metabasis? We see no such consequent, since verse 145 marks the very end of the staged performance.

2§243 Relevant to the structure of the song of Thyrsis as a *humnos* are three different kinds of "refrains" in the song:

A)   ἄρχετε βουκολικᾶς, Μοῖσαι φίλαι, ἄρχετ' ἀοιδᾶς

   Begin [*arkhein*], dear Muses, starting [*arkhein*] from the Cowherd's Song.

   (Theocritus 1 verses 64, 70, 73, 76, 79, 84, 89)

B)   ἄρχετε βουκολικᾶς, Μοῖσαι, πάλιν ἄρχετ' ἀοιδᾶς

   Begin, Muses, starting once again from the Cowherd's Song.

   (Theocritus 1 verses 94, 99, 104, 108, 111, 114, 119, 122)

C)   λήγετε βουκολικᾶς, Μοῖσαι, ἴτε λήγετ' ἀοιδᾶς

   End [*lēgein*] Muses, go and leave off [*lēgein*] from the Cowherd's Song.

   (Theocritus 1 verses 127, 131, 137, 142)

2§244 The term refrain in this context has been explained as follows: Thyrsis's masterpiece, which he now sings at the goatherd's invitation, is divided by refrains or intercalary sections, of which the longest are of five, the shortest of two lines. ... The [manuscripts] show a remarkable unanimity as to their [= the refrains'] position and the tradition on this point appears to be quite firm.[244]

[244] Gow 1952 II 15–16. The highlighting is mine.

Chapter Two

2§245 In terms of this explanation, the "sections" marked off by these refrains cannot be seen as "strophic responsions," since the hexameter is a spoken verse and, consequently, "the 'songs' which T[heocritus] puts in the mouth of his characters can do no more than suggest in another medium the verses which they sang"; in short, "anything in the nature of strophic responsion is not to be looked for."[245]

2§246 I agree that the A/B/C "refrains" of the song of Thyrsis are not markers of "strophes" in "strophic responsion." What, then, do they mark? I propose that these A/B/C "refrains" mark various <u>transitions</u> in the narrative. The most essential of these transitions is the verse I quoted earlier, Theocritus 1.145, which comes at the very end of the song. This transition is signaled by an earlier verse, Theocritus 1.142, which is the last occurrence of the "refrains." That "refrain" is of type "C":

2ⓣ78 Theocritus 1.142

> λ<u>ήγετε</u> βουκολικᾶς, Μοῖσαι, ἴτε λ<u>ήγετ</u>' ἀοιδᾶς.
>
> End [*lēgein*] Muses, <u>go and leave off</u> [*lēgein*] from the Cowherd's Song.

2§247 The same expert whom I quoted earlier has this to say about type "C":

> [The scholia] comment on C at 127, and the [manuscripts] agree in introducing it [= C] at that point and using it [= C] from there on. At 123 Daphnis, who has taken leave of his native haunts, turns to address Pan, and 127 follows the first section of his address. It might seem therefore that if this position for C is correct, <u>T[heocritus] thought of his refrains as belonging to the section which precedes them, not to that which follows</u>, and that <u>the additional refrain thrown in to frame the whole composition is not the last at 142 but the first at 64.</u>[246]

2§248 As I hope to show in what follows, there is no "additional refrain" here, either at the beginning or at the "end." Rather, these "refrains" are introductory formulas that mark the beginning, then the consequent, and then the ending of a *humnos*.

2§249 The word *lēgein* at Theocritus 1.142 and elsewhere, which I translate in two ways within one verse—as both 'end' and 'leave off'—is indicative

---

[245] Gow 1952 II 16.
[246] Gow 1952 II 16. The highlighting is mine.

2⑤20. Theocritus and the mystical circularity of the song of Thyrsis

of two ways of ending a performance. The first and obvious way, of course, is simply to end. The second way, however, is less obvious to us: a performer can end a given performance only to restart it later.

2§250 As the *humnos* of Thyrsis reaches its conclusion, the wording implies that a restarting is anticipated:

2①79 Theocritus 1.137-145

>   λήγετε βουκολικᾶς, Μοῖσαι, ἴτε λήγετ' ἀοιδᾶς.
>   χὠ μὲν τόσσ' εἰπὼν ἀπεπαύσατο· τὸν δ' Ἀφροδίτα
>   ἤθελ' ἀνορθῶσαι· τά γε μὰν λίνα πάντα λελοίπει
> 140 ἐκ Μοιρᾶν, χὠ Δάφνις ἔβα ῥόον. ἔκλυσε δίνα
>   τὸν Μοίσαις φίλον ἄνδρα, τὸν οὐ Νύμφαισιν ἀπεχθῆ.
>   λήγετε βουκολικᾶς, Μοῖσαι, ἴτε λήγετ' ἀοιδᾶς.
>   καὶ τὺ δίδου τὰν αἶγα τό τε σκύφος, ὥς κεν ἀμέλξας
>   σπείσω ταῖς Μοίσαις. ὦ χαίρετε πολλάκι, Μοῖσαι,
> 145 χαίρετ'· ἐγὼ δ' ὔμμιν καὶ ἐς ὕστερον ἅδιον ᾀσῶ.

> End [*lēgein*], Muses, go and leave off [*lēgein*] from the Cowherd's Song.
> Saying this much, he stopped.[247] But him did Aphrodite wish to make stand up straight [*an-orthoûn*].[248] Meanwhile, all the thread had run out
> 140 from the Moirai. And Daphnis went the way of the flow [*rhoos*]. A swirling stream [*dinē*] washed over the man who was near-and-dear [*philos*] to the Muses, the one who was no enemy to the Nymphs.
> End [*lēgein*], Muses, go and leave off [*lēgein*] from the Cowherd's Song.

---

[247] At this point in Theocritus 1, the narrative makes it explicit that Daphnis stops speaking with a human voice. But will he cease being alive? I attempt to address this question in what follows.
[248] The idea of resurrection is intended here, as we will see in what follows.

Chapter Two

> But you, give me the she-goat and the <u>cup</u> [*skuphos*],[249] so that I may milk[250] her
>
> and that I may <u>pour libation</u> [from the cup] to the Muses. O Muses, <u>hail and take pleasure</u> [*khairete*] again and again.
>
> 145 <u>Hail and take pleasure</u> [*khairete*]. As for me, I will sing for you even more sweetly in times to come.

2§251 In the end, there is no immediate restarting after Thyrsis 'leaves off' at verse 142 and pronounces the metabasis at verse 145. Nor is there any counter-starting by the other singer in this poem, a goatherd, once Thyrsis 'leaves off'. Instead, at verses 146-152, which are not quoted here, the other singer responds to the song of Thyrsis by awarding him a prize for the song. That prize, which as we have just seen is anticipated by Thyrsis in his song at verses 143-144, is a wondrous cup described by the goatherd at an earlier point (verses 27-61, which are not quoted here). Are we to conclude, then, that the *humnos* of Thyrsis has simply ended after all and will not be restarted?

2§252 For an answer, I need to reconsider verse 145 in *Idyll* 1 of Theocritus, which signals the metabasis in the *humnos* of Thyrsis. This time, I consider the verse in the context of the wording that leads up to it. In the quotation that I have just given, the wording starts with an earlier "refrain," at verse 137, and proceeds to the last "refrain," at verse 142, and then ends, as it were, with the metabasis at verse 145.

2§253 Verse 137 signals that the performance is heading toward an end, a stopping point, and that the figure of Daphnis is heading toward his own end. The very next verse, 138, makes it explicit that Daphnis stops speaking with a human voice. But will he stop living as well? Yes, he will die, as an earlier verse foretells (135, not quoted here). The death of Daphnis comes to pass at verse 140, when the *dinē* 'swirling stream' washes him away, ἔκλυσε δίνα. But the question remains: will Daphnis stop living after his death? The response is worded in the form of a mystery. The mysticism is signaled already at verses 138-139, where we hear that Aphrodite wished to 'resurrect' Daphnis (verb

---

[249] Earlier, at verse 27 of Theocritus 1, this 'bowl' is called a *kissubion*. At verse 55, it is called a *depas*. Inside this 'bowl', as we learn at verse 32, is the picture of a *gunē* 'woman' who is a *daidalma* 'handiwork' of the gods, and, at verse 33, she is wearing a *peplos* and an *ampux*. At verses 33-34, we see that this woman is flanked on each side by two men who are *etheirazontes* 'wearing long hair' and who are engaged in a *neikos* 'quarrel' over her.

[250] Earlier, at verse 25 of Theocritus 1, we learn that this she-goat is the mother of twin *eriphoi* 'baby-goats'.

2⑤20. Theocritus and the mystical circularity of the song of Thyrsis

anorthoûn).[251] Such opaque references to resurrection (and erection) are typical of wording that signals the process of initiation into a mystery.

2§254 As I noted earlier, the mystical moment of truth comes to pass at verse 140, when Daphnis ἔβα ῥόον 'went the way of the flow [*rhoos*]' as the *dinē* 'swirling stream' washed him away.[252] The context here is comparable with the mystical context of *dinē* 'swirling stream' at verse 21 of Empedocles B 35 DK, which I quoted earlier. The question arises, however, whether the death of Daphnis is truly a mystical theme. According to one view, "the manner of his death remains mysterious, but he may merely have 'wasted away'."[253] The word that is rendered as 'waste away' here in *Idyll* 1 is *tēkesthai* (verse 66 ἐτάκετο), with reference to the mysterious death of Daphnis in the song of Thyrsis. Literally, *tēkesthai* means 'dissolve'.

2§255 In support of the view that Daphnis may merely have 'wasted away', another passage from Theocritus has been cited. In *Idyll* 7 verses 73-77, we find that Daphnis 'dissolved [*tēkesthai*] like snow' (76 εὖτε χιὼν ὥς τις κατετάκετο). The word *tēkesthai*, which I translate here as 'dissolved', has to do basically with liquefaction, as we see most clearly in *Odyssey* xix 205 and 206, where the word is used two times with reference to the melting of snow. In that same Homeric context, the same word *tēkesthai* is also used three more times with reference to the weeping Penelope, who is pictured as physically 'dissolving' in sadness (xix 204, 207, 208).[254] The 'dissolving' of Penelope in her sadness is being metaphorically compared to the dissolving of snow on a mountaintop into the waters of a cold mountain stream.[255]

2§256 With reference to the lovesick Daphnis as pictured in *Idyll* 1 of Theocritus, verse 66 (ἐτάκετο), the application of *tēkesthai* seems to imply the

---

[251] Hunter 1999:104 explains the verb *anorthoûn*: "set him on his feet' . . .; the verb also suggests 'raise him [from death]'."
[252] The scholia for Theocritus 1.140 offer the interpretation: 'went the way of Acheron'.
[253] Hunter 1999:63.
[254] The 'melting' affects the *khrōs* 'complexion' and the *pareiai* 'cheeks' of Penelope: *Odyssey* xix 204 and 208.
[255] I will avoid using the word melt to translate Greek *tēkesthai* because this English word generally implies a transition from cold to warm in metaphors concerning emotions, whereas the Greek word does not necessarily convey that implication. A case in point is the image of cold snow turning into an ice cold mountain stream, as we see it applied here to the 'melting' of Penelope. In this regard, I find most instructive the discussion of Dué 2006:125n18.

idea of 'wasting away' in sadness[256] or in illness.[257] But the basic idea of *tēkesthai* remains 'dissolve' and not merely 'waste away'.[258] And this idea is pertinent to the death of Daphnis. Yes, "the manner of his death remains mysterious," but the ultimate mystery, after all, is not in the way Daphnis died but in the way he may yet come back to life after death. Daphnis lives on by 'going the way of the flow': this expression ἔβα ῥόον at verse 140 evokes the idea of an unfailing 'fluency' emanating from the Muses, as manifested in the Hesiodic expression I quoted earlier from *Theogony* 39-40: τῶν δ' ἀκάματος ῥέει αὐδὴ | ἐκ στομάτων ἡδεῖα 'inexhaustable is the sweet voice that flows from their mouths'. Such 'fluency' is the mark of the *humnos*, as we saw in the usage of the word *rhoos* 'flow' in the *Hymns* of Callimachus, particularly in the *Hymn to Zeus* and in the *Hymn to Apollo*.

2§257 Here I return to an important detail: the song about Daphnis, in verses 64-152 of Theocritus 1, is notionally being performed by a figure called Thyrsis. The song of Thyrsis, as his very name suggests, is driven by the idea of initiation into a mystery. The name Thyrsis is derived from *thursos* / θύρσος, which is a ritual wand of initiation into the mysteries of the god Dionysus, whose ritual name is Bakkhos, that is, Bacchus. This Bacchic wand, the *thursos* / θύρσος, is also known by its metonymic variant *narthēx* / νάρθηξ, which designates the stalk of the wand. Together these words are used to describe the mystical experience of tapping into mysterious sources of wondrous streams:

---

[256] Examples of *tēkesthai* in contexts of sadness: besides the passage just cited from the *Odyssey*, see also *Iliad* III 176 (Helen weeps over her fate in the *Iliad*); *Odyssey* viii 522 (Odysseus weeps in reaction to the third song of Demodokos; at verse 523, he is compared to a woman who is weeping—the verb is *klaiein*—over the dead body of her warrior husband; at verse 527, as she weeps, she is literally *amphi . . . khumenē* 'poured all around' the body; her cheeks 'waste away'—the verb is *phthinesthai*—from all the sorrow); xix 136 (Penelope describes her grief over the absence of Odysseus: the 'dissolving' affects her *ētor* 'heart'); xix 264 (Odysseus describes the grief of Penelope as a 'dissolving' that affects her *thumos*). The wording *amphi . . . khumenē* 'poured all around' (*Odyssey* viii 527) is comparable to other expressions that I will examine at a later point.

[257] Examples of *tēkesthai* in contexts of illness: *Odyssey* v 396 (the suffering here is described as *algea* 'pains' inflicted by a *daimōn*; the sufferer is ultimately 'released'—the verb is *luein*—by the gods), xi 201 (Antikleia says that she died of grief, not of illness, and she describes the hypothetical illness as a *tēkedōn* 'melting away' that depletes the *thumos*).

[258] It is relevant to note that the cognates of *tēkesthai* in other Indo-European languages point to the basic idea of liquefaction: see Chantraine *DELG* s.v. τήκω. For more on the poetic contexts of *tēkesthai*, see Dué 2006:124, especially with reference to Euripides *Hecuba* 433 and 434.

2§20. Theocritus and the mystical circularity of the song of Thyrsis

2Ⓣ80 Euripides *Bacchae* 704-711

θύρσον δέ τις λαβοῦσ' ἔπαισεν ἐς πέτραν, | ὅθεν δροσώδης ὕδατος ἐκπηδᾶι νοτίς· | ἄλλη δὲ νάρθηκ' ἐς πέδον καθῆκε γῆς | καὶ τῆιδε κρήνην ἐξανῆκ' οἴνου θεός· | ὅσαις δὲ λευκοῦ πώματος πόθος παρῆν, | ἄκροισι δακτύλοισι διαμῶσαι χθόνα | γάλακτος ἑσμοὺς εἶχον· ἐκ δὲ κισσίνων | θύρσων γλυκεῖαι μέλιτος ἔσταζον ῥοαί.

One of the them [= women possessed by Bacchus] took a *thursos* and struck it against a rock. | From it sprang forth the moisture of water, looking like dew. | Another one of them lowered her *narthēx* to touch the surface of the earth, and at that spot did the god send up a fountain of wine. | Those women who had a desire for the white drink | pressed the earth with the tips of their fingers | and received jets of milk. Out of the *thursoi*, draped with ivy, emanated sweet streams [*rhoai*] of honey.

2§258 When I say "mystery" in such contexts, I have in mind traditions I describe as Orphic as well as Bacchic. When I say Orphic and Bacchic together, I am following the usage of Herodotus:

2Ⓣ81 Herodotus 2.81.1-2

οὐ μέντοι ἔς γε τὰ ἱρὰ ἐσφέρεται εἰρίνεα οὐδὲ συγκαταθάπτεταί σφι· οὐ γὰρ ὅσιον. ὁμολογέουσι δὲ ταῦτα τοῖσι Ὀρφικοῖσι καλεομένοισι καὶ Βακχικοῖσι, ἐοῦσι δὲ Αἰγυπτίοισι, καὶ <τοῖσι> Πυθαγορείοισι· οὐδὲ γὰρ τούτων τῶν ὀργίων μετέχοντα ὅσιόν ἐστι ἐν εἰρινέοισι εἵμασι θαφθῆναι. Ἔστι δὲ περὶ αὐτῶν ἱρὸς λόγος λεγόμενος.

It is not customary for them [= the Egyptians], however, to wear woolen fabrics for the occasion of sacred rituals or to be buried wearing wool. For it is unholy for them. This is in accordance with rituals that are called Orphic [*Orphika*] and Bacchic [*Bakkhika*], though they are really Egyptian and, by extension, Pythagorean [*Puthagoreia*].[259] I say this because it is unholy for someone who takes part in these [Pythagorean] rituals [*orgia*] to be buried wearing

---

[259] Herodotus thinks that the Pythagoreans were responsible for importing Egyptian customs. I agree with Asheri, Lloyd, and Corcella 2007:296 when they say about the section that reads Βακχικοῖσι … καί: "this section is omitted in all the Florentine mss [as opposed to other mss], but the arguments for postulating an omission in this group are considerably stronger than those for interpolation."

Chapter Two

woolen fabrics. And there is a sacred [*hieros*] discourse [*logos*] that is told [*legesthai*] about that.

2§259 In *Homer the Preclassic*, I analyze the collocation of Orphic and Bacchic elements in such a context.[260] I argue there that the collocation goes back to Athenian traditions dating from the era of the Peisistratidai. Here I simply need to highlight the word used by Herodotus to indicate the Orphic and Bacchic rituals: it is *orgia*, translated in the dictionary of Liddell and Scott as 'secret rites, mysteries'.

2§260 From what I have just quoted, we have seen that Herodotus (2.81.2) links this word *orgia* 'secret rites, mysteries' with *hieros logos* 'sacred discourse', with reference to the wording that accompanies the secret rites. Such wording is attested in the words of Plato's Socrates, where he makes this striking distinction between successful and unsuccessful initiation:

2ⓣ82 Plato *Phaedo* 69c-d

καὶ κινδυνεύουσι καὶ οἱ τὰς τελετὰς ἡμῖν οὗτοι καταστήσαντες οὐ φαῦλοί τινες εἶναι, ἀλλὰ τῷ ὄντι πάλαι αἰνίττεσθαι ὅτι ὃς ἂν ἀμύητος καὶ ἀτέλεστος εἰς Ἅιδου ἀφίκηται ἐν βορβόρῳ κείσεται, ὁ δὲ κεκαθαρμένος τε καὶ τετελεσμένος ἐκεῖσε ἀφικόμενος μετὰ θεῶν οἰκήσει. εἰσὶν γὰρ δή, [ὥς] φασιν οἱ περὶ τὰς τελετάς, "ναρθηκοφόροι μὲν πολλοί, βάκχοι δέ τε παῦροι."

And there is a chance that even these persons who founded the mysteries [*teletai*] for us,[261] whoever they might have been, were not insignificant but were in a real sense saying in enigmatic utterances [*ainittesthai*], back then in those remote times [*palai*], that whoever arrives in the realm of Hades[262] without having been initiated [*amuētos*, from verb *muein*] and without having been ritually inducted [*atelestos*, from the verb of *telos*] will be lodged in the mud,[263] but that he who arrives there after having been purified [= verb of *katharsis*] and having been inducted [= *teleîn*, the verb of

---

[260] *HPC* E§105.

[261] The wording ἡμῖν 'for us' implies that the reference to these unnamed persons who founded the mysteries involves various culture heroes—from the standpoint of the speaker and of his immediate audience. As we will see from the discussion that follows, the most obvious example of such culture heroes is Orpheus.

[262] In the overall logic of this restatement of the mysteries, the realm of Hades figures as a transitional phase, not as an eschatological outcome, not as a final destiny.

[263] I suggest that the wording here evokes the image of frogs lodged in mud; I find it relevant that the chorus of frogs in Aristophanes' *Frogs* is transformed into *mustai* 'initiates'.

2§20. Theocritus and the mystical circularity of the song of Thyrsis

telos] will <u>dwell</u> [= verb of *oikos*] with the gods.[264] "Many," as is said by those concerned with the <u>mysteries</u> [*teletai*], "are the bearers of the *narthēx*, but few are the *bakkhoi* [= devotees of Bacchus]."[265]

2§261 Here we see another dimension of the meaning of *telos*: it is not just the 'outcome' of a process: it is also <u>the successful outcome of a mystical process</u>. In other words, *telos* is a successful 'initiation' into the 'mysteries', that is, into the *teletai*. One such mystery is the 'coming-full-circle' of the Ōkeanos.

2§262 Applying to the song of Thyrsis what we have just learned about <u>Orphic</u> and <u>Bacchic</u> mysteries, I suggest that the dissolving or liquefaction of Daphnis in Theocritus 1 is not only a metaphor for the death of Daphnis: it is also a response to the question posed by the mystery of this death. Daphnis lives on after all, even after his death as a mortal, because he 'went the way of the flow [*rhoos*]', ἔβα ῥόον. This expression ἔβα ῥόον in verse 140 of *Idyll* 1 of Theocritus evokes the metaphor that equates poetry with unfailing 'fluidity', which we saw deployed in the expression (ἀκάματος) ῥέει αὐδὴ ' (unfailing) the voice [*audē*] flows [*rheîn*]' in Hesiod *Theogony* 39. Such 'fluidity', as we saw from the poetry of Hesiod, and of Callimachus as well, is a sign of the *humnos*.

2§263 It is relevant that the singing of Thyrsis is compared at the beginning of *Idyll* 1 of Theocritus, not quoted here, to a stream that 'is poured down [*kataleibesthai*] from the rocks above', in verse 8. So the song of Thyrsis about Daphnis is itself a stream, and Daphnis fuses not only with the stream but also with the song.

2§264 Here is one way of interpreting the closing lines of the song of Thyrsis, in Theocritus 1.143-145: "These lines (143-145) stand outside the song proper, but the promise and hymnic farewell to the Muses which link 144 to 141, the echo of 65 [not quoted here] in 145 (ἐγώ—Θύρσις ὅδ', ἅδιον—ἁδέα), and <u>the fact that the expectation has been created that the refrain of 142 will introduce a new stanza</u> all blur the boundary between the two" (emphasis mine).[266] In terms of this interpretation, "The promise to 'sing a sweeter song in the future' takes the place of the standard αὐτὰρ ἐγὼ καὶ σεῖο καὶ ἄλλης μνήσομ' ἀοιδῆς with which the *Homeric Hymns* close."[267] I offer a different way

---

[264] In other words, the successful initiates experience a transition beyond the realm of Hades into the realm of the gods, whereas the unsuccessful initiates find themselves in a "holding pattern," stuck in the mud.
[265] Compare the Christian aphorism in *Matthew* 22:14: πολλοὶ γάρ εἰσιν κλητοὶ ὀλίγοι δὲ ἐκλεκτοί 'many are called but few are chosen'.
[266] See Hunter 1999:105, who adduces the discussion of Goldhill 1991:245.
[267] Hunter 1999:105.

Chapter Two

of interpreting the closing lines of the song of Thyrsis in Theocritus 1.143-145. Though I agree that the phrasing αὐτὰρ ἐγὼ καὶ σεῖο καὶ ἄλλης μνήσομ' ἀοιδῆς in the *Homeric Hymns* is comparable, I have already argued for a different interpretation of that phrasing: 'as for me, I will keep you in mind along with the rest of the song'—instead of 'another song'. Further, the expression *khairete* in the song of Thyrsis at verses 144 and 145 is more than a mark of 'farewell'. If I am right about this hymnic salutation *khairete*, which I have been translating as 'hail and take pleasure', it activates the onset of a metabasis, which offers an option to continue the performance. As for the wording of the metabasis in the song of Thyrsis, ἐγὼ δ' ὔμμιν καὶ ἐς ὕστερον ἄδιον ᾀσῶ at verse 145, I have been translating it this way: 'as for me, I will sing for you ever more sweetly in times to come'. The wording of the original Greek does not point to a different subject for the song to be sung in the future. As my translation indicates, the wording ἄδιον is most naturally to be taken here as an adverb, 'more sweetly', not as a substantival adjective, 'a more sweet thing [= song]'. The singing that is promised for the future does not point to a different song. Rather, it points to a continuation of the same song with which Thyrsis had begun. The emphasis is placed on the continuum of the song, on its continuity.

2§265 A moment ago, I described the final line of the song of Thyrsis in Theocritus 1.145 as an act of metabasis, activated by the hymnic salutation *khairete*. This same line can also be described as a ritual act of transition, as an initiation into a mystery that tells of a passage from one life into another. Daphnis lives on, transformed into a stream. The song of Thyrsis about Daphnis lives on, transformed into that stream. The A/B/C "refrains" of the song of Thyrsis trace the flow of this song, from beginning (ἄρχετε) to beginning again (πάλιν ἄρχετ') to ending (λήγετε), but the ending can be seem as a circling back to the beginning:

2ⓣ83 Theocritus 1.92-94

τὼς δ' οὐδὲν ποτελέξαθ' ὁ βουκόλος, ἀλλὰ τὸν αὑτῶ
ἄνυε πικρὸν ἔρωτα, καὶ ἐς τέλος ἄνυε μοίρας.
ἄρχετε βουκολικᾶς, Μοῖσαι, πάλιν ἄρχετ' ἀοιδᾶς.

To them no answer made the cowherd, but, as for his own
bitter eros, he continued [= *anuein*] it to the completion [*telos*]
of his share in life [*moira*].
Begin, Muses, starting again from the Cowherd's Song.

2⊚20. Theocritus and the mystical circularity of the song of Thyrsis

2§266 Up to this point in the song of Thyrsis, Daphnis refuses to respond to those who question him; instead, he 'saw his bitter love through to the end [*telos*] appointed by fate [*moira*]'.[268] I have just quoted a leading commentator's translation of τὸν αὐτῶ | ἄνυε πικρὸν ἔρωτα, καὶ ἐς τέλος ἄνυε μοίρας at verses 92-93. My own translation indicates a slightly different interpretation: 'as for his own bitter love, he continued it to the completion [*telos*] of his share in life [*moira*]'. The idea of continuing to the *telos* conveys the idea of continuing to the 'completion' of the continuum that is the narrative (in effect, this completion *is* the *moira*).[269] In terms of a straight line, the 'completion' of the continuum is *telos* in the sense of 'end'; in terms of a circle, however, the 'completion' is a *telos* in the sense of 'coming full circle', which is a further continuum. Thus the 'completion' or fulfillment of the unrequited love (πικρὸν ἔρωτα at verse 93) becomes a transformation of that love. The completion of the life of Daphnis becomes a transformation of that life.[270] The "refrain" (verse 94) says it over and over again: the start is a restarting (ἄρχετε ... πάλιν ἄρχετ' ἀοιδᾶς).

2§267 In this image of the ongoing flow we see the basic idea of the *humnos*. I return to the point I made when we began to look at the song of Thyrsis in Theocritus 1. That song, as we saw at verse 61, calls itself a *humnos*. What makes it a *humnos* is its continuity. And that continuity is in this case circular, not linear.

2§268 To sum up, the hymnic salutation *khairete* of verses 144 and 145 in Theocritus 1 activates the onset of metabasis, which offers an option to continue the performance of song. The song that is promised at the metabasis is not a different song, however, but a continuation—and recycling—of the same song with which Thyrsis had begun:

2①84 Theocritus 1.144-145

ὦ <u>χαίρετε</u> πολλάκι, Μοῖσαι,

<u>χαίρετ'</u>· ἐγὼ δ' ὕμμιν καὶ ἐς ὕστερον ἅδιον ᾀσῶ

O Muses, <u>hail and take pleasure</u> [*khairete*] again and again.

---

[268] Translation by Hunter 1999:63.
[269] On the meaning of *moira* as the 'plot' of the narration, also as 'fate' and even as 'share of sacrificial meat', see BA 7§21n2 (= p. 134); also 2§17 (= p. 40), 5§25n2 (= p. 81), 15§3n9 (= p. 268).
[270] To compare the words of T. S. Eliot, *Four Quartets* (1943): "The end of our exploring takes us back to where we started, and we see it for the first time."

Chapter Two

> Hail and take pleasure [*khairete*]. As for me, I will sing for you even more sweetly in times to come.

2ⓢ21. Redefining the *humnos*

2§269 In the *Homeric Hymns*, I conclude, the continuity that is signaled by metabasis extends beyond the initial subject of the *humnos*. The rest of the performance leads to subjects that extend beyond the subject of the god initially invoked by the performer. Among these subjects is the world of epic, as we saw most clearly in *Homeric Hymn* (32) *to Selene* (verses 17-20). In other words, the metabasis can signal a shift from hymnic subject to epic subject. The entire sequence of subjects, however, remains technically a *humnos*.

2§270 In view of its epic connections, the poetic idea of *humnos* needs to be redefined. The word's technical sense, which as we saw is most evident in the *Homeric Hymns*, is obscured when we translate *humnos* by way of its modern derivative, 'hymn'. From the standpoint of the poetics we see still at work in the *Homeric Hymns*, the *humnos* is not just a 'hymn'—that is, a song sung in praise of gods or heroes—but a song that functions as a connector, a continuator. In this sense, the meaning of the word diverges from the poetic idea of the *prooimion*. Technically, both *humnos* and *prooimion* convey the poetic idea of an authoritative beginning that makes continuity possible. But the word *humnos*, unlike *prooimion*, refers not only to the start of the continuum but also to the continuum itself.

2§271 When the *humnos* leads to epic, as we are about to see from the evidence of Homeric poetry, it is not just a *prooimion* that introduces epic. The *humnos* is also the sequencing principle that connects with epic, then extends into epic, and then finally becomes the same thing as epic itself.

2§272 The *humnoi* of Hellenistic poet-scholars like Callimachus and Theocritus can be seen as alternatives to the *Homeric Hymns*, which are notionally perfect beginnings for epic performance. For example, a Hellenistic *humnos* like the one we find embedded in *Idyll* 1 of Theocritus avoids epic as its hymnic consequent: in fact, in this case, the *humnos* avoids any consequent other than itself—a consequent that thus becomes eternally recycled in performance. Another example is the *Hymn to Zeus* by Callimachus, which as we saw is a notionally perfect beginning not for Homeric performance but for the ever-ongoing process of Homeric scholarship.

2§273 Despite the substitution of alternatives to epic performance as the hymnic consequent of the Hellenistic *humnos*, the idea of poetic authority remains a constant in the Hellenistic usage of the word itself. In all the passages we have considered so far, Hellenistic as well as archaic, this word *humnos* is what signals the perfect beginning, the perfect *arkhē*, of performance. Without the perfect beginning, there can be no perfect sequence leading to the perfect *telos*—whether this *telos* is a linear 'ending' of a narrative or a cyclic 'coming full circle', recycling or looping back to the initial subject. Much more needs to be said about these two senses of *telos*, but here I am simply laying the groundwork for arguing that even the epic of Homeric poetry operates on the principle of starting with a perfect beginning, continuing with the perfect sequence, and finishing off with the perfect *telos*. And the most perfect expression of this perfection is the word *humnos*.

2ⓢ22. The poetics of the *humnos* in Homeric poetry

2§274 At this point, I am at long last ready to show the verse where Homeric poetry refers to itself as *humnos*:

2①85 *Odyssey* viii 429

> δαιτί τε τέρπηται καὶ ἀοιδῆς <u>ὕμνον</u> ἀκούων
>
> ... so that he [= Odysseus] might take delight [*terpesthai*] in the feast [*dais*] and in listening to the <u>humnos</u> of the song.

2§275 Alkinoos, king of the Phaeacians, is the speaker here. He is speaking of an upcoming occasion. The blind singer Demodokos will be performing on this occasion, to which the king refers here as a *dais* 'feast'. The guest of honor at this feast is the yet-unidentified Odysseus. The song that Demodokos will be singing on this occasion is the third of three songs the singer performs in *Odyssey* viii, and the king refers here to this singing as 'the *humnos* of the song'. Each one of the three separate occasions of performance is a part of the *dais* or 'feasting' of the Phaeacians, which has in fact been ongoing throughout the narrative of *Odyssey* viii. This word *dais* in *Odyssey* viii and beyond refers not to any single occasion of feasting: rather, *dais* refers to an ongoing series of occasions for feasting, that is, to a festival.[271] Such a stylized festival is the context for performing an ongoing series of songs, the word for which is *humnos*.

2§276 At verse 429 of *Odyssey* viii, the reference to 'the *humnos* of the singing [*aoidē*]' on the occasion of a *dais* 'feast' involves not only the upcoming

---

[271] *HPC* I§§192 and following.

Chapter Two

third song but also the first and the second songs that preceded it. The word *humnos* is a formal indication that the first, second, and third songs of Demodokos are in the process of becoming connected to each other in the ongoing outer narrative of the *Odyssey*.[272]

2§277 To support the formulation I just made, I start by stating the essentials of my upcoming argumentation. All along, the narrative in *Odyssey* viii makes it implicit that the three songs of Demodokos are intended primarily for Odysseus. But then, as we saw from the wording I just quoted at verse 429, this intentionality is at long last made explicit. As a participant in the audience that is listening to the songs of Demodokos, the hero himself can now become the ultimate point of reference for the audience's reception of these songs, and the hero's perspective will turn out to be the Homeric perspective. For the hero of the *Odyssey*, the poetics of the inner narrative will become the poetics of the outer narrative, since he is the main actor in both narratives. The ongoing outer narrative of the *Odyssey* will put to the test the audience's reception of the inner narrative consisting of the three songs sung by Demodokos. At stake is not only the reception of the singer's three songs but also the reception of Homer.[273]

2§278 A distinctive feature of the outer narrative in *Odyssey* viii is that it separates the three songs of Demodokos from each other: each one of his three songs is represented as having its own separate starting point. And yet, these three separate inner narratives show signs of a narrative continuum connecting the three songs. The connectedness of this continuum will be made evident through the privileged perspective of Odysseus as he listens to the three stories of the inner narrative. The hero will make the mental connections that need to be made by the outer narrative. As we will see, the process of making the *humnos* is the process of making such mental connections. By indicating connections that achieve a narrative continuum in the Homeric *Odyssey*, the word *humnos* is self-referential: in referring to the ongoing *humnos*, Homeric poetry is referring to itself.

2§279 This argument, that *humnos* at verse 429 of *Odyssey* viii expresses the connectedness of a narrative continuum, is consistent with my ongoing argument that the noun *humnos* derives from a verb root that refers to the weaving of a web. In terms of these two arguments combined, the wording

---

[272] For background, I refer to my earlier formulation in *PH* 12§33n77 (= pp. 353–354), following Koller 1956:177. See also Burgess 2001:199n34, with reference to Cook 1999:15n29.
[273] This paragraph has been a summary of my argumentation in *BA* 1§§1–13 (= pp. 15–25); see also the updating at *BA*² Preface §§29–33 (= pp. xvii–xviii).

2ⓢ22. The poetics of the *humnos* in Homeric poetry

that I translate as 'the *humnos* of the singing [*aoidē*]' at verse 429 expresses a metaphor: just as the weaving of a web is a process of making connections, so too is the making of songs. As the argumentation proceeds, the relevance of this metaphor to the context of *humnos* at verse 429 will I hope become ever more evident.

2§280 The use of *humnos* at verse 429 of *Odyssey* viii is parallel to the use of this same word in the *Homeric Hymns*. In both the *Hymns* and the *Odyssey*, *humnos* conveys the idea of making connections to maintain a narrative continuum. Here I turn to a most striking example of parallelism in usage. As in the *Hymns*, the word *humnos* in the *Odyssey* is associated with a technical word that expresses the idea of actually furthering the continuity of the narrative. That word is *metabainein* 'move ahead and shift forward', as used by the still-unidentified Odysseus with reference to what Alkinoos at verse 429 had called the *humnos* to be performed by Demodokos:

2ⓣ86 *Odyssey* viii 485-498

> 485 αὐτὰρ ἐπεὶ πόσιος καὶ ἐδητύος ἐξ ἔρον ἕντο,
> δὴ τότε Δημόδοκον προσέφη πολύμητις Ὀδυσσεύς·
> "Δημόδοκ', ἔξοχα δή σε βροτῶν αἰνίζομ' ἁπάντων·
> ἢ σέ γε Μοῦσ' ἐδίδαξε, Διὸς πάϊς, ἢ σέ γ' Ἀπόλλων·
> λίην γὰρ <u>κατὰ κόσμον</u> Ἀχαιῶν οἶτον ἀείδεις,
> 490 ὅσσ' ἔρξαν τ' ἔπαθόν τε καὶ ὅσσ' ἐμόγησαν Ἀχαιοί,
> ὥς τέ που ἢ αὐτὸς παρεὼν ἢ ἄλλου ἀκούσας.
> ἀλλ' ἄγε δὴ <u>μετάβηθι</u> καὶ <u>ἵππου κόσμον</u> ἄεισον
> <u>δουρατέου</u>, <u>τὸν Ἐπειὸς</u> ἐποίησεν σὺν Ἀθήνῃ,
> <u>ὅν</u> ποτ' ἐς ἀκρόπολιν δόλον ἤγαγε δῖος Ὀδυσσεὺς
> 495 ἀνδρῶν ἐμπλήσας, οἳ Ἴλιον ἐξαλάπαξαν.
> αἴ κεν δή μοι ταῦτα <u>κατὰ μοῖραν</u> <u>καταλέξῃς</u>,
> αὐτίκα καὶ πᾶσιν μυθήσομαι ἀνθρώποισιν,
> ὡς ἄρα τοι πρόφρων θεὸς ὤπασε θέσπιν ἀοιδήν."

> 485 When they had satisfied their desire for drinking and eating,
> then Odysseus, the one with many a stratagem, addressed Demodokos:

Chapter Two

> Demodokos, I admire and pointedly praise you, more than any other human.
> Either the Muse, child of Zeus, taught you, or Apollo.
> All too well, <u>in accord with its <u>kosmos</u></u>, do you sing the fate of the Achaeans
> 490 —all the things the Achaeans did and all the things that were done to them, and they suffered for it -
> you sing it as if you yourself had been present or had heard it from someone else.
> But come now, <u>move ahead and shift forward</u> [<u>metabainein</u>] and sing the <u>kosmos</u> of the <u>horse</u>,
> the <u>wooden</u> horse <u>that</u> <u>Epeios</u> made with the help of Athena,
> <u>the one that</u> Odysseus, the radiant one, once upon a time took to the acropolis as a stratagem,
> 495 having filled it with men, who ransacked Ilion.
> If you can <u>tell</u> me <u>in due order</u> [<u>katalegein</u>], <u>in accord with proper apportioning</u> [<u>moira</u>],[274]
> then right away I will say the authoritative word [*muthos*] to all mortals:
> I will say, and I see it as I say it, that the god, favorably disposed toward you, granted you a divinely sounding song.

2§281 Odysseus here is challenging Demodokos to sing about the Wooden Horse. More specifically, as we see from the use of the technical poetic term *metabainein* 'move ahead and shift forward' at verse 492, he is challenging the poet to perform a hymnic <u>shifting forward</u> or metabasis.

2§282 As we saw in the *Homeric Hymns*, metabasis is a device that activates a hymnic consequent. One such consequent, as we also saw in the *Hymns*, is epic itself. Here in the Homeric *Odyssey*, the hymnic metabasis to be executed by Demodokos will activate as its hymnic consequent the epic narrative about the Wooden Horse. The challenge is formulated in the precise technical language of a poet in the act of performing a *humnos* that leads to the performance of an epic. First, at verse 492, the subject of the consequent

---

[274] Just as the *dais* as a division of the sacrificial body is organically composed of *moirai* 'portions', so also the *humnos* of the *dais* is an organic or organized sequence.

2ⓢ22. The poetics of the *humnos* in Homeric poetry

epic is announced in the accusative: the subject of this epic is to be the Horse. By metonymy, the beginning of the epic subject is to be the cosmic order or *kosmos* inherent in the craft that went into the making of the Horse. The metonymy is inherent in the naming, at verse 493, of the master of this craft: the craftsman, this master joiner of the wooden pieces of the overall construct that is the Wooden Horse, is named *Epeios*. This *Epeios* is a craftsman of *epos* in name as well as a craftsman of woodwork in deed.[275] The etymology of the name of Homer himself is ultimately relevant: as I argued earlier, **hom-āros* is a compound formation meaning 'he who fits [the song] together', composed of the prefix *homo-* (ὁμο-) 'together' and the root *ar-* of the verb *arariskein* (ἀραρίσκειν). As we see from a survey of the oldest attested formations involving the root *ar-*, this form expresses primarily the idea of woodwork and secondarily the idea of other handicrafts that involve the fitting together of distinct pieces into a unified whole.[276] Moreover, this form extends metaphorically to the art of songmaking. As I we have seen, the name *Homēros* in its traditional contexts is linked to all these meanings. The name means literally 'joiner' or 'carpenter'. So, etymologically, *Homēros* is a master joiner of woodwork; and, metaphorically, Homer is a master joiner of song.[277]

2§283 The theme of the Wooden Horse, as Odysseus describes it here, is to be articulated in wording that follows the poetic rules for the beginning of an epic. At verse 493 of *Odyssey* viii, the epithet *douratēos* 'wooden' refers back to the subject of the epic as announced in the previous verse, *hippos* 'horse' at 492. The enjambed position of this epithet is analogous to the wording we find at the beginning of the Homeric *Iliad* as we have it: there the enjambed epithet *oulomenē* 'baneful' at verse 2 of *Iliad* I describes the subject of the epic as announced in the previous verse, *mēnis* 'anger' of Achilles at *Iliad* I 1.[278]

2§284 From what we have seen so far, the technical rules for performing a *humnos* are at work here in *Odyssey* viii. The third song of Demodokos in *Odyssey* viii, to which the word *humnos* refers in advance at verse 429, is about

---

[275] On metaphors of poetry as woodwork, see BA 17§§9–13 (= pp. 296–300), especially 17§11 (= pp. 298–299) with reference to a hero called *Phereklos*, son of a *tektōn* 'carpenter' called *Harmonidēs* at *Iliad* V 59–60: this carpenter made the ships for the abduction of Helen by Paris, and these ships are described as *arkhekakoi* 'beginning the bad events' at *Iliad* V 63. Just as *Epeios* conveys the poetic concept of *epos*, so also *Phereklos* conveys the poetic concept of *kleos* 'fame': the name means 'he who wins *kleos* as a prize'. On *pherein* in the sense of 'win as a prize', see PH 6§87n204 (= p. 194), 7§5n16 (= p. 202). For more on the figure of *Epeios*, see Louden 1996.

[276] PP 74–76.

[277] See 2§43.

[278] We may compare the enjambed position of the epithet at *Iliad* V 63 describing the ships made by the carpenter for the abduction of Helen by Paris.

Chapter Two

to be introduced by a hymnic *metabasis*, a shifting forward, and this *metabasis* will have as its hymnic consequent an epic performance. It remains to be seen, however, what kind of epic will be taking shape.

2§285 Demodokos responds to the poetic challenge of Odysseus, to 'move ahead and shift forward' to epic performance. The beginning of the epic performance of Demodokos turns out to be essential for understanding the content of the epic that he will perform:

2①87 *Odyssey* viii 499-500

ὣς φάθ', ὁ δ' <u>ὁρμηθεὶς θεοῦ ἤρχετο, φαῖνε</u> δ' ἀοιδήν,
<u>ἔνθεν ἑλών, ὥς</u> . . .

Thus he [= Odysseus] spoke. And he [= Demodokos], <u>setting his point of departure [*hormētheis*], started [*arkhesthai*] from the god</u>. And he <u>made visible</u> the song,

taking it <u>from the point where</u> . . .

2§286 What does it mean, to 'make visible' the song, as expressed by the verb *phainein* 'make visible'? The poet is revealing here a vision of his epic narrative. This vision comes from the blind poet's own inner vision of his starting point, that is, of the divinity who authorizes the *humnos* in its entirety. An absolutized hymnic beginning, which comes from the divinity, leads to a perfect visualization of that divinity, which in turn leads to a perfect visualization of whatever follows the hymnic *metabasis*. Such is the theology of the *humnos* as it extends into epic. This theology helps explain why it is that Herodotus defines Homer and Hesiod as the first poets who 'revealed' (*sēmainein*) the 'visible forms' (*eidē*) of the gods to mortals (2.53.2).

2§287 The starting of the epic narration in the third song of Demodokos in *Odyssey* viii is expressed through the technical language of performing a *prooimion* for the projected *humnos* that was mentioned already at verse 429. The performance of that *prooimion* is conveyed by the expression θεοῦ ἤρχετο 'started [*arkhesthai*] from the god' at verse 499. And the technical procedure of performing a *prooimion* to start the projected *humnos* is being equated here metaphorically with the technical procedure of starting the weaving of a web, as marked by the wording *hormētheis* 'setting his point of departure' at verse 499: in effect, the wording predicts the finished web that will have been woven.[279] The root **or-* of the Greek expression *hormētheis* is the same root

---

[279] On the expression *hormētheis*, see PR 25-26, 72.

2⑤22. The poetics of the *humnos* in Homeric poetry

or- that we see in Latin *exordium* 'proemium'; that root, as I pointed out earlier, conveys the idea of an 'initial threading'.[280]

2§288 Once the hymnic *prooimion* is in place, the epic that is part of the projected *humnos* can now start. Demodokos proceeds to perform the equivalent of an *Iliou Persis*, the epic story of Troy's destruction, at verses 500-520 of *Odyssey* viii.

2§289 Just now, I referred to the starting of the epic narration, once the hymnic *prooimion* is in place. It is more accurate, however, to speak of a restarting in this case. The epic about the end of the Trojan War, about to be performed in the third song of Demodokos, is actually a restarting of what had been started already in the first song, which is a story about the beginning of the Trojan War. The starting of that first performance, like the restarting of the third, is expressed through the metaphor of making fabric:

2①88 *Odyssey* viii 62-94

> κῆρυξ δ' ἐγγύθεν ἦλθεν ἄγων ἐρίηρον ἀοιδόν,
> τὸν περὶ Μοῦσ' ἐφίλησε, δίδου δ' ἀγαθόν τε κακόν τε·
> ὀφθαλμῶν μὲν ἄμερσε, δίδου δ' ἡδεῖαν ἀοιδήν.
> 65 τῷ δ' ἄρα Ποντόνοος θῆκε θρόνον ἀργυρόηλον
> μέσσῳ δαιτυμόνων, πρὸς κίονα μακρὸν ἐρείσας·
> κὰδ δ' ἐκ πασσαλόφι κρέμασεν φόρμιγγα λίγειαν
> αὐτοῦ ὑπὲρ κεφαλῆς καὶ ἐπέφραδε χερσὶν ἑλέσθαι
> κῆρυξ· πὰρ δ' ἐτίθει κάνεον καλήν τε τράπεζαν,
> 70 πὰρ δὲ δέπας οἴνοιο, πιεῖν ὅτε θυμὸς ἀνώγοι.
> οἱ δ' ἐπ' ὀνείαθ' ἑτοῖμα προκείμενα χεῖρας ἴαλλον.
> αὐτὰρ ἐπεὶ πόσιος καὶ ἐδητύος ἐξ ἔρον ἕντο,
> Μοῦσ' ἄρ' ἀοιδὸν ἀνῆκεν ἀειδέμεναι κλέα ἀνδρῶν,
> οἴμης, τῆς τότ' ἄρα κλέος οὐρανὸν εὐρὺν ἵκανε,
> 75 νεῖκος Ὀδυσσῆος καὶ Πηληΐδεω Ἀχιλῆος,
> ὥς ποτε δηρίσαντο θεῶν ἐν δαιτὶ θαλείῃ
> ἐκπάγλοισ' ἐπέεσσιν, ἄναξ δ' ἀνδρῶν Ἀγαμέμνων
> χαῖρε νόῳ, ὅ τ' ἄριστοι Ἀχαιῶν δηριόωντο.
> ὡς γάρ οἱ χρείων μυθήσατο Φοῖβος Ἀπόλλων

---

[280] 2§92.

Chapter Two

80 Πυθοῖ ἐν ἠγαθέῃ, ὅθ' ὑπέρβη λάϊνον οὐδὸν
χρησόμενος. τότε γάρ ῥα κυλίνδετο <u>πήματος ἀρχὴ</u>
Τρωσί τε καὶ Δαναοῖσι <u>Διὸς μεγάλου διὰ βουλάς</u>.
ταῦτ' ἄρ' ἀοιδὸς ἄειδε περικλυτός· αὐτὰρ Ὀδυσσεὺς
πορφύρεον μέγα φᾶρος ἑλὼν χερσὶ στιβαρῇσι
85 κὰκ κεφαλῆς εἴρυσσε, κάλυψε δὲ καλὰ πρόσωπα·
αἴδετο γὰρ Φαίηκας ὑπ' ὀφρύσι <u>δάκρυα</u> λείβων.
ἦ τοι ὅτε <u>λήξειεν</u> ἀείδων θεῖος ἀοιδός,
<u>δάκρυ</u>' ὀμορξάμενος κεφαλῆς ἄπο φᾶρος ἔλεσκε
καὶ δέπας ἀμφικύπελλον ἑλὼν σπείσασκε θεοῖσιν·
90 αὐτὰρ ὅτ' <u>ἂψ ἄρχοιτο</u> καὶ ὀτρύνειαν ἀείδειν
Φαιήκων οἱ ἄριστοι, ἐπεὶ τέρποντ' ἐπέεσσιν,
<u>ἂψ</u> Ὀδυσεὺς κατὰ κρᾶτα καλυψάμενος <u>γοάασκεν</u>.
ἔνθ' ἄλλους μὲν πάντας ἐλάνθανε <u>δάκρυα</u> λείβων,
Ἀλκίνοος δέ μιν οἶος ἐπεφράσατ' ἠδ' <u>ἐνόησεν</u>

The herald came near, bringing with him a singer, very trusted,

whom the Muse loved exceedingly. She gave him both a good thing and a bad thing.

For she took away from him his eyes but gave him the sweetness of song [*aoidē*].

65 For him did Pontonoos place a chair, silver studded,

right in the midst of the people who were feasting, propping the chair against a tall column,

and the herald took from a peg the clear-sounding phorminx that was hanging there

above his head, and he presented it to him so he could take it in his hands.

The herald did this. And next to him he [= the herald] put a beautiful basket and a table.

70 He put next to him also a cup of wine to drink from whenever he [= Demodokos] felt in his heart the need to do so.

2ⓢ22. The poetics of the *humnos* in Homeric poetry

And, with hands reaching out swiftly, they made for the good things that were prepared and waiting.

When they had satisfied their desire for drinking and eating,

the Muse impelled the singer to sing the <u>glories [*klea*] of men</u>,

starting from <u>a thread [*oimē*]</u> [of a song][281] that had at that time a fame [*kleos*] reaching all the way up to the vast sky.

75   It was the quarrel of Odysseus and Achilles, son of Peleus,

how they fought once upon a time at a sumptuous feast [*dais*] of the gods

with terrible words, and the king of men, Agamemnon,

was happy in his mind [*noos*] at the fact that the best of the Achaeans were fighting.

<u>For this is the way he</u> [= Agamemnon] <u>was told it would happen by Phoebus Apollo, who uttered an oracle,</u>

80   in holy Delphi, when he [= Agamemnon] crossed the stone threshold,

to consult the oracle. For then it was that the <u>beginning [*arkhē*] of pain [*pēma*]</u> started rolling down [*kulindesthai*]

upon Trojans and Danaans—all <u>on account of the plans of great Zeus</u>.

So these were the things that the singer [*aoidos*] most famed was singing. As for Odysseus,

taking his great purple cloak in his strong hands,

85   he pulled it over his head and covered his beautiful looks.

For he felt ashamed in front of the Phaeacians, as he was pouring out <u>tears [*dakrua*]</u> from beneath his eyebrows.

Whenever the godlike singer [<u>*aoidos*</u>] would <u>leave off [*lēgein*]</u> singing,

he [= Odysseus] would wipe away his <u>tears [*dakrua*]</u> and take off from his head the cloak

---

[281] The metaphorical world of the *oimē* 'initial threading' here is essential for the argumentation that follows.

Chapter Two

>   and, taking hold of a cup that had two handles he would pour
>   libations to the gods.
> 90 But whenever he [= the singer] <u>started</u> [*arkhesthai*] <u>again</u> [*aps*]
>   as he was urged to sing on
>   by the best of the Phaeacians—for they were delighted by his
>   words—
>   Odysseus would start <u>weeping</u> [*goân*] <u>all over again</u> [*aps*],
>   covering his head with the cloak.
>   So there he was, escaping the notice of all while he kept
>   pouring out his <u>tears</u> [*dakrua*].
>   But Alkinoos was the only one of all of them who was aware,
>   and he <u>took note</u> [*noeîn*].

2§290 The word *oimē* here at *Odyssey* viii 74 means the 'thread' or 'threading' of what is pictured metaphorically as the 'weft' or 'plot' of the song—for the semantics, we may compare the French word *trame*, which means both 'weft' and 'plot'.[282] That is, *oimē* is the 'thread' of a story. More important for now, the genitive case of *oimē* here means that the singer starts 'from' a given thread of a given story: in other words, we see the starting thread of the story about to be told. Most important, the syntax of this expression about the *oimē* corresponds to the meaning of a word that is directly linked to the word *oimē*. That word is *prooimion*, which as I have argued is actually derived from *oimos* / *oimē* and means, metaphorically, the 'initial threading'.[283] What the syntax indicates, then, is that the singer is starting his epic performances by performing a *prooimion*. Or, to put it metaphorically, the singer starts from the initial threading of the web to be woven. In this light, we can appreciate more fully the metaphor inherent in the etymology of *humnos*: as I have been arguing all along, this noun derives from a verb root that refers to the weaving of a web. As I have also been arguing, that metaphor is latent in the context of the expression ἀοιδῆς ὕμνον 'the *humnos* of the singing [*aoidē*]' at verse 429: just as the weaving of a web is a process of making connections, so too is the making of songs. The metaphor is also latent in the context of the expression οἶμος ἀοιδῆς at verse 451 of the *Homeric Hymn* (4) *to Hermes*: as I noted earlier, we see here the attestation of both οἶμος ἀοιδῆς and ὕμνος ἀοιδῆς in the manuscript tradition.[284] Both textual variants can be considered formu-

---

[282] PR 79.
[283] 2§92.
[284] 2§93.

laic expressions, and the second of the two, ὕμνος ἀοιδῆς, is evidently cognate with the formulaic expression ἀοιδῆς ὕμνον as attested at verse 429 of *Odyssey* viii. In terms of metaphors comparing the making of song with the making of fabric, I interpret the combinations of *humnos* and *oimos* with *aoidē* 'song' to mean respectively the 'weaving' of song and the 'threading' of song.

2§291 Looking backward from the attestation of *humnos* at verse 429 of *Odyssey* viii, where the speaker looks forward to the singing that will be started in the third song of Demodokos, we have seen that this starting is really a restarting. We can see from the wording and syntax referring to the first song (at verse 74) that the singing in the third song, described as a *humnos* (at verse 429), was already started in the first song.

2§292 The epic singing of the first song of Demodokos in *Odyssey* viii, once it gets started by the *prooimion* as indicated by the syntax at verse 74, keeps getting restarted. Whenever the performer 'leaves off', as indicated by the word *lēgein* at verse 87, he keeps on 'restarting' the epic, as indicated by the wording *aps arkhesthai* 'start again and again' at verse 90. The continual restarting creates the effect of an endless narrative: the epic performance of the first song of Demodokos seems to have no end in sight.

2§293 The use of the word *lēgein* 'leave off' at verse 87 of *Odyssey* viii is relevant to the use of the same word in *Idyll* 1 of Theocritus at verses 127, 131, 137, 142, where it refers to the impending end of an ongoing performance of a stylized *humnos*. At an earlier point in my argumentation, when we were examining a double occurrence of *lēgein* at verse 142 of *Idyll* 1, I translated the word in two ways—both 'to end' and 'to leave off'. As I said before, these two different translations are indicative of two different ways of ending a performance. The obvious way is simply to end, while the alternative way, less obvious to us, is to end the performance only to restart it later.

2§294 When it comes to leaving off and then restarting a song, there is a major difference in the contexts of *lēgein* 'leave off' in *Idyll* 1 of Theocritus and in *Odyssey* viii. In the poem of Theocritus, *lēgein* refers to 'leaving off' while performing a *humnos* that has no epic as a hymnic consequent. To repeat what I said earlier, the *humnos* in *Idyll* 1 of Theocritus has no consequent at all—other than itself. The *humnos* there 'leaves off' only to start itself all over again at the same point where it had started in the first place. There the movement of the *humnos* is circular. In the *Odyssey*, by contrast, the movement of the *humnos* is linear. Here *lēgein* refers to 'leaving off' while performing an epic, which is the hymnic consequent of a *prooimion*. In Homeric terms, the epic is part of the ongoing *humnos*. Each time the performer restarts the epic in the first song of Demodokos, the restarting has moved ahead in the epic, in the ongoing

Chapter Two

humnos, to the point where the performer has last left off. In terms of my argument, the entire sequence of epic performances by Demodokos proceeds within the framework of such an ongoing *humnos*. The *prooimion* of the first song of Demodokos is only the beginning of a *humnos*, and the epic that follows the *prooimion* as its hymnic consequent is technically a continuation of the same ongoing *humnos*. So the act of continually restarting the performance in the first song of Demodokos is not simply a matter of restarting the *prooimion* in and of itself. It is a matter of continually restarting the *humnos*, which in Homeric terms includes the epic that follows the *prooimion*.

2§295 The context of the word *légein* at verse 87 of *Odyssey* viii indicates a recurrent 'leaving off' from the performance, followed by a recurrent starting up at the point where the performance had last left off: every time Demodokos leaves off performing his epic, he comes right back to 'restarting' it where he last left off, as we see from the context of the expression *aps arkhesthai* 'start again and again' at verse 90.

2§296 Once again, the metaphorical world of fabric making is relevant. Comparable to what we have just seen is the meaning of Latin *contexere*, derivative of *texere* 'weave': essentially, *contexere* means 'restart the weaving'—that is, 'restart' it at the point where the weaver had previously left off weaving. Here is a striking example involving the verbs *ordīrī* 'start the weaving' and *contexere* 'restart the weaving':

2ⓣ89 Cicero *Laws* 1.3.9

> cum semel quid <u>orsus</u>, [si] traducor alio, neque tam facile interrupta <u>contexo</u> quam absolvo instituta
>
> Once I have <u>started weaving</u> [*ordīrī*] something, if I get distracted by something else, it is not as easy for me to <u>take up weaving where I left off</u> [*contexere*] than to finish off what I have started.[285]

A weaver may finish a sequence of weaving only to restart it later in a new sequence—at exactly the point where he or she had last left off.[286] There are parallels to be found in other Indo-European languages: in one of the hymns of the *Rig-Veda* (1.110), for example, the singer starts the hymn by saying, at the very beginning of the song (1.110.1a), that this song is like a web stretched on a loom and that the song is getting restarted just as the work of weaving the web

---

[285] *PR* 81.
[286] In the case of Penelope, the restarting is more radical: it is an undoing of everything that has been done up to a point and then doing it all over again. See *PR* 98n88.

2ⓢ22. The poetics of the *humnos* in Homeric poetry

gets restarted: *tatám me ápas tád u tāyate púnar* 'the work that is stretched [on a loom] by me—here it is being stretched again'.[287]

2§297 In the case of performing a song, the performer who restarts a song may be the same performer as the one who started it in the first place, or, alternatively, it may be the next performer who is restarting the song of the previous performer. This alternative kind of restarting is a phenomenon I call relay performance. I have studied this phenomenon in some detail elsewhere, and here I offer only the briefest formulation of the essentials: basically, one performer has to 'leave off' (*lēgein*) singing for another performer to 'start' (*arkhesthai*) again.[288] A prime example is the following passage, describing what I will call the Panathenaic Regulation, which concerns the performing of the Homeric *Iliad* and *Odyssey* at the Athenian feast of the Panathenaia:

2ⓣ90 Dieuchidas of Megara *FGH* 485 F 6 via Diogenes Laertius 1.57

τά τε Ὁμήρου ἐξ ὑποβολῆς γέγραφε ῥαψῳδεῖσθαι, οἷον ὅπου ὁ πρῶτος ἔληξεν, ἐκεῖθεν ἄρχεσθαι τὸν ἐχόμενον

He [= Solon the Lawgiver of the Athenians] has written a law that the words of Homer are to be performed rhapsodically [*rhapsōideîn*], by relay [*hupobolē*], so that wherever the first person left off [*lēgein*], from that point the next person should start [*arkhesthai*].

2§298 I will have more to say in Chapter 3 about *rhapsōidoi* 'rhapsodes' and their relay performances of Homeric poetry at the Athenian festival of the Panathenaia. For now I focus simply on the use of *lēgein* 'leave off' combined with *arkhesthai* 'start' in conveying the idea of relay performance.

2§299 The restartings of the epic of Demodokos, as conveyed by the expression *aps arkhesthai* 'start again and again' at verse 90 of *Odyssey* viii, are linked to the unexpected reaction of Odysseus as the primary audience of the epic—unexpected, that is, in view of the festive occasion. At the start of the epic performance, the hero dissolves into tears: he literally experiences an 'outpouring of tears' (viii 86 *dakrua leibein*), though he tries to hide his reaction from the rest of the audience (83-85). And each time Demodokos restarts his performance of the epic, Odysseus experiences a restarting of his initial reaction: he weeps again and again, and his continually restarted outpouring of tears is expressed by the wording *aps . . . goân* 'lament again and again' (92),

---

[287] See also Durante 1976:175.
[288] *PR* 16–17, 60–61.

Chapter Two

which parallels the wording that expresses the continually restarted epic performance, *aps arkhesthai* 'start again and again' (90).

2§300 The continual restarting of the epic in this first song of Demodokos creates the effect of an endless recycling: although the narration keeps moving ahead with each recycling, there seems to be no end in sight. So far, any ending for the epic seems to be deferred.

2§301 Only Alkinoos, king of the Phaeacians, notices the unexpected reaction of Odysseus to the epic performance in the first song of Demodokos (viii 93-95). The king's own reaction is to defer even further any kind of epic ending. Postponing any more restartings of the ongoing epic performance by Demodokos, Alkinoos announces that the time for dining and drinking and 'the *phorminx*'—a metonym for the singing of Demodokos, who accompanies himself on the string instrument called the *phorminx*—is to be stopped for the moment (98-99).

2§302 What happens after the stopping of the first song of Demodokos is a complex subject. In the twin book *Homer the Preclassic*, I examine in some detail how the Homeric narrative connects the first song with the second song, and the second with the third.[289] I argue there that the second song of Demodokos, although it appears significantly different in form and content from both the first and the third songs, is technically part of an ongoing *humnos* that starts in the first song, continues into the second, and continues from there into the third. In *Homer the Preclassic*, I also argue that the word *humnos* at verse 429 of *Odyssey* viii refers to all three of the songs of Demodokos—as if they constituted a single ongoing narrative. Here, in the next section of Chapter 2, I confine myself to examining two aspects of this ongoing narrative: (1) the transition from the first to the third song and (2) the transition from the second to the third. Both transitions are achieved through the poetics of metabasis.

2ⓢ23. The poetics of metabasis in the making of epic

2§303 In the short term, the word *humnos* at verse 429 in *Odyssey* viii refers to the upcoming third song of Demodokos. In the long term, however, the singing that goes into this third song is an ongoing *humnos*, driven forward by the device of hymnic metabasis. The notion of such an ongoing *humnos* is signaled at verse 492, when the yet-unnamed Odysseus challenges the singer to perform a metabasis, that is, a shift in the current subject. This shift will lead to an epic performance.

[289] *HPC* I§§189-231.

2§23. A poetics of metabasis in the making of epic

2§304 Demodokos responds to the poetic challenge. He performs a metabasis, which will shift forward to a point where the epic that was stopped by Alkinoos can at long last continue. In other words, the forward movement of the metabasis connects the first song of Demodokos with the third, as if the third were a direct continuation of the first. In terms of this continuation, it is as if the second song did not exist. And yet, the continuation from the first to the third song is hardly direct. In terms of the upcoming metabasis, the point where this continuation starts cannot be expected to match the point where it had stopped when the first song of Demodokos was prevented by Alkinoos from restarting any further. The objective of the metabasis is to move ahead and shift forward to a new starting point, and this new starting point is to be situated further ahead than the previous stopping point. Metabasis moves forward the point of restarting the epic narration. In other words, metabasis moves forward the recycling of the epic. As we will see, such use of metabasis is typical of a poetic form that we know as the epic Cycle. Moreover, metabasis is antithetical to the principle of the Panathenaic Regulation, which as we saw requires each successive performer to continue the epic performance at exactly the point where the prior performance left off.

2§305 Odysseus calls for the metabasis at viii 492 (μετάβηθι), in response to the wish expressed by Alkinoos, at viii 429, that Odysseus should 'take delight'—*terpesthai*—in hearing 'the *humnos* of the singing' on the occasion of the feasting (δαιτί τε τέρπηται καὶ ἀοιδῆς ὕμνον ἀκούων). The feasting will continue and the *humnos* will move forward. And what will make the *humnos* move forward is the metabasis. But the singing that follows the metabasis, which is the singing of the third song of Demodokos, will not delight Odysseus: this third song, like the first song that was sung by that singer, causes pain for the hero, not delight. During the singing of the third song, only the king notices the hero's pain (532-533), just as he had been the only one in the audience to notice it during the singing of the first song (94-95). Just as Alkinoos had stopped the singing of the first song (98-99) he now stops the singing of the third (537). And the reason he gives for stopping the third song is that the *kharis* of the singing, that is, the pleasurable beauty it offers, has not pleased his guest: the idea is conveyed by the verb derived from *kharis*, that is, *kharizesthai* (538). It is imperative, the king continues, that everyone at the ongoing feast—especially the yet-unnamed guest of honor—should 'take delight', and the word that is used here to express the delight is once again *terpesthai* (542). It was this same programmatic word that was used earlier to describe the expected response of the audience to the third song of Demodokos: Odysseus as the guest of honor must 'take delight', *terpesthai*, when he listens to the *humnos* at the feast (429). Moreover, the same word *terpesthai* was used even earlier to describe the response of the general audience to the first song of Demodokos: as they listen to the singing, they 'take delight' (91), and they keep on urging the singer to 'restart' his singing, *aps arkhesthai* (90), every time Demodokos 'leaves off' singing, *lēgein* (87). So the ongoing performances of Demodokos are being driven by the imperative of pleasing the audience: the listeners must continue to 'take delight', *terpesthai*.

2§306 But the third song of Demodokos is now causing pain for Odysseus, even though it was he who had called on the singer to start at the point where the singer had started the third song in the first place. The third song is making Odysseus dissolve into tears all over again, just as he dissolved into tears when he heard the first song. When he hears the epic of the third song of Demodokos, Odysseus is described as feeling *akhos* 'sorrow'—indirectly (530) as well as directly (541). As I hope to show, this description signals the form of the epic that is being performed by Demodokos in the third song and, retrospectively, in the first song as well.

2§307 The first and the third songs of Demodokos represent the general epic form that we know as the Cycle, which becomes a foil for the special epic form that will be narrated thereafter by Odysseus—a form represented by what we know as Homeric poetry. In the twin book *Homer the Preclassic*, I focus on the Homeric form of the narration by Odysseus.[290] Here I focus on the form of the epic Cycle.

2§308 The first song of Demodokos in *Odyssey* viii, as we have already seen, keeps on restarting, and, each time it restarts, Odysseus sheds tears all over again: the continually restarted outpouring of tears is expressed by the wording *aps . . . goân* 'lament again and again' at verse 92, which parallels the wording that expresses the continual restarting of the first song of Demodokos, *aps arkhesthai* 'start again and again' at verse 90. Then, in the third song, a connection is established with the first song, as if the third directly followed the first. By way of this connection, the third song will now appear to be a new restarting of the first, which was continually being restarted until Alkinoos stopped it (98-99). The sorrowful themes in the first song are now being recycled in the third song, by way of ring composition. When Odysseus hears the third song, he literally 'dissolves' into tears (522 *tēkesthai*). The hero pours forth 'a tear' (*dakru / dakruon* at 522 / 531) all over again. The wording ἐλεεινὸν . . . δάκρυον εἶβεν 'he poured forth a piteous [*eleeinon*] tear' (531), with reference to the third song, recycles by way of ring composition the earlier

[290] *HPC* I§§232-241.

wording δάκρυα λείβων 'pouring forth tears', with reference to the first song (86). The third song of Demodokos has thus shifted from the 'delight' of the second song—as expressed by the word *terpesthai* (368)—back to the pain of the first song. The ring composition of epic themes centering on pain connects the first and the third songs, creating the effect of a cycle.

2§309 What is it about the first song of Demodokos that keeps on making Odysseus dissolve into tears? The answer is to be found in the formal parallelism that links the hero's continually restarted outpouring of tears, as expressed by the wording *aps . . . goân* 'lament again and again' at verse 92, with the poet's continually restarted epic, as expressed by the wording *aps arkhesthai* 'start again and again' at verse 90. The restartings point back to the starting point of the first song, the beginning of the epic, as retold in *Odyssey* viii 73-83: that beginning is said to be the *pēmatos arkhē* 'beginning of the pain' at viii 81, and that primal pain is equated with the story of the Trojan War. That 'beginning', which leads inexorably to the Trojan War, is equated with what is prophesied by Apollo at viii 79-81—and with what is planned by Zeus at viii 81. As I argue in the twin book *Homer the Preclassic*, the plot of the epic is being equated here with the prophecy of Apollo and the plan of Zeus.[291]

2§310 This way of starting the epic plot of the first song of Demodokos is relevant to the way the third song is started, and I quote the passage again:

2①91 *Odyssey* viii 499-500

> ὣς φάθ', ὁ δ' <u>ὁρμηθεὶς</u> θεοῦ <u>ἤρχετο</u>, <u>φαῖνε</u> δ' ἀοιδήν,
> <u>ἔνθεν</u> ἑλών, ὥς . . .
>
> Thus he [= Odysseus] spoke. And he [= Demodokos], <u>setting his point of departure [*hormētheis*], started [*arkhesthai*]</u> from the god. And he <u>made visible</u> the song,
> taking it <u>from the point where</u> . . .

2§311 When Demodokos started 'from the god' at verse 499 of *Odyssey* viii, he performed a *prooimion* that restarted the ongoing *humnos* to which Alkinoos refers at verse 429 in anticipation of the upcoming third song of Demodokos. The ongoing *humnos*, when it does get restarted in the third song of Demodokos, will shift forward, as prescribed by the hymnic term *metabainein* 'move ahead and shift forward' at verse 492. The *metabasis* achieves the

---

[291] *HPC* I§236.

Chapter Two

effect of continuing the third song from the first song because Demodokos has ostensibly moved ahead to a new starting point.

Excursus at 2§311

Here I stop for a moment, to reflect on the basic meaning of the verb *metabainein*, which means literally 'move ahead and shift forward', as if on a pathway. In the light of the associations we have seen between this word and the word *humnos*, I suggest that the meaning of *metabainein* is relevant to the meaning of *humnos* in the metaphorical sense of making fabric. In combination with *humnos*, this technical term *metabainein* can be understood as a specialization of a general idea. The general idea of moving ahead has been specialized by virtue of being applied to the specific idea of threading a song. The specific idea already has a metaphor built into it: singing is like threading. The application of the general idea of moving ahead to the specific idea of threading a song makes that idea even more specific. Now the specific idea has two metaphors built into it: singing is like threading is like moving from one place to another. Such a metaphorical application of the general idea of moving ahead to the specific idea of threading a song helps account for those contexts of *oimos* and *oimē* that suggest the general meaning of 'way, pathway' for these words.[292] In these contexts, what we see is the metaphorical application of the specific idea of threading a song to the general idea of moving ahead. Conversely, the association of *metabainein* with *humnos* illustrates the metaphorical application of the general idea of moving ahead to the specific idea of threading one's way from one point to another.

2§312 The continuity achieved by the restarting of the third song of Demodokos is not a simple matter. The continuation of the first song by the third leaves a narrative gap between the two. The epic singing about the Trojan War in the third song of Demodokos starts at a point that comes somewhere after the point where the first song of Demodokos last left off when Alkinoos stopped it at verses 96–99. This displacement of the starting point is ostensibly due to metabasis. As we saw, the objective of metabasis is to move the point of restarting further ahead. Such a shifting forward may seem arbitrary from the standpoint of the first song, which was also about the Trojan War. But it is not at all arbitrary from the standpoint of the third song, the epic plot of which is outlined in advance for Demodokos by Odysseus at verses 492–495. I quote again the passage that contains these verses:

---

[292] See 2§92 above.

2§23. A poetics of metabasis in the making of epic

2①92 *Odyssey* viii 485-498

485 αὐτὰρ ἐπεὶ πόσιος καὶ ἐδητύος ἐξ ἔρον ἕντο,
δὴ τότε Δημόδοκον προσέφη πολύμητις Ὀδυσσεύς·
"Δημόδοκ', ἔξοχα δή σε βροτῶν αἰνίζομ' ἁπάντων·
ἢ σέ γε Μοῦσ' ἐδίδαξε, Διὸς πάϊς, ἢ σέ γ' Ἀπόλλων·
λίην γὰρ <u>κατὰ κόσμον</u> Ἀχαιῶν οἶτον ἀείδεις,
490 ὅσσ' ἔρξαν τ' ἔπαθόν τε καὶ ὅσσ' ἐμόγησαν Ἀχαιοί,
ὥς τέ που ἢ αὐτὸς παρεὼν ἢ ἄλλου ἀκούσας.
ἀλλ' ἄγε δὴ <u>μετάβηθι</u> καὶ <u>ἵππου</u> <u>κόσμον</u> ἄεισον
<u>δουρατέου</u>, <u>τὸν</u> <u>Ἐπειὸς</u> ἐποίησεν σὺν Ἀθήνῃ,
<u>ὅν</u> ποτ' ἐς ἀκρόπολιν δόλον ἤγαγε δῖος Ὀδυσσεὺς
495 ἀνδρῶν ἐμπλήσας, οἳ Ἴλιον ἐξαλάπαξαν.
αἴ κεν δή μοι ταῦτα <u>κατὰ μοῖραν</u> <u>καταλέξῃς</u>,
αὐτίκα καὶ πᾶσιν μυθήσομαι ἀνθρώποισιν,
ὡς ἄρα τοι <u>πρόφρων</u> θεὸς ὤπασε θέσπιν ἀοιδήν.

485 When they had satisfied their desire for drinking and eating,
then Odysseus, the one with many a stratagem, addressed Demodokos:
Demodokos, I admire and pointedly praise you, more than any other human.
Either the Muse, child of Zeus, taught you, or Apollo.
All too well, <u>in accord with its *kosmos*</u>, do you sing the fate of the Achaeans
490 —all the things the Achaeans did and all the things that were done to them, and they suffered for it—
you sing it as if you yourself had been present or had heard it from someone else.
But come now, <u>move ahead and shift forward</u> [*metabainein*] and sing the <u>*kosmos*</u> of the <u>horse</u>,
the <u>wooden</u> horse <u>that</u> <u>Epeios</u> made with the help of Athena,
<u>the one that</u> Odysseus, the radiant one, took to the acropolis as a stratagem,

495   having filled it in with men, who ransacked Ilion.

> If you can <u>tell</u> me <u>in due order</u> [<u>katalegein</u>], <u>in accord with proper apportioning</u> [<u>moira</u>],
>
> then right away I will say the authoritative word [*muthos*] to all mortals:
>
> I will say, and I see it as I say it, that the god, <u>favorably disposed</u> toward you, granted you a divinely sounding song.

2§313 The epic of the third song, as we see from the plot outline at verses 492-495, is about the end of the Trojan War, the story of Troy's destruction. To be contrasted is the epic of the first song, which as we saw earlier was about the beginning of this war. The epic in the third song is defined not only by the plot outline given by Odysseus but also by the actual metabasis as signaled at verse 492 (μετάβηθι). The metabasis sets up a distinct starting point for this epic about the Trojan War, which in turn sets up a distinct plot—distinct, that is, from the plot of the epic in the first song. And there is a new *prooimion* that sets up the metabasis that sets up the starting point that sets up the epic. I quote again the relevant verses:

2ⓣ93 *Odyssey* viii 499-500

ὣς φάθ', ὁ δ' <u>ὁρμηθεὶς θεοῦ ἤρχετο</u>, <u>φαῖνε</u> δ' ἀοιδήν,
ἔνθεν ἑλών, ὡς . . .

> Thus he [= Odysseus] spoke. And he [= Demodokos], <u>setting his point of departure</u> [*hormētheis*], started [*arkhesthai*] <u>from the god</u>. And he <u>made visible</u> the song,
>
> taking it <u>from the point where</u> . . .

2§314 Without this new *prooimion* there can be no metabasis, and without the metabasis there can be no new performance of epic. The epic of the third song about the end of the Trojan War cannot simply follow the epic of the first song about the beginning of the war.

2§315 So far, I have considered the distinctions between the first and the third songs of Demodokos in *Odyssey* viii. As we have just seen, the epic of the third song is morphologically distinct from the epic of the first, since it has its own *prooimion* and its own plot. Moreover, as we saw earlier, the metabasis of the third song indicates a narrative gap between the epics of the first and the third songs. Now I turn to considering these same distinctions in terms

2ⓢ23. A poetics of metabasis in the making of epic

of all three songs put together in sequence. What we find is that the existing distinctions are blurred in the overall sequencing, and the key to this blurring is the device of metabasis.

2§316 The metabasis in the third song of Demodokos creates the effect of an ongoing story of Troy that jumps ahead from an epic that starts with the beginning of the whole story—to an epic that ostensibly ends the story. But the effect is even more complex. Since the first and the third songs of Demodokos are physically separated from each other by his intervening second song, the jump from the first to the third song is more visible. Less visible is a shorter jump from the second to the third, which I propose to consider here briefly.

2§317 In terms of an overall epic sequence that tells about the Trojan War from beginning to end, the second song of Demodokos occupies a narrative space that could have been filled with an intervening epic sequence that ostensibly tells about everything that happened between the point where the first song stopped and the third song started again. Such an intervening epic sequence is not needed, however, because the metabasis of the third song makes it possible to jump over the intervening space that would have been occupied by the missing epic sequence.

2§318 Though the poetic content of the second song of Demodokos seems at first sight irrelevant to the narratives of the first and the third songs, it is in fact relevant, as I explain in the twin book *Homer the Preclassic*.[293] Here in Chapter 2, however, I consider the second song only in terms of its poetic form.

2§319 The poetic form of the second song of Demodokos in *Odyssey* viii is hymnic, not epic. What I mean by hymnic here is that the second song is typical of what we have seen so far in the *Homeric Hymns*. That is, the narrative of the second song is typical of an extended hymnic *prooimion* that leads to a hymnic consequent. As we saw earlier, the concept of *humnos* in a *Homeric Hymn* includes both the hymnic *prooimion* and the hymnic consequent that extends from the *prooimion*. The second song of Demodokos is like a *Homeric Hymn* that features a hymnic *prooimion* followed by a hymnic consequent. As we will see in a moment, however, this song is unlike the *Hymns* in having a hymnic consequent that is not epic.

2§320 When the singer, in beginning the third song, 'started from the god' at verse 499 of *Odyssey* viii, the Homeric narrative about the narrative did not name the god who is the hymnic subject of the *prooimion* there, that is, the god who is the starting point of a *prooimion* that features as its hymnic

[293] HPC I§§208–218.

consequent an epic about the end of the Trojan War. Who, then, is that unnamed god? I offer an answer in the twin book *Homer the Preclassic*.[294] Here I confine myself to saying that the name of that divine hymnic subject in the third song of Demodokos is deliberately being withheld in *Odyssey* viii, since the consequent epic is still in the making. That epic is yet to be linked to its hymnic subject.

2§321 There is no withholding of names, however, when it comes to the hymnic subject of the second song of Demodokos, which names the god Ares and the goddess Aphrodite in its hymnic *prooimion* (viii 267). In the twin book *Homer the Preclassic* I focus on the significance of naming Ares and Aphrodite as the hymnic subject in the second song, and I show how this subject fits into the ongoing *humnos* in *Odyssey* viii.[295] Here I focus not on the hymnic subject itself but simply on the fact that this subject is distinct from the hymnic subject of the *prooimion* in the third song. The distinctness of hymnic subjects in the second and the third songs of Demodokos is made clear by the distinctness of the hymnic *prooimia* that lead into these subjects. The second song features a hymnic *prooimion* that leads into virtuoso dancing as its consequent after the actual singing is finished (viii 370-380).[296] The third song, by contrast, features a hymnic *prooimion* that leads into virtuoso singing rather than dancing. That singing is an epic song about the end of the Trojan War.

2§322 As I near the end of this section, I offer a brief summary of the two narrative transitions that are made possible by the metabasis that leads to the third song of Demodokos in *Odyssey* viii. In one transition, the hymnic subject of the second song shifts forward to the hymnic subject of the third. In the other transition, the epic of the first song shifts forward to the epic of the third. In both these transitions, metabasis serves the practical purpose of jumping over the existing gaps in the narrative continuum. One of the two gaps is the space between the stories of the two epics in the first and in the third song, about the beginning and the end of the Trojan War, while the other is the space between the story of the second song, which is about the affair of Ares and Aphrodite, and the story of the third, which as I said is about the end of the Trojan War.

2§323 I close this section by offering a working definition of metabasis as a narrative device. Metabasis is a <u>shifting forward</u> that makes invisible an existing narrative sequence that would otherwise be visible. Potentially, it can

---

[294] *HPC* I§§238–240.
[295] *HPC* I§208.
[296] *HPC* I§§217 and following.

also pretend to make invisible a sequence that never existed. From a practical point of view, the device of metabasis can bridge any logical gap between two given points in a narrative by pretending to shift forward from one point to the next and thus bridging the gap between those two points. The spaces to be bridged can be widened at will, and the bridgings can be multiplied.

2Ⓢ24. The third song of Demodokos

2§324 With this working definition of metabasis in place, I come to the problem of defining the form of epic in the third song of Demodokos, and, retroactively, in the first song. As we have seen so far, the epic of the third song is defined by metabasis, as indicated by the word *metabainein* 'move ahead and shift forward' at verse 492 of *Odyssey* viii. It is also defined prospectively as a *humnos*, at verse 429 in *Odyssey* viii. These two words, *metabainein* and *humnos*, mark the epic of the third song of Demodokos as unique within the epic of Homeric poetry, in that neither word is attested anywhere else in the Homeric *Iliad* and *Odyssey*. The epic of the third song of Demodokos is an exception to the rules of the overall epic of Homeric poetry, even though it is embedded in Homeric poetry.

2§325 The epic of the third song of Demodokos—and, retroactively, of the first song—is not only exceptional but even antithetical to Homeric poetry. When Demodokos restarts his epic in the third song, the device of metabasis frees him to start at a point that is not determined by the point where he had left off in his first song. Such a restarting is antithetical to the poetics of relay performance that typifies Homeric poetry. As I already noted, the performance tradition of Homeric poetry follows the principle of what I called the Panathenaic Regulation, which requires each successive performer to continue the epic performance of Homeric poetry at exactly the point where the prior performance left off. In terms of the Panathenaic Regulation of Homeric poetry, metabasis cannot be allowed. Metabasis frees the performer to start where he sees fit—or where the audience sees fit. There is a danger of inequity in a contest that does not equalize the chances of the contestants.[297]

2§326 What kind of epic, then, is the third song of Demodokos, as restarted from the first song? It is implied that this song is an older kind of epic than the epic of Homeric poetry within which it is embedded. And what kind of epic is the first song of Demodokos? In this case, it is not only

---

[297] On the principle of equalized weighting in the performance traditions of Homeric poetry, see *HQ* 77–80, 82, 88.

Chapter Two

implied but made explicit that this song too is an older kind of epic. At verse 74 of *Odyssey* viii, the *kleos* 'fame' of the *oimē* 'initial threading' that starts the epic of Demodokos is explicitly a thing of the past: the fame of that epic was spreading far and wide *tote* 'at that time'—that is, at the time when it was being narrated, not at the time when the narrator of the *Odyssey* is narrating the *Odyssey*, which would be 'now'. The reference to the past here marks the form of an older story, which was told in the heroic past, as opposed to the form of the newer story that frames the older story. This framing form, which is the Homeric *Odyssey*, belongs to the present time of the telling of Homeric poetry, that is, to the notional present time of Homer, not to the past time that is being narrated by Homeric poetry.

2§327 This older form of epic, as embedded in *Odyssey* viii, is analogous to the kind of epic that would have been introduced by the *Homeric Hymns*. These *Hymns*, as we saw, allow for metabasis, which in turn allows for an epic consequent that starts without regard to any prior epic starts or restarts. As we will now see, such an older form of epic is typical of the epic Cycle. And, in fact, the form of the epic performed by Demodokos in his third song, as we find it represented within the epic of Homeric poetry, is actually attested in the plot summary of an epic that belongs to the epic Cycle.

2§328 To put it more precisely, the plot of the epic narrative in the third song of Demodokos, marked by the word *humnos* at viii 429, corresponds to the plot of the epic narrative of the *Iliou Persis*, attributed to Arctinus of Miletus, which is part of the epic Cycle—and the plot of which is still attested in the summary of Proclus.[298] In Chapter 1, I already quoted the text of this summary in the context of considering a part of the narrative. Now I will quote it again, taking into consideration the narrative in its entirety. Immediately after this quotation, I will also quote the corresponding narrative of the epic of Demodokos as retold in the epic of Homeric poetry. The degree of correspondence between the plot summary of the *Iliou Persis* and the Homeric retelling of the epic of Demodokos is striking:

2①94 Arctinus of Miletus *Iliou Persis* plot summary by Proclus pp. 107-108 ed. Allen

16   Ἕπεται δὲ τούτοις Ἰλίου πέρσιδος βιβλία δύο Ἀρκτίνου
     Μιλησίου περιέχοντα τάδε. ὡς τὰ περὶ τὸν ἵππον οἱ

---

[298] On the overall plot of the narratives of Demodokos in *Odyssey* viii, matching the overall plot of the Cyclic *Iliou Persis*, see again PH 12§33n77 (= pp. 353-354), following Koller 1956:177; also Burgess 2001:199n34, with reference to Cook 1999:15n29.

2⑤24. The third song of Demodokos

Τρῶες ὑπόπτως ἔχοντες περιστάντες βουλεύονται ὅ τι χρὴ
ποιεῖν· καὶ τοῖς μὲν δοκεῖ κατακρημνίσαι αὐτόν, τοῖς δὲ
20 καταφλέγειν, οἱ δὲ ἱερὸν αὐτὸν ἔφασαν δεῖν τῇ Ἀθηνᾷ
ἀνατεθῆναι· καὶ τέλος νικᾷ ἡ τούτων γνώμη. τραπέντες
δὲ εἰς εὐφροσύνην εὐωχοῦνται ὡς ἀπηλλαγμένοι τοῦ πολέμου. ἐν αὐτῷ δὲ τούτῳ δύο δράκοντες ἐπιφανέντες τόν τε
Λαοκόωντα καὶ τὸν ἕτερον τῶν παίδων διαφθείρουσιν. ἐπὶ
25 δὲ τῷ τέρατι δυσφορήσαντες οἱ περὶ τὸν Αἰνείαν ὑπεξῆλθον
εἰς τὴν Ἴδην. καὶ Σίνων τοὺς πυρσοὺς ἀνίσχει τοῖς Ἀχαιοῖς,
πρότερον εἰσεληλυθὼς προσποίητος. οἱ δὲ ἐκ Τενέδου
προσπλεύσαντες καὶ οἱ ἐκ τοῦ δουρείου ἵππου ἐπιπίπτουσι
τοῖς πολεμίοις καὶ πολλοὺς ἀνελόντες τὴν πόλιν κατὰ
30 κράτος λαμβάνουσι. καὶ Νεοπτόλεμος μὲν ἀποκτείνει
Πρίαμον ἐπὶ τὸν τοῦ Διὸς τοῦ ἑρκείου βωμὸν καταφυγόντα.

p. 108 Μενέλαος δὲ ἀνευρὼν Ἑλένην ἐπὶ τὰς ναῦς κατάγει, Δηΐφοβον φονεύσας. Κασσάνδραν δὲ Αἴας ὁ Ἰλέως πρὸς
βίαν ἀποσπῶν συνεφέλκεται τὸ τῆς Ἀθηνᾶς ξόανον. ἐφ'
ᾧ παροξυνθέντες οἱ Ἕλληνες καταλεῦσαι βουλεύονται τὸν
5 Αἴαντα. ὁ δὲ ἐπὶ τὸν τῆς Ἀθηνᾶς βωμὸν καταφεύγει καὶ
διασῴζεται ἐκ τοῦ ἐπικειμένου κινδύνου. ἔπειτα ἐμπρήσαντες τὴν πόλιν Πολυξένην σφαγιάζουσιν ἐπὶ τὸν τοῦ
Ἀχιλλέως τάφον. καὶ Ὀδυσσέως Ἀστυάνακτα ἀνελόντος,
Νεοπτόλεμος Ἀνδρομάχην γέρας λαμβάνει. καὶ τὰ λοιπὰ
10 λάφυρα διανέμονται. Δημοφῶν δὲ καὶ Ἀκάμας Αἴθραν
εὑρόντες ἄγουσι μεθ' ἑαυτῶν. ἔπειτα ἀποπλέουσιν οἱ
Ἕλληνες, καὶ φθορὰν αὐτοῖς ἡ Ἀθηνᾶ κατὰ τὸ πέλαγος
μηχανᾶται.

16 After the preceding [= four scrolls of the *Little Iliad*, by
Lesches of Lesbos] there follow two scrolls of the *Iliou
Persis*, by Arctinus

Chapter Two

of Miletus, containing the following. With regard to the things concerning the Horse, the

Trojans, suspicious about the horse, stand around wondering what they should

do. Some think it should be pushed off a cliff, while others

20   think it should be burned down, and still others say that it should be dedicated as sacred [*hieros*] to Athena.

In the end, the opinion of the third group wins out. They turn

to merriment, feasting as if they had been freed from the war.

At this point two serpents appear and

destroy Laocoön and one of his sons. At the sight of

25   this marvel, Aeneas and his followers get upset and withdraw

to Mount Ida. Sinon lights signal fires for the Achaeans.

He had previously entered the city, using a pretext. And they [= the Achaeans], some of them sailing from Tenedos

[toward Troy] and others of them emerging from the Wooden Horse, fall upon

their enemies. They kill many, and the city

is taken by force. Neoptolemos kills

Priam, who has taken refuge at the altar of Zeus Herkeios.

p. 108   Menelaos finds Helen and takes her back down to the ships, after

slaughtering Deiphobos. Ajax son of Oileus takes Kassandra by

force, dragging her away from the wooden statue [*xoanon*] of Athena. At the sight

of this, the Achaeans get angry and decide to stone

5   Ajax to death, but he takes refuge at the altar of Athena, and so

is preserved from his impending destruction. Then

2⑤24. The third song of Demodokos

the Achaeans put the city to the torch. They slaughter Polyxena on the
tomb of Achilles. Odysseus kills Astyanax,
and Neoptolemos takes Andromache as his prize. The rest
10   of the spoils are distributed. Demophon and Akamas find Aithra
and take her with them. Then the Greeks sail off [from Troy],
and Athena begins to plan destruction for them at sea.

2§329 Now I quote the plot of the "Iliou Persis" as performed by Demodokos and as retold in the epic of Homeric poetry:

2ⓣ95 *Odyssey* viii 499-533

ὣς φάθ', ὁ δ' ὁρμηθεὶς θεοῦ ἤρχετο, φαῖνε δ' ἀοιδήν,
500   <u>ἔνθεν</u> ἑλών, <u>ὡς</u> οἱ μὲν ἐϋσσέλμων ἐπὶ νηῶν
βάντες ἀπέπλειον, πῦρ ἐν κλισίῃσι βαλόντες,
Ἀργεῖοι, τοὶ δ' ἤδη ἀγακλυτὸν ἀμφ' Ὀδυσῆα
εἴατ' ἐνὶ Τρώων ἀγορῇ κεκαλυμμένοι ἵππῳ·
αὐτοὶ γάρ μιν Τρῶες ἐς ἀκρόπολιν ἐρύσαντο.
505   ὣς ὁ μὲν ἑστήκει, τοὶ δ' ἄκριτα πόλλ' ἀγόρευον
ἥμενοι ἀμφ' αὐτόν· τρίχα δέ σφισιν ἥνδανε βουλή,
ἠὲ διατμῆξαι κοῖλον δόρυ νηλέϊ χαλκῷ,
ἢ κατὰ πετράων βαλέειν ἐρύσαντας ἐπ' ἄκρης,
ἢ ἐάαν μέγ' ἄγαλμα θεῶν <u>θελκτήριον</u> εἶναι,
510   τῇ περ δὴ καὶ ἔπειτα τελευτήσεσθαι ἔμελλεν·
αἶσα γὰρ ἦν ἀπολέσθαι, ἐπὴν πόλις ἀμφικαλύψῃ
δουράτεον μέγαν ἵππον, ὅθ' εἴατο πάντες ἄριστοι
Ἀργεῖοι Τρώεσσι φόνον καὶ κῆρα φέροντες.
ᾔειδεν δ' ὡς ἄστυ διέπραθον υἷες Ἀχαιῶν
515   ἱππόθεν ἐκχύμενοι, κοῖλον λόχον ἐκπρολιπόντες.
ἄλλον δ' ἄλλῃ ἄειδε πόλιν κεραϊζέμεν αἰπήν,
αὐτὰρ Ὀδυσσῆα προτὶ δώματα Δηϊφόβοιο

Chapter Two

βήμεναι, ἠΰτ' Ἄρηα, σὺν ἀντιθέῳ Μενελάῳ.
κεῖθι δὴ αἰνότατον πόλεμον φάτο τολμήσαντα
520   νικῆσαι καὶ ἔπειτα διὰ μεγάθυμον Ἀθήνην.
ταῦτ' ἄρ' ἀοιδὸς ἄειδε περικλυτός· αὐτὰρ Ὀδυσσεὺς
<u>τήκετο</u>, δάκρυ δ' ἔδευεν ὑπὸ βλεφάροισι παρειάς.
ὡς δὲ γυνὴ κλαίῃσι φίλον πόσιν ἀμφιπεσοῦσα,
ὅς τε ἑῆς πρόσθεν πόλιος λαῶν τε πέσῃσιν,
525   ἄστεϊ καὶ τεκέεσσιν ἀμύνων νηλεὲς ἦμαρ·
ἡ μὲν τὸν θνῄσκοντα καὶ ἀσπαίροντα ἰδοῦσα
ἀμφ' αὐτῷ χυμένη λίγα κωκύει· οἱ δέ τ' ὄπισθε
κόπτοντες δούρεσσι μετάφρενον ἠδὲ καὶ ὤμους
εἴρερον εἰσανάγουσι, πόνον τ' ἐχέμεν καὶ ὀϊζύν·
530   τῆς δ' ἐλεεινοτάτῳ ἄχεϊ φθινύθουσι παρειαί·
ὣς Ὀδυσεὺς ἐλεεινὸν ὑπ' ὀφρύσι δάκρυον εἶβεν.
ἔνθ' ἄλλους μὲν πάντας ἐλάνθανε δάκρυα λείβων,
Ἀλκίνοος δέ μιν οἶος ἐπεφράσατ' ἠδ' ἐνόησεν

Thus he [= Odysseus] spoke. And he [= Demodokos], setting his point of departure [*hormētheis*], started [*arkhesthai*] from the god. And he made visible the song,
500   taking it <u>from the point where</u> they [= the Achaeans], boarding their ships with the strong benches,
sailed away, setting their tents on fire.
That is what some of the Argives [= Achaeans] were doing. But others of them were in the company of Odysseus most famed, and they were already
sitting hidden inside the Horse, which was now in the meeting place of the Trojans.
The Trojans themselves had pulled the Horse into the acropolis.
505   So there it was, standing there, and they talked a great deal about it, in doubt about what to do,
sitting around it. There were three different plans:

2§24. The third song of Demodokos

to split the hollow wood with pitiless bronze, or to drag it to the heights and push it down from the rocks,

or to leave it, great artifact that it was, a <u>charm</u> [*thelktērion*] of the gods

510 —which, I now see it, was exactly the way it was going to end [*teleutân*],

because it was fate [*aisa*] that the place would be destroyed, once the city had enfolded in itself

the great Wooden Horse, when all the best men were sitting inside it,

the Argives [= Achaeans], that is, bringing slaughter and destruction upon the Trojans.

He sang how the sons of the Achaeans destroyed the city,

515 pouring out of the Horse, leaving behind the hollow place of ambush.

He sang how the steep citadel was destroyed by different men in different places.

—how Odysseus went to the palace of Deiphobos,

how he was looking like Ares, and godlike Menelaos went with him,

and how in that place, I now see it, he [= Demodokos] said that he [= Odysseus] dared to go through the worst part of the war,

520 and how he emerged victorious after that, with the help of Athena, the one with the mighty spirit.

So these were the things that the singer [*aoidos*] most famed was singing. As for Odysseus,

<u>he dissolved</u> [*tēkesthai*][299] into tears. He made wet his cheeks with the tears flowing from his eyelids,

just as a woman cries, falling down and embracing her dear husband,

who fell in front of the city and people he was defending,

---

[299] This image, I argue, is relevant to a theme that is typical of poetry attributed to Orpheus.

Chapter Two

> 525   trying to ward off the pitiless day of doom that is hanging
>   over the city and its children.
>
> She sees him dying, gasping for his last breath,
>
> and she pours herself all over him as she wails with a
>   piercing cry. But there are men behind her,
>
> prodding her with their spears, hurting her back and
>   shoulders,
>
> and they bring for her a life of bondage, which will give her
>   pain and sorrow.
>
> 530   Her cheeks are wasting away with a sorrow [*akhos*] that is
>   most pitiful [*eleeinon*].
>
> So also did Odysseus pour out a piteous tear [*dakruon*] from
>   beneath his brows; there he was, escaping the notice of all
>   while he kept pouring out his tears [*dakrua*].
>
> But Alkinoos was the only one of all of them who was aware,
>   and he took note [*noeîn*].

2§330 On the basis of the correspondences we see between these passages I have just quoted, I am ready to argue that the poetic form of the epic of Demodokos is cognate with the poetic form of the epic Cycle as exemplified by the *Iliou Persis* attributed to Arctinus of Miletus. This poetic form is pre-Homeric, in the sense that it preserves not only epic themes but also epic conventions that are no longer current in the overall poetics of the Homeric *Iliad* and *Odyssey*. These conventions, as we saw, are revealed in the special usage of the word *humnos* with reference to the performance of Demodokos in *Odyssey* viii. This special usage, as we also saw, is marked by the poetic concept of metabasis.

2§331 I used the term pre-Homeric here because Homeric poetry refers to the poetry of Demodokos as an antiquated medium. I have already highlighted the moment when the master narrator begins to narrate how Demodokos begins to narrate his first song: the *kleos* 'fame' of this embedded narration was something that existed *tote* 'at that time' (viii 74). So the master narration is pointedly set apart from the embedded narration, the reception of which is dated to an earlier time. The embedded narration represents an older form of epic.

2§332 I have more to say in the twin book *Homer the Preclassic* about this older form of epic.[300] Here I concentrate on two of its characteristics,

---

[300] *HPC* I§§211 and following.

as represented by the terms *humnos* and *metabasis*. We have seen that the evidence of the *Homeric Hymns* is relevant to these epic characteristics, and that Callimachus understood this relevance in composing his own *Hymns*, even though he thought that these characteristics represented newer rather than older forms of epic. I suspect that Callimachus experimented with the poetic device of metabasis in his *Hymns* precisely because Homer, as the supposedly oldest of poets, makes no metabasis. For Callimachus, this poetic device of metabasis was typical of the supposedly newer poets, as represented by the *Homeric Hymns*.

2§333 It remains to ask: was Callimachus aware of metabasis as a poetic device that was used in the epic Cycle as well? I think so. After all, the Cycle was attributed to newer poets, just like the *Homeric Hymns*. Still, the question may be irrelevant, if it is true that Callimachus was not particularly interested in the Cycle. I recall again the passage where Callimachus declares: ἐχθαίρω τὸ ποίημα τὸ κυκλικόν 'I detest the Cyclic poem' (*Epigram* 28.1).

2ⓢ25. The sorrows of Andromache

2§334 As we have seen so far, the sequencing of the narrative in the third performance by Demodokos is the consequence of a perfectly executed *humnos*. The effects of this perfect execution are demonstrated by the reaction of the audience of Demodokos—in particular, by the tears of Odysseus. As we have also seen, what transforms the third performance into something Cyclic is the correspondence of its story with the story of the *Iliou Persis*. Now, what will transform this same performance into something Homeric is its application to the plot as it is taking shape in the master narrative. The result, which I analyze in the twin book *Homer the Preclassic*, is an actual competition of Homeric form with Cyclic form.[301] In the present book, on the other hand, I analyze the interweaving between the epic of Homer and the epic of Demodokos. And the thread of thought for this interweaving is the story of the sorrows of Andromache.

2§335 Relevant is the fact that the totality of narration in the third performance of Demodokos is achieved not directly but indirectly. It is achieved by way of the outer narrative that frames the third song. In the outer narrative, the reaction of Odysseus to the inner narrative fills out that inner narrative. At the precise moment when Odysseus starts to weep in response to the narration of Demodokos, the weeping of this hero as the foremost participant

[301] *HPC* I§§232–241.

Chapter Two

in the audience is compared by way of a simile to the weeping of an unidentified woman who has just been captured by the enemy. The simile takes up the narration at exactly the point where it was left off by the narrative of Demodokos—and by the outer narrative of the *Odyssey*. That point in the epic Cycle, as we just saw in the Proclus summary of the *Iliou Persis* (p. 108.8-10), is the moment when Odysseus is about to kill Astynanax, son of Andromache and Hector, and Neoptolemos is about to capture Andromache herself as his prize.[302]

2§336 This moment in the Cycle is foreshadowed in the *Iliad*. I quote here the most telling verses, where Hector reveals to Andromache his forebodings about his own death and about its dire consequences for his wife and child:

2ⓣ96 *Iliad* VI 448-464

εὖ γὰρ ἐγὼ τόδε οἶδα κατὰ φρένα καὶ κατὰ θυμόν·
ἔσσεται ἦμαρ ὅτ' ἄν ποτ' ὀλώλῃ Ἴλιος ἱρὴ
450 καὶ Πρίαμος καὶ λαὸς ἐϋμμελίω Πριάμοιο.
ἀλλ' οὔ μοι Τρώων τόσσον μέλει ἄλγος ὀπίσσω,
οὔτ' αὐτῆς Ἑκάβης οὔτε Πριάμοιο ἄνακτος
οὔτε κασιγνήτων, οἵ κεν πολέες τε καὶ ἐσθλοὶ
ἐν κονίῃσι πέσοιεν ὑπ' ἀνδράσι δυσμενέεσσιν,
ὅσσον σεῦ, ὅτε κέν τις Ἀχαιῶν χαλκοχιτώνων
455 δακρυόεσσαν ἄγηται ἐλεύθερον ἦμαρ ἀπούρας·
καί κεν ἐν Ἄργει ἐοῦσα πρὸς ἄλλης ἱστὸν <u>ὑφαίνοις</u>,
καί κεν ὕδωρ φορέοις Μεσσηΐδος ἢ Ὑπερείης
πόλλ' ἀεκαζομένη, κρατερὴ δ' ἐπικείσετ' ἀνάγκη·
καί ποτέ τις εἴπῃσιν ἰδὼν κατὰ δάκρυ χέουσαν·
460 Ἕκτορος ἥδε γυνὴ ὃς ἀριστεύεσκε μάχεσθαι
Τρώων ἱπποδάμων ὅτε Ἴλιον ἀμφεμάχοντο.
ὥς ποτέ τις ἐρέει· σοὶ δ' αὖ νέον ἔσσεται ἄλγος
χήτεϊ τοιοῦδ' ἀνδρὸς ἀμύνειν δούλιον ἦμαρ.
ἀλλά με τεθνηῶτα χυτὴ κατὰ γαῖα καλύπτοι

---

[302] BA 6§§8–9 (= pp. 100–101), Dué 2006:2. An alternative epic version, according to which Astyanax is killed by Neoptolemos, is analyzed in HPC II§193.

2§25. The sorrows of Andromache

For I know well in my thinking, in my heart, that

there will come a day when, once it comes, the sacred city of Ilios [= Ilion = Troy] will be destroyed

450 —and Priam, too, and along with him [will be destroyed] the people of that man with the fine ash spear, that Priam.

But the pain I have on my mind is not as great for the Trojans and for what will happen to them in the future,

or for Hecuba or for Priam the king,

or for my brothers if, many in number and noble as they are,

they will fall in the dust at the hands of men who are their enemies

—no, [the pain I have on my mind is not as great for them] as it is for you when I think of a moment when some Achaean man, one of those men who wear khitons of bronze,

455 takes hold of you as you weep and leads you away as his prize, depriving you of your days of freedom from slavery.

And you would be going to Argos, where you would be weaving [*huphainein*] at the loom of some other woman [and no longer at your own loom at home]

—and you would be carrying water for her, drawing from the spring called Messēís or the one called Hypereia.

Again and again you will be forced to do things against your will, and the bondage holding you down will be harsh.

And someone some day will look at you as you pour out your tears and will say:

460 "Hector is the man whose wife this woman used to be. He used to be the best in battle

—the best of all the Trojans, those horse-tamers, back in those days when they fought to defend Ilion [= Troy]."

That is what someone some day will say. And just hearing it will give you a new sorrow

as the widow of this kind of man, the kind that is able to prevent those days of slavery.

Chapter Two

But, once I am dead, may earth be scattered over me and cover me.

2§337 When the scene of Andromache's capture is about to be retold in the third song of Demodokos, something happens in the overall narrative of the Homeric *Odyssey*. At the point where the retelling is about to happen, it is is blocked. Unlike the *Iliou Persis* of Arctinus, where a high point of the narrative of Troy's destruction is the killing of Astyanax and the capture of Andromache, that high point is missing in the *Odyssey*: instead, the narrator's act of identifying Andromache as a captive woman is screened by a simile about an unidentified captive woman:

2①97 *Odyssey* viii 521-530

      ταῦτ' ἄρ' ἀοιδὸς ἄειδε περικλυτός· αὐτὰρ Ὀδυσσεὺς
      <u>τήκετο</u>, δάκρυ δ' ἔδευεν ὑπὸ βλεφάροισι παρειάς.
      ὡς δὲ γυνὴ κλαίῃσι φίλον πόσιν ἀμφιπεσοῦσα,
      ὅς τε ἑῆς πρόσθεν πόλιος λαῶν τε πέσῃσιν,
525 ἄστεϊ καὶ τεκέεσσιν ἀμύνων νηλεὲς ἦμαρ·
      ἡ μὲν τὸν θνῄσκοντα καὶ ἀσπαίροντα ἰδοῦσα
      <u>ἀμφ' αὐτῷ χυμένη λίγα κωκύει</u>· οἱ δέ τ' ὄπισθε
      κόπτοντες δούρεσσι μετάφρενον ἠδὲ καὶ ὤμους
      εἴρερον εἰσανάγουσι, πόνον τ' ἐχέμεν καὶ ὀϊζύν·
530 τῆς δ' ἐλεεινοτάτῳ ἄχεϊ φθινύθουσι παρειαί·

So these were the things that the singer [*aoidos*] most famed was singing. As for Odysseus,
<u>he dissolved</u> [*tēkesthai*] into tears. He made wet his cheeks with the tears flowing from his eyelids,
just as a woman cries, falling down and embracing her dear husband,
who fell in front of the city and people he was defending,
525 trying to ward off the pitiless day of doom that is hanging over the city and its children.
She sees him dying, gasping for his last breath,
<u>and she pours herself all over him as she wails with a piercing cry</u>. But there are men behind her,

prodding her with their spears, hurting her back and shoulders,

and they bring for her a life of bondage, which will give her pain and sorrow.

535 Her cheeks are wasting away with a sorrow [*akhos*] that is most pitiful [*eleeinon*].

2§338 This sequence of narration in the *Odyssey* achieves an effect of screen memory. An essential phase in the sequence is being screened out by the memory of that narrative. The audience, as foregrounded by Odysseus, is expected to know the sequence, and the sequence is already a reality because the audience already knows where the singer had started. As I have already argued, the beginning of the narration already determines the plot of the narration. So the audience and the singer, in a combined effort, can now all project the image together, projecting it as a flashback on the screen of the mind's eye. But the climax of the action, that is, the capturing of the woman who is yet to be identified as Andromache, has been screened out by a simile about the capturing of a woman who will never be identified.

2§339 I have used here two distinct metaphors involving the concept of screen. The first is the screening or projecting of an image on the screen that is the mind's eye. The second is the screening-out of that image in the overall narrative of the *Odyssey*. It is pertinent that Odysseus is not only the foregrounded audience of the third song of Demodokos: he is also an agent of the plot that is being narrated by the song, since he is the direct cause of Andromache's sorrows.[303]

2§340 The narrative of Demodokos was reaching an outcome that features the capture of Andromache, but such an outcome has been taken over by the outer narrative of the *Odyssey*—once the simile of the captive woman takes over from the inner narrative about the capture of Andromache—an inner narrative that Demodokos would still be performing. But the outer narrative now takes over from the inner narrative. From the standpoint of the outer narrative, the inner narrative remains the same. From the standpoint of the inner narrative, however, its outcome has been preempted.

2§341 As we saw earlier, the sequence of the narrative of the third song of Demodokos in *Odyssey* viii matches the sequence of the narrative we know as the *Iliou Persis* in the epic Cycle, which represents an older form of epic. A distinctive feature of this older form is the poetic device of the metabasis,

---

[303] *BA* 6§9 (= p. 101).

Chapter Two

which links a *humnos* to its hymnic consequent. As we also saw, there is an actual reference to this device in *Odyssey* viii 492, marking the transition that leads into the third song. So the third song of Demodokos, as an older form of epic, is part of a *humnos* by virtue of being a hymnic consequent.

2§342 In the twin book *Homer the Preclassic*, I focus on all three songs of Demodokos as parts of an ongoing *humnos*.[304] In the present book I focus only on the third song. As part of a *humnos*, this song attracts a metaphor traditionally associated with the word *humnos*. It is the metaphor of fluidity, which has been all along the centerpoint of interest in this chapter.

2§343 This metaphor is already signaled in the physical reaction of Odysseus to the first and the third songs of Demodokos, which is linked with his reaction to the third song. I need to repeat here what I said before about these reactions. The first song, as we saw, keeps on restarting, and, each time it restarts, Odysseus sheds tears all over again: the continually restarted outpouring of tears is expressed by the wording *aps . . . goân* 'lament again and again' at verse 92, which parallels the wording that expresses the continual restarting of this first song, *aps arkhesthai* 'start again and again' at verse 90. Then, in the third song, a connection is established with the first song, as if the third directly followed the first. By way of this connection, the third song will now appear to be a new restarting of the first, which was continually being restarted until Alkinoos stopped it (98-99). The sorrowful themes in the first song are now being recycled into the third song, by way of ring composition. When Odysseus hears the third song, he literally 'dissolves' into tears (522 *tēkesthai*). The hero pours forth 'a tear' (*dakru / dakruon* at 522 / 531) all over again. The wording ἐλεεινὸν . . . δάκρυον εἶβεν 'he poured forth a piteous [*eleeinon*] tear' (531), with reference to the third song, recycles by way of ring composition the earlier wording δάκρυα λείβων 'pouring forth tears', with reference to the first song (86).

2§344 As Odysseus weeps, he is compared to an unnamed captive woman who is weeping (*Odyssey* viii 523 *klaiein*) over the dead body of her warrior husband. This woman, within the framework of the third song, would be Andromache.[305] Within the overall framework of the *Odyssey*, however, this woman is not to be identified. As the unidentified captive woman weeps, she is 'poured all around' her dead husband (527 *amphi . . . khumenē*): in effect, she

---

[304] *HPC* I§§232-241.

[305] Again, *BA* 6§9 (= p. 101). Aristotle in the *Rhetoric* (3.1417a14) notes the terror and the pity evoked by the story told by Odysseus to Alkinoos (cf. *Poetics* 1455a2); I suggest that the third song of Demodokos sets the tone, as it were.

dissolves into tears.³⁰⁶ Directly comparable is the primary listener in the audience, Odysseus, who reacts by 'dissolving' (522 *tēkesthai*) into tears.

2§345 Whenever Andromache dissolves into tears and speaks in the mode of lament, it is not only sad for an audience: it is simultaneously erotic.³⁰⁷ The emotional effect achieved in the staging of a grieving Andromache in the *Iliad* is comparable to the emotional effect achieved in the staging of a prima donna singing her song of sorrow in the world of opera.

2§346 There is also an exquisite example of such staging in ancient Greek tragedy. It is an aria of lamentation composed in elegiac couplets and sung as a monody by the actor who plays Andromache in a tragedy of Euripides called the *Andromache*. I quote here the relevant verses, drawing special attention to the association of the word *tēkesthai* 'dissolve', referring to Andromache's tears of lament, with the word *terpsis* 'delight':

2①98 Euripides *Andromache* 91-117

 Αν. ἡμεῖς δ' οἷσπερ ἐγκείμεσθ' ἀεὶ
   θρήνοισι καὶ γόοισι καὶ δακρύμασιν
   πρὸς αἰθέρ' ἐκτενοῦμεν· ἐμπέφυκε γὰρ
   γυναιξὶ τέρψις τῶν παρεστώτων κακῶν
95 ἀνὰ στόμ' αἰεὶ καὶ διὰ γλώσσης ἔχειν.
   πάρεστι δ' οὐχ ἓν ἀλλὰ πολλά μοι στένειν,
   πόλιν πατρῴαν τὸν θανόντα θ' Ἕκτορα
   στερρόν τε τὸν ἐμὸν δαίμον' ὧι συνεζύγην
   δούλειον ἦμαρ ἐσπεσοῦσ' ἀναξίως.
100 χρὴ δ' οὔποτ' εἰπεῖν οὐδέν' ὄλβιον βροτῶν,
   πρὶν ἂν θανόντος τὴν τελευταίαν ἴδηις
   ὅπως περάσας ἡμέραν ἥξει κάτω.
   Ἰλίωι αἰπεινᾶι Πάρις οὐ γάμον ἀλλά τιν' ἄταν
   ἀγάγετ' εὐναίαν ἐς θαλάμους Ἑλέναν.

---

³⁰⁶ We may compare the wording *amphi . . . khumenē* 'poured all around [her husband]' here in the *Odyssey* (viii 527) with the wording *amphikhutheis* 'poured all around [his father]' elsewhere in the *Odyssey* (xvi 214 ἀμφιχυθεὶς πατέρα): there the wording applies to Telemachus, who is *dakrua leibōn* 'pouring tears' as he embraces his father (xxii 498 and 501).

³⁰⁷ On ethnographic investigations of the interchangeability of laments and love songs, see Nagy 1994a/1995:51 and Dué 2006:20n50.

Chapter Two

105 ἃς ἕνεκ', ὦ Τροία, δορὶ καὶ πυρὶ δηϊάλωτον
εἷλέ σ' ὁ χιλιόναυς Ἑλλάδος ὠκὺς Ἄρης
καὶ τὸν ἐμὸν μελέας <u>πόσιν</u> Ἕκτορα, τὸν <u>περὶ τείχη</u>
<u>εἵλκυσε διφρεύων</u> παῖς ἁλίας Θέτιδος·
αὐτὰ δ' ἐκ θαλάμων ἀγόμαν ἐπὶ θῖνα θαλάσσας,
110 δουλοσύναν στυγερὰν ἀμφιβαλοῦσα κάραι.
<u>πολλὰ δὲ δάκρυά μοι κατέβα χροός</u>, ἁνίκ' ἔλειπον
<u>ἄστυ</u> τε καὶ θαλάμους καὶ πόσιν ἐν κονίαις.
<u>ὤμοι</u> ἐγὼ μελέα, τί μ' ἐχρῆν ἔτι φέγγος ὁρᾶσθαι
Ἑρμιόνας δούλαν; ἃς ὕπο τειρομένα
115 πρὸς τόδ' ἄγαλμα θεᾶς ἱκέτις περὶ χεῖρε βαλοῦσα
<u>τάκομαι</u> ὡς πετρίνα πιδακόεσσα λιβάς.

ΧΟΡ.
ὦ γύναι, ἃ Θέτιδος δάπεδον καὶ ἀνάκτορα θάσσεις
δαρὸν οὐδὲ λείπεις,
Φθιὰς ὅμως ἔμολον ποτὶ σὰν Ἀσιήτιδα γένναν, ...

ANDROMACHE:
But I, involved as I am all the time in <u>laments</u> [*thrēnoi*] and
 wailings [*gooi*] and outbursts of tears,
will make them reach far away, as far as the aether. For it is
 natural
for women, when misfortunes attend them, to take <u>pleasure</u>
 [*terpsis*]
90 in giving voice to it all, voicing it again and again, maintaining the voice from one mouth to the next, from one
 tongue to the next.
I have here not one but many things to mourn:
I mourn the city of my fathers. I mourn Hector, <u>dead</u>.
And I mourn the rigid fate allotted to me by an unnamed
 force [*daimōn*], a fate to which I am yoked,
having fallen captive to a life of slavery—so undeserved!

100	You must never call any mortal blessed [*olbios*]
	before he dies and you see him on his last day alive,
	and you see how he lives through that day before he finally goes down below.
	To <u>Ilios</u> [= Troy] <u>with its steep walls</u>[308] did Paris bring not a wedding to be celebrated but some kind of aberration [*atē*]
	when he brought to the wedding chamber, as his partner in bed, Helen herself.
105	Because of her, O Troy, by spear and fire were you captured by the enemy.
	Seized you were by the thousand ships of Hellas sent by swift Ares,
	and so also was my <u>husband</u> Hector taken from me, wretched that I am. <u>Around the walls</u> [of Troy]
	was he <u>dragged from the chariot driven</u> by the son of the sea-dwelling Thetis.
	And then I myself was taken out of my chamber and brought to the shore of the sea.
110	Hateful slavery did I place as headwear upon my head.
	<u>And many a tear came falling, all over the complexion of my face</u> as I left behind
	my <u>city</u> and my chamber and my husband lying in the dust.
	<u>I cry O for me</u>, wretched that I am! Why did I have to see the light of day
	as a slave of Hermione? Worn down by her domination,
115	to this statue of the goddess do I come as a suppliant, embracing it with both hands,
	and I <u>dissolve</u> [*tēkesthai*] [into tears] like a stream that flows from a spring in the rocky heights.

---

[308] The rhythm of the wording here marks an abrupt switch (as marked by the absence of an expected word of syntactical connection) from speaking in iambic trimeter to singing in elegiac couplets. The verse here is a dactylic hexameter, starting a series of elegiac couplets combining dactylic hexameter and pentameter.

Chapter Two

CHORUS

My lady, you who have been sitting there on the sacred
ground and precinct of Thetis[309]
for some time now, unwilling to leave,
I, a woman from Phthia, have come, approaching you,
a woman born in Asia . . .

2§347 This lament sung by Andromache is comparable in its eroticism to the lament sung by the unnamed captive woman in the simile applied to Odysseus when he weeps in reaction to the third song of Demodoklos in *Odyssey* viii. That lament is pointedly left unquoted in the simile about the unidentified captive woman in *Odyssey* viii.

2§348 The lament of Andromache is also comparable to what we saw in *Idyll* 1 of Theocritus, where *tēkesthai* refers to the 'dissolving' (66 ἐτάκετο) of Daphnis in response to his own sad love story. First Daphnis dissolves metaphorically, and then he dissolves literally: in his tears, Daphnis is ultimately absorbed into the waters of the stream (140-141 ἔβα ῥόον. ἔκλυσε δίνα | τὸν Μοίσαις φίλον ἄνδρα).

2§349 So also Odysseus dissolves in response to the sad love story of the lamenting captive woman. As this unnamed woman dissolves into tears in the narrative of the simile, her weeping extends to Odysseus in the outer narrative: he too dissolves into the same world of tears. And, by dissolving into tears, the figure of Odysseus becomes reconfigured as the lamenting woman of the simile. Through the metaphor of fluidity as song, the particles of the picture that is the old song are dissolved and then reassembled in high resolution, thus becoming the newest song.

2§350 The fluidity of performing the third song of Demodokos anticipates the ultimate rigidity of the composition in the end, at the *telos*, once the story is fully told. In *Homer the Preclassic*, I have more to say about this *telos*.[310] In the present book I focus only on the fact that the lamenting woman in the third song of Demodokos is not identified. Relevant is my earlier argu-

---

[309] Here at line 117, the dactylic hexameter of what is expected to be the next elegiac couplet is being picked up as the first line of a choral song that is sung and danced by the chorus. So, line 117 is the first line of the first stanza, strophe α, of this choral song. And, from here on, there will be no more elegiac couplets, since this hexameter at line 117 will not be followed by a pentameter. Instead, the rhythm of elegiac couplets will now be abandoned as the choral song modulates into its own rhythms. There will be no pentameter following the hexameter at line 117, which is the beginning of strophe α, or after lines 126, 135, and 141, which are respectively the beginnings of antistrophe α, strophe β, and antistrophe β.

[310] *HPC* I§§294 and following.

ment about the all-encompassing narration of the Shield of Achilles in *Iliad* XVIII. In the Shield, as in the third song of Demodokos, we see a cross-reference to the totality of an all-encompassing narration. In the third song of Demodokos, the referent is the past that is the Troy story. In the Shield, the referent is the future outcome of a Troy story still in the making. In the third song of Demodokos, the climax of the action is the capturing of Andromache, who is about to be identified by Demodokos. But this climax is screened out by a simile referring to the capture of a woman who will never be identified. The non-identification of the unnamed captive woman in the third song of Demodokos is comparable to the non-identification of the unnamed litigants in the Shield of Achilles. Once the story of the *Iliad* reaches its conclusion, its *telos*, the litigants can be identified as Agamemnon and Achilles. Once the third song of Demodokos reaches its conclusion, the captive woman can be identified as Andromache. The identification of these characters matches the inflexibility and rigidity of the finished composition, while their non-identification matches the flexibility and fluidity of the composition still in progress, still in performance.

CHAPTER THREE

HOMER THE CLASSIC IN THE AGE OF PLATO

3ⓢ1. The Koine of Homer as a model of stability

3§1 The Koine of Homer, as approximated by the base text of Aristarchus in the second century BCE, was more rigid and less fluid than the *Homerus Auctus*, as approximated by the base text of Zenodotus in the age of Callimachus in the third century BCE. This Koine of Homer, as I will now argue, already existed in the age of Plato in the fourth century BCE.

3§2 In this earlier age that I identify here with Plato, the Homeric tradition was more rigid and less fluid than it was—or became—in the later age of Callimachus. Conversely, the Homeric tradition in the later age of Callimachus was less rigid and more fluid. Then, in the still later age of Aristarchus, the Homeric tradition reverted: it became once again more rigid and less fluid. Moreover, as I argued in the Prolegomena, the Homeric tradition reached its ultimate state of rigidity in the age of Aristarchus.

3§3 To put it another way: the age of Plato was a time when the Homeric tradition was relatively stable, but there followed a time of destabilization in the later age of Callimachus, which in turn was followed by a time of restabilization in the still later age of Aristarchus. My concern now is the earliest of these three eras, the age of Plato.

3ⓢ2. Homer and the Panathenaic standard

3§4 The stability of the Homeric tradition in the age of Plato stems from the localization of this tradition in Athens, at the feast of the Panathenaia, which was the premier festival of this city. At this festival, Homeric poetry was performed on a regular basis, season after season. We have already seen one aspect of Homeric performance at the Panathenaia, the Panathenaic

Regulation, which had an effect on the form of Homeric poetry. In general, the ultimate shaping of this form needs to be viewed in the historical context of the Panathenaia. Elsewhere, I have explored this historical context in some detail, keeping track of the relevant evidence to be found in the works of Plato.[1] Here I extend the exploration by concentrating on the actual form of Homeric poetry as Plato must have heard it being performed at the Panathenaia in his time. From here on, I will refer to this form as the Panathenaic Homer.

3§5 Restricting the field of vision to the age of Plato, I start by asking a hypothetical question. Suppose we had access to a transcript of such a Panathenaic Homer—exactly as Plato heard Homeric poetry being performed at the Panathenaia in a given year. The question is, what Homeric text would such a transcript resemble most closely? My answer is this: the closest thing would be the quotations from Homer as we find them in the works of Plato himself. The next closest thing would be the Koine of Homer as approximated by the base text constructed by Aristarchus.

3§6 I follow up with a second question: what poetry was considered to be Homeric—and non-Homeric—in the age of Plato? From the standpoint of the Panathenaia, the answer to this second question is most revealing. As we will see, Homer was assumed to be the poet of the *Iliad* and *Odyssey*—and of nothing else. As we will also see, the *Iliad* and *Odyssey* were the only epics officially performed at the Panathenaia in the age of Plato. From a Panathenaic point of view, Homer was by now the author of only the *Iliad* and *Odyssey*. No other epic qualified as Homeric. Further, what was considered to be Homeric or non-Homeric in the age of Plato was determined by a standard of Panathenaic performance. Here I introduce the concept of a Panathenaic standard as the driving force behind the Panathenaic Homer. What I have been calling the Panathenaic Regulation is a central aspect of this standard.

3§7 Things were different in the subsequent age of Callimachus. By that time, the Homeric tradition had broken free of what I am calling the Panathenaic standard. Texts of the Homeric *Iliad* and *Odyssey* were no longer dominated by the performative norms of the Athenian festival of the Panathenaia. As I started to argue in Chapter 2, texts of Homer in the age of Callimachus accommodated non-Homeric elements—that is, elements differentiated as non-Homeric in other ages. These supposedly non-Homeric elements were recognized in other ages as Cyclic, Hesiodic, and Orphic. What had earlier determined their non-Homeric status was the Panathenaic standard.

[1] PR.

Chapter Three

3§8 Here I return to the model of the <u>Homerus Auctus</u> as I developed it in Chapter 2—the model of an all-encompassing Homer in the age of Callimachus in the third century BCE, accommodating Cyclic, Hesiodic, and Orphic traditions. Such an augmented Homer served as the base text of Zenodotus in the third century BCE. In Chapter 2, I contrasted this model of the <u>Homerus Auctus</u> with the later model of an unagumented Homer, that is, the Koine, which served as the base text of Aristarchus.

3§9 That same model of the Homerus Auctus in the age of Callimachus will now have to be contrasted also with an earlier model of a non-augmented Homer, which I trace back to the age of Plato. That earlier model of a non-augmented Homer in the age of Plato is comparable to the Homeric Koine, that is, to the later model of a non-augmented Homer in the age of Aristarchus. To put it another way, the Koine reconstructed by Aristarchus as his base text for editing Homer approximated the <u>Panathenaic Homer</u>, which embodied the continuation of the old <u>Panathenaic standard</u> for performing Homer.

3§10 The antithesis to an unstable and fluid <u>Homerus Auctus</u> is the stable and relatively rigid <u>Panathenaic Homer</u>, which I argue was later approximated by the <u>Homeric Koine</u> as reconstructed by Aristarchus. To sum up my argument so far: this Homeric text—or, better, this Homeric textual tradition—most closely approximated the Athenian norms for performing the *Iliad* and the *Odyssey* at the feast of the Panathenaia. The Homeric Koine was an Athenian Koine. From here on, I will refer to the Panathenaic Homer simply as the Homeric Koine.

3ⓢ3. The Homerus Auctus as a predecessor of the Homeric Koine

3§11 In Chapter 2, I explored various similarities that linked the Cyclic, Hesiodic, and Orphic traditions embedded in the Homerus Auctus with what we know as the Homeric tradition. Here in Chapter 3 I will concentrate on the dissimilarities. On the basis of these dissimilarities, our first impression is that the Cyclic, Hesiodic, and Orphic augmentations of the Homerus Auctus must come from post-Homeric as well as non-Homeric traditions. In the end, however, I will conclude that they are pre-Homeric—that is, if we define <u>pre-Homeric</u> in terms of earlier periods when the Cyclic, Hesiodic, and Orphic traditions were as yet undifferentiated from what later became the Homeric tradition. In other words, I will conclude that the Cyclic, Hesiodic, and Orphic augmentations predate the Panathenaic standard of performing Homer in the age of Plato.

3§3. The Homerus Auctus as a predecessor of the Homeric Koine

3§12 In Chapter 2, I was using the terms <u>Cyclic</u>, <u>Hesiodic</u>, and <u>Orphic</u> merely as general points of reference to the poetry conventionally attributed in the ancient world to the poets of the epic Cycle, to Hesiod, and to Orpheus. Now I need to refocus on specific points of reference, and I will start with the term <u>Cyclic</u>.

3§13 By <u>Cyclic</u>, I mean the poetry of the epic Cycle as understood by Aristotle, for whom the Cycle was categorically non-Homeric. In his *Poetics*, Aristotle mentions two of the Cyclic epics he knew—the *Cypria* and the *Little Iliad*—and he makes clear his view that the authors of these epics were poets other than Homer; more than that, he chooses not even to name these poets (1459a37–b16). Another source, Proclus, offers specific names and proveniences: for example, the author of the *Cypria* was supposedly Stasinus of Cyprus; of the *Little Iliad*, Lesches of Lesbos; of the *Aithiopis* and the *Iliou Persis*, Arctinus of Miletus.

3§14 Aristotle viewed Homer as the author of only two epics, the *Iliad* and the *Odyssey* (again, *Poetics* 1459a37–b16; cf. 1448b38–1449a1).[2] Plato, as we see in such works as the *Ion*, evidently held the same view. In general, the verses that Plato quotes from 'Homer' are taken from the *Iliad* and the *Odyssey*, not from the epic Cycle.

3§15 This way of thinking is relevant to what I have argued from the start of this chapter: that the *Iliad* and the *Odyssey* were the only two epics being performed at the Panathenaia in the age of Plato. As I will argue in Chapter 4, the same situation holds in the fifth century BCE, the age that preceded the age of Plato: in that earlier age as well, the *Iliad* and the *Odyssey* were the only two epics being performed at the Panathenaia. As we keep moving further back in time to even earlier ages, however, we will need to re-examine the idea of Homer as the author of only two epics, the *Iliad* and the *Odyssey*. Before the age of Plato, and before the earlier age to be surveyed in Chapter 4, there was an even earlier age when Homer could be viewed as the notional author of all epic, as represented by the concept of the epic Cycle before it became historically differentiated from the *Iliad* and *Odyssey*. In that earlier age, as I show in the twin book *Homer the Preclassic*, the traditions represented by what we know as the epic Cycle were not yet excluded from the program, as it were, of the Panathenaia.[3]

---

[2] Aristotle makes one theory-driven exception. In the *Poetics* (1448b30), he theorizes that the author of the mock-epic *Margites* was Homer.

[3] *HPC* I§§169 and following.

Chapter Three

3§16 In that earlier age, the idea of the epic Cycle was simply the idea of epic as a comprehensive totality: the term 'Cycle' or *kuklos* was sustained by metaphors of artistic completeness.[4] In later ages, however, as exemplified by the age of Plato, we find that Cyclic poetry became clearly differentiated from Homeric poetry, and the epic Cycle no longer represented any kind of totality. Newer ideas of completeness had replaced the older idea.

3§17 These newer ideas were determined by the artistic measure of tragedy. In the days of Plato and Aristotle, epic totality was represented only by the Homeric *Iliad* and *Odyssey*, and their completeness was measured according to the standards of tragedy. Aristotle says explicitly that only the Homeric *Iliad* and *Odyssey* are comparable to tragedy because only these epics show a complete and unified structure, unlike the epics of the Cycle (*Poetics* 1459a37–b16). In the works of Plato as well, Homer is measured against the standards of tragedy, and Homer is imagined as a proto-tragedian in his own right (*Theaetetus* 152e; *Republic* 10.595c, 598d, 605c, 607a).[5] For Plato and Aristotle, the Homeric *Iliad* and *Odyssey* measured up to the standards of tragedy, whereas the epics of the Cycle did not.

3§18 The parallelism of Homer and tragedy is evident at the very beginning of the *Poetics* of Aristotle (1447a13–15). There he lists in the following order the forms of composition in verbal art: epic or *epopoiia* (which means literally 'the making of *epos*'), tragedy, comedy, dithyramb, and compositions involving performance on the *aulos* 'reed' or the *kithara* 'lyre'. All these forms listed there at the beginning of Aristotle's *Poetics* correspond to forms of composition that were actually performed at the two major festivals of the Athenians:

(1) the Panathenaia, featuring (a) epic accompanied by no musical instrument, (b) lyric accompanied by *aulos*, (c) lyric accompanied by *kithara*, (d) instrumental music played on the *aulos*, without words, (e) instrumental music played on the *kithara*, without words

(2) the City Dionysia, featuring (a) tragedy, (b) comedy, (c) dithyramb, and (d) satyr drama.[6]

In Aristotle's listing, he ostentatiously pairs the composition of epic with the composition of tragedy (the wording is *epopoiia ... kai hē tēs tragōidias poiēsis*,

---

[4] HQ 38, 89.
[5] In Plato *Republic* 10.595c (also 598d), Homer is described as the *hēgemōn* 'leader' of tragedy. See also the commentary of Murray 1996:188–189.
[6] EH §33 (Nagy 2005a:27); also *PP* 81–82; more recently, Rotstein 2004.

3§3. The Homerus Auctus as a predecessor of the Homeric Koine

which means literally 'the making of *epos* and the making of tragedy').[7] Elsewhere, he says that he views these two particular forms of composition, epic and tragedy, as cognates (*Poetics* 1449a2–6).[8] In the works of Plato as well, epic is viewed as a cognate of tragedy: more than that, Homer is represented as a proto-tragedian (*Theaetetus* 152e; *Republic* 10.595c, 598d, 605c, 607a).

3§19 This pattern of associating tragedy with epic, and epic with tragedy, reflects an institutional reality. The genre of epic, as performed at the festival of the Panathenaia, actually shaped and was shaped by the genre of tragedy as performed at the festival of the City Dionysia. In Athens, ever since the sixth century BCE, these two genres were "complementary forms, evolving together and thereby undergoing a process of mutual assimilation in the course of their institutional coexistence."[9]

3§20 By the time of Plato and Aristotle, such a complementarity of epic and tragedy involved only the epics of the Homeric *Iliad* and *Odyssey*, no longer the epics of the Cycle. This differentiation of the epic Cycle from the Homeric *Iliad* and *Odyssey*, as I show in the twin book *Homer the Preclassic*, can be linked with the obsolescence of performing the poetry of the epic Cycle at the Panathenaia after the age of the Peisistratidai.[10]

3§21 Besides the Cycle, there are two other poetic traditions that are evidently differentiated from Homer in the age of Plato, namely, the Hesiodic and the Orphic. As I also show in the twin book *Homer the Preclassic*, the differentiation of Hesiod and Orpheus from Homer can be linked with the obsolescence of performing Hesiodic and Orphic poetry at the Panathenaia after the age of the Peisistratidai.[11]

3§22 In the case of the Hesiodic tradition, its differentiation from the Homeric tradition is explicit, attested by the textual traditions that culminate in the Hesiodic *Theogony* as well as the *Works and Days*. In the case of the Orphic tradition, on the other hand, the differentiation is only implicit. In Chapter 2, in fact, I have already emphasized some aspects of non-differentiation, focusing on occasional convergences between Orphic and Homeric traditions. Here in Chapter 3, I focus on the divergences, which will help me highlight what was distinct about the Homeric tradition in the age of Plato.

---

[7] *EH* §33 (Nagy 2005a:26–27).
[8] *BA* 14§§1–5 (= pp. 253–255).
[9] *PP* 81.
[10] *HPC* I§§169 and following.
[11] *HPC* I§§178 and following.

Chapter Three

3⒮4. The Panathenaic standard as highlighted by Orphic deviations

3§23 For Plato, what was Orphic was non-Homeric, just as Cyclic and Hesiodic poetry were non-Homeric. Now we will see that whatever Plato considers to be Orphic is a foil for whatever he considers to be Homeric.

3§24 As we consider the dissimilarities between Plato's Orpheus and Plato's Homer, our first impression is that the poetry of Orpheus stems from a post-Homeric tradition that deviated from Homer. This impression is reinforced by Aristotle's view that Orpheus is some kind of post-Homeric invention (*Historia animalium* 563a18, *De generatione animalium* 734a19). In Chapter 2, however, I already began to explore the idea that the poetry associated with Orpheus stems from a pre-Homeric tradition—that is, if we define <u>pre-Homeric</u> in terms of a prehistoric age when Orphic poetry was not yet differentiated from what later became Homeric poetry. As I observed in Chapter 2, this idea applies to Cyclic and Hesiodic poetry as well as to Orphic poetry: all three of these poetic traditions seem at first sight to be post-Homeric, but various aspects turn out to be pre-Homeric. Here in Chapter 3, I follow up on this observation by arguing that the Cyclic, Hesiodic, and Orphic traditions predate the Panathenaic standard of performing Homer in the age of Plato. I will argue further that the anteriority of these traditions became reinterpreted as a deviation from the Homeric Koine. A figure like Orpheus, from the standpoint of Plato's Socrates, was not only non-Homeric: he was deviant in being non-Homeric.

3§25 The idea that Orphic poetry is in some ways older than Homeric poetry can be tested by examining conventional views about Orpheus and Homer in the age of Plato. As we will see, Homer was viewed as a generalist in the realm of poetry, while Orpheus was viewed as a specialist. As we will also see, the poetic categories of <u>generalist</u> and <u>specialist</u> are both defined in terms that conform to the Panathenaic standard of the Homeric Koine.

3§26 In a search for examples, it seems to me best to begin with the idea of the *humnos*. The background has been given in Chapter 2. As we saw there, this word *humnos* is attested only once in the Homeric *Iliad* and *Odyssey*, that is, at *Odyssey* viii 429. Elsewhere, Homer is associated with the *humnos* only to the extent that he is the 'author' of the *Homeric Hymns*, as we saw in Chapters 1 and 2, where I analyzed his role as the notional author of the *Homeric Hymn* (3) *to Apollo*. By contrast, Orpheus is specially associated with the *humnos*, as we saw already in Chapter 2 with reference to the *Humnoi* of Orpheus as cited in the *Derveni Papyrus*. Even in the realm of the *Homeric Hymns*, Orpheus figures as

3§4. The Panathenaic standard as highlighted by Orphic deviations

a rival of Homer, as in the case of the *Homeric Hymn to Demeter*, where the attribution of authorship vacillates between Homer and Orpheus.[12]

3§27 Now we turn to the testimony of Plato. In his usage, Orpheus figures as a specialist in the singing of *humnoi*. In Plato's *Laws* (8.829d-e), for example, there is talk of interdicting a hypothetical *mousa* 'song' that is being sung, 'even if it be sweeter than humnoi that are Orphic [*Orpheioi*] or than [the *humnoi*] of Thamyras' (ᾄδειν ἀδόκιμον μοῦσαν μὴ κρινάντων τῶν νομοφυλάκων, μηδ' ἂν ἡδίων ᾖ τῶν Θαμύρου τε καὶ 'Ορφείων ὕμνων). I draw attention to the fact that Orpheus is implicitly being represented here as a master *kitharōidos* 'citharode', that is, one who sings while playing on the *kithara*, while Thamyras is a master *kitharistēs* 'citharist', that is, one who plays on the *kithara* without singing. These artistic specialties are made explicit in another Platonic passage, which shows most of the central themes that figure in this chapter:

3ⓣ1 Plato *Ion* 533b-c

ΣΩ. Ἀλλὰ μήν, ὥς γ' ἐγὼ οἶμαι, οὐδ' ἐν αὐλήσει γε οὐδὲ ἐν κιθαρίσει οὐδὲ ἐν κιθαρῳδίᾳ οὐδὲ ἐν ῥαψῳδίᾳ οὐδεπώποτ' εἶδες ἄνδρα ὅστις περὶ μὲν 'Ολύμπου δεινός ἐστιν ἐξηγεῖσθαι ἢ περὶ Θαμύρου ἢ περὶ {c} 'Ορφέως ἢ περὶ Φημίου τοῦ 'Ιθακησίου ῥαψῳδοῦ, περὶ δὲ Ἴωνος τοῦ 'Εφεσίου [ῥαψῳδοῦ] ἀπορεῖ καὶ οὐκ ἔχει συμβαλέσθαι ἅ τε εὖ ῥαψῳδεῖ καὶ ἃ μή.

SOCRATES: Here is another thing. As far as I can tell, neither in [1] playing on the *aulos* [= *aulēsis*] nor in [2] playing on the *kithara* [= *kitharisis*] nor in [3] singing and playing on the *kithara* [= *kitharōidia*] nor in [4] performing as a rhapsode [= *rhapsōidia*] have you seen any man who is skilled at explaining about [1] Olympos[13] or about [2] Thamyras[14] or about [3] Orpheus or about [4] Phemios of Ithaca, the rhapsode [= *rhapsōidos*][15]—but who is perplexed about Ion of Ephesus and is unable to formulate what things Ion performs well as a rhapsode [= *rhapsōidein*] and what things he does not.

---

[12] See *Orphic Fragment* 49 ed. Kern and the remarks of Richardson 1974:12.
[13] The figure of Olympos is a prototypical master of the *aulos*; sources and commentary in *PH* 3§§7 (= p. 86), 16–17 (= pp. 90–91), 36 (= pp. 100–101), 39 (= pp. 102–103).
[14] The figure of Thamyras / Thamyris is a prototypical master of the *kithara* in *Iliad* II 594–600; commentary in *PH* 12§71n199 (= p. 376).
[15] The figure of Phemios is a prototypical singer of epic in *Odyssey* i, xvii, and xxii. I will have more to say about him later. On Phemios as a *rhapsōidos* 'rhapsode', see Graziosi 2002:25, 39–40; her interpretation is different from the one I offer in what follows.

Chapter Three

3§28 This passage concerns the ability of specialists to form critical opinions about the crafts in which they specialize. Among these specialists is Orpheus, who is explicitly figured as a master *kitharōidos* 'citharode', that is, one who sings while accompanying himself on the *kithara*; Thamyras is a master *kitharistēs* 'citharist', that is, one who plays on the *kithara*; Olympos is a master *aulētēs* 'aulete', that is, one who plays on the reed or *aulos*; and, finally, Phemios is a master *rhapsōidos*, that is, 'rhapsode'. The types of performers listed in this passage correspond to the types of performers that actually competed at the Panathenaia in the age of Plato. At the Panathenaia, there were separate competitions of *rhapsōidoi* 'rhapsodes', of *kitharōidoi* 'citharodes' (= *kithara*-singers), of *aulōidoi* 'aulodes' (= *aulos*-singers), of *kitharistai* 'citharists' (= *kithara*-players), and of *aulētai* 'auletes' (*aulos*-players), as we learn from an Athenian inscription dated at around 380 BCE (*IG* II² 2311), which records the winners of Panathenaic prizes.¹⁶ We also learn about these categories of competition from Plato's *Laws* (6.764d–e), where we read of rhapsodes, citharodes, and auletes—and where the wording makes it clear that the point of reference is the Panathenaia.¹⁷

3§29 The evidence about these categories of competition at the Panathenaia is supplemented by what we read in the Aristotelian *Constitution of the Athenians* (60.1), where the author refers to these same Panathenaic categories of competition and where the overall competition is specified as the 'competition [*agōn*] in *mousikē*' (τὸν ἀγῶνα τῆς μουσικῆς). We learn further details from this same source: ten magistrates called *athlothetai* 'arrangers of the contests [*athloi*]' were selected by lot every four years to organize the festival of the Panathenaia, and one of their primary tasks was the management of the 'competition [*agōn*] in *mousikē*'. According to Plutarch's *Pericles* (13.9–11), the Athenian statesman Pericles reformed this competition in *mousikē* when he was elected as one of the *athlothetai*.¹⁸ What, then, does the author of the *Constitution of the Athenians* actually mean when he says *mousikē*? In Aristotelian usage, this word *mousikē* is a shorthand way of saying *mousikē tekhnē*, meaning 'craft of the Muses', that is, 'musical craft'. It would be a misreading, however, to think of ancient Greek *mousikē* simply in the modern sense of <u>music</u>, since the categories of 'musical' performers at the Panathenaia included not only *kitharōidoi* 'kithara-singers' and *kitharistai* 'kithara-players'

---

¹⁶ Further discussion in *PR* 38–39, 42n16, 51. The portion of the inscription that deals with rhapsodes is lost, but it is generally accepted that rhapsodic competitions were mentioned in this missing portion. I will return to this inscription at a later point.
¹⁷ *PR* 38, 40, 42.
¹⁸ Background in Rhodes 1981:670–671.

3§4. The Panathenaic standard as highlighted by Orphic deviations

and *aulōidoi* 'aulos-singers' and *aulētai* 'aulos-players' but also *rhapsōidoi* 'rhapsodes'. The performative medium of rhapsodes in the era of Aristotle was recitative and thus not 'musical' in the modern sense of the word. By recitative I mean (1) performed without singing and (2) performed without the instrumental accompaniment of the *kithara* or the *aulos*.[19] In this era, the competitive performances of the Homeric *Iliad* and *Odyssey* by rhapsodes at the Panathenaia were 'musical' only in an etymological sense, and the medium of the rhapsode was actually closer to what we call 'poetry' and farther from what we call 'music' in the modern sense of the word. Still, the fact remains that the performances of rhapsodes belonged to what is called the 'competition [*agōn*] in *mousikē*' (τὸν ἀγῶνα τῆς μουσικῆς), just like the performances of citharodes, citharists, aulodes, auletes, and so on.

3§30 We find in Plato's *Ion* an explicit reference to such 'competition [*agōn*] in *mousikē*':

3①2 Plato *Ion* 530a–c[20]

ΣΩ. Τὸν Ἴωνα χαίρειν. πόθεν τὰ νῦν ἡμῖν ἐπιδεδήμηκας; ἢ οἴκοθεν ἐξ Ἐφέσου;

ΙΩΝ. Οὐδαμῶς, ὦ Σώκρατες, ἀλλ' ἐξ Ἐπιδαύρου ἐκ τῶν Ἀσκληπιείων.

ΣΩ. Μῶν καὶ ῥαψῳδῶν <u>ἀγῶνα</u> τιθέασιν τῷ θεῷ οἱ Ἐπιδαύριοι;

ΙΩΝ. Πάνυ γε, καὶ τῆς ἄλλης γε <u>μουσικῆς</u>.

ΣΩ. Τί οὖν; <u>ἠγωνίζου</u> τι ἡμῖν; καὶ πῶς τι <u>ἠγωνίσω</u>; {b}

ΙΩΝ. Τὰ πρῶτα τῶν ἄθλων ἠνεγκάμεθα, ὦ Σώκρατες.

ΣΩ. Εὖ λέγεις· ἄγε δὴ ὅπως καὶ τὰ Παναθήναια νικήσομεν.

ΙΩΝ. Ἀλλ' ἔσται ταῦτα, ἐὰν θεὸς ἐθέλῃ.

ΣΩ. Καὶ μὴν πολλάκις γε ἐζήλωσα ὑμᾶς τοὺς ῥαψῳδούς, ὦ Ἴων, τῆς τέχνης· τὸ γὰρ ἅμα μὲν τὸ σῶμα κεκοσμῆσθαι ἀεὶ πρέπον ὑμῶν εἶναι τῇ τέχνῃ καὶ ὡς καλλίστοις φαίνεσθαι, ἅμα δὲ ἀναγκαῖον εἶναι ἔν τε ἄλλοις ποιηταῖς διατρίβειν πολλοῖς καὶ ἀγαθοῖς καὶ δὴ καὶ μάλιστα ἐν Ὁμήρῳ, τῷ ἀρίστῳ καὶ θειοτάτῳ τῶν ποιητῶν, καὶ τὴν τούτου διάνοιαν {c} ἐκμανθάνειν, μὴ μόνον τὰ ἔπη, ζηλωτόν ἐστιν. οὐ γὰρ ἂν γένοιτό ποτε ἀγαθὸς ῥαψῳδός, εἰ μὴ συνείη τὰ λεγόμενα ὑπὸ τοῦ

---

[19] PR 36, 41–42.
[20] I have analyzed this passage in earlier work, PR 22, 37–38, 99.

ποιητοῦ. τὸν γὰρ ῥαψῳδὸν ἑρμηνέα δεῖ τοῦ ποιητοῦ τῆς διανοίας γίγνεσθαι τοῖς ἀκούουσι· τοῦτο δὲ καλῶς ποιεῖν μὴ γιγνώσκοντα ὅτι λέγει ὁ ποιητὴς ἀδύνατον. ταῦτα οὖν πάντα ἄξια ζηλοῦσθαι.

SOCRATES: Greetings to Ion. Where from, on this occasion of your visiting us here? Are you coming from your home city, Ephesus?

ION: Not at all, Socrates. I'm coming from Epidaurus, from the festival of Asklepios there.

SOCRATES: You don't mean that the people of Epidaurus also [= like us Athenians] have a custom of holding a <u>competition</u> [<u>agōn</u>] of rhapsodes [*rhapsōidoi*]?

ION: Oh, but they do in fact. And they also have a custom of holding competitions in other kinds of <u>mousikē</u>.

SOCRATES: Well, how about that![21] So you <u>participated in</u> some kind of <u>a competition</u> [<u>agōn</u>] for us?[22] And how did such a <u>competition</u> [<u>agōn</u>] of yours turn out?

ION: We[23] won first prize in the contests [*athloi*], Socrates!

SOCRATES: Well, good for you! So now let's see if we[24] can win first prize at the Panathenaia as well![25]

ION: This will happen, if the god wills it.

SOCRATES: You know, Ion, I for one have always envied you rhapsodes [*rhapsōidoi*] for your craft [*tekhnē*]. I say this because it is envi-

---

[21] Socrates' patronizing tone here implies that there is no reason for Athenians to know whether the people of Epidaurus even have contests of rhapsodes, let alone what the repertoire of these rhapsodes might be. It is also implied that different cities have different *agōnes* 'competitions' in *mousikē*, and that competitions in rhapsodic performance are expected to be included. In PR 39-40, I study the *agōnes* 'competitions' in *mousikē* held at the city of Eretria, as recorded in an inscription (*IG* XII ix 189) dated around 341/0 BCE.

[22] The ethical dative here ('for us') accentuates how indifferent an Athenian would be toward an *agōn* 'competition' that took place elsewhere.

[23] By 'we' Ion means 'I' of course, but this 'we' has a way of potentially including Socrates and all other Athenians.

[24] Socrates patronizingly uses 'we' here to include himself and all Athenians in the potentially inclusive 'we' of Ion. The patronizing use of the first-person plural here matches his earlier patronizing use of the first-person plural pronoun as ethical dative.

[25] For an Athenian, the stakes would be low when the rhapsode competes in an *agōn* 'competition' elsewhere—as compared to the *agōnes* of the Panathenaia in Athens.

3§4. The Panathenaic standard as highlighted by Orphic deviations

able that you are always so physically well put together—as is fitting for your craft [tekhnē]—and that you all look so good, so exceptionally good. And it is enviable at the same time that you rhapsodes have to be well versed in all good poets, especially in the best and most divine of poets, Homer. And that you have to learn not only his verses but also his thinking. For there could never be such a thing as a good rhapsode [rhapsōidos] if he did not understand the things said by the Poet. The rhapsode has to be an interpreter of the thinking of the Poet for his listeners. And to do this well if one does not understand what the Poet says is impossible.[26] So all these things are worthy of envy.

3§31 This passage needs to be seen in the light of the dramatic moment that serves as the setting for this Platonic dialogue. Ion, a rhapsode from Ephesus, has just arrived in Athens, intending to compete for first prize at the festival of the Panathenaia (καὶ τὰ Παναθήναια νικήσομεν, *Ion* 530b). Plato's wording makes it explicit that the occasion for performances by rhapsodes at the Panathenaia was in effect a <u>competition</u> or <u>contest</u> among rhapsodes, an *agōn* (ἀγῶνα *Ion* 530a, picked up by ἠγωνίζου and ἠγωνίσω later on in 530a), and that the agonistic craft of the rhapsodes was included under the general category of *mousikē* (μουσικῆς 530a). When Ion says that he hopes to win first prize at the Panathenaia, he adds that he has just won first prize in an *agōn* of rhapsodes at the feast of the Asklepieia in Epidaurus (530a-b).[27]

3§32 At the *agōn* 'competition' in *mousikē* held at the Panathenaia, the contests of *kitharōidoi* 'citharodes' [= *kithara*-singers], of *aulōidoi* 'aulodes' [= *aulos*-singers], of *kitharistai* 'citharists' [= *kithara*-players], and of *aulētai* 'auletes' [= *aulos*-players] may have varied in content from one season to the next, but the overall content of what the *rhapsōidoi* 'rhapsodes' had to perform was invariable—at least, it had become an invariable by the time we reach the age of Plato. In terms of my overall argumentation, that invariable was the Homeric *Iliad* and *Odyssey*, performed season after season at the Panathenaia. This status of Homer at the Panathenaia is indicated by the wording of Plato's Socrates in the passage I have just quoted. Socrates' emphasis on Homer as

---

[26] The wording of Plato's Socrates assumes that the performance of the poetry of Homer as the Poet par excellence is specially featured at the *agōnes* 'competitions' of the Panathenaia. It seems also assumed, however, that other poems of other poets could be featured at other rhapsodic competitions at other festivals.

[27] PR 22, 37–38, 99.

Chapter Three

the best of poets is parallel to his emphasis on Homer as the featured poet par excellence at the *agōnes* 'competitions' of the Panathenaia.

3§33 Though we know precious little about the actual performances of Homer by rhapsodes at the Panathenaia in the age of Plato, there is sufficient evidence for positing three features: (1) in line with the Panathenaic Regulation, the rhapsodes took turns in performing the narrative sequence of the Homeric *Iliad* and *Odyssey*; (2) each of these two epics was divided into twenty-four rhapsodic performance-units or *rhapsōidiai* 'rhapsodies'; and (3) the rhapsodes were actively competing as well as collaborating with each other in performing the narrative sequence by way of their rhapsodic relay.[28] There is room for debate about the specifics of all three of these posited features,[29] but there is one overall feature, essential to the argument at hand, that seems to me a certainty: in the era of the Athenian democracy, the repertoire of rhapsodes performing at the Panathenaia was confined exclusively to the Homeric *Iliad* and *Odyssey*.[30] There is a reference to this exclusivity in a speech delivered in 330 BCE by the Athenian statesman Lycurgus, *Against Leokrates* (102), which concerns the reperforming of the Homeric *Iliad* and *Odyssey* in their notional entirety on the occasion of the quadrennial festival of the Great Panathenaia:[31]

3①3 Lycurgus *Against Leokrates* 102

βούλομαι δ' ὑμῖν καὶ τὸν Ὅμηρον παρασχέσθαι ἐπαινῶν. οὕτω γὰρ ὑπέλαβον ὑμῶν οἱ πατέρες σπουδαῖον εἶναι ποιητήν, ὥστε νόμον ἔθεντο καθ' ἑκάστην πενταετηρίδα τῶν Παναθηναίων μόνου τῶν ἄλλων ποιητῶν ῥαψῳδεῖσθαι τὰ ἔπη, ἐπίδειξιν ποιούμενοι πρὸς τοὺς Ἕλληνας ὅτι τὰ κάλλιστα τῶν ἔργων προῃροῦντο.

---

[28] PR 36–69. For a comparative perspective on the concept of competition-in-collaboration, see PP 18.
[29] Burgess 2004, with citations.
[30] HTL 28–30.
[31] This passage in Lycurgus *Against Leokrates* (102) is analyzed in PR 10–12; I analyze it further in HPC I§§43–46. I disagree with Graziosi 2002:196 when she says that "this passage does not define Homer as the author of the *Iliad* and the *Odyssey*."

3⒮4. The Panathenaic standard as highlighted by Orphic deviations

I wish to adduce[32] for you Homer, quoting [*epaineîn*] him,[33] since the reception[34] that he had from your [Athenian] ancestors made him so important a poet that there was a law enacted by them that requires, every fourth year of the Panathenaia, the rhapsodic performing [*rhapsōideîn*] of his verses [*epos* plural]—his alone and no other poet's. In this way they [= your (Athenian) ancestors] made a demonstration [*epideixis*],[35] intended for all Hellenes to see,[36] that they made a conscious choice of the most noble of accomplishments.[37]

3§34 To advance the argument further, I adduce three interconnected details. The first two come from the *Ion* of Plato, while the third comes from the *Panegyricus* of Isocrates.

---

[32] The orator Lycurgus, in 'adducing' the various classical authors that he quotes, is doing so in his role as a statesman.

[33] To make his arguments here in *Against Leokrates* 102, Lycurgus is about to adduce a quotation from Homer, the equivalent of what we know as *Iliad* XV verses 494–499. My reasons for translating *epaineîn* as 'quote' will become evident in the analysis that follows. Adducing a Homeric quotation is presented here as if it were a matter of adducing Homer himself. In the same speech, at an earlier point, Lycurgus (*Against Leokrates* 100) had quoted 55 verses from Euripides' *Erekhtheus* (F 50 ed. Austin). At a later point (*Against Leokrates* 107), he quotes 32 verses from Tyrtaeus (F 10 ed. West), whom he identifies as an Athenian (so also does Plato in *Laws* 1.629a). On the politics and poetics of the Athenian appropriation of Tyrtaeus *and* of his poetry, see *GM* 272–273. I suggest that the Ionism of poetic diction in the poetry of Tyrtaeus can be explained along the lines of an evolutionary model of transmission at Ionian festivals: see *PH* 2§3 (= pp. 52–53), 14§41 (= pp. 433–434) and *HQ* 111. See also *PH* 1§13n27 (= p. 23) on Lycurgus *Against Leokrates* 106–107, where the orator mentions a customary law at Sparta concerning the performance of the poetry of Tyrtaeus. For more on *epaineîn*, see now Elmer 2005.

[34] I deliberately translate *hupolambanein* 'receive' here in terms of *reception theory*. In terms of rhapsodic vocabulary, as we see in "Plato" *Hipparkhos* 228b–c, *hupolēpsis* is not just 'reception' but also 'continuation' in the sense of *reception by way of relay* (PR 11n8). Further analysis in *HPC* I§43.

[35] Comparable is the context of *epideigma* 'display, demonstration' in "Plato" *Hipparkhos* 228d, as discussed in *PH* 6§30 (= pp. 160–161); see also *PH* 8§4 (= pp. 217–218) on *apodeixis* 'presentation, demonstration'. The basic idea is this: what is being 'demonstrated' is a *model for performance*. Further observations in *HPC* I§43.

[36] By implication, the Panhellenic impulse of the 'ancestors' of the Athenians in making Homer a "Classic" is mirrored by the impulse of Lycurgus, statesman that he is, to quote extensively from such Classics as Homer, Tyrtaeus, and Euripides. See also "Plutarch" *Lives of the Ten Orators* 841f on the initiatives taken by Lycurgus to produce a *State Script* of the dramas of Aeschylus, Sophocles, and Euripides (commentary in *PP* 174–175, 189n6, 204).

[37] I infer that the *erga* 'accomplishments' include poetic accomplishments: on the mentality of seeing a reciprocity between a noble deed and noble poetry that celebrates the noble deed and thereby becomes a noble deed in its own right, see *PH* 2§35n95 (= p. 70), 8§5 (= pp. 218–219).

Chapter Three

3§35 The first detail has to do with a boast made by the rhapsode Ion in Plato's *Ion*: he claims that he is worthy of being awarded the prize of a golden *stephanos* 'garland' by the *Homēridai* 'descendants of Homer' (530d). The prize that is mentioned here is mentioned again in two later passages of the *Ion* (535d, 541c). In one of these two passages, the golden garland is associated with the words *thusiai* 'feasts' and *heortai* 'festivals' (535d). These words are appropriate designations of the festival of the Panathenaia. Piecing together what we learn from all three contexts (530d, 535d, 541c), I infer that the awarding of a golden garland to Ion by the *Homēridai* is connected with the winning of first prize in the competition of rhapsodes at the Panathenaia.[38] An additional piece of evidence is the inscription I mentioned earlier (*IG* II² 2311) concerning the prizes won at the Panathenaia in Athens for the year 380 BCE: here we read that the first prize in the competition of citharodes is a golden *stephanos* 'garland' valued at 1000 drachmas, which is awarded in addition to a cash prize of silver valued at 500 drachmas. Though the portion of the inscription dealing with the competition of rhapsodes is lost, it is generally agreed that this missing portion indicated that the first prize in the corresponding competition of rhapsodes was likewise a golden *stephanos* 'garland', and that the amount of cash awarded as first prize to the winning rhapsode was comparable to the amount awarded to the winning citharode.[39]

3§36 I infer that Ion is in effect saying: I am not just any rhapsode, I am a tenured Panathenaic rhapsode. The crowning of the rhapsode with a golden garland by the *Homēridai* is a Panathenaic signature, as it were. The fact that the *Homēridai* are linked with the performances of Homeric poetry by rhapsodes at the Panathenaia in Athens is relevant to another fact: as I show in the twin book *Homer the Preclassic*, Homer himself is linked with the performances of the *Iliad* and the *Odyssey* in Athens.[40] Evidence for the linkage comes from myths preserved in the *Life of Homer* traditions, especially in the *Herodotean Life of Homer* (*Vita* 1) and in the *Certamen* or *Contest of Homer and Hesiod* (*Vita* 2).[41] According to the *Certamen*, the people of the island state of Chios claimed that Homer was the ancestor of a *genos* 'lineage' from Chios who called themselves the *Homēridai* (*Vita* 2.13-15). According to the *Herodotean Life of Homer*, Homer composed both the *Iliad* and the *Odyssey* in the city of Chios (*Vita* 1.346-398)

---

[38] In one of these contexts (Plato *Ion* 535d), it is specified that Ion already wears a golden garland while he is performing Homer. Perhaps Ion had already won first prize at the Panathenaia on a previous occasion.
[39] *PR* 51; see also *PR* 99 on the golden garland.
[40] *HPC* I§§55 and following.
[41] My citations from *Vita* 1 and *Vita* 2 follow the line-numbers in the edition of Allen 1912.

3§4. The Panathenaic standard as highlighted by Orphic deviations

and planned to perform both epics in Athens (1.483-484), but he died before he reached his destination (1.484-509). The narrative of the *Herodotean Life* specifies that Homer augments his composition of both the *Iliad* and the *Odyssey* by adding verses that center on the glorification of Athens (1.378-398). Only after he finishes his glorification of Athens does Homer finish composing the *Iliad* and *Odyssey*: only then does he take leave of Chios and set sail to tour the rest of Hellas (1.400), intending ultimately to reach the city of Athens (1.483-484). In *Homer the Preclassic*, I draw the conclusion that these references picturing Athens as the ultimate destination for Homer's would-be performance of his *Iliad* and *Odyssey* are a mythological analogue to the ritual presence of the *Homēridai* at the rhapsodes' actual performances of the Homeric *Iliad* and *Odyssey* at the Panathenaia in Athens.[42]

3§37 I now come to a second interconnected detail in Plato's *Ion*. It has to do with the dramatized circumstances of Ion's dialogue with Socrates, which happens on the eve of the day when this rhapsode enters the *agōn* 'competition' in *mousikē* at the Panathenaia (530a-b). As we saw a moment ago, it is made clear that Ion will be competing with other rhapsodes in the performance of Homeric poetry, and that he expects to win the first prize in that competition.[43] Of special interest here is the term *mousikē* (*tekhnē*), which means literally 'craft (*tekhnē*) of the Muses'. As we saw earlier, it would be anachronistic to translate this term as 'music', since it applies not only to the craft of singing lyric accompanied by the *kithara* or *aulos*, as represented by citharodes and aulodes, but also to the craft of reciting epic without any instrumental accompaniment. That particular craft is represented by rhapsodes at the Panathenaia.

3§38 The third and decisive interconnected detail comes from a passage in the *Panegyricus* of Isocrates, concerning the repertoire of rhapsodes competing with each other in the *athloi* 'contests' in *mousikē* at the Panathenaia:

3①4 Isocrates (4) *Panegyricus* 159

οἶμαι δὲ καὶ τὴν <u>Ὁμήρου</u> <u>ποίησιν</u> μείζω λαβεῖν δόξαν ὅτι καλῶς
τοὺς πολεμήσαντας τοῖς βαρβάροις ἐνεκωμίασεν καὶ διὰ τοῦτο
βουληθῆναι τοὺς προγόνους ἡμῶν ἔντιμον αὐτοῦ ποιῆσαι τὴν

---

[42] HPC I§141.
[43] By implication, Ion was performing Homeric poetry also at the *agōn* 'competition' of rhapsodes at the festival of the Asklepieia in Epidaurus, where it is said that he likewise won the first prize (*Ion* 530a).

τέχνην ἔν τε τοῖς τῆς μουσικῆς ἄθλοις καὶ τῇ παιδεύσει τῶν νεωτέρων, ἵνα πολλάκις ἀκούοντες τῶν ἐπῶν ἐκμανθάνωμεν τὴν ἔχθραν τὴν ὑπάρχουσαν πρὸς αὐτοὺς καὶ ζηλοῦντες τὰς ἀρετὰς τῶν στρατευσαμένων τῶν αὐτῶν ἔργων ἐκείνοις ἐπιθυμῶμεν.

I think that the poetry [*poiēsis*] of Homer received all the more glory because he celebrated so beautifully those who waged war against the barbarians, and it was because of this that our [Athenian] ancestors wanted to make his craft [*tekhnē*] a thing to be honored both in the contests [*athloi*] [of rhapsodes] in *mousikē* and in the education [*paideusis*] of the young, so that we, having the chance to hear often his [= Homer's] verses [*epos* plural], may learn thoroughly the existing hostility against them [= the barbarians], and so that we may admire the accomplishments of those who have waged war and desire to accomplish the same deeds that they had accomplished.[44]

3§39 In the reference that this contemporary of Plato is making here to Homer, the wording assumes that the epics performed at the Panathenaia were totally familiar to all Athenians. Such epics, in the Athens of Isocrates and Plato in the fourth century BCE, can only be the Homeric *Iliad* and *Odyssey*. Even in the general usage of Isocrates (2.48; 10.65; 12.18, 33, 293; 13.2), we find that the term Homer refers to no poet other than the poet of the *Iliad* and *Odyssey*. The same goes for the general usage of Plato himself (a case in point is *Ion* 539d).

3§40 Also relevant in this passage from Isocrates is the designation of Homeric *poiēsis* 'poetic creation' as a *tekhnē* 'craft'.[45] As we see from his wording, Isocrates links the 'craft' of Homer with (1) the Panathenaic *athloi* 'contests' of rhapsodes and (2) the *paideusis* 'education' of the young. In view of the fact that *mousikē* was an appropriate term for designating not only the craft of, say, citharodes performing lyric poetry at the Panathenaia but also the craft of rhapsodes performing the epic poetry of Homer at the same festival, I stress once again that *mousikē* cannot be understood as 'music' in the modern sense of the word.

3§41 Pursuing this idea of the rhapsode as a master of *mousikē*, let us return to the passage in Plato's *Ion* where we saw a list of mythical prototypes corresponding to the categories of performers who compete in the

---

[44] More on this passage in PP 111n24.
[45] I translate *poiēsis* for now as 'poetic creation', but it is more accurate to render it as 'composition' (in the verbal arts).

3§4. The Panathenaic standard as highlighted by Orphic deviations

agōn 'competition' of *mousikē* at the Panathenaia (533b–c). The correspondences were anachronistic—and revealing in their anachronisms. There was Orpheus, master *kitharōidos* 'citharode', that is, one who sings while accompanying himself on the *kithara*. Then there was Thamyras, master *kitharistēs* 'citharist', that is, one who plays on the *kithara* but does not sing.[46] And then there was Olympos, master *aulētēs* 'aulete' that is, one who plays on the reed or *aulos*. Finally, there was Phemios, master *rhapsōidos*, that is, 'rhapsode'. The key figure in this quartet is Phemios the rhapsode. By contrast with the generic rhapsode who recited Homer in the age of Plato, without instrumental accompaniment, the prototypical rhapsode Phemios matches a singing Homer as envisioned in Homeric poetry: inside the narrative of the Homeric *Odyssey*, Phemios is not a reciter but an *aoidos* 'singer' (i 325, 346, 347; xxii 330, 345, 376) who literally 'sings' (*aeidein* i 154, 155, 325, 326, 350; xvii 262; xxii 331, 346, 348; noun *aoidē* i 159, 328, 340, 351) as he performs his epics inside the epic of the *Odyssey* (at i 326, the epic sung by Phemios is a *nostos* 'song of homecoming'), and he even accompanies himself on the equivalent of a *kithara*, the *kitharis* (i 153, 159; elsewhere, his instrument is called a *phorminx* at xvii 262; xxii 332, 340; verb *phormizein* i 155).

3§42 What, then, is the formal difference in Plato's *Ion* between Phemios the 'rhapsode' and Orpheus the 'citharode' or '*kithara*-singer'? After all, Orpheus—just like Phemios—is imagined as singing and accompanying himself on the *kithara*. The difference is that Phemios, as a 'rhapsode', is a worthy point of comparison for Homer as the ultimate poet, whereas Orpheus, as a 'citharode', is not. The 'music' of Phemios as a rhapsode is central at the Panathenaia in the days of Plato, whereas the 'music' of Orpheus is marginalized. Even as a citharode, Orpheus is mockingly marginalized:

3①5 Plato *Symposium* 179d–e

Ὀρφέα δὲ τὸν Οἰάγρου <u>ἀτελῆ</u> ἀπέπεμψαν ἐξ Ἅιδου, φάσμα δείξαντες τῆς γυναικὸς ἐφ' ἣν ἧκεν, αὐτὴν δὲ οὐ δόντες, ὅτι μαλθακίζεσθαι ἐδόκει, ἅτε ὢν <u>κιθαρῳδός</u>, καὶ οὐ τολμᾶν ἕνεκα τοῦ ἔρωτος ἀποθνῄσκειν ὥσπερ Ἄλκηστις, ἀλλὰ διαμηχανᾶσθαι ζῶν εἰσιέναι εἰς

---

[46] The non-singing role of the *kitharistēs* 'citharist' may be aetiologically connected with a myth about a primal 'musical' competition between Thamyras / Thamyris and the Muses (*Iliad* II 594–600). When Thamyris (as he is called in the *Iliad*) challenges the Muses to a duel in singing to the lyre, he is punished for his arrogance by being stuck dumb in the course of the contest (II 599–600). So this proto-citharist is pictured as a citharode who became a citharist by losing his singing voice. In the *Iliad*, Thamyris even forgets how to play the *kitharis* (II 600). So this proto-citharist is prevented even from continuing as a citharist.

Ἅιδου. τοιγάρτοι διὰ ταῦτα δίκην αὐτῷ ἐπέθεσαν, καὶ ἐποίησαν τὸν θάνατον αὐτοῦ ὑπὸ γυναικῶν {ε} γενέσθαι

But the gods sent Orpheus the son of Oiagros back from Hades without his having achieved a successful outcome [*telos*],[47] since they revealed to him a mere phantom [*phasma*] of the woman for whom he came [to Hades], but the woman herself they did not give back to him, since he seemed to them an unmanly man, a typical citharode [*kitharōidos*], who did not have the daring to die for love the way Alcestis did but instead contrived a way to enter Hades while holding on to his life. And that is why the gods imposed their just penalty on him by making him die a death at the hands of women.

3§43 We expect a citharode or *kithara*-singer to be a master of songs about love, but Orpheus here is mocked as a failure in love. Effete and even effeminate, he loses his lady love and then his own life as well. We see him fail here even in his poetic specialty, that is, in his mastery of initiation into the mysteries.[48] Later on, I will have more to say about Orpheus as a specialist in mystical poetry. For now, I merely emphasize that Orpheus in the age of Plato was marginalized by comparison with Homer, who had become centralized as the poet par excellence. By comparison with Homer, Orpheus in the age of Plato seems a deviant.

3§44 The marginalization of Orpheus was in fact well under way before the age of Plato: throughout the era of the Athenian democracy, Orpheus was already being marginalized. He was associated with notionally marginal humans who were not even Hellenes but Thracians. He could even be pictured as a non-Hellene himself, a Thracian in his own right.[49]

3§45 Let us pursue further the idea that Orpheus, the mythical *kitharōidos* 'citharode' of Plato's *Ion*, is a specialist in 'music' and thus a foil for Homer. The same goes for Thamyras the mythical *kitharistēs* 'kithara-player' and for Olympos the mythical *aulētēs* 'aulos-player': they too are specialists and thus foils for Homer.[50] By contrast, Phemios the mythical *rhapsōidos* 'rhap-

---

[47] There is a double meaning to the adjective *atelēs* 'without a *telos*' in this context. On the surface, the idea is that Orpheus failed to achieve the *telos* 'outcome' of rescuing his wife from Hades by bringing her back to the realm of light and life. Underneath the surface, however, Orpheus failed to achieve the *telos* 'outcome' of a successful 'initiation' into the mysteries.

[48] See the previous note.

[49] HPC E§117.

[50] In the case of Thamyras, he is presented by Homeric poetry itself as an implicit foil for Homer.

sode' is a surrogate for Homer as the ultimate generalist in the 'music' of the Panathenaia. Not only the mythical rhapsode but also the contemporary rhapsodes in the days of Plato—as represented by Ion himself—figure as surrogates of Homer in the context of the Panathenaia. As I noted before, the performances of Ion and his colleagues at that festival are restricted to the Homeric *Iliad* and *Odyssey*. As surrogates of Homer, the rhapsodes performing at the Panathenaia must be generalists in 'music' just like Homer, who is viewed as the generalized embodiment of poetry par excellence in the days of Plato. That is why Homer is known as the *poiētēs* 'Poet' *par excellence* and that is why his compositions are known as *poiēsis* 'poetry' or 'poetic creation' *par excellence*.

3§46 Thus the generic rhapsode performing the poetry of Homer at the Panathenaia becomes a generalized representative of poetry as 'music': his identity extends from the prototypical singer who sings Homeric song all the way to the contemporary rhapsode who recites Homeric poetry. By extension, Ion the rhapsode may at first seem like a generalized representative of poetry in his own right, for the simple reason that he is a representative of Homeric poetry. To the extent that Homer the poet is considered a generalist, not a specialist, so too the rhapsode who performs Homer may at first seem like a generalist in poetry.

3⑤5. Plato's attempt to discredit the Panathenaic standard

3§47 If Ion the rhapsode is a generalist in poetry, then he can be held responsible by Plato's Socrates not only for Homeric poetry but also for all poetry. That is Ion's good fortune, from his own standpoint as the most prestigious rhapsode in his time, 'the best rhapsode of the Hellenes' (Plato *Ion* 541b τῶν Ἑλλήνων ἄριστος ῥαψῳδός).[51] That is also Ion's misfortune, from the standpoint of the philosophical agenda built into the dialogue named after him. If Plato's Socrates can succeed in discrediting Ion, he can discredit a man who represents the best of all poetry in the days of Plato.[52] In the process,

---

[51] I accept as a historical fact the preeminent status of Ion in the historical time that corresponds to the dramatized time of his encounter with Socrates. I will have more to say about this in ch. 4. In general, it is important to keep in mind that Plato chooses most worthy opponents for Socrates. When Plato's Socrates predicts that Ion will win first prize in the Panathenaic competitions that follow the day of their encounter with each other (*Ion* 530b), I have no reason to doubt that this detail amounts to a self-fulfilling prophecy, and that the whole dialogue is predicated on the general success of Ion as a rhapsode.

[52] For more on this idea, see PR 9-35.

Chapter Three

Plato is also discrediting the Panathenaic standard of Homeric poetry, which sets the criteria for what is the best of all poetry.

3§48 One way for Socrates to discredit Ion is to show that the rhapsode who performs Homer, unlike Homer, is in fact no generalist in poetry. Plato's Socrates forces Ion to admit that he is a specialist: when Socrates asks Ion whether he is an expert in the poetry of Hesiod or Archilochus, the rhapsode replies that he is not, and that his expertise in Homer is *hikanon* 'sufficient' (*Ion* 531a).[53] Ion is forced to admit that he is an expert in Homer—and Homer only—but he justifies his non-expertise in other poets on the grounds that Homer is superior to all other poets (531a–532c).[54] This formulation suits perfectly a Panathenaic rhapsode, in terms of my argument that Homeric poetry was the only poetry performed by rhapsodes at the Panathenaia in the days of Plato.

3§49 In the context of the Panathenaia, the figure of Homer evolved to the point of becoming the all-sufficient poet, the ultimate generalist in poetry. By the age of Plato, the feast of the Panathenaia could leave no room for any poet other than Homer in the rhapsodic competitions—no Hesiod, no Archilochus—not to mention Orpheus and Musaeus or the poets of the epic Cycle. Only in the citharodic—and the aulodic—competitions at the Panathenaia was there room left for other poets, and these poets had to be non-epic poets, that is, so-called lyric poets like Simonides.

3§50 And yet, all early poets are linked, says Plato's Socrates, to the single and absolute source of poetic or 'musical' inspiration, the Muses. Just as rhapsodes are *hermēneis* 'interpreters' of poets, so also poets are *hermēneis* 'inter-

---

[53] To paraphrase more closely: in Plato *Ion* 531a–532b, when the rhapsode Ion says that he can perform and interpret the poetry of Homer but not the poetry of Hesiod and Archilochus, it is implied that other rhapsodes do indeed perform and interpret the poetry of Hesiod and Archilochus. For further evidence about the rhapsodic performance of Hesiod and Archilochus, see Athenaeus 14.620b-c and the commentary in *PP* (159, 162–163). In the first edition of *PR*, however, I fear I have misled my readers with this phrasing (55): "the rhapsode Ion, who is about to compete in the Panathenaia ([Plato *Ion*] 530b), is represented as a grand master in performing the poetry of Homer and Hesiod, as also of Archilochus (531a)." In the digital edition of *PR*, I rephrase as follows: "the rhapsode Ion, who is about to compete in the Panathenaia (530b), is potentially a grand master in performing Hesiod and even Archilochus, not just Homer (531a); he tells Socrates that he specializes in Homer only because Homer is the best poet and, by implication, the only poet whose poetry is performed by rhapsodes at the Panathenaia (531a–532c)." Then, in the next sentence, I rephrase "The rhapsode is . . ." to read: "As we know from the *Ion* and elsewhere, the generic rhapsode is . . . ."

[54] According to Ion, even where Homer and Hesiod overlap in content, they are different in quality (Plato *Ion* 532a). By contrast, Plato's Socrates is represented as an expert in non-Homeric poetry as well. His expertise in Hesiodic and Orphic traditions is especially to be noted. This expertise, as we will see, shows the mystical side of Socrates, as represented by Protagoras, to be contrasted with his non-mystical side, as represented by Hippias of Elis.

3ⓢ5. Plato's attempt to discredit the Panathenaic standard

preters' of the Muses (*Ion* 535b). I am about to quote a passage from Plato's *Ion* (536a-c) where a collectivized concept of the Muses as a single absolute source of all poetry or 'music'—in the literal sense of *mousikē* 'craft [*tekhnē*] of the Muses'—is expressed by Socrates through the metaphor of the Heraclean or Magnesian stone, that is, the magnet (*Ion* 533d). Poets are imagined as metallic rings directly 'linked' to a prototypical magnet of poetic inspiration, the Muses. Poets, as direct links to the magnet, are the *prōtoi daktulioi* 'first rings'. As we are about to see, Plato's Socrates expresses the direct 'linkage' of the metallic rings to the prototypical magnet by way of the verb *exartân* 'link', which I will translate as 'magnetically link', and he makes it explicit that the poets symbolized by the metallic rings are likewise prototypical, namely, Orpheus, Musaeus, and Homer—in that order:

3ⓣ6 Plato *Ion* 536a-c

> καὶ ὁ μὲν τῶν <u>ποιητῶν</u> ἐξ ἄλλης Μούσης, ὁ δὲ ἐξ ἄλλης <u>ἐξήρτηται</u>. ὀνομάζομεν δὲ <u>αὐτὸ</u> <u>κατέχεται</u>, τὸ δέ {b} ἐστι παραπλήσιον· <u>ἔχεται</u> γάρ. ἐκ δὲ τούτων τῶν <u>πρώτων</u> <u>δακτυλίων</u>, τῶν <u>ποιητῶν</u>, ἄλλοι ἐξ ἄλλου αὖ <u>ἠρτημένοι</u> εἰσὶ καὶ <u>ἐνθουσιάζουσιν</u>, οἱ μὲν ἐξ <u>Ὀρφέως</u>, οἱ δὲ ἐκ <u>Μουσαίου</u>· οἱ δὲ πολλοὶ ἐξ <u>Ὁμήρου</u> <u>κατέχονταί</u> τε καὶ <u>ἔχονται</u>. ὧν σύ, ὦ Ἴων, εἷς εἶ καὶ <u>κατέχῃ</u> ἐξ Ὁμήρου, καὶ ἐπειδὰν μέν τις ἄλλου του ποιητοῦ ᾄδῃ, καθεύδεις τε καὶ ἀπορεῖς ὅτι λέγῃς, ἐπειδὰν δὲ τούτου τοῦ ποιητοῦ φθέγξηταί τις μέλος, εὐθὺς ἐγρήγορας καὶ ὀρχεῖταί σου ἡ ψυχὴ καὶ εὐπορεῖς ὅτι {c} λέγῃς· οὐ γὰρ <u>τέχνῃ</u> οὐδ' <u>ἐπιστήμῃ</u> περὶ Ὁμήρου λέγεις ἃ λέγεις, ἀλλὰ <u>θείᾳ μοίρᾳ</u> καὶ <u>κατοκωχῇ</u>.

> One of the given <u>poets</u> [*poiētai*] is <u>magnetically linked</u> [*exartân*] to one Muse, and another poet [*poiētēs*] to another Muse.[55] And we express <u>this idea</u> [= *auto* 'it' = passive of *exartân* = 'is magnetically linked to'] by saying '<u>is possessed by</u>' [= passive of *katekhein*]. And it [= the idea of 'is possessed by'] is pretty much the same sort of thing, since he [= the poet] is literally '<u>held fast</u>' [= passive of *ekhein*] [by the Muse]. Then, from these <u>first rings</u>, that is, from the <u>poets</u> [*poiētai*], each different person is <u>magnetically linked</u> [*artân*] to a different poet [*poiētēs*], <u>becoming divinely possessed</u> [= *enthousiazein* = becoming *entheos*]: some persons are magnetically linked

---

[55] I translate *poiētēs* as 'poet' for now, but it is more accurate to render it as 'composer' (in the verbal arts). On *poiētēs* as 'composer', I offer an analysis in *HPC* I§62.

375

to <u>Orpheus</u>, some to <u>Musaeus</u>, and the majority, to <u>Homer</u>; they [= these persons] are <u>possessed</u> [= passive of <u>katekhein</u>] [by the poets], and they are literally '<u>held fast</u>' [= passive of <u>ekhein</u>].[56] You, Ion, are one of these persons, and you are <u>possessed</u> [= passive of <u>katekhein</u>] by Homer. When anyone sings the poetry of any other poet, you are asleep and do not know what to say, but when anyone voices the song of this poet [= Homer], then, right away, you are awake and your spirit is dancing and you know very well what to say. For you say what you say about Homer not by means of a <u>craft</u> [<u>tekhnē</u>] or <u>expertise</u> [<u>epistēmē</u>] but rather by means of a <u>god-given legacy</u> [<u>moira</u>] and a <u>state of possession</u> [<u>katokōkhē</u>].

3§51 Of supreme importance is the image of the First Rings (*prōtoi daktulioi*) as visualized here in Plato's *Ion* (536b). The First Rings are symbols for the three First Poets, named here as Orpheus, Musaeus, and Homer—in that order. It is made clear that the performers of Homer outnumber by far the performers of Orpheus and Musaeus in the era of Socrates. One such performer of Homer is Ion the rhapsode, described as a Middle Ring in comparison to Homer. By implication, performers of Orpheus and Musaeus are likewise Middle Rings in comparison to Orpheus and Musaeus themselves, who are First Rings like Homer. As my argumentation proceeds, the image of the First Rings as symbols for First Poets will become ever more significant.

3§52 A figure like Ion, as a rhapsode, is not a prototypical poet. He is no First Ring. He is not even a poet. As a performer, the rhapsode is merely a Middle Ring linked magnetically to one of the First Rings, in this case, to Homer. Performers of epic and of drama are Middle Rings in relation to the poets of epic and of drama, who are First Rings, whereas the audiences watching rhapsodes performing Homer—and the audiences watching actors performing drama in the theater—are the Last Rings:

3①7 Plato *Ion* 535e–536a

ΣΩ. οἶσθα οὖν ὅτι οὗτός ἐστιν ὁ <u>θεατὴς</u> τῶν δακτυλίων ὁ <u>ἔσχατος</u>, ὧν ἐγὼ ἔλεγον ὑπὸ τῆς Ἡρακλειώτιδος λίθου ἀπ' ἀλλήλων τὴν δύναμιν λαμβάνειν; ὁ δὲ <u>μέσος</u> σὺ ὁ {536 a} <u>ῥαψῳδὸς</u> καὶ <u>ὑποκριτής</u>, ὁ δὲ <u>πρῶτος</u> αὐτὸς ὁ <u>ποιητής</u>.

---

[56] Plato's image of three First Rings as three First Poets Orpheus, Musaeus, and Homer (in that order) is relevant, as we will see at a later point, to his image of the Ring of Hippias.

3⑤5. Plato's attempt to discredit the Panathenaic standard

SOCRATES: Of course you know that this person we talked about, the spectator [*theatēs*] in the audience, is the last of the rings—I mean, the rings that get their power from each other through the force of the Heraclean stone. The middle ring is the rhapsode—that's you [= Ion]—as well as the actor [*hupokritēs*]. And the first ring is the Poet [*poiētēs*] himself.

3§53 In introducing this passage, I deliberately used a visual metaphor when I said that the audiences of epic and of drama were 'watching' the performers, not just 'listening' to them. The wording in the passage makes it explicit that the audiences are 'spectators', that is, *theatai*. In using the word *theatēs* 'spectator' here in the *Ion* (535e), Plato's Socrates makes no distinction between the audiences who attend performances of Homeric epic at the Panathenaia and the audiences who attend performances of drama at the City Dionysia and other dramatic festivals.[57] The audiences of both epic and drama are the 'last' ring. Then there is the 'middle' ring, and Socrates places Ion the rhapsode into this category, along with the generic *hupokritēs* 'actor' of drama.

3§54 In order to discredit Ion, Plato's Socrates has in effect disconnected the prestige of Ion as the performer of Homeric poetry from the prestige of Homer as the notional composer of Homeric poetry. This way, the prestige of Homer is not directly challenged, just as the prestige of Homeric poetry as the

---

[57] The theatrical mentality of the Athenians is ostentatiously deplored by Kleon in a speech recreated by Thucydides 3.38.4: in this speech, Kleon criticizes the Athenians as *theatai men tōn logōn . . . akroatai de tōn ergōn* 'spectators of words, audiences of deeds'. The speaker's point here is that theater is so much a part of the lives of Athenians that they treat the real things that people say about real things that people do <u>as if all these things were theatrical spectacles</u>. Thus the Athenians become *theatai* 'spectators' of real things being said as if these things were theatrical lines being delivered by professional performers, and they imagine things done off stage, as it were, by merely hearing these things instead of seeing them for themselves. Significantly, the speaker in this passage from Thucydides (3.38.4) starts the wording of his criticism by saying that the Athenians are acting like perverted *agōnothetai* 'arrangers of the competitions [*agōnes*]' (*kakōs agōnothetountes*). As we saw earlier from the Aristotelian *Constitution of the Athenians* (60.1), ten magistrates called *athlothetai* 'arrangers of the contests [*athloi*]' were elected every four years to organize the festival of the Panathenaia, and one of their primary tasks was the management of 'the *agōn* in *mousikē*'. According to Plutarch's *Pericles* (13.9–11), as we also saw earlier, the Athenian statesman Pericles reformed this competition in *mousikē* when he was elected as one of the *athlothetai*. At a later point in the same speech of Kleon as recreated by Thucydides (3.38.7), there is talk about *theatai* 'spectators' of *sophistai* 'sophists' (σοφιστῶν θεαταῖς). This is the only attestation of *sophistēs* in Thucydides. I am reminded of the scene in Isocrates *Panathenaicus* (12.33) where *sophistai* 'sophists' are pictured as performing and commenting in the Lyceum on the poetry of Homer, Hesiod and others. For more on the passage from Thucydides (3.38.4), I await the forthcoming publication of José González.

Chapter Three

premier poetic event of the Panathenaia cannot be challenged. The idea of Homer as the all-sufficient and all-encompassing Poet is a given. It is already a historical reality.

3§55 The dominant status of Homeric poetry is not the only historical reality relevant to the argument in Plato's *Ion*. Another reality is the dominant status of the actual craft of rhapsodically performing—and interpreting—Homeric poetry at the Panathenaia in the dramatic time of Plato's dialogues. I say craft in view of the explicit designation *rhapsōidikē tekhnē* 'rhapsodic craft' as we see it applied by Plato's Socrates at later stages of his argumentation in the *Ion* (538b, 538c, 538d, 539e, 540a, 540d, 541a). Thus the *rhapsōidikē tekhnē* 'rhapsodic craft' of the Panathenaic rhapsode is another given. It too is already a historical reality.

3§56 At the earliest stages of his argumentation in the *Ion*, however, Plato's Socrates avoids referring to this *tekhnē* of the rhapsode. Instead, he speaks only about the overall craft of the poet, which is designated as *poiētikē tekhnē* 'poetic craft', and he induces Ion to admit that this craft is a *holon*, an integral whole, just like other *tekhnai* (532c). (For the moment, I translate *poiētikē* as 'poetic craft', but it is more accurate to render this word as 'craft of composition', since the *poiētēs* as 'poet' is the composer *par excellence* in the verbal arts.) Then Socrates induces Ion to admit that the craft of painters, *graphikē tekhnē*, is likewise a *holon* 'whole' (532e), and that craftsmen are like painters—and sculptors, he adds—in that they need to be experts in the totality of their respective crafts (532e–533b). By the time he speaks about the craft of sculptors, Plato's Socrates has already omitted the word *tekhnē*. This omission facilitates his transition to the passage I have already quoted about craftsmen such as auletes and citharists and citharodes and rhapsodes (*Ion* 533b–c). Far from speaking of these craftsmen as representatives of separate crafts, Plato's Socrates groups them together as representatives of a single craft, to which he had referred earlier as that integral whole, the *poiētikē tekhnē*. How could it be, asks Socrates, that any one of these craftsmen—auletes and citharists and citharodes and rhapsodes—could fail to be an expert in that integral whole, in that single craft of theirs, that is, in the *poiētikē tekhnē*? Ion, who has already accepted the premise that the *poiētikē tekhnē* is an integral whole, a *holon*, is now forced to admit that he simply cannot claim to be such an expert: instead, Ion is an expert only in one aspect of that craft, that is, in Homeric poetry (533c).

3§57 Next, Plato's Socrates induces Ion to accept the idea that the rhapsode's profession is therefore not even a matter of *tekhnē* but rather, a matter of inspiration (*Ion* 533e). By implication, the rhapsode is an expert only in the

3§5. Plato's attempt to discredit the Panathenaic standard

craft of *mousikē*, the craft of the Muse who inspires poets, not in the craft of the poet himself, that is, in the craft of *poiētikē*. This way, as we have already seen, Ion's authority as a rhapsode can still be validated as 'magnetically' linked to the authority of Homer as poet, which in turn is 'magnetically' linked to the authority of his inspiring Muse as the ultimate source—the ultimate inspiration. Once Ion accepts this idea, however, his authority as a thinker is thereby discredited: he has in effect admitted that, as a rhapsode, he has no mind of his own and simply speaks the mind of Homer. Only after the rhapsode has accepted the idea that he is an inspired performer does Socrates start speaking openly about the 'rhapsodic craft', *rhapsōidikē tekhnē*, in his continued dialogue with the rhapsode. By now it is safe for Socrates to speak this way. Since Ion has already been discredited as a thinker, he cannot invoke his prestigious rhapsodic craft as a source for independent thinking. Even the prestige of Homeric knowledge—to the extent that the rhapsode derives it from his rhapsodic craft—has been diminished: by now the rhapsode's general knowledge seems less impressive than the specialized knowledge that other craftsmen derive from their own specialized crafts.

3§58 From the standpoint of a rhapsode, Ion's mistake in the Platonic dialogue named after him is that he missed the chance of asserting, from the very start, that there was indeed such a thing as a 'rhapsodic craft', a *rhapsōidikē tekhnē*. He also missed the chance of asserting that the prestige of this distinct craft was superior to the prestige of other distinct crafts such as those represented by auletes and citharists and maybe even citharodes—at least, at the Panathenaia.[58]

3§59 As the craft of rhapsodically performing Homeric poetry evolved in the context of 'musical' competitions at the Panathenaia, it had reached a level of prestige that overshadowed other forms of performance as they too evolved in the context of competitions at the same festival. I have already quoted the passage where these other forms are listed alongside the premier form, that is,

---

[58] I mentioned earlier a fourth-century inscription from Eretria that records the awarding of prizes at a festival of Artemis featuring competitions in *mousikē* (*IG* XII ix 189, 341/340 BCE). In this inscription, we find that the first prize awarded to the winner of the competition among citharodes is greater in monetary value than the first prize awarded to the winner of the competition among rhapsodes. (Commentary in *PR* 39-53.) I conjecture that the situation would be different in Athens (and probably only in Athens) in the same era. In Athens, as I have argued, the rhapsodic competition was paramount because it was restricted to Homer—and to the performance of the complete Homer. Here I refer back to my earlier discussion of a fourth-century inscription from Athens that records the awarding of prizes at the Panathenaia (*IG* II² 2311, 380 BCE). As we saw, the part of the inscription that records the awarding of prizes to the winners of the competition among the rhapsodes is unfortunately missing.

Chapter Three

alongside the craft of rhapsodically performing Homeric poetry. Viewing by hindsight the Socratic attempt to shade over the importance of the premier form, I now requote the passage in order to highlight this importance:

3①8 Plato *Ion* 533b-c

ΣΩ. Ἀλλὰ μήν, ὥς γ' ἐγὼ οἶμαι, οὐδ' ἐν αὐλήσει γε οὐδὲ ἐν κιθαρίσει οὐδὲ ἐν κιθαρῳδίᾳ οὐδὲ ἐν ῥαψῳδίᾳ οὐδεπώποτ' εἶδες ἄνδρα ὅστις περὶ μὲν Ὀλύμπου δεινός ἐστιν ἐξηγεῖσθαι ἢ περὶ Θαμύρου ἢ περὶ Ὀρφέως ἢ περὶ Φημίου τοῦ Ἰθακησίου ῥαψῳδοῦ, περὶ δὲ Ἴωνος τοῦ Ἐφεσίου [ῥαψῳδοῦ] ἀπορεῖ καὶ οὐκ ἔχει συμβαλέσθαι ἅ τε εὖ ῥαψῳδεῖ καὶ ἃ μή.

SOCRATES: Here is another thing. As far as I can tell, neither in [1] playing on the *aulos* [= *aulēsis*] nor in [2] playing on the *kithara* [= *kitharisis*] nor in [3] singing and playing on the *kithara* [= *kitharōidia*] nor in [4] performing as a rhapsode [= *rhapsōidia*] have you seen any man who is skilled at explaining about [1] Olympos or about [2] Thamyras or about [3] Orpheus or about [4] Phemios of Ithaca, the rhapsode—but who is perplexed about Ion of Ephesus and is unable to formulate what things Ion performs well as a rhapsode [= verb of *rhapsōidos*] and what things he does not.

3§60 In this catalogue of various crafts of performing various kinds of 'music' at the Panathenaia, Plato's Socrates shades over the historical fact that the repertoire of rhapsodes who competed at the Panathenaia was by this time restricted to Homeric poetry, whereas the repertoire of, say, the citharodes or *kithara*-singers was not restricted to the poetry of any single master of lyric.[59] Plato's Socrates makes it look like a deficiency that Ion the rhapsode performs—and interprets—Homer and only Homer. Philosophically, this specialization may indeed be a deficiency, but, historically, it is a clear indication of the prestige inherent in the craft of performing the epic of Homer in Athens.

3§61 In the passage I just requoted from Plato's *Ion* (533b-c), the wording shows that any rhapsode who competes at the Panathenaia practices the craft of a performer, not the craft of a composer. The same holds for the crafts of the auletes and the citharists and the citharodes. All such craftsmen are being viewed as performers at festivals like the Panathenaia, not as composers. As

---

[59] In *HPC* I§I§47 and following, I consider two lyric masters whose repertoires were sung at the Panathenaia, Anacreon and Simonides.

3§5. Plato's attempt to discredit the Panathenaic standard

we take a closer look at the same passage, we discover that this view extends also to the prototypes of these craftsmen, that is, to Olympos, Thamyras, Orpheus, and Phemios. All four of these prototypical figures are viewed here as performers in their own right, not as composers per se.

3§62 The specialization of these four prototypes of Panathenaic performance is most striking in the case of Phemios, who is being equated in this passage with the figure of an archetypal 'rhapsode'. Plato's Socrates exploits this equation to further his philosophical agenda. We have already seen that the rhapsode can perform and even interpret the content of what he performs at the Panathenaia, that is, the epics of Homer, but he is not the composer of this content. Therefore the rhapsode is not a poet. If Phemios is a rhapsode, then he is not a *poiētēs* 'poet' in the literal sense of this word: he is not the 'maker' of the content. Only Homer can be said to *poieîn* 'make' the content of Homeric poetry.[60]

3§63 From what we have already seen about Phemios, we can picture him as a self-representation of Homer in Homer. And yet, the self that is Homer changes over time. When Phemios is equated with a rhapsode in Plato's *Ion*, this equation implies that Phemios is no longer a poet like Homer, since the rhapsode who competes at the Panathenaia is no composer like Homer but merely a performer of Homer. To equate the Panathenaic rhapsode with the self-represented Homer that is Phemios is to detract from Homer the Poet. If Phemios in the Homeric *Odyssey* is merely performing but not composing, like some rhapsode competing at the Panathenaia, then he has no say about determining the content of what he performs. Such a recreated Homer can only say what Homer is saying. And what exactly is it that Homer is saying? According to Plato's Socrates, Homer in turn can only say what the Muses are saying.

3§64 Thus Plato's Socrates exploits the equating of Phemios with a rhapsode by using it as proof for his argument that the rhapsode has no mind of his own when he performs Homer. This argument, however, can be used to discredit the rhapsode only if the craft of the rhapsode has already been discredited. Plato's Socrates has managed to accomplish that by initially eliding the fact that the rhapsode has his own *tekhnē* 'craft', the *rhapsōidikē tekhnē*. The rhapsode's understanding of Homer, in terms of this *tekhnē*, does not need to be separated from the idea that the rhapsode is inspired by the Muses of Homer. In terms of this *tekhnē*, the professional conceit of the Panathenaic rhapsode is that he reads, as it were, the mind of Homer. The

---

[60] This word *poieîn* 'make' can be used in the sense of 'compose' (in the verbal arts).

rhapsode's mind has learned the 'meaning' or *dianoia* of Homer (*Ion* 530b–c).[61] The living proof of this conceit is the rhapsode's capacity to perform Homer by heart at the Panathenaia and to be the perfect *hermēneus* 'interpreter' of Homer (*Ion* 530c).[62]

3§65 What, then, is the poetry of Homer for the rhapsode? As we saw in the passage I quoted earlier from Isocrates (*Panegyricus* 159), Homeric *poiēsis* 'poetry' is a *tekhnē* 'craft' that is activated in two linked contexts: (1) the Panathenaic *athloi* 'contests' of rhapsodes in *mousikē* 'musical craft' and (2) the *paideusis* 'education' of the young. The wording of Isocrates, as quoted above, makes it clear that Homeric poetry is a *tekhnē* 'craft' in its own right, and that it counts as part of the overall *mousikē* 'musical craft' of the Panathenaic *athloi* 'contests' (*Panegyricus* 159).

3§66 Unlike Isocrates, however, who implicitly identifies the craft of the rhapsode with the craft of Homer, Plato seeks to make a distinction between the two crafts. He does this by implicitly making a distinction between the crafts of *mousikē* and *poiētikē*, as if the rhapsode were an expert only in the craft of *mousikē*, not in the craft of *poiētikē*.

3§67 Already at the very beginning of the *Ion*, Plato's Socrates had drawn Ion's attention away from Homeric poetry as a *tekhnē* 'craft' in its own right by speaking instead about the more general concept of *poiētikē tekhnē* 'poetic craft'. Once Socrates induces Ion to admit that the *poiētikē tekhnē* is a *holon* 'whole' (532c), much like the *tekhnai* 'crafts' of painting and sculpting (532e–533b), he has already succeeded in discrediting the craft of performing and teaching Homeric *poiēsis* 'poetry'. Such performing and teaching is in effect the *rhapsōidikē tekhnē* of Ion. In order to emphasize the universalized importance of Ion's craft, I repeat once again the formulation of Isocrates: the *tekhnē* 'craft' of Homeric *poiēsis* 'poetry' is coextensive with the *paideusis* 'education' of the young. Ion has unwittingly discredited his own *tekhnē* once he admits that he is a specialist in Homer. Moreover, in order to validate his specialty, he is forced to deny that his *tekhnē* is really a *tekhnē*.

3§68 Plato's Socrates has forced Ion to make a choice: the rhapsode's authority comes either from inspiration or from the *poiētikē tekhnē*, the craft of poetry. Ion is forced to choose inspiration as the source of his ultimate authority, since that inspiration comes ultimately from the Muses of Homer. Ion is not allowed to claim the craft of poetry as his ultimate authority because he is forced to admit that he is a master in only one aspect of that craft, that is,

---

[61] PR 29–30.
[62] PR 29.

3⊚5. Plato's attempt to discredit the Panathenaic standard

in Homeric poetry. Moreover, he is a master in only two of three aspects of that poetry, that is, in performing and interpreting it; he not a master in the third aspect, that is, in composing Homeric poetry.

3§69 Plato's *Ion* has to make a choice that a rhapsode need not have had to make, between *tekhnē* and inspiration. Provided the rhapsode insists that his craft is really a craft, a specialized *rhapsōidikē tekhnē* instead of the generalized *poiētikē tekhnē*, he can have his own *tekhnē* and still claim to be inspired by the Muses of Homer. With his specialized craft, he can lay claim to the generalized and even universalized *paideusis* 'education' represented by the *poiēsis* 'poetry' of Homer, since his *rhapsōidikē tekhnē* is part of the overall *mousikē tekhnē* of performing at the Panathenaia.

3§70 The time has come to summarize the distinctions in the meanings of *rhapsōidikē*, *mousikē*, and *poiētikē* as applied to the word *tekhnē* 'craft' in the age of Plato. The *rhapsōidikē tekhnē* is the craft of performing recitative poetry at *agōnes* / *athloi* 'contests, competitions', especially at the Panathenaia. The *mousikē tekhnē* is the craft of performing (1) recitative poetry or (2) song and / or (3) instrumental 'music' (in the modern sense of the word) at these same *agōnes* / *athloi* 'contests, competitions'. The *poiētikē tekhnē* is the craft of composing—but not necessarily performing—in the media of *mousikē tekhnē* that we have seen so far and in other media as well, including tragedy, comedy, dithyramb, satyr drama, and so on. In the opening of Aristotle's *Poetics*, which is, in Greek terms, a discourse about *poiētikē tekhnē*, we see a definition that validates in many ways the working definition that I have just offered:

3①9 Aristotle *Poetics* 1447a8–18

> περὶ <u>ποιητικῆς</u> αὐτῆς τε καὶ τῶν <u>εἰδῶν</u> αὐτῆς, ἥν τινα δύναμιν ἕκαστον ἔχει, καὶ πῶς δεῖ συνίστασθαι τοὺς <u>μύθους</u> εἰ μέλλει καλῶς ἕξειν ἡ <u>ποίησις</u>, ἔτι δὲ ἐκ πόσων καὶ ποίων ἐστὶ μορίων, ὁμοίως δὲ καὶ περὶ τῶν ἄλλων ὅσα τῆς αὐτῆς ἐστι μεθόδου, λέγωμεν ἀρξάμενοι κατὰ φύσιν πρῶτον ἀπὸ τῶν πρώτων. <u>ἐποποιία</u> δὴ καὶ ἡ τῆς <u>τραγῳδίας ποίησις</u> ἔτι δὲ <u>κωμῳδία</u> καὶ <u>ἡ διθυραμβοποιητικὴ</u> καὶ τῆς <u>αὐλητικῆς</u> ἡ πλείστη καὶ <u>κιθαριστικῆς</u> πᾶσαι τυγχάνουσιν οὖσαι <u>μιμήσεις</u> τὸ σύνολον· διαφέρουσι δὲ ἀλλήλων τρισίν, ἢ γὰρ τῷ ἐν ἑτέροις <u>μιμεῖσθαι</u> ἢ τῷ ἕτερα ἢ τῷ ἑτέρως καὶ μὴ τὸν αὐτὸν τρόπον.
>
> Concerning <u>poetic craft</u> [<u>poiētikē (tekhnē)</u>] in and of itself, and its <u>forms</u> [<u>eidos</u> (plural)], and what potential each form has; and how <u>mythical plots</u> [<u>muthoi</u>] must be put together if the <u>poetic composition</u> [<u>poiēsis</u>] is to be good at doing what it does; and how many parts

Chapter Three

it is made of, and what kinds of parts they are; and, likewise, all other questions that belong to the same line of inquiry—let us speak about all these things by starting, in accordance with the natural order, from first principles. So, the composition of epic [*epopoiia* = the *poiēsis* of *epos*] and the composition [*poiēsis*] of tragedy, as well as comedy and the poetic craft [*poiētikē* (*tekhnē*)] of the dithyramb and most sorts of crafts related to the *aulos* and the *kithara*—all of these crafts, as it happens, are instances of re-enactment [*mimēsis*],[63] taken as a whole. There are three things that make these instances of re-enactment different from each other: [1] re-enacting [*mimeîsthai*] things in different media, or [2] re-enacting different things, or [3] re-enacting in a mode [*tropos*] that is different and not the same as the other modes.

3§71 In Aristotle's catalogue of genres of *poiētikē tekhnē* 'poetic craft' we can see the dimension of performance, not only the dimension of composition. Essentially, his catalogue corresponds to the program of performances that took place at the two greatest festivals of the Athenian state. At the City Dionysia of Athens, there were competitions in the performances of tragedies, comedies, dithyrambs, and satyr dramas. At the Panathenaia of Athens, as we have already seen, there were competitions in the performances of epic, of *kithara*-singing and / or -playing, and of *aulos*-singing and / or -playing. From the wording of Aristotle, it is clear that each of these genres is associated with a distinct *tekhnē* 'craft'. That is, the overall *poiētikē tekhnē* 'poetic craft' is subdivided into a variety of specialized *tekhnai*. Among these specialized *tekhnai* is the composition of epic, which as we know corresponds to the performance of epic by rhapsodes at the Panathenaia. The term that Aristotle uses here for the composing of 'epic', *epopoiia* 'making of *epos*', indicates a most general concept, since the word used to designate 'epic,' *epē* (= *epos* plural), is simply the general word for any kind of verbal art created by way of *poiēsis*.[64] And yet, the whole of Aristotle's *Poetics*—and in fact the whole of Aristotle's works in general—operates on the understanding that the only epics of Homer were the *Iliad* and *Odyssey*. So epic as a genre is viewed in a specialized way, even though the wording used to express the idea of epic is expressed in a most generalized way. Even the wording of Aristotle indicates, of and by itself, that the compo-

---

[63] Here the word is in the plural, and I render it as 'instances of re-enactment'.
[64] BA 2§5n2 (= p. 30), 12§15n3 (= p. 236), 12§17 (= p. 237), 14§14n5(= p. 264), 15§§6–8 (= pp. 270–272), 18§4n3 (= p. 304), 20§8n5 (= p. 325).

3§5. Plato's attempt to discredit the Panathenaic standard

sition of Homeric poetry had achieved the most generalized status as poetry par excellence.

3§72 By contrast with the composition of Homeric poetry, we have seen in Plato's *Ion* that the actual performance of this poetry had achieved a most specialized status as the craft of the rhapsode, *rhapsōidikē tekhnē*. For Plato's Socrates, this craft is no craft at all, and only the overall *poiētikē tekhnē* may be considered as a *holon*, a 'whole', comparable to the categories of painting or sculpting, each of which is likewise a craft that may be considered as a whole. As a category, the generalized craft of composing poetry cannot have as a subcategory the specialized craft of composing Homeric poetry—let alone any specialized craft of performing Homeric poetry. Plato's thinking here is contradicted by Aristotle's *Poetics*, where the generalized craft of composing poetry is a category that can in fact have as a subcategory the specialized craft of composing Homeric poetry—though this specialized craft is expressed in a most generalized way.

3§73 Returning to Plato's *Ion*, I conclude that the discrediting of the rhapsode's craft, the *rhapsōidikē tekhnē*, can be countered by reconsidering this craft in its own historical context. The prestige of the rhapsodic *tekhnē* is evidently a threat to the philosophical *tekhnē* of Plato's Socrates. As we saw, the rhapsode is not only a performer of Homer: he is also the *hermēneus* 'interpreter' of Homer (*Ion* 530c).To speak ably about Homer, says Ion, is the most important aspect of his *tekhnē* 'craft' (*Ion* 530c). Homer in turn is recognized as the ultimate source of *paideusis* 'education' for the Hellenes (Plato *Republic* 2.376e–398b; 10.599c–d, 606e).[65] As an exponent of this *paideusis* 'education', the rhapsode is in effect a significant rival of the philosopher. I will have more to say later about this rivalry.

3§74 How, then, can the rhapsode defend himself against the dialectic of Plato's Socrates? In order to maintain Homer as a generalist in the *poiētikē tekhnē*, the rhapsode must insist on being a specialist in the *rhapsōidikē tekhnē*. That way, he maintains a prestige that is coextensive with the prestige of Homer as a universal educator of Hellenes. Since the rhapsode, as a master of the *rhapsōidikē tekhnē*, is a specialist performer but not a specialist composer, he cannot be considered a master of the *poiētikē tekhnē*. Since the rhapsode is a specialist in performing recitative poetry, to the exclusion of other forms of poetry as also of song and 'music' (in the modern sense of the word), he cannot be considered a master of the *mousikē tekhnē*, either.

---

[65] See also the commentary of Murray 1996:205.

Chapter Three

3§75 A qualification is needed here. Though the rhapsode as a master of the *rhapsōidikē tekhnē* cannot be a master of *mousikē tekhnē* in the time of Plato, things must have been different in an earlier time. I have in mind a prehistoric time—back when the craft of the rhapsode could still be understood in a less restricted sense that matched the literal meaning of *mousikē tekhnē*, the 'craft of the Muses'. If the rhapsode of prehistoric time was truly master of the 'craft of the Muses', then surely he was capable of inspiration by the Muses, and, just as surely, he was also capable of composing as well as performing. Even the etymology of the word *rhapsōidos*, 'he who sews the songs together', indicates that the rhapsode of prehistoric time had this capability.[66]

3§76 But Plato has taken away from the rhapsode the *tekhnē* of *mousikē* as a true *tekhnē* or 'craft'. As far as Plato is concerned, the rhapsode cannot really have a *tekhnē* or 'craft' if he is really inspired by the Muses. That craft belongs only to the poet, who is Homer. For Plato, Homer is the inspired creator or poet, whereas the rhapsode is merely an inspired re-creator. The rhapsode is merely a Second Ring to Homer's First Ring, just as the actor of drama is merely a Second Ring to the poets of drama, who are First Rings like Homer. The magnetic force of the Magnesian Stone, which is the source of inspiration by the Muses, attracts rhapsodes and actors only as re-creators, not as the creators who are the poets themselves—poets who have mastered the craft of the Muses as a true craft.

Excursus on Plato's *Laws*

3§77 This magnetic force emanating from the Magnesian Stone in the *Ion* of Plato becomes a virtual reality in the Magnesian State that is taking shape in the *Laws* of Plato. I propose that this ideal state in the making, which is a construct of Plato's *Laws*, is literally named after the magnetic force of inspiration from the Muses, which was a construct of Plato's *Ion*. That is the essence of Magnesia as Plato's chosen name for the virtual reality of this new ideal state, built on the foundation of the old ideal state that was his *Republic*.[67]

3§78 In the old ideal state of Plato's *Republic*, Homer needed to be banned as the primary representative of the *poiētikē tekhnē*, the craft of the Poet. As

---

[66] PP 61–74.
[67] The status of Magnesia as a virtual reality is indicated by the mystical references in Plato's *Laws* to 'the city of the Magnetes' as a new place that is to be 'resurrected'—by way of being relocated in western Crete from an old place that is to exist no more (11.919d Μαγνήτων, οὓς ὁ θεὸς ἀνορθῶν πάλιν κατοικίζει, 12.946b Μαγνήτων ἡ κατὰ θεὸν πάλιν τυχοῦσα σωτηρίας πόλις). Plato's choice of a name for this ideal city is made to seem arbitrary (12.969a σὺ γὰρ τὴν Μαγνήτων πόλιν, ᾗ ᾧ ἂν θεὸς ἐπώνυμον αὐτὴν ποιήσῃ, and also at 4.704a).

3ⓢ5. Plato's attempt to discredit the Panathenaic standard

for the new ideal state of Magnesia in Plato's *Laws*, would Homer need to be banned from here as well? No, not really—not if we think retrospectively in terms of all the works produced by Plato before his final work, the *Laws*. In those previous works, especially in the *Ion*, Homer figured as the primary representative of two crafts—not only the *poiētikē tekhnē*, the craft of poets, but also the *mousikē tekhnē*, the craft of the Muses. So why would there be a need to ban from the city of the inspiring Muses someone who is actually inspired by the Muses?

3§79 Still, even if Homer may not need to be banned from Magnesia, the question remains whether he is any longer really needed there. As Richard Martin argues persuasively, there is really no place left for Homer in the world of *mousikē* that is taking shape in Plato's *Laws*.[68] This magnetic world of *mousikē*, the virtual city of Magnesia, is inspired ultimately by the Muses of philosophy, not by the Muses of poetry and songmaking.

3§80 The *mousikē* of philosophy is all-pervasive in Plato's *Laws* (a shining example is 2.658e–659a). And the pattern has already been set in Plato's earlier works. In the *Phaedrus* (259d), for example, the Muses Kalliope and Ourania are explicitly named as the transcendent Muses of this *mousikē* of philosophy: Plato's cicadas report to these two Muses the good deeds of philosophers, since it is the *mousikē* of Kalliope and Ourania that philosophers hold in honor (τῇ δὲ πρεσβυτάτῃ Καλλιόπῃ καὶ τῇ μετ' αὐτὴν Οὐρανίᾳ τοὺς ἐν φιλοσοφίᾳ διάγοντάς τε καὶ τιμῶντας τὴν ἐκείνων μουσικὴν ἀγγέλλουσιν).

3§81 It is in Plato's *Phaedo* 61a–b that we see the most suggestive reference to this *mousikē* of philosophy. I offer here an analysis of the passage. Plato's Socrates describes philosophy itself as the greatest form of *mousikē* (ὡς φιλοσοφίας μὲν οὔσης μεγίστης μουσικῆς), to be contrasted with any given poetic form of *mousikē*, which is by contrast provincial because it is 'local' or 'popular', that is, *dēmōdēs* (ταύτην τὴν δημώδη μουσικὴν ποιεῖν). As Socrates says, he had a dream in which an oracular voice kept telling him to make this poetic kind of *mousikē*, and he then decided that this *mousikē* would in fact be quite appropriate for marking the occasion of Apollo's *heortē* 'festival'—which was also to be the occasion of his own death. So Socrates proceeded to compose two kinds of poetry as his swan song. One kind was a *Hymn to Apollo*, a form of poetry identified with Homer himself by the *Homēridai* in the era of Plato.[69] And the other kind of poetry was a set of *muthoi* 'myths' by Aesop that Socrates

---

[68] Martin (forthcoming).
[69] In the twin book *Homer the Preclassic*, I argue that the *Homeric Hymn to Apollo* was for the *Homēridai* the authentic signature, as it were, of Homer himself, and that this link between the *Hymn* and the *Homēridai* was well understood in the fifth and fourth centuries BCE.

turned into verse. This terminal gesture that Plato's Socrates makes toward the *mousikē* of poetry puts Homer in his place. The most exalted representative of poetry, Homer the Poet par excellence, is paired here with his lowlife counterpart Aesop: both are described as exponents of *muthos*, which Socrates links with the discourse of poetry, contrasting it with *logos*, which he links with the discourse of philosophy: μετὰ δὲ τὸν θεόν, ἐννοήσας ὅτι τὸν ποιητὴν δέοι, εἴπερ μέλλοι ποιητὴς εἶναι, ποιεῖν μύθους ἀλλ' οὐ λόγους, καὶ αὐτὸς οὐκ ἦ μυθολογικός, διὰ ταῦτα δὴ οὓς προχείρους εἶχον μύθους καὶ ἠπιστάμην τοὺς Αἰσώπου, τούτων ἐποίησα οἷς πρώτοις ἐνέτυχον 'then, after finishing with the god [= after I finished composing my *Hymn to Apollo* in my terminal role as a poet], here is what I did: keeping in mind that the poet must, if he is really going to be a poet, make [*poieîn*] *muthoi* and not *logoi*, and that I was no expert in the discourse of myth [*muthologikos*], I took some *muthoi* of Aesop that I knew and had at hand, and I made poetry [*poieîn*] out of the first few of these that I happened upon'.[70] Once Plato's Socrates performs this terminal gesture toward the *mousikē* of poetry, Homer the Poet par excellence will no longer really be needed for the *mousikē* of philosophy in the works of Plato.

3§82 From the standpoint of the overall philosophical legacy of Plato's Socrates, the *mousikē* of philosophy will survive his death in Plato's *Phaedo*. It will live on in Plato's *Laws*, that is, it will live on in a virtual city named after the magnetic force of inspiration emanating from the Muses of philosophy. And these inspiring Muses of philosophy will surely not need Homer as master of the *mousikē tekhnē*.

3§83 The Cretan setting for the foundation of Magnesia as an ideal city of *mousikē tekhnē* is relevant here. The Cretan speaker in the dialogue of Plato's *Laws*, Kleinias, has already observed that Homer is alien to Crete even before there is any talk about the foundation of Magnesia on that island (*Laws* 3.680c). Richard Martin has drawn attention to this observation made by the Cretan.[71] He notes that the Cretan's reference to Homeric poetry as *xenika poiēmata* 'unfamiliar poems' (again, 3.680c) highlights the Athenocentrism of the anonymous Athenian speaker in the *Laws*, who has just finished making a quotation from Homeric poetry in order to make a point about distinctions between more and less primitive phases of civilization (3.680b). And it also highlights the Athenocentrism of Homer himself, whose poetry is owned by

---

[70] Instead of 'I took some *muthoi* of Aesop that I knew and had at hand', I was tempted to translate 'I took some *muthoi* of Aesop that I knew and had at my fingertips'.

[71] Martin (forthcoming).

3⑤5. Plato's attempt to discredit the Panathenaic standard

the Athenians on the occasion of their premier festival, the Panathenaia. Such a sense of Athenian ownership, as we have seen, is quite evident in Plato's *Ion*.

3§84 In this light, I focus on the adjective used by the Cretan in condescendingly complimenting the poetic abilities of Homer: the Poet, he says, is *kharieis* 'graceful' (*Laws* 3.680c). This term, I argue, is a technical expression used by Athenian intellectuals in the fourth century and thereafter in referring to those poetic qualities of Homer that make him truly Homeric: as we will see later, there is an example of such usage in Isocrates (12) *Panathenaicus* 17-19.[72] How, then, are we to interpret the use of such a term by the Cretan in the *Laws*? I would say that Plato here is playing on a theme of feigned ignorance, which is a proverbial characteristic of Cretans. At the very moment when the Cretan is claiming that Cretans are generally unfamiliar with Homer, he is using a term that demonstrates his own familiarity with Athenian ways of thinking about Homer.

3§85 In Magnesia as their own city of inspiration, the Muses of philosophy will reorganize their craft as the new *mousikē tekhnē* of philosophy. There will now be new poets who will be masters of this new craft (*Laws* 7.801d5). Plato's ideal poet of the future, who is to be synchronically vetted by all, is like the ideal poet of the past, Homer, who has been diachronically vetted by all in the history and prehistory of the *mousikoi agōnes* 'competitions in the craft of *mousikē*' at the Panathenaia.

3§86 Even the genres of song and poetry as represented by the old *mousikē tekhnē* will now be reorganized in terms of the new *mousikē tekhnē*. So the genres of song and poetry will now be reorganized in terms of Plato's philosophical agenda.

3§87 Here I come to a most suggestive passage in Plato's *Laws* dealing with *mousikoi agōnes* 'competitions in the craft of *mousikē*' as reorganized at Magnesia. As we are about to see, the genres of song and dance to be performed at the festivals of Magnesia are recognizable as the same genres of song and dance performed at the festivals of the Panathenaia and the City Dionysia in Athens:

3①10 Plato *Laws* 6.764c–765a

Μουσικῆς δὲ τὸ μετὰ τοῦτο καὶ γυμναστικῆς ἄρχοντας καθίστασθαι
πρέπον ἂν εἴη, διττοὺς ἑκατέρων, τοὺς μὲν παιδείας αὐτῶν
ἕνεκα, τοὺς δὲ ἀγωνιστικῆς. παιδείας μὲν βούλεται λέγειν ὁ
νόμος γυμνασίων καὶ διδασκαλείων {d} ἐπιμελητὰς κόσμου καὶ

---

[72] This passage will be quoted at 3§165 below.

Chapter Three

παιδεύσεως ἅμα καὶ τῆς περὶ ταῦτα ἐπιμελείας τῶν φοιτήσεών τε πέρι καὶ οἰκήσεων ἀρρένων καὶ θηλειῶν κορῶν, ἀγωνίας δέ, ἔν τε τοῖς γυμνικοῖς καὶ περὶ τὴν μουσικὴν <u>ἀθλοθέτας</u> ἀθληταῖς, διττοὺς αὖ τούτους, περὶ μουσικὴν μὲν ἑτέρους, περὶ ἀγωνίαν δ' ἄλλους. ἀγωνιστικῆς μὲν οὖν ἀνθρώπων τε καὶ ἵππων τοὺς αὐτούς, μουσικῆς δὲ ἑτέρους μὲν τοὺς περὶ <u>μονῳδίαν</u> τε καὶ μιμητικήν, οἷον {ε} <u>ῥαψῳδῶν καὶ κιθαρῳδῶν καὶ αὐλητῶν</u> καὶ πάντων τῶν τοιούτων <u>ἀθλοθέτας</u> ἑτέρους πρέπον ἂν εἴη γίγνεσθαι, τῶν δὲ περὶ χορῳδίαν ἄλλους. πρῶτον δὴ περὶ τὴν τῶν χορῶν παιδιὰν παίδων τε καὶ ἀνδρῶν καὶ θηλειῶν κορῶν ἐν ὀρχήσεσι καὶ τῇ τάξει τῇ ἁπάσῃ γιγνομένῃ μουσικῇ τοὺς ἄρχοντας αἱρεῖσθαί που χρεών· ἱκανὸς δὲ εἷς ἄρχων αὐτοῖς, {765a} μὴ ἔλαττον τετταράκοντα γεγονὼς ἐτῶν. ἱκανὸς δὲ καὶ περὶ μονῳδίαν εἷς, μὴ ἔλαττον ἢ τριάκοντα γεγονὼς ἐτῶν, εἰσαγωγεύς τε εἶναι καὶ τοῖς ἀμιλλωμένοις τὴν διάκρισιν ἱκανῶς ἀποδιδούς.

Next, it would be fitting to institute directors [*arkhontes*] of *mousikē* and of athletics, two kinds of each. For one kind, their task is to be education [*paideia*], and, for the other, it is to be the supervision of competitive events [*agōnistikē*]. In connection with education [*paideia*], the law specifies a body of officials who supervise general order [*kosmos*] and the task of teaching in gymnasia and in schools, while at the same time supervising related matters such as going to and from school for boys and girls as well as the maintenance of their school buildings. In connection with competitive activity [*agōnia*], the law specifies two kinds of <u>athlothetai</u>, one kind for contestants [*athlētai*] in athletics and another kind for contestants in *mousikē*; once again there is to be a division into two kinds, the one having to do with *mousikē*, the other with *agōnia* in general [= competition in athletics]. The same ones who set up the athletic contests of men are to set up the contests involving horses; but in *mousikē* it would be fitting that there be one set of <u>athlothetai</u> for <u>solo singing</u> [<u>monōidia</u>] and *mimēsis*—as for example in the case of <u>rhapsodes, citharodes, auletes</u>, and the like—and another set for <u>choral singing</u> [<u>khorōidia</u>]. First and foremost, the *arkhontes* should be chosen for the choruses of boys and men and girls with a view to supervise the playful spontaneity of their dancing and its overall arrangement in terms of *mousikē*. One *arkhōn* will be adequate for

3⑤5. Plato's attempt to discredit the Panathenaic standard

the choruses. He should be not less than forty years of age. One *arkhōn* will also be adequate for the induction of the solo singers and for rendering adequate judgment in selecting from among the competitors. He should be not less than thirty years of age.

3§88 In this passage, I draw special attention to Plato's use of the word *athlothetai*, which I have translated earlier as 'arrangers of the *athloi*', that is, of the contests or competitions. As we have already seen, this term applies to officials at the festival of the Panathenaia in Athens who organized the *athloi* 'contests' among rhapsodes, citharodes, auletes, and so on. Whereas the competitive events at the Panathenaia involved only solo performances of epic or lyric compositions, the competitive events at the City Dionysia involved mostly choral performances of lyric compositions. So the distinction between *monōidia* 'solo singing' and *khorōidia* 'choral singing' in what I have just quoted from the *Laws* replicates an institutional reality grounded in Athens.

3§89 But this reality, as well as other institutional realities grounded in Athens, becomes merely a refraction of reality in the ideal state of Magnesia. The idealized festivals in this ideal state do not match the real festivals of the Panathenaia and the City Dionysia in the real state of Athens. The Olympian gods who are celebrated at those Athenian festivals, Athena and Dionysus, will have to find new places in a new system of idealized festivals that will be redistributed among all twelve Olympian gods. The ideal city of Magnesia will have twelve *heortai* 'festivals', each of them featuring both *khoroi* and *mousikoi agōnes* (as well as athletic events) and each of them celebrating one of the twelve Olympians (*Laws* 8.828b-c; also 7.834d-e). So the existing differentiations between, say, the Panathenaia and the City Dionysia will be undone. If one old festival had only *monōidia* while the other had only *khorōidia*, these two media will now have to coexist in any given new festival. Even if Athens had *mousikoi agōnes* only at the Panathenaia but not at the City Dionysia, or choral competitions only at the City Dionysia but not at the Panathenaia, Magnesia will have both kinds of competition at each one of its twelve festivals. That is why the *athlothetai* of Magnesia, unlike the *athlothetai* of Athens, will supervise the more generalized medium of *khorōidia* as well as the more specialized medium of *monōidia*. And both of these media will now be subsumed under the most general of all media in Magnesia, the medium of *mousikē*.

3§90 In effect, then, Plato has succeeded in diachronically reconstructing the most primal and therefore most undifferentiated sense of *mousikē* as the 'craft of the Muses', but he has reassigned this primal sense by taking it away from poetry and songmaking in general and giving it instead to philosophy. In Magnesia, the magnetic force emanating as inspiration from the Muses is the *mousikē* of philosophy, not the *mousikē* of poetry.

3§91 In the *mousikē* of Magnesia, we can still recognize traces of the ancient poetic craft as preserved in such institutions as the Athenian *mousikoi agōnes* 'competitions in *mousikē*' at the Panathenaia. A prime example is the passage I quoted about the performances of rhapsodes, citharodes, and auletes (*Laws* 6.764c5–e10). But such performances in Magnesia are no longer linked to the old *mousikē* of poetry, since that craft has been replaced by the new *mousikē* of philosophy. True, the medium of the rhapsode can still be associated with Homer in the new world of this new *mousikē* (as in *Laws* 2.658b). But the point is, Homer can no longer be the ultimate standard that he had been once upon a time, back in the old world of the old *mousikē* of poetry.

3§92 The *mousikē* of Plato's *Laws*, even though it is new in terms of its function, is old in terms of its form. As I have just argued, Plato's model of *mousikē* amounts to a diachronic reconstruction of a primal time when the more specialized medium of *monōidia* 'solo singing' and the more general medium of *khorōidia* 'choral singing' were as yet undifferentiated (such a reconstruction is most evident in *Laws* 3.700a–701b and 7.816c–d). Whereas the competitions in *mousikē* at the Panathenaia in Athens centered on the more specialized medium of *monōidia* 'solo singing', the corresponding competitions envisioned for the new state of Magnesia could accommodate the more general medium of *khorōidia* as well. Such *khorōidia* corresponds to what we see in the competitions at the City Dionysia in Athens.

3§93 In Plato's Magnesia, then, the basic idea of *khorōidia* is merged with the even more basic idea of *mousikē*. We see another example of this merger in Plato's vision of *khorōidia* in Egyptian civilization. The Egyptian *khorōidia* is seen as a primal form of *mousikē* (*Laws* 2.656e–657b).

3§94 Such a primal form of *mousikē* is meant to be revived in Magnesia, where *monōidia* and *khorōidia* are to remain undifferentiated. This ideal of undifferentiation avoids the reality of the differentiations we see attested in Athens. We can see only a refraction of that reality in Plato's *Laws*.

3ⓢ6. Orpheus and Homer

3§95 As a specialist in performance, the Panathenaic rhapsode is made to seem closer to Orpheus than to Homer in Plato's *Ion*. As we have already seen, Orpheus himself is envisioned as a specialist in performance, to be contrasted with Homer as the generalist in composition, that is, in *poiēsis* 'poetry'. One

3§6. Orpheus and Homer

aspect of this contrast, as we have also already seen, is the specialization of Orpheus in his association with the *humnos*, whereas Homer's association with this form is general rather than specific. As we are now about to see, there is another dimension in the contrast between Homer the generalist and Orpheus the specialist. It involves the mysticism of Orphic poetry, to be contrasted with the general non-mysticism of Homeric poetry.

3§96 A traditional characteristic of Orpheus is that his language was understood to be mystical, delving into mysteries of initiation, whereas no such special characteristics applied to the language of Homer. In Chapter 2, I already quoted a passage from Plato's *Theaetetus* that illustrates this point (179e–180d). Here I requote only the most relevant portion of that passage:

3①11 Plato *Theaetetus* 180c–d

> ΣΩ. Καὶ μετρίως γε λέγεις. τὸ δὲ δὴ πρόβλημα ἄλλο τι <u>παρειλήφαμεν</u> παρὰ μὲν τῶν <u>ἀρχαίων</u> μετὰ ποιήσεως {d} ἐπικρυπτομένων τοὺς πολλούς, ὡς ἡ <u>γένεσις</u> τῶν ἄλλων πάντων Ὠκεανός τε καὶ Τηθὺς <u>ῥεύματα</u> <ὄντα> τυγχάνει καὶ οὐδὲν <u>ἕστηκε</u>, παρὰ δὲ τῶν <u>ὑστέρων</u> ἅτε <u>σοφωτέρων</u> ἀναφανδὸν ἀποδεικνυμένων, ἵνα καὶ οἱ <u>σκυτοτόμοι</u> αὐτῶν τὴν σοφίαν μάθωσιν ἀκούσαντες καὶ παύσωνται ἠλιθίως οἰόμενοι τὰ μὲν <u>ἑστάναι</u>, τὰ δὲ <u>κινεῖσθαι</u> τῶν ὄντων, μαθόντες δὲ ὅτι πάντα <u>κινεῖται</u> τιμῶσιν αὐτούς;

> SOCRATES: What you say is quite reasonable. As for the problem, isn't it that <u>we have</u> on the one hand <u>a tradition [paralambanein]</u> that derives from the <u>ancient ones [arkhaioi]</u>, who hid their meaning[73] from the *hoi polloi* by way of poetry [*poiēsis*]—a tradition that says that the <u>genesis [genesis]</u> of all things, Ōkeanos and Tethys, happen to be <u>flowing streams [rheumata]</u> and that nothing <u>is static [hestanai]</u>?[74] And that we have, on the other hand, a tradition that derives from the ones who came after [the ancient ones], that is, from the <u>later ones [husteroi]</u>, who are more <u>wise [sophoi]</u> [than the ancient ones] and who make their explanations quite openly, in order that even <u>leatherworkers [skutotomoi]</u> may hear and understand their wisdom [*sophia*] and, abandoning their simple understanding that some things <u>are static [hestanai]</u> while other things

---

[73] Note the mystical language: *epi-kruptesthai* is to 'hide the meaning'.
[74] What is fluid is not rigid or 'static'.

Chapter Three

are in motion [*kineîsthai*], may hold in respect those who teach them that all things are in motion [*kineîsthai*]?

3§97 In this passage, as I argued in Chapter 2, the mystical idea that everything is fluid signals a 'tradition' (as expressed by the wording παρειλήφαμεν at 180c) derived from the *arkhaioi* 'ancient ones', who convey by way of poetry their mystical ideas for the initiated few (180c–d παρὰ μὲν τῶν ἀρχαίων μετὰ ποιήσεως ἐπικρυπτομένων τοὺς πολλούς), to be contrasted with the *husteroi* 'later ones', who express their ideas about fluidity and rigidity for all to hear, without any mystery (180d). Even *skutotomoi* 'leatherworkers' can understand these ideas.[75]

3§98 As I also argued in Chapter 2, the contrast here is between earlier thinkers who depend on mystical sources and later thinkers who depend on non-mystical sources. In contexts where Orpheus and Homer are left undifferentiated, Homer belongs to the earlier mystical sources. In contexts where they are differentiated, however, Homer can be seen as a later non-mystical source, and those thinkers who are Homer's followers can be seen as the *husteroi* 'later ones'. Earlier in Plato's *Theaetetus*, it is made explicit that there are thinkers who are *palaioteroi* 'more ancient' than the thinkers who specialize in Homer (179e Ὁμηρείων καὶ ἔτι παλαιοτέρων).[76] The primary source of such relatively 'more ancient' thinkers, as I argue on the basis of all the relevant Platonic contexts taken together, was supposed to be Orpheus, whose poetry was conventionally ranked as older than the poetry of Homer.

3§99 In the works of Plato, we find that the most ancient poets of the Hellenes are often ranked in chronological order. The sequence proceeds from earlier to later times: Orpheus, Musaeus, Hesiod, and, finally, Homer. In Plato's *Apology* (41a), for example, where Plato's Socrates speaks in mock-mystical style about the prospect of his encountering these four poets in some kind of afterlife after he dies, he mentions them in precisely that order.[77] Such an

---

[75] This reference in Plato *Theaetetus* 180d to *skutotomoi* 'leatherworkers' as notionally lowly craftsmen is evidently an allusion to Hippias of Elis, as I will argue later.

[76] The morphology of *Homēreioi* here is analogous to that of *Kreophuleioi*. On the *Kreophuleioi* see PP 179, 226–227.

[77] I should add that, in contexts where Homer and Hesiod are paired, Hesiod tends to be mentioned before Homer, as happens consistently for example in Plato *Republic* 2.363a, 2.377d, 10.612b. In Plato *Cratylus* 402b–c, the lore about Ōkeanos and Tethys is cited from Homer, Hesiod, and Orpheus, in ascending order of antiquity. According to one tradition, Homer is descended from Orpheus: Pherecydes *FGH* 3 F 167, Hellanicus *FGH* 4 F 5, Damastes 5 *FGH* F 11; according to another, he is traced back to Musaeus: Gorgias 82 B 25 DK.

3⊚6. Orpheus and Homer

ordering is evidently canonical, as we see from the wording of Hippias of Elis, quoted directly by Clement of Alexandria:

3①12 Hippias *FGH* 6 F 4 = DK B 6 via Clement of Alexandria *Stromateis* 6.15 (II pp. 434–435 Stählin)

Ἱππίαν τὸν σοφιστὴν τὸν Ἠλεῖον ... παραστησώμεθα ὧδέ πως λέγοντα· "τούτων ἴσως εἴρηται τὰ μὲν Ὀρφεῖ, τὰ δὲ Μουσαίῳ κατὰ βραχὺ ἄλλῳ ἀλλαχοῦ, τὰ δὲ Ἡσιόδῳ, τὰ δὲ Ὁμήρῳ, τὰ δὲ τοῖς ἄλλοις τῶν ποιητῶν, τὰ δὲ ἐν συγγραφαῖς, τὰ μὲν Ἕλλησι, τὰ δὲ βαρβάροις· ἐγὼ δὲ ἐκ πάντων τούτων τὰ μέγιστα καὶ ὁμόφυλα συνθεὶς τοῦτον καινὸν καὶ πολυειδῆ τὸν λόγον ποιήσομαι."

I will adduce Hippias of Elis, the sophist [*sophistēs*],[78] who said something like the following: "Some of these things may have been said by Orpheus, some by Musaeus—some things briefly by one of them in one place, other things by the other in another place—and some other things were said by Hesiod, some other things by Homer, and still other things were said by others of the poets [*poiētai*], and still other things were said in prose writings—some of those things said by Hellenes and others by barbarians; but of all these things I have combined those that are the greatest and are similar to each other among the classifications [= *phula*] of humanity, and I will now make from all these things the present discourse [*logos*], which is novel and multiform."[79]

3§100 The same sequence of canonical ordering is evident in a passage from the *Frogs* of Aristophanes, where the stage-Aeschylus is speaking in mock-mystical style about the social benefits conferred by the poetry of the four most ancient poets of the Hellenes:

3①13 Aristophanes *Frogs* 1030–1036

1030 ΑΙ. Ταῦτα γὰρ ἄνδρας χρὴ ποιητὰς ἀσκεῖν. σκέψαι γὰρ ἀπ' ἀρχῆς
ὡς ὠφέλιμοι τῶν ποιητῶν οἱ γενναῖοι γεγένηνται.

---

[78] At a later point, I will explore the meaning of the word *sophistēs* 'sophist'. Already at this point, however, I must cite a pathfinding new book by Håkan Tell on Hippias of Elis as *sophistēs* and on the *sophistai* in general.

[79] Compare Xenophon *Memorabilia* 4.4.7, where Hippias is represented as saying: πειρῶμαι καινόν τι λέγειν ἀεί 'I am always trying to say something novel'.

Chapter Three

Ὀρφεὺς μὲν γὰρ <u>τελετάς</u> θ' ἡμῖν κατέδειξε φόνων τ'
ἀπέχεσθαι,
<u>Μουσαῖος</u> δ' ἐξακέσεις τε νόσων καὶ <u>χρησμούς</u>, <u>Ἡσίοδος</u> δὲ
γῆς ἐργασίας, καρπῶν ὥρας, ἀρότους· ὁ δὲ θεῖος <u>Ὅμηρος</u>
1035 ἀπὸ τοῦ τιμὴν καὶ κλέος ἔσχεν πλὴν τοῦδ' ὅτι χρήστ'
ἐδίδαξεν,
τάξεις, ἀρετάς, ὁπλίσεις ἀνδρῶν;

AESCHYLUS:
> Yes, for these are the things that men who are poets should cultivate. Consider how, from the <u>beginning</u> [*arkhē*],
> those of the <u>poets</u> [*poiētai*] who are noble have become by nature useful to society.
> <u>Orpheus</u> showed us the <u>mystic rites</u> [*teletai*] and how to abstain from acts of killing.
> <u>Musaeus</u> showed us the cures for diseases and <u>oracular words</u> [*khrēsmoi*], while <u>Hesiod</u>
> showed us the ways to work the land, and the seasons for harvesting. As for the godlike [*theios*] <u>Homer</u>,
> I want you to tell me what was the source of the honor [*timē*] and the fame [*kleos*] that he had if it was not this, that he taught us things that were useful for society,
> namely, the marshalling of the battle ranks, outstanding deeds of valor, and the ways that men arm themselves?

3§101 In this extract from Aristophanes, we see that the rationale implicit in the sequencing of these four poets is not only chronological, starting 'from the beginning' (ἀπ' ἀρχῆς). The rationale is also qualitative, centering on a contrast between the mystical nature of an earlier Orpheus and the non-mystical nature of a later Homer. Such a contrast is evident elsewhere as well, as we see in a passage from Plato's *Protagoras* where Protagoras of Abdera describes Orpheus and Musaeus as exponents of *teletai* 'mysteries' and *khrēsmōidiai* 'oracular songs', whereas Hesiod and Homer—along with the lyric poet Simonides—are described simply in terms of *poiēsis* 'poetry':

3Ⓢ6. Orpheus and Homer

3①14 Plato *Protagoras* 316c-d

ὀρθῶς, ἔφη, προμηθῇ, ὦ Σώκρατες, ὑπὲρ ἐμοῦ. ξένον γὰρ ἄνδρα καὶ ἰόντα εἰς πόλεις μεγάλας, καὶ ἐν ταύταις πείθοντα τῶν νέων τοὺς βελτίστους ἀπολείποντας τὰς τῶν ἄλλων συνουσίας, καὶ οἰκείων καὶ ὀθνείων, καὶ πρεσβυτέρων καὶ νεωτέρων, ἑαυτῷ συνεῖναι ὡς βελτίους ἐσομένους διὰ {d} τὴν ἑαυτοῦ συνουσίαν, χρὴ εὐλαβεῖσθαι τὸν ταῦτα πράττοντα· οὐ γὰρ σμικροὶ περὶ αὐτὰ φθόνοι τε γίγνονται καὶ ἄλλαι δυσμένειαί τε καὶ ἐπιβουλαί. ἐγὼ δὲ τὴν <u>σοφιστικὴν τέχνην</u> φημὶ μὲν εἶναι παλαιάν, τοὺς δὲ μεταχειριζομένους αὐτὴν τῶν παλαιῶν ἀνδρῶν, φοβουμένους τὸ ἐπαχθὲς αὐτῆς, πρόσχημα ποιεῖσθαι καὶ προκαλύπτεσθαι, τοὺς μὲν <u>ποίησιν</u>, οἷον Ὅμηρόν τε καὶ <u>Ἡσίοδον</u> καὶ <u>Σιμωνίδην</u>, τοὺς δὲ αὖ <u>τελετάς</u> τε καὶ <u>χρησμῳδίας</u>, τοὺς ἀμφί τε <u>Ὀρφέα</u> καὶ <u>Μουσαῖον</u>·

You are thinking ahead correctly, Socrates, on my behalf. For when a man goes as a stranger to great cities, and in them persuades the best of the young men to leave their other associations, relatives, and acquaintances old and young, and associate with him, so that they will be as good as possible through their association with himself, he who does these things must beware. For all kinds of not inconsiderable envy come about concerning these things, and other kinds of ill will, and plots.

I [= Protagoras] declare that the <u>sophistic</u> <u>craft</u> [<u>sophistikē</u> <u>tekhnē</u>] is ancient, but those who had applied it among ancient men were afraid of the opprobrium attaching to it, and disguised and concealed themselves—some in the realm of <u>poetry</u> [<u>poiēsis</u>], like <u>Homer</u> and <u>Hesiod</u> and <u>Simonides</u>, but others in the realm of <u>mysteries</u> [<u>teletai</u>] and <u>oracular songs</u> [<u>khrēsmōidiai</u>], like <u>Orpheus</u> and <u>Musaeus</u> and their followers.[80]

3§102 According to this scheme, Homer and Hesiod—along with Simonides—are generalists in *poiēsis* 'poetry', whereas Orpheus and Musaeus are specialists, that is, experts in mysteries and in specialized poetry concerned with mysteries. This distinction, as it plays out in the *Protagoras* of

---

[80] Translation after Allen 1996:177.

Chapter Three

Plato, evidently extends to the portrayal of Protagoras himself, who claims mastery of a special kind of *tekhnē* 'craft' that aims to conceal and to mystify. He calls it the *sophistikē tekhnē*, the craft of the sophist.

3§103 Before I proceed to explore the distinction being made here between the general poetry of Homer, Hesiod, and Simonides on one hand and the mystical poetry of Orpheus and Musaeus on the other, I pause to comment on the meaning of *sophistikē tekhnē* 'sophistic craft' and *sophistēs* 'sophist' as applied to Protagoras of Abdera and to other 'sophistic' characters in Plato's dialogues. From the very start, the figure of Socrates in Plato's *Protagoras* works at discrediting the words *sophos* and *sophia* as used by 'sophists' in the transcendent sense of what we ordinarily translate as 'wise' and 'wisdom' respectively. By <u>transcendent</u> I mean simply a sense that <u>transcends</u> the practical sense of 'skillful' and 'skill' respectively. As I will argue at a later point, the works of Plato reveal both the transcendent and the practical senses of the words *sophos*, *sophia*, and even *sophistēs*; moreover, some sophists—like Protagoras himself—are represented as preferring the transcendent sense, while others evidently chose the practical sense.[81] Until I reach the point where I follow through on this argument, however, I will postpone making any distinction between transcendent and practical sophists. For the time being, then, I simply translate *sophistēs* and *sophistikē tekhnē* as 'sophist' and 'sophistic craft'.

3§104 Having made this comment on the 'sophistic craft' as applied to Protagoras, I return to the problem at hand, that is, the distinction being made in Plato's *Protagoras* between the general poetry of Homer, Hesiod, and Simonides on one hand and the mystical poetry of Orpheus and Musaeus on the other. As I was saying, this distinction in the *Protagoras* of Plato extends to the portrayal of Protagoras himself, who claims mastery of a special kind of *tekhnē* 'craft' that has the power to conceal and to mystify. As I was also saying, that craft is the craft of the sophist, the *sophistikē tekhnē*.

3§105 Plato's wording pictures Protagoras attended by an ensemble of enthralled followers, devotees recruited from the various cities he visited, who are imagined as a choral ensemble of singers / dancers enchanted by Orpheus himself:

3Ⓣ15 Plato *Protagoras* 314e–315b

ἐπειδὴ δὲ εἰσήλθομεν, κατελάβομεν Πρωταγόραν ἐν τῷ προστῴῳ περιπατοῦντα, ἑξῆς δ' αὐτῷ συμπεριεπάτουν ἐκ μὲν τοῦ ἐπὶ θάτερα

---

[81] I will reach this later point in ch. 4.

Καλλίας ὁ Ἱππονίκου καὶ ὁ ἀδελφὸς αὐτοῦ {315a} ὁ ὁμομήτριος, Πάραλος ὁ Περικλέους, καὶ Χαρμίδης ὁ Γλαύκωνος, ἐκ δὲ τοῦ ἐπὶ θάτερα ὁ ἕτερος τῶν Περικλέους Ξάνθιππος, καὶ Φιλιππίδης ὁ Φιλομήλου καὶ Ἀντίμοιρος ὁ Μενδαῖος, ὅσπερ εὐδοκιμεῖ μάλιστα τῶν Πρωταγόρου μαθητῶν καὶ ἐπὶ τέχνῃ μανθάνει, ὡς σοφιστὴς ἐσόμενος. τούτων δὲ οἳ ὄπισθεν ἠκολούθουν ἐπακούοντες τῶν <u>λεγομένων</u> τὸ μὲν πολὺ ξένοι ἐφαίνοντο οὓς ἄγει ἐξ ἑκάστων τῶν πόλεων ὁ Πρωταγόρας, δι᾽ ὧν διεξέρχεται, <u>κηλῶν</u> τῇ φωνῇ ὥσπερ {b} <u>Ὀρφεύς</u>, οἱ δὲ κατὰ τὴν φωνὴν ἕπονται <u>κεκηλημένοι</u> ἦσαν δέ τινες καὶ τῶν ἐπιχωρίων ἐν τῷ χορῷ.

When we entered, we found Protagoras walking around at the portico. Walking around with him in sequence there were, on one side, Callias son of Hipponikos, and his stepbrother Paralos son of Pericles, and Charmides son of Glaucon; on the other side, there were Pericles' other son, Xanthippos, and Philippides son of Philomelos, and Antimoiros of Mende, the one who is the most highly regarded of the disciples of Protagoras and who is learning the craft [*tekhnē*] with the purpose of becoming a sophist [*sophistēs*] himself. Others followed along behind to hear the things that were being <u>said</u> [*legesthai*]. For the most part they appeared to be non-Athenians whom Protagoras had drawn from every city through which he had passed, <u>enthralling</u> them with his voice like <u>Orpheus</u> while they, <u>enthralled</u>, followed along wherever the voice may lead. And there were also some local people [= fellow Athenians] in the chorus.

3§106 Immediately after this description of Protagoras of Abdera and his enthralled followers, we read a description of another sophist, Hippias of Elis, attended by his own followers. This description presents Hippias as the diametrical opposite of Protagoras. Whereas Protagoras the sophist is mystical and in that sense 'Orphic', Hippias the sophist is non-mystical and in that sense 'Homeric'. Here I proceed to examine the Homeric evocations in the Platonic description applied to Hippias, as spoken by Plato's Socrates:

3ⓣ16 Plato *Protagoras* 315b-c

<u>τὸν δὲ μετ᾽ εἰσενόησα</u>, ἔφη <u>Ὅμηρος</u>, Ἱππίαν τὸν {c} Ἠλεῖον, <u>καθήμενον</u> ἐν τῷ κατ᾽ ἀντικρὺ προστῴῳ <u>ἐν θρόνῳ</u>· περὶ αὐτὸν δ᾽ <u>ἐκάθηντο</u> ἐπὶ βάθρων Ἐρυξίμαχός τε ὁ Ἀκουμενοῦ καὶ Φαῖδρος ὁ Μυρρινούσιος καὶ Ἄνδρων ὁ Ἀνδροτίωνος καὶ τῶν ξένων πολῖταί

Chapter Three

τε αὐτοῦ καὶ ἄλλοι τινές. ἐφαίνοντο δὲ περὶ φύσεώς τε καὶ τῶν μετεώρων ἀστρονομικὰ ἄττα <u>διερωτᾶν</u> τὸν Ἱππίαν, ὁ δ' <u>ἐν θρόνῳ καθήμενος</u> ἑκάστοις αὐτῶν <u>διέκρινεν</u> καὶ διεξῄει τὰ <u>ἐρωτώμενα</u>.

After him [= Protagoras], the next one I noted [eis-noeîn], as Homer says, was Hippias of Elis, seated at the portico across [from the portico of Protagoras] on a throne; and seated around him on benches were Eryximachus son of Akoumenos and Phaedrus of Myrrhinous and Andron son of Androtion as well as some non-Athenians. Among them [= the non-Athenians] were some fellow-citizens [of Hippias of Elis] as well as others. It appeared that they were making a systematic inquiry [di-erōtân] in asking Hippias various astronomical questions concerning the nature [phusis] of heavenly bodies while he, seated on his throne, made critical judgments [dia-krinein] for each one of them as he systematically went through the things about which they had just made inquiries.

3§107 The wording τὸν δὲ μετ' εἰσενόησα 'the next one I noted was . . .' in this Platonic passage, referring to the image of Hippias, evokes a Homeric verse that we know as *Odyssey* xi 601, where Odysseus sees the *eidōlon* 'image' of Herakles in Hades.[82] After Plato's Socrates finishes with his description of Hippias, we find a further Platonic evocation of Homer. Plato's Socrates goes on to say: καὶ μὲν δὴ καὶ Τάνταλόν γε εἰσεῖδον 'the next thing I knew, I saw Tantalos . . .' (*Protagoras* 315c). This time, Plato's wording evokes the Homeric verse at *Odyssey* xi 582, where Odysseus sees Tantalos in Hades. Now the referent is Prodicus of Keos. Plato's pictorial diptych featuring Protagoras and Hippias has now been turned into a triptych featuring Prodicus as the third of three great sophists described by Plato's Socrates (*Protagoras* 315c–316a). The triptych playfully connects all three sophists with mock-mystical visions of great figures from the heroic past. Whereas Protagoras is being compared to Orpheus, Plato's wording links Hippias and Prodicus directly with Homeric poetry, conjuring images seen by Odysseus in his descent to Hades, that is, in the catabasis scene of *Odyssey* xi.[83]

---

[82] The link between Hippias and Herakles may be relevant to the detail about the ring of Hippias in Plato *Hippias Minor* 368b and to the detail about the 'Heraclean' or 'Magnesian' stone in Plato *Ion* 533d.

[83] As Martin 2001 argues, there was a poetic tradition that featured a narrative about the catabasis or descent of Orpheus into the underworld where the first-person narrator was Orpheus himself. See also West 1983.

3Ⓢ6. Orpheus and Homer

3§108 In the passage I just quoted from Plato's *Protagoras*, the opposition between the sophist Hippias of Elis and the sophist Protagoras of Abdera is introduced in spatial terms: Hippias occupies a *prostōion* 'portico' (more literally, 'front part of the stoa') that is positioned right across from a corresponding *prostōion* occupied by Protagoras (*Protagoras* 315b–c). This spatial opposition between the positions occupied by these two sophists prefigures the ideological opposition between the positions they will take concerning poetry: as I have already indicated, Hippias is being associated with the direct wording of Homer, while his counterpart, Protagoras, is compared directly to Orpheus.[84]

3§109 There are further Homeric evocations to be found in the description of Hippias the sophist. Unlike Protagoras, who is mystical, Hippias is decidedly non-mystical. Hippias is described as a straightforward speaker of his own judgments, and the wording of this description in Plato's *Protagoras* matches the Homeric vision of Minos the king of Crete, who is described as the absolute judge in the heroic otherworld of *Odyssey* xi:

3①17 *Odyssey* xi 568–571

> ἔνθ' ἦ τοι Μίνωα ἴδον, Διὸς ἀγλαὸν υἱόν,
> <u>χρύσεον σκῆπτρον ἔχοντα θεμιστεύοντα</u> νέκυσσιν,
> <u>ἥμενον</u>· οἱ δέ μιν ἀμφὶ δίκας <u>εἴροντο</u> ἄνακτα,
> ἥμενοι ἑσταότες τε, κατ' εὐρυπυλὲς Ἄϊδος δῶ.

> There I saw Minos, radiant son of Zeus,
> <u>who was holding a golden scepter as he dispensed justice</u>
>   among the dead.
> He was <u>seated</u>, while they [= the dead] <u>asked</u> the lord for
>   his judgments.
> Some of them [= the dead] were seated, and some were
>   standing, throughout the house of Hades, with its
>   wide gates.

---

[84] We may compare the themes featured in the gigantic picture of the underworld as painted by Polygnotus in the Lesche of the Cnidians at Delphi, dated to the mid-fifth century BCE. From the eyewitness description of Pausanias (10.30.8), we know that this painting pictured Thamyris, sitting blind and dejected after his divine punishment, and Orpheus playing his kithara and surrounded by an attentive audience. See Martin 2001 for details and further citations.

Chapter Three

3§110 From the passage in Plato's *Protagoras* that I quoted just before this Homeric passage, we can see clearly that Plato's vision of Hippias matches the Homeric vision of Minos. Indirectly, it also matches the Homeric vision of Zeus. Minos is not only the son of Zeus but also the underworldly surrogate of the god. Like Minos, Zeus himself is conventionally pictured as sitting on a *thronos* 'throne' (*Iliad* I 536. etc.), and, as the ultimate king, he is the ultimate source of authority for the holding of a *skēptron* 'scepter' (I 234) by kings who dispense *themistes* 'judgments' (I 238–239 οἵ τε θέμιστας | πρὸς Διὸς εἰρύαται). The plural noun *themistes* designates 'judgments' as instantiations of 'justice' as designated by the singular noun *themis*. Like Zeus, Minos is conventionally pictured as sitting on a throne, holding his scepter, and dispensing *themis* or 'divine justice' (*Odyssey* xi 568–571).

3§111 Like the hero Minos, the sophist Hippias is pictured as sitting on a throne (315b καθήμενον ... ἐν θρόνῳ, 315c ἐν θρόνῳ καθήμενος), responding to questions (315c διερωτᾶν ... ἐρωτώμενα) that call for critical judgments, as expressed by the verb *dia-krinein* 'decide [between X and Y]' (315c διέκρινεν). Further, in the *Protagoras*, Hippias is pictured in the act of responding to questions about the natural world, that is, about *phusis* 'nature' in general, and about astronomy in particular (315c ἐφαίνοντο δὲ περὶ φύσεώς τε καὶ τῶν μετεώρων ἀστρονομικὰ ἄττα διερωτᾶν τὸν Ἱππίαν).[85] In Plato's *Hippias Minor*, we see the same Hippias actually responding to questions posed by Socrates, who challenges the sophist to apply various *tekhnai* 'crafts' for the purpose of distinguishing, as empirically as possible, what is true and what is false.[86] Among these *tekhnai*, Hippias singles out the *tekhnē* of astronomy as one of his specialties (*Hippias Minor* 367e).[87] I see in this detail an important link between the portraits of Hippias in Plato's *Protagoras* and *Hippias Minor*.

3§112 As the dialogue in the *Hippias Minor* proceeds, it becomes clear that the expertise of Hippias extends to all *tekhnai* or 'crafts', not just the craft of astronomy, and that these crafts culminate in the craft of poetry and song. As we will see from my upcoming analysis of Plato's *Hippias Minor* as a whole, this dialogue highlights the idea that Hippias the sophist has mastered the craft of poetry in general. In fact, already at the very beginning of the *Hippias Minor*, Hippias is described as an expert in the craft of Homeric poetry in particular:

---

[85] See also Plato *Protagoras* 318d–e.
[86] Aristotle *Metaphysics* 4.1025a2–13 refers to the *Hippias Minor*, criticizing the logic of Plato's argumentation. See Allen 1996:26.
[87] This description of Hippias as a specialist in astronomy in Plato *Hippias Minor* 367e and, as I noted earlier, in *Protagoras* 315c and 318d–e, recurs in other contexts as well. See Plato *Hippias Maior* 285c.

3§6. Orpheus and Homer

3⊕18 Plato *Hippias Minor* 363a–c

ΣΩ. Καὶ μήν, ὦ Εὔδικε, ἔστι γε ἃ ἡδέως ἂν πυθοίμην {b} Ἱππίου ὧν νυνδὴ <u>ἔλεγεν περὶ Ὁμήρου</u>. καὶ γὰρ τοῦ σοῦ πατρὸς Ἀπημάντου ἤκουον ὅτι ἡ Ἰλιὰς κάλλιον εἴη <u>ποίημα</u> τῷ Ὁμήρῳ ἢ ἡ Ὀδύσσεια, τοσούτῳ δὲ κάλλιον, ὅσῳ ἀμείνων Ἀχιλλεὺς Ὀδυσσέως εἴη· ἑκάτερον γὰρ τούτων τὸ μὲν εἰς Ὀδυσσέα ἔφη <u>πεποιῆσθαι</u>, τὸ δ' εἰς Ἀχιλλέα. περὶ ἐκείνου οὖν ἡδέως ἄν, εἰ βουλομένῳ ἐστὶν Ἱππίᾳ, ἀναπυθοίμην ὅπως αὐτῷ δοκεῖ περὶ τοῖν ἀνδροῖν τούτοιν, πότερον {c} ἀμείνω φησὶν εἶναι, ἐπειδὴ <u>καὶ ἄλλα πολλὰ καὶ παντοδαπὰ ἡμῖν ἐπιδέδεικται καὶ περὶ ποιητῶν τε ἄλλων καὶ περὶ Ὁμήρου</u>.

SOCRATES: Now then, Eudikos, there are some things I would like to learn from Hippias. They concern what <u>he was just saying about [*legein peri*] Homer</u>. I used to hear from your father Apemantos that Homer's *Iliad* is a better <u>composition [*poiēma*]</u> than the *Odyssey*, to the extent that Achilles is better than Odysseus. For he said that one of the compositions was <u>composed [*poieîn*]</u> with reference to Odysseus, and the other, with reference to Achilles. If Hippias is willing, I would like to ask what he thinks of these two men,[88] and which of them he says is better, since <u>he has made a display [*epideixis*] of so many other various things to us about other poets, and especially about Homer</u>.

3§113 The expertise of Hippias in the craft of poetry in general is evident not only from an overall reading of Plato's *Hippias Minor* but also from his own words, which I have already quoted and will now quote again here:

3⊕19 Hippias *FGH* 6 F 4 = F 6 DK via Clement of Alexandria *Stromateis* 6.15 (II p. 434 Stählin)

Ἱππίαν τὸν <u>σοφιστὴν</u> τὸν Ἠλεῖον ... παραστησώμεθα ὧδέ πως λέγοντα· "τούτων ἴσως εἴρηται τὰ μὲν <u>Ὀρφεῖ</u>, τὰ δὲ <u>Μουσαίῳ</u> κατὰ βραχὺ ἄλλῳ ἀλλαχοῦ, τὰ δὲ <u>Ἡσιόδῳ</u>, τὰ δὲ <u>Ὁμήρῳ</u>, τὰ δὲ τοῖς ἄλλοις τῶν ποιητῶν, τὰ δὲ ἐν συγγραφαῖς, τὰ μὲν Ἕλλησι, τὰ δὲ βαρβάροις· ἐγὼ δὲ ἐκ πάντων τούτων τὰ μέγιστα καὶ ὁμόφυλα συνθεὶς τοῦτον καινὸν καὶ πολυειδῆ τὸν λόγον ποιήσομαι."

---

[88] The ostentatious use of the dual number here accentuates the complementarity of Achilles and Odysseus as respectively the main heroes of the Homeric *Iliad* and *Odyssey*.

Chapter Three

I will adduce Hippias of Elis, the sophist [*sophistēs*], who said something like the following: "Some of these things may have been said by Orpheus, some by Musaeus—some things briefly by one of them in one place, other things by the other in another place—and some other things were said by Hesiod, some other things by Homer, and still other things were said by others of the poets [*poiētai*], and still other things were said in prose writings—some of those things said by Hellenes and others by barbarians; but of all these things I have combined those that are the greatest and are similar to each other among the classifications [= *phula*] of humanity, and I will now make from all these things the present discourse [*logos*], which is novel and multiform."

3§114 For Hippias, as we will see in what follows, a *logos* is a 'discourse' that includes not only the 'logic' of his discourse but also the actual 'wording'— literally, *logos*—of the poetry or prose that he performs as the basis of this discourse.

3§115 The expertise of Hippias in the craft of poetry in general is evident in Plato's *Protagoras*. I draw attention to a passage where Hippias is represented as claiming expertise in the poetry of Simonides.[89] This expertise of Hippias turns out to be relevant to his expertise in the poetry of Homer. As we have already seen, Plato's *Protagoras* is represented as saying that Simonides is parallel to Homer and Hesiod as exponents of what is called *poiēsis*, which Protagoras distinguishes from the mystical discourse that he associates with himself (*Protagoras* 316c-d). In Plato's *Protagoras*, the wording attributed to Hippias in expressing his own expertise is relevant to such an understanding of *poiēsis*:

3①20 Plato *Protagoras* 347a-b

> καὶ ὁ Ἱππίας, Εὖ μέν μοι δοκεῖς, ἔφη, ὦ Σώκρατες, καὶ σὺ περὶ τοῦ ᾄσματος διεληλυθέναι· ἔστιν μέντοι, ἔφη, καὶ {b} ἐμοὶ λόγος περὶ αὐτοῦ εὖ ἔχων, ὃν ὑμῖν ἐπιδείξω, ἂν βούλησθε.

> And Hippias said: "I think you have gone through the song [of Simonides] very well, Socrates. But I too have a discourse [*logos*] about it that holds up very well, and I will make a public display [*epideixis*] of it, if you-all wish."

---
[89] See Allen 1996:26.

3§116 Hippias is represented here as offering to make a 'display' (*epideixis*)—that is, to perform—a *logos* 'discourse' about a song of Simonides for all the intellectuals assembled in the dramatic setting of Plato's *Protagoras*. That song is what we know as "*Poetae Melici Graeci* (or *PMG*) fragment 542" in Denys Page's collection of archaic Greek lyric fragments. For Hippias, the *logos* 'discourse' that he offers to display about this song includes not only the 'logic' of his own discourse but also the actual 'wording'—literally, *logos*—of the song. In other words, Hippias is ready to perform the song of Simonides while making an argument on the basis of what he performs. The discourse that Hippias offers to perform about "*PMG* 542" would have supposedly rivaled the discourse already performed by Socrates himself about the same song of Simonides. In the preceding section of Plato's *Protagoras*, Socrates is shown in the act of actually performing parts of this song of Simonides in making his own argument (*Protagoras* 342a through 347a).

3§117 It all started when Protagoras challenged Socrates by starting to perform and interpret the initial sequence of that song of Simonides (*Protagoras* 339a-b). Socrates will respond to the challenge by following through on the performing and the interpreting of that song.

3§118 The expertise of Protagoras himself in performing and interpreting Simonides—as opposed to the expertise of Hippias and of Socrates—is shaded over in Plato's *Protagoras*. Although Plato's Protagoras offers to perform the whole song of Simonides for Socrates after adducing the initial sequence from the song, Socrates declines the offer, saying that he knows the song by heart (*Protagoras* 339b). Protagoras gets to perform only the initial sequence of the song (*PMG* 542 lines 1-3 at 339b) and then one more sequence after that (*PMG* 542 lines 11-13 at 339c) before Socrates himself proceeds to perform his own discourse on the whole song, quoting several further sequences from the song as living proof of his claim that he knows it all by heart (*PMG* 542 lines 14-16 at 344c, lines 17-18 at 344e, lines 20-26 at 345c, lines 27-30 at 345d, lines 34-40 at 346c).

3§119 After Socrates is finished with his display of expertise, Hippias gets his chance. But before Hippias can demonstrate his own expertise in poetry by performing a discourse on the song of Simonides in Plato's *Protagoras*, Alcibiades cuts him off, saying that any such performance of a discourse by Hippias on the poetry of Simonides should be postponed for another occasion (*Protagoras* 347a-b). For the present occasion, says Alcibiades, the assembled group is more interested in hearing whether Protagoras has any further question to ask of Socrates or whether he is ready to respond to questions asked by Socrates. By implication, further questioning of Socrates by Protagoras would

Chapter Three

involve challenges to the interpretation of Simonides by Socrates. Instead of such questioning, Plato's Socrates induces Protagoras to stop any further debating of questions in terms of interpreting poetry and song (*Protagoras* 348a–c).[90]

3§120 So we have just missed a chance to hear Plato's Hippias displaying his expertise in poetry. That is, we have missed such a chance in Plato's *Protagoras*. In Plato's *Hippias Minor*, on the other hand, we do in fact have such a chance, and I will return to that dialogue presently in order to explore at length the implications of the dramatized display of Hippias in that other context. For the moment, though, I need to follow through on the implications of what exactly it was that Hippias would have displayed in the context of Plato's *Protagoras*—that is, if he had been allowed by Plato to make such a dramatized display in that dialogue. Let me anticipate my conclusions: the display of Hippias concerning the poetry of Simonides—or concerning the poetry of Homer and Hesiod, for that matter—would have been non-mystifying, non-mystical, as opposed to the stance of Protagoras, which is ostentatiously mystifying, mystical. Correspondingly, the display of Socrates in Plato's *Protagoras* concerning the poetry of Simonides—and concerning the poetry of Homer and Hesiod as well—turns out to be non-mystifying, non-mystical.

3§121 Even before Socrates performs his discourse on the passage adduced for him by Protagoras from the song of Simonides (*PMG* 542), he himself voluntarily adduces passages from Homer and Hesiod (*Iliad* XXI 308–309 at *Protagoras* 340a and *Works and Days* 289–292 at *Protagoras* 340c–d). The motive of Plato's Protagoras had been to test Socrates' general expertise in poetry when he started questioning him about the authorial intent of Simonides, and Socrates remarks that he understands this motive (*Protagoras* 341e–342a). Even after Socrates finishes his discourse about the song of Simonides (*Protagoras* 342a through 347a) and even after he induces Protagoras to move beyond the debating of questions in terms of interpreting poetry and song, he still manages to demonstrate his expertise one last time, adducing yet another passage from Homer (*Iliad* II 224 at *Protagoras* 348c–d).

3§122 In short, what we see in Plato's *Protagoras* is a replacement of Hippias by Socrates as a representative of the craft of performing and interpreting poetry. If Alcibiades had not cut him off, Hippias would have made his own display of this craft.

---

[90] Allen 1996:118: "Having practiced on Simonides an exegetical technique which out-sophists the sophists, Socrates proceeds to dismiss literary criticism as worthless: poets cannot be questioned about what they mean, and the Many, in discussing them, argue about something they cannot test."

3§123 The replacement of Hippias by Socrates in the *Protagoras* is relevant to the dichotomy between Hippias and Protagoras in their attitudes toward the craft of performing and interpreting poetry. I have already quoted the passage in Plato's *Protagoras* where Protagoras specifies Homer, Hesiod, and Simonides as prototypes of sophists who are non-mystical, to be contrasted with Orpheus and Musaeus as prototypes of sophists who are mystical. I quote again here a part of that passage, because the wording it contains turns out to be essential for my further argumentation:

3ⓣ21 Plato *Protagoras* 316d

ἐγὼ δὲ τὴν <u>σοφιστικὴν</u> <u>τέχνην</u> φημὶ μὲν εἶναι παλαιάν, τοὺς δὲ μεταχειριζομένους αὐτὴν τῶν παλαιῶν ἀνδρῶν, φοβουμένους τὸ ἐπαχθὲς αὐτῆς, πρόσχημα ποιεῖσθαι καὶ προκαλύπτεσθαι, τοὺς μὲν <u>ποίησιν</u>, οἷον "<u>Ὅμηρόν</u> τε καὶ <u>Ἡσίοδον</u> καὶ <u>Σιμωνίδην</u>, τοὺς δὲ αὖ <u>τελετάς</u> τε καὶ <u>χρησμῳδίας</u>, τοὺς ἀμφί τε <u>Ὀρφέα</u> καὶ <u>Μουσαῖον</u>·

I [= Protagoras] declare that the <u>sophistic craft</u> [*tekhnē*] is ancient, but those who had applied it among ancient men were afraid of the opprobrium attaching to it, and disguised and concealed themselves—some in the realm of <u>poetry</u> [*poiēsis*], like <u>Homer</u> and <u>Hesiod</u> and <u>Simonides</u>, but others in the realm of <u>mysteries</u> [*teletai*] and <u>oracular songs</u> [*khrēsmōidiai*], like <u>Orpheus</u> and <u>Musaeus</u> and their followers.[91]

3§124 In terms of such a dichotomy between mystical and non-mystical sophists, Socrates is aligned with the non-mystical. That is, Socrates is aligned with Hippias and non-aligned with Protagoras. Like Hippias, Socrates speaks as an expert in poetry when he performs and interprets the poetry of Simonides. By contrast, Plato's Protagoras speaks as an expert in sophistic mysticism. Protagoras looks for hidden meanings, which can elude even great poets like Simonides. Protagoras is saying that the basis of education is not only the understanding of poetry but also the understanding of whatever it is that the poets themselves do not and cannot fully control in their poetry (*Protagoras* 338e–339a). When Protagoras performs two passages from the song of Simonides (*PMG* 542 lines 1–3 at 339b and lines 11–13 at 339c), his intent is to show that a sophist like himself can understand things that even a poet like Simonides fails to understand.

---

[91] Translation after Allen 1996:177.

Chapter Three

3§125 In response to the interpretation claimed by Protagoras concerning the poetry of Simonides, Plato's Socrates playfully confesses a feeling of panic because he too—so he says—fails to understand the hidden meaning that the sophist Protagoras supposedly understands—a hidden meaning that even the poet Simonides himself supposedly fails to understand (*Protagoras* 339d–e). Moments later, having collected his wits, Socrates declares that he will in the end pass the test set by Protagoras. That is, Socrates will now prove his expertise in poetry by attempting to explain fully the meaning of the song of Simonides (*Protagoras* 342a). He then proceeds to present his discourse about the entire song (*Protagoras* 342a through 347a).

3§126 The poetic expertise that Plato's Socrates displays in the *Protagoras* can be used as a model for understanding the kind of poetic expertise that Hippias himself could have displayed and had actually offered to display. Such expertise involves not only the poetry of Simonides but other forms of non-mystical poetry as well, especially Homer.

3§127 To sum up, the divergences between the sophists Hippias and Protagoras as respectively non-mystical and mystical interpreters of Homer and other poets correspond to the divergences between the poetic figures of Homer and Orpheus as respectively non-mystical and mystical poets. Having noted this correspondence, I conclude my consideration of the divergences between Homeric and Orphic poetry in the age of Plato. Before leaving the subject, however, I should note that the alignment of Plato's Socrates with non-mystical interpreters of Homer and other poets, as displayed in Plato's *Protagoras*, is only *ad hoc*, matching the context of the Socratic line of argumentation in that dialogue. In other contexts, Plato's Socrates can align himself with the mystical interpreters of poets, focusing on the ultimate mystical poet, Orpheus. A case in point is Plato's *Phaedo*, where Plato's Socrates explores a variety of mystical models in the quest for initiation into the ultimate mystery that is meant to transcend all other mysteries, the Platonic theory of Forms.

3ⓢ7. Hippias the sophist as master of the Panathenaic standard

3§128 Leaving behind for the moment the mysticism of Protagoras and delving further into the non-mysticism of Hippias in his interpretation of Homer, I turn to the question of describing the overall expertise of Hippias the sophist in the performing and interpreting of Homer. This expertise, I will now argue, corresponds closely to the expertise of Ion the rhapsode in the

3§7. Hippias the sophist as master of the Panathenaic standard

performing and interpreting of Homer. I propose to describe this expertise in terms of the Panathenaic standard. That is to say, I propose that the Homer of Ion and Hippias was essentially the same Homer that was being performed on a seasonally recurring basis at the feast of the Panathenaia in the time of Plato and, by extension, in the earlier time of Ion and Hippias as dramatized by Plato.

3§129 In the *Ion* of Plato, the rhapsode's act of performing at the Panathenaia is directly associated with the act of performing Homer, to the exclusion of other poets. Correspondingly, in the *Protagoras* of Plato, we saw Hippias associated with Homer, while his counterpart, Protagoras, is associated with Orpheus. We also saw that the Socratic vision of Hippias matches the Homeric vision of Minos, and I find it essential at this point to repeat the Homeric details. Hippias too is pictured as seated on a throne (*Protagoras* 315b καθήμενον ... ἐν θρόνῳ, 315c ἐν θρόνῳ καθήμενος), responding to questions (315c διερωτᾶν ... ἐρωτώμενα) that call for critical judgment, as expressed by the verb *dia-krinein* 'decide [between X and Y]' (315c διέκρινεν). In the *Protagoras*, Hippias is pictured in the act of responding to questions about the natural world, that is, about *phusis* 'nature' in general, and about astronomy in particular (315c ἐφαίνοντο δὲ περὶ φύσεώς τε καὶ τῶν μετεώρων ἀστρονομικὰ ἄττα διερωτᾶν τὸν Ἱππίαν). In Plato's *Hippias Minor*, we see the same Hippias actually responding to questions posed by Socrates, who challenges the sophist to apply various *tekhnai* 'crafts' for the purpose of distinguishing, as empirically as possible, what is true and what is false. Among these *tekhnai*, Hippias singles out the *tekhnē* of astronomy as one of his specialties (*Hippias Minor* 367e). As the dialogue proceeds, it becomes clear that Hippias claims to be master of all *tekhnai*, culminating in all the *tekhnai* that relate to poetry and song:

3①22 Plato *Hippias Minor* 368a–369a

> ΣΩ. Ἴθι δή, ὦ Ἱππία, ἀνέδην οὑτωσὶ ἐπίσκεψαι κατὰ {b} πασῶν τῶν ἐπιστημῶν, εἴ που ἔστιν ἄλλως ἔχον ἢ οὕτως. πάντως δὲ πλείστας <u>τέχνας</u> πάντων <u>σοφώτατος</u> εἶ ἀνθρώπων, ὡς ἐγώ ποτέ σου ἤκουον μεγαλαυχουμένου, πολλὴν <u>σοφίαν</u> καὶ ζηλωτὴν σαυτοῦ διεξιόντος ἐν ἀγορᾷ ἐπὶ ταῖς τραπέζαις. ἔφησθα δὲ ἀφικέσθαι ποτὲ εἰς Ὀλυμπίαν ἃ εἶχες περὶ τὸ σῶμα ἅπαντα σαυτοῦ ἔργα ἔχων· πρῶτον μὲν <u>δακτύλιον</u>—ἐντεῦθεν γὰρ ἤρχου—ὃν εἶχες σαυτοῦ ἔχειν {c} ἔργον, ὡς ἐπιστάμενος <u>δακτυλίους γλύφειν</u>, καὶ ἄλλην <u>σφραγῖδα</u> σὸν ἔργον, καὶ στλεγγίδα καὶ λήκυθον ἃ αὐτὸς ἠργάσω· ἔπειτα <u>ὑποδήματα</u> ἃ

Chapter Three

εἶχες ἔφησθα αὐτὸς <u>σκυτοτομῆσαι</u>, καὶ τὸ ἱμάτιον <u>ὑφῆναι</u> καὶ τὸν χιτωνίσκον· καὶ ὅ γε πᾶσιν ἔδοξεν ἀτοπώτατον καὶ <u>σοφίας</u> πλείστης <u>ἐπίδειγμα</u>, ἐπειδὴ τὴν ζώνην ἔφησθα τοῦ χιτωνίσκου, ἣν εἶχες, εἶναι μὲν οἷαι αἱ Περσικαὶ τῶν πολυτελῶν, ταύτην δὲ αὐτὸς <u>πλέξαι</u>· πρὸς δὲ τούτοις <u>ποιήματα</u> ἔχων ἐλθεῖν, καὶ <u>ἔπη</u> καὶ <u>τραγῳδίας</u> {d} καὶ <u>διθυράμβους</u>, καὶ <u>καταλογάδην</u> πολλοὺς <u>λόγους</u> καὶ παντοδαποὺς συγκειμένους· καὶ περὶ τῶν <u>τεχνῶν</u> δὴ ὧν ἄρτι ἐγὼ ἔλεγον ἐπιστήμων ἀφικέσθαι διαφερόντως τῶν ἄλλων, καὶ περὶ <u>ῥυθμῶν</u> καὶ <u>ἁρμονιῶν</u> καὶ <u>γραμμάτων</u> <u>ὀρθότητος</u>, καὶ ἄλλα ἔτι πρὸς τούτοις πάνυ πολλά, ὡς ἐγὼ δοκῶ <u>μνημονεύειν</u>· καίτοι τό γε <u>μνημονικὸν ἐπελαθόμην</u> σου, ὡς ἔοικε, <u>τέχνημα</u>, ἐν ᾧ σὺ οἴει λαμπρότατος εἶναι· οἶμαι δὲ καὶ {e} ἄλλα πάμπολλα <u>ἐπιλελῆσθαι</u>. ἀλλ' ὅπερ ἐγὼ λέγω, καὶ εἰς τὰς σαυτοῦ <u>τέχνας</u> <u>βλέψας</u>—<u>ἱκαναὶ</u> δέ—καὶ εἰς τὰς τῶν ἄλλων εἰπέ μοι, ἐάν που εὕρῃς ἐκ τῶν ὡμολογημένων ἐμοί τε καὶ σοί, ὅπου ἐστὶν ὁ μὲν ἀληθής, ὁ δὲ ψευδής, χωρὶς καὶ οὐχ ὁ αὐτός· ἐν ᾗτινι βούλει <u>σοφίᾳ</u> τοῦτο σκέψαι ἢ πανουργίᾳ {369a} ἢ ὁτιοῦν χαίρεις ὀνομάζων· ἀλλ' οὐχ εὑρήσεις, ὦ ἑταῖρε—οὐ γὰρ ἔστιν—ἐπεὶ σὺ εἰπέ.

SOCRATES: Come, then, Hippias. Consider without any further ado whether or not this point [about the false and the true] holds for all kinds of knowledge. You are absolutely the most <u>skilled</u> [*sophos*] of men in the greatest number of <u>crafts</u> [*tekhnai*] by far, as I once heard you boast when you were describing your great and enviable <u>skill</u> [*sophia*].[92] It was in the agora [= the agora of Athens], near the money-changers' tables [*trapezai*].[93] You were telling how you once upon a time went to Olympia, and everything you wore was your own work: first, your <u>ring</u> [*daktulios*]—you started with that—was your own work because you knew how to <u>engrave</u> <u>rings</u> [*daktulioi*]—and the rest of it [= your ring], that is, its <u>seal</u> [*sphragis*], was your own work,[94] and an athletic scraper, and a *lēkuthion* you had made yourself.

---

[92] I will have more to say in ch. 4 about the usage of *sophos* and *sophia* here in the practical sense of 'skilled' and 'skill'.

[93] Earlier in the *Hippias Minor*, Socrates says that he attended a display by Hippias in Athens that took place within a space that is not yet specified, as we see from the wording ἡνίκα μὲν γὰρ πολλοὶ ἔνδον ἦμεν καὶ σὺ τὴν ἐπίδειξιν ἐποιοῦ 'when there were many of us within that space and you were making your display [*epideixis*]' and ὄχλος τε πολὺς ἔνδον ἦν 'there was a big crowd within that space' (364b). That space, if we are to trust Plato's sense of precision in creating this scene, is the same setting as the one to which Socrates refers here (368b).

[94] The making of this ring, I infer, involved metalwork in general and engraving in particular, and the focus of attention is on the engraved seal of the ring.

3§7. Hippias the sophist as master of the Panathenaic standard

Next, the footwear you had on you—you said you had done the leatherwork [*skutotomeîn*] yourself, and you had woven [*huphainein*] your own *himation* and your own khiton [*khitōn*]. And it seemed dazzling to everyone—a display [*epideigma*] of the greatest skill [*sophia*]⁹⁵ when you said that the cincture of the khiton [*khitōn*] you had on you was made of the costliest Persian kind, and that you had plaited [*plekein*] it yourself. And, on top of all these things, you had come bringing with you compositions [*poiēmata*]⁹⁶—that is, epic [*epos* plural] and tragedies and dithyrambs, and a multitude of discourses [*logoi*] to be performed in the right sequence [*katalogadēn*]⁹⁷ and all kinds of set pieces. And you arrived there as an expert surpassing all others in the knowledge of not only the crafts [*tekhnai*] I just mentioned, but also of the correctness [*orthotēs*] of rhythms [*rhuthmoi*], tunings [*harmoniai*], and letters [*grammata*].⁹⁸ And there were many more things in addition, as I seem to remember [*mnēmoneuein*]. And yet it seems I had almost forgotten [*epilanthanesthai*] about your mnemonic technique [*mnēmonikion tekhnēma*], in which you think you are at your most brilliant. And I suppose I have forgotten [*epilanthanesthai*] a great many other things too. But, as I say, look [*blepein*]⁹⁹ to your own crafts [*tekhnai*]—they are certainly sufficient—and those of others, and tell me if you anywhere find the true man and the false separate and not the same, given what we have agreed. Examine this in terms of any kind of skill [*sophia*] you may want to choose—or in terms of any kind of *panourgia*¹⁰⁰ whatsoever—

---

⁹⁵ I note that *sophia* here conveys a non-transcendent concept, 'skill', instead of the transcendent concept of 'wisdom'. More on this point in the discussion that follows.

⁹⁶ As we see from the context here as we read on, these 'compositions' are the poetic creations not only of Hippias but also of master 'composers' or *poiētai*, including Homer himself as the 'composer' or *poiētēs* par excellence. The concepts of *poiēma* as 'composition' and of *poiētēs* as 'composer' (in the verbal arts) are analyzed in HPC I§62.

⁹⁷ The conventions of performing *katalogadēn* 'in the right sequence, catalogue-style' are relevant to the *mnēmonikon tekhnēma* 'mnemonic technique' of Hippias, a key concept that Plato's Socrates is about to introduce in this same passage (Plato *Hippias Minor* 368d).

⁹⁸ For another passage that emphasizes these specialties of Hippias, see Plato *Hippias Maior* 285d. A relevant term is *grammatistēs*.

⁹⁹ This word *blepein* 'look' highlights the visual aspect of indexing the details associated with the *tekhnai* 'crafts' of Hippias. This same word *blepein* 'look' is used as an index for the perception of Plato's Forms.

¹⁰⁰ I postpone till ch. 4 my analysis of the playful insult implicit in Socrates' use of the word *panourgia* with reference to the *sophia* of Hippias.

or however you would like to call it. You will not find it, my friend, for it does not exist—but you tell me.[101]

3§130 I now focus on Plato's catalogue of skills that are claimed by Hippias in the passage I just quoted, without yet commenting on Plato's usage of *sophos* and *sophia* in referring to these skills.[102] As we examine more closely the structure of this catalogue, we can see that the sophist's skill as an expert in poetry and song takes pride of place. That highlighting can be seen more clearly if we think of Plato's catalogue of skills in terms of two sections. The first section enumerates various kinds of handicraft that Hippias has mastered as a craftsman in his own right, starting with the making of the sophist's ring and going through everything else he wears on his person. Everything is handmade by him. The second section enumerates various kinds of poetry and song that the sophist likewise masters as crafts in their own right. The kinds of poetry and song that the catalogue describes as crafts mastered by Hippias correspond to the kinds of dramatic and 'musical' performance featured at the two premier festivals of Athens, the City Dionysia and the Panathenaia respectively.[103] Among the dramatic performances of the City Dionysia, it is tragedy and dithyramb that are highlighted; among the 'musical' events of the Panathenaia, it is epic. Of all these kinds of poetry and song, epic is mentioned first of all—evidently the epic of Homer. Moreover, as we saw in a passage I quoted earlier from the very beginning of the *Hippias Minor*, Hippias has a special skill in one particular kind of poetry and song: that is, he specializes in the performing and the interpreting of Homer (363b). Relevant to this special skill of Hippias is a term introduced toward the very end of the passage I have just quoted: it is *mnēmonikon tekhnēma* 'mnemonic technique' (368d).

3§131 In this same passage, the status of Hippias as grand master of poetry and song is correlated with the keen interest shown by this sophist in the *orthotēs* 'correctness' of *grammata* 'letters' and in other such matters relating to various *tekhnai* 'crafts' of poetry and song (*Hippias Minor* 368a–e). This interest requires the ability to make critical judgments, as signaled by the verb *dia-krinein* 'decide [between X and Y]' in the description we saw earlier of the sophist seated on a throne and responding to questions (*Protagoras* 315c διέκρινεν). We may compare the interest shown by Ion the rhapsode in making correct critical judgments concerning questions of Homeric verbal artistry—

---

[101] Translation after Allen 1996:36–37.
[102] That commentary is postponed till ch. 4.
[103] When I say musical here, I am referring once again to the competitions in *mousikē* at the Panathenaia.

3Ⓢ7. Hippias the sophist as master of the Panathenaic standard

that is, whether Homer says his epos (plural) 'poetic utterances' orthōs 'correctly' or not (τὰ ἔπη εἴτε ὀρθῶς λέγει Ὅμηρος εἴτε μή Ion 537b-c). In the Ion, when Plato's Socrates asks Ion to tell him what are the things about which the craft of the rhapsode can enable Ion to make critical judgments, that is, dia-krinein 'decide [between X and Y]', the rhapsode replies: 'all things':

3①23 Plato Ion 539d-e

ΣΩ. Καὶ σύ γε, ὦ Ἴων, ἀληθῆ ταῦτα λέγεις. ἴθι δὴ καὶ σὺ ἐμοί, ὥσπερ ἐγὼ σοὶ ἐξέλεξα καὶ ἐξ Ὀδυσσείας καὶ ἐξ Ἰλιάδος ὁποῖα τοῦ μάντεώς ἐστι καὶ ὁποῖα τοῦ ἰατροῦ καὶ {ε} ὁποῖα τοῦ ἁλιέως, οὕτω καὶ σὺ ἐμοὶ ἔκλεξον, ἐπειδὴ καὶ ἐμπειρότερος εἶ ἐμοῦ τῶν Ὁμήρου, ὁποῖα τοῦ ῥαψῳδοῦ ἐστιν, ὦ Ἴων, καὶ τῆς τέχνης τῆς ῥαψῳδικῆς, ἃ τῷ ῥαψῳδῷ προσήκει καὶ σκοπεῖσθαι καὶ διακρίνειν παρὰ τοὺς ἄλλους ἀνθρώπους.

ΙΩΝ. Ἐγὼ μέν φημι, ὦ Σώκρατες, ἅπαντα.

SOCRATES: These things that you say, Ion, are true. But come now and do as I did. I picked out from the Odyssey and the Iliad[104] what sorts of things concern the seer [mantis], and the physician, and the fisherman. Since you are so much more experienced than I am about Homer, Ion, will you in this way also pick out for me what sorts of things belong to the rhapsode and to the rhapsodic craft [rhapsōidikē tekhnē]? What sorts of things are fitting for the rhapsode to consider and to make critical judgments about [dia-krinein], beyond all other humans?

ION: I say it's all things, Socrates.

3§132 Thus the critical judgment of the sophist Hippias in interpreting Homer, as signaled by the verb dia-krinein 'decide [between X and Y]', is matched by the critical judgment of the rhapsode Ion, which is likewise signaled by this same verb dia-krinein. The concept of this kind of critical judgment, I argue, is related to concepts derived from the simple form of this verb, krinein 'decide', as represented most prominently by the designation kritikos 'critic', self-applied by experts of literature in the Hellenistic period.[105]

---

[104] Here in Plato Ion 539d the wording makes it explicit that that the expertise of Ion in 'Homer' is equated with his expertise in the Iliad and Odyssey. So the term Homer here stands for the Iliad and Odyssey. For a similar context, see Xenophon Symposium 3.5.
[105] PH 2§24 (= pp. 61–62), 13§44 (= pp. 402–403).

413

Chapter Three

3§133 I propose to contrast this match between the sophist and the rhapsode with a mismatch deliberately set up by Plato in the *Hippias Minor* and the *Ion*. This mismatch has to do with the different strategies of argumentation used by Plato's Socrates in arguing with the sophist and with the rhapsode. Despite the differentiation between sophist and rhapsode as set up by Plato, I will argue that the actual concept of critical judgment, as signaled by *dia-krinein* 'decide [between X and Y]' and by the simple form *krinein* 'decide' and its derivative *kritikos* 'critic', is in fact not all that different in the craft of the sophist, despite its rivalry with the craft of the rhapsode. A similar argument will apply to other compound formations involving the verb *krinein*, especially *hupokrinesthai* and the noun derived from it, *hupokritēs*.

3§134 As an expert in Homer, Ion the rhapsode is compared by Plato's Socrates to an oracular poet who is inspired, that is, to a *mantis* 'seer' (*Ion* 531b). Hippias the sophist in Plato's *Hippias Minor* is likewise an expert in Homer, but in Plato's terms he would be comparable not to a *mantis* but to a *prophētēs*. In making this point, I have in mind an exceptional passage where Plato's Socrates makes a distinction between two kinds of 'seer', the *mantis* who is inspired and the *prophētēs* who is supposedly uninspired:

3ⓣ24 Plato *Timaeus* 72a–b

> τοῦ δὲ <u>μανέντος</u> ... οὐκ ἔργον τὰ <u>φανέντα</u> καὶ φωνηθέντα ὑφ' ἑαυτοῦ <u>κρίνειν</u>, ... ὅθεν δὴ καὶ τὸ τῶν <u>προφητῶν</u> γένος ἐπὶ ταῖς <u>ἐνθέοις μαντείαις κριτὰς</u> ἐπικαθιστάναι νόμος· οὓς <u>μάντεις</u> αὐτοὺς ὀνομάζουσίν τινες, τὸ πᾶν ἠγνοηκότες ὅτι τῆς δι' αἰνιγμῶν οὗτοι φήμης καὶ φαντάσεως <u>ὑποκριταί</u>, καὶ οὔτι <u>μάντεις</u>, <u>προφῆται</u> δὲ <u>μαντευομένων</u> δικαιότατα ὀνομάζοιντ' ἄν

> But when some person <u>is in a state of mental possession</u> [*manēnai*] ... it is not that person's task to <u>make decisions</u> [*krinein*] about the visions that are <u>made visible</u> [*phanēnai*] to him or about the words that are voiced by him. ... For this reason it is customary to put in charge the class of <u>*prophētai*</u> as <u>decision-makers</u> [*kritai*] presiding over <u>oracular utterances</u> [*manteiai*] that had been <u>made</u> [by others] that are <u>*entheoi*</u> [= <u>in the state of being mentally possessed by the god</u>]. They [= the *prophētai*] are called by some, in ignorance, *manteis*. This is to ignore completely the fact that they [= the *prophētai*] are <u>*hupokritai*</u>, by ways of riddles [*ainigmoi*], of oracular utterance [*phēmē*] and oracular vision [*phantasis*]. So they would be

3⑤7. Hippias the sophist as master of the Panathenaic standard

most justly called not *manteis* but the *prophētai* of things that are uttered by those who function as *manteis*.

3§135 I need to stress that the context here reflects Plato's *ad hoc* philosophical agenda, and that only in this Platonic context is the *prophētēs* assumed to be uninspired.[106] In other Platonic contexts, the *prophētēs* is assumed to be inspired and is synonymous with the *mantis* 'seer' (Plato *Charmides* 173c, etc.). In non-Platonic contexts as well, the *prophētēs* is explicitly inspired (Pindar *Nemean* 1.60, Herodotus 3.37.2, etc.).[107] Generally, if we view the words *mantis* and *prophētēs* outside of Plato's sphere of argumentation, the distinction between them is not a question of being inspired or not inspired. Rather, it is more a question of different degrees of formalization: whereas the words of a *mantis* may or may not be poetic, those of a *prophētēs* are predictably so: a salient example is the wording of Bacchylides (*Epinician* 8.3), who pictures the generic poet as the *prophētēs* of the Muses.[108]

3§136 In the same passage from Plato's *Timaeus* that we have just examined, the *ad hoc* usage of *prophētēs* as an uninspired performer of oracular poetry is matched by the *ad hoc* usage of the agent noun of the verb *hupokrinesthai*, that is, *hupokritēs*. Like *prophētēs*, this word *hupokritēs* is used here in the *ad hoc* sense of designating a performer who is not possessed, not inspired by the god. As we have already seen, however, Plato's Socrates elsewhere actually speaks of the *hupokritēs* as an inspired performer, parallel to the *rhapsōidos*:

3①25 Plato *Ion* 535e–536a

ΣΩ. οἶσθα οὖν ὅτι οὗτός ἐστιν ὁ <u>θεατὴς</u> τῶν δακτυλίων ὁ <u>ἔσχατος</u>, ὧν ἐγὼ ἔλεγον ὑπὸ τῆς Ἡρακλειώτιδος λίθου ἀπ' ἀλλήλων τὴν δύναμιν λαμβάνειν; ὁ δὲ <u>μέσος</u> σὺ ὁ {536a} <u>ῥαψῳδὸς</u> καὶ <u>ὑποκριτής</u>, ὁ δὲ <u>πρῶτος</u> αὐτὸς ὁ <u>ποιητής</u>.

SOCRATES: Of course you know that this person we talked about, the <u>spectator</u> [*theatēs*] in the audience, is the <u>last</u> of the rings—I mean, the rings that get their power from each other through the force of the Heraclean stone. The <u>middle</u> ring is the <u>rhapsode</u>—that's you

---

[106] HR 34–36.
[107] PH 6§§33–35 (= pp. 162–164).
[108] Further examples in PH 6§34 (= p. 163).

Chapter Three

[= Ion]—as well as the actor [*hupokritēs*]. And the first ring is the composer [*poiētēs*] himself.[109]

3§137 As is the case with the word *prophētēs*, so also with *hupokritēs*: we see from the passage just quoted that this word too may be used in the sense of a performer who is possessed, inspired. Plato's wording, as we saw in the *Timaeus* (72a–b), describes *hupokritēs* as one who interprets, by way of performing, the utterance [*phēmē*] and the vision [*phantasis*] of a given oracle. There is no need to follow Plato, however, in assuming that such a *hupokritēs* must be disconnected from the visualization and the verbalization of the oracular vision. Just as the verb *hupokrinesthai* is predicated on the idea of a preexisting vision, so also the noun *hupokritēs*.

3§138 The very act of performing can be considered an act of interpretation, as we see from such modern usages as French *interpréter* in the sense of 'sing' or 'play' a given musical composition. In this light, let us consider the idea inherent in usages of *krinein* ['make decisions'], from which the compound form *hupokrinesthai* is derived. This verb *krinein*, in the active voice, can be translated as 'interpret' when combined with the noun *opsis* 'vision' as its object (Herodotus 7.19.12) or with *enupnion* 'dream' as its object (Herodotus 1.120.1).[110] It is a question of interpreting-in-performance. In the middle voice, *hupo-krinesthai* suggests that the performer is interpreting for himself as well as for others.[111] The basic idea of *hupokrinesthai*, then, is to see the real meaning of what others see, and to quote what this vision is really saying to them.

3§139 Whereas the art of the rhapsode, as conveyed by the word *hupokrinesthai* and related forms, is associated with the idea of responsiveness, Plato seems to associate this art with the idea of unresponsiveness. We may consider in this regard another compound of *krinein*, that is, *anakrinein*, which means 'interrogate [judicially]', as in the usage of Thucydides (1.95). In Plato's *Phaedrus* (277e), we read of *logoi* that are *rhapsōidoumenoi* 'performed rhapsodically' and are exempt from *anakrisis* 'interrogation' (οἱ ῥαψῳδούμενοι ἄνευ ἀνακρίσεως).[112]

3§140 In the case of *hupokrinesthai*, as we saw in Chapter 1, the idea of an oracular vision is evident from the word's conventional associations with such other words as *theōros*, meaning literally 'he who sees [root *hor-*] a vision

---

[109] On *poiētēs* as 'composer', I refer to the analysis in HPC I§62.
[110] Koller 1957:101.
[111] Koller 1957:102.
[112] The last two paragraphs are based on what I already said in HR 37–38.

3§7. Hippias the sophist as master of the Panathenaic standard

[*thea*]'. In the case of *hupokritēs*, as we also saw, the word is associated with *theatron* 'theater', meaning literally 'the vehicle for achieving vision [*thea*]'.

3§141 As I stressed already in Chapter 1, *hupokrinesthai* and *hupokritēs* become the words for 'act' and 'actor' in the language of Athenian State Theater. A case in point is this expression in the usage of Demosthenes (19.246): τὴν Ἀντιγόνην Σοφοκλέους ὑποκέκριται as 'he has performed [*hupokrinesthai*] the *Antigone* of Sophocles'. The definition of *hupokrinesthai* in the dictionary of Liddell and Scott (LSJ s.v., B II) is suggestive: "speak in dialogue, hence play a part on the stage, the part played being put in [accusative]." By metonymy, the part can become the whole (as reflected in the title-style highlighting that I used here for *Antigone*), so that the part being played stands for the whole play.[113] Another relevant example comes from Aristotle (*Rhetoric* 3.1403b23): ὑπεκρίνοντο γὰρ αὐτοὶ τὰς τραγῳδίας οἱ ποιηταὶ τὸ πρῶτον 'in the beginning the poets themselves used to perform [*hupokrinesthai*] their tragedies'.[114] As for the noun *hupokritēs*, it is the standard word for 'performer in theater', 'actor' in the usage of Plato (*Republic* 2.373b, *Symposium* 194b, etc.).[115]

3§142 In the light of the meaning of *hupokritēs* as 'actor' in the usage of Plato, let us return to the context of *Ion* 536a, where Plato's Socrates pictures the generic *hupokritēs* as parallel to the generic *rhapsōidos* in his role as a supposedly inspired performer. This parallelism, though we can justify it from the standpoint of earlier stages in the evolving performance traditions of actors as well as rhapsodes, is anachronistic from the standpoint of these same traditions in the age of Plato. By this time, the idea that actors are inspired performers makes no sense: far from being inspired, they simply learn the words composed by poets. Further, the idea that rhapsodes are inspired performers makes no sense, either, if indeed they are parallel to actors. Thus the parallelism drawn between actors and rhapsodes serves to discredit rhapsodes: it makes them seem to be uninspired.[116] Even further, the idea that actors and rhapsodes are inspired performers suits only the *ad hoc* argumentation of Plato's Socrates in *Ion* 536a—and only to the extent that it serves to discredit the idea that rhapsodes can think for themselves about what they perform. Beyond that, there is no need for Plato's Socrates to maintain the idea that the rhapsode is truly inspired.

3§143 In the end, Plato's portrayal of Ion implies that the rhapsode, like an actor, is simply acting out the words once composed by Homer. The

---

[113] *HR* 36.
[114] *HR* 36.
[115] *HR* 35, 37.
[116] Besides Plato *Ion* 535e, see also 532d.

Chapter Three

moment of truth arrives when Socrates questions Ion whether the rhapsode feels the same emotions felt by the characters in his Homeric performances, such as Andromache, Hector, Hecuba, and Priam:

3ⓣ26 Plato *Ion* 535b–c

> ΣΩ. Ἔχε δή μοι τόδε εἰπέ, ὦ Ἴων, καὶ μὴ ἀποκρύψῃ ὅτι ἄν σε ἔρωμαι· ὅταν εὖ εἴπῃς ἔπη καὶ ἐκπλήξῃς μάλιστα τοὺς θεωμένους, ἢ τὸν Ὀδυσσέα ὅταν ἐπὶ τὸν οὐδὸν ἐφαλλόμενον ᾄδῃς, ἐκφανῆ γιγνόμενον τοῖς μνηστῆρσι καὶ ἐκχέοντα τοὺς ὀιστοὺς πρὸ τῶν ποδῶν, ἢ Ἀχιλλέα ἐπὶ τὸν Ἕκτορα ὁρμῶντα, ἢ καὶ τῶν περὶ Ἀνδρομάχην ἐλεινῶν τι ἢ περὶ Ἑκάβην ἢ περὶ Πρίαμον, τότε πότερον ἔμφρων εἶ ἢ ἔξω {c} σαυτοῦ γίγνῃ καὶ παρὰ τοῖς πράγμασιν οἴεταί σου εἶναι ἡ ψυχὴ οἷς λέγεις ἐνθουσιάζουσα, ἢ ἐν Ἰθάκῃ οὖσιν ἢ ἐν Τροίᾳ ἢ ὅπως ἂν καὶ τὰ ἔπη ἔχῃ;

> SOCRATES: Hold it right there. Tell me this, Ion—respond to what I ask without concealment. When you recite well the epic verses [*epos* plural] and induce a feeling of bedazzlement [*ekplēxis*] for the spectators [*theōmenoi*]—when you sing of Odysseus leaping onto the threshold and revealing himself to the suitors and pouring out the arrows at his feet, or of Achilles rushing at Hector, or something connected to the pitiful things about Andromache or Hecuba or Priam—are you then in your right mind, or outside yourself? Does your *psukhē*, possessed by the god [*enthousiazein*], suppose that you are in the midst of the actions you describe in Ithaca or Troy, or wherever the epic verses [*epos* plural] have it?

3§144 Ion begins his response to the questioning of Socrates by claiming he feels the same emotions of terror and pity that are felt by his audiences in reaction to the actions of his characters (*Ion* 533c). But then, Ion continues his extended response to the question by implying that he is merely acting the words of and about these Homeric characters—and not necessarily experiencing their emotions. If words about sad things composed by Homer make Ion's audiences genuinely sad, then Ion himself can be genuinely happy, he says (*Ion* 535e). Thus Plato's portrait of the rhapsode has ultimately turned this supposedly inspired mouthpiece of the Muses into an uninspired and cynical manipulator of the audience's emotions. While Ion leaves his audiences crying over the grief of Andromache and other such heroic characters, he is "laughing all the way to the bank."

3⒮7. Hippias the sophist as master of the Panathenaic standard

3§145 The parallelism of the *rhapsōidos* and the *hupokritēs* can be taken further. Whereas the *hupokritēs* performs the poetry and songs of drama, primarily at the City Dionysia, the *rhapsōidos* performs the poetry of Homer, primarily at the Panathenaia. Just as the *hupokritēs* acts out his given role in the dramatic performances of the City Dionysia, so too the *rhapsōidos* acts out his given role as the master narrator of the Homeric *Iliad* and *Odyssey* in the epic performances of the Panathenaia. When a rhapsode like Plato's Ion performs Homeric poetry, he is not only quoting the words of heroes and gods, thereby acting both their words and their personalities: he is also quoting the words of Homer, which are the narrative frame of heroic song. That is, the rhapsode is also acting both the words and the persona of Homer himself.[117]

3§146 Whereas the actor represents only the characters made by the poet of drama, the rhapsode represents the poet Homer himself as well as the characters made by Homer. Moreover, when the rhapsode explains the poetry of Homer, he claims to speak for the poet Homer, and he derives his authority from Homer. The actor of drama has no such claim or authority. The actor of drama at the City Dionysia in Athens wears a mask to project the character he represents, whereas the rhapsode of Homeric poetry at the Panathenaia in Athens wears no mask to project the characters that he in turn represents when he quotes their speeches within his narrative. The rhapsode cannot wear the mask of a character because he changes characters in the course of performance. As Aristotle observes in the *Poetics* (1448a22), the representation of a character in Homeric poetry can happen either by narrating about that character or by quoting the character directly. For example, when the words of the priest of Apollo are quoted in *Iliad* I, then Homer assumes the character of the priest. When the priest is answered by Agamemnon, then Homer assumes the character of Agamemnon. Going beyond Aristotle, I add that not only Homer but also the rhapsode himself assumes the character of the priest and then the character of Agamemnon when he quotes Homer who quotes the priest and then Agamemnon. In other words, the rhapsode assumes the character of Homer himself as the master narrator who quotes the voices of the epic past and who thereby assumes the characters that go with the voices. An actor too can assume different characters, but only by way of wearing different masks at different times, and the switching of masks cannot happen within the continuum of performance. For the rhapsode, by contrast, the assuming of different characters must happen within the continuum of performance. And

---

[117] This whole paragraph is based on what I said in *HR* 37.

that continuum is made possible by the rhapsode's assuming the character of Homer himself. Within that continuum, the rhapsode represents both the poet and his poetry. That is why poetry, as a prime target of Plato's Socrates, is primarily represented by the rhapsode, not by the actor.[118]

3§147 I conclude that the authority of the rhapsode is derived from the authority of Homer as the poet par excellence—as the one to whom even Plato's Socrates refers as *ho poiētēs* 'the Poet' (Plato *Ion* 530c, etc.).[119] That is why Socrates must separate the *poiētikē tekhnē* 'craft of the poet' from the *rhapsōidikē tekhnē* 'craft of the rhapsode' in the *Ion*. If the authority of the poetry performed by Ion is merely something derived from the inspiration of and by Homer, then the authority of Ion as a master of the rhapsodic craft can be discredited as insignificant.

3ⓢ8. Sophistic powers of total recall

3§148 The very idea of inspiration or divine 'possession' by the Muses can help Plato undermine the credibility of rhapsodes as representatives of song and poetry. On the other hand, Plato needs different ideas to undermine the credibility of Hippias. As a sophist, Hippias does not represent song and poetry per se.

3§149 Unlike Ion the rhapsode, Hippias the sophist is not overtly inspired or 'possessed'—either by Homer or, ultimately, by the Muses. When Hippias needs to consult Homer, what he needs is not inspiration or possession but memory. As we saw earlier, there is a technical term for this kind of memory, that is, *mnēmonikon tekhnēma* 'mnemonic technique' (*Hippias Minor* 368d). This term is used again in a later passage where Socrates is challenging Hippias to display his all-encompassing knowledge of Homer by responding to the central question of distinguishing between the true and the false man, and the sophist is induced to admit that he will have to use his memory:

---

[118] There is more to be said about the basic difference between the *rhapsōidos* 'rhapsode' and the *hupokritēs* 'actor' as performers. When the actor performs, he is a dramatized character inside the composition of a composer and thus cannot claim any inspiration by the Muses. Only the composer can make such a claim. By contrast, the rhapsode as performer actually represents the composer and can thus claim to be inspired by the Muses. In the case of the rhapsodic craft, the ancient concept of *mousikē* as the 'craft of the Muses' applies to performers as well as composers. That is another reason why rhapsodes, unlike actors, do not wear masks.

[119] On Homer as *ho poiētēs* 'the poet' in Plato *Ion* 530c, see PR 29. On Homer as the *poiētēs* 'composer' par excellence, I offer an analysis in HPC I§61.

3⑤8. Sophistic powers of total recall

3①27 Plato *Hippias Minor* 368e–369b

ἀλλ' ὅπερ ἐγὼ λέγω, καὶ εἰς τὰς σαυτοῦ <u>τέχνας</u> βλέψας—<u>ἱκαναὶ δέ</u>—καὶ εἰς τὰς τῶν ἄλλων εἰπέ μοι, ἐάν που εὕρῃς ἐκ τῶν ὡμολογημένων ἐμοί τε καὶ σοί, ὅπου ἐστὶν ὁ μὲν ἀληθής, ὁ δὲ ψευδής, χωρὶς καὶ οὐχ ὁ αὐτός· ἐν ᾗτινι βούλει <u>σοφίᾳ</u> τοῦτο σκέψαι ἢ πανουργίᾳ {369a} ἢ ὁτιοῦν χαίρεις ὀνομάζων· ἀλλ' οὐχ εὑρήσεις, ὦ ἑταῖρε—οὐ γὰρ ἔστιν—ἐπεὶ σὺ εἰπέ.

ΙΠ. Ἀλλ' οὐκ ἔχω, ὦ Σώκρατες, νῦν γε οὕτως.

ΣΩ. Οὐδέ γε ἕξεις, ὡς ἐγὼ οἶμαι· εἰ δ' ἐγὼ ἀληθῆ λέγω, <u>μέμνησαι</u> ὃ ἡμῖν συμβαίνει ἐκ τοῦ λόγου, ὦ Ἱππία.

ΙΠ. Οὐ πάνυ τι ἐννοῶ, ὦ Σώκρατες, ὃ λέγεις.

ΣΩ. Νυνὶ γὰρ ἴσως οὐ χρῇ τῷ <u>μνημονικῷ</u> τεχνήματι—δῆλον γὰρ ὅτι οὐκ οἴει δεῖν—ἀλλὰ ἐγώ σε <u>ὑπομνήσω</u>. οἶσθα ὅτι τὸν μὲν Ἀχιλλέα ἔφησθα ἀληθῆ εἶναι, τὸν δὲ Ὀδυσσέα {b} ψευδῆ καὶ <u>πολύτροπον</u>;

ΙΠ. Ναί.

SOCRATES (to Hippias): But as I say, look [*blepein*] to your own <u>crafts</u> [*tekhnai*]—they are certainly <u>sufficient</u>—and those of others, and tell me if you anywhere find the true man and the false separate and not the same, given what we have agreed. Examine this in terms of any sort of <u>skill</u> [*sophia*] you may want to choose—or in terms of any kind of *panourgia*[120] whatsoever—or however you would like to call it. You will not find it, my friend, for it does not exist—but you tell me.

HIPPIAS: But I am not able to do so, Socrates, at least not in the present circumstances.

SOCRATES: Nor will you be able, I think. But if I am right, you <u>remember</u> [*memnēsthai*] what follows from the argument, Hippias.

HIPPIAS: I just don't understand what you mean, Socrates, not at all.

SOCRATES: Maybe you are not using your <u>mnemonic technique</u> [*mnēmonikon tekhnēma*] right now—clearly you don't think you need to—but I will <u>give</u> you <u>mnemonic support</u> [*hupo-mnē-*]. You know

---

[120] To repeat, I postpone till ch. 4 my analysis of the playful insult implicit in Socrates' use of the word *panourgia* with reference to the *sophia* of Hippias.

you were saying that Achilles is true but Odysseus false and multi-form [*polutropos*]?

HIPPIAS: Yes.[121]

3§150 In this passage we see again the term *mnēmonikon tekhnēma* 'mnemonic technique' (*Hippias Minor* 369a), which I have already highlighted in the previous passage I quoted (368d). This term is relevant to the notion that the presence of Homer is to be ignored in the dialogue between Hippias and Socrates, and that Hippias is to 'respond' jointly for Homer as well as for himself:

3ⓣ28 Plato *Hippias Minor* 365c–d

ΣΩ. Τὸν μὲν Ὅμηρον τοίνυν ἐάσωμεν, ἐπειδὴ καὶ {d} ἀδύνατον ἐπανερέσθαι τί ποτε νοῶν ταῦτα ἐποίησεν τὰ ἔπη· σὺ δ' ἐπειδὴ φαίνῃ ἀναδεχόμενος τὴν αἰτίαν, καὶ σοὶ συνδοκεῖ ταῦτα ἅπερ φῂς Ὅμηρον λέγειν, ἀπόκριναι κοινῇ ὑπὲρ Ὁμήρου τε καὶ σαυτοῦ.

SOCRATES: Then let us dismiss Homer, since it is impossible to ask him what he intended [*noeîn*] when he made [*poieîn*] these verses [*epos* plural]. But since you are clearly taking up [*anadekhesthai*] his cause [*aitia*][122] and agree with these things you say he is saying [*legein*], I ask you to respond [*apokrinesthai*] in common [*koinēi*] on behalf of Homer and yourself.[123]

3§151 The wording here makes it clear that Plato's Hippias, as a sophist, needs to make no overt claim to the inspiration of and by Homer—unlike Plato's Ion, as a rhapsode. In the case of Hippias, his mastery of Homeric poetry comes from a craft, just as Ion's mastery comes from a craft, but the craft of the sophist is one that transcends the *rhapsōidikē tekhnē*. It transcends even the *poiētikē tekhnē* writ large. I propose that the craft of Hippias the sophist was imagined as a form of *sophistikē tekhnē* 'sophistic craft', which was derived from the *rhapsōidikē tekhnē* but became differentiated from it. Such a transcendent craft, the *sophistikē tekhnē*, was the rival of another transcendent craft, the philosophical dialectic of Socrates himself.

---

[121] Translation after Allen 1996:37.
[122] The use of the word *aitia* 'cause' implies that Hippias must understand the plot of the *Iliad* as a chain of cause-and-effect narrative.
[123] Translation after Allen 1996:33.

3Ⓢ8. Sophistic powers of total recall

3§152 We have already seen this term *sophistikē tekhnē* 'sophistic craft' in a passage that I quoted from Plato's *Protagoras*. Here I requote the part of that passage that features this transcendent *tekhnē* of the sophists:

3①29 Plato *Protagoras* 316d

ἐγὼ δὲ τὴν <u>σοφιστικὴν</u> <u>τέχνην</u> φημὶ μὲν εἶναι παλαιάν, τοὺς δὲ μεταχειριζομένους αὐτὴν τῶν παλαιῶν ἀνδρῶν, φοβουμένους τὸ ἐπαχθὲς αὐτῆς, πρόσχημα ποιεῖσθαι καὶ προκαλύπτεσθαι, τοὺς μὲν <u>ποίησιν</u>, οἷον "<u>Ὅμηρόν</u> τε καὶ <u>Ἡσίοδον</u> καὶ <u>Σιμωνίδην</u>, τοὺς δὲ αὖ <u>τελετάς</u> τε καὶ <u>χρησμῳδίας</u>, τοὺς ἀμφί τε <u>Ὀρφέα</u> καὶ <u>Μουσαῖον</u>·

I [= Protagoras] declare that the <u>sophistic craft</u> [*tekhnē*] is ancient, but those who had applied it among ancient men were afraid of the opprobrium attaching to it, and disguised and concealed themselves—some in the realm of <u>poetry</u> [*poiēsis*],[124] like <u>Homer</u> and <u>Hesiod</u> and <u>Simonides</u>, but others in the realm of <u>mysteries</u> [*teletai*] and <u>oracular songs</u> [*khrēsmōidiai*], like <u>Orpheus</u> and <u>Musaeus</u> and their followers.[125]

3§153 As we see from what I just quoted, the *sophistikē tekhnē* 'sophistic craft' can be mystical, as represented by Protagoras himself. As we can also see in an earlier passage I already quoted from Plato's *Protagoras*, the sophist Protagoras is compared to Orpheus himself (315a-b). Orpheus in the present passage is associated with *teletai* 'mysteries' and *khrēsmōidiai* 'oracular songs' (316d).

3§154 By contrast with Orpheus, Homer in the present passage is associated simply with *poiēsis* 'poetry' (316d). In the earlier passage, the description of Protagoras as Orpheus is being contrasted with the description of the rival sophist Hippias in wording that suits Homer (315b-c). If we apply the term *sophistikē tekhnē* 'sophistic craft' to this sophist, we need to specify that his version of the craft is not mystical, by contrast with the craft of Protagoras.

3§155 The sophistic craft of Hippias the sophist is so non-mystical as to be practical. His craft subsumes various practical crafts. As a living embodiment of his *sophistikē tekhnē*, Hippias the sophist claims personal mastery of practical crafts. In the passage I quoted earlier from the *Hippias Minor*, Socrates tells of Hippias speaking about this mastery. Socrates recalls one particular time

---

[124] Here again I translate *poiēsis* as 'poetry'. But *poiēsis* is more accurately rendered as 'composition' (in the verbal arts).
[125] Translation after Allen 1996:177.

when Hippias came to Athens and spoke in public, in the agora (*Hippias Minor* 368b). Socrates was there and heard him speak, and he tells about Hippias in Athens telling about an earlier time when Hippias spoke in Olympia, in the *hieron* 'sacred precinct' of Zeus (363c-d, 364a). The impression given by Plato is that the performance of Hippias in the agora of Athens is a "replay" of the performance of Hippias in the sacred precinct of Zeus in Olympia.[126] As we saw, Hippias is being pictured in the act of speaking about himself and all his crafts, displaying his mastery of each of those crafts. As we also saw, his catalogue of crafts culminates in the craft of poetry and song, and for Hippias the key to the mastery of that craft is his *mnēmonikon tekhnēma* 'mnemonic technique' (368d, 369a). As I will now argue, that same technique is what differentiates the sophistic craft of Hippias from the rhapsodic craft of Ion.

3§156 Here I need to concentrate on the precise moment when the mnemonic technique of Hippias the sophist is first mentioned in the *Hippias Minor*. In the context of the sophist's display of all the crafts that he has mastered, he starts by highlighting his mastery of the jeweller's craft as a prime example, saying that he himself had hand-made the *daktulios* 'ring' that he wears on his finger—and on that ring is a *sphragis* 'seal' that he himself had specially carved (*Hippias Minor* 368b-c). That ring is the first thing about Hippias that attracts the attention of Plato's Socrates in the *Hippias Minor*. Socrates thinks back to that ring that Hippias was wearing, and he thinks back further: he now remembers that it was Hippias himself who had first drawn attention to the ring. 'You started with that', Socrates says about the ring (Plato *Hippias Minor* 368b).

3§157 So the *daktulios* 'ring' was the first thing that Hippias talked about in the sacred precinct of Zeus in Olympia and, by implication, also later in the agora in Athens. What about that 'first ring'? That all-attractive 'first ring' evokes the image of the magnetic First Rings (*prōtoi daktulioi*) that magnetize performers and their audiences in Plato's *Ion* (536b). This connection between the First Rings in Plato's *Ion* (536b) and the Ring of Hippias in the *Hippias Minor* (368b) will be most relevant in later phases of my argumentation.

3§158 The *daktulios* 'ring' hand-made by the sophist is just the beginning. Hippias then goes on to say that he also hand-made the *himation* and the khiton (*khitōn*) that he is wearing, having woven these fabrics himself. Moreover, Hippias is a master of leatherwork—*skutotomeîn*—in his own right, having hand-made his own shoes. We saw already in another Platonic passage

---

[126] For more on Plato's reference to the public display by Hippias in the agora of Athens, see ch. 4.

that the *husteroi* or 'later' thinkers who are experts in supposedly later poets like Homer—rather than earlier poets like Orpheus—tended to demystify the mysteries, so that even leatherworkers—*skutotomoi*—may understand (Plato *Theaetetus* 180d), to be contrasted with *palaioteroi* or 'earlier' thinkers specializing in supposedly earlier poets like Orpheus, whose mysteries continued to mystify the outsiders (Plato *Theaetetus* 179e–180d). A most valuable independent confirmation comes from Xenophon's *Memorabilia* (4.4.5), where Hippias of Elis is represented as debating with Socrates about the possibilities of teaching even the *skuteus* 'leatherworker' and other specialists (εἰ μέν τις βούλοιτο σκυτέα διδάξασθαί τινα ἢ τέκτονα ἢ χαλκέα ἢ ἱππέα . . .).

3§159 Returning to the point I already made about the *sophistikē tekhnē* 'sophistic craft' as mentioned in the *Protagoras* of Plato, I stress again that this concept is hardly monolithic. The craft of sophists can be either mystical, as represented by Protagoras himself, or decidedly non-mystical, as represented by his rival, Hippias. Also, this craft can subsume other crafts. Among the crafts subsumed by the *sophistikē tekhnē* of Hippias the sophist, the most prominent is the *rhapsōidikē tekhnē*—specifically, the rhapsodic craft of performing and interpreting Homer. That is the craft displayed to the fullest by Hippias the sophist in Plato's *Hippias Minor*.

3§160 By metonymy, this one single craft of the rhapsodes can subsume other crafts. By metonymy, the mastery of Homeric poetry is the mastery of all crafts. We saw this idea proclaimed by the rhapsode Ion in Plato's *Ion*. This stance of Ion the rhapsode is remarkably similar to the stance of Hippias the sophist. The difference is, Hippias does not consider himself a specialist in *rhapsōidikē tekhnē*. Rather, he seems to be a generalist in *sophistikē tekhnē*. The sophist's mastery of the rhapsode's craft is merely the primary example of his mastery of all crafts. Here I return to my argument: what makes all the difference is the sophist's overall mastery of the *mnēmonikon tekhnēma* 'mnemonic technique'.

3§161 In order to show the decisive role of this mnemonic technique, I need to review the two consecutive sections in the catalogue of crafts attributed to Hippias in Plato's *Hippias Minor*. As we saw, the first section enumerated various kinds of handicraft mastered by Hippias, starting with the sophist's ring and going through everything else he wears on his person (368b–c). The second section enumerated the kinds of poetry and song that the sophist has likewise mastered, corresponding to the kinds of dramatic and 'musical' performance featured at the two premier festivals of Athens, the City Dionysia and the Panathenaia respectively (368c–d). It is in this particular context that the mnemonic technique of Hippias is highlighted:

Chapter Three

3①30 Plato *Hippias Minor* 368a–d

ΣΩ. Ἴθι δή, ὦ Ἱππία, ἀνέδην οὑτωσὶ ἐπίσκεψαι κατὰ {b} πασῶν τῶν ἐπιστημῶν, εἴ που ἔστιν ἄλλως ἔχον ἢ οὕτως. πάντως δὲ πλείστας <u>τέχνας</u> πάντων σοφώτατος εἶ ἀνθρώπων, ὡς ἐγώ ποτέ σου ἤκουον μεγαλαυχουμένου, πολλὴν <u>σοφίαν</u> καὶ ζηλωτὴν σαυτοῦ διεξιόντος ἐν ἀγορᾷ ἐπὶ ταῖς τραπέζαις. ἔφησθα δὲ ἀφικέσθαι ποτὲ εἰς Ὀλυμπίαν ἃ εἶχες περὶ τὸ σῶμα ἅπαντα σαυτοῦ ἔργα ἔχων· πρῶτον μὲν <u>δακτύλιον</u>—ἐντεῦθεν γὰρ ἤρχου—ὃν εἶχες σαυτοῦ ἔχειν {c} ἔργον, ὡς ἐπιστάμενος <u>δακτυλίους γλύφειν</u>, καὶ ἄλλην σφραγῖδα σὸν ἔργον, καὶ στλεγγίδα καὶ λήκυθον ἃ αὐτὸς ἠργάσω· ἔπειτα <u>ὑποδήματα</u> ἃ εἶχες ἔφησθα αὐτὸς <u>σκυτοτομῆσαι</u>, καὶ τὸ ἱμάτιον ὑφῆναι καὶ τὸν χιτωνίσκον· καὶ ὅ γε πᾶσιν ἔδοξεν ἀτοπώτατον καὶ σοφίας πλείστης ἐπίδειγμα, ἐπειδὴ τὴν ζώνην ἔφησθα τοῦ χιτωνίσκου, ἣν εἶχες, εἶναι μὲν οἷαι αἱ Περσικαὶ τῶν πολυτελῶν, ταύτην δὲ αὐτὸς <u>πλέξαι</u>· πρὸς δὲ τούτοις <u>ποιήματα</u> ἔχων ἐλθεῖν, καὶ <u>ἔπη</u> καὶ <u>τραγῳδίας</u> {d} καὶ <u>διθυράμβους</u>, καὶ <u>καταλογάδην</u> πολλοὺς λόγους καὶ παντοδαποὺς συγκειμένους· καὶ περὶ τῶν <u>τεχνῶν</u> δὴ ὧν ἄρτι ἐγὼ ἔλεγον ἐπιστήμων ἀφικέσθαι διαφερόντως τῶν ἄλλων, καὶ περὶ <u>ῥυθμῶν</u> καὶ <u>ἁρμονιῶν</u> καὶ <u>γραμμάτων</u> <u>ὀρθότητος</u>, καὶ ἄλλα ἔτι πρὸς τούτοις πάνυ πολλά, ὡς ἐγὼ δοκῶ <u>μνημονεύειν</u>· καίτοι τό γε <u>μνημονικὸν</u> <u>ἐπελαθόμην</u> σου, ὡς ἔοικε, <u>τέχνημα</u>, ἐν ᾧ σὺ οἴει λαμπρότατος εἶναι·

SOCRATES: Come, then, Hippias. Consider without any further ado whether or not this point [about the false and the true] holds for all kinds of knowledge. You are absolutely the most skilled [*sophos*] of men in the greatest number of <u>crafts</u> [*tekhnai*] by far, as I once heard you boast when you were describing your great and enviable <u>skill</u> [<u>*sophia*</u>]. It was in the agora [= the agora of Athens], near the money-changers' tables [*trapezai*]. You were telling how you once upon a time went to Olympia, and everything you wore was your own work: first, your <u>ring</u> [<u>*daktulios*</u>]—you started with that—was your own work because you knew how to <u>engrave rings</u> [<u>*daktulioi*</u>]—and the rest of it [= your ring], that is, its seal [*sphragis*], was your own work, and an athletic scraper, and a *lēkuthion* you had made yourself. Next, the footwear you had on you—you said you had <u>done the leatherwork</u> [<u>*skutotomeîn*</u>] yourself, and you had <u>woven</u> [<u>*huphainein*</u>] your own *himation* and your own *khiton* [*khitōn*]. And it seemed dazzling to everyone—a display [*epideigma*] of the greatest skill [*sophia*] when you said that the cincture of the khiton [*khitōn*] you had on you was made of the costliest Persian kind, and that you had plaited [*plekein*] it yourself. And on top of all these things, you had come bringing with you compositions [*poiēmata*]¹²⁷—that is, epic [*epos* plural] and tragedies and dithyrambs, and a multitude of discourses [*logoi*] performed in the right sequence [*katalogadēn*] and all kinds of set pieces. And you arrived there as an expert surpassing others in the knowledge of not only the crafts [*tekhnai*] I just mentioned, but also of the correctness [*orthotēs*] of rhythms [*rhuthmoi*], tunings [*harmoniai*], and letters [*grammata*]. And there were many more things in addition, as I seem to remember [*mnēmoneuein*]. And yet it seems I had almost forgotten [*epilanthanesthai*] about your mnemonic technique [*mnēmonikon tekhnēma*], in which you think you are at your most brilliant.¹²⁸

3§162 As we see in this passage, the catalogue of crafts in poetry and song is headed by epic, which is mediated by the craft of the rhapsode. Nevertheless, this same passage shows that the sophist's own rhapsodic virtuosity is formulated not in terms of *rhapsōidikē tekhnē* 'rhapsodic craft'. The terms have been reformulated. For Hippias the sophist, rhapsodic virtuosity is treated as an aspect of an overall skill, described here in the *Hippias Minor* as a *mnēmonikon tekhnēma* 'mnemonic technique' (368d). I have already drawn attention to this attestation of the term in the *Hippias Minor*, noting also another attestation (369a). Moreover, there is a valuable independent confirmation of this same term in Xenophon's *Symposium* (4.62), where Hippias is associated with what is called *to mnēmonikon* 'the mnemonic thing'. It is relevant here to note the disparaging reference to the craft of the rhapsodes in Xenophon's *Symposium* (3.6). Such references indicate a distancing on the part of intellectuals who mastered that craft for their own purposes: these intellectuals, as sophists, could consider themselves more sophisticated in their mastery of Homer than the rhapsodes themselves.¹²⁹

3§163 Whenever Hippias of Elis displays his total control of the rhapsodic craft by quoting verses of Homer that are most relevant to his ongoing live dialogues with his interlocutors, it is implied that the credit goes not to the old craft of the rhapsode but to the supposedly new mnemonic technique of

---

[127] I must stress again what I stressed when I first quoted this wording: as we see from the context here, these 'compositions' are the poetic creations not only of Hippias but also of master 'composers' or *poiētai*, including Homer himself as the 'composer' or *poiētēs* par excellence.

[128] Translation after Allen 1996:36–37.

[129] Graziosi 2002:22.

Chapter Three

the sophist. Nevertheless, as we see in Plato's *Hippias Minor*, the rules of the game continue to be set in terms of the old craft. The questions continue to be Homeric questions, debated in a format that corresponds to the ways in which rhapsodes performed and commented on Homer at the Panathenaia.

3§164 I now turn to a passage that shows a remarkable convergence of details we have been considering so far. The context is the feast of the Panathenaia in the age of Plato. The speaker is Isocrates, and the work in question is the last oration that he composed, the *Panathenaicus* or "Panathenaic" speech, issued in 339 BCE, when the author was ninety-seven years old.[130] As the author makes clear, an illness had prevented him from finishing the work earlier (*Panathenaicus* 267–270), and it seems that he had originally intended to issue the work on the occasion of the Great Panathenaia of 342 BCE (*Panathenaicus* 7).[131] We are about to see Isocrates referring negatively to some so-called 'sophists in the Lyceum'.[132] These sophists are described as (1) 'performing rhapsodically' [*rhapsōideîn*] the poetry of Homer, Hesiod, or others and (2) 'mentioning' [*mnēmoneuein*] things concerning this poetry:

3①31 Isocrates (12) *Panathenaicus* 33

> περὶ μὲν οὖν τῶν πεπαιδευμένων τυγχάνω ταῦτα γιγνώσκων. περὶ δὲ τῆς Ὁμήρου καὶ τῆς Ἡσιόδου καὶ τῆς τῶν ἄλλων ποιήσεως ἐπιθυμῶ μὲν εἰπεῖν, οἶμαι γὰρ ἂν παῦσαι τοὺς ἐν τῷ Λυκείῳ ῥαψῳδοῦντας τἀκείνων καὶ ληροῦντας περὶ αὐτῶν, αἰσθάνομαι δ' ἐμαυτὸν ἔξω φερόμενον τῆς συμμετρίας τῆς συντεταγμένης τοῖς προοιμίοις.

> Such, then, are my opinions about educated men. As for the poetry [*poiēsis*] of Homer and Hesiod and the others, I [= Isocrates] do have the desire to speak about it, since I think I could silence those who rhapsodically perform [*rhapsōideîn*] their poems in the Lyceum and speak idly about them,[133] but I sense that I am being carried along beyond the proportion set for the introductory remarks.

---

[130] For Isocrates, as I note in *PP* 122n75, the writing of a speech, expressed by way of *graphein* 'write' (see his *Panathenaicus* 1), is tantamount to the composing and even the notional delivering of a speech. On *graphein* 'write' as a notional speech-act, see *PH* 8§27n86 (= p. 233).
[131] Jebb 1893 II 113.
[132] Although the Lyceum cannot be identified specifically with the school of Aristotle until a later period (after the philosopher's death, when his successor Theophrastus institutionalized the school in the Lyceum), the place was known as a sort of forum for philosophers even before the era of Isocrates (Plato *Lysis* 203a).
[133] We see here a negative version of an idiom derived from rhapsodic discourse: *PR* 29–30.

3Ⓢ8. Sophistic powers of total recall

3①32 Isocrates (12) *Panathenaicus* 18-19

μικρὸν δὲ πρὸ <u>τῶν Παναθηναίων τῶν μεγάλων</u> ἠχθέσθην δι' αὐτούς. ἀπαντήσαντες γάρ τινές μοι τῶν ἐπιτηδείων ἔλεγον ὡς <u>ἐν τῷ Λυκείῳ</u> συγκαθεζόμενοι τρεῖς ἢ τέτταρες τῶν ἀγελαίων <u>σοφιστῶν</u> καὶ πάντα φασκόντων εἰδέναι καὶ ταχέως πανταχοῦ γιγνομένων <u>διαλέγοιντο περί</u> τε τῶν <u>ἄλλων ποιητῶν</u> καὶ <u>τῆς Ἡσιόδου καὶ τῆς Ὁμήρου ποιήσεως</u>, οὐδὲν μὲν παρ' αὐτῶν λέγοντες, <u>τὰ δ' ἐκείνων ῥαψῳδοῦντες</u> καὶ τῶν πρότερον ἄλλοις τισὶν εἰρημένων τὰ <u>χαριέστατα μνημονεύοντες</u>· <u>ἀποδεξαμένων</u> δὲ τῶν περιεστώτων τὴν <u>διατριβὴν</u> αὐτῶν ἕνα τὸν τολμηρότατον ἐπιχειρῆσαί με διαβάλλειν, λέγονθ' ὡς ...

But, a short time before <u>the Great Panathenaia</u>, I [= Isocrates] got very annoyed at them [= Isocrates' detractors]. For, according to what was reported to me by some friends that I happened to meet, there were these run-of-the-mill <u>sophists [sophistai]</u>, sitting together <u>in the Lyceum</u>, three or four of them, the kind who tell you that they know everything, the kind who quickly turn up at every occasion, and here they were <u>discussing various poets [poiētai]</u>, and <u>especially the poetry [poiēsis] of Hesiod and Homer</u>, saying on their own part nothing about them but rather <u>performing rhapsodically [rhapsōideîn] their poems</u> [that is, the poems of Homer, Hesiod, and other poets] and <u>mentioning [mnēmoneuein] things having the most kharis [khariestata]</u> taken from what has previously been said [about the poems] by others. Then, when the bystanders <u>showed their approval [apodekhesthai]</u> of their [= the sophists'] <u>performance [diatribē]</u>, the most audacious one of them [= the sophists] started trying to slander me, saying that ...

3§165 Isocrates is being sarcastic in speaking of these sophists in the act of *mnēmoneuein* 'mentioning' things that are *khariestata* 'having the most *kharis*' about Homer, Hesiod, and other poets—that is, things marked by the greatest beauty and pleasure. There are technical meanings here underneath the surface of the literal meanings. The term *mnēmoneuein* 'mention' is related to the term *hupomnēmata* 'commentary', which as we have seen refers to the discourse of later scholars like Aristarchus in analyzing the text of Homer.[134] And, as we have also seen, the term *khariestata* is actually applied as a criterion

---

[134] See PP 126 on the meaning of *hupomnēma*. See also PP 121 on Aristotle as an early user of the term *diorthōsis*.

by the followers of Aristarchus in describing textual variants that are deemed to be most Homeric in appearance. This specialized term *khariestata*, representing the elitist terminology of sophists, is to be contrasted with the general term *koina*, representing the 'standard' or 'common' usage of rhapsodes.[135] Examples of such standard usage in the Homeric quotations of Plato are αἴ αἴ instead of ὤ μοι for exclamations (as in *Iliad* XVI 433 via *Republic* 3.388c–d)[136] and infinitive -ειν instead of -εμεν before bucolic diaeresis (*Iliad* VIII 107 via *Laches* 191a–b, *Iliad* XIV 97 via *Laws* 4.706e–707a).[137]

3§166 In elitist circles, by contrast, the more refined usages of sophists would be preferred to the more common usages of rhapsodes who actually competed at the Panathenaia. Such preferences are indicated in the works of Xenophon (*Symposium* 3.5–6).[138] In the passage I just quoted from Isocrates, the fact that the sophists are described as including in their repertoire the poet Hesiod and other poets left unnamed is a sign of transcending the Panathenaic standard, which as we have seen was restricted to Homer. In effect, then, Isocrates is portraying the sophists of the Lyceum in the act of second-guessing the Homeric agenda of the Panathenaia on the occasion of that festival. The figure of Hippias himself seems to me an earlier example of such sophists.

3ⓢ9. Rhapsodic powers of total recall

3§167 Hippias seems ideally suited for a rhapsodic debate with Socrates in the *Hippias Minor*. With his rhapsodic powers of total recall, he can not only quote all of Homer, performing relevant Homeric verses to suit relevant debating points in dialogue with his interlocutors: he can also perform dialogic commentaries on Homer, in a mode of delivery equated with epideictic speechmaking (*epideixis*, 363d and 364b). He is portrayed as ready to respond to any question on any subject from anyone in his audience (363d).[139]

3§168 Given that Hippias applies the *rhapsōidikē tekhnē* 'rhapsodic craft' whenever he performs quotations from Homer in his dialogue with Socrates,

---

[135] See PP 124, where I speak of sophistic discourse about the *khariestata* as a precursor of the Aristarchean criteria that privilege those Homeric variants that are supposedly *khariestata*.
[136] Labarbe 1949:183–186.
[137] Labarbe 1949:212–213 and 243 respectively.
[138] Labarbe 1949:422; see also Graziosi 2002:22n23, 45, 224.
[139] In the *Life of Homer* traditions, Homer himself is represented as performing dialogic commentaries. See HPC I§120.

3§9. Rhapsodic powers of total recall

I now propose to test his rhapsodic powers of total recall by comparing the text of his Homeric quotations with the text of Homer as we know it.

3§169 Let us begin at the very beginning of the *Hippias Minor*, where Socrates addresses a most central Homeric question to Hippias: was Achilles really *ameinōn* 'better' than Odysseus (363b)? This question, as we will see presently, has to do with the complementarity of Achilles and Odysseus as the *aristos* 'best' hero of the Achaeans in respectively the *Iliad* and the *Odyssey*. In the *Hippias Minor*, Socrates starts by alluding to this question:

3Ⓣ33 Plato *Hippias Minor* 364b–c

ἀτὰρ τί δὴ λέγεις ἡμῖν περὶ τοῦ Ἀχιλλέως τε καὶ τοῦ Ὀδυσσέως; πότερον ἀμείνω καὶ κατὰ τί φῂς εἶναι; ἡνίκα μὲν γὰρ πολλοὶ ἔνδον ἦμεν καὶ σὺ τὴν ἐπίδειξιν ἐποιοῦ, ἀπελείφθην σου τῶν λεγομένων— ὤκνουν γὰρ ἐπανερέσθαι, διότι ὄχλος τε πολὺς ἔνδον ἦν, καὶ μή σοι ἐμποδὼν εἴην ἐρωτῶν τῇ ἐπιδείξει—νυνὶ δὲ ἐπειδὴ ἐλάττους τέ ἐσμεν καὶ Εὔδικος ὅδε κελεύει ἐρέσθαι, εἰπέ τε καὶ {c} δίδαξον ἡμᾶς σαφῶς, τί ἔλεγες περὶ τούτοιν τοῖν ἀνδροῖν; πῶς διέκρινες αὐτούς;

ΙΠ. Ἀλλ' ἐγώ σοι, ὦ Σώκρατες, ἐθέλω ἔτι σαφέστερον ἢ τότε διελθεῖν ἃ λέγω καὶ περὶ τούτων καὶ ἄλλων. φημὶ γὰρ Ὅμηρον πεποιηκέναι ἄριστον μὲν ἄνδρα Ἀχιλλέα τῶν εἰς Τροίαν ἀφικομένων, σοφώτατον δὲ Νέστορα, πολυτροπώτατον δὲ Ὀδυσσέα.

[SOCRATES:] But what, then, are you saying about [*legein* + *peri*][140] Achilles and Odysseus? Which one of the two do you say is the better [*ameinōn*] one and on what grounds? For when there were many of us inside [= inside an unspecified enclosure, in Athens], and you [= Hippias] were making [*poieîn*] your display [*epideixis*], I could not keep up with what you were saying: for I hesitated to ask questions, because there was a great crowd [*okhlos . . . polus*] inside [= inside the enclosure], also for fear of hindering your display [*epideixis*] by doing so; but now, since we are fewer and Eudikos here urges me to question you, speak and tell us clearly what you said about [*legein* + *peri*][141] these two men [*toutoin toin androin*]. How did you make critical judgments [*dia-krinein*] about them?

---

[140] The combination of the verb *legein* 'speak' with the preposition *peri* 'about' is an idiom typical of the discourse of rhapsodes: see PR 29–30 on Plato *Ion* 530c–d.
[141] See the previous note.

Chapter Three

HIPPIAS: Why, I am glad, Socrates, to go through for you still more clearly what I say about [*legein peri*] these and others also. For I say that Homer has made [*poieîn*] Achilles the best [*aristos*] man of those who went to Troy, and Nestor the most wise [*sophōtatos*], and Odysseus the most multiform [*polutropos*].

3§170 As Socrates proceeds to question Hippias about this formulation, it becomes evident that he also questions Homer:

3ⓣ34 Plato *Hippias Minor* 364e

ἐπειδὴ δὲ τὸν Ὀδυσσέα εἶπες ὅτι πεποιηκὼς εἴη ὁ ποιητὴς πολυτροπώτατον, τοῦτο δ', ὥς γε πρὸς σὲ τἀληθῆ εἰρῆσθαι, παντάπασιν οὐκ οἶδ' ὅτι λέγεις. καί μοι εἰπέ, ἄν τι ἐνθένδε μᾶλλον μάθω· ὁ Ἀχιλλεὺς οὐ πολύτροπος τῷ Ὁμήρῳ πεποίηται;

[SOCRATES:] But when you said that the poet [= Homer] made Odysseus the most multiform [*polutropos*], to tell you the truth, I do not in the least know what you mean by that. Now tell me, and perhaps it may result in my understanding better. Has not Homer made [*poieîn*] Achilles multiform [*polutropos*]?

3§171 This question posed by Socrates undermines a central theme in the Homeric *Iliad*. As I argued in my previous work, the narrative contrasts the latent and dissembling multiformity of Odysseus with the overt and straightforward uniformity of Achilles. In *Iliad* IX, this contrast has to do with a latent and even dissembling multiformity in the actual Homeric narrative that frames the contrast between the dissembling Odysseus and the straightforward Achilles, since the dissembling of Odysseus is not made overt and thus seems to be straightforward on the surface.[142] In Plato's *Hippias Minor*, the strategy of Socrates is to associate this latent and dissembling multiformity of the Homeric framing narrative with the straightforward discourse of Achilles, thus making this hero seem to be a dissembling character; conversely, Socrates pretends to accept the dissembling discourse of Odysseus at face value, as if Odysseus were a straightforward character. In this way, the latent and dissembling multiformity of Socrates undermines the overt and straightforward uniformity of Hippias himself in representing the overt and straightforward uniformity of Achilles. The mistake of Hippias, in terms of the *Hippias Minor* as constructed by Plato, is his failure to perceive the latent and even dissembling

---

[142] BA ch. 3 (= pp. 42–58), HQ 138–145.

multiformity of the narrative—that is, of 'Homer', whose *dianoia* or 'meaning' he claims to represent.[143]

3§172 In the course of their debate over this central Homeric question of the *Iliad*, Hippias and Socrates quote extensively from *Iliad* IX. The first Homeric quotation comes from Hippias:

3①35 Plato *Hippias Minor* 364e

> [ΙΠ.] Ἥκιστά γε, ὦ Σώκρατες, ἀλλ' ἁπλούστατος καὶ ἀληθέστατος, ἐπεὶ καὶ ἐν Λιταῖς, ἡνίκα πρὸς ἀλλήλους ποιεῖ αὐτοὺς <u>διαλεγομένους</u>, <u>λέγει</u> αὐτῷ ὁ Ἀχιλλεὺς πρὸς τὸν Ὀδυσσέα -
>
>> διογενὲς Λαερτιάδη, πολυμήχαν' Ὀδυσσεῦ,
>> χρὴ μὲν δὴ τὸν μῦθον ἀπηλεγέως ἀποειπεῖν,
>> ὥσπερ δὴ <u>κρανέω</u> τε καὶ <u>ὡς τελέεσθαι ὀίω</u>·
>> ἐχθρὸς γάρ μοι κεῖνος ὁμῶς Ἀΐδαο πύλῃσιν,
>> ὅς χ' ἕτερον μὲν κεύθῃ ἐνὶ φρεσίν, ἄλλο δὲ εἴπῃ.
>> αὐτὰρ ἐγὼν ἐρέω <u>ὡς καὶ τετελεσμένον ἔσται</u>
>
> Plato's text of *Iliad* IX 308–314
>
> HIPPIAS: Not at all, Socrates; he [= Homer] made [*poieîn*] him [= Achilles] most simple [*haploûs*][144] and most true [*alēthēs*]; for in "The *Litai*" [= the Embassy Scene of *Iliad* IX] when he makes [*poieîn*] them in the act of <u>talking with one another</u> [*dialegesthai*], Achilles <u>says</u> to him, that is, to Odysseus:
>
>> Descended from Zeus, son of Laertes, you of many resources, Odysseus:
>> I see that I must say what I say back to you without mincing words,
>> just the way I <u>determine</u>, and <u>the way I think it will reach an outcome</u> [*teleîn*].
>> Here is why. Hateful is that man to me, as hateful as the gates of Hades,

---

[143] On the *dianoia* 'thinking' of Homer as a model of authorial intentionality in the discourse of rhapsodes, see Plato *Ion* 530b–c. Commentary in PR 29–30.

[144] The etymology of *haploûs* 'simple, simplex', is analyzed in HPC II§386.

Chapter Three

> the man who hides one thing in his thinking and says another thing.
>
> As for me, I will say it <u>the way it will be when the outcome has been reached</u> [*teleîn*].
>
> Plato's text of Iliad IX 308–314

3§173 These verses as quoted from Plato's text of Homer must be contrasted with the corresponding verses that have come down to us through the medieval manuscript tradition:

3①36 *Iliad* IX 308–314

> διογενὲς Λαερτιάδη πολυμήχαν' Ὀδυσσεῦ
> χρὴ μὲν δὴ τὸν μῦθον ἀπηλεγέως ἀποειπεῖν,
> ᾗ περ δὴ <u>φρονέω τε καὶ ὡς τετελεσμένον ἔσται</u>,
> <u>ὡς μή μοι τρύζητε παρήμενοι ἄλλοθεν ἄλλος</u>.
> ἐχθρὸς γάρ μοι κεῖνος ὁμῶς Ἀΐδαο πύλῃσιν
> ὅς χ' ἕτερον μὲν κεύθῃ ἐνὶ φρεσίν, ἄλλο δὲ εἴπῃ.
> αὐτὰρ ἐγὼν ἐρέω <u>ὥς μοι δοκεῖ εἶναι ἄριστα</u>
>
> Descended from Zeus, son of Laertes, you of many resources, Odysseus:
>
> I see that I must say what I say back to you without mincing words,
>
> just the way I <u>think</u>, and <u>the way it will be that the outcome has been reached</u> [*teleîn*].[145]
>
> <u>So do not try to cajole me, taking turns sitting down next to me.</u>
>
> Here is why. Hateful is that man to me, as hateful as the gates of Hades,

---

[145] In this version, as transmitted in the medieval manuscript tradition, the use of the perfect of *teleîn* at verse 310 of *Iliad* IX indicates that Achilles understands the outcome of the plot as already a *fait accompli*. It is such an understanding that leads to the inference expressed at verse 311: 'so do not try to undo what is already a *fait accompli*'. By contrast, in the version as quoted by Plato, the expression of a *fait accompli* takes place only at the verse that corresponds to verse 312 in "our" Homer. So the equivalent of verse 311 is not needed in the version quoted by Plato, since the equivalent of verse 310 shows not the perfect of *teleîn*, only an imperfective of *teleîn*.

the man who hides one thing in his thinking and says
another thing.

As for me, I will say it <u>the way it seems best to me</u>.

3§174 The differences that we see between the wording of this passage as transmitted in Plato's dialogue and the wording as transmitted in the medieval manuscript tradition can be explained as variations in the formulaic system that typifies Homeric poetry in general. That is to say, the wording as performed by Hippias in this re-enactment by Plato can be considered just as "Homeric" as the wording that has come down to us through the medieval manuscript tradition. That said, I am ready to argue that this wording matches the traditional wording of Homer as he was understood in Plato's time.

3§175 This argument is supported by the internal logic of the whole dialogue that we know as the *Hippias Minor*. That is because the argument of Socrates in this dialogue is actually based on the recognized authority of Hippias as a most accurate transmitter of Homer's *ipsissima verba*. For Socrates to win the argument with Hippias, he has to show that his opponent is trapped and even defeated by these *ipsissima verba*. That is why Socrates has to recognize the sophist's mastery of the same *ipsissima verba*.

3§176 Throughout this dialogue named after him, Hippias makes a dialogic commentary on the Homeric verses that he performs.[146] And this commentary is the essence of the sophist's argumentation:

3①37 Plato *Hippias Minor* 365b

ἐν τούτοις δηλοῖ τοῖς ἔπεσιν τὸν τρόπον ἑκατέρου τοῦ ἀνδρός, ὡς ὁ μὲν Ἀχιλλεὺς εἴη ἀληθής τε καὶ ἁπλοῦς, ὁ δὲ Ὀδυσσεὺς πολύτροπός τε καὶ ψευδής· ποιεῖ γὰρ τὸν Ἀχιλλέα εἰς τὸν Ὀδυσσέα <u>λέγοντα</u> ταῦτα τὰ ἔπη.

[HIPPIAS:] In these verses he [= Homer] makes plain the character of each of the men, that Achilles is true [*alēthēs*] and simple [*haploûs*], and Odysseus multiform [*polutropos*] and false [*pseudēs*], for he figures [*poieîn*] Achilles in the act of <u>saying</u> [<u>*legein*</u>] these verses [*epos* plural] to Odysseus.

3§177 This dialogic commentary of Hippias is countered by the dialogic commentary of Socrates himself, who consistently undermines the words of

---

[146] In the *Life of Homer* traditions, as I noted earlier, with reference to HPC, Homer himself is represented as performing dialogic commentaries.

Homer as faithfully remembered by Hippias. Since Hippias refuses to accept the idea that Homer presents Achilles in an unfavorable light, Socrates challenges Hippias to defend the meaning of these words independently of whatever Homer meant:

3ⓣ38 Plato *Hippias Minor* 365c–d

> [ΣΩ.] Τὸν μὲν Ὅμηρον τοίνυν ἐάσωμεν, ἐπειδὴ καὶ {d} ἀδύνατον ἐπανερέσθαι τί ποτε νοῶν ταῦτα <u>ἐποίησεν</u> τὰ <u>ἔπη</u>· σὺ δ' ἐπειδὴ φαίνῃ ἀναδεχόμενος τὴν αἰτίαν, καὶ σοὶ συνδοκεῖ ταῦτα ἅπερ φῂς Ὅμηρον <u>λέγειν</u>, <u>ἀπόκριναι</u> <u>κοινῇ</u> ὑπὲρ Ὁμήρου τε καὶ σαυτοῦ.
>
> [SOCRATES:] Then let us dismiss Homer, since it is impossible to ask him what he intended [*noeîn*] when he <u>made</u> [<u>*poieîn*</u>] these <u>verses</u> [*epos* plural]. But since you are clearly taking up his cause and agree with these things you say he is <u>saying</u> [<u>*legein*</u>], I ask you to <u>respond</u> [<u>*apokrinesthai*</u>] <u>in common</u> [<u>*koineî*</u>] on behalf of Homer and yourself.[147]

3§178 Socrates bases his argumentation on the premise that Hippias has an exact memory of Homer's exact words—a memory connected with the sophist's expertise in poetry. When Hippias came to Athens to display his many prodigious skills, what impressed Socrates the most was this expertise:

3ⓣ39 Plato *Hippias Minor* 368d–e

> πρὸς δὲ τούτοις <u>ποιήματα</u> ἔχων ἐλθεῖν, καὶ ἔπη καὶ τραγῳδίας καὶ διθυράμβους, καὶ <u>καταλογάδην</u> πολλοὺς <u>λόγους</u> καὶ παντοδαποὺς συγκειμένους· καὶ περὶ τῶν <u>τεχνῶν</u> δὴ ὧν ἄρτι ἐγὼ ἔλεγον ἐπιστήμων ἀφικέσθαι διαφερόντως τῶν ἄλλων, καὶ περὶ ῥυθμῶν καὶ ἁρμονιῶν καὶ γραμμάτων <u>ὀρθότητος</u>, καὶ ἄλλα ἔτι πρὸς τούτοις πάνυ πολλά, ὡς ἐγὼ δοκῶ μνημονεύειν· καίτοι τό γε <u>μνημονικὸν</u> ἐπελαθόμην σου, ὡς ἔοικε, <u>τέχνημα</u>, ἐν ᾧ σὺ οἴει λαμπρότατος εἶναι· οἶμαι δὲ καὶ {e} ἄλλα πάμπολλα ἐπιλελῆσθαι.
>
> SOCRATES: And, on top of all these things [= your displays of other skills], you [= Hippias] had come bringing with you <u>compositions</u> [*poiēmata*][148]—epics as well as tragedies as well as dithyrambs—

---

[147] Translation after Allen 1996:33.
[148] I must stress once again what I stressed when I first quoted this wording: as we see from the context here, these 'compositions' are the poetic creations not only of Hippias but also of master 'composers' or *poiētai*, including Homer himself as the 'composer' or *poiētēs* par excellence.

3§9. Rhapsodic powers of total recall

and a multitude of <u>discourses</u> [*logoi*] <u>to be performed in the right sequence</u> [*katalogadēn*][149] and all kinds of set pieces. And you arrived there as an expert surpassing all others in the knowledge of not only the <u>crafts</u> [*tekhnai*] I just mentioned, but also of the <u>correctness</u> [*orthotēs*] of rhythms [*rhuthmoi*], tunings [*harmoniai*], and letters [*grammata*].[150] And there were many more things in addition, as I seem to remember. And yet it seems I had almost forgotten [*epilanthanesthai*] about your <u>mnemonic technique</u> [*mnēmonikon tekhnēma*], in which you think <u>you</u> are at your most brilliant. And I suppose I have forgotten [*epilanthanesthai*] about a great many other things too.[151]

3§179 It is precisely because Hippias is known for his perfect memory of Homer that Socrates can undermine Homer through Hippias. So when Socrates pretends to be forgetful in the presence of this master of mnemonics, he is ironically accentuating the effectiveness of his own argument against Homer. This effectiveness is all the more accentuated when Socrates proceeds to demonstrate that he too, like Hippias, is a master of mnemonics, and that he too has a perfect memory of Homer. Socrates starts by provoking Hippias, questioning whether the sophist is making use of his vaunted techniques of mnemonics:

3ⓣ40 Plato *Hippias Minor* 369a–369b

[ΣΩ.] Νυνὶ γὰρ ἴσως οὐ χρῇ τῷ <u>μνημονικῷ</u> <u>τεχνήματι</u>—δῆλον γὰρ ὅτι οὐκ οἴει δεῖν—ἀλλὰ ἐγώ σε <u>ὑπομνήσω</u>. οἶσθα ὅτι τὸν μὲν Ἀχιλλέα ἔφησθα ἀληθῆ εἶναι, τὸν δὲ Ὀδυσσέα {360b} ψευδῆ καὶ <u>πολύτροπον</u>;

[ΙΠ.] Ναί.

[ΣΩ.] Νῦν οὖν αἰσθάνῃ ὅτι ἀναπέφανται ὁ αὐτὸς ὢν ψευδής τε καὶ ἀληθής, ὥστε εἰ ψευδὴς ὁ Ὀδυσσεὺς ἦν, καὶ ἀληθὴς γίγνεται, καὶ εἰ ἀληθὴς ὁ Ἀχιλλεύς, καὶ ψευδής, καὶ οὐ διάφοροι ἀλλήλων οἱ ἄνδρες οὐδ' ἐναντίοι, ἀλλ' ὅμοιοι;

---

[149] To repeat, the conventions of performing *katalogadēn* 'in the right sequence, catalogue-style' are relevant to the *mnēmonikon tekhnēma* 'mnemonic technique' of Hippias, a key concept that Plato's Socrates is about to introduce in this same passage (Plato *Hippias Minor* 368d).

[150] For another passage that emphasizes these specialties of Hippias, I cite again Plato *Hippias Maior* 285d. A relevant term is *grammatistēs*.

[151] Translation after Allen 1996:36–37.

Chapter Three

SOCRATES: Maybe you are not using your mnemonic technique [*mnēmonikon tekhnēma*] right now—clearly you don't think you need to—but I will give you mnemonic support [*hupo-mnē-*]. You know you were saying that Achilles is true but Odysseus false and multiform [*polutropos*]?

HIPPIAS: Yes.

SOCRATES: Do you now, then, perceive that the same man has been found to be false and true, so that if Odysseus was false, he becomes also true, and if Achilles was true, he becomes also false, and the two men are not different from one another, nor opposites, but alike?

3§180 Hippias responds to the provocation of Socrates by challenging him to a duel in mnemonics. The two duelists must argue their cases not only by opposing each other's arguments. They must also quote verses from Homer to back up those arguments:

3ⓣ41 Plato *Hippias Minor* 369c

ἐπεὶ καὶ νῦν, ἐὰν βούλῃ, ἐπὶ πολλῶν τεκμηρίων ἀποδείξω σοι ἱκανῷ λόγῳ Ὅμηρον Ἀχιλλέα πεποιηκέναι ἀμείνω Ὀδυσσέως καὶ ἀψευδῆ, τὸν δὲ δολερόν τε καὶ πολλὰ ψευδόμενον καὶ χείρω Ἀχιλλέως. εἰ δὲ βούλει, σὺ αὖ ἀντιπαράβαλλε λόγον παρὰ λόγον, ὡς ὁ ἕτερος ἀμείνων ἐστί· καὶ μᾶλλον εἴσονται οὗτοι ὁπότερος ἄμεινον λέγει.

[HIPPIAS:] Right now, if you want, on the basis of many different pieces of evidence, I will demonstrate to you, using a discourse [*logos*] that is self-sufficient, that Homer has made [*poieîn*] Achilles better than Odysseus and free from falsehood, and [that he has made] Odysseus crafty and a teller of many falsehoods and inferior to Achilles. And, if you want, you should compete by matching discourse [*logos*] against discourse [*logos*], maintaining that one of them is better than the other; and these men here will determine which of us speaks [*legein*] better.

3§181 In the wording of Hippias as re-enacted by Plato, the act of performing Homer's words is expressed not only by the verb *legein* 'speak' but also by the noun *logos* in the general sense of 'speech' or 'discourse', which overlaps with the specific sense of 'argument' in his sophistic discourse. For Hippias, as we are about to see, a *logos* is a 'discourse' that includes not only the 'logic' of his argumentation but also the actual 'wording'—literally, *logos*—of Homer himself. Just as Homer 'speaks' (*legein*), so also Hippias 'speaks' (*legein*) when he performs Homer.

3§182 Socrates responds to the challenge of Hippias by becoming a Homeric performer in his own right. Only, he outdoes Hippias by managing to quote four separate sets of verses from the *Iliad*, not just a single set. The wording that introduces the first set includes numerous instances of *legein* in the sense of 'speaking' the words of Homer as well as 'speaking' the words of the argument supposedly represented by Homer:

3①42 Plato *Hippias Minor* 369d–370a

καὶ γνώσῃ τούτῳ οὓς ἂν ἐγὼ ἡγῶμαι σοφοὺς εἶναι· εὑρήσεις γάρ με λιπαρῆ ὄντα περὶ τὰ {369e} <u>λεγόμενα</u> ὑπὸ τούτου καὶ πυνθανόμενον παρ' αὐτοῦ, ἵνα μαθών τι ὠφεληθῶ. ἐπεὶ καὶ νῦν ἐννενόηκα σοῦ <u>λέγοντος</u>, ὅτι ἐν τοῖς ἔπεσιν οἷς σὺ ἄρτι <u>ἔλεγες</u>, ἐνδεικνύμενος τὸν Ἀχιλλέα εἰς τὸν Ὀδυσσέα <u>λέγειν</u> ὡς ἀλαζόνα ὄντα, ἄτοπόν μοι δοκεῖ εἶναι, εἰ σὺ ἀληθῆ <u>λέγεις</u>, ὅτι ὁ μὲν Ὀδυσσεὺς οὐδαμοῦ {370a} φαίνεται ψευσάμενος, ὁ πολύτροπος, ὁ δὲ Ἀχιλλεὺς πολύτροπός τις φαίνεται κατὰ τὸν σὸν λόγον· ψεύδεται γοῦν. προ<u>ειπὼν</u> γὰρ ταῦτα τὰ ἔπη, ἅπερ καὶ σὺ <u>εἶπες</u> ἄρτι—

ἐχθρὸς γάρ μοι κεῖνος ὁμῶς Ἀΐδαο πύλῃσιν,
ὅς χ' ἕτερον μὲν κεύθῃ ἐνὶ φρεσίν, ἄλλο δὲ εἴπῃ

Plato's text of *Iliad* IX 312–313

SOCRATES: [...] And by this you [= Hippias] will recognize whom I regard as wise; for you will find me persistently asking such a man questions about what he <u>says</u> [*legein*], in order that I may benefit by learning something. Just now I noticed when you were <u>speaking</u> [*legein*] that in the verses [*epos* plural] that you <u>spoke</u> [*legein*] just now to show that Achilles <u>speaks</u> [*legein*] to Odysseus as to a deceiver, it seems to me very strange, if what you <u>say</u> [*legein*] is true, that Odysseus the multiform is nowhere found to have uttered falsehoods [*pseudesthai*], but Achilles is found to be a multiform [*polutropos*] sort of person, according to your own <u>discourse</u> [*logos*]; at any rate, he utters falsehoods [*pseudesthai*]. For he begins by <u>speaking</u> [*legein* / *eipeîn*] these verses [*epos* plural] which you just spoke [*legein* / *eipeîn*]:

Chapter Three

> Hateful is that man to me, as hateful as the gates of Hades,
> the man who hides one thing in his thinking and says another thing.
>
> Plato's text of *Iliad* IX 312–313

3§183 Socrates now proceeds to argue, in opposition to Hippias, that Achilles himself hides one thing in his thinking and says another thing. To back up this argument, he quotes this second set of Homeric verses:

3ⓣ43 Plato *Hippias Minor* 370b–c

> ὀλίγον ὕστερον <u>λέγει</u> ὡς οὔτ' ἂν ἀναπεισθείη ὑπὸ τοῦ Ὀδυσσέως τε καὶ τοῦ Ἀγαμέμνονος οὔτε μένοι τὸ παράπαν ἐν τῇ Τροίᾳ, ἀλλ' –
>
> αὔριον ἱρὰ Διὶ ῥέξας, φησί, καὶ πᾶσι θεοῖσιν,
> νηήσας εὖ νῆας, ἐπὴν ἅλαδε προερύσσω,
> ὄψεαι, αἴ κ' ἐθέλῃσθα καὶ αἴ κέν τοι τὰ μεμήλῃ,
> ἦρι μάλ' Ἑλλήσποντον ἐπ' ἰχθυόεντα πλεούσας
> νῆας ἐμάς, ἐν δ' ἄνδρας ἐρεσσέμεναι μεμαῶτας·
> εἰ δέ κεν εὐπλοΐην δώῃ κλυτὸς Ἐννοσίγαιος,
> ἤματί κεν τριτάτῳ Φθίην ἐρίβωλον ἱκοίμην.
>
> Plato's text of *Iliad* IX 357–363

[…] and a little later he [= Achilles] <u>says</u> [<u>*legein*</u>] that he would not be persuaded by Odysseus and Agamemnon and would not stay at Troy at all, but …

> Tomorrow, when I have sacrificed to Zeus and to all gods,
> and loaded well my ships, and rowed out on to the salt water,
> you will see, if you have a mind to it and if it concerns you,
> my ships in the dawn at sea on the Hellespont where the fish swarm
> and my men manning them with good will to row. If the famed
> shaker of the earth should grant us a favoring passage
> on the third day th ereafter I might reach fertile Phthia.
>
> Plato's text of *Iliad* IX 357-363

3§184 Socrates pursues his argument by quoting a third set of Homeric verses:

3①44 Plato *Hippias Minor* 370c–d

ἔτι δὲ πρότερον τούτων πρὸς τὸν Ἀγαμέμνονα λοιδορούμενος εἶπεν—

νῦν δ' εἶμι Φθίηνδ', ἐπεὶ ἦ πολὺ λώϊόν ἐστιν
οἴκαδ' ἴμεν σὺν νηυσὶ κορωνίσιν, οὐδέ σ' ὀΐω
ἐνθάδ' ἄτιμος ἐὼν ἄφενος καὶ πλοῦτον ἀφύξειν.

Plato's text of Iliad IX 169–171

And even before that, when he [= Achilles] was reviling Agamemnon, he said [*legein* / *eipeîn*]:

Now I am going to Phthia, since it is much better[152]

to go home again with my curved ships, and I have no thought of helping you

by staying here without getting any honor for it as I augment your property and wealth.

Plato's text of Iliad IX 169–171

3§185 On the basis of these Homeric verses, Socrates claims that Achilles too, like Odysseus, is capable of falsehoods, even though both heroes are *aristō*, the 'best' of the Achaeans who came to fight at Troy (Plato *Hippias Minor* 370e).[153] He argues this point even further by quoting a fourth set of Homeric verses:

3①45 Plato *Hippias Minor* 371b–c

[ΣΩ.] Οὐκ οἶσθα ὅτι λέγων ὕστερον ἢ ὡς πρὸς τὸν Ὀδυσσέα ἔφη ἅμα τῇ ἠοῖ ἀποπλευσεῖσθαι, πρὸς τὸν Αἴαντα οὐκ αὖ φησιν ἀποπλευσεῖσθαι, ἀλλὰ ἄλλα λέγει;

---

[152] In Plato's quotation, the wording here is different from what we read in the medieval manuscript tradition.

[153] This way, Plato's Socrates undercuts the complementarity of Achilles and Odysseus as the very best of the Achaeans in the *Iliad* and *Odyssey* respectively, since he seeks to show that these two heroes are undifferentiated in their virtues. The complementarity of Achilles and Odysseus depends on their differentiation in virtues, as I argued at length in *BA* ch. 3 (= pp. 42–58).

[ΙΠ.] Ποῦ δή;

[ΣΩ.] Ἐν οἷς <u>λέγει</u>

οὐ γὰρ πρὶν πολέμοιο μεδήσομαι αἱματόεντος, {371c}
πρίν γ' υἱὸν Πριάμοιο δαΐφρονος, Ἕκτορα δῖον,
Μυρμιδόνων ἐπί τε κλισίας καὶ νῆας ἱκέσθαι
κτείνοντ' Ἀργείους, <u>κατά</u> τε <u>φλέξαι</u> πυρὶ νῆας·
ἀμφὶ δέ μιν τῇ 'μῇ κλισίῃ καὶ νηΐ μελαίνῃ
Ἕκτορα καὶ μεμαῶτα μάχης σχήσεσθαι ὀίω.

Plato's text of Iliad IX 650–655

SOCRATES: Don't you know that he [= Achilles], <u>speaking</u> [<u>legein</u>] at a later point after he declared to Odysseus that he was going to sail away at daybreak, does not in addressing Ajax declare that he [= Achilles] is going to sail away but <u>says</u> [<u>legein</u>] different things?

HIPPIAS: Where is that?

SOCRATES: It is where he [= Achilles] <u>says</u> [<u>legein</u>]:

> For I will not care about the bloody war
> until such time as the son of sharp-thinking Priam, Hector the radiant,
> has reached all the way to the shelters and the ships of the Myrmidons,
> killing the Argives, and until he <u>sets on fire</u> [<u>kata-phlegein</u>][154] the ships.
> But around my own shelter and beside my black ship
> Hector will be held back, no matter how eager he is to fight. That is what I think.

Plato's text of Iliad IX 650–655

3§186 In the case of this Homeric quotation, Plato's text matches the text that has come down to us in the medieval manuscript tradition, except for this variation:

---

[154] In Plato's quotation, the wording here is different from what we read in the medieval manuscript tradition, on which see the next note.

3ⓣ46 *Iliad* IX 653

κτείνοντ' Ἀργείους, <u>κατά</u> τε <u>σμῦξαι</u> πυρὶ νῆας.
killing the Argives, and until he <u>darkens with fire</u>
[<u>kata-smukhein</u>]¹⁵⁵ our vessels.

3§187 Having made his argument against Hippias by performing the words of Homer as part of the argument, Socrates goes out of his way to reaffirm the authority of Hippias as an expert in Homer:

3ⓣ47 Plato *Hippias Minor* 372a–c

[ΣΩ.] Ὁρᾷς, ὦ Ἱππία, ὅτι ἐγὼ ἀληθῆ <u>λέγω</u>, <u>λέγων</u> ὡς {272b} λιπαρής εἰμι πρὸς τὰς ἐρωτήσεις τῶν σοφῶν; καὶ κινδυνεύω ἓν μόνον ἔχειν τοῦτο ἀγαθόν, τἆλλα ἔχων πάνυ φαῦλα· τῶν μὲν γὰρ πραγμάτων ᾗ ἔχει ἔσφαλμαι, καὶ οὐκ οἶδ' ὅπῃ ἐστί. τεκμήριον δέ μοι τούτου ἱκανόν, ὅτι ἐπειδὰν συγγένωμαί τῳ ὑμῶν τῶν εὐδοκιμούντων ἐπὶ σοφίᾳ καὶ οἷς οἱ Ἕλληνες πάντες μάρτυρές εἰσι τῆς σοφίας, φαίνομαι οὐδὲν εἰδώς· οὐδὲν γάρ μοι δοκεῖ τῶν αὐτῶν καὶ ὑμῖν, ὡς ἔπος {372c} εἰπεῖν. καίτοι τί μεῖζον ἀμαθίας τεκμήριον ἢ ἐπειδάν τις σοφοῖς ἀνδράσι διαφέρηται; ἓν δὲ τοῦτο θαυμάσιον ἔχω ἀγαθόν, ὅ με σῴζει· οὐ γὰρ αἰσχύνομαι μανθάνων, ἀλλὰ πυνθάνομαι καὶ ἐρωτῶ καὶ <u>χάριν</u> πολλὴν ἔχω τῷ ἀποκρινομένῳ, καὶ οὐδένα πώποτε ἀπεστέρησα <u>χάριτος</u>. οὐ γὰρ πώποτε ἔξαρνος ἐγενόμην μαθών τι, ἐμαυτοῦ ποιούμενος τὸ μάθημα εἶναι ὡς εὕρημα· ἀλλ' ἐγκωμιάζω τὸν διδάξαντά με ὡς σοφὸν ὄντα, ἀποφαίνων ἃ ἔμαθον παρ' αὐτοῦ.

SOCRATES: Do you see, Hippias, that I <u>say</u> [<u>legein</u>] the truth when I <u>say</u> [<u>legein</u>] that I am persistent in questioning wise men? And this is probably the only good thing I have, since the other things I have are undistinguished; for I am unstable about facts, and do not know what is where. And I have sufficient proof of this in the fact that, whenever I come into contact with one of you who are famous for some expertise, and to whose expertise all the Hellenes bear witness, I show myself to be an expert in nothing; for there is nothing about which you and I have the same opinion; and yet what greater proof

---

¹⁵⁵ This variant, as attested in the medieval manuscript tradition, is explicitly supported by Aristarchus, but he also attests -φλέξαι as a variant of -σμῦξαι. See scholia A^im for *Iliad* IX 653a (Didymus): οὕτως <σμῦξαι> Ἀρίσταρχος. οἶδε <δὲ> καὶ τὴν <u>φλέξαι</u> γραφήν. Also scholia A^int (Aristonicus): ὅτι γράφεται καὶ <u>κατά τε φλέξαι</u>. In the scholia for *Odyssey* iii 195, another variant is reported for *Iliad* IX 653: . . . ἐπισμῦξαι πυρὶ νῆας.

of non-expertise is there than when one disagrees with men who are experts? But I have this one wondrous good quality, which is my salvation; for I am not afraid to learn, but I inquire and ask questions and I show much gratitude [*kharis*] to the person who responds, and I have never deprived anyone of reciprocation [*kharis*];[156] for when I have learned anything I have never denied it, pretending that the thing I learned was a discovery of my own; but I praise as an expert the person who taught me what I learned, making clear the things I learned from him.

3§188 What Socrates ostensibly learns from Hippias is an expertise in a craft that is most highly respected by all Hellenes, that is, the craft of the rhapsode. By ostensibly giving it due respect, Socrates makes that craft a foil for something that demands even more respect, that is, the craft that is not a craft because it transcends all crafts. That non-craft is philosophy, the love of *sophia* as 'wisdom', which transcends *sophia* as 'craft'.

3§189 I have reached the end of my survey of Homeric quotations performed by Hippias—answered by Homeric quotations performed by Socrates himself—in Plato's *Hippias Minor*. We have seen that both Hippias and Socrates are applying the craft of rhapsodes, the *rhapsōidikē tekhnē*, in their dialogue with each other. We have also seen that both of them are in effect performing like rhapsodes, not only in their quotations of Homer but also in their dialogic commentaries about Homer.[157] Finally, we have seen that both the philosopher and the sophist must be reliable sources, given what is at stake in their dialogue with each other. For the philosopher to compete with the sophist, he must apply the same standard of total Homeric recall that the sophist must apply in his own efforts to supersede rhapsodes like Ion who perform Homer at the Panathenaia. That absolute standard of total Homeric recall is a Panathenaic standard. That ideal of Homer is the Panathenaic Homer.

3§10. Panathenaic Homer and the Koine of Aristarchus

3§190 Here I return once more to the question I asked at the beginning of this chapter: if we had access to a transcript of Homer exactly as Plato heard Homeric poetry being performed at the Panathenaia in a given year, what

---

[156] The word implies a pleasurable beauty in the act of reciprocation.
[157] In the *Life of Homer* traditions, as I noted earlier, Homer himself is represented as performing dialogic commentaries.

3⑤10. Panathenaic Homer and the Koine of Aristarchus

Homeric text would such a transcript resemble most closely? My answer was that the closest thing would be the Koine of Homer as represented by the base text of Aristarchus—and by the Homeric quotations of Plato himself. As we saw from the Homeric quotations by Plato's Hippias and Plato's Socrates in Plato's *Hippias Minor*, the Homeric tradition revealed by these quotations does indeed correspond closely—though not exactly—to the Koine of Homer.[158]

3§191 This is not to say that the textual tradition of Homer was monolithic in the age of Plato. We cannot rule out the possibility that non-Koine versions of Homeric poetry were extant. A case in point is a lengthy quotation and exegesis of verses taken from Homer in an oration composed by Aeschines, *Against Timarchus* (133, 141–143, 145–146, 150). In this context, we find verses that are missing in the medieval manuscripts (*Iliad* XXIII 83a and 83b).[159] The motive of the orator in this case may have been to display his learning by quoting a "deluxe" version that transcended the standard version. For Plato's Socrates, on the other hand, the standard version would have been the preferred point of reference. He was after all competing with personalities like Ion and Hippias, who prided themselves on their mastery of the standard Panathenaic Homer.

3§192 It would be going too far, however, to think that Plato's Panathenaic Homer was the same thing as the base text of the Homeric Koine as reconstructed by Aristarchus. That reconstruction was just that, a reconstruction. It could only point toward the reality of the Koine, without ever fully capturing it.

3§193 It may be that Aristarchus himself had access to a copy of Plato's Homer. In the Homeric scholia, we learn that Ammonius, the successor of Aristarchus at the Library of Alexandria, produced a monograph concerning Homeric verses used by Plato. Didymus (via the scholia A for *Iliad* IX 540a1) mentions the title of this monograph, Περὶ τῶν ὑπὸ Πλάτωνος μετενηνεγμένων ἐξ Ὁμήρου 'About the things derived from Homer by Plato'. In this monograph, according to Didymus, Ammonius mentions a variant that Aristarchus found in Plato's Homer for a verse in *Iliad* IX (540): in Plato's Homer, this verse shows the variant ἔρεξεν ἔθων in place of ἔρδεσκεν ἔθων (<ἔρδεσκεν ἔθων>: Ἀμμώνιος ἐν τῷ Περὶ τῶν ὑπὸ Πλάτωνος μετενηνεγμένων ἐξ Ὁμήρου διὰ τοῦ <ξ> προφέρεται, ἔρεξεν). This variant reading from Plato's Homer, ἔρεξεν ἔθων, is attested nowhere in the medieval manuscript

---

[158] Besides the evidence from the Homeric quotations in Plato's *Hippias Minor*, I cite the further evidence of other quotations in other dialogues of Plato, as surveyed by Labarbe 1949. The quotations in other works of Plato do not affect the overall picture that emerges.

[159] Dué 2001a.

Chapter Three

tradition of Homer. Nor is this verse from *Iliad* IX (540) attested anywhere among the verses that Plato actually quotes in his extant works. So it may be that Ammonius inherited from Aristarchus a Homeric text that was used by Plato himself.

3§194 A moment ago, I said that the base text of Homer as edited by Aristarchus was merely his reconstruction of the Homeric Koine, not the Homeric Koine itself. Perhaps it is not too obvious for me to add that Aristarchus could never have fully succeeded in reconstructing what he attempted to reconstruct. Still, the reality of the Homeric Koine came into sharper focus thanks to his efforts in collating Homeric manuscripts, though it became blurred again in the post-Aristarchean age of Didymus, that is, in the age of Virgil, just as it had been blurred earlier in the pre-Aristarchean age of Callimachus.

3§195 To sum up, we can expect to see some differences between "our" Koine and "their" Koine—and by "their" Koine I mean Plato's Homer. These differences are important to the extent that they show not just textual but also formulaic variations, as we saw in Plato's quotations from *Iliad* IX. So Homeric poetry shows some degree of fluidity, however limited, even in the age of Plato.

3§196 Still, as far as differences go, such formulaic variations are relatively minimal—that is, they will seem minimal to us once we compare them to the differences between the Homer quoted by Plato and the Homer that I have been calling the Homerus Auctus. By comparison to the Homerus Auctus, with its Cyclic, Hesiodic, and Orphic accretions, Plato's Homer will seem to be mostly the same as the Homeric Koine, which is "our" Homer. I have more to say about this aspect of the Homerus Auctus in the twin book, *Homer the Preclassic*. For now, however, I focus on the Homeric Koine and on the Panathenaic standard that maintained it. The Homer quoted by Plato is this Homeric Koine.

3§197 I would give anything to hear Homer as quoted by Plato or, even better, to hear the Homeric Koine as performed by rhapsodes heard by Plato at the Panathenaia. I would give anything to hear directly from the rhapsodes their answers to the questions of Socrates—or even their answers to the questions of Plato himself. I would give anything just to overhear their rhapsodic talk, at whatever time and whatever place. Failing that, I need to reconstruct such talk, and I have to go to Plato in order to do it. Even Plato might be sympathetic to such a need. After all, even Plato could not have imagined a world without a Panathenaic festival. Nor could Plato have imagined a world that is truly without a City Dionysia. Granted, he may have wished to ban such a thing from any ideal Republic, but the idea that there would ever be a time when no such thing existed would have seemed unthinkable to him. How to imagine life without a Festival of Dionysus? We who live in such a world need to hear the language of rhapsodes and actors, however indirectly. So we have to reconstruct what it was like to hear the Homeric Koine performed at the Panathenaia. We need the help of witnesses, and the best we can do is to listen to the words of Socrates, as brought back to life each time we read Plato's dialogues. This Socrates is of course Plato's Socrates, and we are in a way fortunate that Plato is the mediator for us, because he has such a good ear for dialogue. This time I don't just mean Socratic dialogue. True, I am sure Plato picked up on Socrates' dialogue and even on Socrates' speech-habits in general, so much so that the real personality of Socrates comes back each time we read Plato. But here I am not talking about Socrates the person. I am talking about Plato the historical person who had a good ear and who listened carefully to the discourse of people in general, and of people of *tekhnē* in particular, such as rhapsodes. We need help in reconstructing the discourse of these rhapsodes. And, like it or not, Plato seems to be the only person who can help us.

3ⓈⒾ11. The sorrows of Andromache

3§198 In Plato's *Ion*, as we saw earlier, Socrates enumerates some highlights of Homeric poetry as performed by a rhapsode like Ion at the Panathenaia (535b-c). The enumeration takes the form of a set of 'accusatives of the rhapsodic subject' following *āidein* 'sing' (ᾄδῃς):[160] (1) Odysseus at the epic moment when he leaps upon the threshold, ready to shoot arrows at the suitors; (2) Achilles at the epic moment when he lunges at Hector; or (3) some other highlighted thing, here unspecified (*ti*, accusative), from epic moments involving Andromache, Hecuba, or Priam. As we are about to see, Plato's precise wording recaptures the precision of the rhapsode's craft in performing Homer.

3§199 Ion, responding to this enumeration by Socrates of highlights from Panathenaic performances of Homer by rhapsodes, says he feels the same emotions of terror and pity felt by the spectators at the Panathenaia as they react to the actions and words of his Homeric characters (*Ion* 533c). As Socrates himself describes it, the rhapsode dazzles his Panathenaic spectators, numbered at 20,000 (*Ion* 535c-d), inducing an overall sense of *ekplēxis*

---

[160] PR 26–27.

Chapter Three

'bedazzlement'.[161] This *eksplēxis* centers on the emotions of terror and pity. We are to imagine 20,000 spectators feeling terrified at one moment of the epic performance and then feeling sorrowful at the next moment (again, *Ion* 535c–d). Socrates recounts five such epic moments of *eksplēxis* as examples, enumerating them in ever-increasing compression and non-specificity:

3①48 Plato *Ion* 535b–c

ΣΩ. Ἔχε δή μοι τόδε εἰπέ, ὦ Ἴων, καὶ μὴ ἀποκρύψῃ ὅτι ἄν σε ἔρωμαι· ὅταν εὖ εἴπῃς ἔπη καὶ ἐκπλήξῃς μάλιστα τοὺς θεωμένους, ἢ τὸν Ὀδυσσέα ὅταν ἐπὶ τὸν οὐδὸν ἐφαλλόμενον ᾄδῃς, ἐκφανῆ γιγνόμενον τοῖς μνηστῆρσι καὶ ἐκχέοντα τοὺς ὀιστοὺς πρὸ τῶν ποδῶν, ἢ Ἀχιλλέα ἐπὶ τὸν Ἕκτορα ὁρμῶντα, ἢ καὶ τῶν περὶ Ἀνδρομάχην ἐλεινῶν τι ἢ περὶ Ἑκάβην ἢ περὶ Πρίαμον, τότε πότερον ἔμφρων εἶ ἢ ἔξω {c} σαυτοῦ γίγνῃ καὶ παρὰ τοῖς πράγμασιν οἴεταί σου εἶναι ἡ ψυχὴ οἷς λέγεις ἐνθουσιάζουσα, ἢ ἐν Ἰθάκῃ οὖσιν ἢ ἐν Τροίᾳ ἢ ὅπως ἂν καὶ τὰ ἔπη ἔχῃ;

SOCRATES: Hold it right there. Tell me this, Ion—respond to what I ask without concealment. When you recite well the epic verses [*epos* plural] and induce a feeling of bedazzlement [*eksplēxis*] for the spectators [*theōmenoi*]—when you sing of [1] Odysseus leaping onto the threshold and revealing himself to the suitors and pouring out the arrows at his feet, or of [2] Achilles rushing at [2->3a] Hector, or [3] something connected to the pitiful things about [3b] Andromache or [3c] Hecuba or [3d] Priam—are you then in your right mind, or outside yourself? Does your *psukhē*, possessed by the god [*enthousiazein*], suppose that you are in the midst of the actions you describe in Ithaca or Troy, or wherever the epic verses [*epos* plural] have it?

3§200 The first two moments have to do primarily with the emotion of terror, and they feature the main heroes of the *Odyssey* and the *Iliad* respectively, [1] Odysseus and [2] Achilles. The next three moments have to do primarily with the emotion of pity, and they feature the main heroes on the other side of the Trojan War: [3b] Andromache, [3c] Hecuba, and [3d] Priam. As I will argue in Chapter 4, the link between the two moments of terror and the three moments of pity is [3a] Hector, who exemplifies the emotion of terror when he is about to be killed by Achilles but who also exemplifies the

---

[161] The number 20,000 seems to be a notional approximation of the size of the Athenian "body politic" (there is a comparable figure of 30,000 in Herodotus 5.97.2).

3ⓢ11. The sorrows of Andromache

emotion of pity through the lamentations of [3b] his wife Andromache. In the wording of Plato's *Ion*, the pairing of [3a] Hector and [3b] Andromache creates a thematic link for the transition from terror to pity.

3§201 The Homeric portrayal of Andromache's lamentations is high theater. As we saw earlier in this dialogue, the *rhapsōidos* who performs such moments at the Panathenaia is parallel to a *hupokritēs* 'actor' who performs similar moments at the City Dionysia. In Chapter 2, I quoted an exquisite example from tragedy: it is an aria sung as a monody by the actor who plays Andromache in the *Andromache* of Euripides (91-117).

3§202 There is an overall parallelism, then, between the scenes of terror and pity in the epic of the Panathenaia and in the drama of the City Dionysia, especially tragedy. Such scenes in tragedy cannot be viewed independently of epic, as if they were intrinsic only to tragedy. Aristotle's formulation about terror and pity as essential ingredients of tragedy extends to epic as well. And his formulation corresponds closely to Plato's earlier formulation about terror and pity as essential ingredients of the epic performed by rhapsodes like Ion at the Panathenaia. There is a tragic way of "reading" Homer.

CHAPTER FOUR

HOMER THE CLASSIC IN THE AGE OF PHEIDIAS

4ⓢ1. Homer as a spokesman for the Athenian empire

4§1 In Chapter 3, my argumentation was limited to showing that Plato's Homer, as reflected in such virtual dialogues as the *Ion* and the *Hippias Minor*, was the Panathenaic Homer of his day, in the fourth century BCE. I used the internal evidence provided by Plato's precise usage of rhapsodic language to argue that he was actually quoting from the Panathenaic Homer in the stylized dialogues he committed to writing in his own historical setting. But what about the earlier historical setting of Socrates himself, in the fifth century BCE? This era, which I have chosen as the chronological cross-section for Chapter 4, is represented by an earlier form of the Panathenaic Homer, and I call this earlier form the imperial Homer. As I will argue, this Homer was the spokesman for what is commonly known as the Athenian empire.[1]

4§2 Before I explain my use of this new terminology, I need to review some points I made in Chapter 3 about the Panathenaic Homer, which need to be linked to the points I will be making here about the imperial Homer. As we saw in Chapter 3, Plato was bent on discrediting not only Homeric poetry in general but the Panathenaic Homer in particular—as represented by the *rhapsōidikē tekhnē* 'rhapsodic craft' of rhapsodes like Ion of Ephesus. As we also saw, the new *sophistikē tekhnē* 'sophistic craft' of sophists like Hippias was derived from this same old *rhapsōidikē tekhnē* 'rhapsodic craft' as practiced by rhapsodes like Ion when they were performing Homer at the festival of the Panathenaia in Athens. The craft of the sophist was becoming a new alternative to the craft of the rhapsode, and the stakes were high not only for rhapsode and sophist but also for the philosopher who presented himself as

---

[1] On the concept of the Athenian empire, I follow the model of Meiggs 1972. As for alternative ways of describing the concept, an example is Smarczyk 1990.

an alternative to both, Socrates. The dialogues of Plato that we have considered, especially the *Ion* and the *Hippias Minor*, dramatize an ongoing struggle to displace the old craft of the rhapsode and the newer craft of the sophist, both of which depended on Homer as a central point of reference, by substituting the newest craft of them all, philosophy. This craft, which is for Plato's Socrates a non-craft that subsumes all crafts, was meant to be independent of Homer. The philosopher's struggle to displace the crafts of the rhapsode and the sophist, as we can see from Plato's own work, began not in the fourth century, in the age of Plato. It began earlier, in the fifth century, in the historical time that corresponds to the dramatic time of these Platonic dialogues.

4§3 The term imperial Homer is apt for the historical period marked by the life and times of Socrates—a period in the fifth century BCE when the Athenian empire was reaching the summit of its prestige as the leading political and cultural force in the ancient Greek-speaking world. Tracing our steps backward in time, we have come to a point in world history when Homer was imagined as a spokesman for the Athenian empire.

4§4 In the title of my chapter, I could have referred to this historical period as the age of Socrates—or even as the age of Pericles, whose name is linked most closely to the Athenian empire at the height of its glory. Instead, I call this period the age of Pheidias. My reason for choosing the sculptor Pheidias and not the philosopher Socrates or the statesman Pericles will be explained as my argumentation proceeds. What cannot wait and needs to be explained without delay, however, is my reason for saying that Homer was a spokesman for the Athenian empire.

4§5 In the Prolegomena, I said I would argue that Homer's poetry gave meaning not only to Athenian civilization in general but to the Athenian empire in particular. For the Athenian empire in the age of Pheidias, Homer was a classic, an Athenian classic. As I now proceed to make this argument in earnest, I will need to reconsider the Panathenaic standard of Homeric poetry. In the fourth century BCE, as we saw in Chapter 3, this Panathenaic standard was primarily a matter of cultural hegemony. In other words, the performance of the Homeric *Iliad* and *Odyssey* at the Athenian festival of the Panathenaia reflected the cultural predominance of Athens in the ongoing evolution of poetry and song. In the fifth century BCE, on the other hand, the Panathenaic standard was a matter of political as well as cultural hegemony. In other words, the Panathenaic Homer reflected the political as well as the cultural predominance of Athens as an imperial power. That is what I mean when I say that Homer was a spokesman for the Athenian empire. That is what I mean by using the term imperial Homer.

Chapter Four

4§6 Already in the Prolegomena, I observed that I could have chosen to describe the historical reality behind the concept of an Athenian empire in a variety of alternative ways, steering clear of the English words empire, imperial, and imperialism. Still, I hope to justify my use of these words precisely because I intend to foreground their Roman source, the Latin word *imperium*. My usage will help highlight the parallels I see between the Roman empire on the one hand and, on the other, what we call the Athenian empire. Although the political causes of the Roman empire were of course different, its poetic effects were noticeably similar to those of the empire ascribed to the Athenians. As we will see later on, the similarities are most striking when we consider the idea of empire as pictured in the epic poetry of Virgil's *Aeneid*. Before we can turn—or rather, return—to Virgil, however, I need to consider the idea of an Athenian empire on its own terms, as pictured by Athenian audiences of the Homeric *Iliad* and *Odyssey* in the age of Pheidias.

4§7 The basic facts about the Athenian empire can be found in the history of Thucydides, who highlights what gradually happened to Athens as a world power in the period extending from the end of the Persian War, with the establishment of the Delian League in 478 BCE, to the outbreak of the Peloponnesian War in the year 431: what had started as a *xummakhia* 'alliance' of the city of Athens with various other cities evolved into an *arkhē* 'rule' by Athens over these cities (Thucydides 1.67.4, 1.75.1, etc.).[2] This 'rule' is the essence of the Athenian empire.[3]

4§8 Of special interest is the *arkhē* 'rule' by Athens over the Ionian cities of Asia Minor and its outlying islands, as distinct from the non-Ionian cities drawn into the political sphere of the evolving empire.[4] The Ionian connection with Athens—as distinct from Dorian or Aeolian connections—was particularly compelling, since the Delian League was conceived as an alliance of Ionians who shared in a common Ionian kinship (Thucydides 1.95.1; Aristotle *Constitution of the Athenians* 23.4).[5] I add this apt formulation: "The reference to

---

[2] Meiggs 1972:376.
[3] This paragraph and the paragraph that follows are repeated in the twin book *Homer the Preclassic*, at the beginning of Part I there.
[4] Meiggs 1972:294.
[5] Most pertinent is the discussion by Meiggs 1972:295 of the *horoi* 'boundary stones' of Samos. See also Barron 1964:39–40, who argues that the Eponymoi to whom the inscriptions on the *horoi* refer are the four sons of Ion, heroes of the four Ionian civic lineages or *phulai*. Barron p. 45 concludes that "the headquarters of the cults of Ion and the Ionic Eponymoi must have been at Athens." Despite the status of Athens as the "headquarters," the four old *phulai* of this notional mother city of the Ionians were ultimately replaced by the ten new *phulai* instituted after the reform of Kleisthenes in 508/7 BCE, as reported by Herodotus 5.66.2.

Ionian kinship [in Thucydides 1.95.1] is a brief allusion to a major element in fifth-century Athenian propaganda, the projection of Athens as mother-city of the whole empire, irrespective of the colonial realities."[6] To put it another way: "the concept of *xungeneia* [kinship] was stretched until it had become almost a metaphor for a relationship of obedience and control."[7]

4⑤2. The imperial Homer of Ion of Ephesus

4§9 This Ionian ideology of the Athenian empire is linked to the Ionian identity of the *rhapsōidos* 'rhapsode' Ion of Ephesus in Plato's *Ion*. That is because Ion's identity as an Ionian is in turn linked to his status as a rhapsode who competes with other rhapsodes in performing Homer at the festival of the Panathenaia in Athens. As a Panathenaic rhapsode, he is an Ionian representative of the imperial Homer, that is, of the Athenian standard of Homeric performance. Even his name is significant: it actually means, appropriately enough, 'the Ionian' (*Iōn*).[8]

4§10 In support of this formulation, I highlight the use of the word *arkhein* 'rule' in Plato's *Ion*. Before I quote the relevant wording, I summarize the context. We are about to read a brief exchange between Plato's Socrates and the rhapsode Ion. Socrates has been questioning the expertise of Ion in the craft of a *stratēgos* 'general'—a craft supposedly derived from Homer's own expertise in matters of war. In response to this questioning, Ion points out that his home city of Ephesus has no generals of its own, since it is 'ruled' (*arkhetai*, from *arkhein*) by Athens:

4①1 Plato *Ion* 541b–c

ΣΩ. Τί δή ποτ' οὖν πρὸς τῶν θεῶν, ὦ Ἴων, ἀμφότερα ἄριστος ὢν τῶν Ἑλλήνων, καὶ στρατηγὸς καὶ ῥαψῳδός, ῥαψῳδεῖς μὲν περιιὼν τοῖς Ἕλλησι, στρατηγεῖς δ' οὔ; ἢ {c} ῥαψῳδοῦ μὲν δοκεῖ σοι χρυσῷ στεφάνῳ ἐστεφανωμένου πολλὴ χρεία εἶναι τοῖς Ἕλλησι, στρατηγοῦ δὲ οὐδεμία;

ΙΩΝ. Ἡ μὲν γὰρ ἡμετέρα, ὦ Σώκρατες, πόλις ἄρχεται ὑπὸ ὑμῶν καὶ στρατηγεῖται καὶ οὐδὲν δεῖται στρατηγοῦ, ἡ δὲ ὑμετέρα καὶ ἡ

---

[6] Hornblower 1996:73.
[7] Hornblower 1996:73.
[8] For more on Ion of Ephesus as a generic 'Ionian', see Porter 2001:281n93 (with reference to Callimachus *Iamboi* 13.30–32; see also the remarks of Hunter 1997:46–47).

Λακεδαιμονίων οὐκ ἄν με ἕλοιτο στρατηγόν· αὐτοὶ γὰρ οἴεσθε ἱκανοὶ εἶναι.

SOCRATES: Why, I swear by the gods! Then how is it—if you are both the best general and the best rhapsode among the Hellenes— that you go around performing rhapsodically for the Hellenes but you are not a general for them? Do you think there is a great need among the Hellenes for a rhapsode garlanded with a golden garland but no need for a general?

ION: It is because our city, Socrates, is ruled [*arkhein*] by you Athenians: it has as its generals *your* generals, and it has no need of its own generals. As for your city, and the same goes for the city of the Spartans,[9] it would not choose me as a general, since you think you can make do with your own generals.

4§11 What Ion is saying here in the dramatic time of Plato's *Ion* matches what was really happening in the corresponding historical time: his native city of Ephesus, like all the other cities on the coast of Asia Minor that came under the control of the Athenian empire between the 460s and 412, had no foreign policy of its own.[10] The dramatic time of this dialogue can be situated in the years immediately preceding the Second Ionian Revolt that started in the year 412, when a number of tributary states revolted from Athens and sided with Sparta. Ephesus is mentioned incidentally by Thucydides in his account of that revolt (8.19.3).[11] The situation before 412 BCE can be described this way: "Ephesus was part of the Delian league, and would have been under Athenian control until the general Ionian uprising against Athens in 412."[12] From the epigraphical evidence of the *Athenian Tribute Lists*, we have precise figures for the assessment of tribute to be paid by Ephesus to Athens in given years: in the year 432 BCE, for example, the tribute is 7 talents and 3000 drachmas;[13] to give

---

[9] Here and everywhere, I translate *Lakedaimōn* 'Lacedaemon' and *Lakedaimonioi* 'Lacedaemonians' as 'Sparta' and 'Spartans' respectively. In ancient Greek usage, the concept of 'Lacedaemon' seems to be inclusive of such subject populations as the Messenians, whereas 'Sparta' is not. In my own usage, however, 'Spartan' is intended as an inclusive cover-term.

[10] For a most helpful summary of the extent of the Athenian empire after the battle at the river Eurymedon around 468 BCE, see Stadter 1989:149–151.

[11] See Moore 1974:426, 431.

[12] Murray 1996:130.

[13] Meiggs 1972:541. As Meiggs argues, p. 240, new assessments of the amount to be paid normally coincided with the quadrennial Great Panathenaia in Athens.

4§2. The imperial Homer of Ion of Ephesus

an idea of the scale, I compare the tribute of 9 talents to be paid in the same year by Aeolian Cyme, another major Hellenic city on the coast of Asia Minor.[14]

4§12 In this historical context, it is significant that Plato stages Ion of Ephesus as saying to Socrates of Athens: 'our city [= Ephesus], Socrates, is ruled [arkhein] by you Athenians: it has as its generals [stratēgoi] your generals, and it has no need of its own generals' (Ion 541c). Here I add a relevant detail from an Athenian inscription recording payments made for public purposes by the treasurers of Athena in the Panathenaic quadrennium of 418–414 BCE (IG I² 302).[15] In this inscription, at a point that follows the recording of payments in 415/4 to the Athenian forces occupying the island state of Melos (lines 69–72) and other payments involving the Sicilian expedition (lines 73–76), we find the recording of two other payments, in spring 414: one is to an unnamed stratēgos 'general' stationed in the Thermaic Gulf (line 78 και στρατεγοι εν τοι Θερμαιοι κολπο [. . .])[16] and another is to an unnamed stratēgos 'general' stationed in Ephesus (line 79 και στρατεγοι εν Εφ[εσοι . . .]).[17]

4§13 In responding to the point made by Ion, Socrates says that Athenians do in fact occasionally choose generals who are non-Athenians (Plato Ion 541d).[18] In the same breath Socrates adds that the people of Ephesus are not even really non-Athenians, since Ephesus, as an Ionian city, is after all a daughter city of Athens, which claims to be the metropolis or 'mother city' of all Ionians (Ion 541c–d). As Socrates puts it, 'after all, you Ephesians were Athenians in ancient times, weren't you?' (Ion 541d· τί δέ; οὐκ Ἀθηναῖοι μέν ἐστε οἱ Ἐφέσιοι τὸ ἀρχαῖον;).

4§14 This idea, that Ephesus is a daughter city of Athens, is not an ad hoc invention by Socrates or by Plato. In the late fifth century, the historical period that corresponds to the dramatic date of Plato's Ion, the idea that Athens was the metropolis or 'mother city' of all Ionian cities was generally accepted by

---

[14] For more figures, see Meiggs 1972:270: "Miletus was never required to pay more than 10 talents tribute before the war and no other Ionian mainland city paid as much. Phocaea's assessment was only 3 talents, and Erythrae paid no more than 7 talents in the third and fourth assessment periods [. . .]; Aeolian [Cyme] alone in the Ionian district paid more than 10 talents, but her first-period assessment of 12 talents was reduced to 9 in the second period and thereafter." As Meiggs notes, the assessments in the Hellespont district are by comparison higher than in the Ionia district, indicating a general trend of "decline" for Ionia in the fifth century BCE.

[15] The text of IG I² 302 is shown by Meiggs / Lewis 1988 no. 77. On this inscription, see in general Meiggs / Lewis pp. 229–236.

[16] This stratēgos 'general' is apparently Euetion, who according to Thucydides 7.9 attacked Amphipolis in the summer of 414 BCE. See Meiggs / Lewis 1988:236.

[17] For more on this unnamed stratēgos, see Meiggs / Lewis 1988:236.

[18] See Moore 1974:433–438 on the services performed for Athens by Herakleides of Klazomenai as stratēgos 'general' (he is mentioned in Plato Ion 541c–d).

Chapter Four

the Greek-speaking world, whether they were allies or enemies of Athens. This idea, as mythologized in the *Ion* of Euripides (1575–1588) and as historicized in both Herodotus (1.147.2) and Thucydides (1.2.6, with qualifications), was generally linked to the political reality of the Athenian empire.[19]

4§15 Of particular relevance to the status of Ion as a rhapsodic performer of Homeric poetry at the Panathenaia is the fact that Ionian cities were actually obliged to participate in the quadrennial celebration of the Great Panathenaia in Athens: for example, they had to send official delegates to attend this festival, and such attendance was considered "an extension of a general tradition linking colony to mother-city."[20]

4§16 Here I return to the remark made by Plato's Socrates when Ion the rhapsode points to the status of his native city of Ephesus as a tributary of Athens. As we have seen, Socrates follows up by remarking that Ephesus is after all a daughter city of Athens. In other words, Ion of Ephesus is a <u>virtual Athenian</u>, since Ion's identity as an Ionian is not only dominated by the Athenians: it is actually determined by them.

4§17 The picturing of Ion as a virtual Athenian is linked to his role as a professional rhapsode who performs Homer at the Panathenaia. And here I return to Ion's assertion that a major opportunity had been missed by the two cities contending for supreme imperial power, Athens and Sparta, since neither had the prudence to enlist his services as *stratēgos* 'general' (*Ion* 541c). Our first impression is that this assertion is absurd, since the rhapsode has no practical knowledge of warfare. On the surface, Plato here is simply undermining the importance of the rhapsode as a public figure. Looking beyond Plato's philosophical motives, however, we need to consider the implicit political realities here. What is elided by Plato in the *Ion* is the fact that the craft of the rhapsode who performs at the festival of the Panathenaia in Athens is politically as well as culturally important. This craft is in fact all-important for Athens, since Ion specializes in performing Homeric poetry, which is the premier form of poetry as performed at the premier festival of the Athenians, the Panathenaia. Ion may seem unimportant as an Ionian, but he becomes all-important as a virtual Athenian in the act of performing Homer for a receptive audience of some 20,000 celebrants attending the festival of the Panathenaia

---

[19] On the *Ion* of Euripides, see especially Barron 1964:48.

[20] Meiggs 1972:294–295. See also his p. 294, with reference to lines 11–13 of *IG* I^2 45 (Meiggs / Lewis 1988 no. 49), where the wording of the inscription specifies that the people of Brea, as a daughter city of Athens, must send a cow along with a panoply to the quadrennial Great Panathenaia and a phallus to the Dionysia. See also Barron 1964:47.

4§2. The imperial Homer of Ion of Ephesus

in Athens (Plato *Ion* 535d).[21] On the occasion of this festival, Athenians are notionally hosting the Ionians of the Delian League in an era marked by the rule of Athens over all Ionians. On this festive occasion, all Ionians are virtual Athenians, assembling in their notional mother city to hear the epics of Homer. On this occasion, Ion the Ionian is re-enacting Homer himself by way of performing Homer.

4§18 By now we see that it is not so absurd for the Athenians, as rivals of the Spartans in their struggle for supreme imperial power, to be competing with their enemy in imagining Ion as their *stratēgos* 'general'. Ion is in fact a virtual general for his Athenian audiences. By re-enacting Homer and explaining Homer to them, he becomes their educator about war.[22] He teaches the Athenians every time he performs at the Panathenaia and tells them the story of the one war that surpasses all other wars, the Trojan War. After all, as we see from the wording of Aristophanes, the Athenians considered Homer to be their foremost educator about war (*Frogs* 1030–1036).

4§19 The fact is, the Athenians considered the figure of Homer to be their universal educator, and Homer's art of teaching was a craft transmitted by the rhapsodes. A case in point is a passage we have already seen in the *Panegyricus* of Isocrates, where the orator refers to the *tekhnē* 'craft' of Homeric poetry as a tradition designed for two central applications: (1) Homeric performances by rhapsodes in *athloi* 'contests', implicitly at the Panathenaia, and (2) Homeric *paideusis* 'education' of the young. I quote the passage again:

4①2 Isocrates (4) *Panegyricus* 159

οἶμαι δὲ καὶ τὴν Ὁμήρου ποίησιν μείζω λαβεῖν δόξαν ὅτι καλῶς
τοὺς πολεμήσαντας τοῖς βαρβάροις ἐνεκωμίασεν καὶ διὰ τοῦτο
βουληθῆναι τοὺς προγόνους ἡμῶν ἔντιμον αὐτοῦ ποιῆσαι τὴν
τέχνην ἔν τε τοῖς τῆς μουσικῆς ἄθλοις καὶ τῇ παιδεύσει τῶν
νεωτέρων, ἵνα πολλάκις ἀκούοντες τῶν ἐπῶν ἐκμανθάνωμεν τὴν
ἔχθραν τὴν ὑπάρχουσαν πρὸς αὐτοὺς καὶ ζηλοῦντες τὰς ἀρετὰς τῶν
στρατευσαμένων τῶν αὐτῶν ἔργων ἐκείνοις ἐπιθυμῶμεν.

---

[21] PR 28.
[22] A point of comparison is the idea that Hippias of Elis is a virtual general for the Spartans when he educates them about war by way of re-enacting and explaining Homer to them, as we read in Plato (*Hippias Maior* 286a–c). Philostratus (*Lives of Sophists* 1.11.3) comments on the political background for the performances of Hippias of Elis in Sparta (*Lives of Sophists* 1.11.3): διὰ τὸ βούλεσθαι ἄρχειν 'through their desire for imperial rule [*arkhein*]'.

Chapter Four

I think that the poetry [*poiēsis*] of Homer received all the more glory because he celebrated so beautifully those who waged war against the barbarians, and it was because of this that our [Athenian] ancestors wanted to make his craft [*tekhnē*] a thing to be honored both in the contests [*athloi*] [of rhapsodes] in *mousikē*[23] and in the education [*paideusis*] of the young, so that we, having the chance to hear often his [= Homer's] verses [*epos* plural], may learn thoroughly the existing hostility against them [= the barbarians], *and* so that we may admire the accomplishments of those who have waged war and desire to accomplish the same deeds that they had accomplished.

4§20 Another case in point is a passage from the *Republic* of Plato where Socrates interrogates the figure of Homer himself about the Poet's expertise in *tekhnai* 'crafts' that involve matters of the greatest importance and beauty. The pratictioners of these crafts are listed as (1) generals, (2) administrators of cities, and (3) educators:

4Ⓣ3 Plato *Republic* 10.599c–d

> μηδ' αὖ περὶ τὰς ἄλλας τέχνας αὐτοὺς ἐρωτῶμεν, ἀλλ' ἐῶμεν· περὶ δὲ ὧν μεγίστων τε καὶ καλλίστων ἐπιχειρεῖ λέγειν Ὅμηρος, πολέμων τε πέρι καὶ στρατηγιῶν καὶ διοικήσεων πόλεων, καὶ {d} παιδείας πέρι ἀνθρώπου, δίκαιόν που ἐρωτᾶν αὐτὸν πυνθανομένους· Ὦ φίλε Ὅμηρε, εἴπερ . . .

> Let's not interrogate them [= the poets] concerning the other *tekhnai*. Let's let those things go. But concerning the greatest and most beautiful things that Homer attempts to speak about—wars and things having to do with generals and administrations of cities and about the education [*paideia*] of a person, it is I should think a just thing if we, seeking answers, interrogate Homer as follows: [The interrogation begins.] "Dear Homer, if indeed . . . ."

4§21 From what we have seen so far, it is evident that the identity of Ion as rhapsode was defined by the Panathenaic Homer, that is, by Homer as performed at the Panathenaia. Now we are about to see that even the identity of Athens as an imperial power was defined by this Panathenaic Homer. The

---

[23] As we have already seen, the *mousikē* 'craft of the Muses' as practiced at the Panathenaia includes the *tekhnē* 'craft' of rhapsodes, not only of citharodes, citharists, aulodes, and auletes. Supporting evidence comes from Aristotle *Constitution of the Athenians* (60.1), Plutarch *Pericles* (13.9-11), and Plato *Ion* (530a).

4§2. The imperial Homer of Ion of Ephesus

Athenian standard for performing Homer at the Panathenaia was a self-expression of the Athenian empire. The Panathenaic Homer was an imperial Homer.

4§22 What I am calling an Athenian standard was simultaneously an Ionian standard. In other words, the Panathenaic Homer was simultaneously an Ionian Homer. That is because the Athenian empire was at least notionally an Ionian empire. The Delian League, as an earlier form of the Athenian empire, was a clear and most forceful expression of Ionian identity. Moreover, the Ionian identity of the Athenian empire could be maintained and even reaffirmed most consistently by invoking the idea that Athens is the metropolis or 'mother city' of all Ionian cities. As we see in Plato's *Ion*, this idea explains how a rhapsode like Ion could be pictured as performing for all Ionians by virtue of performing Homer at the festival of the Panathenaia.

4§23 With the passage of time, however, the Ionian identity of the Athenian empire became blurred as it outgrew its identification with the Delian League. Symptomatic is the fact that the Treasury of the Delian League was ultimately transferred from Delos to Athens, sometime around the middle of the fifth century BCE (Plutarch *Aristeides* 25.2–3).[24] With the blurring of the Ionian identity of the empire, we can expect a concomitant blurring of Homer's own Ionian identity as the model for epic performance at the Panathenaia in the era of the democracy in Athens.

4§24 There was no blurring, however, of the political reality of the Athenian empire, expressed most explicitly by the Athenians' usage of the noun *arkhē* 'rule' and the corresponding verb *arkhein* 'rule' (Thucydides 1.76.1, 1.81.2, etc.). In the words of Pericles himself as re-enacted by Thucydides, the burden, as it were, of this *arkhē*, this empire, had transformed Athens into a *turannis* 'tyranny' over the cities ruled by Athens, even if the city of Athens itself remained a democracy for its own citizens (2.63.1–2).[25]

4§25 A word that most clearly expresses the duality of democracy and empire in Athenian civic discourse is the adjective *koinos*, in the dual sense of 'common' and 'standard'. To be sure, *koinos* in the general sense of 'common'— that is, 'common' to any group of people who have something 'in common'— was used in a wide variety of political and social contexts throughout the history of the ancient Greek-speaking world. What I highlight here, however, is the use of *koinos* in the specific sense of referring to a 'standard' way of thinking. As we are about to see, the 'standard' Athenian way of thinking

---

[24] Thucydides does not mention this transfer at 1.92.2, where we might have expected such a mention, nor anywhere else in his history: see Hornblower 1991:146.
[25] Meiggs 1972:378–379.

Chapter Four

is that the self-interest of the Athenian empire is the 'common' interest of the subject states that are ruled by the Athenian empire. Such usage is clearly attested in the civic discourse of Athenians in the fifth century BCE. The premier example is a passage where Thucydides re-enacts the relevant wording of the statesman Pericles. According to Pericles, it is imperative for the citizens of Athens to promote actively the *sōtēria* 'preservation' of their empire, to which their leader refers simply as *to koinon*, that is, the thing that is 'common' to all (2.60.4, 2.61.4). Ideologically, the Athenian empire is the 'common good' not only for the citizens of the democracy that is Athens but also for all Hellenes under the *arkhē* 'rule' of Athens—Ionians and non-Ionians alike. In other words, what is 'common' to all is 'standard', that is, 'standardized' by Athens.

4§26 This ideology of Athenian self-interest as a common good that must be standardized for all is made explicit in the Melian Dialogue of Thucydides, where the historian dramatizes a debate between a delegation representing the elites of the non-Ionian island-state of Melos and a delegation of Athenian military leaders sent by their city to demand the submission of the Melians to the imperial power of the Athenian state. For the Athenians, such a submission is equivalent to the *sōtēria* or 'preservation' of the Melians, since the alternative to submission is the destruction of those who resist, and this *sōtēria* is equated with the self-interest of the Athenian *arkhē* or 'empire' (5.91.2): ὡς δὲ ἐπ' ὠφελίᾳ τε πάρεσμεν τῆς ἡμετέρας <u>ἀρχῆς</u> καὶ ἐπὶ <u>σωτηρίᾳ</u> νῦν τοὺς λόγους ἐροῦμεν τῆς ὑμετέρας πόλεως 'we will now speak arguments to show that we are here in order to promote the interests of our <u>empire</u> [*arkhē*] and the <u>preservation</u> [*sōtēria*] of your city'. In other words, the *sōtēria* or 'preservation' of the island-state of the Melians is being equated with the self-preservation of the Athenian empire. What is driving the Athenian argumentation here is the principle of expediency, not justice, and this principle is meant to apply to both sides in the debate.

4§27 The Melians, on the other hand, while saying that the Athenian demand for their submission violates the principle of justice, likewise invoke the principle of expediency in arguing that the Athenians should not force them to submit, and in so doing they invoke the ideology of the Athenian empire by resorting to the expression *to agathon koinon* 'the common good' (5.90): μὴ καταλύειν ὑμᾶς τὸ <u>κοινὸν</u> <u>ἀγαθόν</u> '... that you should not destroy the <u>common</u> [*koinon*] good'. In effect, they are saying that the Athenians, by forcing the Melians to submit, will be destroying 'the common good' by virtue of ultimately destroying themselves in the process of forcing others to submit to their will.

4§28 The irony is self-evident: 'the common good', which is presumably *koinon* 'common' to Melians and Athenians alike and, by extension, to all Hellenes, is being equated by the Athenians with the special interests of the Athenian empire. The Athenians know it, and the Melians show that they know it, too, since they too resort to the argument of expediency. The problem is, the Athenians in the Melian Dialogue of Thucydides are not really worried about the self-preservation or *sōtēria* of their empire, despite the warnings of the Melians about its ultimate destruction.

4§29 A spokesman for this ideological world of empire was Homer himself, figured as a universal poet and educator. This Homer was an imperial Homer, ideologized as *koinos* 'common' to all Hellenes—at least, to all Hellenes in the Athenian empire. There is a trace of this ideology to be found in an amalgamated *Life of Homer* story, mediated in part through an Athenian phase of transmission, known as the *Contest of Homer and Hesiod*. In the twin book *Homer the Preclassic* I offer a detailed analysis of this particular "Life" and of other *Life of Homer* traditions as well.[26] Here I focus only on the wording used in the story to describe the reception of Homer: when Homer goes to the island of Delos to participate in a festival celebrated by all Ionians, he is acclaimed by them as the *koinos politēs* 'common citizen' of all their cities (*Contest of Homer and Hesiod* [*Vita 2*] 319–320: οἱ μὲν Ἴωνες πολίτην αὐτὸν κοινὸν ἐποιήσαντο).

4§30 The status of Homer as the *koinos politēs* 'common citizen' of all Ionian cities is linked in this story to his central role in the pan-Ionian festival of the Delia. That festival, as we know independently from Thucydides (3.104.2–3), was reshaped in the late fifth century by the Athenians, who sought to link the myths and rituals of the pan-Ionian Delia with the cultural and political agenda of the Delian League, that is, of the Athenian empire. In the twin book *Homer the Preclassic*, I examine in some detail what Thucydides has to say about Homer and about the pan-Ionian festival of the Delia.[27] Here I confine myself to highlighting the use of the word *koinos* to mark the role of Homer as the spokesman for the Delia and, by extension, for the Delian League. Earlier, we saw the imperial Athenian usage of the same word *koinos* in the sense of 'standard' as well as 'common' to all. Now we are beginning to see how the role of Homer as the *koinos politēs* of all Ionians at the Delia conforms to such an imperial usage. Homer is being imagined as a spokesman for the Athenian empire.

---

[26] *HPC* I§§56 and following.
[27] *HPC* I§§24 and following.

Chapter Four

4Ⓢ3. The imperial Koine of Homer

4§31 The imperial Athenian usage of *koinos* with reference to Homer survives indirectly in the Aristarchean concept of Koine (*koinē*)—in the double sense of 'common' and 'standard'. The sense of 'common', as we saw in the Prolegomena, is appropriate not only to the 'common' manuscripts available to Aristarchus in establishing a base text of Homer in the second century BCE but also to the 'common' usage of Homer as Aristarchus describes it on the basis of the language reflected in the consensus of 'common' manuscripts. As for the sense of 'standard', it is appropriate to an earlier Athenian phase of Homeric textual transmission as presupposed by Aristarchus in his reconstruction of his base text. Such an Athenian phase can be equated with what I am calling the Panathenaic Homer. This equation is pertinent to my overall thesis, which is, to argue that the concept of a Homeric Koine applies to the Panathenaic Homer in the fifth century, at which time the word *koinos* conveyed simultaneously the ideas of democracy and empire. In other words, the reconstructed concept of a Homeric Koine (*koinē*) in the fifth century can be equated with the ideological appropriation of Homer by the Athenian empire. The Homeric Koine was the poetic *lingua franca* of the empire.

4§32 The medieval Latin term *lingua franca*, reflecting the imperial culture of Europe in the days of Charlemagne, King of the Franks, is an apt point of comparison with the ancient Greek term *koinē* as used by Aristarchus, who applied *koinē* not only to the text but also to the language of Homer.[28] The language, like the text, is notionally 'common' to all and is therefore 'standard' for all.

4§33 As we are about to see, Aristarchus imagined the Koine of Homer to be a basic <u>dialect</u>. The Aristarchean idea of the Homeric Koine as an imaginary basic dialect can be traced back to the earlier ideas of Athenians about their actual dialect, Attic. In the fourth century BCE, for example, Isocrates goes on record as saying that the Attic dialect of the Athenians is the universal language of all Greek-speaking people because of its *koinotēs* 'communality' (15.296). In other words, the Attic dialect has a 'standard' quality because it is *koinē* or 'common' to all Hellenes.

4§34 The cultural imperialism of the Attic dialect leaves its mark in the postclassical history of the Greek language. The postclassical form of Greek known as the *koinē*, the language of the Septuagint and the Gospels, was a historical descendant of the Attic dialect as transmitted by the Ionic-speaking

---

[28] There is a relevant discussion in *PP* 184–185.

populations of the former Athenian empire and beyond: in the process of this transmission, the idiosyncrasies of the old Attic dialect were leveled out by the generalities of the Ionic dialects.[29] To restate, the Koine was Attic as generalized by way of Ionic. This new Attic was a regularized Attic, as it were, becoming a frame dialect for all the Ionic dialects. As a regularized dialect, this new Attic was the Koine. As the name Koine indicates, this dialect was a federal language, even an imperial language. It was the *lingua franca* of the Athenian empire.

4§35 Such a modern linguistic reformulation of the Koine is parallel to the ancient philological formulation that I extrapolate from the commentaries of Aristarchus, for whom the 'Koine' patterns found in the Homeric texts represent the *sunētheia* or 'customary usage' of the standard 'dialect' that he associated with Homer, while the non-'Koine' patterns he also found in the Homeric texts represent relatively unaccustomed usages stemming from other 'dialects'.

4§36 As I showed in the Prolegomena, Aristarchus tested his descriptions of *sunētheia* 'customary usage' in the language of 'Homer' by comparing his descriptions of the *sunētheia* 'customary usage' he found in the Greek language as spoken in his own time. I quote again here a particularly telling example:

4①4 Scholia A^im for *Iliad* II 135a (Aristonicus)

<καὶ δὴ δοῦρα σέσηπε νεῶν καὶ σπάρτα λέλυνται:> ὅτι κατὰ τὸν αὐτὸν στίχον καὶ <u>ἑαυτῷ καὶ ἡμῖν συνήθως</u> ἐξενήνοχε τὸ <u>λέλυνται καὶ σέσηπε</u>.

<καὶ δὴ δοῦρα σέσηπε νεῶν καὶ σπάρτα λέλυνται:> [Aristarchus marks this verse in the margin] because he [= Homer] has produced in the same verse, as is customary [*sunēthōs*] both for him [= Homer] and for us, the λέλυνται and σέσηπε.

4§37 In terms of this observation derived from Aristarchus, the Homeric verse in question features a coexistence of 'Koine' and 'Attic' usages in the syntax. The syntactical pattern of combining a plural verb with a neuter plural subject is 'Koine', whereas the pattern of combining a singular verb with a neuter plural subject is 'Attic'. In other words, 'Homer' could accommodate both the 'Koine' and the 'Attic' usages:

---

[29] Meillet 1935:266; Nagy 1972:31.

Chapter Four

4⊕5 Scholia b(BCE³E⁴)T ⁱˡ for *Iliad* II 135b (exegetical scholia)

<καὶ δὴ δοῦρα σέσηπε νεῶν καὶ σπάρτα λέλυνται:> ἐν ἑνὶ στίχῳ ἔθηκε τὴν Ἀτθίδα καὶ κοινὴν χρῆσιν.

<καὶ δὴ δοῦρα σέσηπε νεῶν καὶ σπάρτα λέλυνται:> In the same single verse he [= Homer] placed the Attic and the Koine usage [*khrēsis*].

4§38 According to Aristarchus, what is spoken in the time of Homer *sunēthōs heautōi* 'as is customary for him' can thus include both 'Koine' and 'Attic'. Such an observation on the part of Aristarchus stems from his comparing Homeric diction with what is spoken *sunēthōs hēmīn* 'as is customary for us', that is, in his own time, when the distinction between 'Koine' and 'Attic' is evident. Applying the methods of modern linguistics in analyzing what is 'customary' in the time of Aristarchus, I repeat my working definition: the Koine is Attic as generalized by way of Ionic.

4§39 This relationship of Koine and Attic is indirectly reflected in later ancient commentaries that happen to be derived from Aristarchus: there too the Koine usage is more generalized, in that it represents what Attic and Ionic have in common, whereas the Attic usage is more specialized, in that it represents what is idiosyncratic about Attic as opposed to the Koine. Here are six examples:

4⊕6 Scholia A for *Iliad* I 216a

χρή: ὀξυτονούμενον καὶ ἐν τῇ συντάξει βαρυνόμενον σημαίνει ἐπίρρημα τὸ δεῖ, . . . περισπώμενον δὲ ῥῆμα Ἀττικόν· ἀπὸ γὰρ τοῦ χρῶμαι τὸ δεύτερον τῆς κοινῆς διαλέκτου ἐστὶ χρᾷ Ἰωνικῶς, Ἀττικὸν δὲ χρῇ

χρή: When it [= XPH] is accented with an acute [which is grave when embedded in the syntax], it [= XPH] is an impersonal verb meaning δεῖ. . . . When it [= XPH] is accented with a circumflex, it is the Attic personal verb. Here is how. To conjugate from the verb χρῶμαι: the second person singular in the Koine dialect is χρᾷ. That is the way it is said in Ionic.[30] The Attic way is χρῇ.

---

[30] The comment Ἰωνικῶς is added after the form as mentioned. Such an adding-style is typical of the abbreviated grammatical discourse we find in the Homeric scholia.

4ⓈI3. The imperial Koine of Homer

4①7 Scholia A for *Iliad* II 115a (Aristonicus)

δυσκλέα Ἄργος: ὅτι κατὰ συστολὴν Ὅμηρος τὰ τοιαῦτα ἐκφέρει, δυσκλέα καὶ ἀκλέα, Ἰωνικῶς. οἱ δὲ Ἀττικοὶ ἐκτείνουσιν.

δυσκλέα Ἄργος: [Aristarchus marks this verse in the margin] because Homer produces such forms with a short [final -α], δυσκλέα and ἀκλέα [*Odyssey* iv 728], which is the Ionic way. But the Attic people produce a long [final -α].

4①8 Scholia A for *Iliad* II 532b1

Αὐγειάς: ὡς καλιάς· συνήθης γὰρ ἡ τοιαύτη ἀνάγνωσις παρὰ τῷ ποιητῇ Ἰωνικωτέρα οὖσα.

Αὐγειάς: Like καλιάς. That is because such a reading [*anagnōsis*] is customary [*sunēthēs*] in the Poet, since it is more Ionic.

4①9 Scholia b(BCE³) for *Iliad* II 532b2

... ὡς παρειάς· ἡ γὰρ τοιαύτη ἀνάγνωσις Ἰωνικωτέρα οὖσα συνήθης Ὁμήρῳ ἐστίν.

... or like παρειάς [*Iliad* III 35 etc.]. That is because such a reading [*anagnōsis*], since it is more Ionic, is customary [*sunēthēs*] for Homer.

4①10 Scholia A for *Iliad* I 85c (Herodian)

{θαρσήσας μάλα} εἰπέ: τρία εἰσὶ τὰ ἐν τῇ κοινῇ ὀξυνόμενα, ἐλθέ, εὑρέ, εἰπέ. ἰδίως δὲ καὶ μακρᾷ παραλήγονται. Ἀττικοὶ δὲ καὶ ἐπὶ τῶν βραχυπαραλήκτων ὀξύνουσι τὸ ἰδέ καὶ λαβέ.

{θαρσήσας μάλα} εἰπέ: In the Koine there are these three forms that have acute accent on the ultimate syllable: ἐλθέ, εὑρέ, εἰπέ. They share the property of having a long penultimate syllable. But the Attic people produce acute accent on the last syllable even in forms that have a short penultimate syllable, in the case of ἰδέ and λαβέ.

4①11 Scholia D for *Iliad* VIII 352

νῶϊ. ἡμεῖς. κοινὴ ἡ διάλεκτος. Δωριεῖς δέ φασιν, ἄμμες. Αἰολεῖς, ἄμμε. Ἀττικοὶ δέ, νῶϊ. Ἴωνες, ἡμέες.

Chapter Four

νῶϊ [is the lemma]. ἡμεῖς.[31] <u>The dialect is Koine</u>. The Dorians say ἄμμες and the Aeolians say ἄμμε. But the <u>Attic</u> people say νῶϊ. And the <u>Ionians</u> say ἡμέες.

4§40 The last statement needs special clarification. The point being made here is that the 'Koine' form of Homeric usage would be ἡμεῖς. By implication, the verse-final οὐκέτι νῶϊ as attested at *Iliad* VIII (352) was matched by a variant οὐκέτι ἡμεῖς, featuring the 'Koine' form ἡμεῖς as opposed to the 'Attic' form νῶϊ in the dual (the dual usage is supposedly an aspect of the 'Atticism' here). As a formulaic parallel for οὐκέτι ἡμεῖς I cite verse-final οὐδέ τοι ἡμεῖς at *Iliad* XIX (409).

4§41 In later phases of the commentary tradition, the distinctness of 'Attic' from 'Koine' tends to be forgotten, as we see from this later comment on the same Homeric verse, where 'Attic' is actually being equated with 'Koine':

4①12 Scholia (recentiora) for *Iliad* VIII 352

οὐκέτι νῶϊ] <u>κοινῇ ἡμῖν</u>· Δωριεῖς γάρ φασιν ἄμμες, <u>Ἀττικοὶ</u> δὲ νώ, <u>Ἴωνες</u> ἡμέας.

οὐκέτι νῶϊ [is the *lēmma*]. This is the way it is common [*koinē*] for us. For the Dorians say ἄμμες, the <u>Attic</u> people say νώ, and the <u>Ionians</u> say ἡμέας.

4§42 As I already argued in the Prolegomena, the Aristarchean distinction between 'Koine' and 'Attic' is generally blurred in the post-Aristarchean era, when scholars tend to equate uncritically the ancient usage of Homer with the contemporary usage described by Aristarchus.

4§43 The construction κοινῇ ἡμῖν 'in the way that is common [*koinē*] for us' is comparable to the construction ἡμῖν συνήθως 'in the way that is customary [*sunēthēs*] for us' in the scholia for *Iliad* II 135. The latter construction, as we saw earlier, comes from a description that goes back to the time of Aristarchus, when the distinction was still being made between 'Koine' and 'Attic'.

4§44 From that Aristarchean description in the scholia for *Iliad* II 135, we saw that 'Koine' usage and 'Attic' usage supposedly coexist within the overall 'Homeric' usage. Despite such coexistence, however, the 'Koine' usage is still the overall 'Homeric' usage, not the 'Attic', as I already showed in the exam-

---

[31] At first sight, this form seems to be the definition. On the basis of the comment that follows it, however, I propose that it is an alternative lemma.

ples where the Aristarchean commentary isolates an 'Attic' form as a textual variant of a 'Koine' form and then proceeds to opt for the 'Koine' form.

4§45 To sum up, the Aristarchean commentaries picture a Homer who speaks both 'Koine' and 'Attic', though he mostly defaults to Koine whenever a choice is available between distinct 'Koine' and 'Attic' forms. The presence of Attic forms in Homeric usage fits the overall theory of Aristarchus concerning the origins of Homer himself. Supposedly, Homer was an Athenian who lived in the time of the so-called Ionian Migration, which Aristarchus dated around 1000 BCE (scholia A for *Iliad* XIII 197).[32] Moreover, the scholiastic tradition stemming ultimately from Aristarchus implies that Homer wrote his poems (scholia A for *Iliad* XVII 719) and that Hesiod actually had a chance to read them (scholia A for *Iliad* XII 22a).[33] In Aristarchean terms, then, Homer not only spoke but also wrote a form of Greek that combined 'Koine' and 'Attic' usage.

4§46 Reading the linguistic standards of Aristarchus as indications of an overall cultural standard, I conclude that the Koine of Homer is a form of imperial discourse. It is a standardized Ionic dialect that speaks to the Ionians of the Athenian empire and that overrides even the local dialect of the Athenians. So, linguistically, the Athenian empire is an Ionian construct. And the imperial Homer, as represented by Ionians like Ion of Ephesus, is likewise an Ionian construct.

4⑤4. The imperial Homer of Hippias of Elis

4§47 This imperial Homer is represented not only by Ionians like Ion of Ephesus. An example of a non-Ionian representative is Hippias of Elis, a historical figure who is dramatized in two Platonic dialogues named after him, the *Hippias Maior* and the *Hippias Minor*. The dramatic date of these two dialogues, like that of the *Ion*, highlights the era of the Athenian empire at its apogee. As we will see, both these dialogues make it clear that the Athenian

---

[32] HTL 11-12. As a supplement to scholia A for *Iliad* XIII 197 see Proclus περὶ Ὁμήρου 59–62 ed. Severyns 1938: τοῖς δὲ χρόνοις αὐτὸν οἱ μὲν περὶ τὸν Ἀρίσταρχόν φασι γενέσθαι κατὰ τὴν τῆς Ἰωνίας ἀποικίαν, ἥτις ὑστερεῖ τῆς Ἡρακλειδῶν καθόδου ἔτεσιν ἑξήκοντα, τὸ δὲ περὶ τοὺς Ἡρακλείδας λείπεται τῶν Τρωϊκῶν ἔτεσιν ὀγδοήκοντα. οἱ δὲ περὶ Κράτητα ἀνάγουσιν αὐτὸν εἰς τοὺς Τρωϊκοὺς χρόνους 'As for the dating, Aristarchus and his school situate Homer at the time of the Ionian Migration, supposedly sixty years after the Return of the Herakleidai, which in turn was supposedly eighty years after the era of the Trojan War; by contrast, Crates and his school date him back to the era of the Trojan War'. On the rivalry of Aristarchus and Crates as editors of Homer: PP 151; also Pfeiffer 1968:228; Janko 1992:32n53, 71; Keaney and Lamberton 1996:67n2.

[33] See Porter 1992:83.

Chapter Four

standard of Homeric poetry was politically dominant not only within the Athenian empire but even in places beyond the empire's reach. Among those places was Sparta, the city that figured as the principal enemy of Athens in the Peloponnesian War.

4§48 For background on Hippias of Elis, I look back to the previous chapter, where I compared him directly to Ion the rhapsode. As we saw there, the displays of Homeric performance by the sophist Hippias at the Olympics in Olympia resembled the displays of Homeric performance by the rhapsode Ion at the Panathenaia in Athens. Both kinds of Homeric displays, as we also saw, followed the Panathenaic standard of performing Homer. To that extent, Hippias of Elis rivaled Ion of Ephesus as a performer and interpreter of Homer. Here were two Homeric experts who both considered themselves the absolute best in what they did, immeasurably better, each in his own way, than any of their competitors. Each of the two had worked out his own definition of what exactly it was that they did as Homeric experts. And Homer was for both the absolute measure of perfection.

4§49 The Homeric virtuoso Ion, in terms of his self-definition, is bound both politically and professionally to the Athenian standard of the Panathenaic Homer. He is bound politically as an Ionian and professionally as a rhapsode. By contrast, the Homeric virtuoso Hippias is bound to this standard neither politically, since he is a non-Ionian, nor professionally, since he is a sophist. Rather, the ties that bind Hippias to the Athenian standard of the Panathenaic Homer are simply cultural. Accordingly, Plato's Socrates uses divergent strategies in undermining his two intellectual adversaries: as we saw in Chapter 3, what undermines Ion in Plato's *Ion* is this rhapsode's inability to think independently of Homer; what undermines Hippias in the *Hippias Minor*, as we will now see, is this sophist's inability to think the way Homer really thinks.

4§50 Unlike Plato's Socrates, who focuses on the divergences between Ion as a rhapsode and Hippias as a sophist, we as independent observers can focus on the convergences in their professional claims, and those convergences bring us back to the concept of the Panathenaic signature, that is, the Athenian standard for performing the Panathenaic Homer. The status of Hippias as grand master of poetry and song is correlated with the keen interest shown by this sophist in the *orthotēs* 'correctness' of *grammata* 'letters' and in other such matters relating to various *tekhnai* 'crafts' of poetry and song (*Hippias Minor* 368a–e). This interest requires critical judgment, as signaled by the verb *dia-krinein* 'decide [between X and Y]' in the description we saw of the sophist seated on a throne and responding to questions as if he were Minos himself (Plato *Protagoras* 315c διέκρινεν). We may compare the interest

4§4. The imperial Homer of Hippias of Elis

shown by Ion the rhapsode in making critical judgments concerning questions of Homeric verbal artistry—that is, whether Homer says his *epē* (= *epos* plural) 'verses' *orthōs* 'correctly' or not (*Ion* 537b-c τὰ ἔπη εἴτε ὀρθῶς λέγει Ὅμηρος εἴτε μή). In the *Ion*, when Plato's Socrates asks Ion to tell him what are the things about which the craft of the rhapsode can enable Ion to 'make critical judgments', that is, *dia-krinein*, the rhapsode replies: 'all things' (*Ion* 539e).

4§51 A related point, made in Chapter 3, bears repeating here. By way of metonymy, the craft of the rhapsodes can subsume other crafts. It is as if the mastery of Homeric poetry were the same thing as a mastery of all crafts. We saw this idea proclaimed by the rhapsode Ion in Plato's *Ion*. This stance of Ion the rhapsode is remarkably similar to the stance of Hippias the sophist. Hippias too is a specialist in Homer (*Hippias Minor* 363b-c). The difference is, Hippias does not consider himself a specialist in *rhapsōidikē tekhnē*. Rather, he seems to be a generalist in *sophistikē tekhnē*. The sophist's mastery of the rhapsode's craft is merely the primary example of his mastery of all crafts. What makes all the difference is the sophist's overall mastery of the *mnēmonikon tekhnēma* 'mnemonic technique' (*Hippias Minor* 368d, 369a).

4§52 Hippias was renowned for his prodigious mental powers of recalling any and all Homeric verses. It is in this context that we see him described as a specialist in 'mnemonic technique', *mnēmonikon tekhnēma*. As I have argued in Chapter 3, the supposedly novel mnemonic technique of Hippias was derived from the same old *rhapsōidikē tekhnē* 'rhapsodic craft' as practiced by Ion the rhapsode at the Panathenaia. Unlike Ion, however, Hippias was not politically dependent on Athens. Elis, the home city of Hippias, was independent of the Athenian *arkhē* 'rule'. And it had to deal on its own with another city whose leaders hoped to possess *arkhē* on their own terms, that is, with the city of Sparta.

4§53 I cite a most relevant passage from a later source. Philostratus in the *Lives of Sophists* tells how Hippias, whenever he visited Sparta, made spectacular verbal displays of his mnemonic technique, his *mnēmonikon* (1.11.2 τὸ ... μνημονικόν). I stress the wording that describes the political motive of Hippias when he is performing in Sparta (*Lives of Sophists* 1.11.3): ἐπειδὴ οἱ Λακεδαιμόνιοι διὰ τὸ βούλεσθαι ἄρχειν τῇ ἰδέᾳ ταύτῃ ἔχαιρον '... since the Spartans, through their desire for imperial rule [*arkhein*], took pleasure in this form [*idea*]'.[34] Here I translate *arkhein* in terms of 'imperial rule', not just 'rule', since the Spartans are described as hoping to possess something that

---

[34] A fuller version of this compressed account, which I will quote in its entirety later on, is Plato *Hippias Maior* 284e-286a.

Chapter Four

the Athenians already have, that is, an empire. In other words, the Spartans do have their own imperial ambitions, but these ambitions are formalized in Athenian terms. I infer, then, that the 'form' (in Greek, *idea*) of public verbal displays performed by Hippias does indeed play a part in realizing the imperial ambitions of the Spartans. And such a 'form' derives from the imperial Homer of the Panathenaia.

4§54 In Philostratus' *Lives of Sophists*, we are given two examples of various kinds of verbal displays being performed by Hippias as he applies the 'form' of his mnemonic technique in Sparta.[35] We also find fuller versions of both examples in Plato. I will consider the two examples one by one.

4§55 The first of the two examples is worded by Philostratus as follows (*Lives* 1.11.3): γένη τε διήιει πόλεων καὶ ἀποικίας καὶ ἔργα 'he [= Hippias] would go through [verbally] the genealogies of cities and narratives about how they were founded and about related accomplishments'. Here is Plato's fuller version of this first example:

4Ⓣ13 Plato *Hippias Maior* 285d–e

> ΙΠ. Περὶ τῶν γενῶν, ὦ Σώκρατες, τῶν τε ἡρώων καὶ τῶν ἀνθρώπων, καὶ τῶν κατοικίσεων, ὡς τὸ ἀρχαῖον ἐκτίσθησαν αἱ πόλεις, καὶ συλλήβδην πάσης τῆς ἀρχαιολογίας ἥδιστα {ε} ἀκροῶνται, ὥστ' ἔγωγε δι' αὐτοὺς ἠνάγκασμαι ἐκμεμαθηκέναι τε καὶ ἐκμεμελετηκέναι πάντα τὰ τοιαῦτα.
>
> HIPPIAS: They [= the Spartans] get the greatest pleasure from hearing about the genealogies, Socrates, of both heroes and humans, and about how cities were founded in the past and, taken all together, about all knowledge of the past. So, because of them [= the Spartans], I have been forced to memorize thoroughly and to rehearse thoroughly all such matters.

4§56 The second example of various kinds of verbal displays performed by Hippias in Sparta is related directly to Homeric poetry (Philostratus *Lives of Sophists* 1.11.4): ἔστιν δὲ αὐτῷ καὶ Τρωικὸς διάλογος, οὗ λόγος· ὁ Νέστωρ ἐν Τροίᾳ ἁλούσῃ ὑποτίθεται Νεοπτολέμῳ τῷ Ἀχιλλέως, ἃ χρὴ ἐπιτηδεύοντα ἄνδρα ἀγαθὸν φαίνεσθαι 'he [= Hippias] also has a Trojan *Dialogue*, the plot of which is this: Nestor, in Troy after it is captured, gives instruction to Neoptolemos son

---

[35] On the reception of sophists in Sparta, there is an important reference in Plato *Protagoras* 342b–e.

4§4. The imperial Homer of Hippias of Elis

of Achilles concerning what things one must pursue in order to appear to be a good man'. Here is Plato's fuller version of this second example:

4①14 Plato *Hippias Maior* 286a–c

ΙΠ. Καὶ ναὶ μὰ Δί', ὦ Σώκρατες, περί γε ἐπιτηδευμάτων καλῶν καὶ ἔναγχος αὐτόθι ηὐδοκίμησα διεξιὼν ἃ χρὴ τὸν νέον ἐπιτηδεύειν. ἔστι γάρ μοι περὶ αὐτῶν παγκάλως λόγος συγκείμενος, καὶ ἄλλως εὖ διακείμενος καὶ τοῖς ὀνόμασι· πρόσχημα δέ μοί ἐστι καὶ ἀρχὴ τοιάδε τις τοῦ λόγου. ἐπειδὴ ἡ Τροία ἥλω, λέγει ὁ λόγος ὅτι Νεοπτόλεμος {b} Νέστορα ἔροιτο ποῖά ἐστι καλὰ ἐπιτηδεύματα, ἃ ἄν τις ἐπιτηδεύσας νέος ὢν εὐδοκιμώτατος γένοιτο· μετὰ ταῦτα δὴ λέγων ἐστὶν ὁ Νέστωρ καὶ ὑποτιθέμενος αὐτῷ πάμπολλα νόμιμα καὶ πάγκαλα. τοῦτον δὴ καὶ ἐκεῖ ἐπεδειξάμην καὶ ἐνθάδε μέλλω ἐπιδεικνύναι εἰς τρίτην ἡμέραν, ἐν τῷ Φειδοστράτου διδασκαλείῳ, καὶ ἄλλα πολλὰ καὶ ἄξια ἀκοῆς· ἐδεήθη γάρ μου Εὔδικος ὁ Ἀπημάντου. ἀλλ' ὅπως παρέσῃ {c} καὶ αὐτὸς καὶ ἄλλους ἄξεις, οἵτινες ἱκανοὶ ἀκούσαντες κρῖναι τὰ λεγόμενα.

HIPPIAS: I tell you, Socrates, and I swear by Zeus: I have just recently achieved the greatest celebrity there [= in Sparta] when I went through [verbally] all the studies of fine arts that a young person there has to study. I have a discourse [*logos*] already composed about those things, all beautifully put together in every respect—and that includes the ordering of the words. I have an introductory scheme— that is, a beginning [*arkhē*]—which goes something like this: when Troy was captured, the story [*logos*] says, Neoptolemos asked Nestor what were the studies of fine arts that a young man should study in order to become a celebrity. So, after this, Nestor starts speaking and goes on to give instructions to him [= Neoptolemos] about all manner of fine and lawful things. Now you see: I made a public display of this thing over there [= in Sparta] and I am about to make a public display of it here [= in Athens], three days from now, at the school of Pheidostratos[36]—along with many other things that are worth hearing. That is because Eudikos son of Apemantos asked me

---

[36] This description in the Platonic *Hippias Maior* (286b–c) of the setting for the performance of Hippias in Athens—the *didaskaleion* 'school' of Pheidostratos—leaves it unclear whether this performance should be considered public or private. The wording that follows, however, indicates that anyone interested in hearing Hippias perform is free to come. And the turnout, it is implied, will be huge.

Chapter Four

to do so. So I do hope you [= Socrates] will be present in person and that you will bring others with you—the kind of people who would be capable of judging the things being said when they hear them.

4§57 Toward the end of this passage, we see Hippias in the *Hippias Maior* predicting that the Trojan Dialogue he performed in Sparta will be reperformed in Athens. So now we come to a third example of displays performed by Hippias. The mention here in the *Hippias Maior* of the name of Eudikos (286b), described as the man who invites Hippias the sophist to perform in Athens the same Homeric Trojan Dialogue that he had performed earlier in Sparta, is a signature linking this dialogue with the dramatic setting of the dialogue we know as the *Hippias Minor*, where the same Eudikos is featured as the intermediary of Hippias and Socrates (363a, 363c, 364b, 373b).[37]

4§58 In Plato's *Hippias Minor*, we find three more examples of verbal displays being made by Hippias, and I will now add them to the previous three examples we have just considered in the *Hippias Maior*. By the time we are finished, we will have six Platonic examples in all. Of these six, we will see that the third and the fourth function as alternatives to each other. Whereas the performance of the Trojan Dialogue by Hippias in Athens is viewed prospectively by the speakers in the third example, which is in the *Hippias Maior*, it is viewed retrospectively by the same speakers in the fourth example, which is in the *Hippias Minor*.

4§59 In order to explain my description of the fourth example as an alternative to the third, I need to make a point about the fifth example, which is the actual text of Plato's *Hippias Minor*. In this text, considered in its entirety, we see Hippias engaging in a textually simulated display of a Trojan Dialogue with Socrates in Athens, and the textuality of their dialogue is to be contrasted with the performativity of the corresponding dialogue in the fourth example. That fourth example is mentioned only in passing within the overall *Hippias Minor*. In this passing mention, we see a reference to an earlier display by Hippias of a Trojan Dialogue performed in a public setting in Athens (364b–c)—earlier, that is, than the textually simulated Trojan Dialogue with Socrates that we know as the *Hippias Minor*. Here is the relevant wording in the *Hippias Minor*: ἡνίκα μὲν γὰρ πολλοὶ ἔνδον ἦμεν καὶ σὺ τὴν ἐπίδειξιν ἐποιοῦ 'when there were many of us within that space and you were making your display [*epideixis*]' (364b). Plato's Socrates makes it clear that he had attended that earlier performance

---

[37] For another example of a "signature" linking one Platonic dialogue to another, see PR 56–59 on links between Plato's *Timaeus* and Plato's *Republic*.

4§4. The imperial Homer of Hippias of Elis

of Hippias in Athens but had chosen not to engage in dialogue with Hippias in that setting (364b). And it was definitely a public setting, as we see from this wording: ὄχλος τε πολὺς ἔνδον ἦν 'there was a big crowd within that space' (364b). That space, if we are to trust Plato's sense of precision in creating this scene, is the same setting as the one to which Socrates refers when he says at a later point (368b): πάντως δὲ πλείστας τέχνας πάντων σοφώτατος εἶ ἀνθρώπων, ὡς ἐγώ ποτέ σου ἤκουον μεγαλαυχουμένου, πολλὴν σοφίαν καὶ ζηλωτὴν σαυτοῦ διεξιόντος ἐν ἀγορᾷ ἐπὶ ταῖς τραπέζαις. ἔφησθα δὲ ἀφικέσθαι ποτὲ εἰς Ὀλυμπίαν ἃ εἶχες περὶ τὸ σῶμα ἅπαντα σαυτοῦ ἔργα ἔχων· πρῶτον μὲν δακτύλιον—ἐντεῦθεν γὰρ ἤρχου . . . 'You [= Hippias] are absolutely the most skilled [*sophos*] of men in the greatest number of crafts [*tekhnai*] by far, as I once heard you boast when you were describing your great and enviable skill [*sophia*]. It was in the agora [= the agora of Athens], near the money-changers' tables [*trapezai*]. You were telling how you once upon a time went to Olympia, and everything you wore was your own work: first, your ring [*daktulios*]—you started with that . . .'.

4§60 A moment ago, I described this fourth example, taken from the *Hippias Minor*, as an alternative to the third, that is, to the Trojan Dialogue that Hippias at the beginning of the *Hippias Maior* says he will perform in Athens on the third day after his dialogue with Socrates there. Whereas that particular Trojan Dialogue as viewed prospectively in the *Hippias Maior* seems to be a set piece, the alternative Trojan Dialogue as viewed retrospectively in the *Hippias Minor* seems to be the opposite of a set piece: it is an actual dialogue between Hippias and his audience. I see here a symmetry: the dialogue of Hippias with Socrates in the *Hippias Maior* is imagined as preceding a scheduled public performance of the Trojan Dialogue by Hippias, which is the set piece, whereas the dialogue of Hippias with Socrates in the *Hippias Minor* is imagined as following a spontaneous public performance of an alternative to the Trojan Dialogue, which is not a set piece but a dialogue between Hippias and his audience in the agora of Athens.

4§61 I stress that the textually simulated dialogue between Hippias and Socrates in the *Hippias Minor* writ large—our fifth example—is dramatized as taking place in a setting that seems to have no public to speak of—that is, in comparison to the setting of the fourth example, reporting a public dialogue that took place earlier between Hippias and his audience in the agora of Athens. The absence of a public for Plato's *Hippias Minor* may be viewed as a theatrical illusion induced by the genre we know as the Platonic dialogue. The public for a Platonic dialogue is after all a reading public. In the setting of the *Hippias Minor*, Socrates says, he can feel more confident about asking

Chapter Four

questions of Hippias—and about getting answers—than in the public setting of the earlier dialogue in the agora of Athens (364b–c, 368b). The stage may be smaller, but the rules of the game in staging the questions seem to be analogous: the questions are Homeric questions, debated in a format that corresponds to the ways in which rhapsodes performed and commented on Homer in dialogue with their public.

4§62 Whenever we see Homeric poetry being performed in the format of a dialogue, the poetry takes the exterior form of selected quotations from Homer, interwoven with commentaries that engage with the audience. A simulation of such a dialogue is our text of the encounter between Ion the rhapsode and Socrates in Plato's *Ion*. Another simulation is the text of the fifth of our six examples of verbal displays performed by Hippias, that is, the Trojan Dialogue that takes place between Hippias and Socrates in Plato's *Hippias Minor*, where the sophist engages in a dialogue with Socrates over moral definitions of what it is to be a 'good' man.

4§63 On the basis of the references we have seen so far in Plato's *Ion* and in his *Hippias Minor* I infer that there existed a genre of performance that we may call rhapsodic dialogue—a genre that resembles the Platonic form of philosophical dialogue. The resemblance, I propose, has to do with a metamorphosis of genres. The genre of rhapsodic dialogue is innovatively transformed by sophists like Hippias into the genre of sophistic dialogue, which in turn is transformed by Plato's Socrates into the genre that we know as the Platonic dialogue.[38]

4§64 We can see the existence of such a genre of rhapsodic dialogue from the internal evidence of the wording used in Plato's *Ion*. There we find that the word *dialegesthai*, which means 'have a dialogue, engage in dialectic' in the philosophical terminology of Plato's Socrates, has a similar meaning in the technical language of rhapsodes in referring to their own craft.[39] For a rhapsode like Ion of Ephesus, the standard of reference for such a process of *dialegesthai* is Homer (Plato *Ion* 532b).[40] And, as we can see from Plato's *Hippias Minor*, the same goes for a sophist like Hippias of Elis: his dialogues, like the dialogues of rhapsodes, are based on Homer—on the Panathanaic Homer—as the standard of reference.[41] By contrast, the dialogues of a philosopher like Plato's Socrates, who wishes to distinguish himself from sophists as well as rhapsodes, must be distinguished in their own right from the dialogues

---

[38] PR 31–33.
[39] PR 31.
[40] PR 31.
[41] I refer especially to the analysis in 3§130.

of sophists like Hippias and of rhapsodes like Ion. For Plato's Socrates, the distinction is achieved by rejecting Homer as the standard of reference for finding the truth by way of dialogue.[42]

4§65 At this point, it is important to make a distinction between two forms of Homeric performance. On the one hand, there is a specialized form, the rhapsodic dialogue, where a single rhapsode quotes selectively from Homer in dialogue with his audience. On the other hand, there is the general form of rhapsodic performance at the Panathenaia, where a number of rhapsodes (it is not certain how many) compete with each other in performing, by relay, the totality or notional totality of the Homeric *Iliad* and *Odyssey*. As I show in the twin book *Homer the Preclassic*, this general form must have had a lengthy prehistory, since the traditions of rhapsodic performance at the festival of the Panathenaia in Athens can be traced back to earlier such traditions as they evolved at earlier festivals like the Panionia in Asia Minor.[43]

4§66 For the moment, however, the distinction I am making can be formulated most simply in terms of two kinds of Homeric tradition. The general form, standardized in Athens, represents the first kind. We have here a uniform tradition of Homer, and I will continue to refer to this tradition simply as the Panathenaic Homer. To be contrasted is a specialized form, used *ad hoc* in live exchanges between the rhapsode and his audience in a variety of different settings—even in different cities. For the time being, I will refer to this Homeric tradition as a private Homer—that is, Homer as applied by an individual performer on a case-by-case basis. The private Homer may still be modeled on the Panathenaic Homer, but it is subject to selective variation, fitting a variety of different occasions in different settings. Whereas the Panathenaic Homer is notionally uniform, the private Homer is potentially multiform.

4§67 With this formulation in place, I come to the sixth of our six Platonic examples of verbal displays by Hippias. This one, in Plato's *Hippias Minor*, precedes all the other five in its chronological ordering. Most obviously, this sixth example precedes the fifth, which is the actual text of Plato's *Hippias Minor*. It also precedes the fourth and the third examples, which are two different views of a Trojan Dialogue that Hippias performs in Athens—a retrospective view in the *Hippias Minor*, and a prospective view in the *Hippias Maior*. Moreover, it precedes the two examples of displays performed in Sparta, as mentioned in the *Hippias Maior*, where we see Hippias applying his

---

[42] *PR* 31–33.
[43] *HPC* II§§249 and following.

Chapter Four

mnemonic technique as he dazzles his audiences with his knowledge of antiquity in general and with his performance of a Trojan Dialogue in particular (285d-286c). I repeat what Philostratus says about the motive of Hippias in applying his mnemonic technique in Sparta: ἐπειδὴ οἱ Λακεδαιμόνιοι διὰ τὸ βούλεσθαι ἄρχειν τῇ ἰδέᾳ ταύτῃ ἔχαιρον 'since the Spartans, through their desire for <u>imperial rule</u> [<u>arkhein</u>], took pleasure in this <u>form</u> [<u>idea</u>]' (*Lives of Sophists* 1.11.3).

4§68 The sixth Platonic example not only precedes the other five examples in chronology. It also supersedes them in importance and even subsumes them. Further, the actual setting of this sixth example of displays by Hippias subsumes in its own right all the other settings. It takes place neither in Sparta nor in Athens but in Olympia:

4ⓣ15 Plato *Hippias Minor* 368c-d

> ΣΩ. πρὸς δὲ τούτοις <u>ποιήματα</u> ἔχων ἐλθεῖν, καὶ <u>ἔπη</u> καὶ τραγῳδίας {d} καὶ διθυράμβους, καὶ <u>καταλογάδην</u> πολλοὺς <u>λόγους</u> καὶ παντοδαποὺς συγκειμένους· καὶ περὶ τῶν <u>τεχνῶν</u> δὴ ὧν ἄρτι ἐγὼ ἔλεγον ἐπιστήμων ἀφικέσθαι διαφερόντως τῶν ἄλλων, καὶ περὶ ῥυθμῶν καὶ ἁρμονιῶν καὶ γραμμάτων ὀρθότητος, καὶ ἄλλα ἔτι πρὸς τούτοις πάνυ πολλά, ὡς ἐγὼ δοκῶ μνημονεύειν· καίτοι τό γε <u>μνημονικὸν</u> ἐπελαθόμην σου, ὡς ἔοικε, <u>τέχνημα</u>, ἐν ᾧ σὺ οἴει λαμπρότατος εἶναι·
>
> SOCRATES: And on top of all these things, you had come [to Olympia] bringing with you <u>compositions</u> [<u>poiēmata</u>][44]—that is, <u>epic</u> [<u>epos</u> plural] and tragedies and dithyrambs, and a multitude of <u>discourses</u> [<u>logoi</u>] <u>to be performed in the right sequence</u> [<u>katalogadēn</u>] and all kinds of set pieces. And you arrived there [= at Olympia] as an expert surpassing all others in the knowledge of not only the <u>crafts</u> [<u>tekhnai</u>] I just mentioned, but also of the correctness [<u>orthotēs</u>] of rhythms [<u>rhuthmoi</u>], tunings [<u>harmoniai</u>], and letters [<u>grammata</u>]. And there were many more things in addition, as I seem to remember [<u>mnēmoneuein</u>]. And yet it seems I had almost forgotten [<u>epilanthanesthai</u>] about your <u>mnemonic technique</u> [<u>mnēmonikion tekhnēma</u>], in which you think *you* are at your most brilliant.

---

[44] I must stress once again what I stressed when I first quoted this wording: as we see from the context here, these 'compositions' are the poetic creations not only of Hippias but also of master 'composers' or *poiētai*, including Homer himself as the 'composer' or *poiētēs* par excellence.

4⑤4. The imperial Homer of Hippias of Elis

4§69 Till now, I have not yet emphasized the relevance of Olympia as the setting for such a display by Hippias. This setting, as we will now see, is also relevant to my ongoing examination of the *mnēmonikon tekhnēma* 'mnemonic technique' of Hippias.

4§70 In the passage I just quoted, the mnemonic technique of Hippias figures as the culmination of two consecutive catalogues. The first catalogue, which I quoted earlier in Chapter 3 and will not requote at this point, had enumerated the kinds of handicraft mastered by Hippias, starting with the sophist's ring and going through the other things he wears on his person (Plato *Hippias Minor* 368b–c). Socrates is referring to that first catalogue of crafts when he says in the passage I just quoted (368d): 'and you [= Hippias] arrived there [= at Olympia] as an expert surpassing others in the knowledge of not only the crafts [*tekhnai*] I just mentioned . . .'. Then follows the second part of the statement ('but also . . .'), which begins a second catalogue of crafts. This catalogue, which we saw in the passage I just quoted, enumerates the kinds of poetry and song mastered by Hippias, corresponding to the kinds of dramatic and 'musical' performances featured at the two premier festivals of Athens, the City Dionysia and the Panathenaia respectively.[45]

4§71 The cultural orientation of this second catalogue, where the main genres of poetry and song are viewed in terms of Athenian festivals, can be described as Athenocentric.[46] But can we say the same thing about the political orientation? For an answer, we need to take a closer look at the political implications of the actual setting of this sixth Platonic example of displays by Hippias, that is, Olympia. In the context of this setting, we must also review the wording used in the second catalogue to describe the craft of poetry and song.

4§72 For Hippias (*Hippias Minor* 368c), the first kind of poetry and song mentioned in the second catalogue is *epē* 'epic' (= *epos* plural). For him, this genre comes to life in the rhapsodic craft of Homeric performance and dialogue, as we see from the sophist's subsequent displays in performing and interpreting Homer throughout the *Hippias Minor*. Given the cultural Athenocentrism implied by the kinds of song and poetry listed in the second catalogue, we might have expected the optimal setting for the sixth Platonic example to be Athens. That is, we might have expected Hippias to display his rhapsodic craft of Homeric performance and dialogue in Athens—on the occasion

---

[45] These "kinds of poetry and song," as I have just described them, correspond closely to the genres of poetry as named by Aristotle at the beginning of his *Poetics* (1447a8–18).
[46] I refer again to the analysis in 3§130.

of the feast of the Panathenaia. Instead, the ultimate Homeric display of Hippias takes place in Olympia.

4§73 So the sixth example shows the rhapsodic craft of Hippias being displayed in a context that is decidedly non-Panathenaic. Moreover, the craft itself is being described in terms that are likewise decidedly non-Panathenaic. For Hippias the sophist, the rhapsodic craft of performing Homer or engaging in dialogue about Homer is treated as if it were merely an aspect of an overall virtuosity, which is described in the *Hippias Minor* as a *mnēmonikon tekhnēma* 'mnemonic technique' (368d, 369a).[47]

4§74 I quote here in its entirety a detailed description of this technique, which also provides a valuable synthesis of the life and times of Hippias himself:

4ⓣ16 Philostratus *Lives of Sophists* 1.11.1–8 (= Hippias DK 86 A 2)

> Ἱππίας δὲ ὁ σοφιστὴς ὁ Ἠλεῖος τὸ μὲν <u>μνημονικὸν</u> οὕτω τι καὶ γηράσκων ἔρρωτο, ὡς καὶ πεντήκοντα ὀνομάτων ἀκούσας ἅπαξ <u>ἀπομνημονεύειν</u> αὐτὰ καθ' ἣν ἤκουσε τάξιν, ἐσήγετο δὲ ἐς τὰς <u>διαλέξεις γεωμετρίαν, ἀστρονομίαν, μουσικήν, ῥυθμούς</u>· {2} <u>διελέγετο</u> δὲ καὶ περὶ <u>ζωγραφίας</u> καὶ περὶ <u>ἀγαλματοποιίας</u>· {3} ταῦτα ἑτέρωθι· ἐν Λακεδαίμονι δὲ γένη τε διῄει πόλεων καὶ ἀποικίας καὶ ἔργα, ἐπειδὴ οἱ Λακεδαιμόνιοι διὰ τὸ βούλεσθαι <u>ἄρχειν</u> τῇ <u>ἰδέᾳ</u> ταύτῃ ἔχαιρον. {4} ἔστιν δὲ αὐτῷ καὶ <u>Τρωικὸς διάλογος</u>, οὗ λόγος· ὁ Νέστωρ ἐν Τροίᾳ ἁλούσῃ ὑποτίθεται Νεοπτολέμῳ τῷ Ἀχιλλέως, ἃ χρὴ ἐπιτηδεύοντα ἄνδρα ἀγαθὸν φαίνεσθαι. {5} πλεῖστα δὲ Ἑλλήνων πρεσβεύσας ὑπὲρ τῆς Ἤλιδος οὐδαμοῦ κατέλυσε τὴν ἑαυτοῦ <u>δόξαν</u> δημηγορῶν τε καὶ <u>διαλεγόμενος</u>, ἀλλὰ καὶ χρήματα πλεῖστα ἐξέλεξε καὶ φυλαῖς ἐνεγράφη πόλεων μικρῶν τε καὶ μειζόνων. {6} παρῆλθε καὶ εἰς τὴν Ἰνυκὸν ὑπὲρ χρημάτων, τὸ δὲ πολίχνιον τοῦτο Σικελικοί εἰσιν, οὓς ὁ Πλάτων <ἐν> τῷ Γοργίᾳ ἐπισκώπτει. {7} εὐδοκιμῶν δὲ καὶ τὸν ἄλλον χρόνον ἔθελγε τὴν Ἑλλάδα ἐν Ὀλυμπίᾳ <u>λόγοις ποικίλοις</u> καὶ πεφροντισμένοις εὖ. {8} <u>ἡρμήνευε</u> δὲ οὐκ ἐλλιπῶς ἀλλὰ περιττῶς καὶ κατὰ φύσιν, ἐς ὀλίγα καταφεύγων τῶν ἐκ <u>ποιητικῆς</u> ὀνόματα.

Hippias of Elis, the sophist, had such powers in <u>mnemonics</u> [*mnēmonikon*][48] that, even as he was growing old, if he heard fifty

---

[47] Hippias is associated with the 'mnemonic technique', the *mnēmonikon*, also in Xenophon *Symposium* 4.62.

[48] See further in Plato *Hippias Maior* 285e. The usage of the adjective *mnēmonikon* as a substantive is an elliptic way of saying *mnēmnonikon tekhnēma* 'mnemonic technique'. See the previous note.

4§4. The imperial Homer of Hippias of Elis

words all at once, he could recall [*apo-mnēmoneuein*] them all in the order in which he had heard them.[49] He introduced into his dialogic performances [*dialexeis*] the following: geometry,[50] astronomy,[51] *mousikē*,[52] and rhythms.[53] {2} And he performed dialogues [*dialegesthai*] also about painting [*zōgraphia*] and sculpture [*agalmatopoiia*].[54] {3} He did these things in other places, but in Sparta in particular he did the following: he would go through genealogies of cities and narratives about how they were founded and about related accomplishments,[55] since the Spartans, on account of their desire to achieve supreme power [*arkhein*], took pleasure in this form [*idea*]. {4} He also has a Trojan Dialogue, the plot of which is this: Nestor, in Troy after it is captured, gives instruction to Neoptolemos son of Achilles concerning what things one must pursue in order to appear to be a good man.[56] {5} Acting as ambassador more often than anyone else among all Hellenes, on behalf of Elis, he never failed to maintain his own fame [*doxa*] while speaking in public and performing dialogues [*dialegesthai*]. Far from failing, he collected the greatest amounts of money and got enrolled in the civic lineages [*phulai*] of cities—small cities as well as larger ones. {6} He even visited Inykos in his quest for money—this little city is an aggregate of people called Sikeloi (Plato makes fun of the Sikeloi in the *Gorgias*).[57] {7} Reveling in his glory, he [= Hippias] spent the time he had left over by enchanting the entire Greek world with his discourses [*logoi*] performed at Olympia, which were patterned [*poikiloi*] and well thought out. {8} And he made interpretations

---

[49] See further in Plato *Hippias Maior* 285e. Such a feat of memory, where sequencing is all-important, is relevant to the concept of performing *katalogadēn* 'in the right sequence'.

[50] See further in Plato *Hippias Maior* 285c.

[51] This detail about the expertise of Hippias in astronomy is noted also elsewhere in Plato: *Protagoras* (315c, 318d-e); *Hippias Minor* (367e); *Hippias Maior* (285c).

[52] I stress again that the archaic concept of *mousikē tekhnē* 'craft of the Muses' is not the equivalent of the modern usages of 'music'. The *mousikē* as practiced at the Panathenaia includes the *tekhnē* 'craft' of rhapsodes, not only of citharodes, citharists, aulodes, and auletes.

[53] For more on Hippias' specialty in rhythms, see Plato *Hippias Maior* 285d. See also in general Plato *Hippias Minor* 369c-d, quoted earlier.

[54] The positioning here of the crafts of painting and sculpture is significant.

[55] See further in Plato *Hippias Maior* 285d-e. For more on the close ties between Hippias and the Spartans, see Plato *Hippias Maior* 281b.

[56] The theme of this dialogue corresponds closely to the theme debated by Socrates and Hippias in Plato's *Hippias Minor*: what are the true criteria for defining the 'good man'? For more on this Trojan Dialogue, see Plato *Hippias Maior* 286a-b.

[57] See Plato *Gorgias* 518b.

[*hermēneuein*]⁵⁸ not elliptically but in a full-blown and natural way,⁵⁹ seldom resorting to words taken from the poetic [*poiētikē*] craft.⁶⁰

4§75 This remarkable synthesis in Philostratus' *Lives of the Sophists* concerning the life and times of Hippias of Elis underlines the political importance of Olympia as a setting for verbal displays by the sophist. That importance is underlined even more forcefully in Plato's *Hippias Minor*, where we learn that Hippias performs in Olympia on a sacred occasion. The site of Olympia, where the performances of Hippias take place, can be defined as a notionally neutral space located within the overall political space controlled by Elis, the home city state of Hippias. As we learn from the *Hippias Minor*, Hippias performs before a Panhellenic public assembled in Olympia in a special place that is specially sacred. That place in Olympia is the *hieron* 'sacred precinct' of Zeus (363c–d, 364a). The performance takes place on a seasonally recurring occasion that is also sacred. That occasion is a festival considered to be the greatest of all Panhellenic festivals, the feast of the Olympics (364a). As the wording makes clear in the *Hippias Minor*, Hippias seeks to perform at each quadrennially recurring Olympic festival (364a ἑκάστης Ὀλυμπιάδος). The crowd that heard Hippias perform at the Olympics must have been enormous, if we extrapolate from Socrates' description of a comparable crowd (364b ὄχλος ... πολύς), including Socrates, that heard Hippias perform in the agora of Athens (368b).⁶¹ Enormous too are the effects of the mass psychology linking the crowd with the performer. Hippias is quoted as saying that he actually competes in the Olympics when he performs there, and in making his point he uses the word *agōnizesthai* 'compete', which designates the ritual act of formally engaging in *agōnes* 'competitions': ἐξ οὗ γὰρ ἦργμαι Ὀλυμπίασιν ἀγωνίζεσθαι, οὐδενὶ πώποτε κρείττονι εἰς οὐδὲν ἐμαυτοῦ ἐνέτυχον 'ever since I have begun to compete [*agōnizesthai*] at the Olympics, I have never yet met anyone better than myself in anything' (364a).

4§76 The subjective experience of Hippias in the act of performing at the festival of the Olympics is comparable to the subjective experience of the rhapsode Ion of Ephesus at the festival of the Panathenaia in Athens. Here too we see the effects of mass psychology. I have already quoted the words of

---

⁵⁸ On the term *hermēneus* 'interpreter' as used by Plato with reference to the craft of rhapsodes (*Ion* 530c), see PR 29.

⁵⁹ In other words, the prose of Hippias of Elis sounded like conversation, not like poetry.

⁶⁰ I interpret 'seldom resorting to words taken from the poetic [*poiētikē*] craft' as an explanation of 'in a full-blown and natural way'.

⁶¹ I think that the reference to the large crowd (*Hippias Minor* 364b) is meant as a parallel to the reference to the agora (368b).

4§4. The imperial Homer of Hippias of Elis

Plato's Socrates describing the thrill experienced by the rhapsode as he stands there on a *bēma* 'platform' and performs Homer before an enormous crowd of 20,000 assembled at the feast of the Panathenaia (Plato *Ion* 535d).[62] At that precise moment of Homeric performance, we are in effect witnessing Ion in the act of 'competing', *agōnizesthai*. The actual occasion for the performing of Homer by rhapsodes at the Panathenaia is an *agōn* 'competition' (530a ἀγῶνα) among rhapsodes, and the formal word for 'compete' is *agōnizesthai* (530a ἠγωνίζου ... ἠγωνίσω).[63] Plato's wording makes it explicit that Ion the rhapsode has come to Athens for the express purpose of winning in the competition for first prize at the Panathenaia (530b καὶ τὰ Παναθήναια νικήσομεν 'and we are going to win the Panathenaia').

4§77 The form of performances by Hippias within the sacred precinct of Zeus in Olympia is what I have been calling the rhapsodic dialogue. That is, Hippias can engage in a dialogue with his audience by way of quoting from Homer. In the process, he can also perform a dialogic commentary on Homer, using a mode of delivery that is equated with *epideixis* or epideictic speech-making (*Hippias Minor* 363d and 364b). Homer is explicitly mentioned in the context where Hippias is portrayed as standing ready to answer any questions on any subject from anyone in his audience (363d).[64]

4§78 Although Homer may have been central to the performances of Hippias at Olympia, the sophist has found ways to transcend Homer. We can see signs of this transcendence near the very beginning of Plato's *Hippias Minor*, where Socrates tells Eudikos that he needs to address a question to Hippias, who is at this moment already present but has not yet spoken (363a–b). The question asked by Socrates is explicitly about Homer, focusing on Achilles in the *Iliad* and on Odysseus in the *Odyssey* (*Hippias Minor* 363b). We join the dialogue at the moment when Socrates is about to explain why he seeks a response from Hippias to his question:

4①17 Plato *Hippias Minor* 363c–364a

... ἐπειδὴ καὶ ἄλλα πολλὰ καὶ παντοδαπὰ ἡμῖν ἐπιδέδεικται καὶ περὶ ποιητῶν τε ἄλλων καὶ περὶ Ὁμήρου.

---

[62] See also PR 28.
[63] PR 40, 48.
[64] In the *Life of Homer* traditions, as I noted earlier, Homer himself is represented as performing dialogic commentaries.

Chapter Four

ΕΥ. Ἀλλὰ δῆλον ὅτι οὐ φθονήσει Ἱππίας, ἐάν τι αὐτὸν <u>ἐρωτᾷς</u>, <u>ἀποκρίνεσθαι</u>. ἦ γάρ, ὦ Ἱππία, ἐάν τι <u>ἐρωτᾷ</u> σε Σωκράτης, <u>ἀποκρινῇ</u>; ἢ πῶς ποιήσεις;

ΙΠ. Καὶ γὰρ ἂν δεινὰ ποιοίην, ὦ Εὔδικε, εἰ Ὀλυμπίαζε μὲν εἰς τὴν τῶν Ἑλλήνων πανήγυριν, ὅταν τὰ Ὀλύμπια ᾖ, {d} ἀεὶ ἐπανιὼν οἴκοθεν ἐξ Ἤλιδος εἰς τὸ <u>ἱερὸν</u> παρέχω ἐμαυτὸν καὶ <u>λέγοντα</u> ὅτι ἄν τις βούληται ὧν ἄν μοι εἰς <u>ἐπίδειξιν</u> παρεσκευασμένον ᾖ, καὶ <u>ἀποκρινόμενον</u> τῷ βουλομένῳ ὅτι ἄν τις <u>ἐρωτᾷ</u>, νῦν δὲ τὴν Σωκράτους <u>ἐρώτησιν</u> φύγοιμι. {364 a}

ΣΩ. Μακάριόν γε, ὦ Ἱππία, πάθος πέπονθας, εἰ <u>ἑκάστης Ὀλυμπιάδος</u> οὕτως εὔελπις ὢν <u>περὶ τῆς ψυχῆς</u> εἰς σοφίαν ἀφικνῇ εἰς τὸ <u>ἱερόν</u>· καὶ θαυμάσαιμ' ἂν εἴ τις τῶν <u>περὶ τὸ σῶμα ἀθλητῶν</u> οὕτως ἀφόβως τε καὶ πιστευτικῶς ἔχων τῷ σώματι ἔρχεται αὐτόσε <u>ἀγωνιούμενος</u>, ὥσπερ σὺ φῇς τῇ <u>διανοίᾳ</u>.

ΙΠ. Εἰκότως, ὦ Σώκρατες, ἐγὼ τοῦτο πέπονθα· ἐξ οὗ γὰρ ἦργμαι Ὀλυμπίασιν <u>ἀγωνίζεσθαι</u>, οὐδενὶ πώποτε κρείττονι εἰς οὐδὲν ἐμαυτοῦ ἐνέτυχον.

SOCRATES: . . . since he [= Hippias] has <u>displayed</u> [*epideiknusthai*] so many things about so many <u>poets</u> [*poiētai*]—and especially about Homer.

EUDIKOS: But it is clear that Hippias will not be ungenerous, if you <u>ask</u> him <u>a question</u>, about <u>giving a response</u>. Isn't that right, Hippias? If Socrates <u>asks</u> you <u>a question</u>, you will <u>give a response</u>? You will do it, won't you?

HIPPIAS: I would be doing strange things, Eudikos, if I—as one who always goes to Olympia to the general gathering [*panēguris*] of all Hellenes when the Olympics take place, and, coming from my house in Elis I go into the <u>sacred precinct</u> [*hieron*] and I present myself in person, ready to <u>perform</u> [= literally 'speak', *legein*] whatever anyone wishes to choose from among all the things that I have prepared for <u>display</u> [*epideixis*],[65] and ready to <u>give response</u> to any <u>question</u> that

---

[65] Here the wording delineates one of two forms of performance. This form concerns set pieces.

anyone wishes to ask⁶⁶—I would be doing strange things indeed if I now avoided the questioning of Socrates.

SOCRATES: Blessed, I would say, is the experience that you have experienced, Hippias, if on the occasion of each Olympic festival you go into the sacred precinct [*hieron*] with such good expectations in regard to the skillfulness of your mind [*psukhē*]. And I would be dazzled if any one of those who engage in contests [= *athlētai*] in regard to the body [*sōma*]⁶⁷ is so fearless and confident about his own body [*sōma*] when he goes to the same place in order to compete [*agōnizesthai*] as you say you are fearless and confident about your thinking [*dianoia*].

HIPPIAS: It is likely, Socrates, that I for one have indeed experienced this. For ever since I have begun to compete [*agōnizesthai*] at the Olympics, I have never yet met anyone better than myself in anything.

4§79 A close reading of this passage leads me to make two inferences about the performances of Hippias in Olympia:

(1) Hippias engages in two forms of performance in Olympia. On the one hand, he can perform live dialogues, which resemble in form the simulated live dialogues written down in Plato's *Hippias Minor* and *Ion*. On the other hand, he can perform set pieces, such as the Trojan Dialogue of Nestor and Neoptolemos. (We have already seen a reference to this set piece in Plato *Hippias Maior* 286a-c.) Within the dialogues of Hippias, he can quote set pieces derived from Homer or from other poets.

(2) The content of the performances undertaken by Hippias can be as varied as his areas of expertise are varied. The relationship of Homer to that content depends on the relationship of the *dianoia* 'thinking' of Homer to the *dianoia* 'thinking' of Hippias.

---

[66] Here the wording delineates the other of two forms. This form concerns live dialogues. I have further comments on these two forms in the discussion that follows.

[67] The wording makes it clear that *athlētai* here means 'those who engage in competitions [*athloi*]', where the word *athloi* 'competitions' applies to those who compete in feats of the 'mind' as well as to 'athletes': only the modern word is limited to those who compete in feats of the 'body'. In Isocrates *Panegyricus* 4.159, *athloi* refers to the 'competitions' in *mousikē* at the Panathenaia, with specific reference to the competitions of rhapsodes in the performing of the Homeric *Iliad* and *Odyssey*. See also Isocrates *Antidosis* 295, where *agōnizesthai* is synonymous with *gumnazesthai* 'engage in athletics' in a context that includes any form of competition established by the state of Athens.

4§80 Elaborating on these two inferences, I begin by comparing the performances of Ion the rhapsode. He performs Homer not only on such sacred occasions as the competitions at the Panathenaia in Athens. Like Hippias, Ion too is a performer of rhapsodic dialogue. I recall the quoted words of the rhapsode himself: καὶ οἶμαι κάλλιστα ἀνθρώπων λέγειν περὶ Ὁμήρου, ὡς οὔτε Μητρόδωρος ὁ Λαμψακηνὸς οὔτε Στησίμβροτος ὁ Θάσιος οὔτε Γλαύκων οὔτε ἄλλος οὐδεὶς τῶν πώποτε γενομένων ἔσχεν εἰπεῖν οὕτω πολλὰς καὶ καλὰς διανοίας περὶ Ὁμήρου ὅσας ἐγώ '... and I think I speak about Homer more beautifully than all other men—so that neither Metrodoros of Lampsakos nor Stesimbrotos of Thasos nor Glaukon nor anyone else who has ever yet lived can speak so many and so beautiful commentaries [*dianoiai*] about Homer as I can' (Plato *Ion* 530c–d).[68] The technical rhapsodic word that I translate here as 'commentary', *dianoia*, is the same word that I translated a moment ago as 'thinking' in the earlier passage referring to the confidence of Hippias in his own *dianoia* when he performs in competition at the Olympics (Plato *Hippias Minor* 364a).

4§81 For Ion the rhapsode, his *dianoia* 'thinking' is coextensive with Homer's own thinking about Homeric poetry (*Ion* 530b–d).[69] An occasion for speaking such a *dianoia*—that is, performing such a Homeric 'commentary'—is illustrated by Ion's dialogue with Socrates as dramatized in Plato's *Ion*. Here I reapply to the *Ion* a point I made earlier about the *Hippias Minor*: the fact that this dialogue seems to have no public can be viewed as a theatrical illusion induced by the genre we know as the Platonic dialogue. The public for a Platonic dialogue is after all a reading public.

4§82 What applies to Ion the rhapsode and to his *dianoia* 'thinking' applies also to Hippias the sophist: he too is speaking such a *dianoia*—that is, performing such a Homeric 'commentary' (*Hippias Minor* 364a). As with the thinking of Ion, the thinking of Hippias becomes coextensive with the authorial intent of Homer himself whenever the sophist speaks about Homer (*Hippias Minor* 363b *elegen peri Homērou* 'spoke about Homer').

4§83 Of the five other examples we saw where Hippias makes verbal displays comparable to what we see him doing in Olympia, the most similar is the fourth. It concerns, as we have already seen, a Trojan Dialogue mentioned in the *Hippias Minor*—a dialogue that supposedly took place between Hippias and his audience in the agora of Athens (364b–c). As we saw, Plato's Socrates says that he attended that performance but had chosen not to engage in

---

[68] For more on this passage taken from Plato *Ion* 530c, see PR 30.
[69] PR 29–30.

4§4. The imperial Homer of Hippias of Elis

dialogue with Hippias (364b). To be contrasted is the fifth example, which is the actual text of Plato's *Hippias Minor* and which has no visible public setting. That is, it has no public setting for a live dialogue, because its public is a reading public. The dialogue of Hippias with Socrates in the *Hippias Minor* closely resembles in format the dialogue of Ion with Socrates in the *Ion*. Also to be contrasted is the third example, which is the formal Trojan Dialogue that Plato's Socrates mentions in the passage I quoted earlier from the *Hippias Maior*: that display is less of a dialogue and more of a set piece composed by the sophist himself, featuring a staged dialogue betweeen Nestor and Neoptolemos (286a–c).

4§84 As we review all six Platonic examples of verbal displays by Hippias, we are left with a question of major importance: can we say that Hippias was performing mainly Homer and engaging in dialogues mainly about Homer on the sacred occasion of the Olympics in Olympia? After all, as we saw from the overview of Philostratus, Hippias used to engage in dialogues not only about Homer but also about practically every other craft. For example, we have read that 'he performed dialogues also about painting [*zōgraphia*] and sculpture [*agalmatopoiia*]' (*Lives of Sophists* 1.11.2 διελέγετο δὲ καὶ περὶ ζωγραφίας καὶ περὶ ἀγαλματοποιίας).

4§85 There is an obvious answer to this question. It all depends on how the concept of Homer is understood in the context of saying that Hippias performs Homer or engages in dialogues about Homer. The sophist's choice of Olympia as the definitive place for his ultimate display of expertise in all *tekhnai* 'crafts' is significant. Also significant is the focusing of Socrates on the ring of Hippias, as we will see later. But the most significant choice made by Hippias of Elis is the definitive time for this display. That time is an ultimately sacred time, when all Hellenes celebrate their ultimate festival, the feast of the Olympics (Plato *Hippias Minor* 364a). The place too is an ultimately sacred place, where the *hieron* 'sacred precinct' of Zeus himself is situated (363c–d, 364a). In this context, which is an ultimate context, everything can become absolutized. In this context, Hippias absolutizes the first and foremost of all crafts, the craft that mediates epic, that is, the epic of Homer.

4§86 A Homeric display by Hippias at Olympia is designed to show most definitively his absolute claim to mastery of the rhapsodic craft of Homeric performance and dialogue. The absolutism of this claim matches the absoluteness of Homer himself in the age of Pheidias. Just as Homer is seen as the absolute authority in a rhapsode's performance of Homer or in a rhapsode's dialogue about Homer, so also the master of the rhapsodic craft becomes the absolute authority on Homer and on everything said by Homer. Just as Homer's

Chapter Four

craft subsumes all other crafts, so also the rhapsode as the master craftsman of Homeric performance and dialogue subsumes all other craftsmen.

4§87 Here, then, is an essential difference between Hippias and Ion as craftsmen. For Hippias of Elis, his mastery is expressed not in terms of the rhapsodic craft, as it is for Ion of Ephesus, but in terms of a sophistic craft that subsumes even the rhapsodic craft, which in turn subsumes all other crafts. For Hippias, Homeric performance and dialogue are mediated not by the craft of the rhapsode but by the all-subsuming craft of the sophist, as formalized in the all-subsuming sophistic concept of *mnēmonikon tekhnēma* 'mnemonic technique' (*Hippias Minor* 368d, 369a).

4§88 The sophist's vaunted expertise in all crafts, headed by the craft of Homeric poetry, is viewed as the perfecting of a new unified *sophistikē tekhnē* 'sophistic craft', animated by that supposedly novel creation of his, the *mnēmonikon tekhnēma* 'mnemonic technique'. As I have been arguing all along, this technique that Hippias the sophist uses as part of his *sophistikē tekhnē* 'sophistic craft' is derived from the same *rhapsōidikē tekhnē* 'rhapsodic craft' as practiced by Ion the rhapsode. But the 'sophistic craft' of Hippias as activated on the occasion of the feast of the Olympics in Olympia has become a rival to the 'rhapsodic craft' of the rhapsode as activated on the occasion of the feast of the Panathenaia in Athens.

4§89 Even though the mnemonic technique of Hippias can be derived from a rhapsodic craft centering on the performance of Homeric poetry in a distinctly Athenian setting, that is, at the Panathenaia, the actual applications of this technique are attested primarily in non-Athenian or even anti-Athenian settings. Although Hippias was at least notionally a neutral agent whenever he was sent on missions to other cities from his native city of Elis, he is portrayed as partial to the Spartans instead of the Athenians. He is quoted as saying, at the very beginning of the *Hippias Maior* (281b), that he prefers his frequent visits to the Spartans over his occasional visits to the Athenians. In Sparta, as we saw, he makes use of his Panathenaic craft in order to win the favor of the Spartans, who have their own imperial ambitions: ἐπειδὴ οἱ Λακεδαιμόνιοι διὰ τὸ βούλεσθαι ἄρχειν τῇ ἰδέᾳ ταύτῃ ἔχαιρον 'since the Spartans, through their desire for imperial rule [*arkhein*], took pleasure in this form' (Philostratus *Lives of Sophists* 1.11.3).[70]

4§90 Evidently, Hippias is leaning toward the Spartan side in the struggle for world power between Athens and Sparta. I find it noteworthy that Elis, the city that controls the sacred and therefore notionally neutral space that serves

---

[70] As we have seen, a fuller version of this compressed account is Plato *Hippias Maior* 284e–286a.

4Ⓢ4. The imperial Homer of Hippias of Elis

as the setting of the Olympic Games, sends to Sparta an emissary who gravitates politically toward the Spartan side.[71] To that extent, the Homeric performances and interpretations by Hippias at the *hieron* 'sacred precinct' of Zeus on the occasion of the Olympic *agōnes* 'competitions' in Olympia can be seen as a political counterweight to the Homeric performances and interpretations by rhapsodes like Ion on the occasion of the Panathenaic *agōnes* 'competitions' in Athens. And yet, the actual traditions of performing and interpreting Homer—even in the hostile political space of Sparta and the neutral political space of Olympia—are dominated by the Panathenaic cultural space of Athens. Even in such non-Athenian settings, as we have seen from the parallelisms between Hippias and Ion, there are clear signs of a Panathenaic standard.[72] In Olympia as in Sparta and in Athens, the Homeric performances and dialogues of Hippias stem from a Panathenaic craft—even if the sophist uses this craft primarily to promote the political interests of Sparta.

4§91 Having noted the signs of a Panathenaic standard in the Homeric performances of Hippias at Olympia, I return to the distinction I made earlier between a private Homer and a Panathenaic Homer. The question that arises is whether the Homer of Hippias is one or the other of these two kinds of Homer. From what we have seen so far, the answer must be two-sided. In its applications, the Homer of Hippias is private—that is, Homer is being privatized by a man whose own agenda transcend the political agenda of imperial Athens. Still, even when Hippias performs Homer in Olympia, which is a sacred and therefore notionally neutral space within the political space controlled by Elis, the Homer he performs is a Panathenaic Homer. That is, the Homer of Hippias still conforms to the Panathenaic standard. The statement that I have just made is supported not only by the evidence presented so far. We will see further evidence when we start to examine additional testimony about Hippias. Before we can get to that testimony, however, I need to look more closely at the actual setting for the Homeric performances of Hippias in Olympia.

4§92 The argumentation widens at this point. From here on, I will argue not only that Hippias of Elis conformed to an Athenian standard of performing Homer when he faced his audiences in the sacred precinct of Zeus at Olympia. I will argue also that the Olympian setting for the performance of Homer in this sacred space, removed though it was from the political reach of Athens,

---

[71] This is not to say that Elis was pro-Spartan in its foreign policy. There were open hostilities between Elis and Sparta from 416 BCE onward. Thanks to Douglas Frame on this point.

[72] I refer again to the analysis at 3§130.

4ⓢ5. Pheidias and his Homeric statue of Zeus

4§93 The setting for the Homeric performances of Hippias in Olympia was a building inside the sacred precinct of Zeus in Olympia. The building was a temple of Zeus. Inside the temple was the single most important and prestigious visual attraction of the ancient Greek world. It was a statue of Zeus sculpted by Pheidias of Athens. Retrospectively, I can safely say that this colossal likeness of Zeus, one of the ancient Seven Wonders of the World, was the ultimate center of attention—the metonymic centerpiece—for all Hellenic civilization. As I will argue, the Homeric performances of Hippias in Olympia were linked with this statue made by Pheidias.

4§94 The most vivid description of the statue of Zeus comes from Pausanias. At the very beginning of his self-conscious account, Pausanias conveys most forcefully the foregrounding of the statue against the background of (1) the temple, (2) the sacred precinct of Zeus as a whole, (3) the competition of the Olympics, held within the sacred precinct, and (4) the overall prestige of the Olympics as perceived by all Hellenes:

4ⓣ18 Pausanias 8.10.1–2

> πολλὰ μὲν δὴ καὶ ἄλλα ἴδοι τις ἂν ἐν Ἕλλησι, τὰ δὲ καὶ ἀκοῦσαι θαύματος ἄξια· μάλιστα δὲ τοῖς Ἐλευσῖνι δρωμένοις καὶ ἀγῶνι τῷ ἐν Ὀλυμπίᾳ μέτεστιν ἐκ θεοῦ φροντίδος. τὸ δὲ ἄλσος τὸ ἱερὸν τοῦ Διὸς παραποιήσαντες τὸ ὄνομα Ἄλτιν ἐκ παλαιοῦ καλοῦσι· καὶ δὴ καὶ Πινδάρῳ ποιήσαντι ἐς ἄνδρα ὀλυμπιονίκην ᾆσμα Ἄλτις ἐπωνόμασται {2} τὸ χωρίον. ἐποιήθη δὲ ὁ ναὸς καὶ τὸ ἄγαλμα τῷ Διὶ ἀπὸ λαφύρων, ἡνίκα Πίσαν οἱ Ἠλεῖοι καὶ ὅσον τῶν περιοίκων ἄλλο συναπέστη Πισαίοις πολέμῳ καθεῖλον. <Φειδίαν> δὲ τὸν ἐργασάμενον τὸ ἄγαλμα εἶναι καὶ ἐπίγραμμά ἐστιν ἐς μαρτυρίαν ὑπὸ τοῦ Διὸς γεγραμμένον τοῖς ποσί . . .

> There are many wondrous things to see in the Greek-speaking world and many wondrous things to hear, but the things that are

---

[73] I am deliberately using 'Olympian' as the adjective of the place-name 'Olympia', even though it could also be understood as the adjective of the place-name 'Olympus'. In a future project, I hope to explore the mythological connection between the two places, Olympia and Olympus.

4§5. Pheidias and his Homeric statue of Zeus

absolutely <u>the most closely tied to a divine way of thinking</u> are <u>the rituals [drōmena] in Eleusis</u> and <u>the competition [agōn] in Olympia</u>. The sacred grove [alsos] of Zeus has been called ever since ancient times by its *ad hoc* name, Altis. That is the way the space is called {2} by Pindar in a song he had made for a man who won a victory in the Olympics.[74] The temple and the statue [agalma] dedicated to Zeus were made from the spoils of war—going back to the time when the people of Elis and the rest of the *perioikoi* revolted against the people of Pisa and destroyed Pisa in a war.[75] The fact that <Pheidias> was the one who made the statue [agalma] is proved by an epigram that is written under the feet of Zeus.

4§95 An essential part of my ongoing argument is that this statue of Zeus in the temple of Zeus at Olympia is a distinctly Homeric Zeus. There are many reasons for me to say this, but they can be summed up in a single anecdote about the making of the statue by the sculptor Pheidias. In this anecdote, the verbal art that went into the making of the Homeric *Iliad* converges with the visual art that went into the making of the statue of Zeus by Pheidias. At the moment of convergence, we see the supreme god in the act of expressing his divine will:

4Ⓣ19 Strabo 8.3.30 C354

πολλὰ δὲ συνέπραξε τῷ Φειδίᾳ Πάναινος ὁ <u>ζωγράφος</u>, ἀδελφιδοῦς ὢν αὐτοῦ καὶ συνεργολάβος, πρὸς τὴν τοῦ ξοάνου διὰ τῶν <u>χρωμάτων</u> <u>κόσμησιν</u> καὶ μάλιστα τῆς <u>ἐσθῆτος</u>. δείκνυνται δὲ καὶ <u>γραφαὶ</u> πολλαί τε καὶ <u>θαυμασταὶ</u> περὶ τὸ ἱερὸν ἐκείνου ἔργα. ἀπομνημονεύουσι δὲ τοῦ Φειδίου, διότι πρὸς τὸν Πάναινον εἶπε πυνθανόμενον πρὸς τί <u>παράδειγμα</u> μέλλοι ποιήσειν τὴν <u>εἰκόνα</u> τοῦ Διός, ὅτι πρὸς τὴν Ὁμήρου δι' ἐπῶν ἐκτεθεῖσαν τούτων

ἦ καὶ κυανέῃσιν ἐπ' ὀφρύσι νεῦσε Κρονίων·

ἀμβρόσιαι δ' ἄρα <u>χαῖται</u> ἐπερρώσαντο ἄνακτος

---

[74] Pindar *Olympian* 10.45.
[75] The compressed wording makes it appear that the statue of Zeus by Pheidias goes back to the time of this reported war against Pisa, but the rest of what Pausanias has to say about the temple of Zeus makes it clear that the building of the temple happened well before the making of the statue of Zeus by Pheidias. Pausanias must have meant that the precious material for the making of the statue can be dated back to the time of the war.

Chapter Four

κρατὸς ἀπ' ἀθανάτοιο, μέγαν δ' ἐλέλιξεν Ὄλυμπον.

Iliad I 528–530

Collaborating in many ways with Pheidias was Panainos the painter [zōgraphos].⁷⁶ He was his nephew and his partner in getting the contract [for making the statue]. The collaboration had to do with the adorning [kosmēsis]⁷⁷ of the statue [xoanon], particularly of its fabrics,⁷⁸ with colors [khrōmata]. And many wondrous paintings [graphai],⁷⁹ works of Panainos, are also to be seen all around the temple. There is this recollection about Pheidias: when Panainos asked him after what model [paradeigma] he was going to make the likeness [eikōn] of Zeus, he replied that he was going to make it after the likeness set forth by Homer in these words [epos plural]:

> So spoke the son of Kronos, and with his eyebrows of azure
> he made a reinforcing [= epi-] nod.
> Ambrosial were the locks that cascaded from the lord's
> head immortal. And he caused great Olympus to quake.
>
> *Iliad* I 528–530

4§96 According to this anecdote, the creative impulse that led Pheidias to make the statue of Zeus was a distinctly Homeric impulse. The moment captured by the maker of the statue is a Homeric moment. It is the moment when Zeus nods his head and thus signifies his divine will, that is, the Plan of Zeus, which is coextensive with the plot of the Homeric *Iliad*.

4§97 The Zeus of the temple of Zeus in Olympia is not only a Homeric Zeus. He is also an Athenian Zeus, conforming to a distinctly Athenian standard. It is not only that Zeus was made by an Athenian, Pheidias the sculptor. It is also that this statue of Zeus in Olympia followed the Athenian standard of the statue of Athena Parthenos in the Parthenon on the Acropolis in Athens.⁸⁰ It is known for sure that Pheidias made this Athena Parthenos earlier than he

---

⁷⁶ The *zō-graphos* is literally someone who performs a 'filling in' [*graphein*] of outlines by way of painting, thereby 'animating' or making 'alive' [*zōi-*] what has been filled in.

⁷⁷ At a later point, I will comment on the idea of 'adding' inherent in *kosmeîn* 'adorning'.

⁷⁸ This is a matter of simulating the fabrics by shaping the material that is being sculpted.

⁷⁹ A *graphē* is the result of a filling in of outlines by way of painting.

⁸⁰ Here is my first mention of Athena Parthenos in this section. I stress that Athena Parthenos is a cult figure in her own right, as we see from the evidence gathered by Nick 2002:6. For representations of Athena as a cult statue in vase paintings, I cite the useful analysis of Nick p. 31.

made the Zeus in the temple of Zeus in Olympia.[81] According to Philochorus (*FGH* 328 F 121), the statue of Athena Parthenos was inaugurated in 438/7 BCE, and Pericles himself was an *epistatēs* 'supervisor'.[82]

4§98 The point that I am making so far, that the statue of Athena Parthenos sets an Athenian standard for the statue of Zeus, is connected to another point I will be making in the paragraphs that follow: this standard is linked to the festival of the Panathenaia. In other words, the statue of Zeus is Panathenaic in inspiration, to the extent that the statue of Athena Parthenos is Panathenaic. Here I find it relevant to adduce an argument made by modern historians about the Parthenon: as the sacred space that housed Athena Parthenos, the Parthenon was built to be "a Panathenaic temple."[83]

4§99 By contrast with the statue of Zeus, the temple of Zeus, as it was originally built, did not conform to such an Athenian standard. The Athenian standard applies directly only to the statue of Zeus, not to the temple that housed him. Still, the commissioning of Pheidias of Athens to make the colossal statue of Zeus inside the god's temple led to changes for the temple: in the lengthly process of making the statue, the temple of Zeus was made to conform at least indirectly to the Athenian standard set by the making of his statue. That is to say, the making of the statue of Zeus by Pheidias, which took place in a later era than the making of the statue of Athena, required the remaking of the temple that housed it, since the artistic program of the original builders of the temple stemmed from an earlier era (Pausanias 8.10.1–2). The new statue inside the older temple was enormous—so enormous that it took up the space of one third of the main part of the building, and the fact that the likeness of Zeus was represented as seated and not standing only added to the viewer's sense of the statue's spectacular size.[84] There is an Athenian cultural standard at work here.

4ⓈC6. Pheidias and his Homeric statue of Athena Parthenos

4§100 Having made the point that the statue of Athena Parthenos made by Pheidias was distinctly Athenian and even Panathenaic in inspiration, I now

---

[81] On the priority of the Athena at Athens in comparison with the Zeus at Olympia, see Lapatin 2001:62.

[82] Stadter 1989:176.

[83] So Raubitschek 1984:19, followed by Nick 2002:160n1033. At p. 160n1032, Nick connects the transfer of the Treasury of the Delian League, which she dates to 454 BCE, with the completion of the Parthenon in 433/2 and the completion of the statue of Athena Parthenos in 438. The dates 454 and 438 correspond to years when the festival of the quadrennial Great Panathenaia was celebrated.

[84] Lapatin 2001:81.

Chapter Four

make the further point that it was also Homeric, like the Zeus sculpted by Pheidias. In the case of this statue of Athena Parthenos, we have no surviving anecdote about a Homeric inspiration as we have in the case of the statue of Zeus. But we do have independent evidence that the Parthenos is a Homeric Athena. Just as the statue of Zeus by Pheidias was marked by a Homeric signature, as it were, so too was the statue of Athena by Pheidias. While the statue of Zeus was inspired by the Homeric moment when Zeus nods his head, the statue of Athena was inspired by the moment when Athena goes to war on behalf of the Achaeans. Like the moment of Zeus, the moment of Athena takes place in the Homeric *Iliad*:

4ⓣ20 *Iliad* V 733–747

   Αὐτὰρ Ἀθηναίη κούρη Διὸς <u>αἰγιόχοιο</u>
   <u>πέπλον</u> μὲν κατέχευεν ἑανὸν πατρὸς ἐπ᾽ οὔδει
 735 <u>ποικίλον, ὅν ῥ᾽ αὐτὴ ποιήσατο καὶ κάμε χερσίν</u>·
   ἣ δὲ <u>χιτῶν</u>᾽ ἐνδῦσα Διὸς νεφεληγερέταο
   τεύχεσιν ἐς πόλεμον θωρήσσετο δακρυόεντα.
   ἀμφὶ δ᾽ ἄρ᾽ ὤμοισιν βάλετ᾽ <u>αἰγίδα</u> θυσσανόεσσαν
   δεινήν, ἣν περὶ μὲν πάντῃ Φόβος ἐστεφάνωται,
 740 ἐν δ᾽ Ἔρις, ἐν δ᾽ Ἀλκή, ἐν δὲ κρυόεσσα Ἰωκή,
   ἐν δέ τε <u>Γοργείη κεφαλὴ</u> δεινοῖο πελώρου
   δεινή τε σμερδνή τε, Διὸς τέρας <u>αἰγιόχοιο</u>.
   κρατὶ δ᾽ ἐπ᾽ <u>ἀμφίφαλον</u> κυνέην θέτο <u>τετραφάληρον</u>
   <u>χρυσείην, ἑκατὸν πολίων πρυλέεσσ᾽ ἀραρυῖαν</u>·
 745 ἐς δ᾽ ὄχεα φλόγεα ποσὶ βήσετο, λάζετο δ᾽ ἔγχος
   βριθὺ μέγα στιβαρόν, τῷ δάμνησι στίχας ἀνδρῶν
   ἡρώων, οἷσίν τε κοτέσσεται ὀβριμοπάτρη.

   As for Athena, daughter of Zeus <u>who has the aegis</u>,[85]

---

[85] My translation 'has' not 'shakes' reflects a meaning of *-okhos* that is secondary: this form is derived from the Indo-European root **wegh-* 'shake', which becomes *ekh-* / *okh-* in Greek, homonymous with *ekh-* / *okh-* as in *ekhein* 'have', derived from the distinct Indo-European root **segh-* 'have, hold'. In Greek, the phonological merger of these two distinct roots leads to a semantic shift from 'aegis-shaking' to 'aegis-having' in the epithet *aigiokhos*, as we see from the iconographic representations of the aegis as examined at a later point in my analysis.

4§6. Pheidias and his Homeric statue of Athena Parthenos

she took off her woven peplos [*peplos*] at the threshold of her father,

735   her pattern-woven [*poikilos*] peplos, the one that she herself made and worked on with her own hands.

And, putting on the khiton [*khitōn*] of Zeus the gatherer of clouds,

with armor she armed herself to go to war, which brings tears.

Over her shoulders she threw the aegis, with fringes on it,

—terrifying—garlanded all around by Fear personified.

740   On it [= the aegis] are Strife, Resistance, and the chilling Shout [of victorious pursuers].

On it also is the head of the Gorgon, the terrible monster,

a thing of terror and horror, the portent of Zeus who has the aegis.

On her head she put the helmet,[86] with a *phalos* on each side[87] and with four *phalēra*,[88]

golden, adorned with the warriors [*pruleis*] of a hundred cities.[89]

745   Into the fiery chariot with her feet she stepped, and she took hold of the spear,

---

[86] The helmet, as described here in *Iliad* V 743, is not unique to Athena: the same verse occurs at *Iliad* XI 41, describing the helmet worn by Agamemnon. The helmet of Athena Parthenos as described by Pausanias, with griffins on each side and a sphinx in the middle, does not contradict, in and of itself, the picture of Athena's helmet in the *Iliad*: rather, it shows further elaboration.

[87] Related to the forms *amphiphalos* and *tetraphalēros* in this Homeric verse is the form *tetraphalos*. I propose that the lengthening of the second *a* in *tetraphalos* is a matter of formulaic variation, and that *amphi-phalos* and *tetra-phalos* are related concepts. The sculpture of Pheidias reflects his understanding of such epithets. In LSJ, *amphiphalos kuneē* is explained as a 'helmet with double phalos' (*Iliad* V 743, XI 41). The *phalos* is explained as the 'horn' of a helmet (*Iliad* III 362, etc.).

[88] The two forms as listed in LSJ seem to be formulaic variants: τετραφάληρος 'with four bosses (φάλαρα)' is an epithet of κυνέη 'helmet' at *Iliad* V 743, XI 41, while τετράφαλος 'with four horns' is an epithet of κυνέη / κόρυς 'helmet' at *Iliad* XII 384, XXII 315.

[89] The description of Athena in *Iliad* V 744 here is parallel to the description of Ares in the Hesiodic *Shield of Herakles* 193, Ἄρης . . . πρυλέεσσι κελεύων 'Ares, commanding the warriors [*pruleis*]'. This parallelism of Athena and Ares is comparable to the parallelism of Athena and Ares as depicted on the Shield of Achilles in *Iliad* XVIII 516-519. In that passage as well, the parallelism of these gods is featured in a work of art, the goldsmith's art. See *HPC* II§§408-410.

> heavy, huge, massive. With it she subdues the battle-rows of men—
>
> heroes[90] against whom she is angry, she of the mighty father.

4§101 I note with interest the coextensiveness of the khiton (*khitōn*) and the aegis, metonymically shared by the almighty father with his mighty daughter: the khiton worn by Athena as she goes to war is explicitly said to belong to Zeus, and the aegis that she wears at verse 738 belongs primarily to her father, as we see from the epithet of Zeus at verse 741, *aigiokhos* 'he who has the aegis'. Moreover, the figure of Medusa the Gorgon is explicitly said here to be a *teras* 'portent' that marks Zeus himself.

4§102 At the moment when the goddess begins arming herself for war, she is shown slipping out of her peplos (*peplos*) or 'robe' and slipping into a khiton (*khitōn*) or 'tunic', which is said to belong to her father, Zeus. I should note from the start that the word *peplos* is appropriate for designating masterpieces of weaving meant primarily for display, distinguished by the patterns of images woven into them. It is a specialized artistic term having little to do with everyday wear in the ancient Greek world. The terminology focuses on the art of weaving, not on any utilitarian aspect of the fabric being woven.[91]

4§103 The peplos that Athena takes off connects her to her feminine identity as a weaver, while the khiton she puts on for war connects her to her masculine identity as a warrior. Athena Parthenos wears the armor—and the khiton—of her father, Zeus. This male exterior was highlighted by the sculpture of Pheidias. As we see from the eyewitness description of Pausanias, the statue of Athena Parthenos in the Parthenon wears a khiton:

4ⓣ21 Pausanias 1.24.5–7

> αὐτὸ δὲ ἔκ τε ἐλέφαντος τὸ ἄγαλμα καὶ χρυσοῦ πεποίηται. μέσῳ μὲν οὖν ἐπίκειταί οἱ τῷ κράνει Σφιγγὸς εἰκών […] καθ' ἑκάτερον δὲ τοῦ κράνους {6} γρῦπές εἰσιν ἐπειργασμένοι. […] καὶ γρυπῶν {7} μὲν πέρι τοσαῦτα εἰρήσθω· τὸ δὲ ἄγαλμα τῆς Ἀθηνᾶς ὀρθόν ἐστιν ἐν χιτῶνι ποδήρει καί οἱ κατὰ τὸ στέρνον ἡ κεφαλὴ Μεδούσης ἐλέφαντός ἐστιν ἐμπεποιημένη· καὶ Νίκην τε ὅσον τεσσάρων πηχῶν, ἐν δὲ τῇ χειρὶ δόρυ ἔχει, καί οἱ πρὸς τοῖς ποσὶν ἀσπίς τε κεῖται καὶ πλησίον τοῦ δόρατος δράκων ἐστίν· εἴη δ' ἂν Ἐριχθόνιος οὗτος ὁ δράκων. ἔστι δὲ τῷ βάθρῳ τοῦ ἀγάλματος ἐπειργασμένη Πανδώρας

---

[90] The use of *hērōes* 'heroes' here deflects the hearer's attention from any association with warriors of the here-and-now of Homeric performance.

[91] In making this point, I have benefited from the study of Lee 2004.

4§6. Pheidias and his Homeric statue of Athena Parthenos

γένεσις. πεποίηται δὲ Ἡσιόδῳ τε καὶ ἄλλοις ὡς ἡ Πανδώρα γένοιτο αὕτη γυνὴ πρώτη·

The statue [agalma] itself is made of gold and ivory. In the middle of the helmet is placed a likeness of Sphinx. [Pausanias here gives a cross-reference to a later excursus on the Sphinx.] On each side of the helmet there are griffins worked in. [Pausanias here gives an excursus on griffins.] Enough said about griffins. The statue [agalma] of Athena is standing, wearing a khiton [khitōn] that extends to her feet. On her chest is the head of Medusa, made of ivory. She has [in one hand] a [figure of] Nike, around four cubits in height, and she holds in her [other] hand a spear. A shield [aspis] is positioned at her feet. And near the spear is a serpent [drakōn].[92] Now this serpent [drakōn] would be Erikhthonios. And on the surface of the base of the statue is a relief of the genesis of Pandora. The story of the genesis of this first woman Pandora is told by Hesiod in his poetry as well as by others.

4§104 The wording of Pausanias makes it explicit that Athena Parthenos is wearing not her peplos (peplos) or 'robe' but a khiton (khitōn) or 'tunic', and over her khiton she wears her armor. This image of Athena wearing her khiton and the armor over it matches what we see in the Homeric description of what the goddess wears when she goes to battle against the Trojans in the Trojan War.

4§105 The khiton of Zeus that Athena wears to war marks the coextensiveness between Zeus the father and Athena the daughter who emerged fully formed and fully armed from the head of Zeus at the moment of her birth, as narrated in the Hesiodic *Theogony* (verses 886–900, 924–926) and in the *Homeric Hymn* (28) *to Athena* (verses 4–6). In the *Hymn*, Athena herself is described explicitly as Parthenos (verse 3), and the armor she wears is golden (verse 6). As in the *Iliad* passage I have just quoted, Zeus in this *Hymn* is described as *aigiokhos* 'the one who has the aegis' (verses 7 and 17). Thus the aegis that the statue of Athena Parthenos wears, along with all the armor, is metonymically centered on Zeus.

4§106 In the visual arts, the coextensiveness between Zeus the father and Athena the daughter is most conventionally expressed by the concept of Nike, who is the divine embodiment of *nikē* 'victory' in war. In the work of Pheidias,

---

[92] I draw attention to the wording used by Pausanias here concerning the position of the serpent: 'near the spear', not 'near the shield'.

Chapter Four

both the colossal Zeus and the colossal Athena hold a statue of Nike in the palm of the right hand (Pausanias 1.24.7 and 5.11.1 respectively).

4§107 Moreover, as we see even from the pre-Pheidian art that adorns the temple of Zeus in Olympia, the almighty father is recognized by way of his association with Nike and with the figure of Medusa the Gorgon as the centerpiece of the shield that goes with Nike:

4ⓣ22 Pausanias 5.10.4

ἐν δὲ Ὀλυμπίᾳ λέβης ἐπίχρυσος ἐπὶ ἑκάστῳ τοῦ ὀρόφου τῷ πέρατι ἐπίκειται καὶ Νίκη κατὰ μέσον μάλιστα ἕστηκε τὸν ἀετόν, ἐπίχρυσος καὶ αὕτη. ὑπὸ δὲ τῆς Νίκης τὸ ἄγαλμα ἀσπὶς ἀνάκειται χρυσῆ, Μέδουσαν τὴν Γοργόνα ἔχουσα ἐπειργασμένην.

In Olympia a gilded caldron [*lebēs*] is positioned at each end of the roof [of the temple of Zeus], and a [figure of] Nike, also gilded, stands at the absolute middle of the pediment. Under the statue [*agalma*] of Nike is a golden shield [*aspis*], and it has on it Medusa the Gorgon made in relief.

4§108 Pausanias (5.10.4) goes on to describe the inscription on the golden shield of Nike bearing the image of Medusa the Gorgon, which proclaims that this art treasure was made from spoils won 'from the Argives, Athenians, and Ionians' (Ἀργείων καὶ Ἀθαναίων καὶ Ἰώνων) as the result of a *nikē* 'victory' of the Spartans over these enemies (νίκας εἵνεκα).

4§109 These associations between Zeus and Nike and between Zeus and Medusa the Gorgon in the pre-Pheidian visual art of the temple of Zeus in Olympia are comparable with associations we find in the verbal art of Homeric poetry. As we saw, the aegis, which features Medusa the Gorgon as its centerpiece, belongs primarily to Zeus and only secondarily to Athena by virtue of her being born directly from the head of Zeus.[93] As for Nike, that is, victory incarnate, I should stress that the Plan of Zeus, which is isofunctional with the plot of the *Iliad*, is associated with his awarding *nikē* 'victory' to Trojans or Achaeans in the Trojan War. In Homeric poetry, the role of Zeus in awarding *nikē* is clearly primary, and the role of Athena is just as clearly secondary:

---

[93] For the Aristarcheans, the association of the aegis with Athena, as distinct from Zeus, was a neoteric tradition: see Severyns 1928:34.

4ⓢ6. Pheidias and his Homeric statue of Athena Parthenos

<u>Zeus</u>:

Iliad VII 203: Zeus to give *nikē* to Ajax in the duel of Ajax with Hector—so prays an unnamed Achaean (or, if there is to be no *nikē* for Ajax, he prays for at least an even draw for Ajax and Hector)

Iliad VIII 171: Zeus gives a sign [*sēma*] that he will give *nikē* to the Trojans and not to the Achaeans

Iliad XIII 347: Zeus expresses his plan to give *nikē* to the Trojans and not to the Achaeans

Iliad XVI 121: Zeus expresses his plan to give *nikē* to the Trojans and not to the Achaeans—and Ajax recognizes this

Iliad XVI 362: *nikē* has been given to the Trojans—and Ajax recognizes this; in the battle over the beached ships, Iakhe [personification of the battle-cry] and Phobos [personification of routing the enemy] are compared in a simile to the effects of a storm sent by Zeus (XVI 364–366)

Iliad XVI 844–845: Zeus has given *nikē* to Hector and not to Patroklos—so says the dying Patroklos

Iliad XVII 176–177: Zeus can cause even a valiant warrior to turn and run (*phobeîn*), thus depriving him of *nikē*—so says Hector

Iliad XVII 331–332: Zeus gives *nikē* to the Trojans and not to the Achaeans—so says Apollo (in the guise of a herald) to Aeneas

Iliad XVII 627: Zeus gives *nikē* to the Trojans—and Ajax along with Menelaos recognizes this

Iliad XX 101–102: If the 'god' (*theos*) levels the odds, Achilles will not be able to get *nikē* in his duel with Aeneas, even if Achilles boasts to be 'all-bronze' (*pan-khalkeos*)—says Aeneas

<u>Athena</u>:

Iliad III 439: Menelaos to get *nikē* with the help of Athena

Iliad IV 389: Tydeus got *nikē* with the help of Athena, in an athletic contest with the Thebans

Chapter Four

Iliad VII 26–27: Athena expresses her plan to give *nikē* to the Achaeans—says the god Apollo, whose plan is to give *nikē* to the Trojans (VII 21)

Iliad XXIII 767: Odysseus to get *nikē* with the help of Athena, in an athletic contest—so he prays to her (768–770)

Iliad XXIII 771: Odysseus gets *nikē* with the help of Athena—she heeds his prayer

Odyssey viii 520: Odysseus got *nikē* at Troy with the help of Athena

Odyssey xi 544, 548: Ajax in Hades is angry at Odysseus because he got *nikē* with the direct help of Athena (and with the indirect help of the *paides* 'children' of the Trojans).

4§110 So the Homeric moment of Zeus as sculpted by Pheidias is primary, since the Plan of Zeus is what ultimately achieves victory for the Achaeans over the Trojans in the Trojan War. By contrast, the Homeric moment of Athena Parthenos as sculpted by Pheidias is secondary, since she is only an accessory to the overall Plan of Zeus when she enters the war in her own right.

4§111 As for the pre-Pheidian temple of Zeus at Olympia, it too already bears the markings of a Homeric signature. All the same, the colossal Pheidian statue of Zeus, which holds a statue of Nike in the palm of his hand—and has an aegis—represents the newest and most definitive Homeric signature. And it is a distinctly Athenian version of a Homeric signature, since the colossal Pheidian statue of Athena Parthenos in Athens likewise holds a statue of Nike in the palm of her hand—and has an aegis.

4§112 So, paradoxically, the newer statue of Zeus in Olympia has seniority, as it were, over the older statue of Athena Parthenos in Athens when it comes to the father's authority over Nike as victory personified. From the standpoint of Homeric poetry, Athena is generally involved in the fluctuations of *nikē* in war, but Zeus is specifically involved in the ultimate struggle between the Trojan and the Achaean warriors in their quest for *nikē* in the Trojan War. I repeat, his plan for the Trojan War is in effect the plot of the Homeric *Iliad*. So the newer statue of Zeus is even more Homeric and more definitive than the older statue of Athena Parthenos. The Homeric signature of the statue of Zeus is even more pronounced than the Homeric signature of the statue of Athena.

4§113 In the light of the parallelism we see between the statue of Zeus in the temple of Zeus at Olympia and the statue of Athena Parthenos in the Parthenon at Athens, I am ready to shift the focus of attention from the later

4⑤6. Pheidias and his Homeric statue of Athena Parthenos

to the earlier work of Pheidias. What I said a moment ago about the Zeus of Pheidias in Olympia can now become a restatement of what I can say here about the Athena Parthenos of Pheidias in the Parthenon: this colossal statue of Athena was an ultimate center of attention—a metonymic centerpiece—not only for the entire sacred space of Athena in Athens but also for all Hellenic civilization. Unlike the making of the Zeus of Pheidias, however, which required the remaking of the temple that housed it, the making of the Athena of Pheidias was organically integrated from the start with the making of the temple that housed it, the Parthenon. In other words, the artistic program of the sculptor set the standard for the artistic program of the architects of the temple.

4§114 The synergism of Pheidias with the architects of the temple of Athena Parthenos is narrated in Plutarch's *Pericles*. As we will see, this synergism extends into a larger synergism linking the master sculptor with everyone involved in what modern historians call the Periclean building program. In other words, the artistic program of the architects of the new buildings, as represented by Pheidias, is linked with the political program of the architects of the Athenian empire, as represented by Pericles. As we will also see, Plutarch's narrative is not some anachronistic exercise in restating an imperial ideology current in Plutarch's own day. Rather, the main themes of the narrative go all the way back to the age of Pheidias himself.

4§115 In what follows I offer a close reading of the relevant narrative of Plutarch, concentrating on his description of the relationship between Pheidias as the premier artist and Pericles as the premier statesman of the Athenian empire. In this narrative, Pheidias is portrayed as the grand 'overseer' or *episkopos* who was put in charge of the notional totality of the Periclean building program:

4①23 Plutarch *Pericles* 13.6-15 (abridged)

> Πάντα δὲ διεῖπε καὶ πάντων <u>ἐπίσκοπος</u> ἦν αὐτῷ <u>Φειδίας</u>, καίτοι μεγάλους <u>ἀρχιτέκτονας</u> ἐχόντων καὶ <u>τεχνίτας</u> {7} τῶν ἔργων. τὸν μὲν γὰρ ἑκατόμπεδον <u>Παρθενῶνα</u> Καλλικράτης εἰργάζετο καὶ Ἰκτῖνος, τὸ δ' ἐν Ἐλευσῖνι <u>Τελεστήριον</u> ἤρξατο μὲν Κόροιβος οἰκοδομεῖν, καὶ τοὺς ἐπ' ἐδάφους κίονας ἔθηκεν οὗτος καὶ τοῖς ἐπιστυλίοις ἐπέζευξεν· ἀποθανόντος δὲ τούτου Μεταγένης ὁ Ξυπεταιὼν τὸ διάζωσμα καὶ τοὺς ἄνω κίονας ἐπέστησε, τὸ δ' ὀπαῖον ἐπὶ τοῦ ἀνακτόρου Ξενοκλῆς ὁ Χολαργεὺς ἐκορύφωσε· τὸ δὲ <u>μακρὸν τεῖχος</u>, περὶ οὗ Σωκράτης ἀκοῦσαί φησιν αὐτὸς εἰσηγουμένου γνώμην Περικλέους,

Chapter Four

{8} ἠργολάβησε Καλλικράτης. . . . {9} τὸ δ' <u>Ὠιδεῖον</u>, τῇ μὲν ἐντὸς διαθέσει πολύεδρον καὶ πολύστυλον, τῇ δ' ἐρέψει περικλινὲς καὶ κάταντες ἐκ μιᾶς κορυφῆς πεποιημένον, εἰκόνα λέγουσι γενέσθαι καὶ μίμημα τῆς βασιλέως σκηνῆς, <u>ἐπιστατοῦντος</u> καὶ τούτῳ {10} Περικλέους. [. . .] {11} φιλοτιμούμενος δ' ὁ Περικλῆς τότε πρῶτον ἐψηφίσατο <u>μουσικῆς ἀγῶνα</u> τοῖς <u>Παναθηναίοις</u> ἄγεσθαι, καὶ <u>διέταξεν</u> αὐτὸς <u>ἀθλοθέτης</u> αἱρεθείς, καθότι χρὴ τοὺς <u>ἀγωνιζομένους</u> <u>αὐλεῖν</u> ἢ <u>ᾄδειν</u> ἢ <u>κιθαρίζειν</u>. ἐθεῶντο δὲ καὶ τότε καὶ τὸν ἄλλον χρόνον ἐν <u>Ὠιδείῳ</u> τοὺς <u>μουσικοὺς ἀγῶνας</u>. {12} Τὰ δὲ <u>Προπύλαια</u> τῆς ἀκροπόλεως ἐξειργάσθη μὲν ἐν πενταετίᾳ Μνησικλέους ἀρχιτεκτονοῦντος, τύχη δὲ θαυμαστὴ συμβᾶσα περὶ τὴν οἰκοδομίαν ἐμήνυσε τὴν θεὸν οὐκ ἀποστατοῦσαν, ἀλλὰ <u>συνεφαπτομένην τοῦ</u> <u>ἔργου</u> καὶ {13} <u>συνεπιτελοῦσαν</u>. . . . {14} Ὁ δὲ Φειδίας εἰργάζετο μὲν τῆς θεοῦ τὸ χρυσοῦν <u>ἕδος</u>, καὶ τούτου δημιουργὸς ἐν τῇ στήλῃ [εἶναι] γέγραπται· πάντα δ' ἦν σχεδὸν <u>ἐπ' αὐτῷ</u>, καὶ πᾶσιν ὡς εἰρήκαμεν {15} <u>ἐπεστάτει</u> τοῖς <u>τεχνίταις</u> διὰ φιλίαν Περικλέους. καὶ τοῦτο τῷ μὲν φθόνον, τῷ δὲ βλασφημίαν ἤνεγκεν, ὡς . . .

The man who directed [*diepein*] all the projects for him [= Pericles] and was the <u>overseer</u> [*episkopos*] of everything[94] involved was Pheidias, although individual works were executed by other great master builders [*arkhitektones*][95] and craftsmen [*tekhnitai*] {7} of the various projects. For the hundred-foot Parthenon was executed by Kallikrates and Iktinos. As for the *Telestērion* ['Hall of Initiation'] at Eleusis, it was Koroibos who began the building, and it was this man who had put in place on their foundation the columns and joined them to their architraves. But when he died Metagenes of the deme of Xypete put in place the frieze and the upper columns, while the hearth-opening above the *anaktoron* ['royal space'] received its crowning touch from Xenokles of the deme of Kholargos. For the Long Wall, concerning which Socrates [Plato *Gorgias* 455e] says that he himself heard Pericles make a formal proposal, {8} the contractor was Kallikrates. . . . {9} As for the Odeum, which was designed to have many seats and columns on the inside, and the roofing of

---

[94] When I translate πάντων here as 'of everything', I mean 'of everything and everyone'. I base this translation on the context of section 14 here: 'Almost everything was <u>dependent on</u> [= *epi-* plus dative] him, and, as I have said, he <u>was in charge</u> [*epistateîn*], on account of his friendship with Pericles, of all the other <u>craftsmen</u> [*tekhnitai*]'.

[95] On *arkhitektōn* as 'master builder', see Stadter 1989:167. For example, the inscription *IG* I[3] 474 mentions the *arkhitektōn* as well as the *epistatai* 'overseers' for building the Erekhtheion.

4§6. Pheidias and his Homeric statue of Athena Parthenos

which had a steep slope from the peak downward, they say it was a visual imitation of the Great King's Tent [*skēnē*]—and {10} Pericles was supervising [*epistateîn*] this building project as well. . . .⁹⁶ {11} It was then for the first time that Pericles, ambitious as he was, got a decree passed that there should be a competition [*agōn*] in *mousikē*⁹⁷ at the Panathenaia, and he set up the rules [*diatassein*], having been elected as an *athlothetēs* [= organizer of the *athloi* 'contests'] for those who were competing [*agōnizesthai*]—rules for them to follow about the *aulos*-playing and the singing and the *kithara*-playing. At that point in time and in other periods of time as well, it was in the Odeum that people used to be spectators [*theâsthai*] of competitions [*agōnes*] in *mousikē*. {12} The Propylaea were built within the space of five years, Mnesikles being the architect, and a wondrous event happened in the course of their building, which indicated that the goddess was not just standing back but actively participating [= *sun*-, prefixed to both verbs that follow] in lending a hand to [*sun-haptesthai*] the project and in {13} bringing it to completion [*sun-epi-teleîn*]. . . . {14} Pheidias himself worked on the golden statue [*hedos*] of the goddess, and his name is inscribed as the artist on the stele. Almost everything was dependent on [= *epi*- plus dative] him, and, as I have said, {15} he was in charge [*epistateîn*], on account of his friendship with Pericles, of all the other craftsmen [*tekhnitai*]. This brought envy against one [= Pheidias] and, against the other [= Pericles], defamation, to the effect that . . .

4§116 I consider the narrative in this passage I just quoted from Plutarch's *Pericles* a masterpiece of metonymy.⁹⁸ The relationship of Pericles the statesman to Pheidias the craftsman and artist is being narrated here as a perfect complementarity, a perfect artistic totality in its own right. Just as the leading citizen Pericles leads his fellow citizens in political action, the leading craftsman Pheidias leads his fellow craftsmen in the artistic realization of the same action. I say the same action because I see here an overlapping complementarity, not a mutually exclusive one. The political action and the artistic creativity overlap with each other because the statesman and the

---

⁹⁶ At this point, I omit a quotation that Plutarch adduces from Old Comedy to enhance his remarks about the Odeum. I will include the quotation at a later point where I will repeat this passage in its entirety.

⁹⁷ I emphasize, once again, that the *mousikē* 'craft of the Muses' as practiced at the Panathenaia includes the *tekhnē* 'craft' of rhapsodes, not only of citharodes, citharists, aulodes, and auletes.

⁹⁸ The expression "masterpieces of metonymy" is the title of a forthcoming work of mine.

Chapter Four

craftsman share with each other the political and the artistic credit for their accomplishments.[99] And the unifying force of sharing in all the credit is the goddess of Athens, Athena. Here in Plutarch's *Pericles* (13.13), the goddess is pictured as an active participant in both the art and the politics of the project, and her participation is conveyed in the most physical terms. According to the story, Athena showed her involvement in the overall building program by miraculously 'lending a hand' (*sun-haptesthai*) in the building of the Propylaea, thus 'keeping in touch' (*-haptesthai*) with the craftsmen in their work and making it possible to bring this work to its completion (*sun-epi-teleîn*). This overall building program, to repeat, featured as its highest achievement the making of the statue of Athena. So there was a synergism linking the work of Athena with the work of the craftsman Pheidias and of all the craftsmen he supervised.

4§117 Here it is relevant for me to add a general observation about a most ancient and fundamental connection that exists between the name of Athena and the name of Athens. The very idea of physical contact offered by the goddess to the leaders of Athens and to those they lead is embedded in the grammatical relationship between the name of Athena and the name of Athens. The singular name of the goddess Athena, *Athḗnē*, is coextensive with the plural name of her city of Athens, *Athênai*. This name means, elliptically, 'Athena and everything / everyone connected to her'.[100] In other words, the name of the city of Athens is itself a most ancient metonym that expresses the divine power of integrating and unifying the diversity of all things and all people.

4§118 In the narrative of the passage I just quoted from Plutarch's *Pericles*, there is an inner logic of totality in the sequence of transitions from one highlight to another. Here again are the three phases of the sequence:

(1) the naming of various building projects executed by craftsmen other than Pheidias

(2) the naming of Athena as an active participant and an integrating force in the work to be done

---

[99] There is a precedent for this kind of rhetoric that can be dated as far back as the late sixth century: a case in point is the passage in "Plato" *Hipparkhos* 228b-c, where the tyrant Hipparkhos of Athens takes the artistic credit for Homer's creativity by equating the *sophia* of Homer with his own *sophia*.

[100] *HTL* 163–164.

4§6. Pheidias and his Homeric statue of Athena Parthenos

(3) the climactic naming of Pheidas as the author of the *pièce de résistance*, the project of final integration, which is the statue of Athena Parthenos in the Parthenon on the acropolis.

4§119 Modern historians find it near-impossible to accept the idea that Pheidias the sculptor could have been so important in the age of Pericles. Stories about Pheidias as a close advisor to Pericles are generally mistrusted. Even the idea that Pheidias was overseer of the entire building program is viewed with skepticism.[101] Moreover, the stories about the troubled life of Pheidias, featuring trials, exile from Athens, and even his execution at the hands of the Eleans, seem more mythical than historical in content.[102] I will argue, however, that even the myths framed by the Life of Pheidias traditions have a historical value, in that they serve to explain the historical reality of his colossal prestige. That prestige came from his craft as the sculptor of colossal statues like the Zeus in Olympia and the Athena Parthenos in Athens. As we are about to see, the most visible sign of the prestige inherent in these statues—besides their colossal size—was their chryselephantine surface, that is, the gold and the ivory that adorned their exterior appearance.

4§120 One way to test the historical value of the Life of Pheidias traditions is to look at the negative stories concerning the sculptor, alongside the positive stories concerning his colossal prestige. It turns out that even the negative stories concern that same prestige, and that this colossal prestige is directly connected to the colossal prestige of the Athenian empire. There is a metonymy built into all the stories, positive or negative, that connects the monumental art of Pheidias with the wealth, power, and prestige of the Athenian empire as represented primarily by Pericles. In the stories about Pheidias, he not only shares with Pericles the credit for the glories of the Athenian empire: he also has his own share in the dangers that come with empire. We saw this negative side already in the passage I quoted from Plutarch's *Pericles*, where we read of the *phthonos* 'envy' attracted by Pheidias, matching the *blasphēmia* 'slander' attracted by Pericles (13.9). As Plutarch delves into the grim details of the many instances of 'slander', it becomes clear that both the sculptor and the statesman are plagued by it, though Pericles regularly gets the greater share of the blame (13.9-12). Although the statesman gets the negative privilege of a greater share of blame than the sculptor, the negative privilege of causing the greatest political scandal for Pericles goes to

---

[101] For an effective summary of such modern views, see Stadter 1989:166-167.
[102] For a collection of Life of Pheidias traditions, including the stories in Plutarch's *Pericles*, see Pollitt 1990:53-65.

Pheidias. Not only that, this particular scandal is directly linked to a *pièce de résistance* that stands out as the supreme achievement of Pheidias in Athens, that is, his colossal statue of Athena Parthenos:

4①24 Plutarch *Pericles* 31.2–3

> Ἡ δὲ χειρίστη μὲν αἰτία πασῶν, ἔχουσα δὲ πλείστους μάρτυρας, οὕτω πως λέγεται. Φειδίας ὁ πλάστης ἐργολάβος μὲν ἦν τοῦ ἀγάλματος ὥσπερ εἴρηται, φίλος δὲ τῷ Περικλεῖ γενόμενος καὶ μέγιστον παρ' αὐτῷ δυνηθείς, τοὺς μὲν δι' αὐτὸν ἔσχεν ἐχθροὺς φθονούμενος, οἱ δὲ τοῦ δήμου ποιούμενοι πεῖραν ἐν ἐκείνῳ ποῖός τις ἔσοιτο τῷ Περικλεῖ κριτής, Μένωνά τινα τῶν Φειδίου συνεργῶν πείσαντες ἱκέτην ἐν ἀγορᾷ καθίζουσιν, αἰτούμενον ἄδειαν ἐπὶ μηνύσει {3} καὶ κατηγορίᾳ τοῦ Φειδίου. προσδεξαμένου δὲ τοῦ δήμου τὸν ἄνθρωπον καὶ γενομένης ἐν ἐκκλησίᾳ διώξεως, κλοπαὶ μὲν οὐκ ἠλέγχοντο· τὸ γὰρ χρυσίον οὕτως εὐθὺς ἐξ ἀρχῆς τῷ ἀγάλματι προσειργάσατο καὶ περιέθηκεν ὁ Φειδίας γνώμῃ τοῦ Περικλέους, ὥστε πᾶν δυνατὸν εἶναι περιελοῦσιν ἀποδεῖξαι τὸν σταθμόν, ὃ καὶ τότε τοὺς κατηγόρους ἐκέλευσε ποιεῖν ὁ Περικλῆς·

But the worst accusation of them all [against Pericles], and yet the one that had the most witnesses backing it up, is told in a story that goes something like this. Pheidias the sculptor got the contract, as I said earlier, concerning the statue [*agalma* = of Athena]. Since he had become a friend of Pericles and had the greatest power in his relations with him, he was envied for this and made enemies for himself. Meanwhile, others were using him [= Pheidias] as a test case to see how the people would judge Pericles. So they persuaded someone called Menon, who worked with Pheidias, and they got him to take a seat as a suppliant in the agora. He was asking for immunity in return for reporting on Pheidias {3} and making charges against him. The people accepted the man's plea, and a formal prosecution took place in the assembly. But the charge of theft could not be proved. From the very start, the gold of the Statue had been worked in and around in such a way by Pheidias, at the suggestion of Pericles, that it could all be detached and publicly weighed. And that was exactly what Pericles at that moment told the accusers to do.

4§121 In the logic of this narrative, the importance of the case against Pheidias is measured in terms of the gold attached to and detachable from the statue of Athena Parthenos. This detail about the detachable gold on the

4§6. Pheidias and his Homeric statue of Athena Parthenos

statue of Athena Parthenos turns out to be a historical fact. As we learn from Thucydides, the gold that adorned the statue of Athena Parthenos weighed 40 talents, and all of it was detachable in case any of it was needed by the State for an emergency (2.13.5).[103] In order to appreciate the spectacular value of this amount of gold, I provide here the context that frames this piece of information. Thucydides mentions this reserve sum of 40 talents of gold in the general context of paraphrasing a public speech of Pericles to the Athenians in which the statesman lists all the public funds available to the state of Athens in its preparations for war with the Peloponnesian League (2.13.3-5). First on the list given by Pericles is the annual Tribute paid to Athens by the tributary cities of the Athenian empire, the average yearly amount of which is 600 talents of silver (2.13.3); second on the list is the sum of another 600 talents of coined silver stored on the Acropolis—a sum left over from a larger sum of 9,700 talents of silver spent on (a) the Propylaea, which was the current objective of Pericles' monumental building program, and (b) the current military campaigns in Potidaea (2.13.3); third on the list is a miscellaneous sum of uncoined gold and silver public treasures valued at 500 talents of silver (2.13.4). In the last place on the list, as a last resort for emergency reserves, is the gold that adorns the Athena Parthenos (2.13.5). The climactic mention of the spectacular value of 40 talents of weighed gold, even if we ignore the unreported though doubtless commensurately spectacular value of the ivory that complemented the gold on the statue, is all the more dazzling when we consider the fact that the value of this gold exceeds the value of the 600 talents of silver that were paid as annual Tribute to the Athenian empire.[104] To say it more forcefully, the value of the detachable gold adorning the Athena Parthenos of Pheidias was imperial in its spectacularly colossal dimensions.

4§122 In this reference to the Athena Parthenos of Pheidias, Thucydides is making explicit something that is only implicit in the relevant narrative of Plutarch. That something is the fact that Thucydides represents Pericles himself as saying that the detachable gold of the Athena Parthenos is a visible sign of the wealth, power, and prestige of the Athenian empire. I should add that the narrative of Plutarch's *Pericles* connects the whole building program initiated by Pericles and executed by Pheidias in Athens with the 'income'

---

[103] See Lapatin 2001:65 for other reports besides that of Thucydides. Philochorus *FGH* 328 F 121 gives a more precise accounting of the weight of the gold.

[104] The value of 600 silver talents is 16 silver talents less than the value of 40 talents in gold: Lapatin 2001:65.

(*prosodoi*) of the Athenian empire (*Pericles* 14.1-2).[105] In this light, I return to the words of Pericles as dramatized by Thucydides: since Pericles is quoted as listing the tribute incoming from the tributary states (2.13.3) as a resource that is parallel to the detachable gold adorning the Athena Parthenos (2.13.5), it is implicit that the statue of Pheidias is at least indirectly financed through the resources of Athens <u>as an empire</u>. And so the statue of Athena by Pheidias in the Parthenon can be seen as the metonymic centerpiece not only for the building program of Pericles in Athens but also for the general operation of the entire Athenian empire. The overpowering spectacle of the building program overseen by Pheidias conveys the colossal vastness of the Athenian empire, and it all comes together in one salient detail, which has its own metonymic power. That is the golden statue of Athena Parthenos, a visible sign of the Athenian empire in action.

4§123 With the added perspective of Thucydides in place, I press on with my exploration of the imperial mentality inherent in the making of the statue of Athena Parthenos in Athens. Comparable to what I just said about the gold that was used to make this statue is what can be said about the ivory. Like gold, the ivory that adorned the statues of gods was proverbially priceless (Pliny the Elder *Natural History* 8.30-31). And ivory, like gold, was associated with royalty and empire. A case in point is an anecdote reported by Herodotus about the Ethiopians' tribute of twenty elephant tusks offered to the Great King of Persia (3.97.3).

4§124 The symmetry of gold and ivory as displays of inestimable value is illustrated by the fact that the negative story we read about Pheidias and the gold of the Parthenos is matched by another negative story about Pheidias and the ivory of the Parthenos. In this other story, as reported by Philochorus (*FGH* 328 F 121), Pheidias is accused of embezzling the ivory instead of the gold.[106] Such stories about the sculptor's embezzling either gold or ivory in the course of creating the statue of Athena Parthenos are linked with details about the exile of Pheidias and even about his eventual execution.[107] And what

---

[105] Lapatin 2001:65-66 gives a balanced account. It may be an exaggeration to say, on the basis of what we read in Plutarch *Pericles* 14, that the building program of Pericles on the acropolis was paid for by all the cities that were ruled by Athens: see Kallet-Marx 1989.

[106] The Philochorus passage (*FGH* 328 F 121) is transmitted in the scholia for Aristophanes *Peace* 605. This source gives further details about the Life of Pheidias tradition: how he was supposedly exiled from Athens and sought refuge in Elis, where he was commissioned to create the statue of Zeus, and where he was at some later point supposedly killed by the people of Elis. A translation of the relevant text is given by Pollitt 1990:54-54.

[107] See the previous note.

is reflected in such stories is the colossal prestige that Pheidias derived from the craft of creating colossal statues of inestimable value.

4⒮7. The imperial Homer of Pheidias of Athens

4§125 The prestige inherent in the colossal chryselephantine statues of Zeus and Athena by Pheidias is the prestige of the Athenian empire. To that extent, as I will now argue, the craft of Pheidias himself is imperial. A most revealing point of comparison is the craft of a contemporary, Hippias of Elis. I begin the comparison by considering the Platonic *Hippias Maior*. In the relevant passage I am about to quote, we will see a dramatized description of the chryselephantine art of Pheidias, and the person featured as describing this art will be none other than Hippias himself. We will see Hippias in the act of measuring the greatness of Pheidias in terms of gold and ivory, which he applies as a standard for measuring not just greatness, but absolute greatness. From a historical point of view, Hippias is a most appropriate speaker about the artistry of Pheidias, since the statue of Zeus by Pheidias was the single most important piece of art in his native region of Elis. Contrary to our expectations, however, Hippias will be speaking not about the Zeus of Pheidias in Olympia. Rather, the speaker's focus of attention is on the sculptor's Athena Parthenos in Athens.

4§126 Before I quote the relevant passage, I offer a brief outline of the philosophical context in which it is nested. As we join the dialogue of the *Hippias Maior* in progress, we find three voices in play, as represented by Hippias, Socrates, and a hypothetical third voice, quoted by Socrates, who is questioning or second-guessing Socrates by intruding into the two-voice dialogue between Hippias and Socrates. The three voices are engaged in a free-wheeling dialogue about 'the ideally Beautiful', *to kalon*, and how the 'adding' (*prosgignesthai*) of this absolute beauty to something that is imperfect will transform that imperfect something into perfection on its own terms. The three examples that are being adduced are a beautiful girl, a beautiful horse, and a beautiful lyre. In the everyday world, each of the three will be imperfect. But when 'the ideally Beautiful' is added to each of them, then each of them will become perfect—whether it is a girl or a horse or a lyre. In the case of the 'girl'—the Greek word for which is *parthenos*, conventionally translated as 'maiden' or 'virgin'—the 'adding' (*prosgignesthai*) of 'the ideally Beautiful' transforms her into an ideal *parthenos* who is the perfect beauty. The embodiment of this ideal beauty in the dialogue of the three voices turns out to be the Parthenos par excellence, Athena herself—as sculpted by Pheidias. At least,

Chapter Four

that is how Hippias imagines this ideal: when Pheidias applies his technique of chryselephantine sculpture by adding gold or ivory to the form of his sculpted Athena Parthenos, what the sculptor achieves is the perfect Form of the real Athena, the perfect and absolute Parthenos. I hasten to add that this idea of perfection is a far cry from Plato's own idea of the perfect Form, but it represents here the understanding of Hippias the sophist at this particular point in the three-way dialogue as Plato has staged it. Having given this brief outline of the philosophical context, I proceed to quote the passage:

4①25 Plato *Hippias Maior* 289a–290d

> ΣΩ. Ἄκουε δή. μετὰ τοῦτο γὰρ εὖ οἶδ' ὅτι φήσει· "Τί δέ, ὦ Σώκρατες; τὸ τῶν παρθένων γένος θεῶν γένει ἄν τις {b} συμβάλλῃ, οὐ ταὐτὸν πείσεται ὅπερ τὸ τῶν χυτρῶν τῷ τῶν παρθένων συμβαλλόμενον; οὐχ ἡ καλλίστη παρθένος αἰσχρὰ φανεῖται; ἢ οὐ καὶ Ἡράκλειτος αὐτὸ τοῦτο λέγει, ὃν σὺ ἐπάγῃ, ὅτι "Ἀνθρώπων ὁ σοφώτατος πρὸς θεὸν πίθηκος φανεῖται καὶ σοφίᾳ καὶ κάλλει καὶ τοῖς ἄλλοις πᾶσιν;' ὁμολογήσωμεν, Ἱππία, τὴν καλλίστην παρθένον πρὸς θεῶν γένος αἰσχρὰν εἶναι;"
>
> ΙΠ. Τίς γὰρ ἂν ἀντείποι τούτῳ γε, ὦ Σώκρατες; {c}
>
> ΣΩ. Ἂν τοίνυν ταῦτα ὁμολογήσωμεν, γελάσεταί τε καὶ ἐρεῖ· "Ὦ Σώκρατες, μέμνησαι οὖν ὅτι ἠρωτήθης;" Ἔγωγε, φήσω, <u>ὅτι αὐτὸ τὸ καλὸν ὅτι ποτέ ἐστιν</u>. "Ἔπειτα," φήσει, "ἐρωτηθεὶς τὸ καλὸν ἀποκρίνῃ ὃ τυγχάνει ὄν, ὡς αὐτὸς φῄς, οὐδὲν μᾶλλον καλὸν ἢ αἰσχρόν;" Ἔοικε, φήσω· ἢ τί μοι συμβουλεύεις, ὦ φίλε, φάναι;
>
> ΙΠ. Τοῦτο ἔγωγε· καὶ γὰρ δὴ πρός γε θεοὺς ὅτι οὐ καλὸν τὸ ἀνθρώπειον γένος, ἀληθῆ ἐρεῖ.
>
> ΣΩ. "Εἰ δέ σε ἠρόμην," φήσει, "ἐξ ἀρχῆς τί ἐστι {d} καλόν τε καὶ αἰσχρόν, εἴ μοι ἅπερ νῦν ἀπεκρίνω, ἆρ' οὐκ ἂν ὀρθῶς ἀπεκέκρισο; ἔτι δὲ καὶ δοκεῖ σοι <u>αὐτὸ τὸ καλόν, ᾧ καὶ τἆλλα πάντα κοσμεῖται καὶ καλὰ φαίνεται, ἐπειδὰν προσγένηται ἐκεῖνο τὸ εἶδος, τοῦτ' εἶναι παρθένος ἢ ἵππος ἢ λύρα;"</u>
>
> ΙΠ. Ἀλλὰ μέντοι, ὦ Σώκρατες, εἰ τοῦτό γε ζητεῖ, πάντων ῥᾷστον ἀποκρίνασθαι αὐτῷ τί ἐστι τὸ καλὸν ᾧ καὶ τὰ ἄλλα <u>πάντα κοσμεῖται καὶ προσγενομένου αὐτοῦ καλὰ φαίνεται</u>. {e} εὐηθέστατος οὖν ἐστιν ὁ ἄνθρωπος καὶ οὐδὲν ἐπαΐει περὶ καλῶν κτημάτων. ἐὰν γὰρ αὐτῷ ἀποκρίνῃ ὅτι <u>τοῦτ' ἐστιν ὃ ἐρωτᾷ τὸ καλὸν οὐδὲν ἄλλο ἢ χρυσός</u>,

ἀπορήσει καὶ οὐκ ἐπιχειρήσει σε ἐλέγχειν. ἴσμεν γάρ που πάντες ὅτι ὅπου ἂν τοῦτο προσγένηται, κἂν πρότερον αἰσχρὸν φαίνηται, καλὸν φανεῖται χρυσῷ γε κοσμηθέν.

ΣΩ. Ἄπειρος εἶ τοῦ ἀνδρός, ὦ Ἱππία, ὡς σχέτλιός ἐστι καὶ οὐδὲν ῥαδίως ἀποδεχόμενος.

ΙΠ. Τί οὖν τοῦτο, ὦ Σώκρατες; τὸ γὰρ ὀρθῶς λεγόμενον {290a} ἀνάγκη αὐτῷ ἀποδέχεσθαι, ἢ μὴ ἀποδεχομένῳ καταγελάστῳ εἶναι.

ΣΩ. Καὶ μὲν δὴ ταύτην γε τὴν ἀπόκρισιν, ὦ ἄριστε, οὐ μόνον οὐκ ἀποδέξεται, ἀλλὰ πάνυ με καὶ τωθάσεται, καὶ ἐρεῖ·

"Ὦ τετυφωμένε σύ, Φειδίαν οἴει κακὸν εἶναι δημιουργόν;" καὶ ἐγὼ οἶμαι ἐρῶ ὅτι "Οὐδ' ὁπωστιοῦν."

ΙΠ. Καὶ ὀρθῶς γ' ἐρεῖς, ὦ Σώκρατες.

ΣΩ. Ὀρθῶς μέντοι. τοιγάρτοι ἐκεῖνος, ἐπειδὰν ἐγὼ ὁμολογῶ ἀγαθὸν εἶναι δημιουργὸν τὸν Φειδίαν, "Εἶτα," {b} φήσει, "οἴει τοῦτο τὸ καλὸν ὃ σὺ λέγεις ἠγνόει Φειδίας;" Καὶ ἐγώ· Τί μάλιστα; φήσω. "Ὅτι," ἐρεῖ, "τῆς Ἀθηνᾶς τοὺς ὀφθαλμοὺς οὐ χρυσοῦς ἐποίησεν, οὐδὲ τὸ ἄλλο πρόσωπον οὐδὲ τοὺς πόδας οὐδὲ τὰς χεῖρας, εἴπερ χρυσοῦν γε δὴ ὂν κάλλιστον ἔμελλε φαίνεσθαι, ἀλλ' ἐλεφάντινον· δῆλον ὅτι τοῦτο ὑπὸ ἀμαθίας ἐξήμαρτεν, ἀγνοῶν ὅτι χρυσὸς ἄρ' ἐστὶν ὁ πάντα καλὰ ποιῶν, ὅπου ἂν προσγένηται." ταῦτα οὖν λέγοντι τί ἀποκρινώμεθα, ὦ Ἱππία; {c}

ΙΠ. Οὐδὲν χαλεπόν· ἐροῦμεν γὰρ ὅτι ὀρθῶς ἐποίησε, καὶ γὰρ τὸ ἐλεφάντινον οἶμαι καλόν ἐστιν.

ΣΩ. "Τοῦ οὖν ἕνεκα," φήσει, "οὐ καὶ τὰ μέσα τῶν ὀφθαλμῶν ἐλεφάντινα ἠργάσατο, ἀλλὰ λίθινα, ὡς οἷόν τ' ἦν ὁμοιότητα τοῦ λίθου τῷ ἐλέφαντι ἐξευρών; ἢ καὶ ὁ λίθος ὁ καλὸς καλόν ἐστι;" φήσομεν, ὦ Ἱππία;

ΙΠ. Φήσομεν μέντοι, ὅταν γε πρέπων ᾖ.

ΣΩ. "Ὅταν δὲ μὴ πρέπων, αἰσχρόν;" ὁμολογῶ ἢ μή;

ΙΠ. Ὁμολόγει, ὅταν γε μὴ πρέπῃ. {d}

ΣΩ. "Τί δὲ δή; ὁ ἐλέφας καὶ ὁ χρυσός," φήσει, "ὦ σοφὲ σύ, οὐχ ὅταν μὲν πρέπῃ, καλὰ ποιεῖ φαίνεσθαι, ὅταν δὲ μή, αἰσχρά;" ἔξαρνοι ἐσόμεθα ἢ ὁμολογήσομεν αὐτῷ ὀρθῶς λέγειν αὐτόν;

Chapter Four

ΙΠ. Ὁμολογήσομεν τοῦτό γε, ὅτι ὃ ἂν πρέπῃ ἑκάστῳ, τοῦτο καλὸν ποιεῖ ἕκαστον.

SOCRATES: Listen then. For I know well that he [= the hypothetical third voice who is questioning the voice of Socrates] will next say: "But what about this, Socrates? Suppose someone compares the category of 'girls' [*parthenoi*] with the category of 'gods'. Won't the same thing happen to the category of 'girls' [*parthenoi*] that happened to the category of 'pots' when it was compared with the category of 'girls' [*parthenoi*]? Won't the most beautiful girl [*parthenos*] appear repulsive? Or doesn't even Heraclitus [B 82 DK], whom you cite, say exactly this, that the most wise [*sophos*] of men, when compared to a god, will appear to be a monkey, both in wisdom [*sophia*] and in beauty and in all other things? Shall we agree, Hippias, that the most beautiful girl [*parthenos*] is repulsive when compared with the category of 'gods'?"

HIPPIAS: Yes, for who could contradict this, Socrates?[108]

SOCRATES: If, then, we agree with regard to these things, he [= the third voice] will laugh and say: "so, Socrates, do you remember the question you were asked?" "I do," I will say, "the question was: <u>what on earth is 'the ideally Beautiful' [*to kalon*]</u>?" "Then," he will say, "the moment you are asked about 'the ideally Beautiful' [*to kalon*], what do you say? Do you give a response that goes like this: it is what happens to be, as you yourself say, no more beautiful than repulsive?" "It seems to be the case," I will say; or what do you [= Hippias], my friend, advise me to say?

HIPPIAS: Yes, this *is* what I advise; for, in fact, in saying that the category of 'humans' is not beautiful in comparison with gods, you will be saying what is true.[109]

SOCRATES: "But if I had asked you," he will say, "from the very start what is beautiful and what is repulsive, if you had given in

---

[108] In what follows, Socrates moves Hippias away from this line of thinking, according to which only one category can be perfect while the other categories are imperfect. Socrates will induce Hippias to admit that each category can have its own kind of perfection—whether it is a girl or a horse or a pot.

[109] By now Socrates has induced Hippias to apply a new line of thinking, as summarized in the previous note.

response to me the kind of things you are saying now, would you not have responded correctly? But do you still think that 'the ideally Beautiful' [*auto to kalon*], by means of which all other things are adorned [*kosmeîn*] and appear to be beautiful, when that Form [*eidos* = 'the ideally Beautiful'] is added [*prosgignesthai*] [to the things I mentioned], that this thing [= this thing that results from the addition of 'the ideally beautiful'] is the same thing as a girl [*parthenos*] or a horse or a lyre?"

HIPPIAS: But, Socrates, if this is what he [= the third voice] is seeking, then it is the most easy thing in the world to give a response about what is 'the ideally Beautiful', by means of which all other things are adorned [*kosmeîn*] and by the addition [*prosgignesthai*] of which all other things look beautiful. So I now see that the man is very simple-minded and understands nothing about beautiful possessions. For if you reply to him that "this thing you are asking about, the Beautiful, is nothing other than gold," he will find himself in perplexity [*aporia*] and will not attempt to refute you. For we all know, I think, that wherever this thing is added [*prosgignesthai*], even if earlier it appeared to be repulsive, now it will appear to be beautiful—that is, once it is adorned [*kosmeîn*] with gold.

SOCRATES: You just have no experience with this man, Hippias, and so you do not know how wretched he is, and how he is not about to accept anything easily.

HIPPIAS: What *is* this, Socrates? Surely it is a necessity for him to accept what is said correctly, or, if he does not accept, be worthy of ridicule.

SOCRATES: This response, my most distinguished friend, he will not only not accept, but he will make fun of me in the worst way and say: "Tell me this, you benighted person, do you think that Pheidias is a bad craftsman [*dēmiourgos*]?" And I think I will say: "Not at all."[110]

HIPPIAS: And you will be speaking correctly, Socrates.

---

[110] It is Socrates, not Hippias, who introduces the topic of Pheidias the sculptor. Tradition has it that Socrates himself was the son of a craftsman whose medium was *lithos* 'stone' (*lithourgos*: Diogenes Laertius 2.18).

Chapter Four

SOCRATES: Yes, correctly. So when I agree that Pheidias is a good craftsman [*dēmiourgos*], "well then," he will say, "do you think that Pheidias did not know this thing, 'the ideally Beautiful' [*to kalon*] that you speak of?" And I will say: "Why do you say that in particular"? "Because," he will say, "he did not make the eyes of Athena from gold, nor the rest of her face, nor her feet and hands—if it was really supposed to look most beautiful only if it [= the face] was made of gold, but he made it of ivory; it is clear that he made this mistake through ignorance, not knowing that it is gold which makes all things beautiful, wherever it is added [*prosgignesthai*]." When he says that, what response shall we give him, Hippias?

HIPPIAS: That is not hard at all. For we will say that he [= Pheidias] did it correctly; for ivory, I think, is an absolutely beautiful thing.

SOCRATES: "Why, then," he will say, "did he make the middle parts [= pupils] of the eyes not out of ivory as well, but of [precious] stone, devising as great a similarity as possible between the stone and the ivory? Or is even the beautiful stone a thing of beauty? Shall we say that it is, Hippias?

HIPPIAS: Yes, we shall say so, that is, whenever it [= the (precious) stone] is appropriate."

SOCRATES: And when it is not appropriate, then it is repulsive, right? Shall I agree [with him] or not?

HIPPIAS: Yes, go ahead and agree with him: it is repulsive when it is not appropriate.

SOCRATES: "In that case," he will say, "what about this, you wise [*sophos*] man: do not gold and ivory, when they are appropriate, make things look beautiful, and, when they are not, make them look repulsive?" Shall we deny this or shall we agree with him [= the third voice] that he is speaking correctly?

HIPPIAS: We will agree to this extent: that whatever is appropriate for each thing makes each thing beautiful.

4§127 In summing up what we have just read, I will adopt the standpoint not of Socrates but of Hippias himself as represented here in the Platonic *Hippias Maior*: when Pheidias applies his technique of chryselephantine sculpture by adding gold and ivory to the basic form of his sculpted Athena

Parthenos, what the sculptor achieves is the perfect Form of the real Athena, the perfect and absolute Parthenos. For Hippias, portrayed here as a leading intellectual of his day, such an idea is evidently acceptable and even reasonable, as we see from the line of thinking attributed to him in the *Hippias Maior*.

4§128 It is clear—not only from the portrayal in the *Hippias Maior* but also from the historical realities behind this portrayal, that the ideas of Hippias of Elis must have been most highly valued in his own day and that Hippias was thus a most worthy intellectual opponent of Socrates in the historical context that is being dramatized by Plato. From a purely philosophical point of view, of course, the thinking of Hippias about the statue of Athena can easily be rejected, to the extent that it seems to universalize the privileging of the exterior over the interior. It could be argued, for example, that the reality of anything is what you find on the inside, not on the outside—that the exterior of anything will only conceal the reality of its interior. Such a truism is reflected in the wording of Quintilian when he speaks of 'ornamentation' (*decor*) as something that is added to what is real (*verum*): *decorem addiderit supra verum* (*Institutio oratoria* 12.10.8).[111] The truism espoused by Hippias in the *Hippias Maior* is radically different, however. The gold and ivory exterior of the Athena Parthenos of Pheidias *is* the essence of the goddess, not the wooden interior that gives her form its backbone, as it were.

4§129 The chryselephantine exterior of the goddess, with all the wealth, power, and prestige that it projects, is the essence of empire, the Athenian empire. For an imperial mentality, the Athena Parthenos of Pheidias is the embodiment of absolute beauty—and absolute greatness. The notionally absolute beauty and absolute greatness of Athena Parthenos go together with the notionally absolute power of empire.

4§130 The Athena Parthenos of Pheidias is the classical example of art as a demonstration of imperial power and absolutism. A most striking earlier example of a statue made by Pheidias was a colossal bronze Athena Promakhos standing in the open air near the entrance to the Acropolis—so overpowering in her height that the tip of her spear and the crest of her helmet could be seen from ships coming to and from Athens as they rounded Cape Sounion (Pausanias 1.28.2). The historical context for the making of this statue is most revealing, since it shows a synergism between the making of the Athenian democracy and the making of the Athenian empire:

---

[111] Nick 2002:163, with further citations.

> It may have been at this time [between 461 and 459 BCE] that the Athenians commissioned [Pheidias] to make the great bronze statue of Athena [Promakhos]. It was the first great public monument to be set up since the Persian wars and was to remain the most conspicuous landmark in Athens for those who approached the city by sea. . . . [T]he credit for commissioning Athens' greatest sculptor, still a comparatively young man, to attempt the first colossal bronze statue should be given to the radical democrats. The crucial evidence lies in the public accounts which were inscribed on a marble stele [SEG 10.243] when the work was completed and show that it had lasted nine years. . . . [There] is an entry that recurs in each year's summary of expenditure; it shows that the work was controlled by a board of public commissioners with a secretary and assistant, and that they were paid by the state. Plato in his *Gorgias* [515e] tells us that state pay was first introduced by Pericles. . . . Other sources [Aristotle *Constitution of the Athenians* 27.3] tell us that it was Pericles who introduced pay for the popular law courts; it is reasonable to believe that it was this step which established the precedent and that it was not till later that it was extended to the Boule, magistrates, and other officers of state.[112]

4§131 The sculpture of Pheidias, as a physical manifestation of Athenian imperial prestige, was exportable: already around the middle of the fifth century, as we read in Pausanias, the Athenians sent a group of statues by Pheidias to Delphi (10.10.1).[113] The statue of Zeus at Olympia in Elis is an extreme example of such an imperial export. In this case the imperial craftsman himself came to Elis in order to execute his imperial art on site.

4§8. Hippias and the staging of a perfect Homeric moment

4§132 We would expect Hippias the sophist, native of Elis, to be capable of recognizing a standard of absolute greatness and beauty in the statue of Zeus made in Olympia by Pheidias of Athens. After all, Hippias is represented in the Platonic *Hippias Maior* as someone who is capable of recognizing such a standard of absoluteness in the statue of Athena Parthenos made in Athens by Pheidias. As we will now see, there are two reasons for thinking that Hippias

---

[112] Meiggs 1972:94.
[113] See the commentary of Barron 1964:46.

4§8. Hippias and the staging of a perfect Homeric moment

actually had in mind the statue of Zeus by Pheidias whenever he performed and interpreted Homer in the sacred precinct of Zeus at Olympia. One of these two reasons can be found in a passage I quoted earlier, which captures the classical moment of such a Homeric performance by Hippias:

4①26 Plato *Hippias Minor* 363c–364a (requoted)

... ἐπειδὴ καὶ ἄλλα πολλὰ καὶ παντοδαπὰ ἡμῖν <u>ἐπιδέδεικται</u> καὶ περὶ <u>ποιητῶν</u> τε <u>ἄλλων καὶ περὶ Ὁμήρου</u>.

ΕΥ. Ἀλλὰ δῆλον ὅτι οὐ φθονήσει Ἱππίας, ἐάν τι αὐτὸν <u>ἐρωτᾷς</u>, <u>ἀποκρίνεσθαι</u>. ἦ γάρ, ὦ Ἱππία, ἐάν τι <u>ἐρωτᾷ</u> σε Σωκράτης, <u>ἀποκρινῇ</u>; ἢ πῶς ποιήσεις;

ΙΠ. Καὶ γὰρ ἂν δεινὰ ποιοίην, ὦ Εὔδικε, εἰ Ὀλυμπίαζε μὲν εἰς τὴν τῶν Ἑλλήνων πανήγυριν, ὅταν τὰ Ὀλύμπια ᾖ, {d} ἀεὶ ἐπανιὼν οἴκοθεν ἐξ Ἤλιδος εἰς τὸ <u>ἱερὸν</u> παρέχω ἐμαυτὸν καὶ <u>λέγοντα</u> ὅτι ἄν τις βούληται ὧν ἄν μοι εἰς <u>ἐπίδειξιν</u> παρεσκευασμένον ᾖ, καὶ <u>ἀποκρινόμενον</u> τῷ βουλομένῳ ὅτι ἄν τις <u>ἐρωτᾷ</u>, νῦν δὲ τὴν Σωκράτους <u>ἐρώτησιν</u> φύγοιμι. {364 a}

ΣΩ. Μακάριόν γε, ὦ Ἱππία, <u>πάθος</u> πέπονθας, εἰ <u>ἑκάστης Ὀλυμπιάδος</u> οὕτως εὔελπις ὢν <u>περὶ τῆς ψυχῆς</u> εἰς σοφίαν ἀφικνῇ εἰς τὸ <u>ἱερόν</u>· καὶ θαυμάσαιμ' ἄν εἴ τις τῶν <u>περὶ τὸ σῶμα ἀθλητῶν</u> οὕτως ἀφόβως τε καὶ πιστευτικῶς ἔχων τῷ <u>σώματι</u> ἔρχεται αὐτόσε <u>ἀγωνιούμενος</u>, ὥσπερ σὺ φῂς τῇ <u>διανοίᾳ</u>.

ΙΠ. Εἰκότως, ὦ Σώκρατες, ἐγὼ τοῦτο πέπονθα· ἐξ οὗ γὰρ ἦργμαι Ὀλυμπίασιν <u>ἀγωνίζεσθαι, οὐδενὶ πώποτε κρείττονι εἰς οὐδὲν ἐμαυτοῦ ἐνέτυχον</u>.

SOCRATES: ... since he [= Hippias] has <u>displayed</u> [*epideiknusthai*] so many things about so many <u>poets</u> [*poiētai*]—<u>and especially about Homer</u>.

EUDIKOS: But it is clear that Hippias will not be ungenerous, if you <u>ask</u> him <u>a question</u>, about <u>giving a response</u>. Isn't that right, Hippias? If Socrates <u>asks</u> you <u>a question</u>, you will <u>give a response</u>? You will do it, won't you?

HIPPIAS: I would be doing strange things, Eudikos, if I—as one who always goes to Olympia to the general gathering [*panēguris*] of all Hellenes when the Olympics take place, and, coming from my house

Chapter Four

in Elis I go into the sacred precinct [*hieron*] and I present myself in person, ready to perform [= literally 'speak', *legein*] whatever anyone wishes to choose from among all the things that I have prepared for display [*epideixis*], and ready to give response to any question that anyone wishes to ask—I would be doing strange things indeed if I now avoided the questioning of Socrates.

SOCRATES: Blessed [*makarion*], I would say, is the experience [*pathos*] that you have experienced, Hippias, if on the occasion of each Olympic festival you go into the sacred precinct [*hieron*] with such good expectations in regard to the skillfulness of your mind [*psukhē*]. And I would be dazzled if any one of those who engage in contests [= *athlētai*] in regard to the body [*sōma*] is so fearless and confident about his own body [*sōma*] when he goes to the same place in order to compete [*agōnizesthai*] as you say you are fearless and confident about your thinking [*dianoia*].

HIPPIAS: It is likely, Socrates, that I for one have indeed experienced this. For ever since I have begun to compete [*agōnizesthai*] at the Olympics, I have never yet met anyone better than myself in anything.

4§133 By now we can better appreciate why Plato's Socrates uses sacral terminology when he says *makarion pathos* 'blessed experience' in referring to the Olympic performance staged by Hippias in the *hieron* 'sacred space' of Zeus in Olympia. The exhilarating experience of Hippias in these perfect classical moments of Olympic performances is all-encompassing. He feels he is on top of the world: 'I have never yet met anyone better than myself in anything'.

4§134 Such a perfect classical moment, as staged by Hippias in Olympia, is restaged by Plato in Athens. Plato transfers the performance of Hippias from Olympia to Athens—all for the sake of Plato's Socrates, who gets to be a member of the audience when Hippias performs in the agora of Athens (*Hippias Minor* 368b).

4§135 Now I come to the second of my two reasons for thinking that Hippias actually had in mind the statue of Zeus by Pheidias whenever he performed and interpreted Homer in the sacred precinct of Zeus at Olympia. It has to do with another passage where Socrates gets to see with his own eyes an equivalent of the spectacle of Hippias in the act of Olympic performance. I have quoted the passage before, in Chapter 3, while making another argument, but now I quote it again for the sake of the present argument:

4Ⓢ8. Hippias and the staging of a perfect Homeric moment

4①27 Plato *Protagoras* 315b–c

> τὸν δὲ μετ' εἰσενόησα, ἔφη "Ὅμηρος, Ἱππίαν τὸν {c} Ἠλεῖον, καθήμενον ἐν τῷ κατ' ἀντικρὺ προστῴῳ ἐν θρόνῳ· περὶ αὐτὸν δ' ἐκάθηντο ἐπὶ βάθρων Ἐρυξίμαχός τε ὁ Ἀκουμενοῦ καὶ Φαῖδρος ὁ Μυρρινούσιος καὶ Ἄνδρων ὁ Ἀνδροτίωνος καὶ τῶν ξένων πολῖταί τε αὐτοῦ καὶ ἄλλοι τινές. ἐφαίνοντο δὲ περὶ φύσεώς τε καὶ τῶν μετεώρων ἀστρονομικά ἄττα διερωτᾶν τὸν Ἱππίαν, ὁ δ' ἐν θρόνῳ καθήμενος ἑκάστοις αὐτῶν διέκρινεν καὶ διεξῄει τὰ ἐρωτώμενα.

> After him [= Protagoras], the next one I [= Socrates] noted [*eis-noeîn*], as Homer says, was Hippias of Elis, seated at the portico across [from the portico of Protagoras] on a throne; and seated around him on benches were Eryximachus son of Akoumenos and Phaedrus of Myrrhinous and Andron son of Androtion as well as some non-Athenians. Among them [= the non-Athenians] were some fellow-citizens [of Hippias of Elis] as well as others. It appeared that they were making a systematic inquiry [*di-erōtân*] in asking Hippias various astronomical questions concerning the nature [*phusis*] of heavenly bodies while he, seated on his throne, made critical judgments [*dia-krinein*] for each one of them as he systematically went through the things about which they had just made inquiries.

4§136 What Plato's Socrates sees here is not only a perfect classical moment: it is a perfect Homeric moment. As I noted in Chapter 3, Plato's staging here of Hippias in Athens matches the Homeric staging of Minos son of Zeus. I recall once again the Homeric vision of Minos in the *Odyssey*, where we see the son of Zeus seated in his place of honor, evoking a vision of the god himself as he goes through the motions of acting like Zeus.

4①28 *Odyssey* xi 568–571

> ἔνθ' ἦ τοι Μίνωα ἴδον, Διὸς ἀγλαὸν υἱόν,
> χρύσεον σκῆπτρον ἔχοντα θεμιστεύοντα νέκυσσιν,
> ἥμενον· οἱ δέ μιν ἀμφὶ δίκας εἴροντο ἄνακτα,
> ἥμενοι ἑσταότες τε, κατ' εὐρυπυλὲς Ἄϊδος δῶ.

> There I saw Minos, radiant son of Zeus,
> who was holding a golden scepter as he dispensed justice [*themisteuein*] among the dead.

> He was <u>seated</u>, while they [= the dead] <u>asked</u> the lord for his judgments.
>
> Some of them [= the dead] were seated, and some were standing, throughout the house of Hades, with its wide gates.

4§137 The description in the first three lines of this Homeric passage shows a Minos who matches in appearance the image of a seated Zeus holding a scepter. As I said before, the hero Minos is not only the son of Zeus but also the underworldly surrogate of the god. Like Minos, Zeus himself is conventionally pictured as sitting on a *thronos* 'throne' (*Iliad* I 536, etc.), and, as the ultimate king, he is the ultimate source of authority for the holding of a *skēptron* 'scepter' (I 234) by kings who uphold *themistes* 'judgments' (I 238–239 οἵ τε θέμιστας | πρὸς Διὸς εἰρύαται). As I also said before, the plural noun *themistes* designates 'judgments' as instantiations of 'justice' as designated by the singular noun *themis*.

4§138 Like the son of Zeus, Hippias is pictured as sitting on a throne (*Protagoras* 315b καθήμενον . . . ἐν θρόνῳ / 315c ἐν θρόνῳ καθήμενος), responding to questions (315c διερωτᾶν . . . ἐρωτώμενα) that call for 'making critical judgments', as expressed by the verb *dia-krinein* (315c διέκρινεν). Further, Hippias is pictured in the act of responding to questions about the natural world, that is, about *phusis* 'nature' in general, and about astronomy in particular (315c ἐφαίνοντο δὲ περὶ φύσεώς τε καὶ τῶν μετεώρων ἀστρονομικά ἄττα διερωτᾶν τὸν Ἱππίαν).[114] In Plato's *Hippias Minor*, on the other hand, we see the same Hippias actually responding to similar questions posed by Socrates, who challenges the sophist to apply various *tekhnai* 'crafts' for the purpose of distinguishing, as empirically as possible, what is true and what is false. Among these *tekhnai*, Hippias singles out the *tekhnē* of astronomy as one of his specialties (*Hippias Minor* 367e). This detail, as I argued earlier, is an important link between the portraits of Hippias in Plato's *Protagoras* and *Hippias Minor*.

4§139 Plato's wording suggests that Hippias aspires to an understanding of the cosmos that rivals that of Zeus himself. More than that, Hippias seems to rival Zeus even in his appearance—that is, he rivals the Homeric Zeus of Pheidias. Plato's wording makes it seem as if Hippias himself were seated on the throne in the temple of Zeus in Olympia. Just as Minos the son of Zeus is

---

[114] See also Plato *Protagoras* 318d–e.

going through the motions of Zeus, so also Hippias himself is acting like Zeus. His model is not only the Zeus of Homer but also the Zeus of Pheidias.

4§140 From what we have seen so far, I am led to think that Hippias of Elis actually performed his Homeric displays at the entrance to the temple of Zeus in Olympia. Hippias would be facing his audience while seated on a throne situated in front of the open doors of the temple. As the mind's eye travels up the steps and through the open doors of the temple, it beholds the spectacular vision of Zeus seated on his throne on high. For the audience gathered around the steps leading up to the temple, the line of vision would extend directly from a view of Hippias enthroned outside the temple to a view of Zeus himself enthroned inside the temple. As we saw earlier, the vision of Hippias of Elis sitting on his throne evokes the vision of Minos, son of Zeus, sitting on his own throne: both can be imagined as dispensing responses to all questions addressed to them (Plato *Protagoras* 315b–c). As we also saw in Plato's *Hippias Minor*, Hippias re-enacts in Athens the Homeric displays he had performed at the temple of Zeus in Olympia (363c–d, 364a–b), and it is in this context that Socrates first notices the ring on the sophist's finger (368b). As we saw in Chapter 3, the Ring of Hippias is relevant to the image of the First Rings in Plato's *Ion*, symbols for three First Poets identified as Orpheus, Musaeus, and Homer—in that order (536b). As I show in the twin book *Homer the Preclassic*, this Ring of Hippias is also relevant to another symbol, the Ring of Minos.[115]

4Ⓢ9. Protagoras as a point of comparison for Pheidias and Homer

4§141 So far, I have reconstructed in the works of Plato an implicit link between Homer and Pheidias as masters of the art of picturing Zeus. But Plato himself also makes an explicit link between these two paradigms of artistry. He does it by identifying Homer and Pheidias as craftsmen—professionals who are paid to use the *sophia* 'skill' that makes them experts in whatever *tekhnē* 'craft' they practice. As professionals, Homer and Pheidias are comparable to the most successful of all professionals in the age of Pheidias—to a man who is even more successful than Pheidias himself. That man is Protagoras the sophist. In the passage that follows, I draw special attention to the relevant use of the word *sophistēs* 'sophist':

---

[115] *HPC* E§§158 and following.

Chapter Four

4①29 Plato *Protagoras* 311a–e

Μετὰ ταῦτα ἀναστάντες εἰς τὴν αὐλὴν περιῇμεν· καὶ ἐγὼ {b} ἀποπειρώμενος τοῦ Ἱπποκράτους τῆς ῥώμης διεσκόπουν αὐτὸν καὶ ἠρώτων, Εἰπέ μοι, ἔφην ἐγώ, ὦ Ἱππόκρατες, παρὰ Πρωταγόραν νῦν ἐπιχειρεῖς ἰέναι, ἀργύριον τελῶν ἐκείνῳ μισθὸν ὑπὲρ σεαυτοῦ, ὡς παρὰ τίνα ἀφιξόμενος καὶ τίς γενησόμενος; ὥσπερ ἂν εἰ ἐπενόεις παρὰ τὸν σαυτοῦ ὁμώνυμον ἐλθὼν Ἱπποκράτη τὸν Κῷον, τὸν τῶν Ἀσκληπιαδῶν, ἀργύριον τελεῖν ὑπὲρ σαυτοῦ μισθὸν ἐκείνῳ, εἴ τίς σε ἤρετο· "Εἰπέ μοι, μέλλεις τελεῖν, ὦ Ἱππόκρατες, Ἱπποκράτει {c} μισθὸν ὡς τίνι ὄντι;" τί ἂν ἀπεκρίνω; Εἶπον ἄν, ἔφη, ὅτι ὡς ἰατρῷ. "Ὡς τίς γενησόμενος;" Ὡς ἰατρός, ἔφη. Εἰ δὲ παρὰ Πολύκλειτον τὸν Ἀργεῖον ἢ <u>Φειδίαν</u> τὸν <u>Ἀθηναῖον</u> ἐπενόεις ἀφικόμενος μισθὸν ὑπὲρ σαυτοῦ τελεῖν ἐκείνοις, εἴ τίς σε ἤρετο· "Τελεῖν τοῦτο τὸ ἀργύριον ὡς τίνι ὄντι ἐν νῷ ἔχεις Πολυκλείτῳ τε καὶ <u>Φειδίᾳ</u>;" τί ἂν ἀπεκρίνω; Εἶπον ἂν ὡς <u>ἀγαλματοποιοῖς</u>. "Ὡς τίς δὲ γενησόμενος αὐτός;" Δῆλον ὅτι <u>ἀγαλματοποιός</u>. Εἶεν, ἦν δ' ἐγώ· {d} παρὰ δὲ δὴ Πρωταγόραν νῦν ἀφικόμενοι ἐγώ τε καὶ σὺ ἀργύριον ἐκείνῳ μισθὸν ἕτοιμοι ἐσόμεθα τελεῖν ὑπὲρ σοῦ, ἂν μὲν ἐξικνῆται τὰ ἡμέτερα χρήματα καὶ τούτοις πείθωμεν αὐτόν, εἰ δὲ μή, καὶ τὰ τῶν φίλων προσαναλίσκοντες. εἰ οὖν τις ἡμᾶς περὶ ταῦτα οὕτω σφόδρα σπουδάζοντας ἔροιτο· "Εἰπέ μοι, ὦ Σώκρατές τε καὶ Ἱππόκρατες, ὡς τίνι ὄντι τῷ Πρωταγόρᾳ ἐν νῷ ἔχετε χρήματα τελεῖν;" τί ἂν αὐτῷ {e} ἀποκριναίμεθα; τί ὄνομα ἄλλο γε λεγόμενον περὶ Πρωταγόρου ἀκούομεν; ὥσπερ περὶ <u>Φειδίου</u> <u>ἀγαλματοποιὸν</u> καὶ περὶ <u>Ὁμήρου ποιητήν</u>, τί τοιοῦτον περὶ Πρωταγόρου ἀκούομεν;—<u>Σοφιστὴν</u> δή τοι ὀνομάζουσί γε, ὦ Σώκρατες, τὸν ἄνδρα εἶναι, ἔφη.—Ὡς <u>σοφιστῇ</u> ἄρα ἐρχόμεθα τελοῦντες τὰ χρήματα;—Μάλιστα.

Afterwards, we got up and walked around the open court. And I [= Socrates], testing the powers of Hippocrates, examined him by asking: Tell me, Hippocrates, I said. Here you are trying to go to Protagoras and give him money as a fee on your behalf. So define who exactly this person is that you are going to and who exactly you will become [as a result of going to him]? For example, suppose you were intending to go to your namesake Hippocrates of Cos, the one who belongs to the lineage of the Asklepiadai, and you paid him money as a fee on your behalf. And suppose someone asked you "Tell me, Hippocrates. You are about to pay a fee to Hippocrates because he is functioning as who exactly?" What would you give as a reply?—I would say: because he is a doctor.—"And you are doing this to become who exactly?"—To become likewise a doctor, he said.—Suppose you were intending to go to Polyclitus of Argos or to Pheidias of Athens and you paid them money as a fee on your behalf. And suppose someone asked you "You are intending to pay this money to Polyclitus and to Pheidias because they are functioning as who exactly?" What would you give as a reply?—I would say: because they are sculptors [*agalmatopoioi*].—"And you are doing this to become who exactly?" Clearly, to become a sculptor [*agalmatopoios*].—All right, then, I said, so here is where we are now: you and I have come to Protagoras and we are just about ready to pay money to him as a fee on your behalf—that is, if our resources are up to it, and, if they are not, we would spend in addition the resources of those who are near and dear to us. Now if someone asked us while we were making all this great effort "Tell me, Socrates and Hippocrates, you are intending to pay money to Protagoras because he is functioning as who exactly?" What answer would we give him? What other name do we hear applied to Protagoras? We hear of Pheidias that he is a sculptor [*agalmatopoios*][116] and of Homer that he is a poet [*poiētēs*]: what name of that kind do we hear of Protagoras?—Why, they call the man a sophist [*sophistēs*], Socrates, he said.—So we are going to pay him money because he functions as a sophist [*sophistēs*]?[117]—Yes.[118]

4§142 Here we see Pheidias and Homer being drawn into a single unified category: they are both professionals, like Protagoras. But the profession of Protagoras as *sophistēs* 'sophist' still needs further clarification. First, Socrates establishes that the profession of the *sophistēs* is a *tekhnē* 'craft'. Second, in pursuit of his philosophical agenda, Socrates appeals to the prejudices of his aristocratic listeners. Such aristocrats are repelled by the professionalism of artisans while at the same time feeling attracted to the "gentlemanly" amateurism of a "liberal" education derived from these same artisans:

---

[116] See also Plato *Protagoras* 311c on Pheidias as *agalmatopoios* 'sculptor'.
[117] In Plato *Protagoras* 317b-c, Protagoras makes a point of openly avowing that he is a *sophistēs* 'sophist'.
[118] My translation follows in some details the version of Allen 1996:171-172.

Chapter Four

4⓵30 Plato *Protagoras* 311e–312c (this passage immediately follows the passage previously quoted)

Εἰ οὖν καὶ τοῦτό τίς σε προσέροιτο· {312a} "Αὐτὸς δὲ δὴ ὡς τίς γενησόμενος ἔρχῃ παρὰ τὸν Πρωταγόραν;" Καὶ ὃς εἶπεν ἐρυθριάσας— ἤδη γὰρ ὑπέφαινέν τι ἡμέρας, ὥστε καταφανῆ αὐτὸν γενέσθαι—Εἰ μέν τι τοῖς ἔμπροσθεν ἔοικεν, δῆλον ὅτι <u>σοφιστὴς</u> γενησόμενος. Σὺ δέ, ἦν δ' ἐγώ, πρὸς θεῶν, οὐκ ἂν αἰσχύνοιο εἰς τοὺς Ἕλληνας σαυτὸν <u>σοφιστὴν</u> παρέχων; Νὴ τὸν Δία, ὦ Σώκρατες, εἴπερ γε ἃ διανοοῦμαι χρὴ λέγειν. Ἀλλ' ἄρα, ὦ Ἱππόκρατες, μὴ οὐ τοιαύτην ὑπολαμβάνεις σου τὴν παρὰ Πρωταγόρου {b} μάθησιν ἔσεσθαι, ἀλλ' οἵαπερ ἡ παρὰ τοῦ <u>γραμματιστοῦ</u> ἐγένετο καὶ <u>κιθαριστοῦ</u> καὶ παιδοτρίβου; τούτων γὰρ σὺ ἑκάστην οὐκ ἐπὶ <u>τέχνῃ</u> ἔμαθες, ὡς δημιουργὸς ἐσόμενος, <u>ἀλλ' ἐπὶ παιδείᾳ, ὡς τὸν ἰδιώτην καὶ τὸν ἐλεύθερον πρέπει</u>. Πάνυ μὲν οὖν μοι δοκεῖ, ἔφη, τοιαύτη μᾶλλον εἶναι ἡ παρὰ Πρωταγόρου μάθησις. Οἶσθα οὖν ὃ μέλλεις νῦν πράττειν, ἤ σε λανθάνει; ἦν δ' ἐγώ. Τοῦ πέρι; Ὅτι μέλλεις τὴν ψυχὴν τὴν σαυτοῦ {c} παρασχεῖν θεραπεῦσαι ἀνδρί, ὡς φῄς, <u>σοφιστῇ</u>· ὅτι δέ ποτε ὁ <u>σοφιστής</u> ἐστιν, θαυμάζοιμ' ἂν εἰ οἶσθα. καίτοι εἰ τοῦτ' ἀγνοεῖς, οὐδὲ ὅτῳ παραδίδως τὴν ψυχὴν οἶσθα, οὔτ' εἰ ἀγαθῷ οὔτ' εἰ κακῷ πράγματι. Οἶμαί γ', ἔφη, εἰδέναι.

So if someone asked you this further question "So you yourself are going to Protagoras to become who exactly?" He [= Hippocrates] blushed—there was already enough light of day to see it—and said: if it is anything like the previous examples, then clearly the answer is: to become a <u>sophist</u> [<u>sophistēs</u>].—But then wouldn't you, I said,—and I swear by the gods when I say this—wouldn't you be ashamed in front of all the Hellenes that you would be advertising yourself as a <u>sophist</u> [<u>sophistēs</u>]?—Yes, I swear by Zeus I would be, Socrates, if I may say what is really on my mind.—But then you are assuming, Hippocrates, that the course of study that you take from Protagoras will be this kind of course, and not the kinds of courses of study that you had been taught by, say, an <u>expert in letters</u> [<u>grammatistēs</u>][119] or by a <u>kithara-player</u> [<u>kitharistēs</u>] or by a trainer. But you see, you had taken each one of those courses of study not for the sake of the <u>craft</u> [<u>tekhnē</u>], in order to become an artisan [<u>dēmiourgos</u>], but <u>for the sake</u>

---

[119] This term *grammatistēs* 'expert in letters' is applied to Maiandrios as 'scribe' of the tyrant Polycrates of Samos (Herodotus 3.123.1). On Maiandrios of Samos: PH 11§20n53 (= p. 324), §21n58 (= pp. 324–325).

4§9. Protagoras as a point of comparison...

of your education [*paideia*], as is fitting for a private citizen and a free man.[120]—So then I think it is rather this kind of course, he said, I will be taking from Protagoras.—So do you know what you are about to end up doing, or is it unclear for you?—I said.—About what?—About the fact that you are about to hand over your own *psukhē* to be cared for by a man who is, as you say, a sophist [*sophistēs*]. As for what on earth a sophist [*sophistēs*] is, I would be surprised if you really knew. But if you are ignorant of this, then you don't really know to whom you are handing over your *psukhē*—whether it is to a noble or a base person, or whether it is for a noble or a base purpose.—Well, he said, I *think* I know.[121]

4§143 Why is Protagoras, as a *sophistēs* 'sophist', such a threat to the philosophical agenda of Socrates? It is at least partly because the things he professes rival the things Socrates professes. Protagoras as a professional *sophistēs* professes a *sophia* 'skill' that transcends the skills of all other professionals and can best be defined in transcendent terms. To translate the *sophia* of Protagoras as 'wisdom' rather than 'skill' is apt. But the problem is, this model of *sophia* 'wisdom' rivals the Socratic model of *sophia*, which we translate also as 'wisdom'. In terms of the Socratic model, *sophia* is the transcendent 'wisdom' of *philosophia* or philosophy as attained through the Socratic method. For Plato, the *sophia* professed by Socrates transcends all other crafts, and the philosopher rejects the professionalism of these crafts, including the craft of the *sophistēs*. As for the *sophia* professed by a *sophistēs* like Protagoras, it too transcends all other crafts, but Protagoras does not reject professionalism. The wealth, power, and prestige of a professional like Protagoras are all invested in the title of his profession, *sophistēs*, which for Protagoras designates an expert in the transcendent skill that he calls *sophia*. The objective of Plato's Socrates is to discredit this transcendent *sophia* of the *sophistēs*. By historical hindsight, we may say that the negative connotations of our modern translation, 'sophist', are living proof of Plato's success in achieving such an objective.

4§144 The discrediting of the *sophia* professed by Protagoras as *sophistēs* 'sophist' is pursued further by Socrates in the next passage I am about to quote. We are about to see Socrates undermine the usage of the word *sopha* (neuter plural) in the transcendent 'sophistic' sense of 'things having to do

---

[120] The *paideia* 'education' of the *eleutheros* 'free man' is the aristocratic concept of 'liberal education', as opposed to the 'servile' status of artisans who are educated to make a living as professionals. See also Nagy 1996d on relevant concepts of aristocracy.

[121] Translation after Allen 1996:172–173.

Chapter Four

with wisdom', showing that it really means 'things having to do with technical skill' when it is used by experts in a specific craft (*tekhnē*), that is, by craftsmen (*tekhnitai*) such as *zōgraphoi* 'painters', *tektones* 'builders', and *kitharistai* 'kithara-players':

4①31 Plato *Protagoras* 312c–e (this passage immediately follows the passage previously quoted)

> Λέγε δή, τί ἡγῇ εἶναι τὸν <u>σοφιστήν</u>; Ἐγὼ μέν, ἦ δ' ὅς, ὥσπερ τοὔνομα λέγει, τοῦτον εἶναι τὸν τῶν <u>σοφῶν</u> ἐπιστήμονα. Οὐκοῦν, ἦν δ' ἐγώ, τοῦτο μὲν ἔξεστι λέγειν καὶ περὶ <u>ζωγράφων</u> καὶ περὶ <u>τεκτόνων</u>, ὅτι οὗτοί εἰσιν οἱ τῶν <u>σοφῶν</u> ἐπιστήμονες· ἀλλ' {d} εἴ τις ἔροιτο ἡμᾶς, "Τῶν τί <u>σοφῶν</u> εἰσιν οἱ <u>ζωγράφοι</u> ἐπιστήμονες," εἴποιμεν ἄν που αὐτῷ ὅτι τῶν πρὸς τὴν <u>ἀπεργασίαν</u> τὴν τῶν <u>εἰκόνων</u>, καὶ τἆλλα οὕτως. εἰ δέ τις ἐκεῖνο ἔροιτο, "Ὁ δὲ <u>σοφιστὴς</u> τῶν τί <u>σοφῶν</u> ἐστιν;" τί ἂν ἀποκρινοίμεθα αὐτῷ; ποίας <u>ἐργασίας</u> ἐπιστάτης; Τί ἂν εἴποιμεν αὐτὸν εἶναι, ὦ Σώκρατες, ἢ ἐπιστάτην τοῦ ποιῆσαι δεινὸν λέγειν; Ἴσως ἄν, ἦν δ' ἐγώ, ἀληθῆ λέγοιμεν, οὐ μέντοι ἱκανῶς γε· ἐρωτήσεως γὰρ ἔτι ἡ ἀπόκρισις ἡμῖν δεῖται, περὶ ὅτου ὁ <u>σοφιστὴς</u> δεινὸν ποιεῖ λέγειν· ὥσπερ ὁ {e} <u>κιθαριστὴς</u> δεινὸν δήπου ποιεῖ λέγειν περὶ οὗπερ καὶ ἐπιστήμονα, περὶ <u>κιθαρίσεως</u>· ἦ γάρ; Ναί. Εἶεν· ὁ δὲ δὴ <u>σοφιστὴς</u> περὶ τίνος δεινὸν ποιεῖ λέγειν; Δῆλον ὅτι περὶ οὗπερ καὶ ἐπίστασθαι; Εἰκός γε. τί δή ἐστιν τοῦτο περὶ οὗ αὐτός τε ἐπιστήμων ἐστὶν ὁ <u>σοφιστὴς</u> καὶ τὸν μαθητὴν ποιεῖ; Μὰ Δί', ἔφη, οὐκέτι ἔχω σοι λέγειν.

> So, tell me, what do you think a <u>sophist</u> [<u>sophistēs</u>] is.—I think, he said, that he is someone who is an expert in things that have to do with—just as the word says—<u>sopha</u>.—In that case, I said, it is also possible to say this word in connection with painters [<u>zōgraphoi</u>] and <u>builders</u> [<u>tektones</u>], since these people too are experts in things that have to do with <u>sopha</u>. But if someone asked us "What does <u>sopha</u> mean when you say that <u>painters</u> [<u>zōgraphoi</u>] are experts in things that have to do with <u>sopha</u>?" we would I guess say to him that these people are experts in things that have to do with the <u>production</u> [<u>apergasia</u>] of <u>likenesses</u> [<u>eikones</u>], and the same goes for other cases [= other experts in other things]. But if someone asked us the big question "What about the <u>sophist</u> [<u>sophistēs</u>]? What does <u>sopha</u> mean in that case?" what answer would we give him? What kind of a <u>production</u> [<u>ergasia</u>] is he an expert in?—What other thing could

we say he is, Socrates, other than that he is an expert in making people speak cleverly?—Perhaps we would be saying the truth, but not entirely so, since our answer requires a further question: "About what does the sophist [*sophistēs*] make people speak cleverly?" Is it like the kithara-player [*kitharistēs*], who makes people speak cleverly about the thing that he is an expert in, namely, kithara-playing [*kitharisis*]? Is that it?—Yes.—All right, then, in that case what exactly is this thing about which the sophist [*sophistēs*] makes people speak cleverly?"—Clearly it must be the thing that he is an expert in.—Yes, most likely. But then what exactly is this thing in which the sophist [*sophistēs*] himself is an expert and in which he can make his student an expert?—I swear by Zeus, he said, I just don't have any answer left for me to give you.[122]

4§145 Plato's Socrates is here seeking to disallow the usage of *sopha* (neuter plural) in the transcendent sense of 'wisdom'—but only to the extent that the word is used by 'sophists' like Protagoras. For Socrates, the word *sopha* is allowed to be transcendent—but only when used in the discourse of true philosophy or *philosophia* as he understands it. Otherwise, the word is not allowed by Socrates to extend beyond the technical sense of 'skill'. Correspondingly, Socrates seeks to discredit the *sophistēs* as an expert in *sopha*—if the word *sopha* is allowed to be taken in a transcendent sense. For Socrates, the *sopha* of the sophist must be non-transcendent. In other words, the 'wisdom' of the sophist is not good enough for Socrates. For Socrates, the sophist is a professional who works for pay like other professionals, whether they be painters, builders, or kithara-players. Unlike these professionals, however, who are true craftsmen because they are at least acknowledged experts in their clearly defined crafts, the sophist is not even a true craftsman because his 'craft' eludes any clear definition.

4§146 But the word *sophistēs* 'sophist' as applied by a thinker like Protagoras must have been meant in a transcendent sense corresponding to what we mean by 'wisdom'. Even Plato's own wording in his dramatization of Protagoras bears out this point. I quote again here the passage in Plato's *Protagoras* where the *sophistēs* himself is describing his *sophistikē tekhnē*, the craft of the *sophistēs*:

---

[122] Translation after Allen 1996:173.

Chapter Four

4⓽32 Plato *Protagoras* 316d

ἐγὼ δὲ τὴν <u>σοφιστικὴν τέχνην</u> φημὶ μὲν εἶναι παλαιάν, τοὺς δὲ μεταχειριζομένους αὐτὴν τῶν παλαιῶν ἀνδρῶν, φοβουμένους τὸ ἐπαχθὲς αὐτῆς, πρόσχημα ποιεῖσθαι καὶ προκαλύπτεσθαι, τοὺς μὲν <u>ποίησιν</u>, οἷον <u>Ὅμηρόν</u> τε καὶ <u>Ἡσίοδον</u> καὶ <u>Σιμωνίδην</u>, τοὺς δὲ αὖ <u>τελετάς</u> τε καὶ <u>χρησμῳδίας</u>, τοὺς ἀμφί τε <u>Ὀρφέα</u> καὶ <u>Μουσαῖον</u>·

I [= Protagoras] declare that the <u>sophistic</u> <u>craft</u> [*tekhnē*] is ancient, but those who had applied it among ancient men were afraid of the opprobrium attaching to it, and disguised and concealed themselves—some in the realm of <u>poetry</u> [*poiēsis*], like <u>Homer</u> and <u>Hesiod</u> and <u>Simonides</u>, but others in the realm of <u>mysteries</u> [*teletai*] and <u>oracular songs</u> [*khrēsmōidiai*], like <u>Orpheus</u> and <u>Musaeus</u> and their followers.[123]

4§147 In the Hellenic world of the fifth century, the prestige of Protagoras as a *sophistēs* 'sophist' was still so dominant that he could freely describe his craft as the prototype of Homer and other classics as he knew them. According to the world view of Protagoras as recreated here by Plato, the *sophistēs* in the age of poets like Homer had to conceal his true profession in life, but the value of his skill was already in place, just waiting to be confirmed by the later age of Protagoras in the fifth century BCE. In the old days, a poet like Homer would have been a prototypical *sophistēs* in disguise. In the days of Protagoras, by contrast, the *sophistēs* could finally reveal himself and claim his full value as the highest-paid professional in the world.

4§148 The prestige of Protagoras as a professional is comparable to the prestige of that prototype of all professionals, Homer himself. So says Plato's Socrates in a statement I am about to quote. What I find remarkable about this statement is the mention of Pheidias the sculptor as a second point of comparison to Homer—second only to Protagoras:

4⓽33 Plato *Meno* 91b-92b

ἢ δῆλον δὴ κατὰ τὸν ἄρτι λόγον ὅτι παρὰ τούτους τοὺς ὑπισχνουμένους ἀρετῆς διδασκάλους εἶναι καὶ ἀποφήναντας αὐτοὺς <u>κοινοὺς</u> τῶν Ἑλλήνων τῷ βουλομένῳ μανθάνειν, μισθὸν τούτου ταξαμένους τε καὶ πραττομένους;

ΑΝ. Καὶ τίνας λέγεις τούτους, ὦ Σώκρατες;

---

[123] Translation after Allen 1996:177.

4⑨9. Protagoras as a point of comparison...

ΣΩ. Οἶσθα δήπου καὶ σὺ ὅτι οὗτοί εἰσιν οὓς οἱ ἄνθρωποι καλοῦσι <u>σοφιστάς</u>. {c}

ΑΝ. Ἡράκλεις, εὐφήμει, ὦ Σώκρατες. μηδένα τῶν γ' ἐμῶν μήτε οἰκείων μήτε φίλων, μήτε ἀστὸν μήτε ξένον, τοιαύτη μανία λάβοι, ὥστε παρὰ τούτους ἐλθόντα <u>λωβηθῆναι</u>, ἐπεὶ οὗτοί γε φανερά ἐστι <u>λώβη</u> τε καὶ <u>διαφθορὰ</u> τῶν συγγιγνομένων.

ΣΩ. Πῶς λέγεις, ὦ Ἄνυτε; οὗτοι ἄρα μόνοι τῶν ἀντιποιουμένων τι ἐπίστασθαι εὐεργετεῖν τοσοῦτον τῶν ἄλλων διαφέρουσιν, ὅσον οὐ μόνον οὐκ ὠφελοῦσιν, ὥσπερ οἱ ἄλλοι, ὅτι ἄν τις αὐτοῖς παραδῷ, ἀλλὰ καὶ τὸ ἐναντίον {d} <u>διαφθείρουσιν</u>; καὶ τούτων φανερῶς χρήματα ἀξιοῦσι πράττεσθαι; ἐγὼ μὲν οὖν οὐκ ἔχω ὅπως σοι πιστεύσω· οἶδα γὰρ ἄνδρα ἕνα <u>Πρωταγόραν</u> πλείω χρήματα κτησάμενον ἀπὸ ταύτης τῆς <u>σοφίας</u> ἢ <u>Φειδίαν</u> τε, <u>ὃς οὕτω περιφανῶς καλὰ ἔργα ἠργάζετο</u>, καὶ ἄλλους δέκα τῶν <u>ἀνδριαντοποιῶν</u>. καίτοι τέρας λέγεις εἰ οἱ μὲν τὰ ὑποδήματα ἐργαζόμενοι τὰ παλαιὰ καὶ τὰ ἱμάτια ἐξακούμενοι οὐκ ἂν δύναιντο λαθεῖν τριάκονθ' {e} ἡμέρας μοχθηρότερα ἀποδιδόντες ἢ παρέλαβον τὰ ἱμάτιά τε καὶ ὑποδήματα, ἀλλ' εἰ τοιαῦτα ποιοῖεν, ταχὺ ἂν τῷ λιμῷ ἀποθάνοιεν, <u>Πρωταγόρας</u> δὲ ἄρα ὅλην τὴν Ἑλλάδα ἐλάνθανεν <u>διαφθείρων</u> τοὺς συγγιγνομένους καὶ μοχθηροτέρους ἀποπέμπων ἢ παρελάμβανεν πλέον ἢ τετταράκοντα ἔτη—οἶμαι γὰρ αὐτὸν ἀποθανεῖν ἐγγὺς καὶ ἑβδομήκοντα ἔτη γεγονότα, τετταράκοντα δὲ ἐν τῇ <u>τέχνῃ</u> ὄντα—καὶ ἐν ἅπαντι τῷ χρόνῳ τούτῳ <u>ἔτι εἰς τὴν ἡμέραν ταυτηνὶ εὐδοκιμῶν οὐδὲν πέπαυται</u>, καὶ οὐ μόνον Πρωταγόρας, ἀλλὰ καὶ {92 a} ἄλλοι πάμπολλοι, οἱ μὲν πρότερον γεγονότες ἐκείνου, οἱ δὲ καὶ νῦν ἔτι ὄντες. πότερον δὴ οὖν φῶμεν κατὰ τὸν σὸν λόγον εἰδότας αὐτοὺς ἐξαπατᾶν καὶ <u>λωβᾶσθαι</u> τοὺς νέους, ἢ λεληθέναι καὶ ἑαυτούς; καὶ οὕτω μαίνεσθαι ἀξιώσομεν τούτους, οὓς ἔνιοί φασι σοφωτάτους ἀνθρώπων εἶναι;

ΑΝ. Πολλοῦ γε δέουσι μαίνεσθαι, ὦ Σώκρατες, ἀλλὰ πολὺ μᾶλλον οἱ τούτοις διδόντες ἀργύριον τῶν νέων, τούτων {b} δ' ἔτι μᾶλλον οἱ τούτοις ἐπιτρέποντες, οἱ προσήκοντες, πολὺ δὲ μάλιστα πάντων αἱ <u>πόλεις</u>, ἐῶσαι αὐτοὺς εἰσαφικνεῖσθαι καὶ οὐκ ἐξελαύνουσαι, εἴτε τις ξένος ἐπιχειρεῖ τοιοῦτόν τι ποιεῖν εἴτε ἀστός.

SOCRATES: Or is it clear, then, on the basis of what has just been said: [that we should send Meno] to these men who profess to be teachers of virtue [*aretē*] and who proclaim themselves to be [teachers] common [*koinoi*] to all Hellenes, available to any [Hellene] who wishes to learn from them—that is, available after they set a fee for this and collect the fee?

ANYTUS: And who are these people you are talking about, Socrates?

SOCRATES: Surely you too, like others, are aware that these are the men whom people call sophists [*sophistai*].

ANYTUS: I swear by Herakles! Watch your language, Socrates. I hereby make a solemn wish that none of my relatives or friends, nor any citizen nor even any non-citizen, should experience being seized by such dementia that they should go off to these people and get utterly ruined [*lōbân*], since these people are the utter ruin [*lōbē*] and corruption [*diaphthora*] of those who make contact with them.

SOCRATES: What are you saying, Anytus? Are you really saying that, if you consider all those who strive to understand how to do something good, these are the only ones who are so different from all the rest that they, unlike the rest of them, will not only fail to do any good for anything [= anyone] you hand over to them but will do actually the opposite for it [= whatever you hand over], utterly ruining [*diaphtheirein*] it? And that, in return for these things, they openly charge payment of fees? Well, all I can say is, I don't know how I can believe you. For I know that there was one man, Protagoras, who was making even more money from this skill [*sophia* = being a sophist] than Pheidias [was making from his own *sophia* 'skill'],[124] and he [Pheidias] was creating works of art that were so supremely distinguished—and, in addition to him [Pheidias], you could name ten others of the sculptors [*andriantopoioi*]. And yet, you would be telling me something truly amazing if those who work on old shoes and mend old clothes cannot fool [their customers] and cannot get away with giving back these clothes and shoes to their customers in worse shape than when they got them during the thirty days [of liability for refunding]—since they would soon die of hunger [if they tried to fool their customers]—while, in the meantime, Protagoras

---

[124] Here the *sophia* 'skill' of Pheidias is made parallel to the *sophia* of Protagoras, so that the 'wisdom' of the sophist is reinterpreted in the archaic sense of the 'skill' or 'craft' of a craftsman.

was fooling all of Hellas by getting away with corrupting [*diaphtheirein*] those who made contact with him and sending them back in worse shape than when he got them—during his forty years [of "liability" for refunding the payments of his students]. I say forty years because I think he died when he was close to seventy years old. He was practicing his craft [*tekhnē*] for forty years, and during all that time and even up to this present time he has never in any way stopped having a good reputation.[125] And that goes not only for Protagoras but also for many others, some of whom were born before him while others are still alive today. So what do you say? According to your reasoning, do these people knowingly deceive and ruin [*lōbân*] the young, or are they fooling even themselves? So, shall we posit that these men are demented—the ones that some say are the most *sophoi* of people?

ANYTUS: Far from it. They are not the ones who are demented. It is much more the case that those of the young who give money are demented and, even more so, those who are responsible for instructing these young people, that is, their families, and, most of all, the cities [*poleis*] that allow them [= people like Protagoras] to come in and don't drive them out, whether it is a non-citizen who tries to do such a thing or a citizen.

4§149 The prominent mention of Pheidias here is most telling. Practicing his craft, he makes more money than any other professional—except for the professional *sophistēs* 'sophist' *par excellence*, Protagoras. Not only is the wealth of Pheidias comparable to the wealth of Protagoras. The sculptor's *sophia* is also comparable. Plato's contextualization here forces us to understand *sophia* here as a 'skill' in a given craft. We can see that Plato's Socrates seeks to discredit Protagoras and his *sophia* 'wisdom' by attacking him for being a professional.

4§150 The idea is that professionals like Protagoras are both corrupt and corrupting precisely because they are professionals. Although Protagoras as a *sophistēs* 'sophist' is in theory a man of *sophia* or 'wisdom' *par excellence*, he is in real life a man of *sophia* 'craft', just like the sculptor Pheidias. From a historical point of view, it is not a question of whether these professionals

---

[125] The joke is that, if Anytus is right, then Protagoras as a craftsman is immeasurably worse than a bad shoemaker. As we have noted ever since ch. 3, Plato has a running joke of comparing the craft of a shoemaker with the craft of the sophist.

Chapter Four

were or were not corrupt. It is enough to say that their status as professionals led to suspicions and accusations of corruption. We have already noted the anecdotes about the corruption of Pheidias as the master sculptor (Plutarch *Pericles* 31.2-3, Philochorus *FGH* 328 F 121), and there are comparable anecdotes about other prominent professionals like Simonides in his role as master poet (Aristophanes *Peace* 698, Callimachus F 222). Despite all the potential for suspicions and accusations, however, even Socrates is forced to acknowledge the outstanding reputation of a professionals like Protagoras and Pheidias in their own time. So the fact remains that a celebrity like Protagoras, or like Pheidias, had an overwhelmingly good reputation as a professional, and everybody knew it.

4§151 Plato's Socrates makes the *sophia* 'wisdom' of the *sophistēs* equivalent to the kind of *sophia* 'skill' that comes with the mastery of any and all of the *tekhnai* 'crafts' practiced by professional artisans. The *sophia* 'skill' of these artisans ranges from the most exalted, like the skill of Pheidias the master sculptor, which is rated at the highest level of compensation, to the most humble, like the skill of a leatherworker or shoemaker, which is rated at the correspondingly lowest level of compensation. As we have just seen, Plato's points of comparison for the professional *sophistēs* range all the way from sculptor to shoemaker.

4§152 The prestige of a sculptor like Pheidias, as measured by his wealth, is near-supreme. In other contexts, in fact, we have already seen that his prestige is imperial in its dimensions. It follows, then, that the even greater wealth of a sophist like Protagoras makes his prestige seem even more imperial. Here it is relevant to recall the wording of the claim about Protagoras that I have just quoted from Plato's *Meno* (91b): it is said that sophists of exalted status like Protagoras are teachers who are *koinoi* 'common' to all Hellenes. Such wording evokes a direct comparison between the craft of Protagoras and the craft of a figure acknowledged as the ultimate teacher of all Hellenes. That teacher is Homer himself, in his evolving role as spokesman of the Athenian empire. As we saw earlier, this idea of an imperial Homer who is *koinos* 'common' to all Hellenes—at least, to all Hellenes in the Athenian empire and beyond—is attested in an amalgamated *Life of Homer* story, mediated in part through an Athenian phase of transmission, known as the *Contest of Homer and Hesiod*. Here I highlight again the wording used in the story to describe the reception of Homer: when Homer goes to the island of Delos to participate in a festival celebrated by all Ionians, he is acclaimed by them as the *koinos politēs* 'common citizen' of all their cities (*Contest of Homer and Hesiod* [*Vita* 2] 319-320 οἱ μὲν Ἴωνες πολίτην αὐτὸν κοινὸν ἐποιήσαντο). As we noted earlier, this designation ideologizes Homer as the spokesman of the Delian League and, by extension, of the Athenian empire.

4§153 Returning to the argument at hand, I focus on the wording of the passage I quoted from Plato's *Meno*, where Protagoras and other master sophists are acclaimed as teachers of all Hellenes (91b) by virtue of their *tekhnē* 'craft' as sophists (91d). This idea, I submit, mirrors a more basic idea: Homer himself is such a teacher—because of his own *tekhnē*. In the passage that I quoted earlier from Plato's *Protagoras* (311e), Homer is described as a *poiētēs* 'poet': as such, he is a professional, since he is compared in his professionalism to Pheidias as an *agalmatopoios* 'sculptor' and to Protagoras as a *sophistēs* 'sophist'. The professionalism of all three, as we saw in the same context, is a matter of *tekhnē* (312b).

4ⓢ10. The imperial craft of Homer

4§154 The *tekhnē* of Homer is highlighted in a most revealing passage I quoted earlier from the *Panegyricus* of Isocrates (159). Here the speaker is referring to the *tekhnē* 'craft' of Homeric poetry as a tradition designed for two primary applications: (1) Homeric performances by rhapsodes in *athloi* 'contests', implicitly at the Panathenaia, and (2) Homeric *paideusis* 'education' of the young. The second of these two applications of the *tekhnē* of Homeric poetry concerns the private education provided by the elites for their young while the first application concerns the public education provided by the Athenian state for its citizens—in the form of rhapsodic performances at the Panathenaia. The speaker adds that the art of war is the most important lesson to be learned from Homer. The public and the private functions of Homer as universal educator are indicated in other passages as well (Aristophanes *Frogs* 1034–1036; Plato *Republic* 2.376e–398b; 10.599c-d, 606e).

4§155 As we see from this passage in the *Panegyricus* of Isocrates (159), the *tekhnē* of Homer is the *tekhnē* of rhapsodes who perform in competition at the Panathenaia. Thus the *tekhnē* of Homer is continued metonymically by the *rhapsōidikē tekhnē* of Panathenaic performers. A case in point is Ion of Ephesus. By virtue of his skill as a specialist in Homer, he is a metonymic continuator of Homer, a teacher shared by all Hellenes. Continuing the role of Homer as universal educator, Ion the rhapsode is parallel to Protagoras the sophist, practitioner of the *sophistikē tekhnē*. As such a practitioner, Protagoras is a teacher who is *koinos* 'common' to all Hellenes (Plato *Meno* 91b).

4§156 What I just said about the *rhapsōidikē tekhnē* of Ion the rhapsode is not obvious from Plato's *Ion*. In that dialogue, as I argued in Chapter 3, Plato's

Chapter Four

Socrates seeks to disconnect the *tekhnē* of Homer from the *tekhnē* of Ion. At the earliest stages of his argumentation, Socrates avoids referring to the expertise of the rhapsode in terms of a *tekhnē* 'craft'. Instead, he speaks only about the overall craft of the poet, designated as *poiētikē tekhnē* 'poetic craft', and he induces Ion to admit that this poetic craft is a *holon*, an integral whole, just like other *tekhnai* (*Ion* 532c).[126] Among those other *tekhnai*, he mentions sculpture as a notable example (532e–533b). Plato's Socrates contrasts the expertise of the *poiētēs* 'poet' with the expertise of (1) the *aulos*-player, (2) the *kithara*-player, (3) the *kithara*-singer, and (4) the rhapsode: each of these four different kinds of performer, representing four different forms of performance at the Panathenaia, can claim expertise in only one part of that integral whole, that *poiētikē tekhnē* 'poetic craft' (*Ion* 533b–c). Thus Ion the rhapsode is forced to admit that he has expertise only in Homeric poetry (533c). Next, he is forced to accept the idea that the rhapsode's profession is not even a matter of *tekhnē* 'craft' but rather, a matter of inspiration (*Ion* 533e). As I also argued in Chapter 3, only after the rhapsode has accepted the idea that he is an inspired performer does Socrates start speaking openly about the 'rhapsodic craft', *rhapsōidikē tekhnē* (538b, 538c, 538d, 539e, 540a, 540d, 541a). Plato has thus undermined the dominant status of the actual craft of rhapsodically performing—and interpreting—Homeric poetry at the Panathenaia. Since Ion has already been discredited as a thinker, he cannot invoke his prestigious rhapsodic craft as a source for independent thinking.

4§157 In his effort to discredit Ion, Plato's Socrates has in effect disconnected the prestige of Ion as the performer of Homeric poetry from the prestige of Homer as the notional composer of Homeric poetry. Thus the prestige of Homer himself is not directly challenged, just as the prestige of Homeric poetry as the premier poetic event of the Panathenaia cannot be challenged. The idea of Homer as the all-sufficient and all-encompassing poet is a given. It is already a historical reality. Even in the works of Plato, as we saw, Homer is recognized as the master teacher of all Hellenes (Plato *Republic* 2.376e–398b; 10.599c–d, 606e).

4§158 As I also argued in Chapter 3, the dominant status of Homeric poetry is not the only historical reality relevant to the argument in Plato's *Ion*. Another reality is the dominant status of the *rhapsōidikē tekhnē* 'rhapsodic craft' of performing—and interpreting—Homeric poetry at the Panathenaia. Plato's Socrates makes it look like a deficiency that Ion the rhapsode performs—

---

[126] Up to now, I have been translating *poiētēs* as 'poet' and *poiētikē* as 'poetic craft', but it is more accurate to render these words in terms of 'composition' (in the verbal arts), as we will see.

and interprets—only Homer. Historically, however, the Homeric specialization of Ion is a clear indication of the dominant prestige of performing and interpreting Homer.

4⑤11. Dangerous thoughts about the craft of Homer

4§159 So the prestige of the craft represented by Ion the rhapsode is imperial in scope, as is the prestige of the crafts represented by Pheidias the sculptor and Protagoras the sophist. Such prestige can be undermined, however, by juxtaposing the crafts of rhapsodes, sculptors, and sophists with the craft of, say, a shoemaker. Whereas a *sophistēs* 'sophist' like Protagoras is an artisan of the highest imaginable status, the low social status of professional artisans like shoemakers is enough to make an aristocrat like Hippocrates blush at the very idea of becoming a professional *sophistēs*, as we saw in the passage I quoted earlier from Plato's *Protagoras* (312a). Here is where the difference between a *sophistēs* like Protagoras and a *sophistēs* like Hippias is most telling. Whereas Protagoras considers his craft of *sophistēs* transcendent and even mystical by comparison with the practical crafts of artisans, Hippias demystifies his craft of *sophistēs* by engaging directly in all other crafts. In Plato's catalogue of skills mastered by Hippias, as I quoted it in Chapter 3, Hippias is an expert not only in the sublime crafts, such as poetry (*Hippias Minor* 368c–d). He is also an expert in the everyday crafts: pointedly, Hippias says he is is a master of leatherwork—*skutotomeîn*—in his own right, having hand-made his own shoes (368c). For Plato's Socrates, either way of thinking about the craft of the *sophistēs*—the way of Protagoras or the way of Hippias—is dangerous. And, as we are about to see, both ways of thinking can be applied to the craft of Homer as well.

4§160 We already saw in another Platonic passage that the *husteroi* or 'later' thinkers who are experts in supposedly later poets like Homer—rather than earlier poets like Orpheus—tended to demystify the secrets of mysteries, so that even leatherworkers—*skutotomoi*—may understand these secrets (Plato *Theaetetus* 180d), to be contrasted with *palaioteroi* or 'earlier' thinkers specializing in supposedly earlier poets like Orpheus, whose mysteries continued to mystify the outsiders (Plato *Theaetetus* 179e–180d). A most valuable independent confirmation comes from Xenophon's *Memorabilia* (4.4.5), where Hippias of Elis is represented as debating with Socrates about the possibilities of teaching even the *skuteus* 'leatherworker' and other specialists (εἰ μέν τις βούλοιτο σκυτέα διδάξασθαί τινα ἢ τέκτονα ἢ χαλκέα ἢ ἱππέα . . .).

4§161 Here I focus again on Hippias of Elis. In particular, I focus on his role as a practical *sophistēs* 'sophist'. Hippias makes a point of mastering each *tekhnē*

533

Chapter Four

'craft'—not just transcending them all like Protagoras. With this focal point in mind, I quote again the relevant passage that I quoted already in Chapter 3. There I described this passage, taken from the *Hippias Minor* (368a–e), as Plato's catalogue of *tekhnai* 'crafts' mastered by Hippias. Here I draw special attention to Plato's usage of the words *sophos* and *sophia*. We have just seen Plato use these words in the transcendent sense of 'wise' and 'wisdom', which he associates with Protagoras as a mystical *sophistēs* 'sophist'. This time, I note Plato's usage of these same words *sophos* and *sophia* in the practical sense of 'skilled' and 'skill', which he associates with Hippias as a practical *sophistēs* 'sophist':

4①34 Plato *Hippias Minor* 368a–e

ΣΩ. Ἴθι δή, ὦ Ἱππία, ἀνέδην οὑτωσὶ ἐπίσκεψαι κατὰ {b} πασῶν τῶν ἐπιστημῶν, εἴ που ἔστιν ἄλλως ἔχον ἢ οὕτως. πάντως δὲ πλείστας <u>τέχνας</u> πάντων <u>σοφώτατος</u> εἶ ἀνθρώπων, ὡς ἐγώ ποτέ σου ἤκουον μεγαλαυχουμένου, πολλὴν <u>σοφίαν</u> καὶ ζηλωτὴν σαυτοῦ διεξιόντος ἐν ἀγορᾷ ἐπὶ ταῖς τραπέζαις. ἔφησθα δὲ ἀφικέσθαι ποτὲ εἰς Ὀλυμπίαν ἃ εἶχες περὶ τὸ σῶμα ἅπαντα σαυτοῦ ἔργα ἔχων· πρῶτον μὲν <u>δακτύλιον</u>—ἐντεῦθεν γὰρ ἤρχου—ὃν εἶχες σαυτοῦ ἔχειν {c} ἔργον, ὡς ἐπιστάμενος <u>δακτυλίους γλύφειν</u>, καὶ ἄλλην <u>σφραγῖδα</u> σὸν ἔργον, καὶ στλεγγίδα καὶ λήκυθον ἃ αὐτὸς ἠργάσω· ἔπειτα <u>ὑποδήματα</u> ἃ εἶχες ἔφησθα αὐτὸς <u>σκυτοτομῆσαι</u>, καὶ τὸ ἱμάτιον <u>ὑφῆναι</u> καὶ τὸν χιτωνίσκον· καὶ ὅ γε πᾶσιν ἔδοξεν ἀτοπώτατον καὶ <u>σοφίας</u> πλείστης <u>ἐπίδειγμα</u>, ἐπειδὴ τὴν ζώνην ἔφησθα τοῦ χιτωνίσκου, ἣν εἶχες, εἶναι μὲν οἷαι αἱ Περσικαὶ τῶν πολυτελῶν, ταύτην δὲ αὐτὸς <u>πλέξαι</u>· πρὸς δὲ τούτοις <u>ποιήματα</u> ἔχων ἐλθεῖν, καὶ <u>ἔπη</u> καὶ <u>τραγῳδίας</u> {d} καὶ <u>διθυράμβους</u>, καὶ <u>καταλογάδην</u> πολλοὺς <u>λόγους</u> καὶ παντοδαποὺς συγκειμένους· καὶ περὶ τῶν <u>τεχνῶν</u> δὴ ὧν ἄρτι ἐγὼ ἔλεγον ἐπιστήμων ἀφικέσθαι διαφερόντως τῶν ἄλλων, καὶ περὶ <u>ῥυθμῶν</u> καὶ <u>ἁρμονιῶν</u> καὶ <u>γραμμάτων</u> <u>ὀρθότητος</u>, καὶ ἄλλα ἔτι πρὸς τούτοις πάνυ πολλά, ὡς ἐγὼ δοκῶ <u>μνημονεύειν</u>· καίτοι τό γε <u>μνημονικὸν ἐπελαθόμην</u> σου, ὡς ἔοικε, <u>τέχνημα</u>, ἐν ᾧ σὺ οἴει λαμπρότατος εἶναι· οἶμαι δὲ καὶ {e} ἄλλα πάμπολλα <u>ἐπιλελῆσθαι</u>. ἀλλ' ὅπερ ἐγὼ λέγω, καὶ εἰς τὰς σαυτοῦ <u>τέχνας</u> βλέψας—<u>ἱκαναὶ</u> δέ—καὶ εἰς τὰς τῶν ἄλλων εἰπέ μοι, ἐάν που εὕρῃς ἐκ τῶν ὡμολογημένων ἐμοί τε καὶ σοί, ὅπου ἐστὶν ὁ μὲν ἀληθής, ὁ δὲ ψευδής, χωρὶς καὶ οὐχ ὁ αὐτός; ἐν ᾗτινι βούλει <u>σοφίᾳ</u> τοῦτο σκέψαι ἢ πανουργίᾳ {369a} ἢ ὁτιοῦν χαίρεις ὀνομάζων· ἀλλ' οὐχ εὑρήσεις, ὦ ἑταῖρε—οὐ γὰρ ἔστιν—ἐπεὶ σὺ εἰπέ.

4§11. Dangerous thoughts about the craft of Homer

SOCRATES: Come, then, Hippias. Consider without any further ado whether or not this point [about the false and the true] holds for all kinds of knowledge. You are absolutely the most skilled [*sophos*] of men in the greatest number of crafts [*tekhnai*] by far, as I once heard you boast when you were describing your great and enviable skill [*sophia*]. It was in the agora [= the agora of Athens], near the money-changers' tables [*trapezai*]. You were telling how you once upon a time went to Olympia, and everything you wore was your own work: first, your ring [*daktulios*]—you started with that—was your own work because you knew how to engrave rings [*daktulioi*]—and the rest of it [= your ring], that is, its seal [*sphragis*], was your own work, and an athletic scraper, and a *lēkuthion* you had made yourself. Next, the footwear you had on you—you said you had done the leatherwork [*skutotomeîn*] yourself, and you had woven [*huphainein*] your own *himation* and your own khiton [*khitōn*]. And it seemed dazzling to everyone—a display [*epideigma*] of the greatest skill [*sophia*][127] when you said that the cincture of the khiton [*khitōn*] you had on you was made of the costliest Persian kind, and that you had plaited [*plekein*] it yourself. And on top of all these things, you had come bringing with you compositions [*poiēmata*][128]—that is, epic [*epos* plural] and tragedies and dithyrambs, and a multitude of discourses [*logoi*] to be performed in the right sequence [*katalogadēn*][129] and all kinds of set pieces. And you arrived there as an expert surpassing all others in the knowledge of not only the crafts [*tekhnai*] I just mentioned, but also of the correctness [*orthotēs*] of rhythms [*rhuthmoi*], tunings [*harmoniai*], and letters [*grammata*].[130] And there were many more things in addition, as I seem to remember [*mnēmoneuein*]. And yet it seems I had almost forgotten [*epilanthanesthai*] about your mnemonic technique [*mnēmonikon tekhnēma*], in which you think you are at your most brilliant. And I suppose I have forgotten

---

[127] I note again that *sophia* here conveys a non-transcendent concept, 'skill', instead of the transcendent concept of 'wisdom'.

[128] I must stress once again what I stressed when I first quoted this wording: as we see from the context here, these 'compositions' are the poetic creations not only of Hippias but also of master 'composers' or *poiētai*, including Homer himself as the 'composer' or *poiētēs* par excellence.

[129] The conventions of performing *katalogadēn* 'in the right sequence, catalogue-style', as I noted earlier, are relevant to the *mnēmonikon tekhnēma* 'mnemonic technique' of Hippias).

[130] For another passage that emphasizes these specialties of Hippias, I cite once again Plato *Hippias Maior* 285d. A relevant term is *grammatistēs*.

Chapter Four

[*epilanthanesthai*] a great many other things too. But as I say, look [*blepein*]¹³¹ to your own crafts [*tekhnai*]—they are certainly sufficient— and those of others, and tell me if you anywhere find the true man and the false separate and not the same, given what we have agreed. Examine this in terms of any kind of skill [*sophia*] you may want to choose—or in terms of any kind of *panourgia* whatsoever— or however you would like to call it. You will not find it, my friend, for it does not exist—but you tell me.¹³²

4§162 Not only does Hippias master each *tekhnē* 'craft' that is being catalogued here. For him such mastery is a matter of being *sophos* in the sense of 'skilled' and having *sophia* in the sense of 'skill'. Plato's Socrates ridicules this connectedness with the practical aspect of arts as crafts when he playfully uses the word *panourgia* with reference to the *sophia* of Hippias. This word *panourgia* is derived from the concept of 'the capacity to do any kind of work [*ergon*]'. In terms of this derivation, the word would be appropriate to Hippias. But in actual usage, *panourgia* had developed the morally negative sense of 'the capacity to commit any kind of deed'. Thus Hippias is being implicitly ridiculed as a jack of all trades who supposedly compromises his morals because of his willingness to do just about anything for money. It is the professionalism of Hippias that renders him morally suspect for Plato's Socrates.

4§163 Even the setting that Plato chooses for the use of this word *panourgia* is suggestive. Plato's catalogue of the skills claimed by Hippias is nested in the context of Socratic memories of a most memorable visit by Hippias to Athens. Hippias was speaking in a public space, in the agora of Athens (368b); Socrates was there and heard him speak, and he says that Hippias was telling about an earlier time when he was speaking in a sacred space, in the *hieron* 'sacred precinct' of Zeus in Olympia (363c-d, 364a). As I noted earlier, the impression given by Plato is that the performance of Hippias in the agora of Athens was a "replay" of the performance of Hippias in the sacred precinct of Zeus in Olympia. In Athens, as the phrasing of Socrates pointedly makes clear, Hippias is performing in a public space where the *trapezai* are located, that is, the tables of the money-changers. The venue of Hippias oscillates between the most sacral and the most blatantly commercial

---

¹³¹ This word *blepein* 'look' highlights the visual aspect of indexing the details associated with the *tekhnai* 'crafts' of Hippias. I find it significant that the first detail that catches the eye of Socrates is the *daktulios* 'ring' of Hippias. More on this ring later, as the discussion proceeds. The verb *blepein* 'look', as I noted earlier, is used as an index for the perception of Plato's Forms.
¹³² Translation after Allen 1996:36-37.

4⑤11. Dangerous thoughts about the craft of Homer

settings. In both settings, the primary visual attraction is the ring that Hippias wears on his finger: 'you started with that', says Socrates (368b). That ring is the first thing Hippias says he talked about in the sacred precinct of Zeus in Olympia and again in the "replay," in the agora of Athens, near the tables of the money-changers. That ring is the first thing that catches the Socratic eye, sparking dangerous thoughts of those all-attractive First Rings magnetically drawing performers and audiences closer and closer to the ultimate beauty of Homeric poetry in Plato's *Ion* (536b).

4§164 Beyond the cultural context of Plato's own world, such dangerous thoughts of magnetic beauty evoke for me personally the image of the enchanted diamond ring of Dapertutto in Offenbach's *Tales of Hoffmann*:

4①35 From Act 4, *Les Contes d'Hoffmann*, by Jacques Offenbach, with libretto by Jules Barbier and Michel Carré (Dapertutto sings to the diamond, telling it to gleam or 'sparkle')[133]

> (Tirant de son doigt une bague où brille un gros diamant et le faisant scintiller)
> Tourne, tourne, miroir où se prend l'alouette,
> <u>Scintille</u>, diamant! Fascine, attire-la!
> Femme, oiseau, le chasseur est là!
> Qui vous voit, qui vous guette!
> Le chasseur noir!
> L'alouette ou la femme
> A cet appât vainqueur
> Vont de l'aîle ou du cœur,
> L'une y laisse la vie | et l'autre y perd son âme.

> [He [= Dapertutto] pulls from his finger a ring that has on it a huge shining diamond, and he makes it gleam]
> Turn, turn, mirror in which the skylark is captured.
> <u>Gleam</u>, diamond, fascinate her, draw her near.

---

[133] I quote here the wording of the version known as the "Censor's Libretto" (1881); a facsimile of Acts 4 and 5 has been published by Heinzelmann 1988. The wording in this part of the libretto matches closely the relevant wording in Act 4 Scene 5 of the play by Barbier and Carré, *Les Contes fantastiques d'Hoffmann*, staged in 1851.

Chapter Four

> Woman or bird! The hunter is there.
> The one who sees you, who stalks you.
> The black hunter.
> Skylark or woman
> Toward this irresistible trap
> go by wing or by way of the heart.
> One loses her life there, and the other loses her soul.

4§165 In the course of rereading Plato's catalogue of crafts mastered by Hippias, I have argued that the detail about the ring worn by the sophist is relevant to the artful image of the First Rings of poetry and its attractions as pictured in the *Ion*. I add, in passing, that the image of these rings is relevant to a subject I treat in the twin book *Homer the Preclassic*: it is an enchanted ring of imperial wealth, power, and prestige in Plato's *Republic*—the Ring of Gyges.[134]

4ⓢ12. Sophists, sculptors, and rhapsodes as imperial craftsmen

4§166 Having considered the theme of the *daktulios* 'ring' as a link between Plato's *Hippias Minor* and his *Ion*, I proceed to explore another theme that links these two Platonic dialogues. This theme concerns the craft of the rhapsode, the *rhapsōidikē tekhnē*, which is explicit in the *Ion* but only implicit in the *Hippias Minor*. In Chapter 3, I have already examined what is implied in the *Hippias Minor* when Socrates enumerates the many skills mastered by Hippias the sophist. In the enumeration of these skills, the climax is reached with the skill of performing and interpreting poetry in general and Homeric poetry in particular. This skill is evidently derived from the *tekhnē* 'craft' of performing and interpreting Homeric poetry as it evolved in the context of rhapsodic competitions at the festival of the Panathenaia. And yet, the *tekhnē* professed by Hippias in practicing this skill is not *rhapsōidikē* but *sophistikē*.

4§167 Although I have already elaborated on this point in Chapter 3, I need to return to it here in order to stress the link between the sophist's expertise in using the Homeric art of rhapsodes and his expertise in using another art, the art of the master sculptor Pheidias. As I have argued here in Chapter 4, the craft of sculpting as represented by Pheidias is another most highly valued skill to be used by Hippias, rivaling in value the rhapsodic craft

---

[134] HPC E§159.

4§12. Sophists, sculptors, and rhapsodes as imperial craftsmen

of Homeric poetry. Besides his celebrated dialogues about Homer, Hippias produced comparable dialogues about painting and sculpting. I quote again the wording of Philostratus: 'he [Hippias] performed dialogues also about painting [zōgraphia] and sculpture [agalmatopoiia]' (*Lives of Sophists* 1.11.2 διελέγετο δὲ καὶ περὶ ζωγραφίας καὶ περὶ ἀγαλματοποιίας). The specially high value of Pheidian sculpture for Hippias is reflected in the Platonic *Hippias Maior*, which as we saw shows the sophist in the act of equating the statue of Athena Parthenos by Pheidias with the absolute Form of absolute beauty—with the idea of a perfect artistic totality.

4§168 The art of Pheidias has a value that is absolute for Hippias in the Platonic *Hippias Maior* because it mediates another art that has absolute value for him, the art of Homer. The colossal sculpture of Pheidias the Athenian craftsman, which is featured as the centerpiece of the sacred precinct of Zeus in Olympia, adds a decisively Homeric touch to the performances there by Hippias, the Elean craftsman of all craftsmen. The absolutism of what I have just called the Homeric touch is best conveyed by two crafts that are rivaled by the craft of Hippias the sophist: they are the imperial craft of a sculptor like Pheidias of Athens and the imperial craft of a rhapsode like Ion of Ephesus.

4§169 For the first time, I have described the *rhapsōidikē tekhnē* or 'rhapsodic craft' of Ion of Ephesus as an imperial craft. To justify this description, I start by observing that the term imperial, as I have been using it to describe the craft of Pheidias the sculptor, applies even more to the craft of Ion the rhapsode. An ideal point of comparison for these two traditional crafts is a rival new craft, the *sophistikē tekhnē* or 'sophistic craft' of sophists like Protagoras of Abdera and Hippias of Elis. As we saw, these two sophists typify two different visualizations of their craft: whereas the craft of Protagoras is transcendent, the craft of Hippias is practical. Here I will concentrate, however, on what these visualizations have in common. I will argue that the craft of Protagoras and Hippias as sophists is comparable to the craft of Pheidias as sculptor—and to the craft of Ion as rhapsode.

4§170 In the case of Protagoras, I need to turn back to a passage I already quoted from Plato's *Meno*, where the prestige of Protagoras as sophist is being directly compared to the prestige of Pheidias as an imperial craftsman. As we will see, this comparison involves also the prestige of Homer. As we will also see, the prestige of Homer drives the prestige of Ion the rhapsode as an imperial craftsman in his own right.

4§171 In Plato's comparison of Protagoras and Pheidias, the relative prestige of all craftsmen is being measured in terms of the amount of wealth they have amassed, and only the prodigious wealth of the imperial craftsman

Chapter Four

Pheidias is said to be worthy of comparison to the supreme amount credited to Protagoras (Plato *Meno* 91d). The prestige of Protagoras in Plato's *Meno* is also being compared, albeit indirectly, with the prestige of Homer. The claim of Protagoras is that sophists of his status are teachers who are *koinoi* 'common' to all Hellenes (Plato *Meno* 91b). This status evokes a comparison between the craft of Protagoras and the craft of a figure acknowledged as the ultimate teacher of all Hellenes. That teacher is Homer himself, in his evolving role as spokesman of the Athenian empire.

4§172 I had started this phase of the argumentation by saying that the craft of Protagoras and Hippias as sophists is comparable to the craft of Pheidias as sculptor—and to the craft of Ion as rhapsode. In the case of Hippias, I should add, his actual performances of Homer in Olympia are directly comparable to the performances of Homer by the rhapsode Ion in Athens. The Homeric art of Pheidias the sculptor enhances metonymically the setting for the performances of Homer by Hippias in Olympia, conferring on these performances an imperial aura. The metonymy of such enhancement is what I have been calling the Homeric touch.

4ⓢ13. Making an imperial space for performing Homer in Athens

4§173 Now we are about to see that the rhapsodic performances of Homer at the Panathenaia in Athens are likewise marked by an imperial aura, and again it is the Homeric art of Pheidias that confers this aura.

4§174 Here I return to Plutarch's *Pericles*. In that work, we saw the idea of a perfect artistic totality, that is, the colossal statue of Athena by Pheidias, extended metonymically into an overall idea, that is, the entire building program of Pericles. Now we are about to see that this metonymic extension—from the singularity of the colossal statue to the totality of the buildings all told—involves not only the highlights of the magnificent Athenian building program of Pericles but also some of the major Athenian institutions enhanced by this program. I draw special attention to the details about the building of the new Odeum, which are relevant to the details about the organization of an *agōn* 'competition' at the Panathenaia in the context of the new Odeum as the setting for this competition:

4ⓣ36 Plutarch *Pericles* 13.6–15 (abridged)

Πάντα δὲ διεῖπε καὶ πάντων ἐπίσκοπος ἦν αὐτῷ Φειδίας, καίτοι

4Ⓢ13. Making an imperial space for performing Homer in Athens

μεγάλους <u>ἀρχιτέκτονας</u> ἐχόντων καὶ <u>τεχνίτας</u> {7} τῶν ἔργων. τὸν μὲν γὰρ ἑκατόμπεδον <u>Παρθενῶνα</u> Καλλικράτης εἰργάζετο καὶ Ἰκτῖνος, τὸ δ' ἐν Ἐλευσῖνι <u>Τελεστήριον</u> ἤρξατο μὲν Κόροιβος οἰκοδομεῖν, καὶ τοὺς ἐπ' ἐδάφους κίονας ἔθηκεν οὗτος καὶ τοῖς ἐπιστυλίοις ἐπέζευξεν· ἀποθανόντος δὲ τούτου Μεταγένης ὁ Ξυπεταιὼν τὸ διάζωσμα καὶ τοὺς ἄνω κίονας ἐπέστησε, τὸ δ' ὀπαῖον ἐπὶ τοῦ ἀνακτόρου Ξενοκλῆς ὁ Χολαργεὺς ἐκορύφωσε· τὸ δὲ <u>μακρὸν τεῖχος</u>, περὶ οὗ Σωκράτης ἀκοῦσαί φησιν αὐτὸς εἰσηγουμένου γνώμην Περικλέους, {8} ἠργολάβησε Καλλικράτης. ... {9} τὸ δ' <u>Ὠιδεῖον</u>, τῇ μὲν ἐντὸς διαθέσει πολύεδρον καὶ πολύστυλον, τῇ δ' ἐρέψει περικλινὲς καὶ κάταντες ἐκ μιᾶς κορυφῆς πεποιημένον, εἰκόνα λέγουσι γενέσθαι καὶ μίμημα τῆς βασιλέως σκηνῆς, <u>ἐπιστατοῦντος</u> καὶ τούτῳ {10} Περικλέους. διὸ καὶ πάλιν Κρατῖνος ἐν Θρᾴτταις παίζει πρὸς αὐτόν·

ὁ σχινοκέφαλος Ζεὺς ὅδε

προσέρχεται [Περικλέης] <u>τὠδεῖον</u> ἐπὶ τοῦ κρανίου

ἔχων, ἐπειδὴ τοὔστρακον παροίχεται.

{11} φιλοτιμούμενος δ' ὁ Περικλῆς τότε πρῶτον ἐψηφίσατο <u>μουσικῆς</u> <u>ἀγῶνα</u> τοῖς <u>Παναθηναίοις</u> ἄγεσθαι, καὶ <u>διέταξεν</u> αὐτὸς <u>ἀθλοθέτης</u> αἱρεθείς, καθότι χρὴ τοὺς <u>ἀγωνιζομένους</u> <u>αὐλεῖν</u> ἢ <u>ᾄδειν</u> ἢ <u>κιθαρίζειν</u>. <u>ἐθεῶντο</u> δὲ καὶ τότε καὶ τὸν ἄλλον χρόνον ἐν <u>Ὠιδείῳ</u> τοὺς <u>μουσικοὺς ἀγῶνας</u>. Τὰ δὲ <u>Προπύλαια</u> τῆς ἀκροπόλεως ἐξειργάσθη μὲν ἐν πενταετίᾳ Μνησικλέους ἀρχιτεκτονοῦντος, τύχη δὲ θαυμαστὴ συμβᾶσα περὶ τὴν οἰκοδομίαν ἐμήνυσε τὴν θεὸν οὐκ ἀποστατοῦσαν, ἀλλὰ <u>συνεφαπτομένην τοῦ ἔργου</u> καὶ {13} <u>συνεπιτελοῦσαν</u>. ... {14} Ὁ δὲ Φειδίας εἰργάζετο μὲν τῆς θεοῦ τὸ χρυσοῦν <u>ἕδος</u>, καὶ τούτου δημιουργὸς ἐν τῇ στήλῃ [εἶναι] γέγραπται· πάντα δ' ἦν σχεδὸν <u>ἐπ' αὐτῷ</u>, καὶ πᾶσιν ὡς εἰρήκαμεν {15} <u>ἐπεστάτει</u> τοῖς <u>τεχνίταις</u> διὰ φιλίαν Περικλέους. καὶ τοῦτο τῷ μὲν φθόνον, τῷ δὲ βλασφημίαν ἤνεγκεν, ὡς ...

The man who directed [*diepein*] all the projects for him [= Pericles] and was the <u>overseer</u> [*episkopos*] of everything involved was <u>Pheidias</u>, although individual works were executed by other great <u>master builders</u> [*arkhitektones*] and <u>craftsmen</u> [*tekhnitai*] {7} of the various projects. For the hundred-foot <u>Parthenon</u> was executed by

Chapter Four

Kallikrates and Iktinos. As for the Telestērion ['Hall of Initiation'][135] at Eleusis, it was Koroibos who began the building, and it was this man who had put in place on their foundation the columns and joined them to their architraves.[136] But when he died Metagenes of the deme of Xypete put in place the frieze and the upper columns, while the hearth-opening above the *anaktoron* ['royal space'] received its crowning touch from Xenokles of the deme of Kholargos. For the Long Wall, concerning which Socrates [Plato *Gorgias* 455e] says that he himself heard Pericles make a formal proposal, {8} the contractor was Kallikrates.... {9} As for the Odeum,[137] which was designed to have many seats and columns on the inside,[138] and the roofing of which had a steep slope from the peak downward,[139] they say it was a visual imitation of the Great King's[140] Tent [*Skēnē*]—and {10} Pericles was supervising [*epistateîn*] this building project as well.[141] That is the point of reference when Cratinus—I quote him again—in his *Thracian Women* [CAF I 35 F 71] playfully alludes to him:

---

[135] The interior of the *Telestērion*, which functioned as the Great Hall of Initiation for the Athenian State, can be described as "a forest of columns." Stadter 1989:169 remarks: "Excavations reveal that an original fifth-century design, requiring a forest of 7 x 7 columns, was replaced by a design for 5 x 4 columns, and finally by a 7 x 6 design." The interior of the *Telestērion* at Eleusis, with its capacity for seating enormous crowds, is analogous to the interior of the Odeum of Pericles (mentioned later on in this same passage, at *Pericles* 13.9) on the south slope of the Acropolis. See Stadter 1989:173.

[136] See Stadter 1989:169–170 on the inscription *IG* I³ 32, dated around 450/49, which mentions a board of *epistatai* 'supervisors' appointed for a building project at Eleusis and names Koroibos as the *arkhitektōn* 'master builder'.

[137] Stadter 1989:172 remarks: "Pericles' [Odeum] was on the south slope of the Acropolis, east of the theater of Dionysus. [Plutarch] knew only a reconstruction of the building, which had been burned by the Athenians in 86 [BCE], to prevent its wood from being used by Sulla to besiege the Acropolis" (Appian *Mithridateios* 6.38; see also Vitruvius 5.9.1; Pausanias 1.20.4). As Stadter p. 173 continues: "According to Vitruvius [as cited] the masts and spars of the Persian ships [from Salamis] were used to construct the roof. In his book *Trees*, Meiggs 1982:474 notes that "the roof beams would have been enormous, more than 70 feet (21.3 meters) long."

[138] Stadter 1989:173: "The forest of columns would have been similar to the [*Telestērion*] at Eleusis but covered an even larger area."

[139] Stadter 1989:173 remarks: "Apparently the roof was pyramidal, sloping on four sides."

[140] That is, the King of Kings of Persia: see also Plutarch *Pericles* 10.5.

[141] Pericles is called the *epistatēs* 'supervisor' of the Parthenon and of the *Telestērion* (Strabo 9.1.12 C395) and of the statue of Athena Parthenos (Philochorus *FGH* 328 F 121) and of the Lyceum (Philochorus F 37 via Harpocration s.v.). See Stadter 1989:174.

4§13. Making an imperial space for performing Homer in Athens

> This pin-head ['squill-head'] Zeus,
> this Pericles, is approaching, wearing the Odeum on top of his skull
> as his [head-]wear, [142] now that the time for ostracism has come and gone.

{11} It was then for the first time that Pericles, ambitious as he was, got a decree passed that there should be a competition [*agōn*] in *mousikē* at the Panathenaia,[143] and he set up the rules [*diatassein*], having been elected as an *athlothetēs* [= organizer of the *athloi* 'contests'] for those who were competing [*agōnizesthai*]—rules for them to follow about the *aulos*-playing and the singing and the *kithara*-playing. At that point in time and in other periods of time as well, it was in the Odeum that people used to be spectators [*theâsthai*] of competitions [*agōnes*] in *mousikē*. {12} The Propylaea were built within the space of five years, Mnesikles being the architect, and a wondrous event happened in the course of their building, which indicated that the goddess was not just standing back but actively participating [= *sun*-, prefixed to both verbs that follow] in lending a hand to [*sun-haptesthai*] the project and in {13} bringing it to completion [*sun-epi-teleîn*]. . . . {14} Pheidias himself worked on the golden statue [*hedos*] of the goddess, and his name is inscribed as the artist on the stele. Almost everything was dependent on [= *epi*- plus dative] him, and, as I have said, {15} he was in charge [*epistateîn*], on account of his friendship with Pericles, of all the other craftsmen [*tekhnitai*]. This brought envy against one [= Pheidias] and, against the other [= Pericles], defamation, to the effect that . . .

---

[142] Stadter 1989:174 remarks: "Pericles seems to be wearing the [Odeum] (or its pointed roof) as he did the helmet in the Cresilaus portrait: perhaps Cratinus thought that the pyramidal roof of the [Odeum], with its sharp peak, would be suitable for Pericles' head." So the joke is inspired by the shape of the roof of the Odeum, with its sharp peak, and by the shape of the head of Pericles the 'pin-head'. The metonymic identification of Pericles with the Odeum—a major source of prestige for the statesman—has been comically turned into a metaphoric identification of the 'peak' of Pericles with the 'peak' of the Odeum.

[143] I take it that τότε πρῶτον 'at that point for the first time' refers not to the establishing of an *agōn* 'competition' in *mousikē* but to the fact that there was a formal decree involved. See Stadter 1989:175 for citations of documentation for earlier phases of competitions in *mousikē* in Athens. To repeat what I said earlier: the *mousikē* 'craft of the Muses' as practiced at the Panathenaia includes the *tekhnē* 'craft' of rhapsodes, not only of citharodes, citharists, auloides, and auletes. Supporting evidence comes from Aristotle *Constitution of the Athenians* (60.1), Plato *Ion* (530a), and Isocrates *Panegyricus* (4.159).

Chapter Four

4§175 As we see from this passage, it was Pericles in the fifth century BCE who initiated the legislation creating the institution of performing the Panathenaic Homer as I have reconstructed it so far. Plutarch leaves it unspecified whether the *agōnes* 'competitions' included rhapsodic performances, but we do see a specific reference attested in the ancient dictionary ascribed to Hesychius. In this dictionary we read under the entry *ōideion* 'Odeum': ᾠδεῖον· τόπος, ἐν ᾧ πρὶν τὸ θέατρον κατασκευασθῆναι οἱ ῥαψῳδοὶ καὶ οἱ κιθαρῳδοὶ ἠγωνίζοντο 'Odeum: the place where, before the Theater [of Dionysus] was configured for this purpose, the rhapsodes and the *kithara*-singers used to engage in competition [*agōnizesthai*]'.[144] It follows that Plutarch's elliptic reference to '*aulos*-playing, singing, and *kithara*-playing' does in fact include the 'singing' of rhapsodes.[145]

4§176 As we saw in Chapter 3, the festival of the Panathenaia was the occasion for 'musical' competitions, that is, competitions in the craft of *mousikē*, subdivided into separate events featuring *rhapsōidoi* 'rhapsodes', of *kitharōidoi* 'citharodes' (= *kithara*-singers), of *aulōidoi* 'aulodes' (= *aulos*-singers), of *kitharistai* 'citharists' (= *kithara*-players), and of *aulētai* 'auletes' (*aulos*-players). As I argued on the basis of references dated to the age of Plato, the premier event among these Panathenaic 'musical' competitions was an *agōn* 'competition' among rhapsodes who competed with each other in performing the *Iliad* and the *Odyssey* in their entirety. In Chapter 3, I connected the exclusivity of Ion's Homeric repertoire to the wording at the beginning of Plato's *Ion*, which makes it clear that Ion the rhapsode was set to perform Homeric poetry in the *agōn* 'competition' of *mousikē* at the Panathenaia (*Ion* 530a-b). With this review of the basic facts as a background, I return to the passage I just quoted from Plutarch's *Pericles*. The first time I had quoted this passage, I emphasized the initiative undertaken by the statesman Pericles in reshaping the premier sacred space of Athens, the acropolis, by way of instituting a new building program showcased by the sculpture of Pheidias as the master craftsman of Athens. Now I emphasize the fact that there was a parallel initiative undertaken by Pericles. It was the reshaping of the premier festival of Athens, the Panathenaia, by way of reforming the program of 'musical' competitions showcasing the poetry of Homer as master craftsman of all Hellas.

---

[144] On the use of the Theater of Dionysus for Homeric performances in the late fourth century BCE, see Athenaeus 14.620b-c and my relevant commentary in *PP* 158–163.

[145] The verb *āidein* 'sing', formant of the derivative nouns *kithar-ōidos* and *rhaps-ōidos*, is actually used with reference to the performances of rhapsodes: see Plato *Ion* 535b and my relevant commentary in *PP* 26–27.

4⑤14. Pheidias and the Peplos of Athena

4§177 So we have here a most precious piece of evidence about the Athenian standard of performing the Panathenaic Homer as it existed before the age of Plato, in the age of Pericles—which is seen as coextensive with the age of Pheidias. Further, this piece of evidence indicates that the Panathenaic version of Homer achieved its standard form as a result of the reforms instituted by Pericles concerning the 'musical' competitions at the festival of the Panathenaia. Even further, these Panathenaic reforms are connected with the building program of Pericles and, by extension, of Pheidias. In this metonymic sense, even the Panathenaic Homer can be seen as part of the building program of Pericles and Pheidias, in that the building of the Odeum is coextensive with the Panathenaic *agōn* 'competition' that included Homeric performances by rhapsodes.

4§178 The idea of the Odeum as a visual imitation of the *Skēnē* or 'Tent' of the Great King of the Persian empire, as we have just seen it described in Plutarch's *Pericles*, is a most fitting expression of imperial prestige. The Odeum, as the 'Scene' for the monumental Panathenaic performances of Homer in the age of Pheidias, was monumental in its own right. On the inside, its "forest of columns" matched the spectacular effect achieved at the *Telestērion* or Great Hall of Initiation at Eleusis.[146] In fact, the Odeum was even more spacious than the Great Hall, and the enormous seating capacity of such a monumental building made it a most fitting venue for spectacular events of state, including juridical and political assemblies.[147]

4§179 The macrocosm of the Odeum is metonymically—and comically—evoked by the microcosm sitting on top of the head of Pericles. On top of his comically pointy head is a perfect fit, which is a pointy 'hat'. That pointy 'hat' is the magnificent Odeum, culminating in its magnificent peak. As the most public of all public figures in Athens, Pericles the monumental statesman is wearing his 'hat' as the primary organizer of the Panathenaia, primarily featuring the Panathenaic performances of Homer. Pheidias the monumental sculptor is the secondary organizer, as the metonymic 'hatmaker' of the ultimate venue for the monumental performances of Homeric poetry.

---

[146] I refer again to the mention of the *Telestērion* in Plutarch *Pericles* 13.7, as analyzed in 4§174 above.

[147] Stadter 1989:173 cites Aristophanes *Wasps* 1108-1109 regarding the use of the Odeum as "a court." Citing the testimony of Xenophon *Hellenica* 2.4.9, 24, Stadter adds: "The Thirty used it [= the Odeum] as an assembly point when they were defending their rule in winter 404/3,". Immediately after citing these primary sources, Stadter cites a critical mass of secondary sources.

Chapter Four

4§180 So Pheidias was the notional architect of the setting for Homeric performance at the festival of the Panathenaia. And just as Pheidias was the craftsman primarily responsible for the setting of such performance, Homer was the craftsman primarily responsible for the performance itself.

4ⓢ14. Pheidias and the Peplos of Athena

4§181 So the prestige of Athens and of its premier festival, the Panathenaia, was linked to the prestige of two premier crafts in the age of Pheidias. These crafts were (1) the making of statues by Pheidias himself and (2) the making of poetry by Homer. The prestige of these two crafts was defined by an absolute standard, which was the work of Athena herself as the goddess of all crafts. For Athenians in the age of Pheidias, Athena was the goddess of all work in all crafts. All crafts were notionally derived from her work. As we will see, the work of Athena was primarily visualized as the weaving of her sacred peplos or 'robe', and the primary occasion for this weaving was the festival of the Panathenaia in Athens. In this section, I will show how the Panathenaic craft of weaving the peplos of Athena was linked to the craft of Pheidias. Then, in the next section, I will show how this same Panathenaic craft was linked to the craft of Homer.

4§182 Most relevant to the link between the work of Athena and the work of Pheidias is a story in the passage I quoted from Plutarch's *Pericles* (13.13). This story, as we have seen, shows how the work done by the goddess Athena was imagined as the ultimate model for all craftsmen working on the building program directed by Pericles and supervised by Pheidias. According to the story, Athena showed her involvement in the overall program by miraculously 'lending a hand' (*sun-haptesthai*) in the building of the Propylaea, thus 'keeping in touch' (*-haptesthai*) with the craftsmen in their work and making it possible to bring this work to its completion (*sun-epi-teleîn*). The overall building program of Pericles, as we have also seen, featured as its highest achievement the making of the statue of Athena by Pheidias. There is a synergism linking the work of Athena with the work of the master craftsman Pheidias, standing in for all the craftsmen he supervised.

4§183 Viewed of and by itself, the work done by Athena was represented by the peplos she wears when she is not at war—a peplos she made with her own hands. As we will see in what immediately follows, the metaphorical world of making this peplos was a frame of reference for visualizing the work of Pheidias as a sculptor. And, as we will see at a later point, it was also a frame of reference for visualizing the work of Homer as a poet.

4§14. Pheidias and the Peplos of Athena

4§184 I have already quoted the Homeric passage referring to the peplos made by Athena and worn by her when she is not engaged in warfare. In quoting this passage the last time, however, I highlighted not the peplos of the goddess but rather the khiton of Zeus that is worn by his daughter when she goes to war. This time, I highlight the peplos:

4ⓣ37 *Iliad* V 733–747

    Αὐτὰρ Ἀθηναίη κούρη Διὸς <u>αἰγιόχοιο</u>
    <u>πέπλον</u> μὲν κατέχευεν ἑανὸν πατρὸς ἐπ' οὔδει
735 <u>ποικίλον, ὅν ῥ' αὐτὴ ποιήσατο καὶ κάμε χερσίν·</u>
    ἣ δὲ <u>χιτῶν</u>' ἐνδῦσα Διὸς νεφεληγερέταο
    τεύχεσιν ἐς πόλεμον θωρήσσετο δακρυόεντα.
    ἀμφὶ δ' ἄρ' ὤμοισιν βάλετ' <u>αἰγίδα</u> θυσσανόεσσαν
    δεινήν, ἣν περὶ μὲν πάντῃ Φόβος ἐστεφάνωται,
740 ἐν δ' Ἔρις, ἐν δ' Ἀλκή, ἐν δὲ κρυόεσσα Ἰωκή,
    ἐν δέ τε <u>Γοργείη κεφαλὴ</u> δεινοῖο πελώρου
    δεινή τε σμερδνή τε, Διὸς τέρας <u>αἰγιόχοιο</u>.
    κρατὶ δ' ἐπ' <u>ἀμφίφαλον</u> κυνέην θέτο <u>τετραφάληρον</u>
    <u>χρυσείην, ἑκατὸν πολίων πρυλέεσσ' ἀραρυῖαν·</u>
745 ἐς δ' ὄχεα φλόγεα ποσὶ βήσετο, λάζετο δ' ἔγχος
    βριθὺ μέγα στιβαρόν, τῷ δάμνησι στίχας ἀνδρῶν
    ἡρώων, οἷσίν τε κοτέσσεται ὀβριμοπάτρη.

    But Athena, daughter of Zeus <u>who has the aegis</u>,
    took off her woven <u>peplos</u> [*peplos*] at the threshold of her father,
735 her <u>pattern-woven</u> [*poikilos*] peplos, <u>the one that she herself made and worked on with her own hands</u>.[148]
    And, putting on the <u>khiton</u> [*khitōn*] of Zeus the gatherer of clouds,
    with armor she armed herself to go to war, which brings tears.

---

[148] The verses of *Iliad* V 734–735 were athetized by Zenodotus.

Chapter Four

> Over her shoulders she threw the <u>aegis</u>, with fringes on it,
> —terrifying—garlanded all around by Fear personified.
> 740 On it [= the aegis] are Strife, Resistance, and the chilling Shout [of victorious pursuers].
> On it also is <u>the head of the Gorgon</u>, the terrible monster,
> a thing of terror and horror, the portent of Zeus <u>who has the aegis</u>.
> On her head she put the helmet, <u>with a *phalos* on each side</u> and <u>with four *phalēra*</u>,
> <u>golden, adorned with the warriors [*pruleis*] of a hundred cities</u>.
> 745 Into the fiery chariot with her feet she stepped, and she took hold of the spear,
> heavy, huge, massive. With it she subdues the battle-rows of men—
> heroes against whom she is angry, she of the mighty father.

4§185 At the moment when the goddess begins arming herself for war, she is shown literally slipping out of her peplos, which she is said to have woven with her own hands. The ostentatious reference here to the idea that Athena wove her own peplos with her own divine hands is full of ritual significance. No human handiwork can match the divine handiwork of the goddess. This mentality is comparable to the Greek Christian Orthodox concept of ἀχειροποίητος 'not-made-by-hand'. This word applies to sacred objects of veneration that are believed to be heaven-sent, not made by human hands. The difference is, the goddess Athena was explicitly visualized as setting the absolute standard herself by weaving her own peplos with her own divine hands.

4§186 A word vitally relevant to the work of Athena is *poikilos*, an epithet describing the peplos made by the goddess in the passage I just quoted from *Iliad* V 735. I interpret this epithet as 'pattern-woven' for reasons I will explain as my argumentation proceeds.

4§187 Slipping out of her peplos, the goddess slips into a khiton that belongs to her father Zeus. For a single Homeric moment, there is room for the thought—if not the image—of the goddess in the nude. Some thinkers, like Friedrich Nietzsche, may have held on to that thought. Nietzsche's "theo-

4§14. Pheidias and the Peplos of Athena

retical man" is obsessed with "that one nude goddess," who is truth.[149] Even as the thought flashes by, the Homeric picturing of Athena in motion moves on, without a blink, from a vision of the goddess in a peplos to a vision of the goddess in a khiton. So there is a complementarity in Athena's wearing a peplos at one moment and in her wearing a khiton at the next moment.

4§188 This complementarity of the peplos and the khiton worn by Athena from one moment to the next is matched by the complementarity of the two primary statues of Athena on the acropolis of Athens in the age of Pheidias. On the one hand, there is the archaic Athena Polias. She is housed in the old temple of the goddess. On the other hand, there is the classical Athena Parthenos sculpted by Pheidias. She is housed in her new temple, that is, in the Parthenon. As we have already seen from the eyewitness description of Pausanias, the statue of Athena Parthenos wears not a peplos but a khiton, and this khiton is sculpted into the statue. It does not follow, however, that Athena should wear a peplos that is likewise sculpted into her own statue. As we are about to see, the peplos to be worn by Athena was not sculpted but woven for her.

4§189 Every year, a new peplos was to be woven for Athena to celebrate the occasion of her birthday, which was the climactic final day of the *thusia* 'feast' of the Panathenaia, marked by a spectacular *pompē* 'procession' that culminated in the presentation of this peplos to her statue. In my earlier work, I studied at length the usage of these words *thusia* 'feast' and *pompē* 'procession' with reference not only to the Panathenaia and the Panathenaic Procession but also to the corresponding festivals and processions of other cities.[150] In other cities, there were comparable rituals of weaving robes for the statues of divinities.[151] In Elis, for example, sixteen women representing the sixteen subdivisions of the population wove a peplos for the goddess Hera (Pausanias 5.16.2, 6.24.10). In the city of Argos, a *patos* 'robe' was woven to

---

[149] Nietzsche (1872), Die Geburt der Tragödie, in Section 15: "Es gäbe keine Wissenschaft, wenn ihr nur um jene eine nackte Göttin und um nichts Anderes zu thun wäre." Earlier, in Section 10: "Die Philosophie der wilden und nackten Natur schaut die vorübertanzenden Mythen der homerischen Welt mit der unverhüllten Miene der Wahrheit an: sie erbleichen, sie zittern vor dem blitzartigen Auge dieser Göttin—bis sie die mächtige Faust des dionysischen Künstlers in den Dienst der neuen Gottheit zwingt."

[150] PR ch. 2.

[151] Mansfield 1985:442–487 offers a useful general survey of such rituals. I regret to add that the value of Mansfield's survey—and of his overall work—is consistently undermined by gratuitous insertions of unsupported assumptions about what is supposedly right or wrong about the work of his predecessors.

be presented to the goddess Hera on the occasion of her festival, the Heraia (Callimachus F 66.3, Hesychius s.v.). On this same occasion in Argos, as we see from the scholia for Pindar *Olympian* 7 (152), athletic contests were held, followed by the awarding of prizes; leading up to the awards was a *pompē* 'procession' climaxing in a hecatomb, that is, in a ritual sacrifice of a hundred cattle (in the scholia, the act of sacrifice is indicated by the verb *thuein* 'sacrifice'). The Panathenaic Procession likewise climaxes in a hecatomb, performed on the acropolis of Athens (*IG* II² 334, dated to 335/4 BCE).

4§190 Here I concentrate on the city of Athens and the Athenian ritual of weaving a peplos for Athena, to be presented to the goddess on the occasion of the Panathenaic Procession. From here on, I will distinguish this Panathenaic peplos from other peploi by treating it as a proper noun, Peplos.

4§191 In my earlier work, I reviewed the basic facts we know about the Peplos of Athena, especially the facts reported in the Aristotelian *Constitution of the Athenians* (60.1–3).[152] Here I simply highlight three details most relevant to my current argumentation:

(1) The weaving of the Peplos of Athena was started during the festival of the *Khalkeia*, nine months before the festival of the Panathenaia.

(2) The last day of the Panathenaia was the 28th day of the month of Hekatombaion, Athena's birthday.[153] That was the day of the Panathenaic Procession, which culminated in the presentation of the finished Peplos to the goddess in her aspect as Athena Polias, housed in the old temple of Athena on the acropolis.[154]

(3) The period of time required for the weaving of the Peplos from start to finish was nine months, matching symbolically the period of gestation leading up to the birth of the goddess.[155]

4§192 I draw attention to the name of the festival that inaugurated the weaving of the Peplos, *Khalkeia*, which is derived from the word *khalkos* 'bronze'. This festival celebrated the synergism of the divinities Athena and Hephaistos as models for the work of craftsmen. As the synergistic partner of Hephaistos, Athena was worshipped as *Erganē*, that is, the divinity who

---

[152] PR 86–88.
[153] Rhodes 1981:693 considers a pattern of fluctuation between the 28th and the 27th of Hekatombaion. He also considers the day of the month for the birthday as celebrated for the annual Lesser Panathenaia. In general, Rhodes is vigilant in noting the differences between the quadrennial Great Panathenaia and the annual Lesser Panathenaia.
[154] Rhodes 1981:670 notes that the annual Lesser Panathenaia had a Panathenaic Procession, which is mentioned for the annual Panathenaia in *IG* II² 334, dated to 335/4 BCE.
[155] Scheid/Svenbro 1994:27n43.

presides over the work (*ergon*) of craftsmen.¹⁵⁶ So there was a link between the work of Athena, who practices the craft of weaving her own peplos, and the work of Hephaistos, who practices the craft of metalwork in bronze.

4§193 In the traditions of the city of Argos, there was a comparable link between bronzework and weaving in the context of the festival of Hera, the Heraia. On this occasion, as I noted earlier, a *patos* 'robe' was woven for the goddess Hera (Callimachus F 66.3, Hesychius s.v.). On this same occasion, as we see in the scholia for Pindar (*Olympian* 7.152), prizes made of bronze metalwork were awarded after a *pompē* 'procession' marked by the ritual climax of a *thusia* 'sacrifice' of a hundred cattle (as indicated by the verb *thuein* 'sacrifice'). I consider this festival in more detail in the twin book *Homer the Preclassic*.¹⁵⁷

4§194 How are we to visualize the woven Peplos that was presented to Athena Polias at the ritual climax of the Panathenaic Procession? The following description is most telling:

4①38 Scholia for Aristophanes *Birds* 827

Τῇ Ἀθηνᾷ πολιάδι οὔσῃ πέπλος ἐγίνετο παμποίκιλος, ὃν ἀνέφερον ἐν τῇ πομπῇ τῶν Παναθηναίων.

For <u>Athena</u> in the aspect of <u>Polias</u> there was a <u>peplos</u> made. It was <u>completely pattern-woven</u> [*pan-poikilos*]. And it was ritually carried and presented to her in the <u>procession</u> [*pompē*] of the <u>Panathenaia</u>.

4§195 I highlight the epithet *pan-poikilos*, which describes the Peplos presented to Athena Polias. The same epithet occurs in *Iliad* VI 289 with reference to peploi woven by Phoenician women; the narrative there goes on to say that Hecuba chooses the best and most beautiful of these peploi as an offering to be presented to Athena in the sacred space of the goddess on the acropolis of Troy (VI 293–295).¹⁵⁸ Earlier, I highlighted the epithet *poikilos* 'pattern-woven', which describes the peplos made by Athena herself in the passage I quoted from *Iliad* V 735. For reasons I will explain in what follows, I intepret *pan-poikilos* as 'completely pattern-woven', just as I interpreted *poikilos* as 'pattern-woven'. These words, as we will see, are germane to the identity of the goddess Athena as a model for a special kind of weaving.

---

¹⁵⁶ Parke 1977:92–93.
¹⁵⁷ *HPC* II§§416 and following.
¹⁵⁸ According to a variant reading at *Iliad* VI 289, the epithet *pan-poikila* describes the *erga* 'work' woven by the Phoenician women, where *erga* is in apposition with *peploi*; according to the Koine reading, *pan-poikiloi* describes directly the *peploi*.

4§196 In order to understand the model of weaving that is represented by Athena, we have to confront a historical fact. The activity of weaving the Peplos of Athena was not an exclusively female activity. In the age of Pheidias, weaving in general was a female activity only in the domestic world of non-professional weavers; in the public world of professional weavers, by contrast, weaving was a primarily male activity. In this era, as also in other eras, specialized fabric work was the specialty of professional men.[159] Even in classical poetry, we read of male fabric workers—as signaled by words like *huphantēres* 'weavers' (from *huphainein* 'weave') in the *Epigonoi* of Sophocles (F 771 ed. Radt).[160]

4§197 As I said earlier, the peplos that Athena takes off in *Iliad* V connects her to her feminine identity as a weaver, while the khiton she puts on for war connects her to her masculine identity as a warrior. But there is more to it. As we are about to see, the identity of Athena as a weaver of the peplos is not only feminine. It is also masculine.

4§198 Just as weaving was not an exclusively female activity, the identity of Athena as a prototypical weaver was not an exclusively feminine identity. As we will see, Athena was a prototypical weaver for professional male weavers, not only for non-professional female weavers.

4§199 Linked to the identity of the goddess as weaver are two words I have already highlighted: they are (1) *poikilos* 'pattern-woven', (2) *pan-poikilos* 'completely pattern-woven'. To these words I now add two more: (3) *poikillein* 'pattern-weave' and (4) *poikiltēs* 'pattern-weaver'. The word *poikiltēs*, the plural form of which is *poikiltai*, refers to professional male fabric workers. As we learn from Plutarch's *Pericles* 12.6, the sculptures supervised by Pheidias in the building program of Pericles were influenced by these *poikiltai*.[161] The noun *poikiltēs* is derived from the verb *poikillein* in the sense of 'pattern-weave, weave patterns [into the fabric]', which is in this sense a synonym of *en-huphainein* 'weave patterns [into the fabric]'.[162] Also related is the adjective *poikilos*, which means 'varied, patterned' in general but 'pattern-woven' with specific reference to the Peplos of Athena.

---

[159] Barber 1991:4, 83, 113, 114 (illustration), 115, 270, 283–284, 286 (illustration), 290–291, 299. For an overview of the craft of male weavers and other professional male fabric workers in the Greek-speaking world, see PR 70–73. See also Robertson 1985:288–289 on an aetiological narrative about the first male weavers of the Peplos.

[160] PR 72n7.

[161] See also Mansfield 1985:83n8.

[162] There is a basic discussion in Barber 1991:359n2, which is more useful than the comments offered by Mansfield 1985:88–89n25.

4§14. Pheidias and the Peplos of Athena

4§200 The *poikiltai* are central to my argument not only because their art as 'pattern-weavers' was linked to the art of sculptors in the age of Pheidias. There is an even more important reason for their centrality, which has to do with an all-important ritual in the calendar of the Athenian state—a ritual I highlighted at the start of this argumentation. That ritual is the pattern-weaving of the Peplos of the goddess Athena in her older aspect as Athena Polias, to be contrasted with her newer aspect as Athena Parthenos. As we saw a moment ago, this Peplos was presented to Athena Polias on the occasion of the Panathenaia. As we also saw, this Peplos was *pan-poikilos* 'completely pattern-woven'.

4§201 The 'pattern' that was woven into this Peplos was the equivalent of a myth I examined in Chapter 1. That myth was the Gigantomachy (*Gigantomakhia*), which told of a primal conflict between the gods and the giants (*gigantes*).[163] As I have argued in earlier work, the narrating of this conflict was the equivalent of a charter myth for Athens in the age of Pheidias and beyond.[164] As I will now argue in this work, the ritual of pattern-weaving the Peplos of Athena was the equivalent of narrating this charter myth.

4§202 The charter myth of the Gigantomachy, as a narration, was literally woven into the Peplos of Athena.[165] And there is historical evidence to show that professional male weavers were involved in the weaving—that is, in the performance of this charter ritual.[166] As we are about to see from the wording of Plato, these weavers who wove the story patterns of the Gigantomachy into the Peplos of Athena can be identified as the *poikiltai* mentioned in Plutarch's *Pericles* 12.6. Plato's use of words derived from *poikilos* validates this identification:[167]

4⊕39 Plato *Euthyphro* 6b-c (Socrates is speaking to Euthyphro)

Καὶ πόλεμον ἄρα ἡγῇ σὺ εἶναι τῷ ὄντι ἐν τοῖς θεοῖς πρὸς ἀλλήλους, καὶ ἔχθρας γε δεινὰς καὶ μάχας καὶ ἄλλα τοιαῦτα πολλά, οἷα λέγεταί τε ὑπὸ τῶν ποιητῶν, καὶ ὑπὸ τῶν {c} ἀγαθῶν <u>γραφέων</u> τά τε ἄλλα ἱερὰ ἡμῖν <u>καταπεποίκιλται</u>, καὶ δὴ καὶ <u>τοῖς μεγάλοις Παναθηναίοις</u> ὁ <u>πέπλος</u> μεστὸς τῶν τοιούτων <u>ποικιλμάτων</u> ἀνάγεται εἰς τὴν ἀκρόπολιν; ταῦτα ἀληθῆ φῶμεν εἶναι, ὦ Εὐθύφρων;

---

[163] For a most suggestive introduction to the myth of the Gigantomachy, see Barber 1991:380-382.
[164] *PR* 90-93.
[165] Barber 1992:114, *PR* 90-91.
[166] Barber 1991:361-364.
[167] *PR* 92-93.

Chapter Four

> So do you think that there was really a war among the gods with each other, and that there were terrible hostilities and battles and many other such things as are narrated by poets—sacred things that have been patterned [*kata-poikillein*] for us by noble masters of visual arts [= *grapheus* plural], in particular the Peplos at the Great [= quadrennial] Panathenaia, which is paraded up to the acropolis, and which is full of such pattern-weavings [*poikilmata*]? Shall we say that these things are true?

4§203 It is essential to note the political as well as philosophical significance of this passage. By disparaging the Gigantomachy as a quaint invention that cannot be true for a philosopher, Plato's Socrates is subverting the charter myth of the Athenians and, by extension, he is subverting the state of Athens itself.[168] The subversion is all the more telling because the wording assigned by Plato to Socrates is most accurate in conveying the central importance of this myth of the Gigantomachy to the Athenians. As Socrates himself admits, the things that happened in the course of the battle of the gods and giants are *hiera* 'sacred'. Not only is the content of this myth sacred for the Athenians: so too, by extension, is the form of telling the myth. As we see from Plato's wording, the primary form of narrating the Gigantomachy was to pattern-weave the myth into the Peplos of Athena, which was carried up to the sacred space of the goddess on the acropolis at the ritual climax of the Panathenaic Procession. And the word that is used here in referring to the Peplos of the goddess is the noun *poikilma*, derived from the verb *poikillein* in the specific sense of 'pattern-weave'. So the noun can be interpreted literally as a 'patterned web', that is to say, as a product of pattern-weaving.

4§204 As we also see from Plato's wording, the more general way of narrating the Gigantomachy was to make use of secondary forms of visual arts—secondary, that is, in comparison to the notionally primary form, which was pattern-weaving. In the same passage I just quoted, the verb *poikillein* (in a compounded form, *kata-poikillein*) is used also in the general sense of 'make a patterned picture', and the subject of the verb here is *grapheus* (in the plural, *grapheis*), to be interpreted in the general sense of 'master of the visual arts', not in the specific sense of 'painter' (as in Plato *Phaedo* 110b). There is a rele-

---

[168] PR 92: "Socrates . . . has just remarked that the public resents him for being skeptical about various myths; he then cites as the first object of his skepticism the central myth of the Athenian State, the battle of the gods and giants or Gigantomachy, as represented on the Peplos of Athena herself. The all-importance of this myth is marked here not only by the Peplos itself but also by the occasion that highlights the Peplos, that is, the [quadrennial] Great Panathenaia."

vant attestation of *(en-)graphein* referring to the weaving of patterns into the fabric (scholia for Aristophanes *Knights* 556). The basic idea of *graphein* (verb) / *graphē* (noun) is to fill in a preexisting outline.

4§205 Elsewhere as well in the usage of Plato, the verb *poikillein* in the sense of 'pattern-weave' refers specifically to the act of weaving the narrative of the Gigantomachy into the Peplos of Athena. In Plato's *Republic* 2.378c, the expression *mutholōgēteon* 'to be mythologized' is made parallel to *poikilteon* 'to be pattern-woven', and the subject that is being simultaneously mythologized and pattern-woven is none other than the Gigantomachy (here Plato explicitly uses the noun *gigantomakhiai*, in the plural: 'gigantomachies').[169]

4§206 The professional male weavers known as the *poikiltai* 'pattern-weavers' were evidently hired to weave every four years a spectacularly elaborate and oversized Peplos destined for formal presentation to the statue of the goddess Athena on the occasion of the quadrennial Great Panathenaia. By contrast, on the occasion of the annual Lesser Panathenaia, specially selected young women continued the non-professional ritual custom of weaving a Peplos every year for the statue of Athena; in this case, the fabric was considerably less elaborate in its specifications and perhaps smaller. There is important epigraphical evidence about these young women weavers of the annual Peplos, who were called the *Ergastinai*, and about their primary representatives, called the *Arrhēphoroi*.[170] Here I simply note in passing their centrality in the complex of myths and rituals involving the annual Peplos.

4§207 There are various attested references to the quadrennial Peplos as a gigantic web featured as the sail for an official "ship of state" float that highlighted the parade of the Panathenaic Procession (Plutarch *Demetrius* 10.5, 12.3).[171] To be contrasted are references to the annual Peplos featured as a dress woven for the wooden cult statue (*xoanon*) of Athena.[172] One expert estimates that "the peplos needed to be roughly 5 [feet] by 6 [feet]" in order to dress (literally) this statue.[173] There is an ongoing debate about whether or not to differentiate between the "sail-peplos" of the Panathenaic parade and the "dress-peplos" presented to the cult statue of the goddess.[174] It may be that there were two different sizes for the Peplos and that the two sizes were

---

[169] PR 93. On the Peplos and the *gigantomakhiai* or Gigantomachy woven into it, I find the discussion of Pinney 1988 indispensable (especially p. 471). I interpret the plural of *gigantomakhia* as designating specific "close-ups" of the overall battle of the gods and giants.

[170] Overview by Barber 1991:362, 377. I rely especially on the relevant work of B. Nagy 1972.

[171] Barber 1992:114, with further references.

[172] Ridgway 1992:120–123.

[173] Barber 1992:114.

[174] PR 90.

Chapter Four

proportional to the two different scales of the festival for which it served as centerpiece. The proportionality could be formulated this way: the quadrennial Great Panathenaia is to the annual Lesser Panathenaia as the great quadrennial Peplos is to the smaller annual Peplos. Further, the gigantic scale of the quadrennial Peplos in the era of the Athenian empire is comparable to the gigantic scale of the empire itself.[175] This scale puts into perspective "the philosophical magnitude" of the offense committed by Plato's Socrates in his disparagement of the Gigantomachy:

> As we contemplate the grand Athenian State narrative of luminous *poikilmata* [pattern-weavings] woven into the Peplos of Athena at the Great Panathenaia, we can appreciate all the more the philosophical magnitude of Socrates' challenge to the central myth of this narrative, the *gigantomakhiai*, in Plato's *Euthyphro* and *Republic*. In effect, Plato's Socrates is challenging the State's definition of Athena and even of Athens itself.[176]

4§208 The form and the content of the narrative of the *gigantomakhiai* 'gigantomachies' were evidently regulated by elected state officials who supervised the quadrennial Great Panathenaia, the *athlothetai*, as we see from the Aristotelian *Constitution of the Athenians* (60.1–3). As I noted earlier, these *athlothetai* were directly in charge of all activities concerning the Panathenaia, including the supervision of the making of the Peplos (60.1 *kai ton peplon poiountai*); moreover, they were in charge of approving the *paradeigmata* or 'models' of the patterns to be woven into the Peplos (49.3).[177] Those woven patterns, as I have argued in my previous work, were functional narrations of the "sacred scene" of the Gigantomachy.[178] The responsibility of the *athlothetai* in supervising the narrative woven into Athena's robe is surely relevant to the function of the Peplos as the "raison d'être" of the Panathenaic Procession as well as the "high point" of the whole Panathenaic Festival.[179] The technique of narration by way of weaving such patterns has aptly been described by one expert as a <u>story-frieze</u> style of weaving.[180]

4§209 The question is, why would such important elected state officials be held responsible for the narrative agenda of the story-frieze patterns

---

[175] Parke 1977:38–41 gives an intuitively appealing formulation.
[176] PR 94.
[177] Rhodes 1981:671–672. For more on the interpretation of *paradeigmata* here as referring specifically to the patterns on the fabric, see Rhodes p. 568.
[178] PR 91.
[179] For these apt descriptions, see Neils 1992b:26.
[180] Barber 1992:114–116.

woven into the Peplos of Athena? Evidently, these explicit narrative agenda must have matched in importance the implicit political agenda of the State.[181]

4§210 Some have questioned whether the myth of the Gigantomachy was woven into the smaller web of the Lesser Panathenaia.[182] Such questioning is to my mind unjustified. It reflects a misunderstanding of the relationship between the telling of the myth and the weaving of the Peplos—whether it be the great Peplos of the quadrennial Great Panathenaia or the smaller Peplos of the annual Lesser Panathenaia. As we will see, the very idea of weaving the Peplos of Athena was the ritual equivalent of narrating the Gigantomachy. The myth of the Gigantomachy was intrinsic to and inextricable from the ritual of weaving the Peplos of Athena—both the quadrennial weaving and the annual weaving. To that extent, I agree with those who argue that the pictorial narratives woven into the Peplos of Athena in Athens were variations on one basic theme, the myth of the Gigantomachy.[183]

4ⓢ15. The Peplos of Athena and the sculptures of the Parthenon

4§211 What is narrated by the Peplos of Athena is linked with what is narrated by the various sculptures of the Parthenon. I start with the pièce de résistance, the statue of Athena Parthenos sculpted by Pheidias. Here I need to adjust an observation I made earlier about the passage where Pausanias gives his own eyewitness description of this statue (1.24.5-7). I observed that the Peplos of Athena is missing in the description, since Athena Parthenos is said to be wearing a khiton, not a peplos. But now we will see that the Peplos of Athena was not really missing in the sculptural ensemble of the Athena Parthenos viewed overall.

4§212 Let us take a second look at the armor of the goddess. I said earlier that the male exterior of the goddess is highlighted by her armor. But there is more to it. The female interior of the goddess is likewise highlighted by her armor—specifically, by the interior of her shield. Athena has her shield by her side. The Shield of Athena, like the goddess herself, was made by Pheidias, and the interior of this Shield had something essential to say about the Peplos of Athena.

---

[181] There are also some isolated historical occasions when the political agenda must have been featured explicitly, not just implicitly, on the Peplos itself: I cite again Plutarch *Demetrius* 12.3; also Diodorus 20.46.2.
[182] Mansfield 1985.
[183] Barber 1992:114.

Chapter Four

Figure 13 (as Figure 7 above). Gigantomachy krater by the Pronomos Painter.

4§213 As we see from the description of Pliny the Elder (*Natural History* 36.18), the convex exterior of the Shield of Athena featured a pictorial narrative of the Amazonomachy (*Amazonomakhia*), that is, the primal conflict between the Athenians and the Amazons (*Amazones*); as for the concave interior, it featured a pictorial narrative of the Gigantomachy (*Gigantomakhia*), that is, the primal conflict between the gods and the giants (*gigantes*).[184]

4§214 It has been shown that the pictorial narratives featured on the two sides of the Shield of Athena were not painted by Pheidias, as had once been thought; rather, the Shield was a masterpiece of metalwork.[185] Pliny the Elder (*Natural History* 36.18) says explicitly that Pheidias 'chased', *caelavit*, the surface of the Shield: that is, he worked it in metal (verb *caelare* 'chase').[186] So the metalwork was in bronze, with a gilded surface.

---

[184] Pliny *Natural History* 36.18: *in scuto eius Amazonum proelium caelavit intumescente ambitu, <in> parmae eiusdem concava parte deorum et Gigantum dimicationes* 'on her [= Athena's] Shield he [= Pheidias] chased [*caelare*] the Battle of the Amazons in the convex part, while he chased in the concave part of the same shield the conflicts of gods and giants'.
[185] Leipen 1971:49: the interior as well as the exterior of Athena's Shield was chased, not painted.
[186] Thompson 1939:297–298 comments on what Pliny says: "*Caelavit* means chased and is commonly used for metalwork in relief, certainly not for painting . . . the shield of the great Athena, being of gold, had no reason whatsoever for being painted inside or out."

4§15. The Peplos of Athena and the sculptures of the Parthenon

4§215 The exterior narrative of the Shield, about the Amazonomachy, celebrates the dominance of male over female, which corresponds to the dominance of Athena's male exterior over her female interior. As for the interior narrative, it celebrates the dominance of the Olympian over the earthbound or "chthonic," which corresponds to the dominance of Athena's affinities with the Olympians gods over her affinities with the goddess Earth. Besides the mythological text, as it were, of these two narratives, there was also a political subtext: narratives that were worked into the Shield evoked indirectly the prestige of Pericles and even of Pheidias himself (*Pericles* 31.3-4). Here I concentrate not on that subtext, nor on the narrative of the Amazonomachy, but rather on the myth of the Gigantomachy.

4§216 This myth, as we see from a vase painting I showed already in Chapter 1, narrates the establishment of cosmic order after the defeat of the giants by the gods. I start by showing once more a picture of this vase painting, with its remarkable panorama of the Gigantomachy. The painting has been explained as a copy, as it were, of the masterpiece of metalwork situated inside the concave interior surface of the gigantic Shield of Athena Parthenos in the Parthenon of Athens (Figure 13, as Figure 7 above, Chapter 1).

4§217 As we see from this picture, the myth as painted here and as metalworked by Pheidias narrates how the giants, generated by the primal goddess Earth, rebelled against the gods who live on Mount Olympus. The giants attempted to storm the heavens but were repelled by the Olympians. The Gigantomachy marks the birthday of Athena, that is, the primordial day when the goddess was born fully formed—and armed—from the head of her father Zeus (Hesiod *Theogony* 886-900, 924-926; *Homeric Hymn* [28] *to Athena* 4-6). In other words, Athena's birthday was conceived in mythological terms as the same day on which she joined Zeus and the other Olympians in defeating the giants.[187] As I have already noted, this primordial day was equated with the climactic last day of the festival of the Panathenaia, which was the occasion of the Panathenaic Procession, culminating in the presentation of a newly woven Peplos to the goddess.

4§218 Besides the Shield of Athena made by Pheidias, there is another most telling link with the Peplos of Athena in the Parthenon. If we imagine ourselves standing in the interior of the temple, we see porch colonnades featuring not the expected metopes but instead a continuous frieze of relief sculpture extending along the entire length of the outer walls of the cella.

---

[187] As in ch. 1, I stress here again the mythological synchronicity linking the day of Athena's birth and the day of her defeating the giants.

Chapter Four

Figure 14. Relief sculpture: presentation of the peplos of Athena. Slab 5, East Frieze of the Parthenon, Athens. British Museum, Elgin Collection.

What we are seeing is the Panathenaic Frieze, a visual representation of the Panathenaic Procession sculpted into the interior of the Parthenon under the supervision of Pheidias.

4§219 In my earlier work, I offered this general observation about the Frieze:

> The ritual drama of the Panathenaic Procession, as represented on the Parthenon Frieze, is central to the whole Panathenaic Festival, central to Athena, central to Athens. It is an ultimate exercise in Athenian self-definition, an ultimate point of contact between myth and ritual. The dialectic of such a Classical Moment has us under its spell even to this day. And it is precisely the anxiety of contemplating such a spellbinding moment that calls for the remedy of objective observation, from diachronic as well as synchronic points of view.[188]

4§220 This relief sculpture actually shows the ritual moment when the woven Peplos of Athena is handed over to a representative of the goddess.[189] The Peplos is shown at the moment of its being ritually folded, and its ribbed edge (or selvedge) is visible (Figure 14).[190]

4§221 This frozen motion picture showing the moment of handing over the Peplos at the moment of its ritual folding is a cross-reference. The reference crosses over from the craft of sculpture to the craft of weaving. As we contemplate the sculpting of the fabric of the Peplos on the Parthenon Frieze, I find it relevant to repeat the term story-frieze, applied to the narrative technique of pattern-weaving the Peplos.[191] This term can be applied also to the narrative technique of sculpting the story, as it were, of the Panathenaic Frieze, to the extent that the making of this relief sculpture is an analogue to the making of the Peplos of Athena.

4§222 The positioning of this ritual moment as sculpted into the Parthenon Frieze is comparable to the narrative of the Gigantomachy as metalworked into the concave interior of the Shield of Athena:

> Particularly stressed [in the narrative of the Gigantomachy as sculpted into the Shield] is the presence of Zeus in the centre top

[188] *PR* 90.

[189] There is ongoing debate over whether the Parthenon Frieze depicts the woven robe or Peplos of Athena "realistically." See Barber 1992:114–115, with further citations.

[190] Barber 1992:113; see also Barber 1991:361; see also p. 272, with further illustrations of selvedges as represented in the sculpture of the Parthenon Frieze.

[191] Barber 1992:114–116.

of the heavenly arch: other gods converge toward him symmetrically from either side. [Pheidias] seems to announce in this way to the spectator that Zeus is not only in the centre of the battle but also at its culminating point. The same conception is found on the Panathenaic frieze where the human procession, starting from the south-west corner, proceeds in two directions along the north and south sides of the temple to converge over the east end where the gods are assembled to witness the culmination of the ceremony.[192]

It is at this point of convergence in the narrative of the Panathenaic Frieze that the presentation of the Peplos takes place.

4§223 By now we have seen two links to the Peplos of Athena in the sculptures of the Parthenon. In one case, the pictorial narrative that is sculpted into the Panathenaic Frieze on the interior of the Parthenon refers to the form of the woven Peplos. In the other case, the pictorial narrative that is metalworked into the interior of the Shield of Athena is a myth that matches the pictorial narrative that is woven into the Peplos of Athena, that is, the myth of the Gigantomachy.

4§224 There is also a third link to the Peplos of Athena in the sculptural narratives of the Parthenon. In this case, we find the link on the exterior of the temple. On the surface of this exterior are the grand relief sculptures of the pediments and the metopes, featuring a set of connected mythical and ritual themes. The east and the west pediment show respectively the birth of Athena and her victory over Poseidon in their struggle over the identity of Athens; the metopes show the battle of the gods and giants on the east side, the battle of the Athenians and Amazons on the west, the battle of the Lapiths and Centaurs on the south, and the battle of the Achaeans and Trojans on the north. So once again we see a sculpted narrative that matches the woven narrative of the Peplos of Athena: it is the myth of the Gigantomachy, sculpted into the east metopes, featuring Athena herself battling in the forefront as a *promakhos*.[193] In this case, the Gigantomachy balances the Amazonomachy that is sculpted into the west metopes. Similarly, as we saw earlier, the Gigantomachy that is metalworked into the concave interior of the Shield of Athena balances the Amazonomachy that is metalworked into the convex exterior. So the contents of the east and the west metopes of the Parthenon's exterior correspond respectively to the contents of the concave interior and convex exterior of the

---

[192] Leipen 1971:48.
[193] On the role of Athena in this myth as the central aetiology of the Panathenaia, see especially Pinney 1988.

4⑤15. The Peplos of Athena and the sculptures of the Parthenon

Shield of Athena. Also relevant to the Peplos of Athena, as we will see later, is what we see sculpted into the north metopes of the Parthenon's exterior. It is the battle of the Achaeans and Trojans, the topical centerpiece of the Homeric *Iliad* and *Odyssey*.[194]

4§225 Finally, there is a fourth link to the Peplos of Athena in the sculptural narratives of the Parthenon. It is the Pandora Frieze, sculpted by Pheidias into the base of the statue of Athena Parthenos. In order to appreciate the significance of this sculpture, we must review the first three links in a fixed order. Let us take the perspective of a viewer standing before the entrance to the temple of Athena Parthenos. Facing the east side of the temple and looking for highlights that catch the eye, starting from the top, we would first of all see the birth of Athena sculpted into the pediment on high; next, looking further below, we would see the battle of the gods and giants sculpted into the metopes; next, looking even further below and into the interior, we would see the presentation of the Peplos of Athena sculpted into the Panathenaic Frieze that wraps around this interior above the columns of the porch.[195] Next, ascending the steps of the temple and entering its open doors, we would see the gigantic figure of Athena Parthenos standing on top of a commensurately gigantic base; and we would see sculpted into the surface of this base the Pandora Frieze.

4§226 As we know from Pliny the Elder (*Natural History* 36.19), the relief work of the Pandora Frieze was executed in metal—or 'chased', that is, *caelatum* (verb *caelare* 'chase'). The bronze metalwork must have had a gilded surface, which is to be inferred from what Pausanias says about the corresponding relief work gracing the base of the statue of Zeus in Olympia (5.11.8).[196] Let us continue to follow the perspective of a viewer who has just entered the interior of the temple. As we enter, we see straight ahead the glittering figure of Pandora at the center of the Frieze, her radiance enhanced by her reflection in the pool at the front of the base; this view gives the viewer "a premonition of what, once he had accustomed himself to the semi-darkness in the cella, he would, on directing his gaze upwards, experience in the statue of the Athena Parthenos herself."[197] Even before the viewer "could have been alerted to the astonishing height and polychromatic splendour of the chryselephantine

---

[194] On which see Ferrari 2000.
[195] Berczelly 1992:54.
[196] Berczelly 1992:55.
[197] Berczelly 1992:55.

Chapter Four

Figure 15. Attic red-figure calyx krater: the Birth of Pandora. Attributed to the Niobid Painter, ca. 475-425 BCE. London, British Museum, GR 1856.12-13.1 (Vase E 467).

statue of Athena itself, he would have looked straight ahead and glanced at its base."[198]

4§227 As Pausanias says, the myth that is narrated by the relief work on the base of the statue of Athena Parthenos is the genesis of Pandora (1.24.7). What Pausanias does not say, however, is that Pandora is the first Athenian woman in the Athenian version of the myth, and that she is represented as wearing the first peplos. The narrative of this myth about Pandora, as worked into the frieze of the base of the statue of Athena Parthenos, can be reconstructed primarily on the basis of vase paintings that narrate this myth.[199] In terms of these narrations, Pandora is represented as wearing the first peplos, given to her by the goddess Athena herself:

> This robe, the first peplos, might have been understood in the widest sense of the word as the archetypal peplos, given by Athena to the primordial woman. For that reason its concept was not confined to the bare image of a beautiful garment, but involved women's ability to weave peploi as well.[200] Thus the peplos of Pandora could have represented the mythical pattern or prototype for all the peploi in the world.[201]

---

[198] Berczelly 1992:54–55.
[199] Berczelly 1992:61–67.
[200] The author refers here to Hesiod *Works and Days* 63–64.
[201] Berczelly 1992:61.

4Ⓢ15. The Peplos of Athena and the sculptures of the Parthenon

Figure 16. Attic red-figure cup with white ground: the Creation of Pandora. Attributed to the Tarquinia Painter, ca. 475-425 BCE. London, British Museum, 1885.1-28.1.

4§228 Let us consider in some detail the narratives of two relevant vase paintings. Both paintings are dated to the second quarter of the fifth century BCE; so they predate the Pandora Frieze itself.[202] The first of these paintings shows a frontal view of the newly created Pandora. She is wearing a peplos and is flanked by Athena, who presents her with a garland of flowers (Figure 15).[203]

The second of these two paintings shows Pandora flanked by Athena and Hephaistos on either side. It is the moment when the two divinities have just finished creating this female prototype by way of their combined crafts (Figure 16).

---

[202] Berczelly 1992:61.
[203] On the association of Pandora with garlands of flowers, see also Hesiod *Theogony* 576–580 and *Works and Days* 74–75. See also Blech 1982:34 and Berczelly 1992:63.

Chapter Four

I quote an incisive description:

> We see here only three figures: Hephaistos in company with Athena, respectively on the left (spectator's right) and right side of Pandora. Hephaistos has completed the modelling of Pandora with a small hammer, which he still holds in his left hand. Lifting his right hand over her head he now has a closer look at the results, whereas Athena is engaged in fastening the peplos to Pandora's shoulders. It is not accidental that just these two deities should be flanking her. After all, the part Hephaistos, the creator of Pandora, takes in the myth, is no less significant than that of Athena.[204] As an allusion to his rôle in the artificial birth of Pandora, a cave behind the figures indicates the smithy where Hephaistos and his helpers executed the work. Another reason for his presence in the scene might have been that Hephaistos and Athena *Erganē* very often appear together in Classical Attic art.[205]

4§229 The mention here of Athena *Erganē* is relevant to the Athenian festival that inaugurated the weaving of the Peplos of Athena, the *Khalkeia*, the name of which is derived from the word *khalkos* 'bronze'. This festival, as we saw earlier, celebrated the synergism of the divinities Athena and Hephaistos as models for the work of craftsmen. As the synergistic partner of Hephaistos, Athena was worshipped as *Erganē*, that is, the divinity who presides over the work (*ergon*) of craftsmen.[206] Since the weaving of the Peplos was begun at the festival of the *Khalkeia*, it is relevant that the name for the female weavers of the Peplos was *Ergastinai*.[207]

4§230 Earlier, I argued for a link between the work of Athena, who practices the craft of weaving her own peplos, and the work of Hephaistos, who practices the craft of metalwork in bronze. On the basis of the additional details we have seen since then concerning the myth of Pandora, I now also argue for a link between the work of the weavers who produced the Peplos of Athena and the work of the metalworkers who produced artifacts made of bronze in the sacred space of Athena. The fact that Athena presides over the craft of weaving the Peplos in conjunction with the craft of bronze metalwork is relevant to the fact that the relief work of the Pandora Frieze, which shows Pandora being dressed in a prototypical peplos given to her by Athena,

---

[204] The author refers here to Hesiod *Works and Days* 60–63; also *Theogony* 571 and following.
[205] Berczelly 1992:62.
[206] Parke 1977:92–93.
[207] See 4§206, with reference to the work of B. Nagy 1972.

4§15. The Peplos of Athena and the sculptures of the Parthenon

is an artifact of metalwork in bronze. It is also relevant to the fact that the metalworker who sculpted the narrative about Pandora and her peplos was none other than Pheidias himself, who also metalworked the narrative of the Gigantomachy into the concave interior of the Shield of Athena—matching the narrative of the Gigantomachy woven into the Peplos of Athena.

4§231 By now we have seen four links to the Peplos of Athena in the sculptures of the Parthenon. Taken together, all four show that the Peplos was relevant to Athena Parthenos, the occupant of the Parthenon, not only to Athena Polias, who was the official recipient of the Peplos by virtue of being the occupant of the older temple of the goddess on the acropolis. Moreover, these links show that the making of the Peplos of Athena influenced the making of the sculptures of the Parthenon itself.

4§232 Here I stop to note a basic difference. The metalwork of the Gigantomachy on the concave interior of the Shield of Athena, as performed by Pheidas, was of course a singular historic event. To be contrasted is the weaving of the Gigantomachy, which was a seasonally recurring event. There was the weaving of the annual Peplos, as performed by female weavers, and there was the weaving of the quadrennial Peplos, as performed by professional male weavers called *poikiltai*. Each time the Peplos was woven—or, better, rewoven—it was notionally the same but historically different. So the woven version of the Gigantomachy can be seen as an ongoing classical process in contrast to the metalworked version, which is a single classical moment created by Pheidias.

4§233 The ritual reweaving of Athena's Peplos every year at the Panathenaia—especially every four years at the Great Panathenaia—is a ritual re-enactment of Athena's own weaving of her own peplos, which she wears as a 'robe'. As we saw, Homeric poetry says explicitly, in *Iliad* V (734-735), that the goddess herself had woven—with her own hands—the peplos she is shown as wearing; when she goes to war, she takes off this peplos (V 734) before she puts on a khiton (V 736), over which she wears her suit of armor (V 737).[208] Because it is a divinity who is doing these things, what Athena does or what she makes is absolute and thus permanent. Female and male weavers keep on repeating the absolute and permanent archetype, and their repetition formalizes the permanence. So, while the sculpting of a statue of the goddess is a single act that achieves notional permanence, the weaving of a web for the goddess is an act that has to be reperformed year after year for ever and ever in order to achieve, in the fullness of time, that same kind of notional permanence. The

---

[208] Mansfield 1985:161-162n33.

Chapter Four

woven web of Athena is a multiple and fluid eternity, ever recycled, whereas the sculpted statue of Athena is a single and static moment of that same eternity, ever the same.

4§234 Here I return one last time to the fact that Athena Parthenos in the Parthenon is not wearing her peplos. If the statue of the goddess is viewed as the goddess herself in arrested motion, then Athena herself becomes an appropriate recipient of the Peplos that is forever being ritually rewoven for her. The ritual reweaving is what makes the weaving permanent. So long as the reweaving goes on forever, which is the ideology of ritual, the Peplos is just as permanent as the statue is notionally permanent. The eternity of reweaving makes the rewoven Peplos the same thing, ritually speaking, as the Peplos that Athena had originally woven. She can receive for eternity that same Peplos she once wove because it is rewoven for her by successive generations of weavers weaving into eternity.

4§235 Conversely, Athena can also give the Peplos once and for all to the first woman, Pandora, as we saw from the evidence about relief metalwork of Pheidias known as the Pandora Frieze.[209] In terms of Athenian myth as represented in this relief metalwork created by Pheidias, the Peplos given to Pandora by Athena would have been woven once and for all. In terms of Athenian ritual, on the other hand, women will be weaving a new Peplos for Athena on a seasonally recurring basis, year after year for all time to come. The Peplos given by the goddess to the primal woman will be rewoven and given back to the goddess again and again for the rest of time on the seasonally recurring occasion of the feast of the Panathenaia, which celebrates the genesis of Athena.

4§236 In the age of Pheidias, as we have seen, the reweaving of the Peplos of Athena was no longer restricted to women, so that any idea of Pandora as the first weaver by virtue of being the first woman was neutralized. Still, the craft of weaving the Peplos continued to be associated primarily with the nonprofessional work of women.

4ⓢ16. Reweaving the peplos, retelling the epic

4§237 In the light of what we have seen here in Chapter 4 concerning the differentiation of professional male weavers from nonprofessional female weavers in the age of Pheidias, I will now explore the relevance of this differentiation to the metaphorical world of weaving as epic. As we saw in

---

[209] Berczelly 1992; also Nick 2002:6.

4§16. Reweaving the peplos, retelling the epic

Chapter 2, the general process of weaving as a metaphor is applied by epic to the specific activity of performing epic. The prime example I cited was the word *oimē*, which refers metaphorically to the 'story-thread' that begins the epic performance of the singer Demodokos in *Odyssey* viii 74. Such a beginning of epic, as we saw from the wording of Pindar's *Nemean* 2 (line 3), is a *prooimion*, which is metaphorically the starting point of the threading, of the *oimē*. Comparable to this Greek *prooimion* is the Latin *exordium* 'proemium'. Both words are applicable to the beginning of a song, a poem, or a speech. Like the Greek *prooimion*, the Latin equivalent *exordium* shows a closely comparable etymology: this noun too refers metaphorically to the starting point of the threading, as we see from the meaning of the corresponding verb *ordīrī*, which refers to the actual process of 'threading'.[210] Another semantic parallel is Latin *prīmordia*, which gives us the English word 'primordial'. As we also saw in Chapter 2, the specific meanings of the Greek nouns *oimē* and *prooimion* are related to the general meaning of the noun *humnos*, which I interpreted etymologically as the overall process of weaving as expressed by the verb *huphainein* 'weave'. So the question is, can we say that the performing of epic in the age of Pheidias is visualized metaphorically as the work of male weavers in particular?

4§238 In formulating an answer, I start with the metaphor inherent in the technical poetic term *prooimion*. In terms of this metaphor, a performance started by a singer is like a web started by a weaver. Performing the *prooimion* is like weaving the *exastis*, which is a technical term for the initial phase of the weaving.[211] From the wording of Pindar, we see the application of this metaphor to the start of Homeric performance:

4①40 Pindar *Nemean* 2.1–3

Ὅθεν περ καὶ Ὁμηρίδαι | ῥαπτῶν ἐπέων τὰ πόλλ᾽ ἀοιδοί | ἄρχονται, Διὸς ἐκ προοιμίου.

[starting] <u>from the point where</u> [*hothen*] the Homēridai, singers, most of the time <u>begin</u> [*arkhesthai*] their <u>stitched-together</u> [*rhaptein*] words, from the <u>prooimion</u> of Zeus ...

4§239 The idea of fabric work, implicit in the word *prooimion*, is made explicit here through the word *rhaptein* 'sew, stitch', which conveys the idea of

---

[210] PR 80.
[211] PR 82.

Chapter Four

integrating woven fabric into a totality.[212] The metaphorical world of *rhaptein* 'sew, stitch' is specific to the word *rhapsōidoi* 'rhapsodes', which means etymologically 'stitchers of song'.[213] In the logic of Pindar's wording, the primary fabric workers of song are the *Homēridai*, the 'descendants of Homer' themselves, and the starting point for their fabric work is the web of song that addresses the primary god, Zeus.[214] So the metaphorical fabric workers of epic are specifically male fabric workers. As such, they are analogous to the *poikiltai* mentioned in Plutarch's *Pericles* (12.6).

4§240 In Pindar's *Nemean 2*, Zeus is not only positioned at the starting point of epic: the god is also the starting point himself. That is because Zeus is being celebrated in a notional *prooimion* that is said to invoke him first and foremost. In classical terms, such a *prooimion* is tantamount to a *Hymn to Zeus*. We may compare the wording of Thucydides (3.104.4–5), who uses the word *prooimion* in referring to what we know in classical terms as the *Homeric Hymn (3) to Apollo*. To paraphrase in terms of the analogous Latin word *prīmordia*, Zeus is 'primordial' by virtue of being the initial phase of the weaving. With Zeus as the perfect beginning, a *humnos* to Zeus becomes a perfect web.

4§241 The *prooimion* that is being performed by the *Homēridai* in Pindar's *Nemean 2* (line 3) is the metaphorical equivalent of an *exastis*. As with all matters relating to fabric work, an *exastis* can be linked generically to the work of female weavers. But the artistic *bravura* of creating a *prooimion* can also be linked specifically with professional male fabric workers. In the Pindaric metaphor picturing epic as fabric work, we have just seen that the visual world of weaving as a metaphor includes specialized aspects of fabric work performed by professional male fabric workers, not only the generalized aspect of fabric work performed by women in domestic settings, which remains the standard non-metaphorical poetic visualization. The decisive word in Pindar's *Nemean 2* is *rhaptein* 'sew, stitch' (line 2), which refers to the specialized work of integrating woven fabric into a totality that suits another totality, that is, the body conceived as a whole.[215]

4§242 As we saw in Chapter 2, the overt metaphor of *rhapta epea* 'stitched-together words' in Pindar's *Nemean 2* (line 2) is connected with a latent

---

[212] For more on the metaphorical world of *rhaptein* 'sew, stitch' in the sense of a virtuoso integration of woven fabric, see PR 71. The sewn fabric may in the end suit a body that is not human but divine.

[213] PP 61–76, BA 17§10n5, PH 1§21 (= p. 28), with reference to Schmitt 1967:300–301 and Durante 1976:177–179.

[214] PP 62–64.

[215] For more on *rhaptein* with reference to professional male fabric workers, see PR 71.

4ⓈI6. Reweaving the peplos, retelling the epic

metaphor embedded in the etymology of the word *rhapsōidos* 'rhapsode', a compound formation composed of the morphological elements *rhaptein* 'stitch together' and *aoidē* 'song'. As Pindar's wording indicates, the *rhapsōidoi* 'rhapsodes' who perform the epic of Homer by 'stitching together the words' are comparable to the male fabric workers who create the Peplos of Athena at the quadrennial Great Panathenaia.

4§243 I propose that Pindar's wording here envisions rhapsodes in the act of performing Homer on the occasion of the quadrennial Great Panathenaia just as the male fabric workers who weave the Peplos of Athena weave it for that particular occasion—and not for the annual Lesser Panathenaia. The spectacular size and elaborateness of the quandrennial Peplos woven by professional male fabric workers suited the grandeur of the quadrennial Great Panathenaia.[216] I see an ongoing connection with the spectacular size and elaborateness of the Homeric *Iliad* and *Odyssey* in comparison to other epics.

4§244 The artistry of weaving the quadrennial Peplos is comparable to the spectacular artistry of the woven tapestries of medieval Europe. But the difference is, the Peplos was a self-renewing and self-updating masterpiece, seasonally rewoven. And the occasion for the reweaving was also the occasion for the grandest celebration of the Athenian state, that is, for the quadrennial Great Panathenaia. This festival, rich in lavish prizes, was a most potent new rival to the Olympics and the other grand old festivals of the Peloponnese. And the occasion for the quadrennial reweaving was also the occasion for the quadrennial retelling of the Homeric *Iliad* and *Odyssey*.

4§245 The symmetry of these two Panathenaic insitutions, reweaving the Peplos and retelling the Homeric *Iliad* and *Odyssey*, is evident in the civic discourse of Athens in the fifth and fourth centuries. For illustration, I have in mind two passages where Athenians happen to be speaking about the feast of the Panathenaia, this most important of all festivals in their city's calendar. They speak of two essential features of this festival, both of which are described as most precious heirlooms inherited from their ancestors. One passage, in Aristophanes *Knights* (565-568), concerns the reweaving of Athena's Peplos.[217] The other passage, which comes from a speech delivered in 330 BCE by the Athenian statesman Lycurgus, *Against Leokrates* (102), concerns

---

[216] It also suited the divine body, larger than life, of the goddess Athena. I mean suit figuratively, not literally: there is no need to think that the gigantic quadrennial Peplos was literally draped over any statue of Athena.

[217] Mansfield 1985:51.

Chapter Four

the reperforming of the Homeric *Iliad* and *Odyssey* in their notional entirety on the occasion of the quadrennial festival of the Great Panathenaia.[218]

4§246 Another relevant piece of evidence is the Homeric use of the word *humnos*, which expresses the notion of a continuous narration in the context of a festival.[219] In terms of this notion, we may visualize the sculptural narrative of the east pediment and of the east metopes of the Parthenon as a figurative *Hymn to Athena*. Correspondingly, we may visualize the sculptural narrative of the north metopes as a figurative epic of the Trojan War. In other words, these two sculptural narratives approximate respectively a most grand *prooimion* and the most grand of all epics. In the grand scheme of the sculptural narrative of the Parthenon, *prooimion* and epic connect with each other to become one single continuous and notionally seamless *humnos*.

4§17. The imperial poetics of terror and pity

4§247 Here I focus on the narrative about the battle of the Achaeans and Trojans sculpted into the north metopes of the Parthenon. The central theme of this sculpted narrative is of course parallel to a central theme shared by the spoken narratives of the Homeric *Iliad* and *Odyssey*, that is, the Trojan War. And the parallelism involves not only the Homeric *Iliad* and *Odyssey* but also the epic Cycle. Among the epics of the Cycle, one stands out. It is the epic known as 'The Destruction of Troy' or *Iliou Persis*, attributed to Arctinus of Miletus, the narrative of which focuses on the destruction of Troy. When we compare the ancient plot summary of this epic narrative with what little remains of the sculpted narrative on the north metopes of the Parthenon, we find striking parallels.

4§248 In order to make a comparison with the visual evidence that survives from the reliefs sculpted into the north metopes of the Parthenon, I quote from the work of Gloria Ferrari a summary of this evidence:

> On this [= the north] side, as on the east and west, the sculptures were effaced deliberately, leaving only a few figures and traces of others, but enough remains to be sure of the subject and of the structure of the representation, in a broad sense. With few exceptions (metope D, "Iris" in 31, and "Hera" in 32) all figures face or advance towards right, establishing a strong east-west direction for

---

[218] *PR* 10–12. I quoted this passage in ch. 3.
[219] *PR* 70–98.

4ⓢ17. The imperial poetics of terror and pity

the viewer and a starting point at the east end. The frieze is divided into two unequal sections. The sack of the city is framed by the figures of Helios rising on metope 1 and Selene setting on metope 29. The first scene (metope 2) contains the prow of a ship, from which two nude men disembark, carrying objects. [Considered here is metope 3; there is considerable uncertainty about the reading of the representations here.] Of the next twenty metopes only fragments survive, for the most part small and unreadable, whose place in the sequence is uncertain. One (metope A) probably held the representation of a bull led to sacrifice. Metope D shows a man, nude except for a mantle, leading away a female figure in peplos, perhaps Polyxena. The scene of the recovery of Helen by Menelaus stretches over metopes 24 and 25. Helen runs to a shrine, toward an ancient statue, while Aphrodite—a small Eros perched on her shoulder—stands between her and her vengeful former husband. 26 is lost. [Considered here is a suggestion that metope 26 was part of a two-metopes sequence showing the rescue of Aithra and Klymene, who might be the woman following a man on metope 27.] Aeneas's escape with Ascanius [/ Iulus] is recognizable in metope 28. [...] Situated beyond and outside the depiction of the events at Troy, the last three metopes form a self-contained whole. [Considered here is a suggestion that the scene being depicted is a council of the gods, with Zeus and Iris at the center in metope 31.] Although the identity of the goddesses in metope 32 is far from secure, it is possible that the seated one is Hera and the one that is standing is Athena.[220]

4§249 Now I repeat here from Chapter 2 my translation of the ancient plot-summary of the *Iliou Persis* attributed to Arctinus of Miletus. This time, I highlight with asterisks those details in the summary that correspond or at least seem to correspond to details in the narrative of the north metopes of the Parthenon:

4ⓣ41 Arctinus of Miletus *Iliou Persis* plot summary by Proclus pp. 107–108 ed. Allen

    16   After the preceding [= four scrolls of the *Little Iliad*, by Lesches of Lesbos] there follow two scrolls of the *Iliou Persis*, by Arctinus

---

[220] Ferrari 2000:130–131.

Chapter Four

of Miletus, containing the following. With regard to the things concerning the Horse, the

Trojans, being suspicious, stand about wondering what they should

do. Some think it should be pushed off a cliff, while others

20 think it should be burned down, and still others say that it should be dedicated as sacred [*hieros*] to Athena.

In the end, the opinion of the third group wins out. They turn

to merriment, feasting as if they had been freed from the war.

At this point two serpents appear and

destroy Laocoön[221] and one of his sons. At the sight of

25 this marvel, Aeneas[222] and his followers become disquieted, and they withdraw

to Mount Ida. Sinon lights signal fires for the Achaeans.

He had previously entered the city, using a pretext. And they [= the Achaeans], some of them sailing from Tenedos

[toward Troy] and others of them emerging from the Wooden Horse, fall upon

their enemies. They kill many, and the city

is taken by force. Neoptolemos kills

Priam, who has taken refuge at the altar of Zeus Herkeios.

p. 108 Menelaos[223] finds Helen[224] and takes her back down to the ships, after

slaughtering Deiphobos. Ajax son of Oileus takes Kassandra by

force, dragging her away from the wooden statue [*xoanon*] of Athena. At the sight

of this, the Achaeans get angry and decide to stone

---

[221] The north metopes picture the sacrifice of a bull; perhaps this is the bull being sacrificed by Laocoön.
[222] The north metopes picture both Aeneas and his son Ascanius, still in Troy.
[223] The north metopes picture Menelaos in the act of taking back Helen.
[224] See the previous note.

4⒮17. The imperial poetics of terror and pity

5   Ajax to death, but he takes refuge at the altar of Athena, and so
    is preserved from his impending destruction. Then
    the Achaeans put the city to the torch. They slaughter Polyxena[225] on the
    tomb of Achilles. Odysseus kills Astyanax,
    and Neoptolemos takes Andromache as his prize. The rest
10 of the spoils are distributed. Demophon and Akamas find Aithra[226]
    and take her with them. Then the Greeks sail off [from Troy],
    and Athena[227] begins to plan destruction for them at sea.

4§250 In analyzing the convergences between these sculptural and epic narratives, I refer to both as *Iliou Persis* without intending to imply any one-on-one relation between the two. It is important to note that the *Iliou Persis* narrative of the north metope sculptures, completed in 432 BCE, was preceded by the *Iliou Persis* narrative of the wall paintings of Polygnotus in the Stoa Poikilē (described by Pausanias 1.15.1-3; Plutarch *Kimon* 4.5-6), completed sometime between 460 and 450 BCE.[228] Instead of assuming that any single text influenced the painting and the sculpting of the *Iliou Persis* narratives in the age of Pheidias, I find it more accurate to speak of mutual influence between the visual arts and the verbal arts.

4§251 In the age of Virgil, by contrast, we find evidence that the epic of the *Aeneid* was directly influenced by the epic of the *Iliou Persis* attributed to Arctinus of Miletus. As we saw in Chapter 1, Virgil's *Aeneid* makes pointed references to this epic *Iliou Persis*. And, as we are about to see, Virgil's *Aeneid* also makes pointed reference to relief sculptures such as the ones we find adorning the north metopes of the Parthenon. It happens when Aeneas, while waiting for an audience with the queen Dido at the temple of Juno in Carthage, looks up and sees the artwork adorning the face of the temple. I propose that this artwork is meant to be understood as relief sculpture. More precisely, it

---

[225] The north metopes picture Polyxena being led to her sacrificial slaughter, though this reading is not certain.
[226] The north metopes show Aithra at the moment she is found.
[227] The north metopes show Athena attending a council of the gods.
[228] Ferrari 2000. On the *Iliou Persis* of the Stoa Poikilē, see Dué 2006:99-102. On the Iliou Persis of the Lesche of the Cnidians, especially the visual details described by Pausanias 10.25.4, 10.25.9-11, and 10.26.1-2, see Dué pp. 102-106.

Chapter Four

is meant to be understood as a poetic allusion to the relief sculptures of the Parthenon, especially to those sculptures that adorn the north face of the building. Aeneas recognizes his own picture inside the picture of the Trojan War as it is narrated on the face of the temple of Juno. There he is, pictured in the midst of the battle of the Achaeans and Trojans:

4ⓣ42 Virgil *Aeneid* 1.488

> se quoque <u>principibus permixtum</u> agnovit <u>Achivis</u>
>
> Himself, too, all <u>mixed</u> into the thick of battle with the <u>Achaean princes</u>, he [= Aeneas] recognized.

4§252 Similarly, as we saw in the description of the north face of the Parthenon, Aeneas is pictured inside the picture of the Trojan War as it is narrated there. Captured by the picture is a moment when Aeneas himself and his son Ascanius (/ Iulus) are still in Troy, about to escape from the city before its ultimate destruction.

4§253 The emotions evoked by this picture narrating the destruction of Troy on the face of the temple of Juno are terror and pity:

4ⓣ43 Virgil *Aeneid* 1.462

> <u>sunt lacrimae rerum</u> et mentem mortalia tangunt.
>
> <u>There are tears that connect with the universe</u>, and things mortal touch the mind.

4ⓣ44 Virgil *Aeneid* 1.463

> <u>solve metus</u>; feret haec aliquam tibi fama salutem.
>
> <u>Dissolve your fears</u>: this fame will bring for you a salvation of some kind.

4§254 As I argued in Chapter 1, the emotions of terror and pity in this scene from Virgil's *Aeneid* are being experienced by Aeneas as the heroic prototype of the Roman Empire. The picture of the terror and the pity seen by Aeneas is just a picture, but this picture becomes a reality because there are real emotions that correspond to it—the emotions of terror and pity as experienced by Aeneas himself in the war of the Achaeans and Trojans. The terror and the pity are viewed and projected through the lens of epic—not only the epic of the *Aeneid* but also the entire epic tradition about the destruction of Troy.

4Ⓢ17. The imperial poetics of terror and pity

4§255 As I also argued in Chapter 1, the poetics of terror and pity can be seen as a hallmark not only of Roman imperial poetry but also of Homeric poetry. Here in Chapter 4, I have been arguing that Homeric poetry too became imperial in its own right. The Athenian empire, in appropriating Homeric poetry, made it imperial. In the process, the poetics of terror and pity became a hallmark of Athenian imperial poetry, and here I mean not only Homeric poetry but also the epic tradition reflected by the *Iliou Persis* attributed to Arctinus of Miletus. Closely related to this epic tradition was the iconographic tradition of the *Iliou Persis* as reflected in the north metopes of the Parthenon. Also closely related was the *Ilious Persis* tradition as reflected in paintings. One example is the picture of the *Ilious Persis* by the Kleophrades Painter: "The central scene of sacrilege [that is, the killing of Priam by Neoptolemos] is framed on either side by paragons of filial piety: the departure of the Trojan Aeneas from the burning city, carrying Anchises on his shoulder, and the Athenian Demophon and Acamas turning a helping hand to old [Aithra]."[229]

4§256 Obviously, there are significant differences in the imperial poetics of Athens and Rome, conditioned by the many historical differences between the Athenian and the Roman empires. But there is one most significant similarity that stands out. Like the imperial poetics of Rome, which favored the Trojans over the Achaeans in its retrospective on the Trojan War, the imperial poetics of Athens was likewise partial to the Trojans. This partiality is evident in the *Iliou Persis* narrative sculpted into the north metopes of the Parthenon, as Gloria Ferrari has argued:

> The [*Iliou Persis*] was deployed on the Parthenon precisely because it was the paradigm of wrongful conquest. The images invited comparison with the Persian invasion of Greece, not, however, in the sense that the Trojans prefigure the Persians. Rather, the recent sack of Athens is seen through the image of the epic sack of Troy. The comparison is reinforced and acquires special poignancy by the position of this subject on the north side of the temple, overlooking the site of the old temple of Athena that had been burned by the Persians.[230]

4§257 As we saw already in the description of the representations surviving from the pictorial narrative of the north metopes, a prominent

---

[229] Ferrari 2000.
[230] Ferrari 2000. See also Dué 2006:96–97. On the idiosyncratic attitude of Isocrates (as in *Panegyricus* 159), see Dué p. 98n26.

Chapter Four

figure in that sorrowful narrative was the Trojan hero Aeneas. His prominence there is comparable to his prominence in Virgil's epic narrative about the equally sorrowful pictorial narrative adorning the temple of Juno. As I argue in *Homer the Preclassic*, the Athenian appropriation of Aeneas and the Aeneas theme actually started not in the era of the democracy but far earlier, and I make a parallel argument about the Athenian appropriation of Hector and his immediate family.[231]

4§258 So the poetics of terror and pity, centering on the sufferings of the Trojans, suits the cultural and political agenda of both the Roman empire in the age of Virgil and the Athenian empire in the age of Pheidias. I find it striking that this poetics can serve as an expression of imperial power. But I find it even more striking that Homeric poetry can be appropriated by the Athenian empire as a primary form of its own self-expression.

4Ⓢ18. The sorrows of Andromache

4§259 In this poetics of terror and pity, two victims of the Trojan War stand out: Hector and Andromache. To make this point, I start by returning to a most revealing passage I already quoted in Chapter 3:

4Ⓣ45 Plato *Ion* 535b–c

> ΣΩ. Ἔχε δή μοι τόδε εἰπέ, ὦ Ἴων, καὶ μὴ ἀποκρύψῃ ὅτι ἄν σε ἔρωμαι· ὅταν εὖ εἴπῃς ἔπη καὶ ἐκπλήξῃς μάλιστα τοὺς θεωμένους, ἢ τὸν Ὀδυσσέα ὅταν ἐπὶ τὸν οὐδὸν ἐφαλλόμενον ᾄδῃς, ἐκφανῆ γιγνόμενον τοῖς μνηστῆρσι καὶ ἐκχέοντα τοὺς ὀιστοὺς πρὸ τῶν ποδῶν, ἢ Ἀχιλλέα ἐπὶ τὸν Ἕκτορα ὁρμῶντα, ἢ καὶ τῶν περὶ Ἀνδρομάχην ἐλεινῶν τι ἢ περὶ Ἑκάβην ἢ περὶ Πρίαμον, τότε πότερον ἔμφρων εἶ ἢ ἔξω {c} σαυτοῦ γίγνῃ καὶ παρὰ τοῖς πράγμασιν οἴεταί σου εἶναι ἡ ψυχὴ οἷς λέγεις ἐνθουσιάζουσα, ἢ ἐν Ἰθάκῃ οὖσιν ἢ ἐν Τροίᾳ ἢ ὅπως ἂν καὶ τὰ ἔπη ἔχῃ;

> SOCRATES: Hold it right there. Tell me this, Ion—respond to what I ask without concealment. When you recite well the epic verses [*epos* plural] and induce a feeling of bedazzlement [*ekplēxis*] for the spectators [*theōmenoi*]—when you sing of [1] Odysseus leaping onto the threshold and revealing himself to the suitors and pouring out the arrows at his feet, or of [2] Achilles rushing at [2->3a] Hector, or [3]

---

[231] *HPC* II§§202 and following.

something connected to the pitiful things about [3b] Andromache or [3c] Hecuba or [3d] Priam—are you then in your right mind, or outside yourself? Does your *psukhē*, possessed by the god [*enthousiazein*], suppose that you are in the midst of the actions you describe in Ithaca or Troy, or wherever the epic verses [*epos* plural] have it?

4§260 In this passage, Socrates is enumerating some highlights of Homeric poetry as performed by rhapsodes like Ion at the Panathenaia. As we saw in Chapter 3, the enumeration takes the form of a set of accusatives of the rhapsodic subject following the verb *āidein* 'sing' (ᾄδῃς): [1] Odysseus at the epic moment when he leaps upon the threshold, ready to shoot arrows at the suitors; [2] Achilles at the epic moment when he lunges at Hector; or [3] some other highlighted thing, here unspecified (*ti*, accusative), from epic moments involving Andromache, Hecuba, or Priam.

4§261 As I noted in Chapter 3, there are five epic moments recounted here in ever-increasing compression and non-specificity. The first two moments have to do primarily with the emotion of terror, and they feature the main heroes of the *Odyssey* and the *Iliad* respectively, [1] Odysseus and [2] Achilles. The next three moments have to do primarily with the emotion of pity, and they feature the main heroes on the other side of the Trojan War: [3b] Andromache, [3c] Hecuba, and [3d] Priam. The link between the two moments of terror and the three moments of pity is [3a] Hector, who exemplifies the emotion of terror when he is about to be killed by the one who hates him most of all, his enemy Achilles, but who also exemplifies the emotion of pity when he says his last farewell to the one who loves him most of all, that is, [3b] his wife Andromache. In the wording of Plato's *Ion*, the pairing of [3a] Hector and [3b] Andromache creates a thematic link for the transition from terror to pity.

4§262 Plato's reference to 'something connected to the pitiful things about Andromache' indicates that the epic character of Andromache is specially connected to the emotion of pity.[232] In the language of epic, this emotion is formally expressed by way of lamentation. In all three of Andromache's appearances in the *Iliad*, there is an element of lament. When we hear her speak in *Iliad* XXIV (725-745), she is performing a formal lament for Hector; when we hear her in *Iliad* XXII (477-514), much of what she says corresponds morphologically to the words of a formal lament.[233] Already in

---

[232] For a most intuitive study of the rhetoric of pity, I single out the work of Konstan 2001.

[233] In the case of epic as well as tragedy, I agree with the formulation of Dué 2006:112: "the laments of the Trojan women are fundamentally Greek in form and theme"—even if the Trojans are imagined as non-Greeks.

Chapter Four

Figure 17a. Attic red-figure neck-amphora: Hector parting with Priam and Hecuba. Attributed to the Peleus Painter, ca. 475-425 BCE. Vatican Museums, Museo Gregoriano Etrusco Vaticano, 16570.

her first appearance, in *Iliad* VI (407–439), the language of lament is evident in her words as she and Hector part forever, she going back to her weaving at the loom while he goes off to his death. In short, the Homeric character of Andromache displays a distinct virtuosity in the art of lamentation.

4§263 So Plato's understanding of Andromache as the primary example of the poetics of pity in the Homeric performances of rhapsodes corresponds to an understanding already built into Homeric poetry itself. This poetry actively expresses the emotion of pity by highlighting the lamentations of Andromache. More than that, it highlights the sorrowful occasions that induce these lamentations. To review the three occasions, they are, first, the scene in *Iliad* VI when Andromache says her final farewell to Hector; second, the scene in *Iliad* XXII when Andromache is told the news of Hector's death; and, third, the scene in *Iliad* XXIV when Andromache sings her formal lament over the dead body of Hector. I refer to these three sorrowful occasions as <u>scenes</u> because all of them are theatrical—virtually operatic, as I noted in Chapter 2. In

4§18. The sorrows of Andromache

Figure 17b. Amphora, Departure of Hector, detail: Priam in tears.

Figure 17c. Amphora, Departure of Hector, detail: Hector, juxtaposed with the inscribed erotic reaction: ΚΑΛΟΣ.

Chapter Four

the age of Pheidias, the theatrical power of Andromache's laments in epic is reflected in corresponding laments staged in theater. As an example, I quoted in Chapter 2 an aria of lamentation composed in elegiac couplets and sung as a monody by the actor who plays Andromache in a tragedy of Euripides called the *Andromache*. Here I quote from the lines that introduce the aria:

4ⓣ46 Euripides *Andromache* 91–95

> Αν.   ἡμεῖς δ' οἷσπερ ἐγκείμεσθ' ἀεὶ
> θρήνοισι καὶ γόοισι καὶ δακρύμασιν
> πρὸς αἰθέρ' ἐκτενοῦμεν· ἐμπέφυκε γὰρ
> γυναιξὶ τέρψις τῶν παρεστώτων κακῶν
> 95 ἀνὰ στόμ' αἰεὶ καὶ διὰ γλώσσης ἔχειν.

> ANDROMACHE: But I, intent as always on laments [*thrēnoi*]
> and wailings [*gooi*] and outburst of tears,
> will direct these toward the aether. For it is natural
> for women to take pleasure [*terpsis*], when sufferings happen to them,
> 95 in voicing these [sufferings] again and again, maintaining the voice from one mouth to the next, from one tongue to the next.

4§264 We see here a reference to mixed feelings of sadness and erotic pleasure in response to a sorrowful song.[234] Such mixed feelings are also evident in fifth-century Athenian vase paintings that focus on the sorrowful family of Priam, Hecuba, Hector, and Andromache. A case in point is a painting that shows Hector and his parents Priam and Hecuba at the moment of their final parting (Figures 17a, 17b, 17c).

4§265 In the foreground is a profile view of Hector and his mother Hecuba facing each other for the last time, and, next to the figure of Hector, we see an inscription that eroticizes him in this saddest of moments. The inscription reads simply ΚΑΛΟΣ (*kalos*), meaning 'beautiful'. In the conventions of vase painting, such an inscription indicates the subjective reaction of the intended

---

[234] I see a reference to such mixed feelings also in *Iliad* VI 411–413: there Andromache refers to her laments, that is, to the expression of her *akhē* (plural of *akhos*) 'sorrows', as a *thalpōrē* 'comforting warmth' (on the erotic associations of *thalpein* 'make warm', see for example Aeschylus *Prometheus* 590). For more on the *terpsis* 'pleasure' of lament in tragedy, see Fantuzzi 2007b.

582

viewer of the picture. That reaction is meant to be erotic as well as esthetic. Hector is a beautiful object of desire in this sorrowful moment, and that desire is the force of the inscribed word ΚΑΛΟΣ 'beautiful'. In the background, off to the side, is a frontal view of Priam wiping away a tear. In the conventions of vase painting, a frontal view of a figure evokes the subjective reaction of the viewer, since the viewed figure is notionally making eye contact with the viewer. Whereas a profile view is the equivalent of a narrative in the third person, a frontal view is the equivalent of an eye contact between the viewer and the viewed, whose exchange of looks corresponds to an exchange of words between a first person and a second person. The overt theme of the painting, then, is the sorrow and the pity of the story of Hector. And the latent theme is the pleasure that the story brings to the viewer. That pleasure is both esthetic and erotic.

4§266 Such a combination of estheticism and eroticism in referring to Hector is already built into Homeric poetry. It all comes together in *Iliad* XXIV, when Hector is lamented at his funeral by the three women closest to him, in descending order of closeness. The lamentation is led off by Andromache, followed by Hecuba and then by Helen. Through their laments, Hector becomes estheticized and eroticized as the ultimate object of desire, the primary *beau mort* of the *Iliad*.[235]

4§267 The focus of the *Iliad* on Hector as the primary *beau mort* is evident at the conclusion of this epic. The *Iliad* as we know it ends with the funeral of Hector, not of Achilles. It is Hector, not Achilles, who is lamented at the end. Even the very last word of the *Iliad* as we have it is a signature for Hector: it is his ornamental epithet *hippodamos*, the 'horse-tamer' (*Iliad* XXIV 804).[236] So the Panathenaic tradition of the Homeric *Iliad* evolved in such a way as to highlight Hector as the primary point of interest in the poetics of terror and pity. To be contrasted is an alternative epic like the *Aithiopis*, attributed to Arctinus of Miletus, where the focus at the end is evidently on Achilles as the primary *beau mort*. Pindar's reference to the dead Achilles in *Isthmian* 8 (56–60) alludes to this alternative epic tradition.[237] In the *Iliad*, the doomed figure of Hector has been substituted for the equally doomed figure of Achilles, who is the ultimate *beau mort* of epic. Hector in the *Iliad* prefigures Achilles as that ultimate *beau mort*.

---

[235] See Vernant 1982 on the heroic concept of *le beau mort* as a complement to *la belle mort*. See also Dué 2006:80n66, with further citations.
[236] Sacks 1987.
[237] *PH* 7§6 (= pp. 204–206).

Chapter Four

4§268 This foregrounding of Hector in the *Iliad* as we know it is a matter of politics as well as esthetics. The beautiful death of Hector, his *belle mort*, is for Athenians an expression of their empire. The Athenian statesman Lycurgus says it best when he refers to the willingness of Athenian citizens to die in war not only for their own *patris* 'fatherland' but also for all of Hellas as a *patris* 'fatherland' that is *koinē* 'common' to all Hellenes (*Against Leokrates* 104 οὐ μόνον ὑπὲρ τῆς αὐτῶν πατρίδος, ἀλλὰ καὶ πάσης <τῆς> Ἑλλάδος ὡς κοινῆς <πατρίδος> ἤθελον). Lycurgus invokes as his prime example the *belle mort* of the Athenian citizen-warriors who fought at Marathon and who thereby won for Hellas a freedom from terror, an *adeia* 'security' that is *koinē* 'common' to all Hellenes (104 κοινὴν ἄδειαν ἅπασι τοῖς Ἕλλησι κτώμενοι). The Athenian statesman is making this reference to the imperial interests of Athens in the context of actually quoting the words of Hector in the *Iliad*, who says that he is willing to die for his fatherland in order to protect it against the Achaeans (Lycurgus *Against Leokrates* 103 lines 4–9, corresponding to *Iliad* XV 494–499), and Lycurgus quotes these heroic words in the larger context of saying that the Homeric *Iliad* and *Odyssey*, as performed at the quadrennial Panathenaia, are the ancestral heritage of the Athenians and the primary source of their education as citizen-warriors (*Against Leokrates* 102). In this invocation of Homeric poetry as the most sublime expression of the Athenian empire, the statesman is quoting the words of a Trojan, not the words of an Achaean. It is the *belle mort* of Hector that motivates the Athenians to live up to the heroic legacy they learn from Homer.

4§269 This Homeric *belle mort* of Hector, estheticized and eroticized through the laments of Andromache, was understood by the master artisan Pheidias when he sculpted the statue of Zeus in the temple of Zeus at Olympia. I started this chapter by highlighting Strabo's anecdote about the creative impulse that led Pheidias to sculpt this statue (8.3.30 C354). According to this anecdote, the creative impulse was a distinctly Homeric impulse. The moment captured by the sculptor is a Homeric moment. It is the moment in *Iliad* I (528–530) when Zeus nods his head and thus signifies the Plan of Zeus, which is coextensive with the plot of the Homeric *Iliad*. When I quoted this Iliadic passage, I held off saying that there is also another Iliadic passage where the god nods his head and thus signifies his Plan. This time, the Plan of Zeus is expressed not in terms of the overall plot, as in *Iliad* I, but in terms of one specific theme that pervades the plot. That theme is a picture of Hector that is animated by the sorrows of Andromache. It is a picture of Hector as a *beau mort* who takes the place of Achilles as the ultimate *beau mort* of the *Iliad*. Like some director of a grand theatrical production, Zeus pictures Andromache waiting

4§18. The sorrows of Andromache

for Hector to return to her from battle. It is the Plan of Zeus that Andromache will be kept waiting, because Hector will never return to Andromache:

4ⓣ47 *Iliad* XVII 195–214

        ὃ δ' ἄμβροτα τεύχεα δῦνε
195 Πηλεΐδεω Ἀχιλῆος ἅ οἱ θεοὶ οὐρανίωνες
      πατρὶ φίλῳ ἔπορον· ὃ δ' ἄρα ᾧ παιδὶ ὄπασσε
      γηράς· ἀλλ' οὐχ υἱὸς ἐν ἔντεσι πατρὸς ἐγήρα.
      τὸν δ' ὡς οὖν ἀπάνευθεν ἴδεν νεφεληγερέτα Ζεὺς
      τεύχεσι Πηλεΐδαο κορυσσόμενον θείοιο,
200 <u>κινήσας ῥα κάρη</u> προτὶ ὃν μυθήσατο θυμόν·
      ἆ δείλ' οὐδέ τί τοι θάνατος καταθύμιός ἐστιν
      <u>ὅς δή τοι σχεδὸν εἶσι</u>· σὺ δ' ἄμβροτα τεύχεα δύνεις
      ἀνδρὸς ἀριστῆος, τόν τε τρομέουσι καὶ ἄλλοι·
      τοῦ δὴ ἑταῖρον ἔπεφνες ἐνηέα τε κρατερόν τε,
205 τεύχεα δ' <u>οὐ κατὰ κόσμον</u> ἀπὸ κρατός τε καὶ ὤμων
      εἵλευ· ἀτάρ τοι νῦν γε μέγα κράτος ἐγγυαλίξω,
      τῶν <u>ποινὴν</u> ὅ τοι οὔ τι μάχης ἐκνοστήσαντι
      <u>δέξεται Ἀνδρομάχη</u> κλυτὰ τεύχεα Πηλεΐωνος.
      Ἦ καὶ κυανέῃσιν ἐπ' ὀφρύσι <u>νεῦσε</u> Κρονίων.
210 Ἕκτορι δ' ἥρμοσε τεύχε' ἐπὶ χροΐ, δῦ δέ μιν Ἄρης
      δεινὸς ἐνυάλιος, πλῆσθεν δ' ἄρα οἱ μέλε' ἐντὸς
      ἀλκῆς καὶ σθένεος· μετὰ δὲ κλειτοὺς ἐπικούρους
      βῆ ῥα μέγα ἰάχων· <u>ἰνδάλλετο</u> δέ σφισι πᾶσι
      τεύχεσι λαμπόμενος μεγαθύμου Πηλεΐωνος.

      He [= Hector] put on the immortalizing armor
195 of Achilles son of Peleus, which the skydwelling gods
      gave to his father [= Peleus] near and dear. And he had given it to his son [= Achilles]
      when he grew old. But the son himself never reached old age wearing the armor of his father.
      He [= Hector] was seen from afar by Zeus, gatherer of clouds.

Chapter Four

>   There he [= Hector] was, all fitted out in the armor of the
>   godlike son of Peleus.
> 200 Then he [= Zeus] <u>moved his head</u> and spoke to himself [= to
>   his own *thumos*]:
>   "Ah, you [= Hector] are a pitiful wretch. Your own death is
>   not on your mind [*thumos*]—
>   —<u>a death that is coming near</u>.[238] There you are, putting on the
>   immortalizing armor
>   of a man who is champion, one who makes all others
>   tremble.
>   It was his comrade you killed, gentle he was and strong,
> 205 and his armor, in a way that went <u>against the order</u> [<u>*kosmos*</u>]
>   <u>of things</u>, from his head and shoulders
>   you took. All the same, I will for now put in your hands great
>   power [*kratos*].
>   As a <u>compensation</u> [<u>*poinē*</u>] for this, you will never return
>   home from the battle.
>   Never will you bring home, <u>for Andromache to receive</u>, the
>   famed [*kluta*] armor of Peleus' son."
>   So spoke the son of Kronos, and with his eyebrows of azure
>   he made a reinforcing [= *epi*-] nod.
> 210 He [= Zeus] fitted the armor to Hector's skin, and he
>   [= Hector] was entered by Ares
>   the terrifying, the Enyalios. And his [= Hector's] limbs were
>   all filled inside
>   with force and strength. Seeking to join up with his famed
>   allies
>   he went off, making a great war cry. <u>He was quite the picture</u>
>   for them all.
>   He was shining in the armor of the man with the great heart
>   [*thumos*], the son of Peleus.

---

[238] In the scholia A (Aristonicus) for *Iliad* XVII 202, we learn that the variant reading ὃς δή τοι σχεδὸν εἶσιν 'that is coming near' was preferred by Aristarchus: <ὃς δή τοι σχεδόν ἐστι:> ... αἱ δὲ Ἀριστάρχου <u>ὃς δή τοι σχεδὸν εἶσιν</u>. In scholia A^im (Didymus), we read: Ἀρίσταρχος <u>εἶσιν</u>.

4ⓈI8. The sorrows of Andromache

4§270 So the sorrows of Andromache are willed by Zeus. The Plan of Zeus prioritizes these sorrows in the plot of the Homeric *Iliad*, which foregrounds the terrible and pitiful fate of Hector and Andromache. The poetry of terror and pity, brought to life in the lamentations of Andromache over the fate of her husband and over her own fate, is distinctly Homeric. More than that, this poetry is distinctly imperial in the age of Pheidias, an age of Athenian imperial power. For an Athenian master craftsman like Pheidias, this imperial poetry of terror and pity comes to life in the moment when Zeus nods his head to signify what will happen to Hector and Andromache in the Homeric *Iliad*. It is this Homeric moment that must be captured by the imperial sculptor, to be preserved forever in all its rigid beauty.

CONCLUSIONS

C⊛1. Five centuries of Homeric transmission

C§1. I propose to outline here the overall chronology of Homeric transmission as I have reconstructed it in this book. The basis for my overall reconstruction is the <u>Homeric Koine</u>, which I have equated with the Panathenaic Homer in the era of the Athenian democracy. This Koine was relatively unaugmented. To be contrasted is the <u>Homerus Auctus</u>, which I have defined as an augmented or expanded Homer. As I showed in Chapters 2 and 3, the themes that differentiate the poetry of the Homerus Auctus from the poetry of the Homeric Koine are characteristic of Cyclic, Orphic, and Hesiodic traditions. As I also showed, these traditions are pre-Homeric—that is, if we define <u>pre-Homeric</u> in terms of earlier periods when the Cyclic, Orphic, and Hesiodic traditions were as yet undifferentiated from what later became the Homeric tradition. In other words, the Cyclic, Hesiodic, and Orphic variants of the Homerus Auctus predate the Homeric Koine. I reconstruct a succession of five phases corresponding roughly to five successive centuries:

Phase A. The augmented Homer or Homerus Auctus took shape in an era that preceded the fifth century BCE. This version of Homer may be considered Panathenaic, but only in terms of the sixth century BCE. This phase is reconstructed in the twin book *Homer the Preclassic*.

Phase B (as introduced in Chapter 4). The Homerus Auctus was ultimately replaced as the Panathenaic Homer by an unaugmented Homer in the era of the democracy in the fifth century BCE. This new Panathenaic Homer is what I have been calling the Homeric Koine.

Phase C (as introduced in Chapter 3). The Homeric Koine persisted as the Panathenaic Homer into the age of Plato, in the fourth century BCE.

Phase D (as introduced in Chapter 2). The Homerus Auctus resurfaced, but not as a Panathenaic Homer, in the later age of Callimachus, in the third century BCE.

Conclusions

Phase E (as introduced in Chapter 1). The Homerus Auctus was suppressed and replaced by the unaugmented Homeric Koine in the still later age of Aristarchus in the second century BCE. This unaugmented Koine of Homer, as edited by Aristarchus, was no longer simply a Panathenaic Homer. In editing the unaugmented Homer, Aristarchus reported in his commentaries a mass of non-Koine variants that had gone unreported in earlier editions of the unaugmented Koine of Homer, and many of these non-Koine variants eventually infiltrated the textual transmission of the unaugmented Homer.

C§2. In the age of Plato, the Athenian Koine was the dominant version of Homer. Later on, in the age of Callimachus, the Homerus Auctus became the dominant version—so much so that I never needed to use the word *koinē* in Chapter 2, which I devote to that later age. Still later, in the age of Aristarchus, the Athenian Koine became once again the dominant version of Homer.

C§3. What I just said about the age of Aristarchus is a one-sided formulation, however. In order to show the other side, I highlight a basic fact. The age of Aristarchus, director of the Library in Alexandria, was also the age of Crates, director of the Library in Pergamon. And while the base text of Homer used by Aristarchus was the Athenian Koine, the base text used by Crates was the Homerus Auctus.

C⑤2. An example of significant differences in theme between the Koine and the Homerus Auctus

C§4. There is a reference made by Callimachus to Scheria, the mythical island of the Phaeacians in the *Odyssey*. In his poetry, Callimachus equated this mythical place with a historical place, the island of Corcyra (*Aetia* Book 1 F 12, 13, 15). In making this equation, he was following a traditional theme already known to Thucydides, who says explicitly that the people of Corcyra claimed to be descended from the Phaeacians (1.25.4).[1] This theme differs from what we find in the text of Homer as we know it, which I identify with the Homeric Koine. This different theme, I argue, stems from the textual tradition that I identify with the Homerus Auctus.

C§5. The wording of this different theme is actually attested at verse 158 of *Odyssey* xiii. In the scholia linked to this verse (at xiii 152), we learn that Aristophanes of Byzantium reported a reading that differed from the reading

---

[1] Nagy 2001c:89, with reference to Thucydides 3.70.4 as well as 1.25.4.

he found in the Homeric Koine.[2] The difference in meaning has to do with an equation of the mythical Scheria, island of the Phaeacians, with the historical Corcyra. This equation was possible in terms of the variant reading, but it was impossible in terms of the reading found in the Homeric Koine, that is, in the Athenian Homer stemming from the new era of the democracy. In the Koine version of the *Odyssey*, the Phaeacians are cut off from the world outside their mythical past after Poseidon interposes a huge mountain that seals them off forever. In this particular version, the wording at verse 158 of *Odyssey* xiii is μέγα δέ σφιν ὄρος πόλει ἀμφικαλύψαι 'and make the huge mountain envelop their city'. In the non-Koine version favored by Callimachus, by contrast, Zeus enjoins Poseidon not to interpose the mountain. As we know from the testimony of Aristophanes of Byzantium, the variant wording is μηδέ σφιν ὄρος πόλει ἀμφικαλύψαι 'but do not make the mountain envelop their city'.[3]

C§6. In terms of the Koine version heard by Athenians in the new era of the democracy, the mythical place of Scheria cannot be identified with the historical place of Corcyra, since Scheria had been sealed off forever. In terms of the non-Koine version favored by Callimachus, by contrast, the possibility of such an identification is not sealed off but left open. Thus the Phaeacians are saved from the fate of losing contact with the real world of their future, and they retain the alternative fate of becoming the ancestors of the people of Corcyra.[4]

C§7. But the Koine version of Homer negates such an identification of Scheria with Corcyra. I interpret this negation in terms of politics as well as poetics. The political terms correspond to the imperial design of Athens in the era of the democracy. If the mythical Scheria can be sealed off from the historical Corcyra, it is owned by Athens; if it is not sealed off, it is owned by Corcyra.[5] The Athenians may be said to own the mythical place of Scheria because of a political reality, that is, because they actually controlled the Homeric Koine in the era of the democracy. In the undifferentiated Homerus Auctus as emulated

---

[2] Nagy 2001c:93n65.
[3] Nagy 2001c:83–84.
[4] Nagy 2001c:84–91.
[5] Douglas Frame notes that we may see traces here of converging Athenian and Panionian agenda.

Conclusions

by Callimachus and his contemporaries, by contrast, the imperial designs of the Athenians were not so clearly foregrounded.⁶

C⑤3. On the Homerus Auctus in the age of Virgil

C§8. In the twin book *Homer the Preclassic*, I argue that Virgil in the first century BCE drew on the Homerus Auctus as a source for his own epic, the *Aeneid*.⁷ In drawing on the Homerus Auctus, he was emulating Callimachus and his contemporaries in the third century BCE. Like Callimachus, Virgil was a neoteric poet in that he based his poetry on the Homerus Auctus. Like Callimachus, he was drawing on a form of Homer that seemed to him newer than the supposedly real Homer. This seemingly newer Homer, however, was really the oldest available Homer of them all. As I also argue in *Homer the Preclassic*, the Homerus Auctus of Virgil preserved some of the oldest recoverable phases of Homer.⁸

C§9. As I argued in Chapters 1 and 2 of the present book, the Homerus Auctus was antithetical to the Homer of Aristarchus, whose edition represented the most limited and the most rigid of all Homers. This Homer of Aristarchus was the equivalent of scripture for the premier Aristarchean in the era of Virgil, Didymus. From the standpoint of an Aristarchean scholar like Didymus, the using of the Homerus Auctus by any poet would be the equivalent of abusing Homer. Such an attitude is not confined to the ancient world. Even today Virgil is occasionally criticized as an unworthy imitator of Homer on the grounds that he infuses his own epic with elements judged to be Cyclic, Hesiodic, and Orphic. Such criticism, I submit, is based on the same kinds of criteria that produced the most rigid Homer of them all, the quasi scriptural Homer of Aristarcheans like Didymus in the first century BCE.

---

⁶ Nagy 2001c:84–91. The politics and poetics of identifying Corcyra with the land of the Phaeacians are comparable, I think, to the politics and poetics of identifying the historical Ithaca of the first millennium BCE with the homeland of Odysseus. An essential place-marker for the latter identification was the "Cave of the Nymphs" in the Bay of Polis on the northwestern coast of Ithaca, which was a stopping point for travelers sailing from the Corinthian Gulf to Corcyra and back. On the links between this cave, which is the location of a hero-cult for Odysseus, and the Cave of the Nymphs in *Odyssey* xiii 363, where we see Odysseus in the act of hiding the tripods given to him by the Phaeacians, see Malkin 1998:64–67, 95–107. On the epic poetry of the *Odyssey* as a form of "merchandise," see the pertinent analysis of Dougherty 2001:53–68. For an earlier localization of Ithaca, dating back to the second millennium BCE, see Bittlestone 2005.

⁷ *HPC* E§§145 and following.

⁸ *HPC* E§§154 and following.

C⒮3. On the Homerus Auctus in the age of Virgil

C§10. In Chapter 1, I was already saying that the Homer of Aristarchus was too rigid a Homeric model for Virgil. But now the question is, what kind of Homeric model could Virgil have chosen instead? Clearly, the most useful Homer for Virgil would have been the Homer of Zenodotus. This text of Homer was the text used by Callimachus and other neoteric poets, including Apollonius and Theocritus.[9] And Virgil's poetry is modeled on their neoteric poetry.

C§11. It is common knowledge, of course, that Callimachus, Apollonius, and Theocritus—all three—represent major influences in the shaping of Virgil and his poetic repertoire. Virgil, after all, imitated these three poets as much as he imitated Homer, if not more so. To the extent that Virgil did indeed choose these neoteric poets as his models, he too was a neoteric poet.

C§12. But my argument goes further. Virgil had access not only to neoteric poets like Callimachus but also to the Homerus Auctus. To say this much is not the same thing as saying that the Homerus Auctus in the age of Virgil was represented by the base text once used by Zenodotus in the age of Callimachus. In the age of Virgil and already in the age of Aristarchus, that base text had been replaced by a narrower base text representing the unaugmented Athenian version. How, then, did Virgil have access to a Homerus Auctus? Here it is essential to recall the fact that the age of Aristarchus in Alexandria was also the age of Crates in Pergamon. This Crates, as I argued in Chapter 2, used for his edition of Homer a base text that still represented the Homerus Auctus.[10] Further, Crates as editor of this Homerus Auctus happened to privilege many of the same elements that neoteric poets in the age of Callimachus considered to be neoteric. What I am arguing, then, is that Virgil preferred the Homerus Auctus as represented by the Homer of Crates, not the Homeric Koine as represented by the Homer of Aristarchus. Virgil's epic *Aeneid* was based on the inclusive Homer of Crates, not on the exclusive Homer of Aristarchus.

C§13. Just as the base text used by Aristarchus for his edition of Homer in Alexandria was inherited rather than created by that editor, the same can be said about the augmented base text used by Crates in Pergamon – and, a century earlier, by Zenodotus in Alexandria. The Homerus Auctus, which was the basis of the texts used by Crates and by Zenodotus before him, was not an editorial creation resulting from arbitrary additions of Cyclic, Hesiodic, and Orphic elements to an original Homer. Rather, as I argue in *Homer the Preclassic*,

---

[9] See ch. 2 on the neoterism of Callimachus and his contemporaries.
[10] See also LP (Nagy 1998) 215, 222–223.

Conclusions

the Homerus Auctus was a poetic creation resulting from organic accretions later judged to be non-Homeric and therefore neoteric, that is, Cyclic, Hesiodic, and Orphic.

C⑤4. The Shield of Aeneas in the *Aeneid* of Virgil

C§14. A prime example of Virgil's use of the Homerus Auctus is his narrative of the Shield of Aeneas in *Aeneid* 8. This narrative is based not only on the narrative of the Shield of Achilles in *Iliad* XVIII. As Philip Hardie has shown, it is based also on the work of Crates himself in editing and commenting on this Iliadic narrative.[11] In the Epilegomena of *Homer the Preclassic*, I explore at some length the ways in which Virgil's poetry not only emulates the Homerus Auctus but also refers to the edition and commentary of Crates. Here in this Appendix, I simply offer my own translation of relevant portions of Virgil's narrative, along with a brief commentary of my own.

C§15. To narrate the Shield of Aeneas is to narrate the imperial power of Rome.[12] Such power is not only imperial but cosmic, thus transcending the conventional forms of epic narration. It is Virgil's ultimate poetic formulation of <u>cosmos and imperium</u>:[13]

Virgil *Aeneid* 8.615–629, 729–731

    615   dixit, et amplexus nati Cytherea petivit,

            <u>arma</u> sub aduersa posuit radiantia quercu.

            ille deae donis et tanto laetus honore

            expleri nequit atque <u>oculos per singula volvit</u>,

            miraturque interque manus et bracchia versat

    620   terribilem cristis galeam flammasque vomentem,

            fatiferumque ensem, loricam ex aere rigentem,

            sanguineam, ingentem, qualis cum caerula nubes

            solis inardescit radiis longeque refulget;

            tum levis ocreas electro auroque recocto,

    625   hastamque et <u>clipei</u> non enarrabile <u>textum</u>.

---

[11] Hardie 1986.

[12] In Virgil *Aeneid* 8.640, the wording *Iovis ante aram* 'in front of the altar of Jupiter' may imply a mental association with the Altar of Zeus at Pergamon.

[13] For this term, see especially Hardie 1986:339.

C⒮4. The Shield of Aeneas in the *Aeneid* of Virgil

illic res Italas Romanorumque triumphos
haud vatum ignarus venturique inscius aevi
fecerat ignipotens, illic genus omne futurae
stirpis ab Ascanio pugnataque in ordine bella.
...

Talia per clipeum Volcani, dona parentis,
730 miratur rerumque ignarus imagine gaudet
attollens umero famamque et fata nepotum.

615 She spoke, and the goddess of the island Cythera sought the embrace of her son,
and she placed the arms [*arma*], radiant, under the shade of an oak that faced her.
And he, rejoicing at the gifts of the goddess and at such a great honor,
cannot get his fill as he lets his eyes turn them over, over and over again, one by one,[14]
and he looks in wonder at them, handles them, and turns them over and over in his arms,
620 the helmet's crest, with its look of terror, which belches bursts of flame,
and the sword that brings doom, and the rigid breastplate made of bronze,
blood-red and huge, like some bluish cloud
that is set on fire by the rays of the sun and reflects them from afar.
Then there were the polished shin-guards, made of amber and refined gold,
625 and the spear and the shield, the weaving [*textus*] of which is beyond all power to narrate.
It was there [= on the shield of Aeneas] that the story of Italy and the triumphs of the Romans

---

[14] The visual sequencing of the metalwork is made parallel to the verbal sequencing of the poetry.

Conclusions

      had been made by one <u>who is not at all without knowledge of
what seers know, not without knowledge of the age that
was yet to come</u>,[15]

      made by the master of fire, yes, there was the entire lineage
of the future

      descendants of Ascanius [/ Iulus], and the wars to be fought,
to be fought <u>in due order</u>, those wars.[16]

      ...

      Such things, through Vulcan's <u>shield</u> given by his mother,

730   he <u>gazes at with wonder</u> [*mirārī*] and, having no knowledge
of the <u>universe</u> that is there, he rejoices in the <u>image</u>
[*imāgō*][17]

      and <u>lifts it up on his shoulder</u>. There is was, what was to be
the fame and the destinies of his descendants.

C§16. The Shield of Aeneas is signaled here in *Aeneid* 8.616 with *arma* 'armor, arms' as the first word, which corresponds to the first word of the epic, at *Aeneid* 1.1: *arma virumque cano* 'armor I sing, and the man'. But now, in the first reference to arma 'armor' in *Aeneid* 8.616, the description of the Shield as a shield has not yet happened. So far, only the armor in general is being described. But there is more to it: the word *arma* 'armor' here in *Aeneid* 8.616, by way of cross-referring to the initial use of *arma* in *Aeneid* 1.1, stands metonymically for the whole epic, not only for the 'armor' of Aeneas. The *arma* 'armor' at the beginning of *Aeneid* 1.1 can apply here in *Aeneid* 8.616 if we understand the deployment of *arma* in *Aeneid* 1.1 as a masterstroke of metonymy. What is being signaled by the arma in *Aeneid* 8.616 is a description of the Shield that becomes coextensive with the overall narration of the epic that is the *Aeneid* in its entirety. But when the actual description of the Shield begins in *Aeneid* 8.625, the wording makes it clear that this description defies any immediate narration: *clipei non enarrabile textum* 'the <u>shield</u>, the

---

[15] In *Aeneid* 8.627, Vulcan is *haud vatum ignarus* 'not at all without knowledge of what seers know'. Thus the metalworker is conscious of an equation between the metalworking that creates the Shield and the songmaking that creates the description that defies narration. The choice of the word *vates* instead of *poeta* is appropriate to the Augustan poetics of a romanized <u>Homerus Auctus</u>, containing elements that critics like Zenodotus would have considered non-Homeric and therefore Orphic.

[16] See my earlier remark on the visual sequencing of the metalwork.

[17] The character of Aeneas cannot yet 'read' the prophecy woven into the description that cannot be narrated as a narration, only as a weaving.

C⓼4. The Shield of Aeneas in the *Aeneid* of Virgil

Figure 18. Sculpture: the "Farnese Atlas." Roman marble copy of a Hellenistic Greek original. Naples, Museo Archeologico Nazionale, 6374.

Conclusions

weaving [<u>textus</u>] of which is beyond all power to narrate'. To describe such a cosmic power will require an overall epic narration, from beginning to end, which cannot be successful until the story is fully told. Such a narration calls for a metaphor to substitute for the narration: instead of a tale that is being told, the narration is reconfigured as a web that is being woven, a *textus*. The story has to be told from beginning to end, just as a web has to be woven from beginning to end. Further, the metaphor of the woven web is itself a crossover from the world of weaving to the world of metalwork, as performed by the god Vulcan. There is a comparable crossover in *Iliad* XVIII 590, where the word *poikillein* 'pattern-weave' refers to the metalwork performed by the god Hephaistos in making the Shield of Achilles.[18] Virgil must have had this reference in mind in *Aeneid* 8.625, describing the ineffable *textus* or web that is the Shield of Aeneas. The ineffable power of this web, cosmic and imperial, is ultimately realized as the epic that is the *Aeneid*. It is simultaneously realized as the universal globe that is the Shield of the Aeneas, the description of which defies immediate narration but becomes coextensive with the ultimate narration of the *Aeneid*. As the description of the Shield reaches completion, the hero of the *Aeneid* shoulders its massive orb as his own burden.

C§17. As Hardie has shown, the Shield of Aeneas is not only a picturing of the globe that is the universe. The Shield is meant to be the globe itself. For Aeneas, carrying the Shield in *Aeneid* 8.730–731 is the same thing as carrying the weight of the whole world on his shoulder. The shouldering of this titanic burden by Aeneas matches the shouldering of the universal globe by Atlas the Titan. Here I find it relevant to show an evocative image. It is the statue of the Farnese Atlas. The sculpture pictures the Titan in the act of shouldering a celestial sphere, which is an idealization of the earthly sphere (Figure 18).

C§18. Such a visualization of Atlas struggling underneath the massive burden of a cosmic and imperial globe was inspired by theories about a spherical world, and these theories were in turn inspired by allegorizing traditions stemming from the Homerus Auctus, that is, from a text that combined—or recombined—the world of Orpheus with the world of Homer. The burden that weighs so heavily on the shoulder of this primordial Atlas is analogous to the cosmic and imperial burden of an augmented and theoretically all-inclusive Homer.

---

[18] *HPC* II 413. Also, in *HPC* E§148, I argue that the use of the word *triplax* 'three-fold' or 'triple' with reference to the Shield of Achilles at *Iliad* XVIII 480 shows another comparable pattern of crossover from weaving to metalwork.

C§4. The Shield of Aeneas in the *Aeneid* of Virgil

C§19. Aeneas does not yet know what it means for him to shoulder the Shield that was made for him by the divine metalworker—and, ultimately, by the poet of his own epic, which is the *Aeneid*. But the poetic description of what is pictured on the Shield has already prophesied that meaning. We may compare the poetic image of the petrified serpent in *Iliad* II verse 319, in the context of verses 299–332, as I analyzed it in Chapter 1: that stop-motion picture of terror and pity turns out to be a prophecy of the Troy story—once that story is fully told from beginning to end. So also the stop-motion picture of the Shield of Aeneas prophesies the story of Rome.

C§20. The Shield of Achilles, as a globe, was simply Homeric as far as Crates was concerned. Since it was evidently the model for the Shield of Aeneas, it must have been Homeric for Virgil as well. Evidently, Virgil's Homer was the Homerus Auctus of Crates, to be distinguished from the narrower Homer of Aristarchus, for whom the Ōkeanos was a fresh-water river encircling an earth that was flat. Virgil's Homer is also to be distinguished from the supposedly real Homer as edited by Zenodotus, for whom the verses about the Ōkeanos—and in fact all the verses about the Shield of Achilles—were Orphic accretions that needed to be athetized in his base text of Homer.

C§21. From all we have just seen, I conclude that the idea of <u>cosmos and imperium</u> in Virgil's *Aeneid* was derived from the Homerus Auctus—as mediated by the Homeric edition and the Homeric commentaries of Crates in Pergamon. This Cratetean Homer was the source for the imperial design of Virgil's *Aeneid*.

ABBREVIATIONS

BA – *The Best of the Achaeans: Concepts of the Hero in Archaic Greek Poetry* = N 1979; BA^2 = N 1999
EH – "The Epic Hero" = N 2005a
GM – *Greek Mythology and Poetics* = N 1990b
HQ – *Homeric Questions* = N 1996b
HR – *Homeric Responses* = N 2003a
HTL – *Homer's Text and Language* = N 2004a
LP – "The Library of Pergamon as a Classical Model" = N 1998
N – Nagy, G.
PH – *Pindar's Homer: The Lyric Possession of an Epic Past* = N 1990a
PP – *Poetry as Performance: Homer and Beyond* = N 1996a
PR – *Plato's Rhapsody and Homer's Music: The Poetics of the Panathenaic Festival in Classical Athens* = N 2002

BIBLIOGRAPHY

Alexiou, M. 2002. *After Antiquity: Greek Language, Myth and Metaphor.* Ithaca, NY.
Allen, R. E., ed. 1996. *Ion, Hippias Minor, Laches, Protagoras.* New Haven.
Allen, T. W., ed. 1912. *Homeri Opera. Vol. 5, Hymni, Cyclus, Fragmenta, Margites, Batrachomyomachia, Vitae.* Oxford.
———. 1924. *Homer: The Origins and the Transmission.* Oxford.
Allen, T. W., and Monro, D. B., eds. 1920. *Homeri Opera I–V.* 3rd ed. Oxford.
Aloni, A. 1986. *Tradizioni arcaiche della Troade e composizione dell'Iliade.* Milan.
———. 1989. *L'aedo e i tiranni: Ricerche sull'Inno omerico ad Apollo.* Rome.
———. 2006. *Da Pilo a Sigeo: Poemi cantori e scrivani al tempo dei Tiranni.* Alessandria.
Anderson, M. J. 1997. *The Fall of Troy in Early Greek Poetry and Art.* Oxford.
Antonelli, L. 2000. "I Pisistratidi al Sigeo. Instanze pan-ioniche nell'Atene tirannica." *Anemos* 1:9–58.
Apthorp, M. J. 1980. *The Manuscript Evidence for Interpolation in Homer.* Heidelberg.

Armstrong, R., and Dué, C., eds. 2006. *The Homerizon: Conceptual Interrogations in Homeric Studies.* Classics@ 3, http://chs.harvard.edu/publications.sec/classics.ssp.
Asheri, D., Lloyd, A., and Corcella, A. 2007. *A Commentary on Herodotus Books I-IV* (ed. O. Murray and A. Moreno; tr. B. Graziosi et al.). Oxford.
Austin, R. G., ed. 1964. *P. Vergili Maronis Aeneidos liber secundus.* Oxford.
Bader, F. 1989. *La langue des dieux, ou l'hermétisme des poètes indo-européens.* Pisa.
Bakker, E. J. 1997. *Poetry in Speech: Orality and Homeric Discourse.* Ithaca, NY.
———. 2005. *Pointing at the Past: From Formula to Performance in Homeric Poetics.* Hellenic Studies 12. Washington, DC.
Bakker, E. J., and Kahane, A., eds. 1997. *Written Voices, Spoken Signs: Tradition, Performance, and the Epic Text.* Cambridge, MA.
Barber, E. J. W. 1991. *Prehistoric Textiles: The Development of Cloth in the Neolithic and Bronze Ages, with Special Reference to the Aegean.* Princeton.
———. 1992. "The Peplos of Athena." In Neils 1992a:103–117, with notes at 208–210.
Barrett, W. S., ed. 1966. *Euripides: Hippolytos.* Corrected reprint of 1964 ed. Oxford.
Barron, J. P. 1964. "Religious Propaganda of the Delian League." *Journal of Hellenic Studies* 84:35–48.
Bassett, S.E. 1938. *The Poetry of Homer.* Berkeley. 2nd ed. 2003 by B. Heiden. Lanham, MD.
Beck, D. 2005. *Homeric Conversation.* Hellenic Studies 14. Washington, DC.
Benveniste, E. 1948. *Noms d'agent et noms d'action en indo-européen.* Paris.
Berczelly, L. 1992. "Pandora and Panathenaia: The Pandora Myth and the Sculptural Decoration of the Parthenon." *Acta ad archaeologiam et artium historiam pertinentia* 8:53–86.
Berenson Maclean, J. K., and Aitken, E. B., eds. 2001. *Flavius Philostratus, Heroikos.* Atlanta.
Bernabé, A., ed. 1987–2007. *Poetae Epici Graeci: Testimonia et Fragmenta.* I–II (1–3). Berlin.
Bidez, J., ed. 1924. *L'empereur Julien. Oeuvres complètes.* Vol. 1, pt. 2, *Lettres et fragments.* Paris.
Bird, G. D. 1994. "The Textual Criticism of an Oral Homer." *Nile, Ilissos and Tiber: Essays in Honour of Walter Kirkpatrick Lacey* (ed. V. J. Gray). Special issue, *Prudentia* 26:35–52.
Bittlestone, R. 2005. *Odysseus Unbound: The Search for Homer's Ithaca.* With J. Diggle and J. Underhill. Cambridge.
Blanc, A. 2008. *Les contraintes métriques dans la poésie homérique. L'emploi des thèmes nominaux sigmatiques dans l'hexamètre dactylique.* Leuven and Paris.
Blech, M. 1982. *Studien zum Kranz bei den Griechen.* Berlin and New York.

Blegen, C. W. 1958. *Troy.* Vol. 4, *Settlements VIIa, VIIb and VIII.* With C. Boulter, J. Caskey, and M. Rawson. Princeton.
Boedeker, D., and Sider, D., eds. 2001. *The New Simonides: Contexts of Praise and Desire.* Oxford.
Böhme, R. 1988. "Homer oder Orpheus?" *Zeitschrift für Papyrologie und Epigraphik* 71:25–31.
———. 1989. "Neue Orpheusverse auf dem Derveni-Papyrus." *Emerita* 57:211–238.
Bollack, J. 1969. *Empédocle.* Vol. 3, pt. 1, *Les Origines. Commentaire.* Paris.
———. 1994. "Une action de restauration culturelle. La place accordée aux tragiques par le décret de Lycurgue." *Mélanges Pierre Lévêque* (eds. M.-M. Mactoux and E. Geny) 13–24. Paris.
Brelich, A. 1958. *Gli eroi greci: un problema storico-religioso.* Rome.
Broggiato, M. 1998. "Cratete di Mallo negli Scholl. A ad *Il.* 24.282 e ad *Il.* 9.169a." *Seminari Romani di Cultura Greca* 1:137–143.
———, ed. 2001. *Cratete di Mallo.* La Spezia.
Bundy, E. L. 1972. "The 'Quarrel between Kallimachos and Apollonios' Part I: The Epilogue of Kallimachos's 'Hymn to Apollo'." *California Studies in Classical Antiquity* 5:39–94.
———. 1986. *Studia Pindarica.* Berkeley and Los Angeles.
Burgess, J. S. 2001. *The Tradition of the Trojan War in Homer and the Epic Cycle.* Baltimore.
———. 2004. "Performance and the Epic Cycle." *Classical Journal* 100:1–23.
———. 2006. "Tumuli of Achilles." In Armstrong and Dué 2006, http://chs.harvard.edu/publications.sec/classics.ssp.
———. 2008. *The Death and Afterlife of Achilles.* Baltimore.
Burkert, W. 1960. "Das Lied von Ares und Aphrodite. Zum Verhältnis von Odyssee und Ilias." *Rheinisches Museum für Philologie* 103:130–144. Trans. by G. M. Wright and P. V. Jones in *Homer: German Scholarship in Translation* 249–262. 1997. Oxford.
———. 1979. "Kynaithos, Polycrates, and the Homeric Hymn to Apollo." *Arktouros: Hellenic Studies Presented to B. M. W. Knox* (eds. G. W. Bowersock, W. Burkert, and M. C. J. Putnam) 53–62. Berlin.
Calame, C. 2001. *Choruses of Young Women in Ancient Greece: Their Morphology, Religious Role, and Social Function.* Trans. D. Collins and J. Orion. 2nd ed. Lanham, MD.
———. 2005. *Masks of Authority: Fiction and Pragmatics in Ancient Greek Poetics.* Trans. P. M. Burk. Ithaca, NY.
Cameron, A. 1990. "Isidore of Miletus and Hypatia: On the Editing of Mathematical Texts." *Greek, Roman and Byzantine Studies* 31:103–127.
———. 1995. *Callimachus and His Critics.* Princeton.
Carlisle, M., and Levaniouk, O., eds. 1999. *Nine Essays on Homer.* Lanham, MD.

Cassio, A. C. 2003. "Ospitare in casa poeti orali: Omero, Testoride, Creofilo e Staroselac ([Herodot.] *vita Hom.* 190 ss. Allen; Plat. *Resp.* 600b)." *Quaderni dei Seminari Romani di Cultura Greca* 6:35–46.

Càssola, F., ed. 1975. *Inni Omerici*. Milan.

CEG. See Hansen 1983.

Chantraine, P. 1953. *Grammaire homérique*. Vol. 2, *Syntaxe*. Paris.

———. 1958. *Grammaire homérique*. Vol. 1, *Phonétique et morphologie*. 3rd ed. Paris.

———. 2009. *Dictionnaire étymologique de la langue grecque: histoire des mots* (eds. J. Taillardat, O. Masson, and J.-L. Perpillou). Includes supplement "Chroniques d'étymologie grecque" (eds. A. Blanc, C. de Lamberterie, and J.-L. Perpillou) 1–10. Paris. Abbreviated DELG.

Citti, V. 1966. "Le edizioni omeriche 'delle città'." *Vichiana* 3:227–267.

Clader, L. L. 1976. *Helen: The Evolution From Divine to Heroic in Greek Epic Tradition*. Mnemosyne Supplement 42. Leiden.

Clay, D. 1988. "The Archaeology of the Temple of Juno in Carthage (*Aen.* I. 446–93)." *Classical Philology* 83:195–205.

———. 1991. "Alcman's *Partheneion*." *Quaderni Urbinati di Cultura Classica* 39:47–67.

———. 1992. "The World of Hesiod." *Ramus: Critical Studies in Greek and Roman Literature* 21:131–155.

———. 1998. "The Theory of the Literary Persona in Antiquity." *Materiali e Dicussioni per l'analisi dei testi Classici* 40:9–40.

Clay, J. S. 1997. "The Homeric Hymns." In Morris and Powell 1997:489–507.

Colbeaux, M. A. 2005. "Raconter la vie d'Homère dans l'antiquité: Édition commentée du traité anonyme, 'Au sujet d'Homère et d'Hésiode, de leurs origines et de leur joute,' et de la 'Vie d'Homère' attribué à Hérodote." Doctoral diss., Université Charles de Gaulle—Lille III.

Collins, D. 2004. *Master of the Game: Competition and Performance in Greek Poetry*. Hellenic Studies 7. Washington, DC.

Collins, L. 1988. *Studies in Characterization in the Iliad*. Frankfurt.

Cook, E. 1995. *The Odyssey at Athens: Myths of Cultural Origins*. Ithaca, NY.

———. 1999. "'Active' and 'Passive' Heroics in the *Odyssey*." *Classical World* 93:149–167.

Cook, J. M. 1973. *The Troad: An Archaeological and Topographical Study*. Oxford.

———. 1984. "The Topography of the Plain of Troy." In Foxhall and Davies 1984:163–172. Bristol.

Cooper, J. M., and Hutchinson, D. S. 1997. *Plato: Complete Works*. Indianapolis.

Crane, G. 1988. *Calypso: Backgrounds and Conventions of the Odyssey*. Frankfurt.

Csapo, E., and Miller, M. C., eds. 2007. *The Origins of Theater in Ancient Greece and Beyond: From Ritual to Drama*. Cambridge.

Cuillandre, J. 1944. *La droite et la gauche dans les poèmes homériques en concordance avec la doctrine pythagoricienne et avec la tradition celtique.* Paris.
Currie, B. 2005. *Pindar and the Cult of Heroes.* Oxford.
D'Alessio, G. B. 2004. "Textual Fluctuations and Cosmic Streams: Ocean and Acheloios." *Journal of Hellenic Studies* 124:16–37.
———. 2005a. "The Megalai Ehoiai: A Survey of the Fragments." In Hunter 2005a:176–216.
———. 2005b. "Pindar, Bacchylides, and Hesiodic Genealogical Poetry." In Hunter 2005a:217–238.
Davidson, O. M. 2001a. "Some Iranian Poetic Tropes as Reflected in the 'Life of Ferdowsi' Traditions." *Philologica et Linguistica. Historia, Pluralitas, Universitas. Festschrift für Helmut Humbach zum 80. Geburtstag am 4. Dezember 2001* (eds. M. G. Schmidt and W. Bisang) supplement, 1–12. Trier.
———. 2001b. "La 'publication' des textes arabes sous forme de lectures publiques dans les mosquées." In Giard and Jacob 2001:401–411.
Davies, M. 1994. "The Tradition about the First Sacred War." In Hornblower 1994:193–212.
Day, J. W. 1989. "Rituals in Stone: Early Greek Grave Epigrams and Monuments." *Journal of Hellenic Studies* 109:16–28.
DELG. See Chantraine 2009.
Detienne, M. 1973. *Les maîtres de vérité dans la Grèce archaïque.* 2nd ed. Paris.
Deutsche Akademie der Wissenschaften zu Berlin. 1873–. *Inscriptiones Graecae.* Berlin. Abbreviated *IG.*
de Vet, T. 2005. "Parry in Paris: Structuralism, Historical Linguistics, and the Oral Theory." *Classical Antiquity* 24:257–284.
Diels, H., and Kranz, W., eds. 1951/1952. *Die Fragmente der Vorsokratiker.* 6th ed. Berlin. Abbreviated DK.
DK. See Diels and Kranz 1951/1952.
Dougherty, C. 2001. *The Raft of Odysseus: The Ethnographic Imagination of Homer's Odyssey.* Oxford.
Drachmann, A. B., ed. 1903–1927. *Scholia Vetera in Pindari Carmina I–III.* Leipzig.
Dué, C. 2000. "Poetry and the *Dêmos*: State Regulation of a Civic Possession." *Dēmos: Classical Athenian Democracy* (ed. C. Blackwell). Stoa Consortium (eds. R. Scaife and A. Mahoney), http://www.stoa.org/projects/demos/home.
———. 2001a. "Achilles' Golden Amphora in Aeschines' *Against Timarchus* and the Afterlife of Oral Tradition." *Classical Philology* 96:33–47.
———. 2001b. "*Sunt Aliquid Manes*: Homer, Plato, and Alexandrian Allusion in Propertius 4.7." *Classical Journal* 96:401–413.
———. 2002. *Homeric Variations on a Lament by Briseis.* Lanham, MD.
———. 2006. *The Captive Woman's Lament in Greek Tragedy.* Austin.

Durante, M. 1976. *Sulla preistoria della tradizione poetic greca*. Vol. 2, *Risultanze della comparazione indoeuropea*. Incunabula Graeca 64. Rome.
Dyer, R. 2006. *Suda On Line: Byzantine Lexicography* (eds. D. Whitehead et al.), s.v. "Homeros" (Note 9), http://www.stoa.org/sol.
Easton, D. et al. 2002. "Troy in Recent Perspective." *Anatolian Studies* 52:75–109.
Ebbott, M. 1999. "The Wrath of Helen: Self-Blame and Nemesis in the *Iliad*." In Carlisle and Levaniouk 1999:3–20.
———. 2003. *Imagining Illegitimacy in Classical Greek Literature*. Lanham, MD.
Elmer, D. F. 2005. "Helen *Epigrammatopoios*." *Classical Antiquity* 24:1–39.
Erbse, H. 1959. "Über Aristarchs Iliasausgaben." *Hermes* 87:275–303.
———. 1960. *Beiträge zur Überlieferung der Iliasscholien*. Zetemata 24. Munich.
———, ed. 1969–1988. *Scholia Graeca in Homeri Iliadem* I–VII. Berlin.
Erskine, A. 2001. *Troy between Greece and Rome: Local Tradition and Imperial Power*. Oxford.
Fantuzzi, M. 2007a. "Dioscoride e la storia del teatro." *La cultura ellenistica: persistenza, innovazione, trasmissione; atti del convegno COFIN 2003, Università di Roma, Tor Vergata, 19–21 settembre 2005* (eds. E. Dettori and R. Pretagostini) 105–123. Rome.
———. 2007b. "La mousa del lamento in Euripide, e il lamento della Musa nel *Reso* ascritto a Euripide." *Eikasmos* 18:173–199.
Fantuzzi, M., and Pretagostini, R., eds. 1995, 1996. *Struttura e storia dell'esametro greco* I, II. Rome.
Fearn, D. 2003. "Mapping Phleious: Politics and Myth-making in Bacchylides 9." *Classical Quarterly* 3:347–367.
Ferrari, G. 1997. "Figures in the Text: Metaphors and Riddles in the *Agamemnon*." *Classical Philology* 92:1–45.
———. 2000. "The *Ilioupersis* in Athens." *Harvard Studies in Classical Philology* 100:119–150.
FGH. See Jacoby 1923–.
Figuiera, T. J. 1981. *Aegina, Society and Politics*. New York.
———. 1985. "The Theognidea and Megarian Society." *Theognis of Megara: Poetry and the Polis* (eds. T. J. Figueira and G. Nagy) 112–158. Baltimore.
———. 1991. *Athens and Aigina in the Age of Imperial Colonization*. Baltimore.
———. 1993. *Excursions in Epichoric History: Aeginetan Essays*. Lanham, MD.
Finkelberg, M. 2000. "The *Cypria*, the *Iliad*, and the Problem of Multiformity in Oral and Written Tradition." *Classical Philology* 95:1–11.
Flashar, H. 1958. *Der Dialog Ion als Zeugnis platonischer Philosophie*. Berlin.
Ford, A. 2002. *The Origins of Criticism: Literary Culture and Poetic Theory in Classical Greece*. Princeton.
Fowler, R. 1998. "Genealogical Thinking, Hesiod's Catalogue, and the Creation of the Hellenes." *Proceedings of the Cambridge Philological Society* 44:1–19.

Foxhall, L., and Davies, J. K., eds. 1984. *The Trojan War: Its Historicity and Context, Papers of the First Greenbank Colloquium, Liverpool, 1981*. Bristol.
Frame, D. 1978. *The Myth of Return in Early Greek Epic*. New Haven.
———. 2009. *Hippota Nestor*. Hellenic Studies 37. Washington, DC.
Fraser, P. M. 1972. *Ptolemaic Alexandria* I–III. Oxford.
Frazer, J. G., ed. 1929. *Publius Ovidius Naso, Fastorum libri sex* I–V. London.
Freedman, D. G. 1998. "Sokrates: The Athenian Oracle of Plato's Imagination." PhD diss., Harvard University.
Friedländer, L., ed. 1850. *Nicanoris Peri Iliakēs stigmēs reliquiae emendatiores*. Königsberg.
———, ed. 1853. *Aristonici Peri sēmeiōn Iliados reliquiae emendatiores*. Göttingen.
Funghi, M. S. 1997. "The Derveni Papyrus." In Laks and Most 1997:25–37.
Gaede, R., ed. 1880. *Demetrii Scepsii quae supersunt*. Greifswald.
Gentili, B. 1988. *Poetry and its Public in Ancient Greece: From Homer to the Fifth Century*. Trans. A. T. Cole. Baltimore.
Gérard-Rousseau, M. 1968. *Les mentions religieuses dans les tablettes mycéniennes*. Incunabula Graeca 29. Rome.
Giard, L., and Jacob, C., eds. 2001. *Des Alexandries*. Vol. 1, *Du livre au texte*. Paris.
Giovannini, A. 1969. *Étude historique sur l'origine du Catalogue des vaisseaux*. Bern.
Goh, M. 2004. "The Poetics of Chariot Driving and Rites of Passage in Ancient Greece." PhD diss., Harvard University.
Goldhill, S. 1991. *The Poet's Voice: Essays on Poetics and Greek Literature*. Cambridge.
Gomme, A. W. 1956. *A Historical Commentary on Thucydides*. Vol. 2, *Books II–III*. Oxford.
González, J. M. 2000. "*Mousai Hypophetores*: Apollonius of Rhodes on Inspiration and Interpretation." *Harvard Studies in Classical Philology* 100:269–292.
Gow, A. S. F., ed. 1952. *Theocritus*. I, II. 2nd ed. Cambridge.
Grafton, A., Most, G. W., and Zetzel, J. E. G., eds. 1985. *F. A. Wolf, Prolegomena to Homer*. Princeton.
Graziosi, B. 2002. *Inventing Homer: The Early Reception of Epic*. Cambridge.
Grethlein, J. 2007. "The Poetics of the Bath in the *Iliad*." *Harvard Studies in Classical Philology* 103:25–49.
Griffith, M. 1995. "Brilliant Dynasts: Power and Politics in the *Oresteia*." *Classical Antiquity* 14:62–129.
Gruen, E. 1990. *Studies in Greek Culture and Roman Policy*. Leiden.
———. 1992. *Culture and National Identity in Republican Rome*. Ithaca, NY.
Habinek, T. 1998. "Singing, Speaking, Making, Writing: Classical Alternatives to Literature and Literary Studies." *Stanford Humanities Review* 6:65–75.
Hall, J. M. 1997. *Ethnic Identity in Greek Antiquity*. New York.

———. 2002. *Hellenicity: Between Ethnicity and Culture*. Chicago.
Hansen, P. A., ed. 1983. *Carmina epigraphica Graeca saeculorum viii-v a. Chr. n.* Berlin and New York. Abbreviated CEG.
Hansen, W. F. 2002. *Ariadne's Thread: A Guide to International Tales Found in Classical Literature*. Ithaca, NY.
Hardie, P. 1985. "Imago Mundi: Cosmological and Ideological Aspects of the Shield of Achilles." *Journal of Hellenic Studies* 105:11–31.
Hardie, P. 1986. *Virgil's Aeneid: Cosmos and Imperium*. Oxford.
Haslam, M. 1997. "Homeric Papyri and Transmission of the Text." In Morris and Powell 1997:55–100.
Haubold, J. 2000. *Homer's People: Epic Poetry and Social Formations*. Cambridge.
Hedreen, G. 2001. *Capturing Troy: The Narrative Functions of Landscape in Archaic and Early Classical Greek Art*. Ann Arbor.
Heinze, R. 1915. *Virgils epische Technik*. 3rd ed. Leipzig.
Heinzelmann, J. 1988. "Offenbachs Hoffmann: Dokumente anstelle von Erzählungen," with "Faksimile der Akte IV und V des Pariser Zensurlibrettos vom Januar 1881 der 'Contes d'Hoffmann'." *Jacques Offenbachs Hoffmanns Erzählungen: Konzeption, Rezeption, Dokumentation* (ed. G. Brandstetter) 421–463. Laaber.
Heitsch, E. 1965. *Aphroditehymnus, Aeneas und Homer*. Hypomnemata 15. Göttingen.
Helck, H. 1905. *De Cratetis Mallotae studiis criticis quae ad Iliadem spectant*. Leipzig.
Heldmann, K. 1982. *Die Niederlage Homers im Dichterwettstreit mit Hesiod*. Hypomnemata 75. Göttingen.
Henrichs, A. 1993. "Response." *Images and Ideologies: Self-definition in the Hellenistic World* (eds. A. W. Bulloch et al.) 171–195. Berkeley and Los Angeles.
Hirschberger, M. 2004. *Gynaikōn Katalogos und Megalai Ēhoiai. Ein Kommentar zu den Fragmenten zweier hesiodeischer Epen*. Beiträge zur Altertumskunde 198. Munich and Leipzig.
Hodot, R. 1990. *Le dialecte éolien d'Asie: La langue des inscriptions VIIe s. a.C. - IVe s. p.C.* Paris.
Hornblower, S. 1991. *A Commentary on Thucydides*. Vol. 1, Books I-III. Oxford.
———, ed. 1994. *Greek Historiography*. Oxford.
———. 1996. *A Commentary on Thucydides*. Vol. 2, Books IV-V.24. Oxford.
Horrocks, G. 1987. "The Ionian Epic Tradition: Was There an Aeolic Phase in Its Development?" *Minos* 20–22:269–294.
———. 1997. "Homer's Dialect." In Morris and Powell 1997:193–217.
Householder, F. W., and Nagy, G., eds. 1972. *Greek: A Survey of Recent Work*. Janua Linguarum Series Practica 211. The Hague.

How, W. W., and Wells, J. 1912. *A Commentary on Herodotus* I, II. Revised ed. 1928. Oxford.
Hunter, R. L. 1997. "(B)ionic Man: Callimachus' Iambic Program." *Proceedings of the Cambridge Philological Society* 43:41–51.
———, ed. 1999. *Theocritus: Idylls, Selections.* Cambridge.
———, ed. 2005a. *The Hesiodic Catalogue of Women: Constructions and Reconstructions.* Cambridge.
———. 2005b. "The Hesiodic Catalogue and Hellenistic Poetry." In Hunter 2005a:239–265.
IG. See Deutsche Akademie der Wissenschaften zu Berlin 1873–.
Jacoby, F., ed. 1923–. *Die Fragmente der griechischen Historiker.* Leiden. Abbreviated *FGH.*
Janko, R. 1982. *Homer, Hesiod, and the Hymns: Diachronic Development of Epic Diction.* Cambridge.
———, ed. 1987. *Aristotle: Poetics.* Indianapolis.
———, ed. 1992. *The Iliad: A Commentary.* Vol. 4, Books 13–16. Cambridge.
Jebb, R. C. 1893. *The Attic Orators* I, II. 2nd ed. London.
Jensen, M. Skafte. 1980. *The Homeric Question and the Oral-Formulaic Theory.* Copenhagen.
Jowett, B., ed. 1895. *The Dialogues of Plato.* New York.
Kallet-Marx, L. 1989. "Did Tribute Fund the Parthenon?" *Classical Antiquity* 8:252–266.
Kassel, R. 1973. "Antimachos in der *Vita Chisiana* des Dionysios Periegetes." *Catalepton: Festschrift für Bernhard Wyss zum 80. Geburtstag* (ed. C. Schäublin) 69–76. Basel.
Kayan, I. 1991. "Holocene Geomorphic Evolution of the Beşik Plain and Changing Environment of Ancient Man." *Studia Troica* 1:79–92.
———. 1995. "The Troia Bay and Supposed Harbour Sites in the Bronze Age." *Studia Troica* 5:211–235.
———. 1996. "Holocene Stratigraphy of the Lower Karamenderes-Dumrek Plain and Archaeological Material in the Alluvial Sediments to the North of the Troia Ridge." *Studia Troica* 6:239–249.
———. 1997. "Geomorphological Evolution of the Ciplak Valley and Archaeological Material in the Alluvial Sediments to the South of the Lower City of Troia." *Studia Troica* 7:489–507.
———. 2003. "Geoarchaeological Interpretations of the 'Troian Bay'." With E. Öner et al. *Troia and the Troad: Scientific Approaches* (eds. G. A. Wagner, E. Pernicka, and H.-P. Uerpmann) 379–401. Berlin and New York.
Kazazis, J. N., and Rengakos, A., eds. 1999. *Euphrosyne: Studies in Ancient Epic and Its Legacy in Honor of Dimitris N. Maronitis.* Stuttgart.
Keaney, J. J., and Lamberton, R., eds. 1996. *Essay on the Life and Poetry of Homer.* American Classical Studies 40. Atlanta.

Kirk, G. S., ed. 1985. *The Iliad: A Commentary*. Vol. 1, Books 1-4. Cambridge.
———, ed. 1990. *The Iliad: A Commentary*. Vol. 2, Books 5-8. Cambridge.
Koller, H. 1956. "Das kitharodische Prooimion: Eine formgeschichtliche Untersuchung." *Philologus* 100:159-206.
———. 1957. "Hypokrisis und Hypokrites." *Museum Helveticum* 14:100-107.
Konstan, D. 2001. *Pity Transformed*. London.
Kosslyn, S. M. 1994. *Image and Brain: The Resolution of the Imagery Debate*. Cambridge, MA.
Kouremenos, T., Parássoglou, G., and Tsantsanoglou, K., eds. 2006. *The Derveni Papyrus*. Firenze.
Kraft, J. C. 1980. "Geomorphic Reconstructions in the Environs of Ancient Troy." With I. Kayan and E. Oğuz. *Science* 209, no. 4458:776-782.
———. 1982. "Geology and Paleogeographic Reconstructions of the Vicinity of Troy." With I. Kayan and E. Oğuz. *Troy: The Archaeological Geography* (eds. G. Rapp and J. A. Gifford). Troy, Supplementary Monograph 4:11-41. Princeton.
———. 2001. "A Geologic Analysis of Ancient Landscapes and the Harbors of Ephesus and the Artemision in Anatolia." With I. Kayan, H. Brückner, and G. Rapp. *Jahreshefte des Österreichischen Archäologischen Institutes in Wien: Verlag der Österreichischen Akademie der Wissenschaften* 69:175-233.
———. 2003a. "Sedimentary Facies Patterns and the Interpretation of Paleogeographies of Ancient Troia." With I. Kayan, H. Brückner, and G. Rapp. *Troia and the Troad. Scientific Approaches. Natural Science in Archaeology* (eds. G. A.Wagner, E. Pernicka, and H.-P. Uerpmann) 361-377. Berlin and New York.
———. 2003b. "Harbor Areas at Ancient Troy: Sedimentology and Geomorphology Complement Homer's *Iliad*." With G. Rapp, I. Kayan, and J. V. Luce. *Geology* 31/32:163-166.
Kullmann, W. 1960. *Die Quellen der Ilias*. Hermes Einzelschriften 14. Wiesbaden.
Kurke, L. 1991. *The Traffic in Praise: Pindar and the Poetics of Social Economy*. Ithaca, NY.
Labarbe, J. 1949. *L' Homère de Platon*. Liège.
Laks, A., and Most, G. W., eds. 1997. *Studies on the Derveni Papyrus*. Oxford.
Lamberterie, C. de. 1997. "Milman Parry et Antoine Meillet." In Létoublon 1997:9-22. Trans. by A. Goldhammer as "Milman Parry and Antoine Meillet" in Loraux, Nagy, and Slatkin 2001:409-421.
Lapatin, K. D. S. 2001. *Chryselephantine Statuary in the Ancient Mediterranean World*. Oxford.
Leaf, W. 1923. *Strabo on the Troad*. Cambridge.
Lee, M. M. 2004. "Evil Wealth of Raiment: Deadly πέπλοι in Greek Tragedy." *The Classical Journal* 99:253-279.
Lehrs, K. 1882. *De Aristarchi Studiis Homericis*. 3rd ed. Leipzig.

Leipen, N. 1971. *Athena Parthenos: A Reconstruction*. Toronto.
Lepschy, A. 1998. "Il colore della porpora." *La porpora: realtà e immaginario di un colore simbolico; atti del convegno di studio, Venezia, 24 e 25 ottobre 1996* (ed. O. Longo) 53–66. Venice.
Lessing, G. E. 1766. *Laokoon, oder Über die Grenzen der Mahlerey und Poesie*. Trans. by E. A. McCormick as *Laocoön: An Essay on the Limits of Painting and Poetry*. 1962. Revised ed. 1984. Baltimore.
Létoublon, F., ed. 1997. *Hommage à Milman Parry: le style formulaire de l'épopée et la théorie de l'oralité poétique*. Amsterdam.
Levaniouk, O. 1999. "Penelope and the *Pēnelops*." In Carlisle and Levaniouk 1999:95–136.
———. 2000a. "*Aithōn*, Aithon, and Odysseus." *Harvard Studies in Classical Philology* 100:25–51.
———. 2000b. "Odyssean Usages of Local Traditions." PhD diss., Harvard University.
Liddell, H. G., Scott, R., and Stuart Jones, H., eds. 1940. *Greek-English Lexicon*. 9th ed. Oxford. Abbreviated LSJ.
Lohmann, D. 1988. *Die Andromache-Szenen der Ilias*. Spudasmata 42. Hildesheim.
Loraux, N. 1987. "Le lien de la division." *Le Cahier du Collège International de Philosophie* 4:101–124.
Loraux, N., Nagy, G., and Slatkin, L., eds. 2001. *Antiquities*. Vol. 3 of *Postwar French Thought*. New York.
Lord, A. B. 1960. *The Singer of Tales*. Harvard Studies in Comparative Literature 24. 2nd ed. 2000 by S. Mitchell and G. Nagy. Cambridge, MA.
———. 1995. *The Singer Resumes the Tale* (ed. M. L. Lord). Ithaca, NY.
Louden, B. 1996. "Epeios, Odysseus, and the Indo-European Metaphor for Poet." *Journal of Indo-European Studies* 24:277–304.
———. 2002. "Eurybates, Odysseus, and the Duals in Book 9 of the *Iliad*." *Colby Quarterly* 38:62–76.
Lowenstam, S. 1997. "Talking Vases: The Relationship between the Homeric Poems and Archaic Representations of Epic Myth." *Transactions of the American Philological Association* 127:21–76.
LSJ. See Liddell, Scott, and Jones 1940.
Ludwich, A. 1884, 1885. *Aristarchs Homerische Textkritik nach den Fragmenten des Didymos* I, II. Leipzig.
———. 1898. *Die Homervulgata als voralexandrinisch erwiesen*. Leipzig.
Lührs, D. 1992. *Untersuchungen zu den Athetesen Aristarchs in der Ilias und zu ihrer Behandlung im Corpus der exegetischen Scholien*. Beiträge zur Altertumswissenschaft 11. Hildesheim.
Lyne, R. O. A. M., ed. 1978. *Ciris: A Poem Attributed to Vergil*. Cambridge.
McNamee, K. 1981. "Aristarchus and Everyman's Homer." *Greek, Roman and Byzantine Studies* 22:247–255.

———. 1992. *Sigla and Select Marginalia in Greek Literary Papyri*. Brussels.
Malkin, I. 1998. *The Returns of Odysseus: Ethnicity and Colonization*. Berkeley and Los Angeles.
Mansfield, J. M. 1985. "The Robe of Athena and the Panathenaic Peplos." PhD diss., University of California at Berkeley.
Martin, J., ed. 1974. *Scholia in Aratum vetera*. Stuttgart.
Martin, R. P. 1989. *The Language of Heroes: Speech and Performance in the Iliad*. Ithaca, NY.
———. 1992. "Hesiod's Metanastic Poetics." *Ramus* 21:11–33.
———. 1993. "Telemachus and the Last Hero Song." *Colby Quarterly* 29:222–240.
———. 2000a. "Wrapping Homer Up: Cohesion, Discourse, and Deviation in the *Iliad*." *Intratextuality: Greek and Roman Textual Relations* (eds. A. Sharrock and H. Morales) 43–65. Oxford.
———. 2000b. "Synchronic Aspects of Homeric Performance: The Evidence of the *Hymn to Apollo*." *Una nueva visión de la cultura griega antigua hacia el fin del milenio* (ed. A. M. González de Tobia) 403–432. La Plata.
———. 2001. "Rhapsodizing Orpheus." *Kernos* 14:23–33.
Meiggs, R. 1972. *The Athenian Empire*. Oxford.
Meiggs, R., and Lewis, D. 1988. *A Selection of Greek Historical Inscriptions to the End of the Fifth Century B.C.* Revised ed. Oxford.
Meillet, A. 1935. *Aperçu d'une histoire de la langue grecque*. 4th ed. Reissued 7th ed. 1965 with bibliography by O. Masson. Paris.
Montanari, F. 1979. *Studi di filologia omerica antica* I. Pisa.
———. 1998. "Zenodotus, Aristarchus and the *Ekdosis* Of Homer." In Most 1998:1–21.
———. 2002a. "Alexandrian Homeric Philology: The Form of the *Ekdosis* and the *Variae Lectiones*." *ΕΠΕΑ ΠΤΕΡΟΕΝΤΑ: Beiträge zur Homerforschung* (eds. M. Reichel and A. Rengakos) 119–140. Stuttgart.
———. 2002b. "Filologia ed erudizione antica." *Da Aiōn a eikasmos: Atti della giornata di studio sulla figura e l'opera di Enzo Degani. Eikasmos, Studi* 8:73–88. Bologna.
———. 2004a. "La filologia Omerica antica e la storia del testo Omerico." *Antike Literatur in neuer Deutung* (eds. A. Bierl, A. Schmitt, and A. Willi) 127–143. Munich.
———. 2004b. "The PAWAG Project (Poorly Attested Words in Ancient Greek): Ancient Greek Lexicography on Line." *Euphrosyne* 32:75–78.
———. 2008. "Aristotele, Zenodoto, Aristarco e il serpente pietrificato di *Iliade* II 319." *Studi offerti ad Alessandro Perutelli* II (eds. P. Arduini et al.) 237–243. Rome.
Moore, J. D. 1974. "The Date of Plato's *Ion*." *Greek, Roman and Byzantine Studies* 15:421–439.
Morris, I., and Powell, B., eds. 1997. *A New Companion to Homer*. Leiden.

Most, G. W., ed. 1998. *Editing Texts = Texte edieren*. Aporemata 2. Göttingen.
Muellner, L. 1976. *The Meaning of Homeric EYXOMAI through Its Formulas*. Innsbruck.
———. 1990. "The Simile of the Cranes and Pygmies: A Study of Homeric Metaphor." *Harvard Studies in Classical Philology* 93:59–101.
———. 1996. *The Anger of Achilles: Mênis in Greek Epic*. Ithaca, NY.
Murray, P., ed. 1996. *Plato on Poetry: Ion, Republic 376e-398b, Republic 595-608b*. Cambridge.
Nagy, B. 1972. "The Athenian Ergastinai and the Panathenaic Peplos." PhD diss., Harvard University.
———. 1978a. "The Ritual in Slab-V East of the Parthenon Frieze." *Classical Philology* 73:137–141.
———. 1978b. "The Athenian Athlothetai" *Greek, Roman and Byzantine Studies* 19:307–314.
———. 1980. "A Late Panathenaic Document." *Ancient World* 3:106–111.
———. 1983. "The Peplotheke." Studies Presented to Sterling Dow (ed. K. Rigsby) 227–232. Greek, Roman, and Byzantine Monographs 10. Durham, NC.
———. 1991. "The Procession to Phaleron." *Historia* 40:288–306.
———. 1992. "Athenian Officials on the Parthenon Frieze." *American Journal of Archaeology* 96:55–69.
———. 1994. "Alcibiades' Second Profanation." *Historia* 43:275–285.
Nagy, G. 1969. Review of J. Chadwick, *The Decipherment of Linear B*, 2nd ed. (Cambridge 1967). *General Linguistics* 9:123–132.
———. 1974. *Comparative Studies in Greek and Indic Meter*. Harvard Studies in Comparative Literature 33. Cambridge, MA.
———. 1979. *The Best of the Achaeans: Concepts of the Hero in Archaic Greek Poetry*. Revised ed. with new introduction 1999. Baltimore. http://www.press.jhu.edu/books/nagy/BofATL/toc.html. Trans. by J. Carlier and N. Loraux as *Le meilleur des Achéens: La fabrique du héros dans la poésie grecque archaïque*. 1999. Paris.
———. 1985. "Theognis and Megara: A Poet's Vision of His City." *Theognis of Megara: Poetry and the Polis* (eds. T. J. Figueira and G. Nagy) 22–81. Baltimore.
———. 1990a. *Pindar's Homer: The Lyric Possession of an Epic Past*. Baltimore. http://www.press.jhu.edu/books/nagy/PHTL/toc.html.
———. 1990b. *Greek Mythology and Poetics*. Ithaca, NY.
———. 1993. "Alcaeus in Sacred Space." *Tradizione e innovazione nella cultura greca da Omero all' età ellenistica: Scritti in onore di Bruno Gentili* (ed. R. Pretagostini) 221–225. Rome.
———. 1994a/1995 "Transformations of Choral Lyric Traditions in the Context of Athenian State Theater." *Arion* 3:41–55.

———. 1994b/1995. "A Mycenaean Reflex in Homer: *phorênai*." *Minos* 29/30:171–175
———. 1994c/1995. "Genre and Occasion." ΜΗΤΙΣ: *Revue d'Anthropologie du Monde Grec Ancien* 9/10:11–25.
———. 1996a. *Poetry as Performance: Homer and Beyond.* Cambridge.
———. 1996b. *Homeric Questions.* Austin.
———. 1996c. "Metrical Convergences and Divergences in Early Greek Poetry and Song." In Fantuzzi and Pretagostini 1996 (II):63–110.
———. 1998. "The Library of Pergamon as a Classical Model." *Pergamon: Citadel of the Gods* (ed. H. Koester) 185–232. Harvard Theological Studies 46. Philadelphia.
———. 2000a. Review of West 1998b. *Bryn Mawr Classical Review* 00.09.12 (2000), http://ccat.sas.upenn.edu/bmcr/2000/2000-09-12.html.
———. 2000b. "Epic as Music: Rhapsodic Models of Homer in Plato's *Timaeus* and *Critias*." *The Oral Epic: Performance and Music* (ed. K. Reichl) 41–67. Berlin. Rewritten as Ch. 2 in Nagy 2002.
———. 2000c. "Homeric *humnos* as a Rhapsodic Term." *Una nueva visión de la cultura griega antigua hacia el fin del milenio* (ed. A. M. González de Tobia) 385–401. La Plata.
———. 2000d. "Distortion diachronique dans l'art homérique: quelques précisions." *Constructions du temps dans le monde ancien* (ed. C. Darbo-Peschanski) 417–426. Paris.
———. 2000e. "Reading Greek Poetry Aloud: Evidence from the Bacchylides Papyri." *Quaderni Urbinati di Cultura Classica* 64:7–28.
———. 2000f. "'Dream of a Shade': Refractions of Epic Vision in Pindar's *Pythian 8* and Aeschylus' *Seven against Thebes*." *Harvard Studies in Classical Philology* 100:97–118.
———. 2001a. "Homeric Poetry and Problems of Multiformity: The 'Panathenaic Bottleneck.'" *Classical Philology* 96:109–119. Rewritten as Ch. 2 in Nagy 2004a.
———. 2001b. "The Textualizing of Homer." *Inclinate Aurem—Oral Perspectives on Early European Verbal Culture* (eds. J. Helldén, M. S. Jensen, and T. Pettitt) 57–84. Odense.
———. 2001c. "Reading Bakhtin Reading the Classics: An Epic Fate for Conveyors of the Heroic Past." *Bakhtin and the Classics* (ed. R. B. Branham) 71–96. Evanston, IL.
———. 2001d. "Éléments orphiques chez Homère." *Kernos* 14:1–9.
———. 2001e. "The Sign of the Hero: A Prologue." *Flavius Philostratus, Heroikos* (eds. J. K. Berenson Maclean and E. B. Aitken) xv–xxxv. Atlanta.
———. 2001f. "Η ποιητική της προφορικότητας και η ομηρική έρευνα." Νεκρά γράμματα· οι κλασσικές σπουδές στον 21ο αιώνα (ed. A. Rengakos) 135–146. Athens.

———. 2001g. "Introductions and Bibliographies." http://chs.harvard.edu/chs/online_books_list. Electronic Publication of Introductions and Bibliographies for Nagy 2001h. Center for Hellenic Studies.

———, ed. 2001h1. *Greek Literature*. Vol. 1, *The Oral Traditional Background of Ancient Greek Literature*. New York.

———, ed. 2001h2. *Greek Literature*. Vol. 2, *Homer and Hesiod as Prototypes of Greek Literature*. New York.

———. 2002. *Plato's Rhapsody and Homer's Music: The Poetics of the Panathenaic Festival in Classical Athens*. Cambridge, MA and Athens.

———. 2003a. *Homeric Responses*. Austin.

———. 2003b. Review of West 2001. *Gnomon* 75:481–501.

———. 2004a. *Homer's Text and Language*. Urbana and Chicago.

———. 2004b. "Transmission of Archaic Greek Sympotic Songs: From Lesbos to Alexandria." *Critical Inquiry* 31:26–48.

———. 2004c. "Poetics of Repetition in Homer." In Yatromanolakis and Roilos 2004:139–148.

———. 2004d. "Homeric Echoes in Posidippus." *Labored in Papyrus Leaves: Perspectives on an Epigram Collection Attributed to Posidippus (P.Mil.Vogl. VIII 309)* (eds. B. Acosta-Hughes, E. Kosmetatou, and M. Baumbach) 57–64. Hellenic Studies 2. Washington, DC.

———. 2004e. "L'aède épique en auteur: la tradition des Vies d'Homère." *Identités d'auteur dans l'Antiquité et la tradition européenne* (eds. C. Calame and R. Chartier) 41–67. Grenoble.

———. 2005a. "The Epic Hero." *A Companion to Ancient Epic* (ed. J. M. Foley) 71–89. Oxford. Expanded version at http://chs.harvard.edu/chs/online_books_list.

———. 2005b. Review of Boedeker and Sider 2001. *Classical Review* 55:407–409.

———. 2005c. "An Apobatic Moment for Achilles as Athlete at the Festival of the Panathenaia." *Imeros* 5:311–317.

———. 2006a. "Homer's Name Revisited." *La langue poétique indo-européenne: actes du Colloque de travail de la Société des Études Indo-Européennes (Indogermanische Gesellschaft / Society for Indo-European Studies), Paris, 22-24 octobre 2003* (eds. G.-J. Pinault and D. Petit) 317–330. Collection linguistique de la Société de Linguistique de Paris 91. Leuven and Paris.

———. 2006b. "Hymnic Elements in Empedocles (B 35 DK = 201 Bollack)." *Revue de Philosophie Ancienne* 24:51–61.

———. 2007a. "Emergence of Drama: Introduction and Discussion." *The Origins of Theater in Ancient Greece and Beyond: From Ritual to Drama* (eds. E. Csapo and M. C. Miller) 121–125. Cambridge.

———. 2007b. "Did Sappho and Alcaeus ever meet?" *Literatur und Religion: Wege zu einer mythisch-rituellen Poetik bei den Griechen* I (eds. A. Bierl, R. Lämmle, and K. Wesselmann) 211–269. MythosEikonPoiesis 1.1. Berlin and New York.
———. 2007c. "Lyric and Greek Myth." *The Cambridge Companion to Greek Mythology* (ed. R. D. Woodard) 19–51. Cambridge.
———. 2007d. "Homer and Greek Myth." *The Cambridge Companion to Greek Mythology* (ed. R. D. Woodard) 52–82. Cambridge.
———. 2009. "Hesiod and the Ancient Biographical Traditions." *Brill's Companion to Hesiod* (eds. F. Montanari, A. Rengakos, and C. Tsagalis) 271–311. Leiden.
———. 2010. Homer the Preclassic. Berkeley and Los Angeles. Online edition published 2009 at http://chs.harvard.edu/publications.
Nagy, J. F. 1985. *The Wisdom of the Outlaw: The Boyhood Deeds of Finn in Gaelic Narrative Tradition*. Berkeley and Los Angeles.
———. 1986. "Orality in Medieval Irish Narrative." *Oral Tradition* 1:272–301.
———. 1990a. "Hierarchy, Heroes, and Heads: Indo-European Structures in Greek Myth." *Approaches to Greek Myth* (ed. Lowell Edmunds) 199–238. Baltimore.
———. 1990b. *Conversing with Angels and Ancients: Literary Myths of Medieval Ireland*. Ithaca, NY.
Nails, D. 2002. *"The People of Plato: A Prosopography of Plato and Other Socratics."* Indianapolis and Cambridge.
Neils, J., ed. 1992a. *Goddess and Polis: The Panathenaic Festival in Ancient Athens*. Princeton.
———. 1992b. "The Panathenaia: An Introduction." In Neils 1992a:13–27, with notes at 194–195.
Neuschäfer, B. 1987. *Origenes als Philologe* I, II. Schweizerische Beiträge zur Altertumswissenschaft 18.1, 18.2. Basel.
Nick, G. 2002. *Die Athena Parthenos: Studien zum griechischen Kultbild und seiner Rezeption*. Mitteilungen des Deutschen Archäologischen Instituts. Athenische Abteilung. Beiheft 19. Mainz.
Nickau, K. 1977. *Untersuchungen zur textkritischen Methode des Zenodotos von Ephesos*. Berlin and New York.
Nietzsche, F. 1870. "Der Florentinische Tractat über Homer und Hesiod, ihr Geschlecht und ihren Wettkampf." *Rheinisches Museum* 25:528–540.
———. 1872. *Die Geburt der Tragödie aus dem Geiste der Musik*. Leipzig.
O'Sullivan, N. 1992. *Alcidamas, Aristophanes and the Beginning of Greek Stylistic Theory*. Hermes Einzelschriften 60. Stuttgart.
Obbink, D. 1997. "Cosmology as Initiation vs. the Critique of Orphic Mysteries." In Laks and Most 1997:39–54.

———. 2001. "The Genre of *Plataea*: Generic Unity in the New Simonides." In Boedeker and Sider 2001:65–85.
Oettinger N. 1976. *Die militärischen Eide der Hethiter*. Wiesbaden.
Onians, R. B. 1951. *The Origins of European Thought about the Body, the Mind, the Soul, the World, Time, and Fate*. Cambridge.
Özgünel, C. A. 2003. "Das Heiligtum des Apollon Smintheus und die Ilias." *Studia Troica* 13:261–291.
Page, D. L. 1955. *Sappho and Alcaeus: An Introduction to the Study of Ancient Lesbian Poetry*. Oxford.
———. 1959. *History and the Homeric Iliad*. Berkeley and Los Angeles.
Page, T. E., ed. 1894. *The Aeneid of Virgil I–VI*. London.
Pagliaro, A. 1953. *Saggi di critica semantica*. Messina and Firenze.
Palmer, L. R. 1980. *The Greek Language*. Atlantic Highlands, NJ.
Papadopoulou-Belmehdi, I. 1994. *Le chant de Pénélope: Poétique du tissage féminin dans l'Odyssée*. Paris.
Parke, H. W. 1977. *Festivals of the Athenians*. Ithaca, NY.
Parry, A. 1966. "Have We Homer's *Iliad*?" *Yale Classical Studies* 20:177–216.
———, ed. 1971. *The Making of Homeric Verse: The Collected Papers of Milman Parry*. Oxford.
Parry, M. 1932. "Studies in the Epic Technique of Oral Versemaking. II. The Homeric Language as the Language of Oral Poetry." *Harvard Studies in Classical Philology* 43:1–50. Republished in Parry 1971:325–364.
Pasquali, G. 1962. *Storia della tradizione e critica del testo*. Firenze.
Patton, K. C. 1992. "When the High Gods Pour Out Wine: A Paradox of Ancient Greek Iconography in Comparative Context." PhD diss., Harvard University.
Pelliccia, H. N. 1997. "As Many Homers As You Please." *New York Review of Books* 44, no. 18:44–48.
Peponi, A. E. 2004. "Initiating the Viewer: Deixis and Visual Perception in Alcman's Lyric Drama." *The Poetics of Deixis in Alcman, Pindar, and Other Lyric* (ed. N. Felson). *Arethusa* 37:295–316.
———. 2009. "*Choreia* and Aesthetics in the *Homeric Hymn to Apollo*: The Performance of the Delian Maidens (lines 156–64)." *Classical Antiquity* 28:39–70.
Petropoulos, J. C. B. 1993. "Sappho the Sorceress: Another look at fr. 1 (LP)." *Zeitschrift für Papyrologie und Epigraphik* 97:43–56.
Pfeiffer, R. 1968. *History of Classical Scholarship from the Beginnings to the End of the Hellenistic Age*. Oxford.
Pinney, G. F. 1988. "Pallas and Panathenaea." *Proceedings of the Third Symposium on Ancient Greek and Related Pottery* (eds. J. Christiansen and T. Melander) 465–477. Copenhagen.
Pollitt, J. J. 1990. *The Art of Ancient Greece: Sources and Documents*. 2nd ed. Cambridge.

Porter, J. I. 1992. "Hermeneutic Lines and Circles: Aristarchus and Crates on the Exegesis of Homer." *Homer's Ancient Readers: The Hermeneutics of Greek Epic's Earliest Exegetes* (eds. R. Lamberton and J. J. Keaney) 67–114. Princeton.

———. 2001. "Ideals and Ruins: Pausanias, Longinus, and the Second Sophistic." *Pausanias: Travel and Memory in Roman Greece* (eds. S. E. Alcock, J. F. Cherry, and J. Elsner) 63–92, 273–283. Oxford.

Pucci, P., ed. 2007. *Inno alle Muse (Esiodo, Teogonia, 1-115)*. Pisa and Rome.

Questa, C., and Rafaelli, R., eds. 1984. *Atti del Convegno internazionale Il libro e il testo, Urbino, 20-23 settembre 1982*. Urbino.

Rabinowitz, N. 1998. "Slaves with Slaves: Women and Class in Euripidean Tragedy." *Women and Slaves in Greco-Roman Culture: Differential Equations* (eds. S. Joshel and S. Murnaghan) 56–68. New York.

Race, W. H. 1990. *Style and Rhetoric in Pindar's Odes*. Atlanta.

Rapp, G., and Gifford, J. A., eds. 1982. *Troy: The Archaeological Geography*. Supplementary Mongraph 4. Princeton.

Raubitschek, A. E. 1984. "Die historisch-politische Bedeutung des Parthenon und seines Skulpturenschmuckes." *Parthenon-Kongreß Basel: Referate und Berichte 4. bis 8. April 1982* I (ed. E. Berger) p. 19 (one-page note). Mainz.

Rengakos, A. 1993. *Der Homertext und die Hellenistischen Dichter*. Hermes Einzelschriften 64. Stuttgart.

———. 2000. "Aristarchus and the Hellenistic Poets." *Seminari Romani di Cultura Greca* 3:325–335.

———. 2001. "Apollonius Rhodius as a Homer Scholar." *A Companion to Apollonius Rhodius* (eds. T. D. Papanghelis and A. Rengakos) 193–216. Leiden.

———. 2002. Review of West 2001. *Bryn Mawr Classical Review* 02.11.15. (2002), http://ccat.sas.upenn.edu/bmcr/2002/2002-11-15.html.

Revermann, M. 1998. "The Text of *Iliad* 18.603-6 and the Presence of an ΑΟΙΔΟΣ on the Shield of Achilles." *Classical Quarterly* 48:29–38.

Rhodes, P. J. 1981. *A Commentary on the Aristotelian Athenaion Politeia*. Oxford.

———, ed. 1994. *Thucydides History* III. Warminster.

Richardson, N. J., ed. 1974. *The Homeric Hymn to Demeter*. Oxford.

Ridgway, B. S. 1992. "Images of Athena on the Acropolis." In Neils 1992a:119–142.

Riedweg, C. 2002. *Pythagoras: Leben, Lehre, Nachwirkung*. Munich.

Ritoók, Z. 1970. "Die Homeriden." *Acta Antiqua* 18:1–29.

Robert, L. 1960. "Recherches épigraphiques, V: Inscriptions de Lesbos." *Revue des études grecques* 73:285–315. Republished in *Opera Minora Selecta* II 816-831. 1969. Amsterdam.

Robertson, N. 1970. "Laomedon's Corpse, Laomedon's Tomb." *Greek, Roman and Byzantine Studies* 11:23–26.
———. 1978. "The Myth of the First Sacred War." *Classical Quarterly* 28:38–73.
———. 1985. "The Origin of the Panathenaea." *Rheinisches Museum für Philologie* 128:231–295.
———. 1996. "Athena's Shrines and Festivals." *Worshipping Athena* (ed. J. Neils) 27–77. Madison.
Rose, C. B. 1999. "The 1998 Post-Bronze Age Excavations at Troia." *Studia Troica* 9:35–71.
———. 2000. "The 1999 Post-Bronze Age Research at Troia." *Studia Troica* 10:53–71.
———. 2006. "Ilion." *Stadtgrabungen und Stadtforschung im westlichen Kleinasien: Geplantes und Erreichtes* (ed. W. Radt) 135–158. Istanbul.
Rosen, R. M. 1988. *Old Comedy and the Iambographic Tradition*. American Classical Studies 19. Atlanta.
———. 1990. "Poetry and Sailing in Hesiod's *Works and Days*." *Classical Antiquity* 9:99–113.
Rotstein, A. 2004. "Aristotle, *Poetics* 1447a13–16 and Musical Contests." *Zeitschrift für Papyrologie und Epigraphik* 149:39–42.
Rousseau, P. 1996. "*Dios d' eteleieto boulê*: Destin des héros et dessein de Zeus dans l'intrigue de *l'Iliade*." Doctoral diss., Université Charles de Gaulle—Lille III.
———. 2001. "L'intrigue de Zeus." *Europe* 865:120–158.
Russell, D. A., and Winterbottom, M., eds. 1972. *Ancient Literary Criticism: The Principal Texts in New Translations*. Oxford.
Rusten, J. S. 1982. *Dionysius Scytobrachion*. Papyrologica Coloniensia 10. Opladen.
Rutherford, I. 2005. "Mestra at Athens." In Hunter 2005a:99–117.
Sacks, R. 1987. *The Traditional Phrase in Homer: Two Studies in Form, Meaning and Interpretation*. Leiden.
Saussure, F. de. 1916. *Cours de linguistique générale*. Critical ed. 1972 by T. de Mauro. Paris.
Scarry, E. 1999. *Dreaming by the Book*. New York.
Scheid, J., and Svenbro, J. 1994. *Le Métier de Zeus: Mythe du tissage et du tissu dans le monde gréco-romain*. Paris.
Schliemann, H. 1884. *Troja. Results of the Latest Researches and Discoveries on the Site of Homer's Troy*. New York.
Schmitt, R. 1967. *Dichtung und Dichtersprache in indogermanischer Zeit*. Wiesbaden.
Schrader, H., ed. 1880–1882. *Porphyrii Quaestionum Homericarum ad Iliadem pertinentium reliquiae*. Leipzig.

———, ed. 1890. *Porphyrii Quaestionum Homericarum ad Odysseam pertinentium reliquiae*. Leipzig.
Schuler, E. von. 1965. *Die Kaskäer*. Berlin.
Schultz, P. 2007. "The Iconography of the Athenian *apobates* Race: Origins, Meanings, Transformations." *The Panathenaic Games* (eds. A. Choremi and O. Palagia) 59–72. Oxford.
Schwartz, E., ed. 1887, 1891. *Scholia in Euripidem*. I, II. Berlin.
Schwartz, M. 1982. "The Indo-European Vocabulary of Exchange, Hospitality, and Intimacy." *Proceedings of the Berkeley Linguistics Society* 8:188–204.
Scodel, R. 1982. "The Achaean Wall and the Myth of Destruction." *Harvard Studies in Classical Philology* 86:33–50.
Seaford, R., ed. 1984. *Euripides: Cyclops*. Oxford.
———. 1994. *Reciprocity and Ritual: Homer and Tragedy in the Developing City-State*. Oxford.
Segal, C. 1971. "Andromache's Anagnorisis: Formulaic Artistry in *Iliad* 22.437–76." *Harvard Studies in Classical Philology* 75:33–57.
Severyns, A. 1928. *Le cycle épique dans l'école d'Aristarque*. Bibliothèque de la Faculté de Philosophie et Lettres de l'Université de Liège 40. Paris.
———. 1938. *Recherches sur la Chrestomathie de Proclos* I, II. Paris.
Sevinç, N. 1996. "A New Sarcophagus of Polyxena from the Salvage Excavations at Gümüşçay." *Studia Troica* 6:251–264.
Shankman, S. 1983. "Led by the Light of the Maeonian Star: Aristotle on Tragedy and *Odyssey* 17.415–444." *Studies in Classical Lyric: A Homage to Elroy Bundy* (eds. T. D'Evelyn, P. N. Psoinos, and T. R. Walsh). Special issue, *Classical Antiquity* 2, no. 1:108–116.
Shaw, P. J. 2001. "Lords of Hellas, Old Men of the Sea: The Occasion of Simonides' Elegy on Plataea." In Boedeker and Sider 2001:164–181.
Sherratt, E. S. 1990. "'Reading the Texts': Archaeology and the Homeric Question." *Antiquity* 64:807–824.
Signore, S. 2006. "Andromache's Aristeia: The Poetic Resonance of *mainadi isē* in *Iliad* 22.460." Paper presented at the 102nd Annual Meeting of the Classical Association of the Middle West and South, Gainesville, FL, April 6–8, 2006.
Sinos, D. S. 1980. *Achilles, Patroklos, and the Meaning of Philos*. Innsbrucker Beiträge zur Sprachwissenschaft 29. Innsbruck.
Slatkin, L. 1987. "Genre and Generation in the Odyssey." *METIS: Revue d'anthropologie du monde grec ancien* 2:259–268.
Smarczyk, B. 1990. *Untersuchungen zur Religionspolitik und politischen Propaganda Athens im Delisch-Attischen Seebund*. Munich.
Smith, P. M. 1981. "Aineiadai as Patrons of *Iliad* XX and the *Homeric Hymn to Aphrodite*." *Harvard Studies in Classical Philology* 85:17–58.
Sodano, A. R., ed. 1970. *Porphyrii Quaestionum Homericarum liber* I. Naples.

Stadter, P. A. 1989. *A Commentary on Plutarch's* Pericles. Chapel Hill, NC.
Stähler, K. P. 1967. *Grab und Pysche des Patroklos: Ein schwarzfiguriges Vasenbild.* Münster.
Stallbaum, J. G., ed. 1825. *Eustathii Commentarii ad Homeri Odysseam* I, II. Leipzig.
Steinhart, M. 2004. *Die Kunst der Nachahmung.* Mainz.
———. 2007. "From Ritual to Narrative." *The Origins of Theater in Ancient Greece and Beyond: From Ritual to Drama* (eds. E. Csapo and M. C. Miller) 196–220. Cambridge.
Strassler, R. B., ed. 1996. *The Landmark Thucydides: A Comprehensive Guide to the Peloponnesian War.* New York.
Svenbro, J. 1988. *Phrasikleia: Anthropologie de la lecture en Grèce ancienne.* Paris. Trans. by J. Lloyd as *Phrasikleia: An Anthropology of Reading in Ancient Greece.* 1993. Ithaca, NY.
Tarrant, R. 2005. "Roads not Taken: Untold Stories in Ovid's Metamorphoses." *Materiali e discussioni per l'analisi dei testi classici* 54:65–89.
Thiel, H. van, ed. 1991. *Homeri Odyssea.* Hildesheim.
———, ed. 1996. *Homeri Ilias.* Hildesheim.
Thompson, D. B. 1939. "Mater Caelaturae, Impressions from Ancient Metalwork." *Hesperia* 8:285–316.
Tsagalis, C. 2004. *Epic Grief: Personal Laments in Homer's Iliad.* Berlin.
Tsantsanoglou, K., and Parassoglou, G. M. 1988. "Heraclitus in the Derveni Papyrus." *Aristoxenica, Menandrea, Fragmenta Philosophica* (eds. A. Brancacci et al.) 125–133. Firenze.
Usher, S., ed. 1974. *Dionysius of Halicarnassus: The Critical Essays* I, II. Cambridge, MA.
Vermeule, E. 1965. "The Vengeance of Achilles: The Dragging of Hektor at Troy." *Bulletin of the Museum of Fine Arts, Boston* 63:34–52.
———. 1987. "Baby Aigisthos and the End of the Bronze Age." *Proceedings of the Cambridge Philological Society* 1987:122–152.
Vernant, J.-P. 1982. "La belle mort et le cadavre outragé." *La mort, les morts dans les sociétés anciennes* (eds. G. Gnoli and J.-P. Vernant) 45–76. Cambridge and Paris. Reprinted in *L'individu, la mort, l'amour: Soi-même et autre en Grèce ancienne* 41–79. 1989. Paris.
Villoison, J. B. G. d'Ansse de, ed. 1788. *Homeri Ilias ad veteris codicis Veneti fidem recensita.* Venice.
Vine, B. 1999. "On 'Cowgill's Law' in Greek." *Compositiones Indogermanicae in memoriam Jochem Schindler* (eds. H. Eichner and H. C. Luschützky) 555–599. Prague.
Vogt, E. 1959. "Die Schrift vom Wettkampf Homers und Hesiods." *Rheinisches Museum* 102:193–221.

Wace, A. 1948. "Weaving or Embroidery?" *American Journal of Archaeology* 52:51–55.
Wachsmuth, C. 1860. *De Cratete Mallota*. Leipzig.
Wachter, R. 2000. "Grammatik der homerischen Sprache." *Homers Ilias: Gesamtkommentar. Prolegomena* (ed. J. Latacz) 61–108. Munich and Leipzig.
———. 2001. *Non-Attic Greek Vase-Inscriptions*. Oxford.
West, M. L., ed. 1966. *Hesiod: Theogony*. Oxford.
———. 1967. "The Contest of Homer and Hesiod." *Classical Quarterly* 17:433–450.
———, ed. 1978. *Hesiod: Works and Days*. Oxford.
———. 1983. *The Orphic Poems*. Oxford.
———. 1985. *The Hesiodic Catalogue of Women*. Oxford.
———. 1988. "The Rise of the Greek Epic." *Journal of Hellenic Studies* 108:151–172.
———. 1995. "The Date of the *Iliad*." *Museum Helveticum* 52:203–219.
———. 1998a. "The Textual Criticism and Editing of Homer." In Most 1998:94–109.
———, ed. 1998b. *Homeri Ilias* I. Stuttgart and Leipzig.
———. 1999. "The Invention of Homer." *Classical Quarterly* 49:364–382.
———, ed. 2000a. *Homeri Ilias* II. Munich and Leipzig.
———. 2000b. "The Gardens of Alcinous and the Oral Dictated Text Theory." *Acta Antiqua Academiae Scientiarum Hungaricae* 40:479–488.
———. 2000c. *The East Face of Helicon: West Asiatic Elements in Greek Poetry and Myth*. Oxford.
———. 2001. *Studies in the Text and Transmission of the Iliad*. Munich and Leipzig.
———. 2002. "The View from Lesbos." *Beiträge zur Homerforschung: Festschrift Wolfgang Kullmann* (eds. M. Reichel and A. Rengakos) 207–219. Stuttgart.
———, ed. 2003a. *Homeric Hymns. Homeric Apocrypha. Lives of Homer*. Cambridge, MA.
———. 2003b. "*Iliad* and *Aethiopis*." *Classical Quarterly* 53:1–14.
———. 2007. *Indo-European Poetry and Myth*. Oxford.
West, S. 1967. *The Ptolemaic Papyri of Homer*. Cologne and Opladen.
———. 1988. "The Transmission of the Text." *A Commentary on Homer's Odyssey* I (eds. A. Heubeck, S. West, and J. B. Hainsworth) 33–48. Oxford.
Wilamowitz-Moellendorff, U. von. 1929. *Vitae Homeri et Hesiodi*. 2nd ed. Berlin.
Williams, R. D., ed. 1972. *The Aeneid of Virgil. Books 1-6*. Basingstoke and London.
Wilson, N. G. 1967. "A Chapter in the History of Scholia." *Classical Quarterly* 59:244–256.
———. 1984. "The Relation of Text and Commentary in Greek Books." In Questa and Rafaelli 1984:105–110.
Winter, J. G. 1925. "A New Fragment on the Life of Homer." *Transactions of the American Philological Association* 56:120–129.

Wolf, F. A. 1795. *Prolegomena ad Homerum, sive de operum Homericorum prisca et genuina forma variisque mutationibus et probabili ratione emendandi.* Halle.
———, ed. 1804, 1807. *Homerou epe. Homeri et Homeridarum opera et reliquiae* I–IV. Leipzig.
Yatromanolakis D., and Roilos, P., eds. 2004. *Greek Ritual Poetics.* Hellenic Studies 3. Washington, DC.
Zeitlin, F. I. 1970. "The Argive Festival of Hera and Euripides' *Electra.*" *Transactions of the American Philological Association* 101:645–669.
Zumthor, P. 1983. *Introduction à la poésie orale.* Paris.

Index Locorum

Aeschines 3§191
Aeschylus 2§92n, 4§264n
Alcaeus 1①20n(1§119), 1①23n(1§139)
Alcman 2§31
Apollodorus of Athens 2§187, 2§187n, 2§193n
"Apollodorus" 1§87n, 1§90, 1§98, 1§138
Apollonius of Perga P①3(P§77), P§86
Apollonius of Rhodes 1§170n, 2§18n, 2§167, 2①69(2§167), 2§194, 2§216, 2§236
Appian 1§113, 1§113n, 4①36n(4§174)
Σ Aratus 2①6n(2§27)
Archilochus 2①20(2§68), 2§69, 2①21(2§70)
Arctinus of Miletus 1§86, 1§102, 1§117, 1§145 [see also Proclus]
Aristophanes
  Frogs 1030-1036 3①13(3§100), 4§18
  Frogs 1034-1036 4§154
  Knights 565-568 4§245
  Lysistrata 759 1§137, 1①22n(1§137)
  Peace 698 4§150
  Wasps 1108-1109 4§178n
  Σ Aristophanes Birds 827 4①38(4§194), Knights 556 4§204, Peace 605 4§124n, Wasps 438 1§132n

Aristotle
  Constitution of the Athenians 23.4 4§8
  Constitution of the Athenians 49.3 4§208
  Constitution of the Athenians 60.1 3§29, 3§53n, 4①2n(4§19), 4①36n(4§174)
  Constitution of the Athenians 60.1-3 4§191, 4§208
  De generatione animalium 734a19 3§24
  Historia animalium 563a18 3§24
  Metaphysics 4.1025a2-13 3§111n
  Poetics 1447a8-18 3①9(3§70), 4§70n
  Poetics 1447a13-15 3§18
  Poetics 1448a1-2 2§56, 2§64
  Poetics 1448a22 3§146
  Poetics 1448a26-27 2§56, 2§64
  Poetics 1448b25-27 2①17(2§55), 2§67
  Poetics 1448b27 2§56
  Poetics 1448b30 3§14n
  Poetics 1448b34-36 2§56, 2§64
  Poetics 1448b38-1449a1 3§14
  Poetics 1449a2-6 3§18
  Poetics 1449a10-11 2§65, 2§68
  Poetics 1449a12-14 2§65
  Poetics 1449a19-21 2①19(2§66)
  Poetics 1449a22-24 2§69
  Poetics 1449b9-10 2§56, 2§64
  Poetics 1449b17-20 2§56, 2§64
  Poetics 1449b24-28 1§10, 1§176, 2§56, 2§64

625

INDEX LOCORUM

Poetics 1455a2 2§344n
Poetics 1459a37-b16 1§176, 3§13,
   3§14, 3§17
Rhetoric 3.1403b23 3§141
Rhetoric 3.1404a31-33 2§69
Rhetoric 3.1417a14 2§344n
F 145 1§32n
Athenaeus 2①24n(2§74), 2§180,
   3§48n, 4§175n

Bacchylides 1§87n, 2§91n, 3§135

Callimachus
   Aetia 1.F12 C§4
   Aetia 1.F13 2§193n, C§4
   Aetia 1.F15 C§4
   Aetia 4.F112.7-9 2①74(2§229)
   Epigram 28.1 2§217, 2§333
   Hymn to Apollo 28-31 2①1(2§11)
   Hymn to Apollo 31 2§12, 2§13, 2§22
   Hymn to Apollo 108 2§14n
   Hymn to Zeus 10 2§14
   Hymn to Zeus 17 2§14
   Hymn to Zeus 19 2§14
   Hymn to Zeus 20 2§14
   Hymn to Zeus 32 2§14n
   Hymn to Zeus 91-94 2①55(2§118),
      2§119
   Iamboi 13.30-32 4§9n
   F 66.3 4§189, 4§193
   F 177.8-8 2§216
   F 222 4§150
CEG 286 1①10(1§40), 1①10n(1§40),
   2§28
Crates 2§152, 2§152n, 2§208
Cratinus 4①36(4§174)

Damastes 3§99

Demosthenes P§178n, 1①11(1§44),
   1①11n(1§44), 2§58n, 3§141
Derveni Papyrus 2§135, 2§135n,
   2§140, 2§140n
Dictys of Crete 1§90n
Dieuchidas of Megara 2①90(2§297)
Diodorus 4§209n
Diogenes Laertius P§58n,
   2①90(2§297), 4①25n(4§126)
Dionysius of Halicarnassus
   On Lysias 10 P①5(P§115)
   On Lysias 11 P①6(P§115)
   Roman Antiquities 1.45.4-1.48.1
      1§108
   Roman Antiquities 1.48 1§86n
   Roman Antiquities 1.69 1§95n
   Roman Antiquities 1.69.2 1§95, 1§104
   Roman Antiquities 1.69.3 1§102,
      1①19(1§103)
   Roman Antiquities 2.66.4 1§97n
   Roman Antiquities 2.66.5 1§95n,
      1§104n
Dioscorides 1§48n

Empedocles 2①75(2§233),
   2①75n(2§233), 2§234,
   2①76(2§235), 2①76n(2§235),
   2§236, 2§237, 2§254
Euripides
   Andromache 91-95 4①46(4§263)
   Andromache 91-117 2①98(2§346),
      3§201
   Andromache 117 2①98n(2§346)
   Andromache 126 2①98n(2§346)
   Andromache 135 2①98n(2§346)
   Andromache 141 2①98n(2§346)
   Bacchae 704-711 2①80(2§257)
   Erekhtheus F 50 3①3n(3§33)
   Hecuba 433 2§256n

Hecuba 434 2§256n
Hecuba 939 1§210n
Hippolytus 121-130 2§155n
Hippolytus 742-751 2§145n
Ion 1575-1588 4§14
Trojan Women 146-151 1§11n
Trojan Women 740-779
  1①38n(1§190)
Trojan Women 826-830 1§11n
Trojan Women 1218-1220
  1①38n(1§190)
Eustathius P①14(P§137),
  P①30(P§160), P①34(P§162),
  P§164n
Eutocius of Ascalon P①2(P§76),
  P①35(P§166)
Galen P①4(P§80)
Gorgias 3§99n

Harpocration 1§94n
Hellanicus 1§108, 1§112, 3§99n
Heraclitus 2§132, 2①57n(2§132),
  2§135n
Herodotus
  1.23-24 2§61
  1.31.3-5 1①12(1§46)
  1.31.5 1§47, 1§48
  1.120.1 1§158, 3§138
  1.147.2 4§14
  2.53.2 2§286
  2.81.1-2 2①81(2§258)
  2.81.2 2§260
  3.37.2 3§135
  3.97.3 4§123
  3.123.1 4①30n(4§142)
  5.66.2 4§8n
  5.97.2 3§199n
  7.19.1-2 1§158
  7.19.12 3§138
  8.41.2 1§137

Hesiod
Theogony
  1 2§25
  1-2 1§169, 2§16, 2§25
  3 1§169
  3-4 1§169, 2§16, 2§32
  5 P§58n
  7 2§17
  7-8 1§169, 2§16, 2§43
  7-11 2§17
  8 1§169
  8-10 2§17
  10 1§169, 2§16, 2§43
  11 2§16, 2§17, 2§25
  11-21 2§16
  14 2§16
  22 1§169, 2§16, 2§25, 2§43
  22-34 2§35
  29 2①9(2§42), 2§43
  33 1§169, 2§16, 2§25, 2§113
  34 1§169, 2§16, 2§25
  35 2§16n, 2§25
  35-45 1§172, 2①2(2§16), 2§20
  36 2§25
  37 1§169, 2§17
  39 1§169, 2§17, 2①8(2§42), 2§43,
    2§256
  39-40 1§169, 2§17, 2§256
  41 1§169, 2§17
  43 1§169, 2§17, 2§43
  44 2§17, 2§113
  45 2§17
  47 2§17
  50 2§17
  51 2§17
  52 2§35
  52-62 2§17, 2§25
  63 2§43
  65 2§43
  67 2§43
  68 2§17
  69 2§17

70 2§17, 2§32
71-93 1§170, 2§18
83-84 1①29(1§170), 2①3(2§18)
94-95 2§33
94-97 1①30(1§171), 2①4(2§19)
97 1§172, 2§20
99-101 2§35, 2§35n, 2①52(2§112)
100 2§30n, 2§34n, 2§113
101 2§20
100-101 2①52n(2§112)
104 2§15, 2§21, 2§22, 2§33, 2§34
120 1§146
142 P§58n
201 1§146
337 2①57n(2§132)
337-370 2§144n
571 4§228n
576-580 4§228n
791 2§166, 2①68n(2§167)
886-900 4§105, 4§217
924-926 4§105, 4§217
965 2§113
987 1§147
Works and Days
 1-10 2§115n
 60-63 4§228n
 63-64 4§227n
 74-75 4§228n
 289-292 3§121
 290 2§92n
Shield of Herakles
 193 4①20n(4§168)
 314-315 2①70(2§168)
F 70.23 1§166

Hesychius 1①22(1§137), 2§4, 2①6n(2§27), 2§92n, 4§175, 4§189, 4§193

Hippias 3①12(3§99), 3①19(3§113), 4①16(4§74)

Hippon 2§208

Homer
Iliad
 I 1-2 2§283
 I 5 1§163
 Σ I 69ab P§48n
 Σ I 85c 4①10(4§39)
 Σ I 216a 4①6(4§39)
 I 234 3§110, 4§137
 I 238-239 3§110, 4§137
 I 299 P①9(P§128)
 Σ I 465b P§65
 Σ I 465b1 P①19(P§142)
 Σ I 465b2 P①20(P§142), P①21(P§142)
 I 528-530 4①19(4§95), 4§269
 I 536 3§110, 4§137
 I 544 2§156
 Σ II 12a P§66
 Σ II 53a1 P§39, P§63, P§114
 Σ II 53a2 P§39
 Σ II 53c P①24(P§149)
 Σ II 111b P§72, P§107n
 Σ II 115a 4①7(4§39)
 Σ II 133a P§73, P§73n, P§107n
 II 135 P§132, P§137
 Σ II 125 4§43, 4§44
 Σ II 135a P①12(P§133), P§139, 4①4(4§36)
 Σ II 135b P①11(P§131), P§137, 4①5(4§37)
 Σ II 196c2 P§114
 II 224 3§121
 II 299-332 1①1(1§8), C§19
 II 299-310 1①17(1§82)
 II 305-324 1§11
 II 308 1§83, 1§84, 1§121
 II 309 1§83
 II 318 1①5(1§19), 1§26, 1§27, 1§28, 1①7(1§29), 1§30, 1§31, 132, 1①13(1§53), 1§57, 2§170, 2§171
 Σ II 318 1§24, 1§24n, 1§27, 1§28

II 318-319 1⊕8(1§30), 1§31,
　　1§32n
II 319 1§19, 1⊕6(1§20), 1§21,
　　1§23, 1§24, 1§25, 1§30, 1§32,
　　1§37, 1§ 83, C§19
Σ II 319a1 1§21
II 322 1⊕3(1§16)
II 323-329 1§17, 1§19
II 324-325 1⊕16(1§62)
II 325 1§12
II 326-329 1§12
II 330 1§12, 1⊕4(1§18),
　　1⊕15(1§61), 1§63
Σ II 397a P§144
Σ II 397b P§144
Σ II 532b1 4⊕8(4§39)
Σ II 532b2 4⊕9(4§39)
II 547 1§138
II 548 1§138
Σ II 579 P§39, P§66
II 594-600 3⊕1n(3§27), 3§41n
II 600 3§41n
II 662 P§126
Σ II 662a1 P⊕7(P§125), P§157
Σ II 665a P§61n
Σ II 807 P⊕16(P§140)
III 10 P§36n
III 18 P§153
Σ III 18a P⊕27(P§152)
Σ III 18b1 P⊕25(P§151)
Σ III 18b2 P⊕26(P§151)
III 35 4⊕9(4§39)
Σ III 99a P⊕18(P§140)
III 176 2§256n
Σ III 206a P⊕17(P§140)
Σ III 338a P§48n
III 362 4⊕20n(4§100)
Σ III 406a1 P§107
III 439 4§109
Σ IV 170 P§36
IV 319 P⊕7(P§125)
IV 389 4§109

IV 59-60 2§282n
V 63 2§282n, 2§283n
V 87 2⊕70n(2§168)
V 228 P⊕31(P§162), P⊕33(P§162)
Σ V 228 P§162n
Σ V 385 2§188n
Σ V 461b P§121
V 733-747 4⊕20(4§100),
　　4⊕37(4§184)
V 734-735 4⊕37n(4§184), 4§233
V 735 4§186, 4§195
V 736 4§233
V 737 4§233
V 738 4§101
V 741 4§101
V 743 4⊕20n(4§100)
V 744 4⊕20n(4§100)
Σ V 808 P§48n
Σ V 881a1 P§36
VI 64 P⊕7(P§125)
VI 289 4§195, 4§195n
VI 293-295 4§195
VI 355 P§127, P§147
Σ VI 355a1 P⊕8(P§127),
　　P⊕9(P§128), P§131,
　　P⊕22(P§146), P§148
Σ VI 355a2 P⊕10(P§130), P§131,
　　P⊕23(P§147), P§148
VI 389 1§205n
VI 407-439 4§262
VI 411-413 4§264n
VI 429-430 1⊕43(1§208)
VI 448-464 2⊕96(2§336)
VI 484 1⊕44n(1§209)
VI 490-491 1⊕43(1§208)
VI 496 1⊕44(1§209)
VI 510-511 P⊕34(P§162)
Σ VI 510-511a1 P⊕33(P§162),
　　P§164n
VI 511 P§162, P§164
Σ VI 511 P§162n

Iliad (continued)
Σ VI 511a P§158, P⊕31(P§162), P§162n, P§164n
Σ VI 511b P⊕32(P§162)
VII 21 4§109
VII 26-27 4§109
VII 203 4§109
Σ VII 428a1 P§39, P§66
Σ VIII 52a-d P§48n
VIII 107 3§165
VIII 171 4§109
Σ VIII 276a1 P⊕27n(P§152)
VIII 352 4§40
Σ VIII 352 4⊕11(4§39), 4⊕12(4§41)
IX 169-171 3⊕44(3§184)
Σ IX 222b P§61n
IX 308-314 3⊕35(3§172), 3⊕36(3§173)
IX 310-312 3⊕36n(3§173)
IX 312-313 3⊕42(3§182)
IX 357-363 3⊕43(3§183)
IX 540 3§193
Σ IX 540a1 3§193
IX 650-655 3⊕45(3§185)
IX 653 3⊕46(3§186), 3⊕46n(3§186)
Σ IX 653a 3⊕46n(3§186)
Σ X 349 P§48n
Σ X 397-399a P§67, P§68, P§69, P§79
Σ X 461c P⊕15(P§139)
XI 41 4⊕20n(4§100)
XI 492 2⊕70n(2§168)
Σ XII 22a 4§45
XII 228 1⊕2(1§14)
Σ XII 382a1 P§114
XII 384 4⊕20n(4§100)
Σ XII 404a P§65, P§93, P§104, P§106
Σ XII 404a1 P§121
XIII 23-31 1⊕24(1§148)

Σ XIII 28b P§144
Σ XIII 197 4§45, 4§45n, P§144n
XIII 343 1§121
XIII 347 4§109
XIII 435 1§121
XIII 632 2§154n
XIII 808a P§48n
XIV 97 3§165
Σ XIV 136a P§48n
XIV 200-207 2§145n
XIV 201 2⊕57(2§132), 2⊕57n(2§132), 2§134, 2§140, 2⊕59(2§140), 2§144n, 2⊕64(2§146)
XIV 245-246 2§150
XIV 246 2⊕62(2§144), 2§144n, 2⊕65(2§149), 2§153, 2§156n, 2§178
XIV 246-246a 2§153, 2§156, 2§160, 2§163, 2§182, 2§183
XIV 246a 2⊕65(2§149), 2§150n, 2§153, 2§154, 2§155, 2§156n, 2§178, 2§214
Σ XIV 246a P§47n, 2§152, 2§153, 2§190
XIV 302 2⊕57(2§132), 2⊕57n(2§132), 2§134, 2§140, 2⊕59(2§140), 2⊕64(2§146)
XV 405 P⊕31(P§162)
XV 494-499 4§268, 3⊕3n(3§33)
XVI 121 4§109
Σ XVI 313 P§113
XVI 362 4§109
XVI 364-366 4§109
XVI 433 3§165
XVI 446-467 P⊕25(P§151)
Σ XVI 467c1 P§61n
XVI 844-845 4§109
XVII 75 P§159
XVII 75-76 P⊕30(P§160)
Σ XVII 75a P§143, P§158, P⊕29(P§159)

XVII 176-177 4§109
XVII 195-214 4⓪47(4§269)
Σ XVII 202 4⓪47n(4§269)
XVII 207 1⓪41n(1§203)
XVII 331-332 4§109
Σ XVII 456a P§48n
XVII 627 4§109
Σ XVII 719 4§45
Σ XVIII 156a P§48n
XVIII 399 2§165
XVIII 478-609 2⓪67(2§164)
XVIII 479 2§165
XVIII 480 C§16n
XVIII 481-489 2§152n
XVIII 482-485 2§165
XVIII 482-608 2§173
XVIII 483-608 2§195, 2§198
Σ XVIII 483a 2§195n
XVIII 490-491 2⓪71(2§173)
XVIII 491-508 2§174
XVIII 497-501 2⓪72(2§174)
XVIII 516-519 1⓪14(1§54), 4⓪20n(4§100)
XVIII 519 1§55, 2§170, 2§171
XVIII 590 C§16
XVIII 590-604 2⓪24(2§74)
XVIII 604-605 2⓪24n(2§74)
XVIII 606 2⓪24n(2§74)
XVIII 607-608 2§165, 2§168, 2§195, 2§198
XVIII 608 2§165
Σ XIX 365-368a P§67, P§71, P§73, P§79
Σ XIX 386b1 P§36n
XIX 409 4§40
XX 7 2§204n, 2§212
XX 65 2§165
XX 101-102 4§109
Σ XX 188b1 P§113
Σ XX 307-308a1 1§108, 1§112
XXI 158 2§154n

XXI 194-197 2§196, 2§196n, 2§211
XXI 195 2§206, 2§207, 2§207n, 2§208, 2§209, 2§213, 2§214, 2§198, 2§198n
Σ XXI 195 2§196n, 2§207, 2§208, 2§209, 2§212, 2§152n
XXI 195-197 2§155n
XXI 196-197 2§144
Σ XXI 221 P⓪28(P§154)
Σ XXI 221b1 P⓪28n(P§154)
Σ XXI 221b2 P⓪28n(P§154)
Σ XXI 221c1 P⓪28n(P§154)
Σ XXI 221c2 P⓪28n(P§154)
XXI 308-309 3§121
XXI 323 2§204n
XXI 483 P⓪8(P§127), P⓪22(P§146)
XXII 315 4⓪20n(4§100)
XXII 437-515 1⓪41(1§203)
XXII 441 1⓪41n(1§203)
XXII 444 1⓪41n(1§203)
XXII 460 1§205
XXII 466-474 1§205
XXII 477-514 4§262
XXIII 83a 3§191
XXIII 83b 3§191
XXIII 767 4§109
XXIII 768-770 4§109
XXIII 771 4§109
XXIV 28-30 1§145n
XXIV 527-528 2§135n
XXIV 580-581 1⓪41n(1§203)
XXIV 601-620 1⓪9(1§33)
XXIV 611 1§35
Σ XXIV 613a1 1§35
XXIV 614-617 1§35
Σ XXIV 614-617a1 1§35
XXIV 684 P⓪8(P§127), P⓪22(P§146)
XXIV 725-745 4§262
XXIV 804 1⓪31n(1§178), 4§267

Odyssey
 i 153 3§41
 i 154 3§41
 i 155 3§41
 i 159 3§41
 i 325 3§41
 i 326 3§41
 i 328 3§41
 i 340 3§41
 i 346 3§41
 i 347 3§41
 i 350 3§41
 i 351 3§41
 Σ i 356 P§36, P§53
 iii 88 2⊕6n(2§27)
 iii 132-135 1§118
 iii 184 2⊕6(2§27)
 Σ iii 195 3⊕46n(3§186)
 iii 432 1§67n
 iv 17-18 2⊕24n(2§74)
 iv 18 2⊕24n(2§74)
 Σ iv 727 P§66, P§85
 iv 728 4⊕7(4§39)
 v 47 1§121
 v 396 2§256n
 vii 81 1§138
 Σ vii 132 P⊕13(P§136), P§137
 viii 62-94 2⊕88(2§289)
 viii 73-83 2§309
 viii 74 2§29n, 2§93, 2§290, 2§291, 2§292, 2§326, 2§331, 4§237
 viii 79-81 2§309
 viii 83-85 2§299
 viii 86 2§299, 2§308, 2§343
 viii 87 2§292, 2§293, 2§295, 2§305
 viii 90 2§292, 2§295, 2§299, 2§305, 2§308, 2§309, 2§343
 viii 91 2§305
 viii 92 2§299, 2§308, 2§309, 2§343
 viii 93-95 2§301
 viii 94-95 2§305
 viii 96-99 2§312
 viii 98-99 2§301, 2§305, 2§308, 2§343
 viii 256-266 2⊕24n(2§74)
 viii 267 2§321
 viii 335 2§135n
 viii 368 2§308
 viii 370-380 2§321
 viii 429 2§93, 2⊕85(2§274), 2§276, 2§277, 2§279, 2§280, 2§284, 2§287, 2§290, 2§291, 2§302, 2§303, 2§305, 2§311, 2§324, 2§328, 3§26
 viii 485-498 2⊕86(2§280), 2⊕92(2§312)
 viii 492 2⊕76n(2§235), 2§281, 2§282, 2§283, 2§303, 2§305, 2§311, 2§313, 2§324, 2§341
 viii 492-495 2§312, 2§313
 viii 493 2§282, 2§283
 viii 499 2⊕76n(2§235), 2§287, 2§311, 2§320
 viii 499-500 2⊕87(2§285), 2⊕91(2§310), 2⊕93(2§313)
 viii 499-533 2⊕95(2§329)
 viii 500-520 2§288
 viii 504-512 1§119, 1⊕20(1§119)
 viii 509 1§121, 1§122, 1§123
 viii 510 1§120
 viii 510-512 1§120
 viii 520 4§109
 viii 521-530 2⊕97(2§337)
 viii 522 2§256n, 2§308, 2§343, 2§344
 viii 523 2§256n, 2§344
 viii 527 1⊕1n(1§8), 2§256n, 2§344, 2§344n
 viii 530 2§306
 viii 531 2§308, 2§343
 viii 532-533 2§305
 viii 537 2§305
 viii 538 2§305
 viii 541 2§306

viii 542 2§305
ix 372-374 P⊕27(P§152)
xi 196 P§36
xi 201 2§256n
xi 239 2§154n
xi 410 P⊕7(P§125)
xi 544 4§109
xi 548 4§109
xi 568-571 3⊕17(3§109), 3§110, 4⊕28(4§136)
xi 582 3§8107
xi 601 3§107
xiii 23-31 1⊕24(1§148)
xiii 27-28 2⊕24n(2§74)
Σ xiii 152 C§5
xiii 158 C§5
xiii 160-164 1§19n
xiii 228 P⊕8(P§127), P⊕22(P§146)
xiii 363 C§7n
xv 277 P⊕8(P§127), P⊕22(P§146)
xvi 214 2§344n
xvii 150 P⊕1(P§37)
xvii 150-165 P§38
Σ xvii 160 P⊕1(P§37), P§53
xvii 160-161 P⊕1(P§37), P§38
xvii 165 P⊕1(P§37)
xvii 262 3§41
xvii 415-444 1§10n
xvii 521 1§121
xix 136 2§256n
xix 204 2§255, 2§255n
xix 205 2§255
xix 206 2§255
xix 207 2§255
xix 208 2§255, 2§255n
xix 264 2§256n
xix 547 1§63
xxii 165 1§27n
xxii 330 3§41
xxii 331 3§41
xxii 332 3§41
xxii 340 3§41
xxii 345 3§41
xxii 346 3§41
xxii 347 2§92n
xxii 348 3§41
xxii 376 3§41
xxii 498 2§344n
xxii 501 2§344n
xxiii 246 1§147
xiv 3 1§121

Homeric Hymns
  Homeric Hymn to Demeter 2.1 2⊕31(2§88); HH Demeter 2.494-495 2⊕35(2§101), 2§102n
  Homeric Hymn to Apollo 3.14 2⊕5n(2§23), 2§104, 2§106, 2§119; 3.16-20 2§26; 3.19 2⊕5(2§23), 2⊕5n(2§23), 2§25, 2⊕16n(2§52), 2⊕47(2§104), 2⊕47n(2§104), 2§106, 2§107, 2§119; 3.156 2§37; 3.156-178 2⊕6(2§27); 3.157 2§33, 2§34n; 3.158 2§36, 2⊕11(2§46), 2§89; 3.158-159 2§46; 3.160-161 2⊕12(2§46); 3.161 2§36, 2§47, 2§89; 3.163 2§29, 2§29n, 2§57, 2⊕6n(2§27), 2§34n; 3.164 2⊕7(2§41), 2⊕10(2§44); 3.165-166 2§33; 3.166 2⊕5n(2§23), 2⊕6n(2§27), 2§34, 2§104, 2§104n, 2§106, 2§107, 2§107n, 2§119; 3.167-179 2§39; 3.168 2§39n; 3.169 2§36; 3.169-175 2§37, 2§38; 3.171 2⊕6n(2§27), 2§28, 2§29, 2§47, 2§57, 2§58; 3.172 2§36; 3.172-173 2⊕14(2§47); 3.173-175 2§36; 3.177 2§107, 2§107n, 2§108, 2§108n; 3.177-178 2⊕13(2§46), 2⊕15(2§49), 2§51, 2⊕48(2§107); 3.178 2§89; 3.186-203 2§51; 3.207 2⊕5(2§23), 2⊕5n(2§23), 2§25, 2§26, 2⊕16(2§52), 2⊕16n(2§52), 2⊕47(2§104),

Index Locorum

2①47n(2§104), 2§106, 2§107,
  2§108n, 2§119; 3.502-513
  2§71; 3.514-523 2①22(2§71);
  3.545-546 2①36(2§101), 2§108,
  2①49(2§108), 2§119
Homeric Hymn to Hermes 4.172
  2①76n(2§235); 4.451 2§93, 2§290;
  4.579-580 2①37(2§101)
Homeric Hymn to Aphrodite 5.292-
  293 2①32(2§98), 2§101
Homeric Hymn to Aphrodite 6.19-20
  2§102n; 6.19-21 2①38(2§101)
Homeric Hymn 7.58 2§103
Homeric Hymn to Artemis 9.1
  2①33n(2§98); 9.7-9 2①33(2§98),
  2§101; 9.8 2①26(2§78)
Homeric Hymn to Aphrodite 10.4-5
  2§102n; 10.4-6 2①39(2§101)
Homeric Hymn 11.5 2§103
Homeric Hymn 13.1-3 2§103n; 13.3
  2§103
Homeric Hymn 14.6 2§103
Homeric Hymn 15.9 2§103
Homeric Hymn 16.5 2§103
Homeric Hymn 17.5 2§103
Homeric Hymn to Hermes 18.10-12
  2①34(2§98), 2§100n, 2§101;
  18.11-12 2§103n; 18.12 2§100
Homeric Hymn to Pan 19.48-49
  2①40(2§101)
Homeric Hymn 20.8 2§103n
Homeric Hymn 21.5 2§103
Homeric Hymn 22.7 2§103
Homeric Hymn 23.1-4 2①54(2§117);
  23.4 2§103n
Homeric Hymn to Hermes 24.5 2§100,
  2§103n
Homeric Hymn to Muses & Apollo
  25.6-7 2①41(2§101)
Homeric Hymn to Dionysus 26.11
  2§103; 26.11-13 2§100
Homeric Hymn to Artemis 27.11-20

2①25(2§76); 27.15-19 2§77;
  27.21-22 2①42(2§101)
Homeric Hymn to Athena 28.4-6
  4§105, 4§217; 28.7 4§105; 28.17
  4§105; 28.17-18 2①43(2§101)
Homeric Hymn to Hestia 29.13-14
  2①44(2§101)
Homeric Hymn to Gaia 30.17-18
  2§102n; 30.17-19 2①45(2§101)
Homeric Hymn to Helios 31.17-19
  2①50(2§110); 31.18 2§111, 2§113;
  31.18-19 2①50n(2§110); 31.19
  2§111, 2§113
Homeric Hymn to Selene 32.17-20
  2①51(2§110), 2§269; 32.18 2§111;
  32.19 2§111, 2§113
Homeric Hymn to Dioskouroi 33.18-19
  2①46(2§101)

IG
  I³ 32 4①36n(4§174)
  I² 45 4§15n
  I² 302 4§12, 4§12n
  I³ 474 4①23n(4§115)
  II² 334 4§189, 4§191n
  II² 2311 3§28, 3§35
  XII ix 189 3①2n(3§30), 3§58n
Isaeus P§178n
Isocrates
  Antidosis 295 4①17n(4§78)
  Panathenaicus 1 3§164n
  Panathenaicus 7 3§164
  Panathenaicus 17-19 3§84
  Panathenaicus 18-19 3①32(3§164)
  Panathenaicus 33 3§53n,
    3①31(3§164)
  Panathenaicus 267-270 3§164
  Panegyricus 159 4§154, 4§155,
    3①4(3§38), 3§65, 4①2(4§19),
    4①17n(4§78), 4①36n(4§174),
    4§256n

2.48 3§39, 4§33
10.65 3§39
12.18 3§39
12.33 3§39
12.293 3§39
13.2 3§39
15.296 4§33

"Life of Homer" narratives 3§36, 4§29, 4§152

Σ Lycophron 1§87n, 1§90n

Lycurgus P§178n, 3§33, 3§33n, 3①3(3§33), 3①3n(3§33), 4§245, 4§268

Orphic Hymn 2①60(2§142), 2§166n

Orphic Fragments 1§146n, 2①57(2§132), 2§142n, 2①63(2§145), 3§26n

Ovid 1§90n, 1§90n, 1§101, 1①25(1§152), 1①25n(1§152), 1§154n, 1§167n

Oxyrhynchus Papyri 221 P①28(P§154), 2§198n

Pausanias
  1.2.6 1§138
  1.5.3 1§138
  1.14.6 1§138
  1.15.1-3 4§250
  1.20.4 4①36n(4§174)
  1.24.5-7 1①23(1§139), 4①21(4§103), 4§211
  1.24.7 2§4, 4§106, 4§227
  1.26.4 1§98
  1.26.6 1§98
  1.26.5 1§138
  1.28.2 4§130
  1.28.8-9 1§94n
  2.23.5 1§93, 1§95n
  2.31.10 2§155n
  5.10.4 4①22(4§107), 4§108
  5.11.1 4§106
  5.11.8 4§226
  5.16.2 4§189
  6.24.10 4§189
  8.10.1-2 4①18(4§94), 4§99
  8.38.10 2§196n
  10.10.1 4§131
  10.25.4 4§250n
  10.25.9-11 4§250n
  10.26.1-2 4§250n
  10.27.3 1§79n
  10.30.8 3§108n

Pherecydes 2§14n, 2§145n, 3§99n

Philochorus 4§97, 4§121n, 4§124, 4§124n, 4§150, 4①36n(4§174)

Philostratus 4§18n, 4§53, 4§55, 4§56, 4§67, 4①16(4§74), 4§84, 4§89, 4§167

Photius 1§137, 2§4

Phylarchus 1§137, 1§142, 2§4

Pindar
  Isthmian 8.56-60 4§267
  Nemean 1.60 3§135
  Nemean 2.1 2§87n
  Nemean 2.1-3 2①28(2§80), 2①29(2§84), 2①53(2§115), 4①40(4§238)
  Nemean 2.2 4§241, 4§242
  Nemean 2.3 4§237, 4§241
  Nemean 2.23-25 2①23(2§72), 2①27(2§79), 2①30(2§86)
  Olympian 10.45 4①18n(4§94)
  Olympian 13.18-19 2①18n(2§63)
  F 194 2§173n
  Σ Pindar Olympian 7.152 4§189, 4§193, Olympian 13.26b 2①18(2§63)

Plato
  Apology 41a 3§99
  Charmides 173c 3§135

  Cratylus 402a 2§132
    402a-c 2§145, 2§146
    402a-d 2①57(2§132), 2§136
    402b-c 3§99n
  Euthyphro 6b-c 4①39(4§202)
  Gorgias 518b 4①16n(4§74)
    455e 4①23(4§115)
  Hipparkhos 228b-c 3①3n(3§33),
    4§116 n
    228d 3①3n(3§33)
  Hippias Maior 281b 4①16n(4§74),
    4§89
    284e-286a 4§53n, 4§89n
    285c 3§111n, 4①16n(4§74)
    285d 3①39n(3§178),
      4①16n(4§74), 4①34n(4§161)
    285d-e 4①13(4§55), 4①16n(4§74)
    285d-286c 4§67
    285e 4①16n(4§74)
    286a-b 4①16n(4§74)
    286a-c 4§18n, 4①14(4§56), 4§79,
      4§83
    286b-c 4①14n(4§56)
    286b 4§57
    289a-290d 4①25(4§126)
  Hippias Minor 363a 4§57
    363a-b 4§78
    363a-c 3①18(3§112)
    363b 3§130, 3§169, 4§78, 4§82
    363b-c 4§51
    363c 4§57
    363c-d 3§155, 4§75, 4§85, 4§140,
      4§163
    363c-364a 4①17(4§78),
      4①26(4§132)
    363d 3§167, 4§77
    364a 3§155, 4§75, 4§75n, 4§80,
      4§82, 4§85, 4§163

    364a-b 4§140
    364b 3①22n(3§129), 3§167, 4§57,
      4§59, 4§75, 4§77, 4§83
    364b-c 3①33(3§169), 4§59, 4§61,
      4§83
    364e 3①34(3§170), 3①35(3§172)
    365b 3①37(3§176)
    365c-d 3①28(3§150),
      3①38(3§177)
    367e 3§111, 3§111n, 3§129,
      4①16n(4§74), 4§138
    368a-d 3①30(3§161)
    368a-e 3§131, 4§50, 4§161,
      4①34(4§161)
    368a-369a 3①22(3§129)
    368b 3§107n, 3①22n(3§129),
      3§155, 3§156, 3§157, 4§59,
      4§61, 4§75, 4§75n, 4§134,
      4§140, 4§163
    368b-c 3§156, 3§161, 4§70
    368c 4§72
    368c-d 3§161, 4①15(4§68), 4§159
    368d 3①22n(3§129), 3§130,
      3§149, 3§150, 3§155, 3§162,
      3①39n(3§178), 4§51, 4§70,
      4§73, 4§87
    368d-e 3①39(3§178)
    368e-369b 3①27(3§149)
    369a 3§150, 3§155, 3§162, 4§51,
      4§73, 4§87
    369a-369b 3①40(3§179)
    369c 3①41(3§180)
    369c-d 4①16n(4§74)
    369d-370a 3①42(3§182)
    370b-c 3①43(3§183)
    370c-d 3①44(3§184)
    370e 3§185
    371b-c 3①45(3§185)
    372a-c 3①47(3§187)
    373b 4§57
  Ion 530a 3§31, 3§37n, 4①2n(4§19),
    4§76, 4①36n(4§174)

530a-b 3§31, 3§37, 4§176
530a-c 3①2(3§30)
530b 3§31, 3§47n, 3§48n, 4§76
530b-c 2§135, 3§64, 3§171n
530b-d 4§81
530c 3§64, 3§73, 3§147, 3§147n,
    4①16n(4§74), 4§80n
530c-d 3①33n(3§169), 4§80
530d 2§95n, 3§35
531a 3§48
531a-532b 3§48n
531a-532c 3§48, 3§48n
531b 3§134
532a 3§48n
532b 4§64
532c 3§56, 3§67, 4§156
532d 3§142n
532e 3§56
532e-533b 3§56, 3§67, 4§156
533b-c 3①1(3§27), 3§41, 3§56,
    3①8(3§59), 3§61, 4§156
533c 3§56, 3§144, 3§199, 4§156
533d 3§50, 3§107n
533e 3§57, 4§156
535b 3§50, 4§175n
535b-c 3①26(3§143), 3§198,
    3①48(3§199), 4①45(4§259)
535c-d 3§199
535d 3§35, 3§35n, 4§17, 4§76
535e 3§53, 3§142n, 3§144
535e-536a 3①7(3§52),
    3①25(3§136)
536a 3§142
536a-c 3①6(3§50)
536b 3§51, 3§157, 4§140, 4§163
537b-c 3§131, 4§50
538b 3§55, 4§156
538c 3§55, 4§156
538d 3§55, 4§156
539d 3§39, 3①23n(3§131)
539d-e 3①23(3§131)
539e 3§55, 4§50, 4§156

540a 3§55, 4§156
540d 3§55, 4§156
541a 3§55, 4§156
541b 3§47
541b-c 4①1(4§10)
541c 3§35, 4§12, 4§17
541c-d 4§13, 4§13n
541d 4§13
Laws 1.629a 3①3n(3§33)
  2.656e-657b 3§93
  2.658b 3§91
  2.658e-659a 3§80
  3.680b 3§83, 3§84
  3.680c 3§83, 3§84
  3.700a-701b 3§92
  4.704a 3§77n
  4.706e-707a 3§165
  6.746c5-e10 3§91
  6.764c-765a 3①10(3§87)
  6.764d-e 3§28
  7.805d5 3§85
  7.816c-d 3§92
  7.834d-e 3§89
  8.828b-c 3§89
  8.829d-e 3§27
  11.919d 3§77n
  12.946b 3§77n
  12.969a 3§77n
Lysias 203a 3§164n
Laches 191a-b 3§165
Meno 91b 4§152, 4§153, 4§155,
    4§171
  91b-92b 4①33(4§148)
  91d 4§153, 4§171
Phaedo 60d 2§89
  60d-61b 2§89n
  61a-b 3§81
  69c-d 2①82(2§260)
  110b 4§204
  112d 2①68(2§167), 2①68n(2§167)
  112e 2①56(2§131), 2①66(2§161)

Phaedrus 259d 3§80
  277e 3§139
Protagoras 311a-e 4①29(4§141)
  311c 4①29n(4§141)
  311e 4§153
  311e-312c 4①30(4§142)
  312a 4§159
  312b 4§153
  312c-e 4①31(4§144)
  314e-315b 3①15(3§105)
  315a-b 3§153
  315b 3§111, 3§129, 4§138
  315b-c 3①16(3§106), 3§108,
    3§154, 4①27(4§135), 4§140
  315c 3§107, 3§111, 3§111n,
    3§129, 3§131, 4§50,
    4①16n(4§74), 4§138
  315c-316a 3§107
  316c-d 3①14(3§101), 3§115
  316d 3①21(3§123), 3①29(3§152),
    3§153, 3§154, 4①32(4§146)
  317b-c 4①29n(4§141)
  318d-e 3§111n, 4①16n(4§74),
    4§138n
  338e-339a 3§124
  339a-b 3§117
  339b 3§118, 3§124
  339d-e 3§125
  340a 3§121
  340c-d 3§121
  341e-342a 3§121
  342a 3§125
  342a-347a 3§116, 3§121 3§125
  342b-e 4§54n
  344c 3§118
  344e 3§118
  345c 3§118
  345d 3§118
  346c 3§118
  347a-b 3①20(3§115), 3§119
  348a-c 3§119
  348c-d 3§121

Republic 2.363a 3§99n
  2.373b 3§141
  2.376e-398b 3§73, 4§154, 4§157
  2.377d 3§99n
  2.378c 4§205
  3.388c-d 3§105
  10.595c 3§17, 3§17n, 3§18
  10.598d 3§17, 3§17n, 3§18
  10.599c-d 3§73, 4①3(4§20),
    4§154, 4§157
  10.605c 3§17, 3§18
  10.607a 3§17, 3§18
  10.606e 3§73, 4§154, 4§157
  10.612b 3§99n
Symposium 179d-e 3①5(3§42)
  194b 3§141
Theaetetus 152e 2①59(2§140), 3§17,
    3§18
  179d 2①58n(2§137)
  179e 2§138, 3§98
  179e-180d 2①58(2§137), 3§96,
    3§158, 4§160
  180c-d 2§138, 3①11(3§96), 3§97
  180d 3§97n, 3§158, 4§160
Timaeus 21a 2§58n
  40d-41a 2①61(2§143)
  72a-b 3①24(3§134), 3§137
Plutarch
  Aristeides 25.2-3 4§23
  Brutus 23.2-5 1①42(1§207)
  Brutus 23.5-6 1①43(1§208)
  Camillus 20 1§95n
  Demetrius 10.5 4§207
  Demetrius 12.3 4§207, 4§209n
  Kimon 4.5-6 4§250
  Pericles 10.5 4①36n(4§174)
  Pericles 12.6 4§199, 4§202, 4§239
  Pericles 13.6-15 4①23(4§115),
    4①36(4§174)
  Pericles 13.7 4§178n
  Pericles 13.9 4§120, 4①36n(4§174)
  Pericles 13.9-11 3§29, 3§53n,

4①2n(4§19), 4§120
Pericles 13.9-12 4§120
Pericles 13.13 1①31n(1§78), 4§116, 4§182
Pericles 14.1-2 4§122
Pericles 31.2-3 4①24(4§120), 4§150
Pericles 31.3-4 4§215
Lives of the Ten Orators 841f P§178n, 3①3n(3§33)
On the face in the moon 938d 2①65(2§149)
On the glory of the Athenians 346f 1§127

Polyaenus 1§94n

Porphyry 1§32n, 2§188n

Proclus 1①18(1§85), 1§86, 1§93, 1§100, 1§111, 1§117n, 2①94(2§328), 2§335, 4①41(4§249), 4§45n

Quintus of Smyrna 1§87n, 1§136n

SH 903A 2§187

Simonides 2§232, 2§232n, 3§121, 3§124

Solon 2§24n

Sophocles 1§34, 1§79n, 1§86n, 1§87n, 1§146, 4§196

Strabo
  1.2.31 C38 P§101n
  1.2.37 C44 2§193n
  8.3.30 C354 4①19(4§95), 4§269
  9.1.12 C395 4①36n(4§174)
  13.1.27 C594-595 1§96, 1§110n, 1§113n
  13.1.46 C604 1§87n
  13.1.52 C607 1§107
  13.1.53 C608 1§105
  14.5.16 C676 2§180

Suda P§105, P§25n, 1§94n, 2§62

Theocritus
  1.8 2§263
  1.25 2①79n(2§250)
  1.27 2①79n(2§250)
  1.27-61 2§251
  1.32 2①79n(2§250)
  1.33 2①79n(2§250)
  1.33-34 2①79n(2§250)
  1.35-40 2§253
  1.42-52 2§251
  1.55 2①79n(2§250)
  1.61 2§242, 2§242n, 2§267
  1.64 2§243
  1.64-152 2§257
  1.66 2§255, 2§348
  1.70 2§243
  1.73 2§243
  1.76 2§243
  1.79 2§243
  1.84 2§243
  1.89 2§243
  1.92-93 2§266
  1.92-94 2①83(2§265)
  1.94 2§243, 2§266
  1.99 2§243
  1.104 2§243
  1.108 2§243
  1.111 2§243
  1.114 2§243
  1.119 2§243
  1.122 2§243
  1.127 2§243, 2§293
  1.131 2§243, 2§293
  1.137 2§243, 2§252, 2§293
  1.137-145 2①79(2§250)
  1.140 2§254, 2§256, 2§262
  1.140-141 2§348
  1.142 2§243, 2①78(2§246), 2§249, 2§252, 2§293

1.143-145 2§264
1.144-145 2§268, 2①84(2§268)
1.145 2①77(2§238), 2§240, 2§241, 2§242, 2§246, 2§252, 2§265, 2§268
7.73-77 2§255
Σ Theocritus 1.140 2§254n

Theon of Alexandria P①36(P§168), P①37(P§169)

Thucydides
1.2.6 4§14
1.25.4 C§4, C§4n
1.67.4 4§7
1.75.1 4§7
1.76.1 4§24
1.81.2 4§24
1.92.2 4§23n
1.95 3§139
1.95.1 4§8
2.13.3 4§122
2.13.3-5 4§121
2.13.5 4§122
2.60.4 4§25
2.61.4 4§25
2.63.1-2 4§24
3.38.4 3§53n
3.38.7 3§53n
3.70.4 C§4n
3.104.2-3 4§30
3.104.4 2§27, 2§33, 2§43, 2§89
3.104.4-5 4§240
3.104.5 2①6n(2§27), 2§34n, 2§39n
5.90 4§27
5.91.2 4§26
7.9 4§12n
8.19.3 4§11

Tyrtaeus 3①3n(3§33)

Virgil
Aeneid 1.1 C§16
Aeneid 1.441-493 1①31(1§178)
Aeneid 1.459-465 1①34(1§182)
Aeneid 1.461 1§183
Aeneid 1.462 1§181, 1§182, 1§183, 1§193, 4①43(4§253)
Aeneid 1.463 4①44(4§253)
Aeneid 1.464 1§179, 1§181, 1§182, 1§183, 1§192, 1§194, 1§195, 1§196
Aeneid 1.476 1§185
Aeneid 1.488 4①42(4§251)
Aeneid 2.162-175 1§99
Aeneid 2.182 1§99
Aeneid 2.183-184 1§117
Aeneid 2.189 1§116n
Aeneid 2.199-227 1§79, 1§80
Aeneid 2.202 1§79n
Aeneid 2.203 1§79n, 1§84, 1§145
Aeneid 2.218-219 1§128
Aeneid 2.225-227 1①21(1§135)
Aeneid 2.259 1§86n
Aeneid 3.293 1§199
Aeneid 3.294-355 1§199
Aeneid 3.302 1§200
Aeneid 3.303-305 1①38(1§190), 1①39(1§199)
Aeneid 3.304 1§195
Aeneid 3.306-309 1§205
Aeneid 3.307 1§79n
Aeneid 3.313 1§205
Aeneid 3.343 1§202
Aeneid 3.482-491 1①40(1§200)
Aeneid 3.483 1§201
Aeneid 3.495 1§202
Aeneid 4.449 1①36(1§186)
Aeneid 6.11 1§181n
Aeneid 6.851 1§174n
Aeneid 7.450 1§79n
Aeneid 8.289 1§79n
Aeneid 8.615-629 C§15
Aeneid 8.616 C§16
Aeneid 8.625 C§16
Aeneid 8.627 C§15

Aeneid 8.640 C§15n
Aeneid 8.697 1§79n
Aeneid 8.729-731 C§15
Aeneid 8.730-731 C§17
Eclogues 6.11 1§167
Georgics 2.475-477 1①28(1§167)
Georgics 2.477-486 1①28n(1§167)
Georgics 2.483-484 1①28n(1§167)
Georgics 2.485-486 1①28(1§167), 1①28n(1§167)

Xenophon 3①12n(3§99), 3①23n(3§131), 3§158, 3§162, 3§166, 4§73n, 4§160, 4§178n